W9-BLK-081

Health, Safety,
AND
Nutrition
FOR THE
Young Child

SEVENTH EDITION

Health, Safety,

AND

Nutrition

FOR THE

Young Child

SEVENTH EDITION

Lynn R. Marotz

DELMAR
CENGAGE Learning

Australia • Brazil • Japan • Korea • Mexico • Singapore • Spain • United Kingdom • United States

Health, Safety, and Nutrition for the Young Child, Seventh Edition
Lynn R. Marotz

Vice President, Career Education SBU: Dawn Gerrain

Director of Learning Solutions: John Fedor

Managing Editor: Robert L. Serenka, Jr.

Acquisitions Editor: Christopher Shortt

Editorial Assistant: Alison Archambault

Director of Content and Media Production: Wendy A. Troeger

Production Manager: Mark Bernard

Content Project Manager: Angela Iula

Technology Project Manager: Sandy Charette

Director of Marketing: Wendy E. Mapstone

Senior Channel Manager: Kristin McNary

Marketing Coordinator: Scott A. Chrysler

Art Director: Dave Arsenault

© 2009 Delmar, Cengage Learning

ALL RIGHTS RESERVED. No part of this work covered by the copyright herein may be reproduced, transmitted, stored or used in any form or by any means graphic, electronic, or mechanical, including but not limited to photocopying, recording, scanning, digitizing, taping, Web distribution, information networks, or information storage and retrieval systems, except as permitted under Section 107 or 108 of the 1976 United States Copyright Act, without the prior written permission of the publisher.

For product information and technology assistance, contact us at
Cengage Learning Customer & Sales Support, 1-800-354-9706

For permission to use material from this text or product,
submit all requests online at **www.cengage.com/permissions**
Further permissions questions can be emailed to
permissionrequest@cengage.com

Library of Congress Control Number: 2007043982

ISBN-13: 978-1-4283-2070-3

ISBN-10: 1-4283-2070-9

Delmar
5 Maxwell Drive
PO Box 8007
Clifton Park, NY 12065-2919
USA

Cengage Learning is a leading provider of customized learning solutions with office locations around the globe, including Singapore, the United Kingdom, Australia, Mexico, Brazil, and Japan. Locate your local office at **international.cengage.com/region**

Cengage Learning products are represented in Canada by Nelson Education, Ltd.

For your lifelong learning solutions, visit **www.cengage.com/delmar**

Visit our corporate website at **www.cengage.com**

Notice to the Reader

Publisher does not warrant or guarantee any of the products described herein or perform any independent analysis in connection with any of the product information contained herein. Publisher does not assume, and expressly disclaims, any obligation to obtain and include information other than that provided to it by the manufacturer. The reader is expressly warned to consider and adopt all safety precautions that might be indicated by the activities described herein and to avoid all potential hazards. By following the instructions contained herein, the reader willingly assumes all risks in connection with such instructions. The publisher makes no representations or warranties of any kind, including but not limited to, the warranties of fitness for particular purpose or merchantability, nor are any such representations implied with respect to the material set forth herein, and the publisher takes no responsibility with respect to such material. The publisher shall not be liable for any special, consequential, or exemplary damages resulting, in whole or part, from the readers' use of, or reliance upon, this material.

Printed in the United States of America
2 3 4 5 XXX 12 11 10 09 08

Brief Contents

Contents

UNIT 3
Safety for the Young Child / 185

UNIT 4
Foods and Nutrients: Basic Concepts / 335

- **Web Links**—An annotated list of Web links is provided for your reference and further research.
- **Sample Quizzes**—Questions are provided online to let you practice and test your knowledge of the material presented in each chapter.
- **Printable Forms and Charts**—Many of the forms and charts that appear in this book are available online for download in PDF format.
- **Educational Resources**—Many of the associations and organizations that support the health, safety, and nutrition of young children are detailed in the Online Companion, including addresses and Web site URLs.
- **Online Early Education Survey**—This survey gives you the opportunity to respond to what features you like and what features you would like to see improved in the Online Companion.

 The Online Companion icon appears at the end of each chapter to prompt you to go online and take advantage of the many features provided.

You can find the Online Companion at *http://www.EarlyChildEd.delmar.cengage.com*.

THE ULTIMATE GOAL

The effect of a child's health, safety, and nutrition on development has been proven beyond a doubt! However, each of these subject areas was once viewed and discussed as separate entities. Research has shown the correlation among them is so intertwined that they must be considered as a collective whole. This notion has also changed our views about health and approaches to health care. We have witnessed a dramatic shift away from the treatment of disease to its prevention—an approach that recognizes the direct relationships which exist among health status, safety, nutrition, social and environmental factors, and informed individuals who accept personal and social responsibility for improving their own health as well as that of others.

ABOUT THE AUTHOR

Lynn R. Marotz received a Ph.D. from the University of Kansas, an M.Ed. from the University of Illinois, and a B.S. in nursing from the University of Wisconsin. She has served as the health and safety coordinator and associate director of the Edna A. Hill Child Development Center (University of Kansas) for 30 years. In addition, she teaches undergraduate and graduate courses in the Department of Applied Behavioral Science that include issues in parenting, health/safety/nutrition for the young child, administration, and foundations of early childhood education. She also provides training in these areas for students in the Early Childhood Teacher Education program. She has contributed chapters in several early childhood and law books and is the co-author of *Developmental Profiles—Pre-Birth to 12 years* and *Motivational Leadership*.

She has also contributed to several articles which have appeared in national parenting magazines. Her research activities focus on childhood obesity and children's health, safety, and nutrition. Her professional contributions include numerous conference presentations, appointments to national, state, and local committees and initiatives, and membership in community organizations and programs that advocate on children's and families' behalf. However, it is her daily interactions with children and their families, students, colleagues, and the endearing qualities of her own family that bring true insight, meaning, and balance to the material in this book.

ACKNOWLEDGMENTS

A special thank you is extended to the instructors, students, and colleagues who use *Health, Safety, and Nutrition for the Young Child* in their classes and continue to offer suggestions for its improvement. I would also like to recognize the contributions of teachers and families who are dedicated to improving the lives of children everywhere.

I also wish to acknowledge Teri Varuska for her commitment to young children and the field of early childhood education and her innovative contributions to the Classroom Corner feature.

I am also grateful to the many "behind-the-scene" people whose encouragement and technical assistance continue to make this book a valued resource for teachers and families. And a big thank you goes out to Robin Reed and the editorial and production staff at Delmar for their insight and expertise in making this an even better edition.

I would also like to express my sincere appreciation to the following reviewers for sharing many valuable comments and suggestions in both this edition and the previous edition of the text:

Seventh Edition Reviewers

Linda Aiken
Southwestern Community College
Sylva, NC

Marla Osband
Santa Monica College
Santa Monica, CA

Marcia Broughton
Angelo State University
San Angelo, TX

Karen Roth
National-Louis University
Skokie, IL

Denise Binkley
Oklahoma City University
Oklahoma City, OK

Patricia Weaver
Fayetteville Technical College
Fayetteville, NC

Kathy Ann Betters
Genesee Community College
Batavia, NY

Mary Clare Munger
Amarillo College
Canyon, TX

Ithel Jones
Florida State University
Tallahassee, FL

Sixth Edition Reviewers

Linda S. Estes, Ed.D.
St. Charles Community College
St. Peters, MO

Teresa Frazier
Thomas Nelson Community College
Hampton, VA

Jennifer Gutowsky, M.Ed.
San Jacinto College North
Houston, TX

Judith Ann Schust
Professor Emeritus
Harold Washington College
Chicago, IL

Cynthia Waters
Upper Iowa University
Fayette, IA 52142

Becky Wyatt
Murray State College
Tishomingo, OK 73460

THE ORIGINAL IN A SEVENTH EDITION

The seventh edition of *Health, Safety, and Nutrition for the Young Child* continues to build on the success of previous editions. This best-selling, full-color text was the first of its kind to address all three essential components of children's wellness in one book:

- promoting children's **health** through awareness, effective practices, and health education
- creating and maintaining *safe learning environments*
- meeting children's essential *nutritional needs* through thoughtful meal planning and nutrition education

THE INTENDED AUDIENCE

First and foremost, *Health, Safety, and Nutrition for the Young Child* is written on behalf of young children everywhere. Ultimately, it is the children who benefit from having families and teachers who understand and know how to protect and promote their safety and well-being. In the seventh edition, the term *families* refers to the many different caring environments in which children are currently being raised and that may or may not include their biological parents. The term *teachers* is used inclusively to describe all adults who care for and work with young children—including educators, therapists, coaches, camp leaders, administrators, legislators, and concerned citizens, whether they work in early education centers, home-based programs, community recreation activities, public schools, or after-school programs. The term *teacher* also acknowledges the important educational role that families play in their children's daily lives. Its use also acknowledges the educators who dedicate their lives to children's learning.

Health, Safety, and Nutrition for the Young Child is intended for students, new and experienced teachers, families, and colleagues who work in any role that touches children's lives. The material is based on the most current research and reflects the latest developments in health, safety, and nutrition as well as their application in multiple settings. It is the author's hope that, after reading and studying the material addressed in this text, teachers, families, and professional colleagues will understand and value the important role they play in fostering children's wellness.

ORGANIZATION AND CONTENT

Three major topical areas are addressed in this new edition: children's health; safety concerns and management; and nutrition (basic and applied). This arrangement offers individual instructors maximum flexibility in designing their courses and personalizing content. However, the interrelatedness of these three areas cannot be overlooked despite their artificial separation. The seventh edition of *Health, Safety, and Nutrition for the Young Child* continues to emphasize collective ways in which families and teachers promote and influence children's well-being. Information on many topics included in previous editions, such as asthma, allergies, SIDS, childhood obesity, fetal alcohol syndrome, the Food Guide Pyramid, food safety, and menu planning has been expanded and updated to reflect the latest research developments and applications. Several topics of recent concern have also been addressed, such as West Nile virus, sun safety, bullying, building resiliency in children, improving security, and food allergies. Additional information on children with special needs and school-aged children has been incorporated throughout the book to address the interest and needs of teachers who work with children of all ages and abilities.

This new edition is written in a clear, concise, and thought-provoking manner. Extensive checklists, tables, and lesson plans are included in each chapter to help students recognize and grasp fundamental concepts. These features also make it easy for busy teachers to access and use this information in their own programs. Additional learning activities have also been included in each chapter to encourage teachers and families to devote more time to educating children about important health, safety, and nutrition issues. As always, emphasis is placed on establishing quality learning environments and best practices that respect the diversity of settings, families, and teachers who care for young children. This comprehensive book is a resource that no teacher (new or experienced) should be without!

NEW TO THIS EDITION

Front-of-Book CD:

The CD bound in the front of the book contains both Word® and PDF files of the forms found in the text. These can be printed and filled in as part of classroom exercises or used as illustrations of the concepts in the text.

SPECIAL FEATURES

Several special features are included in this seventh edition to improve the reader's understanding of fundamental concepts and their application in contemporary educational settings:

- Focus on Families—This feature is designed to assist teachers in offering more family/parent education and to reinforce the collaborative efforts of families and teachers in promoting children's health, safety, and nutrition. The information and suggestions included in this feature will help teachers bridge the gap between knowledge and its application, and can be used in a variety of ways, such as in newsletters or program handbooks; for discussion during conferences or family/parent meetings; or posting the information on bulletin boards or a program's Web site.

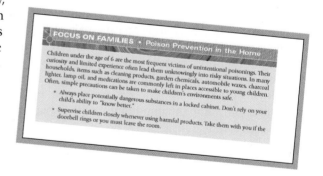

Although topics showcased in this feature have been chosen to address select issues and problems, teachers are encouraged to identify others that are unique to the children, families, and communities they serve. The author also hopes this feature will serve as a model and that teachers will continue their efforts to provide families with information about new developments.

■ Fast Foods and Children—Concerns about the increasing incidence of adult and childhood obesity and type 2 diabetes continue to raise questions about the relationship between health problems and fast food consumption. Web addresses for many of the largest fast-food chains are included in Appendix A to provide the reader with easy access and up-to-date nutrient information. The need to counter the negative effects of media persuasion that is often aimed at young children is also addressed.

■ New Food Pyramid—Information on the new Food Pyramid and other nutritional tools has been updated to reflect the latest developments. Greater emphasis has also been placed on the importance of increasing children's physical activity given the continued upward trends in childhood and adult obesity.

■ Teacher Checklists—are included in every chapter. They provide teachers with an efficient way to access critical information about key issues and best practices. Beginning practitioners will find these resource lists especially efficient and helpful.

■ National Health Education Standards for Students (Grades K–4)—The concept of preventive health is built on a foundation of sound, ongoing education. The national standards listed in Appendix C are part of a unified framework for guiding children's educational experiences in the areas of health, safety, and nutrition.

■ Classroom Corner .... Teacher Activities—This resource feature reinforces the need to provide children with ongoing health, safety, and nutrition learning experiences as an integral part of their everyday education. Lesson plans are included in each chapter (except in 12 and 21 where lesson plans already abound) to help teachers translate chapter content into meaningful lessons for children.

■ Monthly Calendar of National Health, Safety and Nutrition Observances—A month-by-month listing of national observances and Web site resources are included in this feature to help teachers plan corresponding learning experiences for children.

■ Epilogue—This final section acknowledges that many new developments and opportunities for improving children's wellness still need to be addressed.

■ A Children's Book List—Reading to children not only enhances their literacy skills but can also be an effective method for teaching about health, safety, and nutrition. A list of book titles is included in Appendix G and address topics such as dental health, mental health, self-care, safety, and nutrition to reinforce learning in these areas and encourage families and teachers to read often to children.

■ Reflective Thoughts—This feature is designed to encourage students and teachers to examine their personal attitudes and practices based on the concepts presented in each chapter. Thought-provoking questions are included to stimulate individual reflection and/or class discussion.

- **Issues to Consider**—This feature showcases current events and is designed to help the reader relate basic principles of health, safety, and nutrition presented in each chapter to everyday situations and settings. A series of questions is provided to stimulate individual thought and/or group discussion.

- **Case Studies**—Case studies have been provided in each chapter to encourage the application of basic concepts to everyday practice. Questions are designed to guide individual thought and/or group discussion.

- **Helpful Web Resources**—The important role that the Internet and technology play in today's world is recognized in this feature. Web addresses are provided at the end of each chapter for readers who wish to continue exploring topics presented in the text.

PEDAGOGY

Each chapter includes pedagogical features based on sound educational principles that support student learning and facilitate mastery. They also acknowledge that students have different needs, abilities, and learning styles:

1. **Terms to Know** are listed in order of appearance at the beginning of each chapter, in color where they appear within the chapter, in a running glossary at the bottom of the page on which they appear, and again in the glossary at the back of the book. Reinforcement and cross-referencing enhance comprehension.

2. **Objectives** appear at the beginning of each chapter to help the reader focus on key issues and areas of learning.

3. Bulleted lists alert the reader to important information and provide easy access to specific examples.

4. Real-life, colorful photographs taken on location at centers and schools show children as they work and play in developmentally appropriate settings.

5. Full-color illustrations and tables reinforce important chapter content.

6. **Reflective Thoughts** encourage the reader to examine personal attitudes and practices based on the concepts presented in each chapter. Thought-provoking questions are included.

7. **Issues to Consider** is a feature that showcases current events

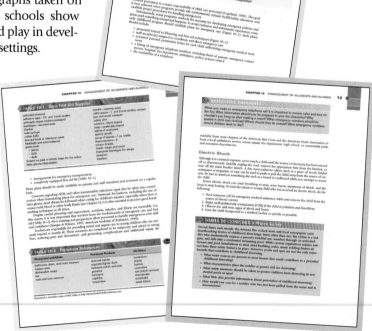

e-Resource

This feature is new to the seventh edition and contains the Instructor's Manual, Computerized Test Bank, Image Library and PowerPoint Slides.

- Instructor's Manual – The Instructor's Manual on the e-Resource is an electronic version of the print Instructor's Manual.
- Computerized Text Bank – The e-Resource includes a Computerized Test Bank containing multiple-choice, true-false, short answer and completion questions for each chapter. Instructors have immediate access to the questions in a format that is versatile and easy to use for creating customized printed tests, online tests, or computer-based tests.
- PowerPoint Presentations – This feature provides instructors with an additional resource tool that can reduce preparation time and support student mastery, especially for the visual learner. Chapter content is presented in an organized and attractive format and instructors can customize their presentations by adding or deleting slides.
- Image Library – An Image Library of 35 photos and tables from the seventh edition can be added to PowerPoint presentations or exported into other documents for handouts or overheads.

Web Tutor

The Web Tutor to accompany the seventh edition of *Health, Safety, and Nutrition for the Young Child* allows you to take learning beyond the classroom. This online courseware is designed to complement the text and allows students to better manage their time, prepare for exams, organize their notes, communicate, and much more. Special features include Chapter Learning Objectives, Online Course Preparation, Study Sheets, Glossary, Discussion Topics, Frequently Asked Questions, Online Class Notes, Online Chapter Quizzes, and Web Links related to chapter content. Printing features allow students to print their own customized study guides.

A benefit for instructors as well as students, the Web Tutor allows for online discussion with the instructor and other class members, real-time chat to enable virtual office hours and encourage collaborative learning environments, a calendar of syllabus information for easy reference, e-mail connections to facilitate communication among classmates and between students and instructors, and customization tools that help educators tailor their course to fit their needs by adding or changing content.

WebTutor allows you to extend your reach beyond the classroom and is available on either the WebCT or Blackboard platform. Your students may also access sample quizzes created by Delmar, a part of Cengage Learning, from its Web site for Online Companion for Students at *http://www. EarlyChildEd.delmar.cengage.com.*

Online Companion

The Online Companion to accompany the seventh edition of *Health, Safety, and Nutrition for the Young Child* is your link to early childhood education on the Internet. The Online Companion contains many features that integrate technology with opportunities to reinforce and expand your understanding of children's health, safety, and nutrition and include:

- **Critical Thinking Forum**—In this section you have the opportunity to respond to "Reflective Thoughts" and "Issues to Consider" concepts. Various health, safety, and nutrition scenarios and thought-provoking questions test your understanding of the content provided in the text. You can share your ideas with classmates and communicate informally with your instructor online.
- **Web Activities**—These activities direct you to a Web site(s) where you can conduct additional research, broaden your understanding of contemporary issues, and learn to apply information about children's health, safety, and nutrition to everyday settings.

and is designed to help you apply basic principles of health, safety, and nutrition to real-life situations. Questions are included to stimulate individual thought or group discussion.

8. **Classroom Corner** showcases lesson plans that reflect the application of chapter content. Step-by-step procedures, materials lists, and discussion questions are included.

9. The **Summary**, presented in a bulleted list format, concludes each chapter and is followed by:
   - **Application Activities**—individual and group projects to reinforce learning
   - **Chapter Review Questions**—allow students to test their own comprehension
   - **References**—for additional reading and research
   - **Helpful Web Resources**—provide links to additional information sources and materials

10. **Appendices**, designed to be used in conjunction with all 21 chapters, include:
    - *Appendix A:* Nutrient Information: Fast-Food Vendor Web Sites
    - *Appendix B:* Growth and BMI Charts for Boys and Girls
    - *Appendix C:* National Health Education Standards for Students (Grades K-4)
    - *Appendix D:* Federal Food Programs
    - *Appendix E:* Monthly Calendar: Health, Safety & Nutrition Observances
    - *Appendix F:* One-Week Sample Menu
    - *Appendix G:* Children's Book List

A comprehensive glossary and index conclude the text with reader-friendly cross-references.

DESIGN

We were proud to present the first full-color, early childhood textbook and we continue that tradition with a beautiful contemporary design in this edition. All new colors and attractive unit and chapter openers invite the reader into the book. Multicultural photographs, all taken on location at early childhood centers and schools, plus accompanying graphic illustrations contribute to the visual appeal of this text.

ANCILLARIES

Instructor's Manual

The Instructor's Manual that accompanies the seventh edition includes answers to chapter review questions and case studies. Additional questions are provided to guide class discussions or to be used for testing purposes. A list of multimedia resources is also included.

CHAPTER 1

Interrelationship of Health, Safety, and Nutrition

OBJECTIVES

After studying this chapter, you should be able to:

- Describe how health, safety, and nutrition are interrelated.
- Explain why a person's state of well-being is continually changing.
- Describe ways that teachers can promote children's health.
- Discuss how adults influence children's early attitudes and health practices.
- Identify three factors that affect children's safety.
- Discuss three current health initiatives designed to improve children's well-being.

TERMS TO KNOW

prevention	health	nutrients
preventive health	heredity	resistance
habits	predisposition	malnutrition
food insecurity	sedentary	obesity

Recall for a moment the special memories you have of a recent trip. Perhaps they are of majestic mountain scenery, a crimson sunset, brilliant turquoise waters, the aroma of salt marsh or pine forest, or an especially tasty meal in a special restaurant. Such experiences inevitably change us in some way. They may cause us to question, think, and/or act differently than we did prior to the experience.

We intend to take you on one of those memorable journeys as you read through the pages of this book—one that will change what you may already know about children's health, safety, and nutrition needs and one that is likely to change the way in which you view and address these areas in the future. It is our goal to illustrate and emphasize the important and influential role you play in shaping children's lives.

Many of you may already be familiar with some of the topics that will be discussed as a result of personal interest or work experiences. We hope to build on this foundation and to expand your

Health, Safety, and Nutrition: An Introduction

understanding of issues critical to children's well-being and their ability to become productive citizens. We also want to provoke your curiosity about these topics so that you will continue to explore and learn about new developments as they unfold. And, ultimately, we want to challenge you to use this information to implement changes in your teaching practices and programs. So, if you are ready, let our journey begin!

THE PREVENTIVE HEALTH CONCEPT

Our ideas about disease and our reliance on the health care system have undergone a significant shift in recent years. Rising medical costs and the realization that doctors are not able to cure every disease and health condition have contributed to an interest in **prevention**. Conclusive research evidence has also demonstrated that adapting healthy lifestyles and behaviors can lead to improved health (Kennedy, 2006; Bhargava, 2002; U.S. Department of Health and Human Services, 2002; Kavanagh, 2001).

The concept of **preventive health** recognizes that individuals are able to influence many factors that affect personal health (Figure 1–1). It implies that children and adults must begin to assume greater responsibility for developing and maintaining attitudes, **habits**, behaviors, and

FIGURE 1–1

Examples of preventive health practices.

A preventive health approach involves a combination of personal practices and national initiatives.

On a personal scale, these include:
- eating a diet low in animal fats
- consuming a wide variety of fruits, vegetables, and grains
- exercising on a daily basis
- practicing good oral hygiene
- using proper hand washing techniques
- avoiding substance abuse (e.g., alcohol, tobacco, drugs)
- keeping immunizations up-to-date

On a national scale, these include:
- regulating vehicle emissions
- preventing chemical dumping
- inspecting food supplies
- measuring air pollution
- providing immunization programs
- fluoridating drinking water
- monitoring disease outbreaks

---

prevention – *measures taken to avoid an event such as an accident or illness from occurring; implies the ability to anticipate circumstances and behaviors.*
preventive health – *engaging in behaviors that help to maintain and enhance one's health status; includes concern for certain social issues affecting the populations' health and environment.*
habits – *the unconscious repetitions of a particular behavior.*

FIGURE 1–2

Children can begin to develop preventive health behaviors.

choices that promote good health (Earls, 1998). This includes practices such as establishing good dietary habits (eating more fruits and vegetables), practicing safety behaviors (wearing seat belts and limiting sun exposure), exercising regularly, and seeking early treatment for occasional illness and injury.

The early years are an ideal time for children to begin establishing preventive behaviors that will encourage a healthy lifestyle (Figure 1–2). Teachers and families can capitalize on children's endless curiosity and take advantage of learning opportunities throughout the day—planned as well as spontaneous—to teach good health, safety, and nutrition practices.

The concept of health promotion also implies that individuals will assume some responsibility for social and environmental issues that affect the short- and long-term quality of everyone's health, safety, and nutritional well-being, including:

- poverty and homelessness
- **food insecurity**
- inequitable access to medical and dental care
- adverse effects of media advertising
- substance abuse (e.g., alcohol, tobacco, drugs)
- pesticides and chemical additives in food
- child abuse and neglect
- air and water pollution
- discrimination based on diversity
- unsafe neighborhoods

In addition to helping children learn about these complex issues, adults must also demonstrate their commitment by supporting social actions, policies, and programs that contribute to healthier environments and lifestyles for society as a whole.

National Health Initiatives

The benefits of preventive health care continue to attract increased public attention. This change has been particularly notable with respect to young children. Poor standards of health, safety, and nutrition are seen as significant barriers to children's ability to learn and to ultimately become healthy, productive adults. As a result, several large-scale programs have been established in recent years to improve children's access to preventive service. Descriptions of several initiatives follow; information about federal food programs for children is located in Appendix D.

Healthy People 2010 In 1990, the U.S. Department of Health and Human Services issued an agenda entitled *Healthy People 2000: National Health Promotion and Disease Prevention Objectives,* which outlined 22 national health priorities, many of which addressed the needs of children (Office of Disease Prevention & Health Promotion, 2000). This document was originally designed to improve the nation's standard of health through increased public awareness,

food insecurity – *uncertain or limited access to a reliable source of food.*

dissemination of health information, interagency collaboration, and community participation. It also placed significant emphasis on the need for individuals to assume active responsibility for their personal health. Many states adopted these early objectives and modified their programs to meet the unique needs of their local populations. Government agencies also used these objectives for funding purposes, monitoring the health status of the U.S. population and reporting measurable improvements in their well-being.

Healthy People 2010 is an updated version of the original document that continues to reinforce the philosophy of health promotion for achieving improved well-being. Goals and objectives are inclusive and target individuals of all ages and backgrounds (Figure 1–3). They continue to emphasize personal responsibility and the need for coordinating the efforts of public and private organizations and agencies (Pamuk, Wagener, & Molia, 2004) (Table 1–1). Individual states are expected to assume a critical role in this process through expansion of current programs and implementation of new initiatives. Many of the 2010 goals and objectives have direct application for schools and early childhood programs and can easily be incorporated into existing efforts to protect and enhance children's health. For example, teaching children positive ways of expressing anger or frustration and maintaining environments respective of individual differences contribute directly to the promotion of children's mental health. Serving nutritious foods, making physical activity a daily priority, and creating safe learning environments also reflect teachers' understanding and commitment to promoting children's healthy growth and development.

FIGURE 1–3

Healthy People 2010.

National Children's Agenda A similar Canadian initiative aimed at health promotion for children is outlined in a report titled *A National Children's Agenda: Developing a Shared Vision.* This document presents a comprehensive agenda of goals and objectives for addressing children's critical health care and safety needs. It also embraces the importance of the early years and supports the vision of creating a unified approach to helping children achieve their full potential.

State Children's Health Insurance Program (SCHIP) Legislation included in the Balanced Budget Act of 1997, also know as Title XXI, established a national health insurance program for uninsured income-eligible children. This program is administered by individual states through annual appropriations. To qualify for funding, states must submit a Child Health Plan that describes how the program will be administered, how eligibility will be determined, and how eligible children will be located.

TABLE 1–1 Healthy People 2010 Objectives

Areas targeted for improving children's health include the following:

• physical activity and fitness	• unintentional injury
• nutrition—overweight and obesity	• immunizations
• substance abuse	• oral health
• mental health	• maternal and infant health
• violent and abusive behavior	• access to health care
• elimination of lead poisoning	

Approximately 6.1 million children were enrolled in SCHIP in 2005, although many more children are eligible to participate in this program (Centers for Medicare & Medicaid Services, 2006). Services covered by this plan include free or low-cost medical and dental care, immunizations, prescriptions, mental health treatment, and hospitalization. Improving children's access to preventive health care contributes to a better quality of life and ability to learn. It also results in significant cost-saving benefits that can be attributed to early identification and treatment of children's medical and developmental problems (Davidoff, Kenny, & Dubay, 2005). The 2007 reauthorization of SCHIP requested additional funding to serve more low-income children, improve the quality of health care, increase accessibility, and encourage communities to improve their outreach efforts.

Healthy Child Care America   The primary objective of the Healthy Child Care America (HCCA) Initiative is quality improvement in early childhood programs. HCCA, supported by the U.S. Department of Health and Human Services, the Child Care Bureau, and the Maternal and Child Health Bureau, was established in 1995 to coordinate the mutual interests of health professions, early education professionals, and families in addressing children's health and safety needs in out-of-home programs. The program is administered by the American Academy of Pediatrics (AAP) and has been instrumental in launching several large-scale educational campaigns, including Moving Kids Safely in Child Care, Back to Sleep (for parents), and Back to Sleep in Child Care Settings (2003). Grant-supported offices, located in every state, have been established to evaluate and strengthen existing community infrastructure and to assist with new initiatives for improving children's health and safety in early childhood programs and access to preventive health care.

National Health and Safety Performance Standards for Child Care
National concern for children's welfare also resulted in a collaborative project between the American Academy of Pediatrics (AAP) and the American Public Health Association (APHA) to develop health, safety, and nutrition guidelines for out-of-home child care programs. The resulting document, *National Health and Safety Performance Standards: Guidelines for Out-of-Home Child Care Programs,* provides detailed quality standards and procedures for ensuring children's health and safety while they are in organized care (Table 1–2) (American Public Health Association & American Academy of Pediatrics, 2002). The current system of child care regulation allows individual states to establish their own licensing standards, which has contributed to significant differences in quality.

TABLE 1–2 National Health and Safety Performance Standards

Comprehensive guidelines address the following areas of child care:

- staffing – child staff ratios, credentials, and training
- activities for healthy development – supervision, transportation, behavior management, partnerships with families, health education
- health promotion and protection – sanitation, special medical conditions, illness management
- nutrition and food services – nutritional requirements, food safety, nutrition education
- facilities, supplies, equipment, and transportation – space and equipment requirements, indoor/outdoor play, maintenance, transportation
- infectious diseases – respiratory, bloodborne, skin
- children with special needs – inclusion, IDEA eligibility, facility modifications, assessment
- administration – health/safety policies, personnel policies, documentation, contracts
- recommendations for licensing and community action – regulatory agencies, policy

The word *diversity* appears frequently in the media and conversation. What does the term *diversity* mean to you? What biases do you have that would influence your attitudes toward people of diverse backgrounds? Why do you think you have developed these feelings? Consider how you might go about changing any personal biases. What steps can you take to help children develop positive attitudes toward all people?

This project was an attempt to develop and recommend standards that would improve uniformity and consistency. The National Association for the Education of Young Children (NAEYC) has developed similar guidelines for their quality accreditation program (NAEYC, 2006).

No Child Left Behind The importance of children's health and learning during their earliest years received one of its strongest acknowledgments with the passage of the No Child Left Behind Act of 2001. This bill authorized significant reforms of the K–12 educational system and strengthens partnerships with Head Start, Even Start, and early education programs in center- and home-based settings. It recognizes families as children's first and most important teachers, the valued contribution of early childhood care and education programs, and the need to foster early literacy skills (understanding and using language) to ensure children's success in school. In addition, this bill authorized additional funding to cover child care costs for low-income families and to expand prenatal services for pregnant women and children's health services for improved well-being. Parent education programs and subsidized research are also important components of this initiative designed to improve the quality of children's care and education. Some of the law's controversial features were addressed with the 2007 reauthorization.

The National Children's Study One of the most comprehensive studies of children's health ever undertaken in the U.S. is currently in progress (National Children's Study, 2006). The National Institutes of Child Health and Human Development is conducting this longitudinal study which will follow over 100,000 children from birth to age 21 to examine environmental effects on children's health and how they might contribute to disease. The study will eventually yield a large information database about children's growth and development, differences in access to health care, and the incidence of disease that will be useful for policy formulation and service interventions.

Many states and professional organizations, such as Head Start, Parents as Teachers, and Zero to Three have also developed programs that focus on young children's health and nutrition needs. National concerns about childhood obesity have prompted many schools and school districts to develop similar programs that target improved nutrition and physical activity (Figure 1–4).

FIGURE 1–4

Many schools have developed programs to improve children's eating and physical activity.

HEALTH

Definitions of **health** are as numerous as the factors that affect it. Historically, the term has referred only to an individual's physical well-being and the medical treatment of disorders. Today's broader concept of health encompasses more than the absence of illness and disease. International groups such as the World Health Organization recognize health as a state or quality of complete physical, emotional, social, economic, cultural, and spiritual well-being. Each element is assumed to make an equally important contribution to health. Furthermore, factors affecting the quality of one element are known to have an effect on the others. For example, a stressful home environment may contribute to a child's frequent illnesses, stomachaches, or headaches. Also, a child's chronic illness or disability may have a profound effect on the family's emotional, financial, social, and physical well-being.

This new definition of health also recognizes that children and adults do not live in isolation but are important members of multiple groups, including family, peer, neighborhood, ethnic, cultural, recreational, and community. Social interaction and participation in these groups often affects, and is affected by, the state of an individual's health. Consider, for example, the recent outbreaks of measles and whooping cough and how quickly these communicable illnesses spread through daily contacts and the ease of modern-day travel. In each case, the environment served as an important and influential factor in both the spread and control of the disease.

Factors Influencing Children's Health

Health is a complex state determined by ongoing interactions between biological material inherited at conception and environmental factors (Figure 1–5). For example, a baby's immediate

FIGURE 1–5

Health is an interactive process.

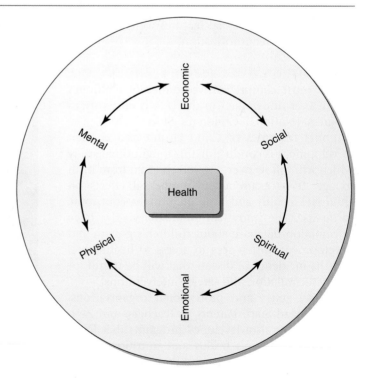

---

health – *a state of wellness. Complete physical, mental, social, and emotional well-being; the quality of one element affects the state of the others.*

FIGURE 1–6

Heredity sets the limits for growth, development, and health potential.

and long-term health is affected by the mother's personal health practices and state of health during pregnancy: her diet; use or avoidance of alcohol, tobacco, and certain medications; routine medical supervision; and exposure to communicable illnesses. Mothers who do not follow healthy practices during pregnancy are more likely to give birth to babies who are born prematurely, have low birth weight, or experience a range of special needs (Kotelchuck, 2006; Dillard, 2004). These children face a significantly greater risk of lifelong health problems and early death. In contrast, a child who grows up in a nurturing family and experiences a nutritious diet, safe environment, and opportunities for learning and recreation is more likely to enjoy good health.

Heredity   Characteristics transmitted from parents to their children at the time of conception determine all of the genetic traits of a new, unique individual. **Heredity** sets the limits for growth, development, and health potential (Figure 1–6). It explains, in part, why children in one family are short while those from another family are tall or why some individuals have allergies or need glasses while others do not.

Understanding how heredity influences health can also be useful for predicting an inherited tendency, or **predisposition**, to certain health problems, such as heart disease, deafness, cancer, diabetes, allergies, or mental health disorders. However, it should be noted that having a family history of heart disease or diabetes, for example, does not necessarily mean that a child will develop these conditions. Many lifestyle factors, including physical activity, diet, sleep, and stress levels, interact with genetic material (genes) to determine whether a child will ultimately develop heart disease or any number of other chronic health disorders.

Environment   Although heredity provides the basic building materials that determine one's health, environment plays an equally important role. Environment encompasses a combination of physical, psychological, social, economic, and cultural factors. Collectively, these factors influence the way individuals perceive and respond to their surroundings. In turn, these responses affect one's physical, social, emotional, and economic choices and behaviors (Charlesworth, 2004). For example, two bicyclists set off on a ride: one wears a helmet, the other does not. The choices each has made could potentially have quite different outcomes if they were to be involved in a collision. In turn, if the cyclist sustained injuries as the result of her decision not to wear a helmet, this could have significant health, economic, social, and psychological consequences.

Examples of environmental factors that promote healthy outcomes include:

■ following a healthful diet
■ participating in physical activity and recreation
■ getting adequate rest
■ having access to medical and dental care

---

heredity – *the transmission of certain genetic material and characteristics from parents to child at the time of conception.*

predisposition – *having an increased chance or susceptibility.*

- reducing stress
- residing in homes, child care facilities, schools, and workplaces that are clean and safe
- having opportunities to form stable and respectful relationships

There are also many factors that have a negative effect on health. For example, exposure to chemicals and pollution, abuse, illness, obesity, prenatal alcohol, **sedentary** lifestyles, poverty, stress, food insecurity, violence, unhealthy dietary choices, and lack of medical and dental care can interfere with optimal growth and development.

SAFETY

Safety refers to the behaviors and practices that protect children and adults from risk or injury. Safety is of special concern with young children because their well-being is often directly affected by environmental conditions. Unintentional injury is the single leading cause of death among children birth to 14 years in the United States and Canada (Birken, et al., 2006; NCIPC, 2006). Sadly, many of these injuries are preventable. As greater numbers of children with special needs and diverse abilities are included in early education programs, the need for high standards of safety management becomes increasingly important. Efforts to prevent unintentional injury and death must be a major responsibility of every adult who works with, or cares for, young children (Garzon, 2005; Marotz, 2000).

Accidents resulting in even minor injuries have an immediate effect on a child's health. Serious injury can cause an extended absence and temporarily interrupt a child's learning and participation in daily activities. It may also result in added medical expense and increased stress for the child's family. Guidelines for creating and maintaining safe environments will be discussed in Chapters 8 and 9.

Factors Affecting Children's Safety

Providing for children's safety requires a keen awareness of the skills and abilities typical of each developmental stage (Allen & Marotz, 2007; Berk, 2005). Teachers can use this information to identify and correct sources of potential harm in children's environments (Aronson, 2002). For example, knowing that an infant enjoys hand-to-mouth activities should alert teachers to continuously monitor the environment for small objects or poisonous substances that could be ingested. Recognizing the toddler's curiosity and desire to explore should make adults concerned about such things as children wandering away, pedestrian safety, unsupervised sources of water, and availability of unsafe play materials. Adults should also be alert to children's health and sensory problems (especially vision and hearing) that may contribute to unintentional injury.

Limits or rules offer another important form of protection. Rules stated in simple terms are easy for children to understand and provide the type of positive guidance that encourages mastery of personal safety skills. Frequent reminders and consistent enforcement also make rules more meaningful for young children. However, teachers must never become overly trusting of a child who has supposedly "learned the rules." Children's spontaneity often takes precedence over their learned behaviors. Consequently, awareness and efforts to protect children's safety are a continuous adult responsibility. It also requires families and teachers to be aware of personal limitations and circumstances that could interfere with their ability to effectively protect children from injury.

---

sedentary – *unusually slow or sluggish; a lifestyle that implies a general lack of physical activity.*

❈ NUTRITION

Nutrition can be defined as "all processes used by an adult or child to take in food and to digest, absorb, transport, utilize, and excrete food substances" (Endres, Rockwell & Mense, 2004). What children and adults eat has a direct effect on their nutritional status, behavior, and health. Food yields chemical components called **nutrients** that are essential for life. Nutrients play critical roles in a variety of essential functions, including:

- supplying energy
- growth and development
- normal behavior
- resistance to illness and infection
- tissue repair

A daily intake of essential nutrients depends on eating a variety of foods in adequate amounts. However, the quality of one's diet can be affected by a number of environmental factors, such as financial resources and availability, transportation, geographical location, cultural preferences, convenience, and knowledge of good nutrition. Most children in the United States live in a time and place where food is reasonably abundant. Yet, there is increasing concern about the number of children who may not be getting enough to eat or whose diets do not include the right types of foods (Forum on Child and Family Statistics, 2006; Rose & Bodor, 2006). Also, because many young children spend the majority of their waking hours in out-of-home child care arrangements or school classrooms, special efforts must be made to provide essential nutrients that are needed for optimal growth and good health. Programs can meet this goal by serving meals and snacks that include a variety of nutrient-dense foods and encouraging adults to model healthful eating habits.

Children's Nutrition and Its Effect on Behavior and Illness

Children's nutritional status also affects their behavior (Figure 1–7). Well-nourished children are more alert, attentive, and better able to benefit from physical activity and learning experiences (Jyoti, Frongillo, & Jones, 2005). Poorly nourished children may be quiet and withdrawn, or hyperactive and disruptive during class activities (Whitaker, et al., 2006). They are also more prone to accidental

FIGURE 1–7

Nutritional status also affects children's behavior.

nutrients – *the components or substances that are found in food.*

injury because they are less alert and have poorer response times. Children who are overweight may face a range of social, emotional, and physical problems (Braet, Mervielde, & Vandereycken, 2003). They often have difficulty participating in physical activities and may be subjected to ridicule, emotional stress, and exclusion by peers (Belfield, 2003; Latner & Stunkard, 2003; Davidson & Birch, 2001).

Children's **resistance** to infection and illness is also directly influenced by their nutritional status (Trahms & Pipes, 2000). Well-nourished children are more resistant to illness and recover more quickly when they are sick (Kennedy, 2006). Children who are poorly nourished are more susceptible to infections and illness and often take longer to get well. Repeated illness can lessen children's appetites which, in turn, limits their intake of nutrients important for the recovery process. Thus, poor nutrition creates a cycle of illness, poorer nutritional status, and lowered resistance to illness.

Malnutrition **Malnutrition** is always a serious problem, but it is especially harmful for infants and young children. A lack of essential nutrients and adequate calories can severely interfere with a child's early growth and brain development. These harmful effects cannot be entirely reversed even when children are fed a healthy diet later on (Bryan, et al., 2004; Gordon, 1997). Although malnutrition is commonly thought to be associated with poverty, food insecurity, and ignorance, this is not always true. Even children of middle- and upper-income families may be malnourished simply because of poor food choices. Frequent fast food meals, snacking habits, unrealistic concerns regarding weight control, and skipped meals limit the variety of foods and nutrients that are consumed (Satter, 2006). However, there are some children who may develop malnutrition as a result of a chronic health condition or disease.

Obesity

Another significant nutritional concern is the recent and dramatic increase in childhood **obesity**. Studies indicate that approximately 25 percent of school-aged children are either overweight or obese (Haque, et al, 2006; Johnson, et al., 2006). Excessive intake of calories, sugars, and dietary fat, coupled with a significant decrease in physical activity, has spelled trouble for many young children (Mendoza, et al., 2006). Not only do overweight children experience immediate health and psychological consequences, but many are also developing serious long-term health problems, such as type 2 diabetes and heart disease which are conditions not previously seen at this age (Daniels, 2006; Hannon, et al., 2006).

▓ HEALTH, SAFETY, AND NUTRITION: AN INTERDEPENDENT RELATIONSHIP

Health, safety, and nutrition are closely related and dependent on one another. The status of each has a direct effect on the quality of the others. For example, children who get all of their essential nutrients from a healthful diet will have energy for active play, exploration, and social interaction, and a decreased risk of serious injury and illness. In contrast, a child whose diet lacks adequate iron may develop anemia. This can result in a diminished alertness that affects their safety and ability to learn, fatigue, and loss of appetite. A lack of interest in food may

---

resistance – *the ability to avoid infection or illness.*
malnutrition – *prolonged inadequate or excessive intake of nutrients and/or calories required by the body.*
obesity – *a condition characterized by an excessive accumulation of fat.*

further compromise the child's intake of iron. In other words, nutritional status affects the quality of children's health which, in turn, influences nutritional requirements needed to restore and maintain good health.

Good nutrition also plays an important role in injury prevention. The child or adult who arrives at school having eaten little or no breakfast may experience low blood sugar. This can result in decreased alertness and slowed reaction times which can cause an individual to be more accident prone and less able to avoid serious injury. Children and adults who are overweight are also more likely to experience accidental injury. Excess weight can restrict physical activity, slow reaction times, and cause children and adults to tire more quickly.

IMPLICATIONS FOR TEACHERS

Today, more than 70 percent of all children younger than age six have mothers who are currently working outside of the home (U.S. Department of Labor, 2006). As a result, early childhood and after-school programs serve more children now than at any other time in history. Because many children spend the majority of the day away from their families, it is important that teachers be knowledgeable about children's health, safety, and nutrition needs. Activities, environments, meal planning, and supervision should reflect a strong commitment to promoting each child's optimal growth and development (Gupta, et al., 2005). Programs can fulfill this commitment to children by providing the following:

- protection
- services
- education

Protection

Educational programs and teaching professionals have a moral and legal obligation to protect the children in their care. The physical arrangement of all spaces occupied by children should receive utmost attention. Planning of indoor and outdoor areas must be carried out carefully to provide environments that are safe, stimulating, and designed to meet children's developmental needs. Daily inspections of indoor and outdoor areas, prompt removal of hazardous materials, and careful selection of developmentally appropriate equipment and learning activities help to prevent accidents. Appropriate supervision and the establishment of rules also reduce the chances for unintentional injury.

Programs must also establish policies and procedures that address and safeguard children's health, safety, and nutritional needs. These policies should reflect the goals and philosophy of an individual program, and address important issues such as:

- Who is responsible for providing first aid?
- What types of emergency information should be obtained from families?
- When and how are emergency procedures, such as fire and tornado drills, earthquake preparedness, and building security, practiced with children and staff?

State child care licensing requirements often require programs to adopt additional health policies, such as:

- How are sanitary conditions in the classrooms and food preparation areas to be monitored?
- Which staff members will be permitted to administer medications? Will a physician's prescription be required before over-the-counter medications can be given?
- How will children's medical procedures, such as nebulizer treatments, catheter irrigations, or dressing changes, be handled? Who will perform these routines?

ISSUES TO CONSIDER • Teacher's Role in Children's Health Care

Legislation has opened classrooms to children with a diverse range of abilities and disabilities. Recently, the family of a student who requires continuous monitoring for his complex physical needs challenged school officials in the U.S. Supreme Court for refusing to cover the cost of these services. School officials believed the boy's medical needs were beyond their expertise, financial capabilities, and time limitations. However, the courts upheld the student's right to attend school and to have all necessary services provided by the school district. As increasing number of children who require some form of medical assistance are being served in inclusive programs, teachers are beginning to ask serious questions about their role in, and responsibility for, administering these procedures:

- What laws address children with disabilities and protect their right to an education?
- Should teachers be required to administer medications and medical treatments?
- What rights does a teacher have in these situations? Where would a teacher go to learn about his or her rights?
- What steps can teachers take in these situations to protect themselves from legal problems? Can a teacher legally refuse to perform certain medical treatments?

For legal protection, programs may also establish policies that explicitly address:

- What types of activities require special parental permission?
- What information concerning a child can be released and to whom? What steps must be taken before such information can be released?
- What pick-up procedures must be followed before a child can be released? Special identification? Permission forms?

To be most useful, policies must be written in clear, concise terms that teachers and families can easily understand. Policies should describe the expectations, actions, and consequences for noncompliance. New policies should be explained fully and copies distributed to families and staff members.

Teachers are responsible for implementing practices to protect young children from unnecessary illness and disease. Adherence to good sanitary standards and personal health practices such as disinfecting tables after each diaper change and careful handwashing are important for controlling the spread of infectious disease in group settings. Ongoing educational programs for children and adults are also necessary to ensure long-term success.

Services

Changes in social and family structure have made it increasingly important for teachers and families to address children's health needs through collaborative efforts. However, teachers must respect the fact that families are ultimately responsible for approving and obtaining children's health care. For example, parental consent must always be gotten before arrangements are made for any special testing, screening procedures, or treatment or if information about the child is to be shared with other programs. In addition, teachers must have up-to-date information; a sound understanding of health, safety, and nutrition issues that affect young children; an ability to establish cooperative partnerships with families; and, knowledge of community resources.

FIGURE 1-8

Learning is meaningful when it is part of children's everyday experiences.

Early identification of health impairments is critical to the optimal realization of a child's growth and development potential (Allen & Marotz, 2007). Teachers occupy an ideal position for observing children's health and identifying children who require professional evaluation. They can assist in making arrangements for basic screening tests, such as vision, hearing, and speech evaluations, for the early detection of problems. They can also be instrumental in making referrals and assisting families in locating appropriate community services.

Education

Early childhood is an ideal time to promote health, safety, and nutrition education. It is also a time when teachers can help young children begin to develop an awareness of social and environmental issues that affect their well-being. Teachers have a professional and ethical obligation to provide children with accurate information and to help them learn good habits and attitudes. Many health, safety, and nutrition behaviors become well established during the early years and are typically carried over into adulthood (Hendricks et al., 1988). For these reasons, it is important that families and teachers capitalize on teachable moments and children's developmental readiness to learn. Helping children to establish positive behaviors and practices during the early years is more effective than attempting to reverse poor habits later in life.

Health, safety, and nutrition educational experiences should appeal to children's developmental interests and help them to see their immediate application. Learning becomes meaningful when it is woven into children's everyday experiences (Figure 1–8). For example, physical activities can be incorporated into the music curriculum, healthy nutrition can be reinforced during snacktime and science activities, and the importance of good handwashing can be combined with cooking and art activities.

Educational experiences must gradually go beyond simply teaching children basic facts and rules. Teachers must also help children develop problem-solving skills and learn to apply practices in a variety of settings and situations. For example, children may know how to wash their hands and do so while they are at school, but the true mark of success is whether they practice good handwashing outside of the school environment.

It is also important to remember that children are more likely to pattern their behaviors and attitudes after those being modeled by adults. Thus, setting good examples of positive health, safety, and nutrition practices is one of the most important responsibilities that teachers and families share. When children see adults wearing their safety belts, eating a variety of foods, washing their hands, and engaging in physical activities they too will gradually learn to assume responsibility for their own well-being.

FOCUS ON FAMILIES • Healthy Living

A healthy body often leads to positive effects on attitude, self-confidence, interest, and energy levels. A nutritious diet and participation in regular physical activity are necessary to maintain a healthy body and to keep it performing at its best. Families play a key role in this process and help shape children's early attitudes and habits about the value of good nutrition and daily exercise.

- Be a good role model! Eat a variety of foods and engage in daily physical activity with your children.

- Start the day with breakfast and encourage children to eat. Studies show they will be more alert, better able to learn, and have more energy for play.

- Serve healthy meals that are low in fat and refined sugars. Include a variety of fruits and vegetables, whole grains, and low-fat dairy products each day.

- Encourage children of all ages to help with meal preparation. Involvement often improves children's interest in eating. Very young children can help by putting napkins and utensils on the table; older children can assist with washing fruits and vegetables or stirring.

- Turn off the television and eat meals together. Use the opportunity to engage children in conversation.

- Involve children in 60 minutes of physical activity each day. Plan family activities that are enjoyable and that everyone can do together, such as walking the dog, swimming, riding bicycles, skating, playing golf or baseball, or playing kickball or badminton in the backyard.

- Let children know they are loved. Acknowledge the positive things they do and minimize criticism.

- Assign children age-appropriate responsibility around the house, such as feeding the dog, bringing in the newspaper, dusting furniture, vacuuming, or folding clothes. Encourage their efforts, even if the results aren't perfect.

CASE STUDY

Jose, seven years old, and his mother live alone in a one-bedroom apartment close to his school. Most afternoons Jose walks home alone from school, lets himself into their apartment, and watches television until his mother gets home from work. His favorite after-school snack consists of potato chips and a soda or fruit drink. For dinner, Jose's mother usually brings something home from a local fast food restaurant because she is "too tired to cook." She knows this isn't good for either one of them. She is currently being treated for high blood pressure and Jose's health care provider has expressed concern about his continued weight gain. However, his mother doesn't see how she can change anything given her work schedule and limited income.

1. How would you describe Jose's short- and long-term health potential?

2. What concerns would you have about Jose's safety?

3. What potential health problems is Jose likely to develop if he does not change his current behavior?

4. What environmental risk factors may be contributing to the family's health problems?

5. If you were working with this family, what suggestions would you have for improving their health?

CLASSROOM CORNER • Teacher Activities

Apples Make a Healthy Snack...

Concept: Your body needs healthy snacks, and apples are a healthy snack. There are a variety of apple products to try.   (Pre-2)

Learning Objectives

- Children will learn that apples are a healthy snack.
- Children will experience tasting a variety of apples and apple products.

Supplies

- One Red Delicious apple; one Granny Smith apple; one Gala apple; one can of applesauce; one jar of apple butter; slices of bread (enough to give each child one-quarter of a slice); one jug of apple cider or apple juice (make sure it is pasteurized); hand wipes; plates; napkins; spoons; small cups

Learning Activities:

- Read and discuss one of the following books:
  - *Up, Up, Up! It's Apple-Picking Time* by Jody Fickes Shapiro
  - *Let's Visit an Apple Orchard* by Melissa G. Daly
- Talk with the children about the importance of eating healthy snacks.
- Show them the different kinds of apples and apple products and ask them if they know the names of them and if they have tasted them before.
- Have all the children wash their hands with wipes and then pass out a napkin, a plate, a cup, and a spoon to each child. Provide each child with a small bite or each item (this can be done one at a time, or the plate can be served with some of everything on it and given to each child).
- Give the children the opportunity to taste each item. Discuss how each item is made from apples. Talk about the different tastes and textures of each apple product.

Evaluation

- Children can name several kinds of apples and explain how different apple products are made.
- Children will name apples as a healthy snack choice.

SUMMARY

- Preventive health care is a relatively new concept.
  - It recognizes that health attitudes and practices are learned behaviors.
  - It encourages individuals to assume an active role in developing and maintaining practices that promote good health.
  - It suggests a need to begin teaching children about good health in the early years.
- Health is determined by one's genetic makeup and environment.
  - It is a dynamic state of physical, mental, and social well-being that is continuously changing as a result of lifestyle decisions.
- Children's growth and development potentials are influenced by the interactions of health, safety, and nutrition.

APPLICATION ACTIVITIES

1. Contact local law enforcement, fire, public school authorities, or service agencies in your community. Learn more about the types of safety programs they offer for young children. Invite several representatives to present their programs to your class. Discuss how appropriate and effective you thought the programs were based on the children's developmental stage and particular needs.

2. Observe a child eating lunch or dinner. What foods does the child eat? What foods are refused? Based on your observation, do you think the child is developing healthy eating habits? If there is an adult present, observe the adult's eating practices. Do you think the adult is modeling healthy eating habits? Do the adult's food likes and dislikes seem to have any influence on what the children eat? Explain.

3. Review a menu from an early childhood center. Are children served a variety of foods? Are meals and snacks offered at times when children are likely to be hungry? Are foods nutritious and appealing to children? Are the children likely to eat the food?

4. Contact your local public health department. Make arrangements to observe a routine well-child visit. What preventive health information was given to the families?

5. Compile a list of early care and education programs available in your community. Note the variety of schedules and services offered. Select five programs at random; check to see if they have waiting lists. If there is a waiting list, how long can families expect to wait for placement of their child? How many of these programs provide services for children with special needs, such as physical disabilities, behavior problems, giftedness, or learning disabilities? What adaptations are made for these children in their programs?

6. Research and read more about the national health initiatives described in this chapter. Find out if they are available in your area and what services are provided. Continue your research to learn about other child health programs that may be offered in your state.

CHAPTER REVIEW

A. **By Yourself:**

1. Define each of the *Terms to Know* listed at the beginning of this chapter.

2. Identify the six components of health and provide an example for each.

3. Explain how genetics and environment influence the quality of a person's well-being.

B. **As a Group:**

1. Discuss how an individual's lifestyle decisions can have either a positive or negative effect on health.

2. Describe how early education teachers can use their knowledge of children's development for health promotion.

3. Discuss why it is important to involve and include families in children's health education activities. What steps can a teacher take to be sure that children's cultural beliefs are respected?

4. Explain why an abundant food supply does not always assure good nutrition.

5. Discuss how illness might affect a child's nutritional needs.

REFERENCES

Allen, K. E., & Marotz, L. R. (2007). *Developmental profiles: Pre-birth through twelve* (5th ed.). Clifton Park, NY: Thomson Delmar Learning.

American Public Health Association & American Academy of Pediatrics. (2002). Caring for our children. National health and safety performance standards: Guidelines for out-of-home care. Washington, DC.

Aronson, S. (2002). *Healthy young children: A manual for programs.* (4th ed.). Washington, DC: NAEYC.

Belfield, J. (2003). Childhood obesity—a public health problem. *School Nurse News, 20*(1), 20, 22, 24.

Berk, L. E. (2005). *Child development* (7th ed.). Boston: Allyn & Bacon.

Bhargava, A. (2003). A longitudinal analysis of the risk factors for diabetes and coronary heart disease in the Framingham Offspring Study. *Population Health Metrics, 1*(1), 3.

Birken, C., Parkin, P., To, T., & Macarthur, C. (2006). Trends in rates of death from unintentional injury among Canadian children in urban areas: Influence of socioeconomic status. *Canadian Medical Association Journal, 175*(8), 845, 847.

Braet, C., Mervielde, I., & Vandereycken, W. (2003). Psychological aspects of childhood obesity: A controlled study in a clinical and nonclinical sample. *Journal of Pediatric Psychology, 22*(1), 59–71.

Bryan, J., Osendarp, S., Hughes, D., Calvaresi, E., Baghurst, K., & van Klinken, J. (2004). Nutrients for cognitive development in school-aged children. *Nutrition Reviews, 62*(8), 295–306.

Centers for Medicare & Medicaid Services (CMS). (2006). *FY 2005 SCHIP Annual Report.* Washington, DC: U.S. Department of Health and Human Services. Accessed October 1, 2006, from www.cms.hhs.gov.

Charlesworth, R. (2004). *Understanding child development* (6th ed.). Clifton Park, NY: Delmar Learning.

Daniels, S. (2006). The consequences of childhood overweight and obesity. *The Future of Children, 16*(1), 47–67.

Davison, K., & Birch, L. (2001). Weight status, parent reaction, and self-concept in five-year-old girls. *Pediatrics, 107*(1), 46–53.

Dillard, R. G. (2004). Improving pre-pregnancy health is key to reducing infant mortality. *North Carolina Medical Journal, 65*(3), 147–148.

Davidoff, A., Kenney, G., & Dubay, L. (2005). Effects of the State Children's Health Insurance Program expansions on children with chronic health conditions. *Pediatrics, 116*(1), e34–42.

Earls, F. (1998). The era of health promotion for children and adolescents—a cross-sectional survey of strategies and new knowledge. *American Journal of Public Health, 88*(6):869–871.

Endres, J., Rockwell, R., & Mense, C. (2004). *Food, nutrition, and the young child* (5th ed.). New York: Prentice Hall.

Forum on Child and Family Statistics. (2006). *America's children: Key national indicators of well-being, 2006.* Washington, DC: National Center for Health Statistics. Accessed October 1, 2006, from http://www.child-stats.gov/amchildren05/eco4.asp.

Garzon, D. L. (2005). Contributing factors to preschool unintentional injury. *Journal of Pediatric Nursing, 20*(6), 441–447.

Gordon, N. (1997). Nutrition and cognitive function. *Brain Development, 19*(3), 165–170.

Gupta, R., Shuman, S., Taveras, E., Kulldorff, M., & Finkelstein, J. (2005). Opportunities for health promotion education in child care. *Pediatrics, 116*(4), 499–505.

Hannon, T., Rao, G., & Arslanian, S. (2006). Childhood obesity and type 2 diabetes mellitus. *Pediatrics, 116*(2), 473–80.

Haque, F., de la Rocha, A., Horbul, B., Desroches, P., & Orrell, C. (2006). Prevalence of childhood obesity in northeastern Ontario: A cross-sectional study. *Canadian Journal of Dietetic Practice and Research, 67*(3), 143–147.

Hendricks, C., Peterson, F., Windsor, R., Poehler, D., & Young, M. (1988). Reliability of health knowledge measurement in very young children. *Young Children, 58*(1), 21–25.

Johnson, D., Gerstein, D., Evans, A., & Woodward-Lopez, G., (2006). *Journal of the American Dietetics Association, 106*(1), 97–102.

Jyoti, D., Frongillo, E., & Jones, S. (2005). Food insecurity affects school children's academic performance, weight gain, and social skills. *Journal of Nutrition, 135*(12), 2831–2839.

Kavanagh, T. (2001). Exercise in the primary prevention of coronary artery disease. *Canadian Journal of Cardiology, 17*(2), 155–161.

Kennedy, E. (2006). Evidence for nutritional benefits in prolonging wellness. *American Journal of Clinical Nutrition, 83*(2), 410s–414s.

Kotelchuck, M. (2006). Pregnancy risk assessment monitoring system (PRAMS): possible new roles for a national MCH data system. *Public Health Reports, 121*(1), 74–83.

Latner, J. D., & Stunkard, A. J. (2003). Getting worse: The stigmatization of obese children. *Obesity Research, 11*(3), 452–456.

Marotz, L. R. (2000). Childhood and classroom injuries. In J. L. Frost (Ed.), *Children and injuries.* Tucson, AZ: Lawyers & Judges Publishing Co., Inc.

Mendoza, J., Drewnowski, A., Cheadle, A., & Christakis, D. (2006). Dietary energy density is associated with selected predictors of obesity in U.S. Children. *Journal of Nutrition, 136*(5), 1318–1322.

National Association for the Education of Young Children (NAEYC). (2006). NAEYC accreditation criteria. Accessed on December 15, 2006, from http://www.naeyc.org/accreditation.

National Center for Injury Prevention and Control (NCIPC). (2006). *Unintentional injury deaths and rates 2003.* Accessed October 1, 2006, from http://www.cdc.gov/ncipc.

National Children's Study. (2006). Accessed on October, 1, 2006, from http://www.nationalchildstudy.gov.

Office of Disease Prevention and Health Promotion. (2000). *Healthy People 2010.* Washington, DC: Office of Disease Prevention and Health Promotion. U.S. Department of Health and Human Services. Accessed June 9, 2003, from http://www.healthypeople.gov.

Pamuk, E., Wagener, D., & Molia, M. (2004). Achieving national health objectives: The impact on life expectancy and on healthy life expectancy. *American Journal of Public Health, 94*(3), 378–383.

Rose, D., & Bodor, J. N. (2006). Household food insecurity and overweight status in young school children: Results from the Early Childhood Longitudinal Study. *Pediatrics, 117*(2), 464–473.

Satter, E. (2006). Secrets of feeding a healthy family. Madison, WI: Kelcy Press.

Trahms, C. M., & Pipes, P. L. (2000). *Nutrition in infancy and childhood.* Columbus, OH: McGraw-Hill.

U.S. Department of Labor. Bureau of Labor Statistics. (2006). *Women in the labor force: A Databook. May 2005.* Retrieved October 1, 2006, from http://www.bls.gov/cps/wlf-table5–2005.pdf.

U.S. Department of Health and Human Services. (2002). *Health, United States, 2002 with Chartbook on Trends in the Health of Americans.* Washington, DC.

Whitaker, R., Phillips, S., & Orzol, S. (2006). Food insecurity and the risks of depression and anxiety in mothers and behavior problems in their preschool-aged children. *Pediatrics, 118*(3), 859–68.

HELPFUL WEB RESOURCES

Canadian Institute of Child Health (CICH)	http://www.cich.ca
Canadian Pediatric Society	http://www.cps.ca
Children's Defense Fund	http://www.childrensdefense.org
Healthy People 2010	http://www.healthypeople.gov
National Center for Health Statistics	http://www.cdc.gov
National Resource Center for Health and Safety in Child Care & Early Education	http://nrc.uchsc.edu
No Child Left Behind	http://www.ed.gov
Office of Disease Prevention and Health Promotion (Dept. of Health and Human Services)	http://odphp.osophs.dhhs.gov
Centers for Medicare & Medicaid Services (State Children's Health Insurance Program)	http://www.cms.hhs.gov

For additional health, safety, and nutrition resources, go to http://www.EarlyChildEd.delmar.cengage.com

Children's Health: Maximizing the Child's Potential

CHAPTER **2**

Promoting a Healthy Lifestyle

After studying this chapter, you should be able to:

- Identify typical growth and developmental characteristics of the infant, toddler, preschool, and school-age child.
- Describe how teachers can provide for the different safety needs of infants, toddlers, and preschool children.
- Describe at least four practices that contribute to a child's improved dental health.
- Explain what teachers can do to promote children's mental health.

⊞ TERMS TO KNOW

autonomy	head circumference	well child
norms	bonding	characteristics
normal	deciduous teeth	resilient
growth	development	

The period of infancy is truly a marvel when one considers the dramatic changes in growth and development that occur in a relatively short span of time. The infant progresses from a stage of dependency and relative passiveness to one that enables the child to explore the environment and communicate with others. The spectacular changes in growth and development that occur during this first year will never again be repeated throughout the entire life span.

The toddler years are characterized by an explosive combination of improved locomotion, seemingly unending energy, delightful curiosity, and an eagerness to become independent. Driven by the desire for **autonomy**, or personal identity, toddlers display an intense determination to do things for themselves. As a result, special attention to safety and accident prevention must be a prime concern for teachers and families.

The preschool years are a time of increased awareness and competence. As children pass through this stage of life, they continue to explore the world around them, but with an added

---

autonomy – *a state of personal or self-identity.*

dimension of understanding. Their efforts and skills become increasingly sophisticated, while concentration on basic needs such as eating, sleeping, mobility, and communicating grows less intense. Moving toward a sense of independence becomes a major task. Unlimited energy is united with a spirit of curiosity, imagination, and adventurous instincts. This creates a dynamic child who continues to need careful adult supervision and guidance.

School-age children have mastered the basics of self-care, language, and motor development. They are generally content with themselves, thoughtful toward others and bubbling with enthusiasm. They are curious, eager for new challenges, and can find humor in nearly everything they do (Figure 2–1). Although they enjoy spending time alone, friends and friendships are becoming more important. School-age children seek out organized games and activities and learn how to become a team player. However, they still experience periods of self-doubt, disappointment, and frustration when faced with increasingly complex demands and expectations at home and in school.

FIGURE 2–1

School-age children enjoy new challenges.

GROWTH AND DEVELOPMENT

When teachers understand children's typical growth and development, they are able to appreciate and work more effectively to address their diverse needs (Charlesworth, 2008). They are better prepared to help children master critical skills and behaviors at each developmental level. They can create learning experiences and set goals for children that are developmentally appropriate and foster positive self-esteem. They are able to design quality environments that are safe and encourage children's mastery of new skills. Teachers can also use this knowledge to promote children's well-being by identifying health problems and abnormal behaviors and teaching healthy practices.

Discussions of growth and development often refer to the "average" or "normal" child; such a child probably does not exist. Every child is a unique individual—a product of different experiences, environments, interactions, and heredity. These factors lead to considerable variation in the rate at which children grow and acquire various skills and behaviors (Allen & Marotz, 2007). As a result, each child differs in many ways from every other child.

Norms have been established for children's growth and development to serve as useful frames of reference. These norms represent the average or approximate age when the majority of children demonstrate a given behavior or skill. Therefore, the term **normal** implies that while many children can perform a particular skill, some will be more advanced and others may be somewhat slower, yet they are still considered within the normal range.

---

norms – *an expression (e.g., weeks, months, years) of when a child is likely to demonstrate certain developmental skills.*
normal – *average; a characteristic or quality that is common to most individuals in a defined group.*

Growth

The term **growth** refers to the many physical changes that occur as a child matures. Although the process of growth takes place without much conscious control, there are many factors that affect both the quality and rate of growth:

- genetic potential
- level of emotional stimulation and bonding
- cultural influences
- socioeconomic factors
- adequate nutrition
- parent responsiveness
- health status (i.e., illness)

Infants (0–12 months)   The average newborn weighs approximately 7 to 8 pounds (3.2–3.6 kg) at birth and is approximately 20 inches (50 cm) in length. Growth is rapid during the first year; an infant's birth weight nearly doubles by the fifth month and triples by the end of the first year (Berk, 2005). An infant who weighs 8 pounds (3.6 kg) at birth will weigh approximately 16 pounds (7.3 kg) at 5 months and 24 pounds (10.9 kg) at 12 months.

An infant's length increases by approximately 50 percent during the first year. For example, an infant measuring 21 inches (52.5 cm) at birth should reach an approximate length of 31.5 inches (78.7 cm) by 12 months of age. A larger percentage of this gain occurs during the first six months when an infant may grow as much as 1 inch (2.5 cm) per month.

Rapid growth of the brain causes the infant's head to appear large in proportion to the rest of the body. Thus, measurements of **head circumference** are important indicators of normal growth. Measurements should increase steadily and equal the chest circumference by the end of the first year.

Additional physical changes that occur during the first year include the growth of hair and eruption of teeth (four upper and four lower). The eyes begin to focus and move together as a unit by the third month, and vision becomes more acute. Special health concerns for infants include the following:

- nutritional requirements
- adequate provisions for sleep
- **bonding** or maternal attachment
- early brain development
- safety and injury prevention
- identification of birth defects and health impairments

During the weeks and months following birth, a baby's brain undergoes rapid change as the result of maturation and experience. Genetic makeup and maternal practices during pregnancy (such as diet, smoking, ingestion of alcohol or drugs, infections) also have a significant effect on babies' brain development. The quality of attachment that infants establish with their primary caregivers can have a positive or negative effect on this process. Early learning experiences provide critical stimulation within the brain that forces it to begin establishing, organizing, and maintaining complex electrical connections (Gallagher, 2005). Gradually, through new and repetitive learning experiences, the baby's brain is transformed from an otherwise disorganized system to

---

growth – *increase in size of any body part or of the entire body.*
head circumference – *the distance around the head obtained by measuring over the forehead and bony protuberance on the back of the head; it is an indication of normal or abnormal growth and development of the brain and central nervous system.*
bonding – *the process of establishing a positive and strong emotional relationship between an infant and his or her parent; sometimes referred to as attachment.*

one capable of profound thought, emotions, and learning. Most of this transformation occurs during the first three years, when the brain appears to be more receptive to shaping and change. Researchers have also discovered what they believe to be certain "critical periods," or windows of opportunity, when some forms of learning and sensory development are more likely to occur (Bailey, et al., 2001). Families and teachers can use this knowledge to provide infants and young children with environments and experiences that are enriching and will foster healthy brain development. For example, hanging pictures and mobiles where babies can see helps to promote their visual and cognitive development.

Toddlers (12–30 months) The toddler continues to make steady gains in height and weight, but at a much slower rate than during infancy. A weight increase of 6 to 7 pounds (2.7–3.2 kg) per year is considered normal and reflects a total gain of nearly four times the child's birth weight by the age of two. The toddler grows approximately 3 to 5 inches (7.5–12.5 cm) in height per year. Body proportions change and result in a more erect and adultlike appearance.

Eruption of "baby teeth," or **deciduous teeth**, is completed by the end of the toddler period. (Deciduous teeth consist of a set of 20 temporary teeth.) Toddlers can learn to brush their new teeth as an important aspect of preventive health care, although considerable adult supervision is still needed. Special attention should also be paid to providing foods that promote good dental health; are colorful, appealing, and easily chewed; and include all of the essential nutrients since toddlers typically have smaller appetites. Foods from all food groups—fruits, vegetables, dairy, protein, whole-grains—should be part of the toddler's daily meal pattern.

High activity levels require that the toddler get at least 10 to 12 hours of uninterrupted night-time sleep. In addition, most toddlers continue to nap one to two hours each day. Safety awareness and injury prevention continue to be major concerns that demand careful adult attention (Figure 2–2).

FIGURE 2–2

Toddlers need plenty of sleep to meet their high energy demands.

---

deciduous teeth – *a child's initial set of teeth; this set is temporary and gradually begins to fall out at about five years of age.*

Preschoolers/Early School-age (2 1/2–8 years)   During the preschool and early school-age years, a child's appearance becomes more streamlined and adultlike in form. Head size remains approximately the same, while the child's trunk (body) and extremities (arms and legs) continue to grow. Gradually, the head appears to separate from the trunk as the neck lengthens. Legs grow longer and at a faster rate than the arms, adding extra inches to the child's height. The characteristic chubby shape of the toddler is gradually lost as muscle tone and strength increase. These changes are also responsible for the flattening of the abdomen, or stomach, and straighter posture.

Gains in weight and height are relatively slow but steady throughout this period. By three years of age, children weigh approximately five times their weight at birth. An ideal weight gain for a preschool child is approximately 4 to 5 pounds (1.8–2.3 kg) per year. However, children grow more in height than in weight during this period, gaining an average of 2 to 2.5 inches (5.0–6.3 cm) per year. By the time children reach six years of age, they have nearly doubled their original birth length (from approximately 20 inches to 40 inches [50–100 cm]). By age seven, girls are approximately 42–46 inches (105–115 cm) tall and weigh 38–47 pounds (19.1–22.3 kg); boys are 44–47 inches (110–117.5 cm) tall and weigh 42–49 pounds (17.3–21.4 kg). This combination of growth and muscle development causes children to appear longer, thinner, and more adultlike.

Adequate nutrition continues to be a prime consideration (Satter, 2000). High activity levels replace the rapid growth of earlier years as the primary demand for calories. A general rule for estimating a child's daily caloric needs is to begin with a base of 1,000 calories and add an additional 100 calories per birthday. (For example, a seven-year-old would need approximately 1,700 calories.) However, the preschool years are often marked by decreased appetite and poor eating habits. Consequently, families and teachers must be aware of children's actual food intake and work to encourage healthy eating habits.

Sleep is also required for optimal growth and development. When days are long and tiring or unusually stressful, children's need for sleep may be even greater. Most preschool and school-aged children require 8 to 12 hours of uninterrupted nighttime sleep in addition to daytime rest periods. However, bedtime and afternoon naps often become a source of conflict between children and adults. Preschool children have a tendency to become so involved in play activities that they are reluctant to stop for sleep. Nevertheless, young children benefit from brief rest breaks during their normal daytime routine. Planned quiet times, with books, puzzles, quiet music, or a small toy, may be an adequate substitute for older children.

By the time children reach school-age, they begin to enjoy one of the healthiest periods of their lives. They generally experience fewer colds and upper respiratory infections due to improved resistance and physical maturation. Their visual acuity also continues to improve, resulting in a gradual decrease of farsightedness. Once again, children will undergo fairly rapid growth as height and muscle mass increase to give them a more adultlike appearance.

Development

In the span of one year, remarkable changes take place in the infant's **development**. The child progresses from a stage of complete dependency on adults to one marked by the acquisition of language and the formation of rather complex thought patterns. Infants also become more social and outgoing near the

 REFLECTIVE THOUGHTS

Adequate sleep is important for children during their early years. What strategies could you use to encourage children to rest quietly during naptime? What suggestions would you have for families to improve children's compliance with bedtimes?

---

development – *commonly refers to the process of intellectual growth and change.*

end of the first year and seemingly enjoy and imitate the adults around them (Allen & Marotz, 2007).

The toddler and preschool periods reflect a continued refinement of language, perceptual, motor, cognitive, and social achievements. Improved motor and verbal skills enable the toddler to explore, test, and interact with the environment for the purpose of determining personal identity, or autonomy.

Developmental gains enable the preschool-aged child to perform self-care and fine motor tasks with improved strength, speed, accuracy, control, and ease (Figure 2–3). The beginning of a conscience slowly emerges. This is an important step in the process of socialization because it allows children to exercise control over some of their emotions. Friendships with peers become increasingly important as preschool children begin to extend their sphere of acquaintances beyond the limit of family members.

Six-, seven-, and eight-year-olds are motivated by a strong desire to achieve. Participation in sports and other vigorous activities help children improve their motor skills. Rewards and adult approval continue to be important and help children build self-esteem. During this stage, children also begin to sort out gender identity through increased social contacts.

A summary of major developmental achievements is presented in Table 2–1. It should be remembered that such a list represents accomplishments that a majority of children can perform at a given age. It should also be noted that not every child achieves all of these tasks. Many factors, including nutritional adequacy, opportunities for learning, access to appropriate medical and dental care, a nurturing environment, and parental support, exert a strong influence on children's skill acquisition.

FIGURE 2–3

Preschoolers can manage most of their own self-care.

PROMOTION OF GOOD HEALTH

Today, concern for children's health and welfare is a shared vision. Changes in current lifestyles, trends, and expectations have shifted some responsibilities for children's health to the collaborative efforts of families, teachers, and service providers. Communities are also valued members of this partnership and must be proactive in creating environments that are safe, enriching, and healthy places for children to live.

How can families and teachers determine whether children are healthy? What qualities or indicators are commonly associated with being a healthy or **well child**? **Characteristics** of normal growth and development can be helpful in evaluating children's overall health status and developmental progress. However, there is much variation within the so-called normal range, so they must be used cautiously. Table 2–2 identifies a sampling of physical and developmental expectations for the healthy preschool child based on these norms. Similar lists can be generated for infants and toddlers based on characteristics of growth and development (Allen & Marotz, 2007).

---

well child – *a child in a good physical, mental, social, and emotional state.*
characteristics – *qualities or traits that distinguish one person from another.*

TABLE 2-1 Major Developmental Achievements

Age	Achievements
2 months	lifts head up when placed on stomach follows moving person or object with eyes imitates or responds to smiling person with occasional smiles turns toward source of sound begins to make simple sounds and noises grasps objects with entire hand; not strong enough to hold on enjoys being held and cuddled
4 months	has good control of head reaches for and grasps objects with both hands laughs out loud; vocalizes with coos and giggles waves arms about holds head erect when supported in a sitting position rolls over from side to back to stomach recognizes familiar objects (e.g., bottle, toy)
6 months	grasps objects with entire hand; transfers objects from one hand to the other and from hand to mouth sits alone with minimal support deliberately reaches for, grasps and holds objects (e.g., rattles, bottle) plays games and imitates (e.g., peek-a-boo) shows signs of teeth beginning to erupt prefers primary caregiver to strangers babbles using different sounds raises up and supports weight of upper body on arms
9 months	sits alone; able to maintain balance while changing positions picks up objects (e.g., bits of cracker, peas) with pincer grasp (first finger and thumb) begins to crawl attempts to say words such as "mama" and "dada" is hesitant toward strangers explores new objects by chewing or placing them in mouth
12 months	pulls up to a standing position may "walk" by holding on to objects stacks several objects one on top of the other responds to simple commands and own name babbles using jargon in sentence-like form uses hands, eyes, and mouth to investigate new objects can hold own eating utensils (e.g., cup, spoon)
18 months	crawls up and down stairs one at a time walks unassisted; has difficulty avoiding obstacles in pathway is less fearful of strangers enjoys being read to; likes toys for pushing and pulling has a vocabulary consisting of approximately 5–50 words, can name familiar objects helps feed self; manages spoon and cup
2 years	runs, walks with ease; can kick and throw a ball; jumps in place speaks in two- to three-word sentences (ex; -Dada bye-bye-); asks simple questions; knows about 200 words displays parallel play achieves daytime toilet training voices displeasure

TABLE 2-1 Major Developmental Achievements (continued)

Age	Achievements
3 years	climbs stairs using alternating feet can hop and balance on one foot feeds self can help dress and undress; washes own hands and brushes teeth with help is usually toilet trained is curious; asks and answers questions enjoys drawing, cutting with scissors, painting, clay, and make-believe can throw and bounce a ball states name; recognizes self in pictures
4 years	dresses and undresses self; helps with bathing; manages own toothbrushing enjoys creative activities: paints, draws with detail, models with clay, builds imaginative structures with blocks rides a bike with confidence, turns corners, maintains balance climbs, runs, and hops with skill and vigor enjoys friendships and playing with small groups of children enjoys and seeks adult approval understands simple concepts (e.g., shortest, longest, same)
5 years	expresses ideas and questions clearly and with fluency has vocabulary consisting of approximately 2,500–3,000 words substitutes verbal for physical expressions of displeasure dresses without supervision seeks reassurance and recognition for achievements engages in active and energetic play, especially outdoors throws and catches a ball with relative accuracy cuts with scissors along a straight line; draws in detail
6 years	plays with enthusiasm and vigor develops increasing interest in books and reading displays greater independence from adults; makes fewer requests for help forms close friendships with several peers exhibits improved motor skills; can jump rope, hop and skip, ride a bicycle enjoys conversation sorts objects by color and shape
7 and 8 years	enjoys friends; seeks their approval shows increased curiosity and interest in exploration develops greater clarity of gender identity is motivated by a sense of achievement begins to reveal a moral consciousness
9–12 years	uses logic to reason and problem-solve energetic; enjoys team activities, as well as individual projects likes school and academic challenge, especially math learning social customs and moral values is able to think in abstract terms enjoys eating anytime of the day

Adapted from Allen K. E., & Marotz, L. R. (2007). *Developmental profiles* (5th ed.). Clifton Park, NY: Delmar Learning.

TABLE 2–2   Characteristics of the Healthy Preschool Child

	Yes	No
A. Physical Characteristics		
1. alert and enthusiastic	X	
2. enjoys vigorous, active play		X
3. appears rested		
4. firm musculature		
5. growth—slow, steady increases in height and weight		
6. not easily fatigued		
7. inoffensive breath		
8. legs and back straight		
9. teeth well formed—even, clean, free from cavities		
10. lips and gums pink and firm		
11. skin clear (color is important) and eyes bright		
12. assumes straight posture		
13. large motor control well developed		
14. beginning to develop fine motor control		
15. good hand-eye coordination		
B. Social Behaviors		
1. enthusiastic		
2. curious—interested in surroundings		
3. enters willingly into a wide range of activities		
4. happy and friendly; cheerful most of the time		
5. developing self-confidence; anticipates success, copes with failure		
6. shares in group responsibilities		
7. works and plays cooperatively with peers		
8. respects other's property		
9. appreciates and understands other's feelings		
10. adapts to new situations		
11. enjoys friends and friendships		
12. participates in cooperative play		
13. understands language; can express thoughts and feelings to adults and peers		
14. demonstrates courage in meeting difficulties; recovers quickly from upsets		
15. begins to exercise self-control		
C. Characteristic Work Behaviors		
1. attentive		
2. begins to carry tasks through to completion		
3. increasing attention span		
4. is persistent in activities; is not easily frustrated		
5. can work independently at times		
6. demonstrates an interest in learning; curiosity		
7. shows originality, creativity, imagination		
8. accepts responsibility		
9. responds quickly and appropriately to directions and instructions		
10. works and shares responsibilities with others		
11. accepts new challenges		
12. adaptable		

Download this form online at http://www.EarlyChildEd.delmar.cengage.com

SPECIAL AREAS OF CONSIDERATION

Teachers, in cooperation with families, have considerable influence on children's well-being. In addition to providing safe environments, nutritious meals, health supervision, stimulating learning experiences, and valuable guidance, teachers have many opportunities throughout the day to promote children's health and development of healthy behaviors (Marcon, 2003). Again, knowledge of children's growth and development serves as an important guide for understanding the special needs associated with each stage. Four areas of concern will be addressed here: injury prevention, posture, dental health, and mental health.

Injury Prevention

Unintentional injuries, especially those involving motor vehicles, pose the greatest threat to the lives of young children (Schwebel, Brezausek, & Belsky, 2006; Garzon, 2005). They are responsible for more than one-half of all deaths among children under five years of age in the United States. Each year an additional one million children sustain injuries that require medical attention, and many are left with permanent disabilities (Hammig & Ogletree, 2006; National Center for Health Statistics, 2004).

An understanding of normal growth and development is particularly useful when planning for children's safety. Many characteristics that make children delightful to work with are the same qualities that make them likely to sustain injury. Children's skills are seldom as well developed as their determination, and in their zealous approach to life, they often fail to recognize inherent dangers. Their inability to judge time, distance, and speed accurately contributes to many injuries, including those resulting from falls, as a pedestrian, or riding toys out into the street (Crawley-Coha, 2002; Marotz, 2000). Limited experience also makes it difficult for children to always anticipate the consequences of their actions. The inclusion of infants and children with developmental disabilities raises additional safety concerns. For these reasons, safety awareness and injury prevention must be given prime consideration in any group care setting and in a child's home (Figure 2–4). Approaches to safety management will be discussed in Chapter 9.

FIGURE 2–4

Teachers must always be aware of hazards in children's environments.

Posture and Physical Activity

Good posture, balance, and correct body *alignment* are necessary for many of the physical activities that children engage in, such as walking, jumping, running, skipping, standing, and sitting. Teaching and modeling good body mechanics can help children avoid chronic problems related to poor posture that often develop later in life. Early recognition and treatment of ear infections is also important because they can affect children's balance and coordination.

Orthopedic problems (those relating to skeletal and muscular systems) are not common among young children. However, there are several conditions that warrant early diagnosis and treatment:

- birth injuries, such as hip dislocation, fractured collarbone
- abnormal or unusual walking patterns, such as limping, walking pigeon-toed
- bowed legs
- knock-knees
- flat feet
- unusual curvature of the spine
- unequal length of extremities (arms and legs)

Some irregularities of posture disappear spontaneously as young children mature. For example, it is not uncommon for infants and toddlers to have bowed legs or to walk slightly pigeon-toed. By age three or four, these problems should correct themselves. However, if they persist beyond the age of four, children should be evaluated by a health professional. Early detection and treatment can prevent many long-term or permanent deformities.

Good posture is an excellent topic for classroom discussion, demonstrations, rhythm and movement activities, games, and art projects (Bronson, 2003; Arnsdorff, 2001). Information about what children are learning should also be shared with families so they can reinforce these practices at home. Parent newsletters can include suggestions for good posture, children can illustrate basic posture concepts in pictures, and families can be invited to attend a class demonstration of good body alignment.

Children can begin to learn good body mechanics, including:

- Sitting squarely in a chair, resting the back firmly against the chair back with both feet flat on the floor.
- Sitting on the floor with legs crossed (in front) or with both legs extended out in front. Children should be discouraged from kneeling or sitting in a "W" position because this places stress on developing hip joints and can interfere with proper development overtime (Figure 2–5). Have children sit in a chair with feet planted firmly on the ground or provide them with a small stool that can be straddled (one leg on each side); this eliminates adult nagging and forces children to sit in a correct position. Alternative seating supports may be required for children who have muscular or neurological disabilities.
- Standing with the shoulders square, the chin up, and the chest out. Distribute body weight evenly over both feet to avoid placing added stress on one or the other hip joints.
- Lifting and carrying heavy objects using the stronger muscles of the arms and legs rather than weaker back muscles. Standing close to an object that is to be lifted with feet spread slightly apart to provide a wider support base. Stooping down to lift (with your legs); bending over when lifting stresses back muscles and increases the risk of injury.

FIGURE 2–5

Children should be discouraged from sitting in the "W" position.

TABLE 2-3 Good Body Mechanics For Adults

- Use proper technique when lifting children; flex the knees and lift using leg muscles; avoid lifting with back muscles, which are weaker.
- Adjust the height of children's cribs and changing tables to avoid bending over.
- Provide children with step stools so that they can reach water fountains and faucets without having to be lifted.
- Bend down by flexing the knees rather than bending over at the waist; this reduces strain on weaker back muscles and decreases the risk of possible injury.
- Sit in adult-sized furniture with feet resting comfortably on the floor to lessen strain on the back and knees.
- Transport children in strollers or wagons rather than carrying them.
- Exercise regularly to improve muscle strength, especially back muscles, and to relieve mental stress.
- Lift objects by keeping arms close to the body versus extended; this also reduces potential for back strain.

Good posture and body mechanics are also important for parents and teachers to practice (Table 2–3). Because they perform many activities each day that involve lifting and bending, following proper technique can help reduce chronic fatigue and work-related injury. Exercising regularly also helps to improve muscle strength, makes demanding physical tasks easier to manage, and reduces the risk of injury.

Vigorous physical activity should also be an essential part of every child's daily routine. Evidence continues to establish a strong correlation between declining rates of physical activity, especially among children, and increasing obesity (Sorte & Daeschel, 2006; He & Beynon, 2006). Because children are establishing lifelong habits, it is an ideal time to help them develop practices that will promote good health. Frequent opportunities for vigorous indoor and outdoor play should be planned throughout the day. Current guidelines recommend that children get a minimum of 30 to 60 minutes of moderate physical activity daily (NASPE, 2006; Huettig, et al., 2006). These periods are important for children's physical and mental well-being and are also effective for relieving excess energy, stress, and boredom. Families and teachers can serve as good role models for children by engaging in physical activity each day (Pica, 2006).

Dental Health

Children's dental health has been targeted as a major goal in the *Healthy People 2010* objectives (Figure 2–6). Dental problems affect children's general health, appearance, and self-esteem in addition to causing considerable pain and expense. Advancements in pediatric dentistry and ongoing

FIGURE 2–6

Children's oral health is a major goal of *Healthy People 2010*.

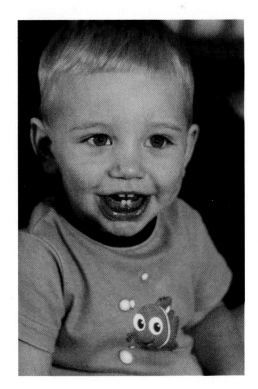

educational efforts have improved children's dental health. The importance of good nutrition during pregnancy, scheduling dental visits for children before age two, addition of fluoride to water supplies, and application of sealants have contributed to a significant decrease in dental caries in children's permanent teeth and gum disease (CDC, 2007; Jones, et al., 2005). Yet, there are still many children who have never been treated by a dentist because their families cannot afford dental insurance or costly preventive dental care. Children from low-income and minority groups are twice as likely to experience tooth decay and a lack of treatment (CDC, 2007). Also, many adults erroneously believe that "baby teeth," or deciduous teeth, are relatively unimportant because they will eventually fall out (Riedy, 2001). This belief is unfortunate because temporary teeth are necessary for:

- chewing
- the spacing of permanent teeth
- influencing the shape of the jaw bone
- the development of speech

Children's behavior and ability to learn can also be affected by the condition of their teeth. Neglected dental care can result in painful cavities and infected teeth, making it difficult for children to concentrate and maintain interest in tasks and activities. Proper dental care must be practiced from birth, with special attention given to the following:

- diet
- hygienic practices—e.g., toothbrushing, flossing
- regular dental examinations
- prompt treatment of dental problems

A child's first visit to the dentist should be scheduled before age two (ADA, 2006). Initial visits should be a pleasant experience and allow the child to become acquainted with the dentist, routine examinations, and cleanings without the discomfort of painful dental work. Hopefully, such positive experiences will foster a healthy attitude toward dental care and discourage children from anticipating future dental examinations with fear and anxiety. Routine checkups at 6- to 12-month intervals are generally recommended as part of a preventive dentistry program.

Diet has an unquestionable effect on children's dental health (Satter, 2000). Proper tooth formation depends on an adequate intake of protein and minerals, particularly calcium and fluoride. One of the most devastating influences on diet, however, is the consumption of large amounts of highly refined and sticky carbohydrates. These are commonly found in cakes, cookies, candies, gum, soft drinks, sweetened cereals, and dried fruits (for example, raisins, dates, and prunes). Families and teachers can help children begin to adopt good dietary habits by limiting the frequency and amounts of sweets they are served and by substituting foods that are nutritious. Because many children's medications and chewable vitamins are sweetened with sugars, toothbrushing should always be encouraged following their ingestion.

A daily routine of good oral hygiene is also essential for the promotion of good dental health. An infant's teeth should be wiped with a small, wet washcloth to remove food particles. Most toddlers can begin learning how to brush their teeth at around 15 months of age. Several steps teachers and families can take to increase children's interest in brushing their own teeth include:

- purchasing a small, soft toothbrush in the child's favorite color
- storing the toothbrush where the child can reach it
- providing a footstool or chair so that the child can reach the sink

Caution: **Supervise the child closely to prevent slipping or falling.**

- demonstrating the toothbrushing procedure so that the child knows what to expect

- helping the child to brush at least twice daily—once in the morning and again before going to bed
- constructing a simple chart where children can place a check each time they brush their teeth; this provides a good method for reinforcing regular toothbrushing habits

Toddlers can be taught to brush their teeth with an adult's help. At this age, toothbrushing can be accomplished by using a soft brush and water to clean the teeth. The use of toothpaste is not recommended before age two; most toddlers do not like its taste and are unable to spit it out after brushing. When a child is first learning toothbrushing skills, it is a good idea for an adult to brush over the teeth after at least one of the brushings each day to be sure all areas are clean. Children can also be taught alternative methods for cleaning teeth between brushings. These methods include rinsing out the mouth with water after eating, and eating raw foods such as apples, pears, and celery which provide a natural cleansing action on the teeth. Some cheeses, such as cheddar, Swiss, and Monterey Jack, have also been found beneficial for reducing dental decay (Kashket & DePaola, 2002).

Preschool children are usually able to brush with minimal adult supervision. Although their technique may not always be perfect, children are establishing a lifelong habit of good toothbrushing. In addition to proper technique, the use of a toothpaste containing fluoride has proven to be effective in reducing dental cavities. However, children should be cautioned not to swallow the toothpaste: too much fluoride can be harmful and cause small white spots to develop on the teeth.

The question of whether young children should learn to floss their teeth is best answered by the child's dentist. Although the practice is regarded as beneficial, much depends on the child's maturity and fine motor skills. Flossing is often not stressed until after permanent teeth begin erupting and the spaces between teeth disappear. If children are too young to floss their own teeth, parents can provide assistance.

Regular dental supervision also contributes to good dental health. However, it cannot replace daily attention to good nutrition and hygiene. During routine examinations, dentists look for signs of any dental problems and also review the child's toothbrushing technique, diet, and personal habits that may have an effect on the teeth (such as thumbsucking or grinding the teeth). Cleaning and an application of fluoride are generally included with routine examinations. Fluoride added to city water supplies has also been shown to significantly reduce tooth decay (ADA, 2006). Preventive treatments, such as sealants (a plasticlike material applied over the grooves of permanent molars to protect them from decay) and fluoride applications are also effective in reducing children's dental problems (Jones, et al., 2006; Weintraub, et al., 2006).

 REFLECTIVE THOUGHTS

Baby bottle tooth decay (BBTD) is a preventable condition that occurs when a baby's teeth are exposed to sugary substances, including juices, formula, and breast milk, for prolonged periods. Practices such as putting a baby to bed with a bottle, nursing a baby frequently or for extended periods at night, and giving a toddler a bottle or sippy cup with fruit juice to carry around are harmful to children's teeth (Gilmore & Stumbo, 2003). Because saliva flow is decreased during sleep, it is less effective in rinsing the teeth.

- What cautions would you offer to new parents who want to prevent their infants from developing bottle mouth syndrome?
- What practices can a mother who wants to feed her infant on demand use to avoid BBTD?
- What practices can parents use with older children to encourage good dental health?

Social-Emotional Competence

Children's social-emotional competence and mental health have received increasing attention as problems of juvenile delinquency, school dropout rates, substance abuse, violence, gang membership, and child suicide escalate. Approximately 15 to 22 percent of children in the United States experience mental health problems that seriously interfere with learning and their ability to become productive adults (Kessler, et al., 2005). Children who live in dysfunctional or low-income families or who have disabilities are at highest risk for developing such problems.

Teachers play a major role in promoting children's social-emotional development (Kaiser & Rasminsky, 2007; Collins, et al., 2003). They can accomplish this by:

- practicing good mental health principles—creating classroom environments that are supportive, responsive, and respectful.
- preventing emotional problems—teaching children effective social, communication, and problem-solving skills (Gillespie & Seibel, 2006).
- identifying and referring children who may exhibit signs of emotional problems, such as excessive anger, aggressive behavior, or difficulty making and keeping friends; working collaboratively with families to find appropriate community resources (Ruffolo, Kuhn, & Evans, 2006).

Children's Basic Needs The preventive health care model recognizes that a close relationship exists between children's emotional and physical well-being (Dawson, Ashman, & Carver, 2000). To achieve sound emotional health, children must first have their basic needs for food, water, shelter, sleep, love, security, and achievement satisfied (Maslow, 1970). Without this, children will be challenged in their quest to achieve positive self-esteem and meaningful relationships with others (Casey, et al., 2005).

However, teachers are in a strategic position to help children develop positive attitudes and socially acceptable behaviors despite some of these challenges (Reddy & Richardson, 2006). They can create opportunities and environments where children practice and learn communication skills and how to control impulsive and aggressive behaviors, express feelings and emotions, develop independence, handle success and failure, respond with ease to new situations, solve problems, and feel good about themselves (Serna, Nielsen, & Mattern, 2003; Parlakian, 2002). In other words, teachers' understanding of basic needs can be used to foster children's development of effective social-emotional skills.

Adults as Role Models Adults must never overlook their importance as role models for young children. Their personal behaviors and response styles exert a powerful and direct influence on children's social-emotional development.

Teachers must carefully examine their own emotional state if they are to be successful in helping children achieve positive emotional health. They, too, must have a strong sense of self-worth and confidence in what they are doing. They should be aware of personal prejudices, be able to

REFLECTIVE THOUGHTS

Making friends is an important part of growing up. Gaining acceptance and respect from peers helps shape one's sense of self-esteem. However, friendships are not always easy for children to establish. What social skills are required for making friends? What behaviors are likely to alienate friends? Should families get involved in their children's friendships? As a parent, what would you do if your child became friends with someone you didn't care for?

accept constructive criticism, and recognize their strengths and limitations. They must have effective communication skills and be able to work collaboratively with families, community service providers, health care professionals, and other members of the child's educational team.

If teachers are to serve as positive role models, they must be able to exercise the same control over their emotions that they expect of children. Personal problems and stressors must be left at home so that full attention can be focused on the children. Teachers must respect children as individuals—who they are, and not what they are able or not able to do—because every child has qualities that are endearing and worthy of recognition. Teachers must also be impartial in their treatment of children; favoritism cannot be tolerated.

Working with young children can be rewarding, but it can also be stressful and demanding in terms of the patience, energy, and stamina required. Noise, children's continuous requests, long hours, staff shortages, low wages, and occasional conflicts with families or co-workers are everyday challenges. Physical demands and unresolved stress can gradually take their toll on teachers' health, commitment, and daily performance. This can eventually lead to negative interactions with colleagues and children and job burnout (Noble & Macfarlane, 2005). For this reason, teachers should try to identify sources of stress in their jobs and take steps to address, reduce, or eliminate them to the extent possible (Marotz & Lawson, 2007; Kunitz, 2000) (Table 2–4).

Emotional Climate The emotional climate of a classroom—the positive or negative feelings one senses—has a significant impact on children's social-emotional development. Consider the following situations and decide which classroom you would find most inviting:

> Kate enters the classroom excited and eager to tell her teacher about the tooth she lost last night and the quarter she found under her pillow from the "tooth fairy." Without any greeting, the teacher hurries to check Kate in and informs her that she is too busy to talk right now, "but maybe later." When they are finished, the teacher instructs Kate to find something to do without getting into trouble. Kate quietly walks away to her cubbie.

> Ted arrives and seems reluctant to leave his mother for some reason this morning. The home provider immediately senses his distress and walks over to greet Ted and his mother. "Ted, I am so glad that you came today. We're going to learn about farm animals and build a farm with the wooden blocks. I know that blocks are one of your favorite activities. Perhaps you'd like to build something small for your mother before it's time for her to go home." Ted eagerly builds a barn with several "animals" in the yard around it and proudly looks to his mother for approval. When Ted's mother is ready to leave, he waves good-bye.

TABLE 2-4 Strategies for Managing Teacher Stress

- Seek out training opportunities where you can learn new skills and improve your work effectiveness.
- Learn and practice time management techniques.
- Develop program policies and procedures that will increase efficiency and reduce sources of tension and conflict.
- Join professional organizations; expand your contacts with other child care professionals, acquire new ideas, advocate for young children.
- Take care of your personal health—get plenty of sleep, eat a nutritious diet, and participate in some form of physical exercise several times each week.
- Develop new interests, hobbies, and other outlets for releasing tension.
- Practice progressive relaxation techniques. Periodically, concentrate on making yourself relax.
- Plan time for yourself each day—read a good book, watch a movie or favorite TV program, go for a long walk, paint, go shopping, play golf, or participate in some activity that you enjoy.

FIGURE 2–7

The classroom atmosphere has a direct effect on children's behavior and development.

Clearly, the teacher's actions in each example create a classroom atmosphere that has a different effect on each child's Ted's behavior (Figure 2–7). Children are generally more receptive and responsive to teachers who are warm, nurturing, and sensitive to their needs. Exposure to negative adult responses, such as ridicule, sarcasm, or threats is harmful to children's emotional development and simply teaches inappropriate behaviors. However, an emotional climate that encourages and supports mutual cooperation, respect, trust, acceptance, and independence will encourage children to develop positive social-emotional skills.

A teacher's communication style and understanding of cultural differences also affects the emotional climate of a classroom. Treating all children as if they were the same is insensitive and can encourage failure, especially if a teacher's expectations are inconsistent or incompatible with the child's cultural background. For example, children in some Hispanic cultures are taught primarily through non-verbal instruction (modeling); a child who is only given verbal directives may not be responsive to this approach (Stanton-Salazar, 2001). Some children may be reluctant to participate in group activities or to answer a teacher's question because this is counter to the way they have been raised. Unless the teacher understands these cultural differences such behaviors could easily be misinterpreted as defiance or inattention. When teachers make an effort to learn about individual children and their families they are able to create a climate that supports learning and healthy social-emotional development.

The way in which curriculum is planned and implemented also contributes to the emotional climate. Learning activities that are developmentally appropriate and matched to children's individual needs and abilities improve children's chances for achieving success (Fallin, Wallinga, & Coleman, 2001).

Stress Prolonged or intense stress in children's lives will sooner or later affect their emotional and physical well-being. Stressful situations, such as abusive treatment, poverty, unrealistic parental demands, chronic illness, unsafe neighborhoods, being left alone for long periods, or natural disasters (floods, tornadoes), can have a serious impact on children's emotional states (Murray, 2006; Galea, Nandi, & Valhov, 2005; Jewett & Peterson, 2002). Poverty, food insecurity, maternal depression, and parental substance abuse are also strongly correlated with an increase in mental health problems among children (Whitaker, Orzol, & Kahn, 2006; Whitbeck, et al., 2006). They may also experience feelings of undue tension, anxiety, and stress in response to many everyday experiences such as:

- separation from families
- new experiences—for example, moving, enrollment in a new early childhood program, mother going to work, birth of a sibling, having a new teacher, being left with a sitter
- chronic illness and hospitalization
- divorce of parents
- death of a pet, family member, or close friend
- conflict of ideas; confrontations with family, friends, or teachers
- overstimulation due to hectic schedules, participation in numerous extracurricular activities
- learning problems

Inexperience and immature development of defense mechanisms challenge children's ability to handle stressful events in a healthy manner (Berk, 2005). Sudden behavior changes may be an early indication that a child is experiencing undue stress, anxiety, or inner turmoil (Parlakian, 2002; Honig, 1986). Signs of behavior disturbances can range from those that are less serious—nail biting, hair twisting, excessive fear, prolonged sadness, anxiety—to more serious problems—repeated aggressiveness, destructiveness, withdrawal, depression, nightmares, psychosomatic illnesses, or poor performance in school.

Childhood Depression   Some children are unsuccessful or unable to cope with chronic stress and turmoil. They may develop a sense of extreme and persistent sadness and hopelessness that begins to affect the way they think, feel, and act. Some early signs of childhood depression include:

- apathy or disinterest in activities or friends
- loss of appetite
- difficulty sleeping
- complaints of physical discomforts, such as headaches, stomachaches, vomiting, diarrhea, ulcers, repetitive tics (twitches), or difficulty breathing (Cullinan, et al., 2003; Luby, et al., 2003)
- lack of energy or enthusiasm
- indecision
- poor self-esteem
- uncontrollable anger

Children who have learning and behavior disorders are known to experience an increased risk of also developing depression (National Institutes of Mental Health, 2000). Having a family history of mental health problems also places some children at higher risk. Even children as young as three may show early signs of depression particularly when their mothers are also suffering from this condition (Whitaker, Phillips, & Orzol, 2006).

The onset of childhood depression may occur abruptly following a traumatic event, such as parental divorce, death of a close family member or friend, abusive treatment, or chronic illness (Hopkins, 2002). However, it can also develop slowly over time, making the early signs more difficult to notice. In either case, teachers must be knowledgeable about the behaviors commonly associated with childhood depression so that they can refer children for evaluation and diagnosis. Depression requires early recognition and treatment to avoid serious and debilitating effects on children's social, emotional, and cognitive development and long-term mental health disorders (Chrisman, et al., 2006).

Childhood Fears   Most childhood fears and nightmares are a normal part of the developmental process and are eventually outgrown as children mature. Basic fears are relatively consistent across generations, although they vary from one developmental stage to the next (King, et al., 2005). For example, a three-month-old infant is seldom fearful, whereas a three-year-old may awake during the night because of "monsters under the bed." Five- and six-year-olds tend to experience fears that reflect real-life events, such as fire, kidnapping, thunderstorms, or homelessness, whereas ten- and eleven-year-olds express fears related to appearance and social rejection (Allen & Marotz, 2007). Some fears are unique to an individual child and stem from personal experiences, such as an earthquake, tornado, witness to a shooting, car accident, abuse, or abandonment (Cjte, et al., 2002).

Fears and nightmares are often accentuated during the preschool years, a time when children have a heightened imagination and are trying to make sense of their world (Figure 2–7). Children's literal interpretation of the things they see and hear can easily lead to misunderstanding and fear. For example, children may believe an adult who says, "I'm going to give you away if you misbehave one more time." Some childhood fears also develop as the result of witnessing adult reactions or having previous bad experiences, such as being frightened by a large dog.

It is important that adults acknowledge children's fears and understand they are real to the child. Although it may be difficult to remain patient and caring when a child wakes up repeatedly at 2 AM, children need consistent adult reassurance and trust to overcome their fears. Children may also find comfort in talking about the things that frighten them or rehearsing what they might do, for example, if they got lost at the supermarket or if it began to thunder.

Poverty and Homelessness Nearly 42 percent of U.S. children younger than age six currently live in poor-low income families (NCCP, 2006). Most of these children live in families that have recently immigrated to the United States, are categorized as minorities (especially Hispanic, Native American, and African American), or are headed by a single parent—usually a mother. Living in a single versus two-parent family places children at the highest economic risk for poverty. Children living in rural areas also comprise an often overlooked group who are increasingly being affected by poverty. Difficult economic times and lack of employment opportunities have placed many rural families in jeopardy. Consequently, families with young children represent a large segment of today's homeless population.

Poverty places additional burdens on the already challenging demands of parenting. Struggles simply to provide basic food, clothing, shelter, health care, and adult attention for children are often compromised by increased stress, fear, conflict, and even violence. Economic hardship also forces many families into undesirable housing and living arrangements. There is often increased parental tension, domestic violence and abusive treatment of children, and inability to provide the nurturing and support children require.

ISSUES TO CONSIDER • Children and Television

In a policy statement titled "Children, Adolescents, and Television," the American Academy of Pediatrics recommends that children younger than two years be discouraged from watching television and that viewing time for older children be limited to no more than two hours of "quality programming" per day. Increasing concerns regarding television's negative impact on children's emotional, social, and physical well-being, including its effect on aggressive behavior and obesity, have prompted the AAP and other professional groups to issue guidelines and recommendations for children's television viewing. Although they recognize that parents are unlikely to discontinue children's access to television and other media forms (for example, movies, videos, and computer games), they encourage families to engage in more activities, such as reading together, conversing with one another, and playing together to foster children's early brain development and promote learning. In addition, parents are encouraged to watch television programs with their children and to monitor their exposure to media violence.

- What are your thoughts about the role of television for very young children? Is it inappropriate for children younger than two years?
- Should families prevent children from watching violence on television or playing games that involve violence?
- What other factors might contribute to children's violent behavior?
- How can families help children to view television and other media in a healthy context?

Unfortunately, the impact of poverty has both immediate and long-term consequences for children's growth and development. Children born into poverty have a higher rate of birth defects, early death, and chronic illnesses, such as anemia and lead poisoning (Allen & Marotz, 2007). Often the quality of their diets, access to health and dental care, and mental health status are also compromised (Hood, 2005; Woolf, Johnson, & Geiger, 2005). Consequently, children are more likely to experience child abuse, learning and behavior problems in school, teen pregnancy, and reduced earning potential as adults (Krieger, et al., 2003). Ultimately, poverty threatens their chances of growing up to become healthy, educated, and productive adults (Currie, 2005).

Violence Children today live in a world where daily exposure to violence is common. Neighborhood crime, substance abuse, the presence of gangs, and access to guns are often associated with poverty and have created poor urban environments where children's personal safety may be at risk. Many of these children have also witnessed family violence or are themselves victims of child abuse. Their families are more likely to exhibit dysfunctional parenting skills, be less responsive and supportive, and use discipline that is either lacking, inconsistent, or punitive and harsh (Evans, 2004). They are also less likely to become involved in their children's education or schools. As a result, many of these children are at greater risk for becoming violent adults and/or developing serious mental health disorders (Burns, et al., 2004). Teachers who understand this potential must reach out to children and help them develop skills to improve their resilience (see Table 2–5).

Children growing up in disadvantaged environments not only face challenges at home, but also at school (Ryan, Fauth, & Brooks-Gunn, 2006). Child care programs in lower-income neighborhoods are often of poorer quality than those found in higher income areas (National Institute of Child Health & Human Development Early Child Care Research Network, 1997). In addition, children may have fewer opportunities to participate in learning and enriching experiences at home. Researchers have observed that children from disadvantaged households typically have poorer language development and literacy skills due to a lower rate of parent-child interaction and lack of available reading materials (Stanton-Chapman, et al., 2004; Hoff, 2003). This combination sets many children up for early school failure.

Children are also exposed to violence and death in movies, video games, cartoons, and on television (Browne & Hamilton-Giachritsis, 2005; Bushman & Cantor, 2003). Studies have concluded that children do not necessarily become aggressive or engage in criminal activity simply from observing

---

TABLE 2-5 Strategies for Increasing Children's Resilient Behaviors

- Be a good role model for children; demonstrate how you expect them to behave.
- Accept children unconditionally; avoid being judgmental.
- Help children develop and use effective communication skills.
- Listen carefully to children to show that you value their thoughts and ideas.
- Use discipline that is developmentally appropriate and based on natural or logical consequences.
- Use and enforce discipline consistently.
- Help children understand and express their feelings; encourage them to have empathy for others.
- Avoid harsh physical punishment and angry outbursts.
- Help children establish realistic goals, set high expectations for themselves, and have a positive outlook.
- Promote good problem-solving skills; help children make informed decisions.
- Reinforce children's efforts with praise and encouragement.
- Give children responsibility; assign household tasks.
- Involve children in activities outside of their home.
- Encourage children to believe in themselves, to feel confident rather than seeing themselves as failures or victims.

violence in the media. However, the dynamics are considerably different for children who grow up in environments where violence is part of their daily lives. Because young children have limited ability to understand the dysfunctional nature of these events, they can have lasting and damaging psychological effects. In addition, repeated media exposure to violence and death has been shown to desensitize children to their significance (Funk, 2005). To limit these effects, families are encouraged to limit children's media viewing, monitor what they are watching, and help children to understand that media is not reality.

Resilient Children

Children face many challenges while growing up in this complex world. Stress, violence, uncertainty, and negative encounters are everywhere. What makes some children more vulnerable to the negative effects of stress and aversive treatment or more likely to develop inappropriate behaviors? Many factors have been suggested, including genetic predisposition, malnutrition, prenatal exposure to drugs or alcohol, poor attachment (bonding) to primary caregivers, physical or learning disabilities, and an irritable personality. Children's home environments can also contribute to this problem. Chaos, inconsistent responsiveness, and unsupportive relationships make it difficult for children to achieve normal developmental tasks and positive self-esteem (Marcenko, 2006).

Why are some children better able to survive the negative effects of an impoverished, traumatic, violent, or stressful life? Researchers continue to study this question in an effort to learn what qualities make some children more **resilient** in the face of such adversity. Although much remains to be understood, several important protective factors have been identified. These include having certain personal characteristics (such as above-average intelligence, positive self-esteem, and good social and problem-solving skills), having a strong and dependable relationship with a parent or parent substitute, and having a social support network outside of one's immediate family (such as a church group, local recreation center, organized sports, Boys and Girls clubs, or youth groups).

Competent parenting is, beyond a doubt, the most important and critical factor in helping children manage adversity and avoid its potentially damaging consequences (Table 2–5). Children who grow up in an environment where families are caring and emotionally responsive, provide meaningful supervision and discipline that is consistent and developmentally appropriate, offer encouragement and praise, and help their children learn to solve problems in a peaceful way are more likely to demonstrate resilient behavior (Thompson, 2006; Brooks & Goldstein, 2002). Teachers, likewise, can facilitate children's development of resiliency skills through nurturing environments and relationships that are consistent and supportive.

Management Strategies Understandably, all children undergo occasional periods of emotional instability or undesirable behavior. Short-term or one-time occurrences are usually not cause for concern. However, when a child consistently demonstrates abnormal or antisocial behaviors, an intervention program or counseling therapy may be necessary.

At times, it may be difficult for families to recognize abnormal behaviors in their own children. Some emotional problems develop slowly over time and therefore may be difficult to distinguish from normal behaviors. Some families may find it difficult to talk about or admit that their child has an emotional disturbance. Others, unknowingly, may be contributing to their children's problems because of dysfunctional (e.g., abusive, unrealistic, inconsistent, or absent) parenting styles.

For whatever reasons, it may be teachers who first identify children's abnormal social and emotional behaviors. Teachers occupy an ideal position for observing children's mental health status and documenting inappropriate conduct. They can also be effective in helping children develop behaviors that are functional, more appropriate, and socially acceptable. Teachers can also use their expertise to help families become more aware of children's problems, counsel them in appropriate behavior management techniques, and/or help them arrange for professional counseling or other needed services.

---

resilient – *the ability to withstand or resist difficulty.*

Teachers can also be instrumental in promoting children's emotional health and resiliency by recognizing early changes in behavior, providing stable and supportive environments, and fostering children's communication and problem-solving skills. They can also help children learn how to cope with stressful events by practicing strategies such as (Wittmer & Honig, 1994):

- the use of music for relaxation
- progressive relaxation techniques—the process of contracting and relaxing various body parts, beginning at one end of the body and moving toward the other
- relaxation activities—the use of imagery and visualization, make-believe, let's pretend, books and stories, movement activities
- short periods of vigorous physical activity followed by rest
- art activities—water play, clay and play dough, painting
- dramatic play—using dolls and puppets to act out feelings of fear, anger, or frustration

There are also many books available to read and discuss with children (see Appendix F).

Thus, teachers have many opportunities to promote children's development of positive mental health skills. Children who learn conflict resolution, problem-solving, and effective communication skills will have powerful resources available to help them cope with daily problems in an effective manner. Parent–child relationships can also be strengthened by sharing information and providing similar training to families. Although most parents welcome an opportunity to improve their parenting skills, the benefit to high-risk or dysfunctional families may be even greater.

FOCUS ON FAMILIES • Helping Children Cope with Trauma

Children are exposed to violence on many levels—from viewing events on television and hearing others talk about it to witnessing traumatic acts in their own neighborhoods or even being personally involved. Their reactions to these experiences can range from a heightened concern or expressed fear to serious and prolonged behaviors, such as withdrawal, nightmares, aggression, sadness, complaints of physical ailments (such as headache, stomachache, sleep disturbances, and loss of appetite), excessive fear, and depression. When children have a supportive environment and caring adults in their lives, they are often able to gradually recover from negative experiences.

- Examine your own personal reactions and responses. Children often imitate adult behaviors. If adults appear to lack self-control, children are likely to exhibit similar characteristics.
- Provide added attention and comfort; reassure children that they will be safe.
- Foster open communication without judgment. Encourage children to talk about the experiences and acknowledge their feelings. Let them know these are normal. Do not call children "sissies" or tell them to "grow up" because of the way they are reacting.
- Maintain regular schedules, routines, and rules to help children feel more secure.
- Restrict children's media exposure. Monitor what they listen to and see.
- Avoid temporary separations. Children may be afraid to sleep alone at night; allowing them to stay in the same room with you may be helpful in overcoming their fear.
- Involve children in outside activities to minimize focusing on a traumatic event.
- Obtain the help of a mental health counselor if children continue to experience problems.
- Help children develop and practice effective social, communication, and problem-solving skills.
- Build children's resilience through positive self-esteem.

CASE STUDY

Azumi's family recently moved to the community when her father was transferred to another company location. This was the family's second move this year. Azumi's mother, a librarian, was successful in finding a job at the local library soon after they arrived. She contacted the local resource and referral agency for help in locating child care for Azumi. After visiting several programs, she chose one that was only a few blocks from her workplace and felt comfortable that her daughter would receive quality care. However, Azumi's mother also knew that her three-year-old daughter would probably have difficulty adjusting to new teachers and children once again.

1. What are some of the feelings a "new" child is likely to experience?
2. What strategies can teachers use to help integrate a "new" child into an existing group?
3. What personal qualities make this transition easier for some children than others?
4. What can teachers do to help the other children begin to make the "new" child feel welcomed and accepted?
5. How can teachers help families with this transition?

CLASSROOM CORNER • Teacher Activities

The Importance of Friendship

Concept: It is fun to do things with friends. (Pre-2)

Learning Objectives

- Children will learn that there are many activities to do with friends.
- Children will learn that friendship requires sharing and turn taking.
- Children will learn that working together can be a lot of fun.

Supplies

- a variety of colors of construction paper cut into large hearts (each heart should then be cut in half in a variety of ways so that the two heart pieces can be put back together to form a large heart); glue sticks; various art supplies (glitter, feathers, puff balls, foam shapes, etc.); scotch tape; large piece of bulletin board paper (large enough to display all of the hearts)

Learning Activities

- Read and discuss one of the following books:
  - *What Is a Friend?* by Josie Firmin
  - *Winnie the Pooh Friendship Day* by Nancy Parent
  - *I Can Share* by David Parker
  - *Pooh Just be Nice . . . to Your Little Friends!* by Caroline Kenneth
- Explain to the children that they are going to make a friendship quilt.
  - Have the children come up and pick a heart half. After they have all selected half of a heart, pair the two children together whose heart halves fit together. Provide art supplies

CLASSROOM CORNER • Teacher Activities (continued)

and one glue stick per pair of children to encourage sharing and cooperation. When each pair of children has finished decorating their heart half, tape the two halves together. Label each heart set with the names of both children. Arrange the completed hearts on a large sheet of bulletin board paper to create a friendship quilt that can be hung up in your classroom.

- Talk about the experience, including what it means to work with a partner and to make a friendship quilt.

Evaluation

- Children will work together and take turns.
- Children will name activities they like to do with their friends.

SUMMARY

- Growth is rapid during infancy; the rate slows considerably during the preschool years.
- Preschoolers can manage most of their own personal care, but they may still need some adult assistance.
  - Good dental hygiene is important for all children once they have teeth.
  - A baby's gums and teeth can be wiped with a damp cloth to remove food particles.
  - Parents should brush a toddler's teeth at least once each day.
- Changes in socialization are dramatic from infancy to early school years.
  - Friendships and group interaction become important to older children.
  - Some children continue to experience difficulty separating from families.
- Children's mental health requires special adult attention and consideration to promote healthy development and prevent emotional problems.
  - Positive self-esteem is a key component of good mental health.
  - Sudden changes in children's behavior may be an indication of stress.
  - Childhood fears are common during the preschool years.
  - Poverty, homelessness, violence, and other social ills contribute to increasing concerns about the quality of children's mental health.

APPLICATION ACTIVITIES

1. Observe a small group of preschool-aged children during free-play or outdoor times for two 15-minute intervals. For each observation, select a different child and record the number of times that child engages in cooperative play. Repeat this observation procedure with a group of toddler or school-age children. Note any differences.

2. Select and read 10 children's books from the Mental Health section in Appendix F. Prepare a brief annotation of the theme and content for each book. Describe how you might use each book to promote children's positive mental health skills or as part of a classroom learning activity.

3. Visit the American or Canadian Dental Association Web site or contact a local dentist and request information on children's dental care. Design a lesson plan on dental health. Implement and evaluate the lesson. What improvements might you make the next time?

4. Invite a child mental health specialist to speak to your class. Find out what types of problems are treated most often and what teachers might do to help families avoid these problems in the future.

5. Develop a checklist, similar to the one in Table 2–2, identifying appropriate characteristics for infants and for toddlers.

6. Visit your Public Health Department. What services/programs would be available to you if you were a single, unemployed parent of two children, ages six months and two-and-one-half-years-old?

CHAPTER REVIEW

A. **By Yourself:**

1. Answer the following questions by filling in the blanks. Take the first letter of each answer and place it in the appropriate square that follows Question 6 to form an important word.

a. Major gains in the preschool child's growth are due to increases in _____.

b. A comprehensive health program should include services, _____, and provisions for a healthy environment.

c. _____ are the leading cause of death among children younger than age 14.

d. Teachers can promote children's mental health by planning activities that are appropriate for their _____ of skill.

e. _____ have a professional and ethical responsibility to protect the safety of young children in their programs.

f. Good dental care depends on a nutritious diet, good oral _____, and routine dental examinations.

2. How many hours of sleep are recommended for the toddler each day?

3. What methods might a parent or teacher use to encourage a child who refuses to sleep, relax, or rest quietly?

4. How much can an infant be expected to grow in weight and length during the first year?

5. What is another term used to describe "baby teeth"?

B. **As a Group:**

1. Discuss how environment affects or contributes to children's mental health.

2. Explain the relationship between good dental health and learning.

3. Would it be realistic to expect an 11-month-old infant to be toilet trained? Should parents be concerned if their nine-month-old infant cannot sit up without support? Explain.

4. Identify and discuss at least five ways that families and teachers can help children to become more resilient when faced with stressful or adverse situations.

5. Discuss why a teacher's mental health state is important to monitor and consider. What potential effect(s) might it have on the children in a classroom?

REFERENCES

Allen, K. E., & Marotz, L. R. (2007). *Developmental profiles: Pre-birth through twelve* (5th ed.). Clifton Park, NY: Delmar Learning.

American Dental Association (ADA). (2006). Life stages: Caring for children's teeth. Accessed on December 10, 2006, from http://www.ada.org/public/manage/stages/parents.asp.

Arnsdorff, M. (2001). *Pete the posture parrot*. Annapolis, MD: Body Mechanics, Inc.

Bailey, D., Bruer, J. R., Symons, F., & Lichtma, J. (Eds.). (2001). *Critical thinking about critical periods*. Baltimore: Paul H. Brookes.

Berk, L. (2005). *Child development* (7th ed.). Boston: Allyn & Bacon.

Bronson, M. B. (2003). Choosing play materials for primary school children (ages 6–8). *Young Children, 58*(3), 24–25.

Brooks, R., & Goldstein, S. (2002). Nurturing resilience in our children: Answers to the most important parenting questions. New York: McGraw-Hill/Contemporary Books.

Browne, C., & Hamilton-Giachritsis, C. (2005). The influence of violent media on children and adolescents: A public-health approach. *Lancet, 365*(9460), 702–710.

Burns, B., Phillips, S., Wagner, H., Barth, R., Kolko, D., Campbell, Y., & Yandsverk, J. (2004). Mental health need and access to mental health services by youths involved with child welfare: A national survey. *Journal of the American Academy of Child and Adolescent Psychiatry, 43*(8), 960–970.

Bushman, B. J., & Cantor, J. (2003). Media ratings for violence and sex. Implications for policymakers and parents. *American Psychologist, 58*(2), 130–141.

Casey, P., Szeto, K., Robbins, J., Stuff, J., Connell, C., Gossett, J., & Simpson, P. (2005). Child health-related quality of life and household food security. *Pediatric & Adolescent Medicine, 159*(1), 51–56.

Centers for Disease Control and Prevention. (2007). Oral health improving for most Americans, but tooth decay among preschool children on the rise. Accessed on September 24, 2007 from http://www.cdc.gov/nchs/pressroom/07newsreleases/oralhealth.htm.

Charlesworth, R. (2008). Understanding child development: For adults who work with young children. (7th ed.). Clifton Park, NY: Delmar Learning.

Chrisman, A., Egger, H., Compton, S., Curry, J., & Goldstein, D. (2006). Assessment in childhood depression. *Child and Adolescent Mental Health, 11*(2), 111–116.

Cjte, S., Tremblay, R. E., Nagin, D., Zoccolillo, M., & Vitaro, F. (2002). The development of impulsivity, fearfulness, and helpfulness during childhood: Patterns of consistency and change in the trajectories of boys and girls. *Journal of Child Psychology & Psychiatry, 43*(5), 609–701.

Collins, R., Mascia, J., Kendall, R., Golden, O., & Schock, L. (2003). Promoting mental health in child care settings: Caring for the whole child. *Zero to Three, 23*(4), 39–45.

Crawley-Coha, T. (2002). Childhood injury: A status report, part 2. *Journal of Pediatric Nursing, 17*(2), 133–136.

Cullinan, D., Evans, C., Epstein, M., & Ryser, G. (2003). Characteristics of emotional disturbance of elementary school students. *Behavioral Disorders, 28*(2), 94–110.

Currie, J. (2005). Health disparities and gaps in school readiness. *The Future of Children, 15*(1), 117–138.

Dawson, G., Ashman, S. B., & Carver, L. J. (2000). The role of early experience in shaping behavioral and brain development and its implications for social policy. *Developmental Psychopathology, 12*(4), 695–712.

Evans, G. (2004). The environment of childhood poverty. *The American Psychologist, 59*(2), 77–92.

Fallin, K., Wallinga, C., & Coleman, M. (2001). Helping children cope with stress in the classroom setting. *Childhood Education, 78*(1), 17–24.

Funk, J. (2005). Children's exposure to violent video games and desensitization to violence. *Child and Adolescent Psychiatric Clinics of North America, 14*(3), 387–404.

Galea, S., Nandi, A., & Vlahov, D. (2005). The epidemiology of post-traumatic stress disorder after disasters. *Epidemiologic Reviews, 27*(1), 78–91.

Gallagher, K. (2005). Brain research and early childhood development: A primer for developmentally appropriate practice. *Young Children, 60*(4), 12–20.

Garzon, D. (2005). Contributing factors to preschool unintentional injury. *Journal of Pediatric Nursing, 20*(6), 441–447.

Gillespie, L., & Seibel, N. (2006). Self-regulation: A cornerstone of early childhood development. *Young Children, 61*(4), 34–39.

Gilmore, J., & Stumbo, P. (2003). Patterns of beverage consumption during the transition stage of infant nutrition. *Journal of the American Dietetic Association, 103*(10), 1350–1353.

Hammig, B., & Ogletree, R. (2006). Burn injuries among infants and toddlers in the United States, 1997–2002. *American Journal of Health Behavior, 30*(3), 259–267.

He, M., & Beynon, C. (2006). Prevalence of overweight and obesity in school-aged children. *Canadian Journal of Dietetic Practice & Research, 67*(3), 125–129.

Hoff, E. (2003). The specificity of environmental influence: Socioeconomic status affects early vocabulary development via maternal speech. *Child Development,* **74**(5), 1368–1378.

Honig, A. (1986). Stress and coping in children (part I). *Young Children, 41*(4), 50–63.

Honig, A. (1986). Stress and coping in children (part II). *Young Children, 41*(5), 47–59.

Hood, E. (2005). Dwelling disparities: How poor housing leads to poor health. *Environmental Health Perspectives, 113*(5), A310–A317.

Hopkins, A. R. (2002). Children and grief: The role of the early childhood educator. *Young Children, 57*(1), 40–47.

Huettig, C., Rich, J., Engelbrecht, S., Sanborn, E., Essery, N., DiMarco, L., Velez, L, & Levy, L. (2006). Growing up with EASE: Eating, Activity, and Self-Esteem. *Young Children, 61*(3), 26–30.

Jewett, J., & Peterson, K. (2002). Stress and young children. *ERIC Digests, #EDO-PS-02–20.* Accessed June 6, 2003, from http://ericeece.org/pubs/digests/2002/jewett02.html.

Jones, K., Griffin, S., Moonesinghe, R., Jaramillo, F., & Vousden, C. (2005). Reducing dental sealant disparities in school-aged children through better targeting of informational campaigns. *Preventing Chronic Disease, 2*(4), A21.

Kaiser, B., & Rasminsky, J. (2007). Challenging behavior in young children: Understanding, preventing, and responding effectively. (2nd ed.). Boston, MA: Allyn & Bacon.

Kashket, S. & DePaola, D. (2002). Cheese consumption and the development and progression of dental caries. *Nutrition Reviews, 60*(4), 97–103.

Kessler, R., Beglund, P., Demler, O., Jin, R., & Walters, E. (2005). Lifetime prevalence and the age-of-onset distributions of DSM-IV disorders in the National Comorbidity Survey replication. *Archives of General Psychiatry, 62*(6), 593–602.

King, N., Muris, P., Ollendick, T., & Gullone, E. (2005). Childhood fears and phobias: Advances in assessment and treatment. *Behaviour Change, 22*(4), 199–211.

Krieger, N., Chen, J. T., Waterman, P. D., Soobader, M. J., Subramanian, S. V., & Carson, R. (2003). Choosing area based socioeconomic measures to monitor social inequalities in low birth weight and childhood lead poisoning: The Public Health Disparities Geocoding Project (US). *Journal of Epidemiology & Community Health, 57*(3), 186–199.

Kunitz, J. (2000). Avoiding provider burnout. *Child Care Health Connections, 13*(6), 9.

Luby, J., Heffelfinger, A., Mrakotsky, C., Brown, K., Hessler, M., Wallis, J., & Spitznagel, E. L. (2003). The clinical picture of depression in preschool children. *Journal of the American Academy of Child and Adolescent Psychiatry, 42*(3), 340–348.

Marcenko, M. (2006). Parenting in poor environments: Stress, support, and coping. *Children and Youth Services Review, 28*(7), 857–858.

Marcon, R. A. (2003). Growing children: The physical side of development. *Young Children, 58*(1), 80–87.

Marotz, L, & Lawson, A. (2007). *Motivational leadership.* Clifton Park, NY: Thomson Delmar Learning.

Marotz, L. (2000). Childhood and classroom injuries. In J. L. Frost (Ed.), *Children and injuries.* Tucson: Lawyers & Judges Publishing Co.

Maslow, A. H. (1970). *Motivation and personality* (2nd ed.). New York: Harper & Row.

Murray, J. (2006). Addressing the psychosocial needs of children following disasters. *Journal for Specialists in Pediatric Nursing, 11*(2), 133–137.

National Association for Sport and Physical Education (NASPE). (2006, May). Active start-physical activity guidelines for children birth to five years. *Beyond the Journal.* Accessed on September 23, 2007 from http://www.journal.naeyc.org/btj/200605/.

National Center for Children in Poverty (NCCP). (2006). Basic facts about low-income children: Birth to age 18. Accessed on December 9, 2006, from http://www.nccp.org/pub_lic06b.html.

National Center for Health Statistics (NCHS). (2004). NCHS Data on injuries. Accessed on December 11, 2006, from http://www.cdc.gov/nchs/data/factsheets/injury.pdf.

National Institute of Child Health & Human Development Early Child Care Research Network. (1997). Poverty and patterns of child care. In G. J. Duncan & J. Brooks-Gunn (Eds.), *Consequences of growing up poor* (pp. 100–131). NY: Russell Sage Foundation.

National Institutes of Mental Health (NIMH). (2000). *Depression in children and adolescents.* Bethesda, MD: Author.

Noble, K, & Macfarlane, K. (2005). Romance or reality? Examining burnout in early childhood teachers. *Australian Journal of Early Childhood, 30*(3), 53–58.

Parlakian, R. (2002). Building strong foundations: Practical guidance for promoting the social/emotional development of infants and toddlers. Herndon, VA: Zero to Three.

Pica, R. (2006). Physical fitness and the early childhood curriculum. *Young Children, 61*(3), 12–19.

Reddy, L., & Richardson, L. (2006). School-based prevention and intervention programs for children with emotional disturbance. *Education & Treatment of Children, 29*(2), 379–404.

Riedy, C. A., Weinstein, P., Milgrom, P., & Bruss, M. (2001). An ethnographic study for understanding children's oral health in a multicultural community. *International Dental Journal, 51*(4), 305–312.

Ruffolo, M., Kuhn, M., & Evans, M. (2006). Developing a parent-professional team leadership model in group work: Work with families with children experiencing behavioral and emotional problems. *Social Work, 51*(1), 39–47.

Ryan, R., Fauth, R., & Brooks-Gunn, J. (2006). Childhood poverty: Implications for school readiness and early childhood education. In B. Spodak & O. Saracho (Eds.), *Handbook of research on the education of young children* (2nd ed.). Mahwah, NJ: Erlbaum.

Satter, E. (2000). *Child of mine: Feeding with love and good sense.* Palo Alto, CA: Bull Publishing Co.

Schwebel, D., Brezausek, C., & Belsky, J. (2006). Does time spent in child care influence risk for unintentional injury? *Journal of Pediatric Psychology, 31*(2), 184–193.

Serna, L., Nielsen, E., & Mattern, N. (2003). Primary prevention in mental health for Head Start classrooms: Partial replication with teachers and intervenors. *Behavioral Disorders, 28*(2), 124–129.

Sorte, J, & Daeschel, I. (2006). Health in action: A program approach to fighting obesity in young children. *Young Children, 61*(3), 40–48.

Stanton-Chapman, T., Chapman, D., Kaiser, A., & Hancock, T. (2004). Cumulative risk and low-income children's language development. *Topics in Early Childhood Special Education, 24*(4), 227–237.

Stanton-Salazar, R. (2001). *Manufacturing hope and despair: The school and kin support networks of U.S.-Mexican youth.* New York: Teachers College, Columbia University.

Thompson, R. (2006). *Nurturing future generations: Promoting resilience in children and adolescents through social, emotional and cognitive skills.* New York: Routledge/Taylor & Francis Group.

Weintraub, J., Ramos-Gomez, F., Jue, B., Hoover, C., Featherstone, J., & Gansky, S. (2006). Fluoride varnish efficacy in preventing early childhood caries. *Journal of Dental Research, 85*(2), 172–176.

Whitaker, R., Orzol, S., & Kahn, R. (2006). Maternal mental health, substance use, and domestic violence in the year after delivery and subsequent behavior problems in children at age 3 years. *Archives of General Psychiatry, 63*(5), 551–560.

Whitaker, R., Phillips, S., & Orzol, S. (2006). Food insecurity and the risks of depression and anxiety in mothers and behavior problems in their preschool-aged children. *Pediatrics, 118*(3), e859–868.

Whitbeck, L., Johnson, K., Hoyt, D., & Walls, M. (2006). Prevalence and comorbidity of mental disorders among American Indian children in the Northern Midwest. *Journal of Adolescent Health, 39*(3), 427–434.

Wittmer, D., & Honig, A. (1994). Encouraging positive social development in young children. *Young Children, 49*(5), 4–12.

Woolf, S., Johnson, R., & Geiger, H. (2006). The rising prevalence of severe poverty in America: A growing threat to public health. *American Journal of Preventive Medicine, 31*(4), 332–341.

HELPFUL WEB RESOURCES

American Academy of Pediatric Dentistry	http://www.aapd.org
American Institute of Stress	http://www.stress.org
Children's Television Workshop Online	http://www.ctw.org
Council for Exceptional Children	http://www.cec.sped.org
Indian Health Service	http://www.ihs.gov
KidsHealth	http://www.kidshealth.org
National Academy for Child Development	http://www.nacd.org

National Center for Children in Poverty	http://asp.cumc.columbia.edu
National Mental Health Association	http://www.nmha.org
National SAFE KIDS Campaign	http://www.safekids.org

 For additional health, safety, and nutrition resources, go to http://www.EarlyChildEd.delmar.cengage.com

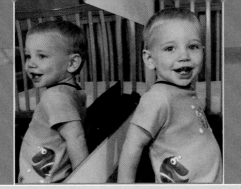

CHAPTER **3**

Health Appraisals

❊ OBJECTIVES

After studying this chapter, you should be able to:

- State why it is important for teachers to observe children's health.
- Explain the relationship between health and learning.
- List four sources where information about a child's health can be obtained.
- Identify five health specialists who may be called upon to evaluate children's health.
- Describe how to conduct a health check.
- Discuss how good family-teacher communication can enhance children's health.

❊ TERMS TO KNOW

impairment	atypical	anecdotal
chronic	observations	diagnosis
health assessment	symptoms	

T he *Healthy People 2010* national initiative reinforces the important relationship between a child's health and ability to learn (U.S. Department of Health & Human Services, 2006). It also recognizes that not all children have equal access to medical and dental care or to environments that promote long-term well-being. It underscores the collaborative effort necessary for assuring children's health and educational success, and challenges communities to address these problems. Teachers and health professionals play a critical role in this process through their early identification of children's health problems, assistance in helping families obtain appropriate medical treatment, and collaboration with families to encourage a healthy lifestyle.

When children enjoy good health, they are more likely to benefit from participation in learning experiences. However, an acute or chronic illness, undetected health **impairment**, or emotional problem can interfere with a child's interest, level of involvement, and performance in school. For example, a mild hearing loss may distort a child's perception of letter sounds, pronunciations, and

---

impairment – *a condition or malfunction of a body part that interferes with optimal functioning.*

responsiveness. If left undetected, it can have a profound and long-term effect on a child's ability to learn. However, health problems do not have to be obvious or complex to have a negative effect. Even a simple cold, toothache, allergic reaction, or chronic tonsillitis will disrupt a child's energy level, cooperation, attention span, interest, and enjoyment of learning. Thus, it is imperative that teachers be continuously aware of children's health status. Recognizing the early signs of health conditions and arranging for early intervention can limit the negative impact these problems would otherwise have on children's development and learning ability.

❊ PROMOTING CHILDREN'S HEALTH

Early care and education programs make a significant contribution to children's well-being through their provision of health services, educational programs, safe and healthy learning environments, and good nutrition. Quality programs employ a variety of techniques, including teacher observations and daily health checks, to continually monitor children's health status and identify potential health needs. It is important that this process be ongoing because children's health status changes continuously, as illustrated in the following example:

Joshua bounded into the classroom and greeted his classmates with the usual "Hi guys." However, by 10:00 AM his teacher noticed that Joshua had retrieved his blanket and was lying quietly in the book area. Despite several minutes of coaxing, Joshua vehemently refused to budge. His teacher continued to observe Joshua for the next few minutes and noted that he was holding his hand over his left ear and whimpering. When the teacher took Joshua's temperature, it was 103°F and he complained of an earache.

FIGURE 3–1

Teachers should be alert to changes in children's appearance and behavior.

Teachers must be alert to changes in children's appearance and behavior throughout the day (Figure 3–1). These early signs may be the first indication of an impending acute illness or **chronic** health problem and should prompt the teacher to take action.

Gathering Information

Information about children's health can be gathered from a variety of sources, including:

- dietary assessment
- health histories
- results of medical examinations
- teacher observations and health checks
- dental examinations
- family interviews
- vision and hearing screenings
- speech evaluations

---

chronic – *frequent or repeated incidences of illness; can also be a lengthy or permanent status, as in chronic disease or dysfunction.*

- psychological testing
- developmental evaluations

Several of these assessment tools can be administered by teachers or volunteers, while others require the skills of specially trained health professionals. Often, the process of identifying a specific health impairment requires the cooperative efforts of specialists from several different fields:

- pediatric medicine
- nursing
- speech
- dietetics
- dentistry

- psychology
- education
- ophthalmology
- social work
- audiology

Health information should always be collected from a variety of sources before any final conclusions about the child's condition are reached. Relying on the results of a single **health assessment** may present a biased and unrealistic picture of the child's problem (Allen & Cowdery, 2005). Children sometimes behave or respond in ways that are **atypical** when confronted with new surroundings or an unfamiliar adult examiner, thereby making it difficult to obtain reliable results. By gathering information from multiple sources, a more accurate assessment of the illness or impairment and its effect on the child can be formed. For example, combining teacher and parent observations with the results of a hearing evaluation may confirm the need to refer a child to a hearing specialist.

OBSERVATION AS A SCREENING TOOL

Teachers are valuable members of a child's comprehensive health team. Their knowledge of children's developmental patterns and involvement with children in a classroom setting places them in an excellent position for observing potential health problems (Figure 3–2). Information obtained from daily **observations** provides a useful baseline for determining what is typical behavior and appearance for each child. When combined with an understanding of normal growth and development, this information allows teachers to quickly note any changes or deviations (Bentzen, 2005).

FIGURE 3–2

Teachers have an excellent opportunity to see children functioning in different settings and to note any health problems.

---

health assessment – *the process of gathering and evaluating information about an individual's state of health.*
atypical – *unusual; different from what might commonly be expected.*
observations – *to inspect and take note of the appearance and behavior of other individuals.*

Health observations are a simple and effective screening tool readily available to teachers. Many of the skills necessary for making objective health observations are already at their disposal. Sight, for example, is one of the most important senses; much can be learned about children's health by merely watching them in action. A simple touch can detect a fever or enlarged lymph glands. Odors may indicate lack of cleanliness or an infection. Careful listening may reveal breathing difficulties or changes in voice quality. Problems with peer relationships, eating habits, self-esteem, or abuse in the child's home may be detected during a conversation. Utilizing one's senses to the fullest—seeing children as they really are, hearing what they really have to say, and responding to their true needs—is a skill that requires time, patience, and practice to perfect.

As with any form of evaluation, conclusions drawn from teacher observations should be made with caution. It must always be remembered that a wide range of normal behavior and skill attainment exists at each developmental stage. Norms merely represent the average age at which most children are able to perform a given skill. For example, many three-year-olds can reproduce the shape of a circle, name and match primary colors, and walk across a balance beam. There will also be some three-year-olds, however, who will not be able to perform these tasks. This does not imply that they are not "normal." Some children simply take longer than others to master certain skills. Developmental norms are useful for identifying children who may be experiencing health problems, as well as those who may simply require additional time and help in acquiring these skills. However, an abrupt change or prolonged delay in a child's developmental progress should be noted and prompt further evaluation.

DAILY HEALTH CHECKS

Evaluating children's health status on a daily basis provides valuable information about their well-being and readiness to learn. Health checks require only a minute or two to complete. They enable teachers to detect early signs and symptoms of many illnesses and health impairments and should, therefore, be conducted as part of ongoing observations. Daily health checks also help teachers become familiar with each child's typical appearance and behavior so that changes are easily recognized. This is especially important for teachers who have children with chronic health conditions or other special needs in their classrooms (French, 2004). Because these children are often more susceptible to infections and communicable illnesses, daily health checks can be beneficial for the early identification and removal of sick children.

Parents should be encouraged to remain with their child until the health check has been completed. Children may find comfort in having a family member nearby. Families are also able to provide information about conditions or behaviors the teacher has observed. Parents may also be less apprehensive if they have an opportunity to witness health checks firsthand and to ask their own questions. However, if a parent is unavailable, it may be advisable to have a second teacher witness the procedure so as to avoid any allegations of misconduct.

Method

A quiet area set aside in the classroom is ideal for conducting health checks. A teacher may choose simply to sit on the floor with the children or provide a more structured setting with a table and chairs. Health checks should be conducted in the same area each day, so children become familiar with the routine.

Conducting health checks in a systematic manner can improve the teacher's efficiency and assure that the process will be consistent and thorough each time. Table 3–1 illustrates a simple observation checklist that can be used for this purpose. It is organized so that observations are conducted from head to foot, first looking at the child's front- and then backside. However, this procedure can easily be modified to meet a program's unique needs in terms of setting and children being served. For example, teachers who work with school-age children might use the

TABLE 3-1 Health Observation Checklist

1. *General appearance*—note changes in weight (gain or loss), signs of fatigue or unusual excitability, skin tone (pallor or flushed), and size for age group.
2. *Scalp*—observe for signs of itching, head lice, sores, hair loss, and cleanliness.
3. *Face*—notice general expression (e.g., fear, anger, happy, anxious), skin tone, and any scratches, bruises, or rashes.
4. *Eyes*—look for redness, tearing, puffiness, sensitivity to light, frequent rubbing, styes, sores, drainage, or uncoordinated eye movements.
5. *Ears*—check for drainage, redness, and appropriate responses to sounds or verbal requests.
6. *Nose*—note any deformity, frequent rubbing, congestion, sneezing, or drainage.
7. *Mouth*—look inside at the teeth; note cavities, malformations, sores, or mouth-breathing.
8. *Throat*—observe for enlarged or red tonsils, red throat, white patches on throat or tonsils, drainage, or unusual breath odors.
9. *Neck*—feel for enlarged glands.
10. *Chest*—watch the child's breathing and note any wheezing, rattles, shortness of breath, coughing (with or without other symptoms).
11. *Skin*—lift up clothing and observe the chest and back for color (pallor or redness), rashes, scratches, bumps, bruises, scars, unusual warmth, and perspiration.
12. *Speech*—listen for clarity, stuttering, nasality, mispronunciations, monotone voice, and appropriateness for age.
13. *Extremities*—observe posture, coordination; note conditions such as bowed legs, toeing-in, or arms and legs of unequal length.
14. *Behavior and temperament*—note any changes in activity level, alertness, cooperation, appetite, sleep patterns, toileting habits, irritability, or uncharacteristic restlessness.

checklist as a guide for observing signs and symptoms in children rather than for conducting a hands-on health check.

A teacher should begin the daily health checks by observing children as they first enter the classroom. Clues about their well-being, such as personal cleanliness, weight changes, signs of illness, facial expressions, posture, skin color, balance and coordination, can be quickly noted. The nature of parent–child interactions and their relationship with one another can also be noted and may help to explain why some children exhibit certain behaviors. For example, does the parent have a tendency to do everything for the child—take off boots, hang up coats, pick up items the child has dropped—or is the child encouraged to be independent? Is the child allowed to answer questions or does the parent provide all of the answers?

Following these initial observations, a flashlight can be used to inspect inside of the mouth and throat (Figure 3–3). A quick look inside alerts the teacher to any child with an unusually red throat, swollen or infected tonsils, dental cavities, sores, or unusual breath odors. Observations of

 REFLECTIVE THOUGHTS

Daily health checks serve many important functions. They help teachers monitor children's health, and can also be a valuable teaching tool. How can teachers involve children in the process? What can children learn from this experience? What are some health and safety topics that teachers might discuss with children during health checks? What strategies can a teacher use to improve a child's cooperation? How might families be involved?

FIGURE 3–3

Teachers' observations can provide valuable clues about a child's well-being.

the hair and face, including the eyes, ears, and nose, can provide clues about the child's general hygiene as well as any communicable illness.

Next, the child's clothing can be lifted and any rashes, unusual scratches, bumps or bruises, and skin color on the chest, abdomen, and arms noted. Patches of blue discoloration, called Mongolian spots, are sometimes visible on the lower back of children with darker skin pigment, particularly children of Asian, Native American, and Middle Eastern origin. These spots appear similar to bruises, but do not undergo the color changes typical of an injury. Mongolian patches gradually disappear as children approach eight or nine years of age. Because many rashes associated with communicable disease begin on the warmer areas of the body, such as the chest, back, neck, and forearms, these parts should be inspected carefully (Figure 3–4). Finally, the child is asked to turn around and similar checks are made of the head, hair, and back.

Teachers should continue their observations after the health check has been completed. For example, balance, coordination, and posture can easily be noted as an infant crawls away or an older child walks over to join their friends. Information gathered from health checks and teacher observations contributes to a well-rounded picture of a child's health status—physical, mental, emotional, and social well-being (Table 3–2).

With time and practice, teachers become skilled in conducting daily health checks and making valuable observations. They are able to recognize the early signs and **symptoms** of illnesses and health conditions that may be cause for concern or require further evaluation.

Recording Health Observations

Teachers are indispensable as observers and recorders of information concerning children's health. Through their skilled questioning, careful listening, keen observation, understanding of children's development, and precise recording skills, they contribute information that can be useful to health care professionals. Observations should be recorded immediately following the health check and placed in each child's permanent health file or notebook designated for this purpose. Programs may develop a form similar to the one illustrated in Figure 3–5, or use daily attendance records to record **anecdotal** health information. Checklists can also be useful for conducting and recording observations in a systematic manner. Throughout the day, any additional changes in a child's condition, such as a seizure, uncontrollable coughing, or episode of diarrhea, should also be noted and reported to the family.

---

symptoms – *changes in the body or its functions that are experienced by the affected individual.*
anecdotal – *a brief note or description that contains useful and important information.*

FIGURE 3-4

Checklists are useful for conducting systematic observations and recording information about children's health.

Observations must be recorded in an accurate and precise manner in order to be meaningful to others. To say that a child "looks sick" is vague and open to individual interpretation. However, stating that a child is flushed, has a fever of 101°F (38.3°C), and is covered with a fine red rash on his torso is definitive and less likely to be confusing. A meaningful description is also helpful to families who may need to convey this information to the child's physician (Dailey, 1999).

Confidentiality of Health Information

Information obtained from daily health checks and teacher observations should be treated with utmost confidentiality and not left out where it may be accessible to other families or staff members. Anecdotal records and health checklists should be kept in a notebook or folder to protect children's identity until the information can be transferred to their personal files. Additionally, this

TABLE 3-2 Checklist of Potential Warning Signs of Mental Health Problems

Occasional responses to stress and change are to be expected. However, children who experience excessive or frequent episodes of the following behaviors may need to be referred for professional evaluation and treatment:

- *tearfulness or sadness*
- *preference for being alone*—is withdrawn; reluctant to play with others
- *hostility or excessive* anger—overreacts to situations; has frequent tantrums
- *difficulty concentrating*—has trouble staying focused, remembering, or making decisions
- *aggressiveness*—initiates fights; hurts animals or others; destroys property
- *irritability*—seems anxious, restless or overly worried; continuous fidgeting
- *unexplained change in eating and/or sleeping habits*—refusal to eat; compulsive eating; persistent nightmares; difficulty sleeping
- *excessive fear*—exhibits fear that is excessive or unwarranted
- *feelings of worthlessness*—self-critical; fear or failure; unwilling to try new things
- *refusal to go to school*—*repeatedly* fails to complete work; performs poorly in school
- *complains of physical ailments*—experiences stomachaches, headaches, joint aches, or fatigue without any reasonable cause
- *engages in substance abuse* (for older children)—uses drugs and/or drinks
- *talks about suicide*—overly curious about suicide

Sunny Days Child Care Center

Daily Health Check Recording Form

Week of: _____

Observations and Comments

Child's Name	Monday	Tuesday	Wednesday	Thursday	Friday

FIGURE 3-5

Daily health check form

Download this form online at http://www.EarlyChildEd.delmar.cengage.com

information must never be released to another individual or organization without first obtaining written parental permission (HHS, 2003). However, federal law guarantees families the right to access information in their child's health file at anytime and to request correction of errors or mistakes.

Benefits of Health Observations

Monitoring children's health status on a regular basis offers several distinct advantages. First, teachers are obligated, professionally and morally, to protect the health of other children in a group setting (Aronson, 2002). Observations and daily health checks provide an effective way to achieve this goal. For example, a teacher may note changes in a child's appearance or behavior that signal the onset of a communicable illness. This information can be used to determine if a child is too ill to remain in the classroom based on the program's exclusion policies. Sending a sick child home reduces unnecessary exposure to other children.

Daily health checks and teacher observations provide several additional benefits. Teachers' descriptive records can be helpful to health care professionals when they are evaluating a child's condition. A teacher's perspective adds a unique dimension in the identification and understanding of how a health problem may be affecting a child's development. The earlier health impairments, such as a hearing loss, allergy, or diabetes, are recognized and treatment is begun, the less negative the impact will be on a child's ability to learn.

> *Caution:* **Responsibility for interpreting signs and symptoms of an illness or health condition and arriving at a final diagnosis always belongs to trained health care professionals.**

Children also benefit from the individualized attention given to their well-being and to the informal health education that can take place during health checks. This daily routine also enhances children's awareness of their personal health and may help them become more comfortable with visits to their health care provider.

Patterns of illness or significant behavioral changes can also be noted by examining daily health records. For example, knowing that children have been exposed to chicken pox or that there has been a reported outbreak of head lice in the community should alert teachers to be even more vigilant in the coming weeks.

FAMILY INVOLVEMENT

Daily health checks provide an excellent opportunity for involving families in children's preventive health care. Frequent contact with families helps build a relationship of understanding and trust with staff (Wright & Stegelin, 2003; File, 2001; Turbiville, Umbarger, & Guthrie, 2000) (Figure 3–6).

REFLECTIVE THOUGHTS

Family involvement in children's education has been shown to have a positive effect on their development. Finding ways to increase family participation is, therefore, important.

How do children benefit from family involvement? What are some ways that families can become more involved in children's programs? What strategies can teachers use to successfully increase family participation? How can we help families who are uncomfortable in a school setting feel more welcomed?

---

diagnosis – *the process of identifying a disease, illness, or injury from its symptoms.*

FIGURE 3–6

Effective communication builds a relationship of trust and understanding between families and teachers.

Some families may be hesitant, at first, to initiate contacts with the teacher regarding their child's health needs. However, through repeated encouragement, interest, and assistance, effective lines of communication can gradually be established (Lundgren & Morrison, 2003).

During the health check procedure, parents should be encouraged to ask questions and voice concerns about their child's behavior, physical condition, habits, or adjustment to care. In addition, parents may be able to provide simple explanations for problems the teacher observes. For example, a child's fatigue or aggressiveness may be the result of a new puppy, a grandmother's visit, a new baby in the home, or a seizure the night before. Allergies or a red vitamin taken at breakfast may be the cause of a questionable red throat. Without this direct sharing of information, such symptoms might otherwise be cause for concern.

Contacts with families during health checks are also a good time to alert them to outbreaks of communicable illnesses. Letting them know what signs and symptoms to watch for will help them to avoid bringing sick children to school.

The Family's Responsibility

Primary responsibility for a child's health care *always* belongs to the family. They are ultimately responsible for maintaining their child's health, following through with recommendations, and obtaining any necessary evaluations and treatments.

Often families are the first to sense that something is wrong with their child (Allen & Marotz, 2007). However, they may delay seeking professional advice, either denying that a problem exists or hoping the child will eventually outgrow it. Some parents may not realize the serious consequences that health problems can have on their child's development and learning potential. Others may not be able to determine the exact nature of a child's problem or know where to go to obtain appropriate diagnosis and treatment.

Occasionally, families fail to take the initiative to provide for any type of routine health care. Some parents find it difficult to understand the need for medical care when a child does not appear to be sick, while others simply cannot afford preventive health care. With today's rising medical care costs, it is easy to understand why this might occur. Cost, however, must not discourage parents from obtaining necessary medical attention. Health insurance is now available for income-eligible children through the national State Children's Health Insurance Program (SCHIP) to help improve their access to health care. In addition, most communities offer a variety of free or low-cost health services for young children, including:

- Head Start
- Child Find screening programs
- Medicaid assistance
- Well-child clinics
- University-affiliated training centers and clinics
- Public health immunization centers
- Community centers
- Interagency Coordinating Councils

These agencies and services can generally be located in the telephone directory or by contacting the local public health department.

Teachers can be supportive and instrumental in helping parents understand the importance of scheduling routine health care for children. They can also become familiar with community resources and assist families in securing appropriate health care services (Allen & Cowdery, 2005).

HEALTH EDUCATION

Daily health checks also provide many opportunities for teaching children about good health. Teachers can begin to encourage children's interest in practices that promote a healthy lifestyle.

Simple questions about topics, such as dental hygiene, nutrition, physical activity, and sleep, can be discussed with even very young children. For example:

- "Sandy, did you brush your teeth this morning? Brushing helps to keep teeth healthy and chases away the mean germs that cause cavities."
- "Mario, have you had a drink of water yet today? Water helps our body grow and stay healthy just like the plants in the classroom."

ISSUES TO CONSIDER • The Impact of Health on Learning

High drop-out rates among school-age children continue to attract national attention. According to several recent studies, many of these children have undiagnosed health problems, such as vision and hearing impairments, allergies, asthma, and anemia, which interfere with their ability to learn and perform adequately in school. After years of struggle and failure, some children simply choose to abandon the source of their frustration.

The visionary founders of Head Start clearly understood the importance of early identification of children's health problems to assure that they were ready and able to learn upon entering school. This fundamental principle was again recognized in the *Goals 2000* and reiterated in the *Healthy People 2010* initiatives. Together, these programs continue to reinforce the essential role teachers play in assessing and promoting children's health.

- Should inservice and teacher education programs include more training about children's health needs? Explain.
- Do state child care licensing regulations support this important role?
- What rights does a teacher have in terms of making sure that children receive treatment for their health problems?
- What health care options exist for children whose families cannot afford needed treatments?

FOCUS ON FAMILIES • Children's Oral Health

Good oral health and a bright smile are important components of children's well-being. Teeth are necessary for chewing, speech, maintaining proper space for permanent teeth, and appearance. Decay and infection can cause discomfort and make it difficult for children to focus on school. Unfortunately, tooth decay continues to affect many young children today despite increased public education and improved dental treatments. However, families can do many things at home to promote children's dental health.

- Keep baby's gums clean by wiping them with a damp washcloth after each feeding.
- Dampen a soft toothbrush and use twice daily to clean baby's first teeth.
- Don't put babies to bed with a bottle containing juice, formula, or breast milk. These solutions can pool around gums and teeth and lead to early decay. Offer water if your baby takes a bottle to bed. Also, stop breastfeeding once baby falls asleep.
- Apply a pea-sized dab of toothpaste to a soft brush and encourage toddlers to begin brushing their own teeth. Be sure to follow their efforts by "going around the block" once again.
- Purchase fluoride toothpaste to help reduce dental decay. Fluoride is also added to the water supply in many cities. Your doctor or dentist may prescribe fluoride drops or tablets if your local water supply does not contain adequate fluoride.
- Continue to supervise preschool children's twice-daily tooth brushing. Discourage children from swallowing too much fluoride toothpaste; this can cause spots to develop on children's permanent teeth.
- Schedule your child's first routine dental check between one and two years of age. If you can't afford dental care, contact local public health personnel for information about free or low-cost options in your community. Reduced-cost dental insurance is also available to low income families in some states.
- Serve nutritious meals and snacks. Include fresh fruits and vegetables, whole-grain breads, crackers and cereals, and dairy products and limit sugary foods and drinks.
- Offer children water when they are thirsty. Limit their consumption of carbonated beverages, fruit drinks, and sport drinks, which tend to be high in sugars.

School-age children can be engaged in discussions that are more advanced. For example:

- "Yolanda, how many different fruits and vegetables have you eaten today? Eating a variety of fruits and vegetables provides different vitamins that our body needs to stay healthy."
- "Raja, did you put on sunscreen before playing outdoors? The sun has special rays that can damage our skin.

Utilizing everyday situations for ongoing health education can capture children's interest and help them begin to understand the importance of taking good care of themselves.

Family Education

Daily health checks also provide an effective opportunity for sharing information with families. Many topics related to children's health care and education lend themselves to informal discussions with parents during the daily health check assessment, such as:

- new safety alerts and concerns
- the importance of eating breakfast
- nutritious snack ideas
- getting children involved in physical activity
- handwashing
- dressing children appropriately for the weather
- dental hygiene
- new vaccines

Including families in health education programs brings about an improved understanding of the health principles and goals that a program shares with the children. It also assures greater consistency in terms of information and practices between school and the child's home.

CASE STUDY

Lynette's teacher recently became concerned about her ability to see. He has noticed that during group story time, Lynette quickly loses interest, often leaves her place in the circle, and crawls closer to him in order to see the pictures he holds up. The teacher has also observed that Lynette lowers her head close to puzzles and books. Lynette's parents have also expressed some concern about her clumsiness at home. The results of two vision screening tests, administered by the school nurse on different days, suggest that Lynette's vision is not within normal limits. These findings were shared with her parents who were encouraged to take Lynette to an eye specialist for further evaluation.

1. What behaviors did Lynette exhibit that made her teacher suspect some type of vision disorder?

2. Identify the sources from which information concerning Lynette's vision problem was obtained before she was referred to an eye specialist.

3. If the teacher suspected a vision problem, why didn't he just go ahead and recommend that Lynette get glasses?

4. What responsibilities do teachers have when they believe that a child has a health impairment?

CLASSROOM CORNER • Teacher Activities

I Hear With My Ears...
Concept: You use your ears to hear sounds. (Pre-2)

Learning Objectives
- Children will learn that ears are used for hearing sounds.
- Children will learn that there are many sounds all around.

Supplies
- various musical instruments (need two of each); a divider or a barrier

(continued)

CLASSROOM CORNER • Teacher Activities (continued)

Learning Activities

- Read and discuss one of the following books:
  - *You Hear with Your Ears* by Melvin and Gilda Berger
  - *The Ear Book* by Al Perkins
- Tell the children that their ears are for hearing sounds. Ask them some of the sounds that they hear.
- Place the musical instruments where the children can see them and play each one so they can become familiar with the sound each instrument makes.
- Next, place one of each instrument in front of the barrier/divider and one of each behind the barrier/divider.
- Call up one child to go behind the divider and pick an instrument to play. While he/she is playing the instrument, call on another child to come up and pick the instrument which makes the matching sound to the instrument the child is playing behind the barrier.
- Continue until each child has had a turn, and then have the children play all the instruments at once.
- Talk about why it is important to take good care of our ears so we can hear.

Evaluation

- Children can name which body part is used for hearing.
- Children will name some different sounds in their environment.
- Children can match sounds.

SUMMARY

- Good health is essential for effective learning.
  - Health problems can interfere with children's ability to learn.
- Teachers play a valuable role in promoting children's health.
  - Their observations provide information about children's physical, mental, social, and emotional well-being.
  - Their daily health checks yield additional information that is useful for identifying changes in children's health status, including communicable illness.
  - They must never attempt to diagnose children's health problems; this is the health professional's responsibility.
  - They can help families understand the need for professional health care, and assist them in locating appropriate and affordable community services.
- Information gathered from daily health checks and teacher observations can be useful to health professionals for diagnosing and/or ruling out children's health problems.
- Families must always be involved in children's health care and health education.

APPLICATION ACTIVITIES

1. With another student, role-play the daily health check procedure. Record your findings and discuss the experience. Do you have any suggestions for the "teacher" conducting the procedure?

2. Invite a public health nurse from a well-child clinic or a local pediatrician to speak to the class about preventive health care for children birth to 12 years.

3. Visit several early education programs in your community. Note whether health checks are conducted as children arrive. Describe the method you observed at each center. Also, briefly discuss how this information was recorded.

4. Develop a list of resources available in your community and state for children with vision impairments, speech impairments, deafness, cerebral palsy, autism, and learning disabilities. Be creative in your search; consider child care options, schools, special equipment needs, availability of special therapists, transportation needs, family financial assistance, etc.

CHAPTER REVIEW

A. **By Yourself:**

1. Define each of the *Terms to Know* listed at the beginning of this chapter.

2. Explain how a child's health and ability to learn influence each other.

3. List the reasons why teachers should conduct daily health checks.

4. Describe how an elementary teacher might modify the health check procedure to use with older children.

B. **As a Group:**

1. Describe the sources available to teachers for gathering information about a child's health.

2. Discuss how you might respond to a parent who objects to the daily health checks conducted by her child's teacher.

3. What benefits do daily health checks have for the child?

4. What are some things teachers can do to get families more involved in their child's preventive health care?

5. Describe the health check routine. What are some of the health problems/conditions that teachers should be looking for?

6. What suggestions would you have for a preschool teacher who says he is too busy to conduct daily health checks?

REFERENCES

Allen, K. E., & Cowdery, G. (2005). *The exceptional child: Inclusion in early childhood education.* (5th ed.). Clifton Park, NY: Thomson Delmar Learning.

Allen, K. E., & Marotz, L. R. (2007). *Developmental profiles: Pre-birth through twelve.* (5th ed.). Clifton Park, NY: Thomson Delmar Learning.

Aronson, S. (2002). *Healthy young children: A manual for programs.* (4th ed.). Washington, DC: NAEYC.

Bentzen, W. R. (2005). *Seeing young children: A guide to observing and recording behavior.* (5th ed.). Clifton Park, NY: Thomson Delmar Learning.

Dailey, L. (1999). Communicating health, safety, and developmental concerns to parents. *Child Care Health Connections, 12*(5), 4.

File, N. (2001). Family-professional partnerships: Practice that matches philosophy. *Young Children, 56*(4), 70–74.

French, K. (2004). Supporting a child with special health care needs. *Young Children, 59*(2), 62–63.

Lundgren, D., & Morrison, J. W. (2003). Involving Spanish-speaking families in early education programs. *Young Children, 58*(3), 88–95.

Turbiville, V. P., Umbarger, G. T., & Guthrie, A.C. (2000). Father's involvement in programs for young children. *Young Children, 55*(4), 74–79.

U.S. Department of Health & Human Services (HHS). (2006). *Healthy people 2010.* Office of Disease Prevention and Health Promotion. Accessed October 5, 2006, from http://www.healthypeople.gov.

U.S. Department of Health & Human Services (HHS). (2003). Fact sheet: Protecting the privacy of patients' health information. Accessed May 25, 2003, from http://www.hhs.gov/news/facts/privacy.html.

Wright, K. & Stegelin, D.A. (2003). *Building school and community partnerships through parent involvement.* Upper Saddle River, NJ: Merrill/Prentice Hall.

HELPFUL WEB RESOURCES

Canada Health Portal	http://www.chp-pcs.gc.ca
Child Development Institute	http://www.cdipage.com
Early Head Start National Resource Center	http://www.ehsnrc.org
Office of Head Start	http://www.acf.hhs.gov
Tuft's University	http://www.cfw.tufts.edu
Zero to Three; National Center for Infants, Toddlers, and Families	http://www.zerotothree.org

For additional health, safety, and nutrition resources, go to http://www.EarlyChildEd.delmar.cengage.com

CHAPTER 4

Health Assessment Tools

After studying this chapter, you should be able to:

- List five screening procedures that can be used to assess a child's health status.
- Name and describe three vision impairments that can be detected through screening.
- Match the recommended screening test to the condition or behavior that indicates its need.
- Identify the physical signs of three common nutritional deficiencies.
- Describe two methods used for dietary assessment.

❈ **TERMS TO KNOW**

intervention	myopia	misarticulations
referrals	hyperopia	pallor
skeletal	language	lethargy
neurological	audiologist	mottling
ophthalmologist	conductive loss	nutrient intake
optometrist	sensorineural loss	skinfold
amblyopia	mixed hearing loss	
strabismus	speech	

Teachers understand that health problems can interfere with a child's ability to learn and that early detection improves the success of many interventions. Screening instruments are available to help teachers identify children who may require additional evaluation. Several are described in this chapter. Information collected in an objective manner and from a combination of screening procedures yields: (1) reliable data for health promotion, (2) the early detection of potentially disabling conditions that can affect children's growth and development, and (3) an opportunity to adjust programs and environments to meet a child's unique needs.

HEALTH RECORDS

Careful recordkeeping is not always a priority in many early childhood programs. However, when information in children's files is current and sufficiently detailed, it can be used to promote their well-being (Table 4–1). The types of records schools are required to maintain are usually mandated by state departments of education. Child care licensing divisions in each state issue similar regulations for licensed centers and home-based programs. However, because these regulations typically reflect only minimal standards, programs may want to consider keeping additional sources of documentation. Unlicensed programs are not obligated to maintain any type of records.

Forms and records should be designed to gather information that is consistent with a program's goals and philosophy and that protects the legal rights of the children and staff. This information can serve many purposes, including:

- determining children's health status
- identifying patterns and potential problem areas
- developing **intervention** programs
- evaluating the outcome of special services, e.g., speech therapy, occupational therapy
- coordinating services
- making **referrals**
- following a child's progress
- research

Health records often include private information about children and their families. Only information that a teacher requires to work effectively with a child should be shared. Personal details about a child or family should remain confidential and must never serve as topics of conversation outside of the classroom. No portion of a child's health record should ever be released to another agency, school, health professional, or clinician until written permission has been obtained from the child's parent or guardian. A special release form, such as the one shown in Figure 4–1, can be used for this purpose. The form should clearly indicate the nature of information to be released and the agency or person to whom it is to be sent. It must also be dated and signed by the parent or guardian, and a copy retained in the child's folder.

Recordkeeping is most efficient when one person is responsible for maintaining all health-related records. However, input from all members of a child's teaching team is important for

---

TABLE 4–1 Children's Health Records

Children's permanent health records should include:

- child/family health history
- copy of a recent medical assessment (physical examination)
- immunization records
- emergency contact information
- record of dental examinations
- attendance data
- school-related injuries
- documentation of family conferences concerning the child's health
- screening results, e.g., vision, hearing, speech, developmental
- medications administered while the child is at school

---

intervention – *practices or procedures implemented to modify or change a specific behavior or condition.*
referrals – *directing an individual to other sources, usually for additional evaluation or treatment.*

FIGURE 4–1

A sample information release form.

INFORMATION RELEASE FORM

I understand the confidentiality of any personally identifiable information concerning my child shall be maintained in accordance with the Family Education Rights and Privacy Act (P.L.93-380), federal and state regulations, and used only for the educational benefit of my child. Personally identifiable information about my child will be released only with my written consent. With this information, I hereby grant the

_____
(Name of program, agency, or person)

permission to release the following types of information:

Medical information	_____
Assessment reports	_____
Child histories	_____
Progress reports	_____
Clinical reports	_____
(Other)	_____

to:_____
(Name of agency or person to whom information is to be sent)

regarding _____ _____ _____
                 Child's Name   Birthdate   Gender

_____
Signature of Parent or Guardian

_____
Relationship of Representative

_____
Date

determining the overall impact of health problems and for monitoring progress. Because health records are legal documents, schools and programs should keep them on file for at least five years.

Child Health Histories

Health histories include information about children's backgrounds, past medical conditions, as well as current developmental status and health problems. Questions about family history are generally included to provide a better understanding of the child's strengths and special needs. Families should complete the health history form at the time of enrollment and update it annually to reflect any changes.

The nature of information requested on health history forms varies from program to program. Unless a standardized form is required by a licensing agency or school district, programs may wish to develop their own format. Sample forms can often be obtained from other programs or state agencies and modified to meet a program's specific needs. However, questionnaires should gather certain basic information including:

- circumstances related to the child's birth
- family structure, e.g., siblings and their ages, family members, predominant language spoken, legal custody issues
- major developmental milestones
- previous injuries, illnesses, surgeries or hospitalizations
- daily habits, e.g., toileting, eating habits, napping
- family concerns about the child, e.g., behavior problems, social development, speech delays
- any special health conditions, e.g., allergies, asthma, seizures, diabetes, poor vision, hearing loss

Information included in health histories contributes to a better understanding of each child's uniqueness, including past health events and potential health risks. It can also be helpful for assessing a child's current state of health and aid teachers in establishing appropriate goals and expectations for individual children. It also enables teachers to modify children's environments and activities to accommodate their special needs, such as a hearing loss, fatigue due to anemia, the use of a wheelchair, or a mild heart condition. However, caution must be exercised not to set expectation levels unnecessarily low for children based on this information alone. A child's potential for learning must never be discounted unless an impairment is definitely known to restrict the educational process or performance. Lowering goals and expectations may limit what a child is willing to try, for often children will achieve only what is expected and may not be encouraged to progress or achieve their true potential.

Child health histories also provide teachers with insight into the type of medical supervision a child receives. This information may reflect the value a family places on preventive health care and can be useful when making future referrals.

Medical and Dental Examinations

Most states require children to have a complete health assessment and current immunizations before they can attend school or an early education program. Some states require an annual examination, while others request it only at the time of admission. Health care providers recommend that infants have well-child checkups every two to three months. Families are encouraged to have their two- and three-year-olds examined by a physician every six months; children four and older should be examined annually. More frequent medical supervision may be necessary if children have existing health problems or new conditions develop.

Current information is obtained from the family and child during the course of the health examination. Families may also be asked to complete a brief developmental questionnaire to better help medical personnel assess all aspects of the child's health. The child's immunization record is reviewed and additional doses are administered as indicated. Body parts and systems, such as the heart, lungs, eyes, ears, **skeletal** and **neurological** development, and gastrointestinal function (stomach and intestines) are carefully examined. Head circumference is routinely measured on all infants and children until 36 months of age to be certain that head size continues to increase at an acceptable rate. Height, weight, and blood pressure readings (after age three) are also recorded and compared to prior measurements to determine if a child's growth is progressing satisfactorily. Lack of growth may be an indication of other health problems. Specialized tests, such as blood tests for anemia, sickle cell disease, or lead poisoning, may be ordered to identify or rule out any

---

skeletal – *pertaining to the bony framework that supports the body.*
neurological – *pertaining to the nervous system, which consists of the nerves, brain, and spinal column.*

of these conditions. Urinalysis, tuberculin testing, vision screening, and hearing evaluation may also be completed.

Although dental examinations are seldom required for enrollment in early education programs, their benefits are unquestionable. Parents are encouraged to take children in for routine dental checks and preventive care, including a visual inspection of the teeth, cleaning, and an application of fluoride, every 6 to 12 months.

SCREENING PROCEDURES

Screening tests are also an essential component of the comprehensive health assessment process. They reflect the philosophy of preventive care by ensuring that health problems and physical impairments do not interfere with a child's ability to learn.

A variety of screening tools are available for assessing children's health. Most are relatively quick, inexpensive, and efficient to administer to groups of young children. Some tests can be conducted by teachers, while others require the services of professional clinicians. Screening tests should only be used to identify children who may have an impairment that requires professional evaluation, *never* to diagnose or confirm specific conditions. Test results simply provide additional information about a child that can be used in combination with family and teacher observations, assessments of growth and development, and the results of daily health checks.

Measurements of Height and Weight

The first five years of life are an important period of rapid growth. Increases in height and weight are most dramatic during infancy, and continue at a slower, but steady, rate throughout the preschool and school-age years (Allen & Marotz, 2007). Measurements of height are particularly important because they are a reliable indicator of a child's general health and nutritional status (see Appendix B for growth curves that show norms by children's age and gender). Weight, on the other hand, fluctuates in response to short-term events, such as a recent illness, infection, emotional stress, or overeating.

Teachers and families must understand that a child's growth potential is ultimately governed by genetics. This is especially important to remember when working with children from different cultures and ethnic backgrounds. New growth charts, released by the Centers for Disease Control & Prevention (CDC) in 2000, more accurately represent the diverse child population in the U.S. although they still lack height and weight measures that are appropriate for all ethnicities. The World Health Organization (WHO) has since released new international Child Growth Standards for children birth to 19 years (WHO, 2006) (www.who.int/childgrowth/en). The standards also include developmental milestones (Windows of Achievement) based on an extensive study of children, birth to age five, from around the world and may more accurately reflect the growth and developmental patterns typical of today's children.

Ideally, height and weight should be measured at four- to six-month intervals and recorded in the child's permanent health file. A single measurement is unlikely to identify the child who is experiencing a growth disturbance related to physical illness, stress, or an eating disorder. Rather, what is more important is the pattern of changes that occur over a period of time. Measurements recorded on standardized growth charts allow comparisons to be made with previous data and can be useful for determining if a child's growth is progressing satisfactorily (Figure 4–2). Growth charts are available from the National Centers for Health Statistics or they can be downloaded from their Web site: http://www.cdc.gov/growthcharts/ (see Appendix B).

The Body Mass Index (BMI) is a newer tool that provides a height-for-weight ratio and is replacing the standard weight and height tables (see Appendix B). It can be used with children two years and older to determine their risk of being underweight, healthy weight, at risk of overweight, or overweight. Gender-specific charts are available for plotting children's BMI-for-age and can also

FIGURE 4–2

Measurements of height and weight provide a good index of children's health.

be accessed from the National Centers for Health Statistics' Web site. Examples of BMI-for-age charts are also included in Appendix B.

SENSORY DEVELOPMENT

The sensory system affects all parameters of a child's growth and development. Five special senses comprise the sensory system: vision, hearing, smell, touch, and taste. Children depend on these senses to receive, interpret, process, and respond to information in their environment. Optimal functioning

REFLECTIVE THOUGHTS

Children enjoy being weighed and measured. Monitoring their growth is important for assuring good health. Teachers can use this activity for periodic assessment of children's well-being and to reinforce their learning of good health practices. However, ethnic differences must be taken into consideration when using standardized tables (such as Appendix B) to evaluate children's measurements of height and weight. Data in these tables are based on middle-class, Caucasian children and do not account for ethnic variations in body structure. How could you determine if an Asian or Hispanic child's growth was appropriate? How does nutrition influence a child's growth? What classroom activities (science, art, language, motor) could you plan to help children understand the concept of good health? In what ways can teachers include children's families in health education activities? What Internet sites provide reliable health and nutrition information for young children?

of the sensory system is, therefore, of critical importance, especially during the early stages of growth and development. Of the five senses, vision and hearing are most critical for young children, since much of their early learning is dependent on what they are able to see and hear (Allen & Cowdery, 2005; MMWR, 2005).

❈ VISION SCREENING

It is often falsely assumed that because children are young and healthy they naturally have good vision. Approximately one in 20 preschoolers and one in four school-age children has a vision impairment that interferes with learning (Prevent Blindness America, 2006). Some conditions, such as cataracts or blindness, may be present at birth. Others can develop as the result of an injury or infectious illness, such as meningitis. Vision problems are also more common in children who have other disabilities, such as cerebral palsy, Down syndrome, or fetal alcohol syndrome (FAS) (Erin, 2000; Topor, 1999; Lewis & Russo, 1998). For this reason, an infant's eyes should be examined for abnormalities and muscle imbalance during routine well-child checkups to reduce the risk of permanent vision loss (Teplin, 1995). It is also recommended that all children have a professional eye evaluation by an **ophthalmologist** or **optometrist** before starting kindergarten. Early detection of vision impairments improves the success of medical treatments and a child's readiness for school.

Often, it is the teacher who first notices clues in a child's behavior that suggest a vision disorder (Figure 4–3). As greater demands are placed on a child to perform tasks accurately, vision problems become more apparent. Also, it is unlikely that young children will recognize when their vision is not normal, especially if they have never experienced good vision. A careful comparison of screening results and adult observations can provide reliable information about a child's vision and the need for professional referral.

Special attention should be paid to children who have other known physical disabilities or who are repeatedly unsuccessful in achieving tasks that depend on visual cues (Allen & Cowdery, 2005).

FIGURE 4–3

Often it is the teacher who first notices signs of a child's vision problem.

---

ophthalmologist – *a physician who specializes in diseases and abnormalities of the eye.*
optometrist – *a specialist (nonphysician) trained to examine eyes and prescribe glasses and eye exercises.*

Delays in identifying vision problems can seriously affect the learning process and reduce the chance for successful treatment. Undiagnosed vision problems can lead to the inappropriate labeling of children as cognitively delayed or mentally retarded when, in fact, they simply cannot see well enough to learn (Allen & Marotz, 2007). The following case study illustrates the point:

> In many ways, Tina is a typical four-year-old. However, the teachers have been puzzled by some of her recent behaviors. Tina seems easily frustrated and unable to complete many of the preacademic tasks that her peers enjoy, such as puzzles, tracing, threading beads, and simple object labeling. She seems to be quite clumsy and is often reluctant to join in outdoor games with the other children. Her teachers are concerned that she may have a learning disability and have begun developmental testing. They also contacted the school health consultant to have Tina's vision checked and were surprised to learn that it was only 20/100. Tina's mother was encouraged to make an appointment with an eye specialist and, after further testing, it was determined that Tina needed corrective glasses. The teachers are amazed by the changes that Tina's glasses have made in both her behavior and academic progress.

Methods of Assessment

Early detection of visual impairments requires observing children carefully for specific behavioral indicators (Tables 4–2 and 4–3). Any concerns should be discussed with a child's family and may confirm a teacher's suspicions. Some vision problems are more difficult to detect because there are no visible signs or symptoms. Vision problems are also not outgrown, nor do they usually improve without treatment (Figure 4–4). Therefore, routine screenings are essential for monitoring children's vision and making sure that it continues to develop properly (Greenwald, 2003).

An infant's vision can be tested by holding an object, such as a rattle, 10 to 12 inches away and observing the infant's ability to focus on (fixation) and track (follow) the object as it is moved in a 180° arc around the child's head. The infant's eyes should also be observed carefully for any uncoordinated movements as the object is brought closer (convergence) and farther away from the face. In addition, the blink reflex (sweep hand quickly in front of the eyes; observe for blinking), and pupil response (shine a penlight, held four to six inches away, into the eye; pupil should become smaller) should also be checked. A child showing abnormal responses should be referred for professional evaluation.

Teachers and volunteers can be trained by health professionals to administer many of the standardized visual acuity tests (Table 4–4) (The Vision in Preschoolers Study Group, 2005). Printable versions of the Eye Tests for Children (HOTV charts for near and distance vision) are also available on the Prevent Blindness America Web site (www.preventblindness.org) or by contacting the

---

TABLE 4–2 Early Signs of Visual Abnormalities in Infants and Toddlers

Observe the infant closely for:

- roving eye movements that are suggestive of blindness
- jerky or fluttering eye movements
- eyes that wander in opposite directions or are crossed (after three months)
- inability to focus or follow a moving object (after three months)
- pupil of one eye larger than the other
- absence of a blink reflex
- drooping of one or both lids
- cloudiness on the eyeball
- chronic tearing

TABLE 4-3 Signs of Visual Acuity Problems in Older Children

- rubs eyes frequently
- attempts to brush away blurs
- is irritable with close work
- is inattentive to distant tasks, e.g., watching a movie, catching a ball
- strains to see distant objects; squints; or screws up face
- blinks often when reading; holds books too close or far away
- is inattentive with close work; quits after a short time
- closes or covers one eye to see better
- tilts head to one side
- appears cross-eyed at times
- reverses letters, words
- stumbles over objects; runs into things
- complains of repeated headaches or double vision
- poor eye–hand coordination
- experiences repeated styes, redness, or watery eyes

organization's headquarters (211 West Wacker Drive, Chicago, IL, 60606). Children's eyes should also be checked for:

- convergence
- depth perception (Titmus Fly test)
- binocular fusion (Worth 4-Dot test; Random Dot E)
- deviations in pupil position (test by holding a penlight 12 inches from the child's face, direct light at the bridge of the nose; the light reflection should appear in the same position on both pupils; any discrepancy requires professional evaluation.)

Photoscreening is a relatively new option that is increasingly being used with young children, especially those who are preverbal or nonverbal or have developmental delays or disabilities that would make it difficult for them to complete conventional screening procedures (Leman, et al., 2006;

FIGURE 4-4

Early detection and treatment of vision problems improves children's learning success.

⁂ **TABLE 4–4 Examples of Acuity Tests for Preschool Children**
• Denver Eye Screening Test (DEST) • HOTV Symbols Visual Acuity Test • Screening Test for Young Children and Retardates (STYCAR); (this test can be used with children who have developmental delays) • Snellen Illiterate E • Allen Card Test • Cover-Uncover Test • Lea Symbols Visual Acuity Test • Random Dot E Stereoacuity Test

AAP, 2002). A special camera records a small beam of light as it is reflected on the eye, and is especially useful for the early detection of amblyopia and strabismus. Although it is an efficient and effective screening technology, the equipment is relatively expensive and the test requires special training to administer.

Whenever screening tests are administered to children, it is important that they understand the instructions and expected method of response, or the results may be invalid. Children who fail an initial screening should be retested within two weeks. If a second screening is failed, testing results should be shared with the child's family and a referral made to a professional eye specialist for a comprehensive assessment.

The early detection and successful treatment of vision impairments in children has been targeted as a major goal in the *Healthy People 2010* initiative. Efforts to increase public awareness and to reach children in medically underserved areas are aimed at combating unnecessary and irreversible vision loss. Valuable information concerning symptoms of visual impairments, testing procedures, and treatments is also available on the Web sites of many professional organizations, including Prevent Blindness America (http://www.preventblindness.org), American Academy of Ophthalmology (http://www.aao.org), American Academy of Pediatrics (http://www.aap.org), and the American Association of Pediatric Ophthalmology and Strabismus (http://www.aapos.org).

Common Disorders

Vision screening programs are designed to detect three common disorders in young children, including:

- amblyopia
- strabismus
- myopia

Amblyopia, or "lazy eye," affects approximately 2 percent of all children younger than 10 years. Children born to mothers who smoke seem to be at higher risk for developing this condition (Lempert, 2005). Amblyopia is caused by a muscle imbalance or childhood cataracts that result in blurred or double vision. The child's brain finds this distortion confusing and begins to only recognize images received from the stronger eye while ignoring (suppressing) those from the weaker or "lazy" eye. Sight is gradually lost in the weaker eye as a result of disuse. This also causes a loss of depth perception which depends on having equal sight in both eyes.

---

amblyopia – *a condition of the eye commonly referred to as "lazy eye"; vision gradually becomes blurred or distorted due to unequal balance of the eye muscles. The eyes do not present any physical clues when a child has amblyopia.*

Early identification and treatment of amblyopia is critical for preventing a permanent loss of vision. If the condition is diagnosed before the age of six or seven, a significant portion of the child's eyesight can often be restored. Treatment is even more successful when this condition is diagnosed between six months and two years of age (National Eye Institute, 2006; Mittelman, 2003). However, new research suggests that children as old as 17 may regain some sight with treatment (Scheiman, et al., 2005).

Early diagnosis requires early detection (Leman, et al., 2006). Unfortunately, there are no observable signs in the child's appearance or behaviors which would suggest this condition. Children are seldom aware that anything is wrong with their vision and, therefore, unable to tell an adult. Consequently, amblyopia too often goes undetected. However, routine vision screening is effective for detecting this condition.

Amblyopia is commonly treated by having the child wear a patch over the stronger (unaffected) eye until the muscle strength in the weaker (affected eye) gradually improves. Additional methods for treating amblyopia include corrective glasses, eye drops, and special eye exercises (Repka, et al., 2003; Healthlink, 2002). Teachers may be asked to administer treatments while children are in school. They must understand the importance of maintaining a child's treatment schedule and be supportive when children resist or are embarrassed by having to wear special glasses or a patch. Teachers may need to take added precautions during treatments, such as clearing obstacles from pathways and holding children's hands to guide them around new spaces. Teachers can also use these opportunities to help other children develop empathy and acceptance for individuals with special needs.

Strabismus, commonly referred to as crossed eyes, is another vision impairment occasionally seen in young children. Strabismus causes an observable misalignment of the child's eyes (e.g., both eyes may turn inward, one eye may turn inward or outward) that occurs intermittently or consistently (Figure 4–5). As a result, children's eyes are not able to work together as a unit and they may experience symptoms similar to those of amblyopia, including double or blurred vision, images from the weaker eye being ignored by the brain, and gradual loss of vision.

FIGURE 4–5

Strabismus interferes with children's ability to see properly.

Early recognition and treatment of strabismus is essential for restoring normal vision. Today, even infants are being treated aggressively for this condition. Although uncoordinated eye movements are common in very young infants, by four months of age an infant's eyes should move together as a unit. Several methods are used to treat strabismus, including surgical correction, patching of the unaffected eye, and eye exercises.

Myopia, or nearsightedness can affect young children, but is more common in school-aged children. A child who is nearsighted can see near objects, but has poor distant vision. This condition is especially problematic for young children because they move about quickly and engage in play that is primarily large motor such as running, jumping, and climbing. As a result, children with myopia may appear clumsy, and repeatedly stumble or run into objects. Squinting is

---

strabismus – *a condition of the eyes in which one or both eyes appear to be turned inward (crossed) or outward (walleye).*
myopia – *nearsightedness; an individual has good near vision but poor distant vision.*

also common as children attempt to bring distant objects into focus. Teachers can be instrumental in noting these behaviors and referring children for screening.

Farsightedness, or **hyperopia**, is thought to be a normal occurence in children under the age of five, and is caused by a shortness of the eyeball. This condition often corrects itself as children mature and their eyeballs change shape. Children who are farsighted can see objects clearly at a distance but have difficulty focusing on near objects. Older children may struggle academically, be poor readers, have a short attention span, and complain of headaches, tired eyes, or blurred vision following periods of close work. Hyperopia cannot be easily detected with most routinely administered screening procedures. Teacher and parent observations often provide the best clues to this disorder. A child who exhibits signs of hyperopia should be referred to a professional eye specialist for evaluation.

Color blindness affects a small percentage of children and is generally limited to males. Females are carriers of this hereditary defect but are rarely affected themselves. The most common form of color blindness involves the inability to discriminate between red and green. Testing young children for color blindness is difficult and often omitted, since learning is not seriously affected and there is no treatment.

Management

When a child is suspected of having vision problems, families should be counseled and encouraged to arrange for professional screening (Kimel, 2006). Teachers can assist families in locating services and help them to understand why it is important to follow through with any recommendations. Arrangements for vision testing can often be made through pediatricians' offices, "well-child" clinics, public health departments, professional eye doctors, and public schools. Local service organizations, such as the Lions Clubs, may help qualified families with the costs of professional eye examinations and glasses.

Children who do not pass an initial vision screening should be retested. Failure to pass a second screening necessitates referral to a professional eye specialist for more extensive evaluation and diagnosis. However, results obtained from routine vision testing should be viewed with some caution because they do not guarantee that a child does or does not have a problem. Most routine screening procedures are not designed to test for all types of vision impairments. Consequently, there will always be some overreferral of children who do not have any problems, while other children with vision defects will be missed. It is for this reason that the observations of teachers

 REFLECTIVE THOUGHTS

Children who experience vision problems may require extra care and direction in the classroom (Li, 2004; Koenig & Holbrook, 2000; Desrochers, 1999). They may not be able to complete tasks as quickly or precisely as other children. Some children have difficulty tolerating treatments, such as patching or wearing modified glasses for amblyopia, because their visual field is temporarily distorted. Daily application and removal of adhesive patches can cause skin irritation and also attract peer attention and curiosity. How can teachers turn this opportunity into a learning experience for young children? What strategies can teachers use in the classroom to help a child with vision problems? How might vision problems affect children in outdoor settings? What observable behaviors would suggest to a parent or teacher that a child may have vision problems?

---

hyperopia – *farsightedness; a condition of the eyes in which an individual can see objects clearly in the distance but has poor close vision.*

and families are extremely important. Visual acuity also changes over time, so it is important for teachers and families to be continuously vigilant of children's visual performance.

HEARING SCREENING

A child's ability to hear is essential for the development of speech patterns, **language**, and many other facets of learning. Undetected hearing impairments can also affect the quality of a child's social interactions, emotional development, and performance in school (Niles, et al., 2006; Kaderavek & Pakulski, 2002). When children cannot hear properly, they may respond and behave in seemingly unacceptable ways and end up being labeled as slow learners, retarded, or behavior problems. Early diagnosis of any chronic hearing problem or loss is, therefore, extremely critical.

Methods of Assessment

Inappropriate responses and behaviors may be the first indication that a child is not hearing properly (Guralnick, 2000; Chen, 1998). Signs of hearing loss range from very obvious problems to those that are subtle and more difficult to identify (Table 4–5).

Hospitals in many states now comply with Universal Infant Hearing Screening recommendations (see Reflective Thoughts) (Connolly, et al., 2005). Trained hospital staff test infants' hearing shortly after birth to detect deafness. An infant's hearing can also be evaluated informally by checking for responses such as eye blinking and turning of the head or interruption of sucking in an attempt to locate sounds (Table 4–6). Older infants and toddlers can be tested by observing as they turn to locate sounds (often emitted through speakers in formal testing procedures), as well as by the appropriateness of their responses and language development. Although these procedures can be useful for identifying some children with hearing problems, they are not effective for detecting all forms of hearing loss.

Children's hearing should be tested by a trained specialist at least once during the preschool and school-age years and more often if a hearing problem is suspected. Hearing tests are conducted

TABLE 4–5 Indicators of Potential Hearing Loss

Parents and teachers may observe behaviors that suggest a possible hearing loss, such as:
- frequent mouth breathing
- failure to turn toward the direction of a sound
- delays in acquiring language; development of poor speech patterns
- difficulty understanding and following directions
- asking to have statements repeated
- rubbing or pulling at ears
- mumbling, shouting, or talking loudly
- reluctant to interact with others; quiet or withdrawn
- using gestures rather than words
- excelling in activities that do not depend on hearing
- imitating others at play
- responding to questions inappropriately
- mispronouncing many word sounds
- having an unusual voice quality—one that is extremely high, low, hoarse, or monotone
- failing to respond to normal sounds and voices

language – *form of communication that allows individuals to share feelings, ideas, and experiences with one another.*

TABLE 4–6 Early Signs of Hearing Abnormalities in the Infant and Toddler

Observe the infant closely for:

- absence of a startle response to a loud noise
- failure to stop crying briefly when adult speaks to baby (three months)
- failure to turn head in the direction of sound, such as a doorbell or a dog barking (four months)
- absence of babbling or interest in imitating simple speech sounds (six–eight months)
- no response to adult commands, such as "no"

by trained paraprofessionals, nurses, and **audiologists** to assess a child's ability to hear the normal range of tones used in everyday conversation (Figure 4–6).

Most children are able to complete routine hearing screening with little trouble. However, an unfamiliar situation involving new people, instruments and equipment, a novel task, a lack of understanding, or failure to cooperate may occasionally interfere with the child's performance and cause unreliable test results. These problems must be taken into consideration whenever children fail an initial screening. Children should always be retested to be sure that screening results are valid. Families and teachers should continue to monitor the child who passes a hearing test yet continues to exhibit behaviors suggestive of a hearing loss.

Teachers and families can be extremely helpful by preparing and training young children in advance for a hearing screening (Katz & Schery, 2006). Children can practice concentrated listening for short periods of time. They can also be involved in play activities that use headphones—telephone operators, airplane pilots, radio announcers, or musicians—to become more comfortable

FIGURE 4–6

Hearing tests are conducted by audiologists or trained personnel.

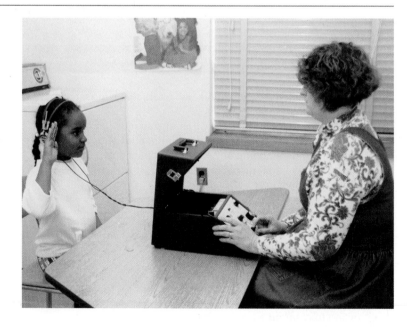

audiologist – *a specially prepared clinician who uses nonmedical techniques to diagnose hearing impairments.*

REFLECTIVE THOUGHTS

Universal Newborn Hearing Screening and Intervention programs are currently available in 45 states and the District of Columbia (ASHA, 2006). Many other countries around the world are making efforts to adapt and implement similar screening initiatives. These programs are designed to evaluate newborn infants for significant hearing loss before they leave the hospital nursery or maternity center so that arrangements can be made for additional testing and medical intervention if indicated (Widen, Bull & Folsom, 2003). Trained staff administer the test in a matter of minutes. Small electrodes, placed on the scalp, measure the baby's response (brain waves) to soft sounds emitted through a tiny earpiece. Babies experience no discomfort during this test, and parents can learn the results within minutes. The average cost for this testing is approximately $30 to $40 and is often covered by insurance plans. Numerous studies have demonstrated the unquestionable advantage of identifying infants with hearing loss and initiating appropriate intervention before six months of age (Grosse & Ross, 2006; Thompson, et al. 2001). Yet not every hospital offers this type of screening; some reserve it only for babies considered to be at high risk for having a hearing impairment (e.g., low birth weight, prematurity, family history, maternal infection during pregnancy, presence of other disabilities). Why is the early identification of hearing loss so important to young children's development? Why are hearing impairments often not diagnosed before the age of two to three years? What areas of development are most likely to be affected by hearing loss? What community resources are typically available to families who may have concerns about their child's hearing? Should all insurance companies be required to pay for newborn hearing screening? Explain.

when they are asked to wear headphones for screening purposes. Teachers should try to determine what response method (e.g., raising one hand, pressing a button, pointing to pictures, or dropping a wooden block into an empty can) children will be expected to use and practice this activity in the classroom. If a special room will be used for testing purposes, teachers should arrange for children to visit the facilities and look at the equipment beforehand. These special preparations will make hearing screening less frightening for young children and increase the reliability of test results.

Common Disorders

Children who are born with any physical disability are at greater risk of also having hearing problems (Allen & Marotz, 2007; Chen, 1998). Temporary and permanent hearing losses are more commonly associated with:

- a family history of hearing problems
- prenatal exposure to maternal infections, e.g., herpes, German measles, cytomegalovirus
- prematurity, low birthweight
- bacterial meningitis, measles, mumps
- allergies
- frequent colds and ear infections (otitis media)
- birth defects, such as Down syndrome, Fetal Alcohol syndrome (FAS), cleft lip/cleft palate, cerebral palsy
- head injuries

Any parent who expresses concern about their child's hearing should always be listened to carefully and encouraged to seek professional advice. The most common forms of hearing loss are:

- **Conductive loss** affects the volume of word tones. For example, this child will be able to hear loud, but not soft sounds. Conductive hearing loss occurs when sound waves are not being transmitted properly from the external ear to structures in the middle ear (Figure 4–7). Fluid accumulation in the child's middle ear following an infection is a common cause of conductive hearing loss.
- **Sensorineural loss** results when the structures of the inner ear (cochlea) or the auditory nerve (which connects to the brain) have been damaged or do not function properly. This type of hearing loss is permanent and affects a child's ability to understand speech and to hear softer sounds. Children who have a sensorineural loss are considered to have a learning disability that requires special educational management.
- **Mixed hearing loss** refers to a disorder that involves a combination of conductive and sensorineural hearing losses. Structures in both the outer or middle ear and the inner ear or auditory nerve have either been damaged or are not functional.

Management

Some hearing impairments can be successfully treated if they are identified in the early stages. Treatment depends on the underlying cause, and ranges from ear drops and antibiotic therapy to surgery (Katz & Schery, 2006; Paradise, et al., 2005). Some children benefit from hearing aids, while others eventually learn sign language.

A child who experiences a sudden or gradual hearing loss should be referred to a family physician for medical diagnosis or to an audiologist for a thorough hearing evaluation. Families can arrange for this testing through the child's doctor, a speech and hearing clinic, public health department, public schools, or an audiologist.

A teacher who understands how different impairments affect children's ability to hear, can take appropriate steps to improve communication and learning conditions (Table 4–7). Additional

FIGURE 4–7

Diagram of the ear.

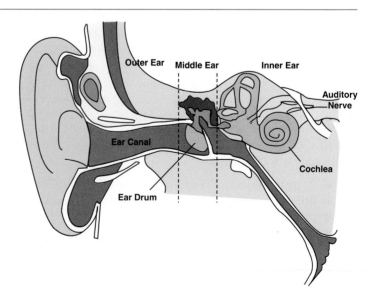

---

conductive loss – *affects the volume of word tones heard, so that loud sounds are more likely to be heard than soft sounds.*
sensorineural loss – *a type of loss that occurs when sound impulses cannot reach the brain due to damage of the auditory nerve, or cannot be interpreted because of prior brain damage.*
mixed hearing loss – *a disorder that involves a combination of conductive and sensorineural hearing losses.*

TABLE 4-7 Teacher Checklist: Strategies for Improved Communication with Hearing-Impaired Children

- reduce background noises, such as musical tapes, radio, motors, or fans that can interfere with a child's limited ability to hear
- provide individualized versus group instructions
- face and stand near the child when speaking
- bend down to the child's level; this makes it easier for the child to hear and understand what is being said
- speak slowly and clearly
- use gestures or pictures to illustrate what is being said, e.g., point to the door when it is time to go outside
- demonstrate what the child is expected to do, e.g., pick up a bead and thread it on a shoestring

information about hearing impairments, testing procedures, and resources for families can be obtained from:

American Association of Speech-Language-Hearing
10801 Rockville Pike
Rockville, MD 20852
www.asha.org

SPEECH AND LANGUAGE EVALUATION

Throughout the early years, children make impressive gains in both the number of words they understand (receptive vocabulary) and use to express themselves (expressive vocabulary) (Table 4–8). Children's receptive vocabulary develops earlier and is usually more extensive than their expressive vocabulary. For example, most toddlers can understand and follow simple directions long before they can use words to express themselves. Children's language gradually becomes increasingly fluent and complex with time and practice.

Many factors influence children's **speech** and language development. Their ability to hear is most important during the early years when children are beginning to learn and imitate sounds, words, and word patterns (Swanwick & Watson, 2005). Hearing disorders can jeopardize the normal acquisition of speech and language development and lead to long-term speech impairments. Whenever there is concern about the progress of a child's language development, a comprehensive hearing evaluation is always recommended.

It is also important to consider a child's home environment when evaluating language development (Leung & Kao, 1999). Families who engage children in conversation, read stories to their children, and support children's efforts to express themselves are encouraging early literacy and language development. Homes where these opportunities are lacking may limit children's ability to experience and practice important verbal and learning skills.

Young children also acquire early speech and language skills by imitating speech that is heard in their homes (Jaffe, 1997). For example, children who have a parent with an unusual voice inflection or speech impairment are more likely to exhibit similar qualities. Children who live in bilingual homes may also be slower to develop language skills because they must learn to think and speak in two different languages. Cultural values and variations also exert a strong influence on children's language usage, style, and speech patterns (Trawlick-Smith, 2006).

---

speech – *the process of using words to express one's thoughts and ideas.*

TABLE 4–8 Speech and Language Developmental Milestones

Infants

birth–4 months
- turns to locate the source of sound
- begins to coo and make babbling sounds, *(baa, aah, ooh)*
- imitates own voice and sounds

4–8 months
- repeats syllables in a series: *ba, ba, ba*
- "talks" to self
- responds to simple commands: "no" and "come"

8–12 months
- recognizes labels for common objects: shoe, blanket, cup
- "talks" in one word sentences to convey ideas or requests: "cookie"
  (meaning "I want a cookie")

Toddlers

12–24 months
- follows simple directions
- knows and uses 10–30 words
- points to pictures and body parts on request
- asks frequently, "What's that?" "Why?"
- enjoys being read to
- understands 200–300 words
- speaks in two–three word sentences
- 65–70% of speech is intelligible

24–36 months
- refers to self as "me": "Me do it myself."
- uses language to get desired attention or object
- understands simple concepts when asked: "Find the small ball."
- follows simple directions: "It's time to get dressed."
- understands and uses 50–300 new words
- 70–80% of speech is intelligible

Preschoolers

3–6 years
- answers simple questions appropriately
- describes objects, events, and experiences in fairly detailed terms
- sings simple songs and recites nursery rhymes
- carries on detailed telephone conversations
- enjoys making up and telling stories; acquires a vocabulary of
  approximately 10,000–14,000 words by age six
- uses verb tenses and word order correctly

School-age

6–8 years
- enjoys talking and conversing with adults
- uses language, in place of physical aggression, to express feelings
- loves to tell jokes and riddles
- understands complex statements and performs multistep requests
- finds pleasure in writing stories, letters, and e-mail messages
- expresses self fluently and in elaborate detail

9–12 years
- talks nonstop
- understands grammatical sequences and uses them appropriately
- speaks in longer, complex sentences
- uses and understands irony and sarcasm
- achieves mastery of language development
- becomes a thoughtful listener

Adapted from: *Developmental profiles: Pre-birth through twelve,* by K. Eileen Allen & L. Marotz, 2007, Clifton Park, NY: Delmar Learning.

Methods of Assessment

Families are often aware of their child's speech problems but may not know what to do about them. Many adults also believe erroneously that children will eventually outgrow these impairments so they take no action. Indeed, some children have developmentally appropriate **misarticulations** that will improve. For example, many three-year-olds mispronounce "r" as "w" as in "wabbit" (rabbit) or "s" as "th" as in "thong" (song); by age four or five they are able to pronounce these letter sounds correctly. Nevertheless, children who demonstrate speech or speech patterns that are not developmentally appropriate should be referred to a speech therapist for a thorough evaluation. A hearing test should be included in this evaluation to rule out the possibility of a hearing loss that could be affecting the child's speech. Speech and hearing clinics are often affiliated with colleges and universities, medical centers, child development centers, public health departments, public schools, and Head Start programs. A listing of certified speech and hearing specialists can also be found in most local telephone directories or by checking with local school districts or the American Speech, Language, and Hearing Association.

Common Disorders

The term *speech impairment* has many different meanings to persons working with children. For some, the term refers only to more obvious problems, such as stuttering, lisping, or unintelligent speech patterns. For others, a wide range of conditions are cause for concern, for example, a monotone voice, nasality, improper pitch of the voice, a voice tone that is too high or too low, omissions of certain letter sounds, or misarticulations of word sounds.

The range of speech and language disorders is as great as the variations in normal speech and language development (Venn, 2004; Hamaguchi, 2001). Abnormal speech patterns that continue for more than a few months should be evaluated, and include:

■ no speech by two years of age
■ stuttering
■ substitution of word sounds
■ rate of speech that is too fast or unusually slow
■ monotone voice
■ no improvement in speech development
■ unintelligent speech by three years of age
■ inattentive behavior or ignoring others

Management

Families and teachers are important role models in a child's speech and language development. Early language experiences and opportunities encourage children's effective use of language. However, teachers should never hesitate to refer children for professional evaluation if their speech and language patterns interfere with effective communication. Early recognition and treatment can help young children overcome many speech impairments.

NUTRITIONAL ASSESSMENT

There is no question that the quality of children's diets has a direct effect on their behavior and state of health. Problems related to over- and underconsumption of food and nutrients are of increasing concern. Rising food costs and economic struggles force many families to sacrifice the quality and quantity of food they purchase and serve (Kumanyika & Grier, 2006). Furthermore, television

---

misarticulations – *improper pronunciations of words and word sounds.*

advertising, increased consumption of fast foods, and availability of prepackaged and convenience foods have also contributed to a further decline in the quality of children's diets (Connor, 2006; Francis & Birch, 2006).

A preliminary assessment of children's nutritional status and general health can be obtained through direct observation of their behavior and physical appearance. Many of these indicators can be noted during daily health checks. For example, facial **pallor**, dry skin, or **lethargy** may reflect poor eating habits. Healthy, well-nourished children typically exhibit the following physical signs:

- height appropriate for age
- weight appropriate for height
- bright, clear eyes—no puffiness, crusting, or paleness of inner lids
- clear skin—good color; no pallor or scaliness
- teeth—appropriate number for age; no caries or **mottling**
- gums—pink and firm; not puffy, dark red, or bleeding
- lips—soft, moist; no cracking at corner of mouth
- tongue—pink; no cracking, smooth spots, or deep red color

Assessment Methods

Selecting an appropriate method for assessing children's nutritional status depends upon the child's age, reason for evaluation, type of information desired, and available resources. The methods most commonly used include:

- dietary assessment—is used to determine adequacy of nutrient intake and other nutritional deficiencies. The child's eating patterns are monitored for various lengths of time (24 hours, one to seven days) and actual food intake is recorded (Figure 4–8). Dietary information is then analyzed for nutritional content according to one of several methods, e.g., Food Guide Pyramid, nutrient analysis, RDIs (see Chapter 13) to determine if **nutrient intake** is adequate.
- anthropometric assessment—is based on simple measurements of height, weight, and head circumference. Comparisons are made with standardized norms (see Appendix B). Additional measurements of **skinfold** thickness and mid-arm circumference are sometimes also taken (Trahms & Pipes, 2000). These measurements yield specific information about a child's growth.
- clinical assessment—involves observing a child for signs of nutritional deficiency (Table 4–9). This is not considered a reliable method because of its subjective nature and the fact that physical symptoms often do not appear until a deficiency is severe.
- biochemical assessment—involves laboratory testing of various body tissues and fluids, such as urinalysis or hemoglobin (testing for iron level) to validate concerns related to over- or underconsumption of nutrients. These tests are usually ordered by a health care provider and performed by trained laboratory technicians.

Common Disorders

Teachers and families should be alert to several nutritional problems that may affect children's health. Poor dietary habits, resulting in inadequate intake of essential nutrients, can lead to

---

pallor – *paleness.*
lethargy – *a state of inaction or indifference.*
mottling – *marked with spots of dense white or brown coloring.*
nutrient intake – *consumption of foods containing chemical substances (nutrients) essential to the human body.*
skinfold – *a measurement of the amount of fat under the skin; also referred to as fat-fold measurements.*

FIGURE 4–8

Sample questionnaire for obtaining information about a child's eating habits.

NUTRITIONAL ASSESSMENT

Dear Parent:

Nutrition is a very important part of our program. In order for us to plan appropriate nutrition-education activities and menus to meet your child's needs, we need to know your child's eating patterns. This information will also help us obtain an overview of the eating habits of young children as a group. Please take the time to fill out the questionnaire carefully.

NAME _____ AGE _____ DATE _____

1. How many days a week does your child eat the following meals or snacks?
   a morning meal _____ a midafternoon snack _____
   a lunch or midday meal _____ an evening snack _____
   an evening meal _____ snack during the night _____
   a midmorning snack _____

2. When is your child most hungry?
   morning _____
   noon _____
   evening _____

3. What are some of your child's favorite foods? _____

4. What foods does your child dislike? _____
   _____

5. Is your child on a special diet? Yes _____ No _____
   If yes, why? _____
   Describe diet _____
   Diet prescribed by whom? _____

6. Does your child eat things not usually considered food e.g., paste, dirt, paper? _____
   If yes, how often? _____
   What is eaten? _____

7. Is your child taking a vitamin or mineral supplement?
   Yes _____ No _____ If yes, what kind? _____

8. Does your child have any dental problems that might create a problem when eating certain foods? _____

9. Has your child ever been treated by a dentist? _____

10. Does your child have any diet-related health problems?
    Diabetes _____ Allergies _____ Other _____

11. Is your child taking any medication for a diet-related health problem?
    _____

12. How much water does your child normally drink throughout the day?
    _____

13. Please list as accurately as possible what your child eats and drinks on a typical day. If yesterday was a typical day, you may use those foods and drinks.

TIME	PLACE	FOOD	AMOUNT

 Download this form online at http://www.EarlyChildEd.delmar.cengage.com

✿ TABLE 4–9   Physical Signs of Malnutrition

Tissue	Sign	Cause
Face	Pallor	Niacin, iron deficiency
	Scaling of skin around nostrils	Riboflavin, B_6 deficiency
Eyes	Hardening of cornea and lining: pale lining	Iron deficiency
	Foamy spots in cornea	Vitamin A deficiency
Lips	Redness; swelling of mouth and lips; cracking at corners of mouth	Riboflavin deficiency
Teeth	Decayed or missing	Excess sugar (or poor dental hygiene)
	Mottled enamel	Excess fluoride
Tongue	Red, raw, cracked, swollen	Niacin deficiency
	Magenta color	Riboflavin deficiency
	Pale	Iron deficiency
Gums	Spongy, red, bleeding	Vitamin C deficiency
Skin	Dry, flaking	Vitamin A deficiency
	Small underskin hemorrhages	Vitamin C deficiency
Nails	Brittle, ridged	Iron deficiency

malnutrition over a period of time. Nutrients most commonly missing from children's diets today include vitamins A and C, iron, and calcium. Long-term use of certain medications, such as steroids, aspirin, antibiotics, and laxatives, can interfere with the absorption of critical nutrients. Many children are also undernourished simply because they do not get enough to eat. These children are often below average in height and weight, irritable, anemic, and listless (see Appendix B). Their poor state of nutrition can severely limit their ability to learn.

However, not all malnourished children are thin and emaciated. Children who are overweight can also be malnourished. Because the bulk of their diet often consists of sugars and refined starches, these children may appear to be well fed, yet lack many of the nutrients essential for good health. Inactivity also contributes significantly to their weight problems.

Another serious nutritional health problem is that of obesity. Approximately 20 to 25 percent of all children in the United States are considered overweight for their age (CDC, 2006). Inactivity and poor eating habits are the primary causes of this current childhood epidemic (Anderson & Butcher, 2006; Nelson, Carpenter, & Chiasson, 2006).

Children who are overweight or obese are likely to remain so as adults. They are also at greater risk for developing life-threatening health problems including heart disease, stroke, sleep apnea, asthma, and diabetes.

Management

Obesity in young children cannot be ignored. Prevention is always the most effective method. However, promising results can also be obtained by taking action while a child is young and still in the process of establishing lifelong eating and activity habits (Anderson, 2006; Sorte & Daeschel, 2006; Dehghan, Akhtar-Danesh, & Merchant, 2005). For maximum success, weight control programs must include the cooperation of the child, family, teachers, and health care personnel, and target:

- meal planning and nutritious eating habits.
- strategies for increasing children's daily activity level (Figure 4–9). (For example, children can be asked to run errands, walk a pet, help with daily household chores, or ride their bike to school.)
- acquainting children with new outside interests, hobbies, or activities, such as swimming, dance, neighborhood baseball, or learning to ride a bike. (Involvement in fun activities can divert children's attention away from food.)
- finding ways to help children experience success and develop a positive self-image.

(For example, praise received for simple achievements can make children feel good about themselves—"Lonnie, you did a nice job of sweeping all the sand off the sidewalk." For many children, praise replaces food as an important source of satisfaction.)

FIGURE 4–9

Increasing children's activity levels can help to control their weight.

ISSUES TO CONSIDER • Children's Health

The U.S. Census Bureau has redefined the term *poverty* so that it more accurately reflects today's economic standards (U.S. Census Bureau, 2005). However, current guidelines exclude many families whose income is often not adequate to meet even minimal requirements for food, clothing, shelter, and health care. Data show that the adults in a majority of these families are employed, but often in jobs paying minimum wages. Health care and insurance are luxuries that many cannot afford. Eligibility changes in various government assistance programs (food, cash, and housing) have further reduced access to resources that affect children's health. Increased poverty has also contributed to an increase in homelessness, especially for families with children—currently the fastest growing segment of the homeless population (U.S. Conference of Mayors, 2005).

- Why is it important for teachers to be aware of changes in national fiscal policy and federal programs?
- How does increasing poverty and homelessness affect a teacher's role in monitoring children's health?
- How can teachers become stronger advocates for children?
- What types of partnerships with families can help improve children's health status?

Long-term weight management is achieved by attending to all aspects of a child's well-being, physical, emotional, and social (Plourde, 2006; Satter, 2005). Children should not be placed on weight reduction programs unless they are under a doctor's supervision. Weight reduction programs must be designed carefully to meet all the nutritional needs of children to ensure normal growth and development. Education and positive role modeling are also important factors in the management of good nutrition and promotion of healthier lifestyles.

REFERRALS

The initial step in making successful referrals involves gaining the family's trust and cooperation. Referrals are of little use unless families are willing and able to follow through with recommendations. Knowing something about their beliefs, customs, habits, and community will improve a teacher's ability to make effective referrals. For example, mistrust of the medical profession,

FOCUS ON FAMILIES • Children's Eye Safety

Each year, thousands of children sustain eye injuries as the result of hazardous conditions at home or school. The majority of these eye injuries are preventable through appropriate supervision, selection of toys and equipment, and protection. Families play a major role in identifying potentially dangerous situations and taking measures to eliminate children's exposure to unnecessary risk. They should also take similar precautions to protect their own eye safety and serve as a positive role model for children.

- Never shake a baby! Vigorous shaking can cause serious eye damage and blindness.
- Insist that children wear sunglasses whenever they play outdoors to limit exposure to ultraviolet (UV) light. Over time, UV exposure increases the risk of developing a number of serious eye conditions, including macular degeneration and cataracts. Purchase sunglasses that fit closely, cover the entire eye area, and provide UV protection.
- Keep children indoors whenever mowing or edging the lawn. Stones, sticks, and small debris can easily become dangerous projectiles.
- Select toys and play equipment based on your child's age and abilities. Avoid toys with projectile parts, such as darts, slingshots, pellet guns, and missile-launching devices.
- Stones, rubber bands, balls, wire coat hangers, and fish hooks also pose a serious eye danger.
- Supervise children closely whenever they are using a sharp item, such as a fork, pencil, toothpicks, wire, paperclips, scissors, or small wooden dowels.
- Keep children away from fireworks. Do not allow them to light fireworks or to be near anyone who is doing so.
- Lock up household cleaners, sprays, paints, paint thinners, and chemicals such as garden fertilizers and pesticides that could injure children's eyes.
- Make sure children wear appropriate protective eyewear, such as goggles or a helmet with a face guard, when participating in sports.
- Don't allow children to shine a laser pointer or aim a squirt gun or spray nozzle toward someone's eyes.
- Remind children to avoid touching their eyes with unwashed hands.

poverty, job conflicts, religious beliefs, a lack of transportation, or limited education will undoubtedly affect a family's capacity and willingness to follow through with recommendations.

Meeting with the child's family, or calling them on the telephone, is often the most effective method for making referrals:

> Teacher: "I am concerned about Ryan's vision. On several occasions, I have noticed that his right eye turns inward more than the left eye and that he holds his head close to materials when he is working. Have you observed any of these behaviors at home?"

> Parent: "Yes, but we didn't think it was anything to worry about. We thought it would go away when he was older."

> Teacher: "I cannot be sure if Ryan has anything wrong with his eyes, but the behaviors I have observed can sometimes be an indication of vision problems and should be checked carefully by an eye specialist. If you need help locating a doctor or making an appointment, I will be glad to help you. I will also give you a written copy of my observations to take along. Please let me know the date of Ryan's appointment after you have made it."

Although a face-to-face meeting with parents is preferable, a well-written letter may be the only way to reach some families today. Parents should be given copies of screening test results, which they can forward to the specialist who will be evaluating their child. This step also improves the efficiency of the referral process. Familiarity with various community services, such as hospitals, clinics, health departments, medical specialists, public and private service agencies, volunteer organizations, and funding sources, also improves teachers' ability to assist families in securing appropriate help for the child and alleviate some of their frustration in the process.

Follow-up contact should be made after several days to determine if families have been successful in arranging for professional evaluation or to learn the outcome of diagnostic testing. Teachers can use these findings to make adjustments in the child's instructional program or learning environment. Follow-up contacts can also be beneficial for reinforcing a family's efforts to obtain necessary services for the child and to convey the teacher's genuine interest in the child's well-being.

 CASE STUDY

A friend encouraged Mrs. Howard to take her son to the developmental screening clinic being held at the community recreation center. Parker was nearly two-years-old and spoke only a few words that were understandable. Because he spent most days with his grandmother while his mother worked at the local hospital, Parker had few opportunities to play with other children his age. The developmental screening team checked his height, weight, vision, hearing speech, cognitive abilities, and motor skills. The team leader noted that Mrs. Howard had indicated on the history intake form that Parker had several food allergies and frequent upper respiratory and ear infections. His hearing tests revealed a significant loss in one ear and a moderate loss in the other.

1. Is Parker's speech development appropriate for his age?

2. What significance do Parker's ear infections have to his hearing loss?

3. Should the screening team's recommendation for Parker include a referral to his physician? Why?

4. What strategies can Parker's mother and others use to improve his communication skills?

5. What things can Parker's mother do to encourage his speech development?

CLASSROOM CORNER • Teacher Activities

My Five Senses...

Concept: Seeing, hearing, tasting, touching, and smelling are your five senses. (Pre-2)

Learning Objectives

- Children will learn to name all five senses.
- Children will learn which body parts go with which senses: see with eyes, hear with ears, taste with tongue, touch with fingers and skin, and smell with nose.

Supplies

- Small blanket; various objects (items that children can label—plastic foods, animals, people, etc); small paper cups; tin foil; various scents or foods (vanilla, orange peel, ketchup, peppermint, chocolate, ranch dressing, green pepper, etc); tape recording of children's and teachers' voices; feely box; various items with shapes that children can recognize (ball, pine cone, banana, block, plate, cup, etc); salty (crackers), sweet (mandarin orange), sour (lemon) and bitter (unsweetened chocolate) items; hand wipes; plates; forks

Learning Activities

- Read and discuss the following book:
  - *Your Five Senses* by Bobbi Katz
- Each day discuss one of the senses and have the children participate in an activity.
- Seeing—Tell the children that you are going to play a game called "What's Missing?" This is a game that uses their sense of seeing. Place four to five objects out on the floor in front of the children. Name each item, and then line the items up in a way so that all the children can see them. Place the towel over the items. Remove one of the items and wrap it in the towel. Ask children to guess which item is missing. Call on children one at a time; if they name the missing item, they can come up and hide the next item. Continue until all children have had a turn. Vary the toys to keep children interested.
- Smelling—Tell the children that you are going to do an activity to learn about their sense of smell. Make "smelling cups": for liquid scents, put a few drops on a cotton ball and place it in the cup. Cover the cup with tin foil in which holes have been poked. Pass the cups around. Have children smell each cup and try to guess what the smell is. After each child has had a chance to smell each cup, remove the foil so they can see if they were correct.
- Hearing—Make a recording of the teachers and children while they are playing. On another day, tell the children that they will use their sense of hearing for this activity. Play the tape and see if the children can guess whose voices they are hearing on the tape.
- Feeling—Tell the children that this activity will involve using their sense of touch. Place various items in a feely box. Have each child reach in and use their sense of touch to determine what the object is.
- Tasting—Tell the children you are going to have them taste some different items to see if they are sweet, sour, salty, or bitter. Tell them that their tongue has little things called taste buds on it that help them know what a food tastes like. Next, have all the children wash their hands with a wipe. Place a cracker, a mandarin orange, a small piece of lemon, and bit of unsweetened chocolate on each plate, and set a plate in front of each child. Have the children taste one item at a time and talk about the different tastes.

Evaluation

- Children can name each of the five senses.
- Children can name which body parts are associated with each sense.

SUMMARY

- Teachers play an important role in the health assessment of young children.
  - They can use a variety of information to evaluate children's health status, including observations, health records, screening procedures, daily health checks, and interactions with families.
- Results of screening procedures are not always accurate and can be affected by children's ability to respond.
- Teachers can initiate the referral process after gathering and evaluating data from multiple sources.
  - Referrals should be followed up to make certain that recommendations have been carried out and to learn how teachers can implement suggestions in the classroom.

APPLICATION ACTIVITIES

1. Locate and read instructions for administering the Snellen E and one additional acuity screening test. With another student, practice testing one another. What were the advantages of each test? Disadvantages? Did you encounter any problems in administering the test? How would you modify your instructions to a child as a result?

2. Devise a monitoring system for recording the daily food intakes of individual children in a group setting. Be sure to address the following questions:

   a. What nutritional information do you want to collect? In what form?

   b. Who will be responsible for collecting this data?

   c. How can this information be obtained efficiently?

   d. How can teachers and families use this data to improve children's eating habits?

   e. What other ways might teachers use this information to promote children's health?

3. Collect samples of child history forms from several schools and/or early childhood programs in your area. Review the type of information that is requested most often. Design your own form.

4. Attend a signing class. Learn to say "hello" and "good-bye" and 10 additional words in sign language.

5. Make arrangements with a local school or early childhood program to conduct a comparison study of children's growth. Measure and record the heights and weights of 15 children, ages three to six years, on the standard Growth Charts (Appendix B). Then, determine their BMI and plot this information on the BMI-for-age charts. Which method provides the most accurate information about children's growth? What did you learn about the children's potential risk for becoming overweight? Learn more about the BMI measure and initiatives for preventing childhood obesity (http://www.cdc.gov/nccdphp/dnpa/bmi/index.htm).

6. Obtain an audiometer. Have a nurse or audiologist demonstrate the technique for testing hearing. Locate a partner and practice administering the test with one another.

7. Research the Internet or contact the American Heart Association for educational programs designed to improve cardiovascular health. Are the materials/programs developmentally appropriate? How is improvement determined?

CHAPTER REVIEW

A. By Yourself:

1. Define each of the *Terms to Know* listed at the beginning of this chapter.

2. Select the screening test that is recommended for children with the following behaviors, signs, or symptoms. Place the appropriate code letter in each space for questions 1–15.

H	Hearing screening	Dt	Dental screening
V	Vision screening	S	Speech evaluation
D	Developmental screening	N	Nutrition evaluation
HW	Height and weight		

_____ 1. frequent blinking; often closes one eye to see

_____ 2. stutters whenever tense and in a hurry to speak

_____ 3. usually listless; appears very small for her chronological age

_____ 4. stumbles over objects in the classroom; frequently walks into play equipment in the play yard

_____ 5. very crooked teeth that make his speech difficult to understand

_____ 6. seems to ignore the teacher's requests; shouts at the other children to get their attention

_____ 7. awkward; has great difficulty running and climbing; tires easily because of obesity

_____ 8. a five-year-old who has trouble catching a ball, pedaling a bicycle, and cutting with scissors

_____ 9. appears to focus on objects with one eye while the other eye looks off in another direction

_____ 10. multiple cavities; in recent weeks has not been able to concentrate on any task

_____ 11. is extremely shy and withdrawn; spends the majority of her time playing alone, imitating the actions of other children

_____ 12. seems extremely hungry at snack time; always asks for extra servings and takes food left on other children's plates when the teacher isn't looking

_____ 13. becomes hoarse after shouting and yelling during outdoor time

_____ 14. arrives at school each morning with potato chips, candy, or a cupcake

_____ 15. a four-and-a-half-year-old who whines and has tantrums to get his own way

B. As a Group:

1. Identify and describe the vision disorders that are most common among young children. How is each typically treated? What indicators might a teacher observe?

2. Discuss how health records can be used to assess children's health.

3. Describe several strategies that teachers can use to evaluate the adequacy of a child's diet.

4. What recommendations could a teacher offer to the family of an obese child for managing this condition?

5. If a family asks you where they can get their two-year-old's hearing tested, what resources in your community would you recommend?

REFERENCES

Allen, K. E., & Cowdery, G. (2005). *The exceptional child: Inclusion in early childhood education.* (5th ed.). Clifton Park, NY: Thomson Delmar Learning.

Allen, K. E., & Marotz, L. R. (2007). *Developmental profiles: Pre-birth through twelve.* (5th ed.). Clifton Park, NY: Thomson Delmar Learning.

American Academy of Pediatrics (AAP). (2002). Use of photoscreening for children's vision screening. *Pediatrics, 109*(3), 524–525.

American Speech-Language-Hearing Association (ASHA). (2006). Status of State universal newborn and infant hearing screening legislation and laws. Accessed October 8, 2006, from http://www.asha.org/about/legislation-advocacy/state/issues/.

Anderson, J. (2006). A comprehensive approach to addressing childhood obesity in early childhood programs. *Exchange, 169*, 41–45.

Anderson, P., & Butcher, K. (2006). Childhood obesity: Trends and potential causes. *The Future of Children, 16*(1), 19–45.

CDC. (2006). *Childhood overweight.* National Center for Chronic Disease Prevention and Health Promotion. Accessed October 19, 2006, from http://www.cdc.gov/HealthyYouth/overweight/index.htm.

Chen, D. (1998). Early identification of infants who are deaf-blind: A systematic approach for early interventionists. *Deaf-Blind Perspectives, 5*(3), 1–5.

Connolly, J., Carron, J., & Roark, S. (2005). Universal newborn hearing screening: Are we achieving the Joint Committee on Infant Hearing (JCIH) objectives? *Laryngoscope, 115*(2), 232–236.

Connor, S. (2006). Food-related advertising on preschool television: Building brand recognition in young viewers. *Pediatrics, 118*(4), 1478–1485.

Dehghan, M., Akhtar-Danesh, N., & Merchant, A. (2005). Childhood obesity, prevalence and prevention. *Nutrition Journal* (online), September 2, 24.

Desrochers, J. (1999). Vision problems—How teachers can help. *Young Children, 54*(2), 36–38.

Erin, J. N. (2000). Students with visual impairments and additional disabilities. In A. J. Koenig & M. C. Holbrook (Eds.), *Foundations of education: Instructional strategies for teaching children and youths with visual impairments* (Vol. 2, pp. 720–752). New York: American Foundation for the Blind.

Francis, L., & Birch, L. (2006). Does eating during television viewing affect preschool children's intake? *Journal of the American Dietetic Association, 106*(4), 598–600.

Greenwald, M. J. (2003). Refractive abnormalities in childhood. *Pediatric Clinics of North America, 50*(1), 197–212.

Grosse, S., & Ross, D. (2006). Cost savings form universal newborn hearing screening. *Pediatrics, 118*(2), 844–845.

Guralnick, M. J. (Ed.) (2000). Interdisciplinary clinical assessment of young children with developmental disabilities. Baltimore, MD: Paul H. Brookes.

Hamaguchi, P. (2001). *Childhood speech, language & listening problems.* (2nd ed.). Indianapolis, IN: John Wiley & Sons.

Healthlink. (2002). Amblyopia: Eye drops could be as effective as patching. Accessed May 24, 2003, from http://healthlink.mcw.edu/article/1030635385.html.

Jaffe, M. (1997). *Understanding parenting.* Dubuque, IA: William C. Brown.

Kaderavek, J. N., & Pakulski, L. A. (2002). Minimal hearing loss is not minimal. *Teaching Exceptional Children, 34*(6), 14–18.

Katz, L., & Schery, T. (2006). Including children with hearing loss in early childhood programs. *Young Children, 61*(1), 86–95.

Kimel, L. (2006). Lack of follow-up exams after failed school vision screenings: An investigation of contributing factors. *Journal of School Health, 22*(3), 156–162.

Koenig, A., & Holbrook, M. (2000). *Foundations of education: Instructional strategies for teaching children and youths with visual impairments.* New York: American Foundation for the Blind.

Kumanyika, S., & Grier, S. (2006). Targeting interventions for ethnic minority and low-income populations. *The Future of Children, 16*(1), 187–207.

Leman, R., Clausen, M., Bates, J., Stark, L., Arnold, K., & Arnold, R. (2006). A comparison of patched HOTV visual acuity and photoscreening. *Journal of School Nursing, 22*(4), 237–243.

Lempert, P. (2005). Amblyopia prevalence and cigarette smoking by women. *Ophthalmic & Physiological Optics, 25*(6), 592–595.

Leung, A., & Kao, C. (1999). Evaluation and management of the child with speech delay. *American Family Physician, 59*(11), 3121–3135.

Lewis, S., & Russo, R. (1998). Educational assessment for students who have visual impairments and other disabilities. In S. Sacks & R. Silberman (Eds.), *Education of students who have visual impairments and other disabilities* (pp. 39–71). Baltimore, MD: Paul H. Brookes.

Li, A. (2004). Classroom strategies for improving and enhancing visual skills in students with disabilities. *Teaching Exceptional Children, 36*(6), 38–46.

Mittelman, D. (2003). Amblyopia. *Pediatric clinics of North America, 50*(1), 189–196.

Morbidity & Mortality Weekly Report (MMWR). (2005, May 6). Visual impairment and use of eye-care services and protective eyewear among children—United States, 2002. Accessed October 8, 2006, from http://www.cdc.gov/mmwr/preview/mmwrhtml/mm5417a2.htm.

National Eye Institute. (2006). Amblyopia. Accessed on October 8, 2006, from http://www.nei.nih.gov/health/amblyopia/index.asp.

Nelson, J., Carpenter, K., & Chiasson, M. (2006). Diet, activity, and overweight among preschool-age children enrolled in the Special Supplemental Nutrition Program for Women, Infants, and Children (WIC). *Prevention of Chronic Disease* (online Journal), 3(2), A49.

Niles, M., Reynolds, A., & Nagasawa, M. (2006). Does early childhood intervention affect the social and emotional development of participants? *Early Childhood Research & Practice, 8*(1). Accessed on September 21, 2007 from http://ecrp.uiuc.edu/v8n1/niles.html.

Paradise, J., Campbell, T., Dollaghan, C., Feldman, H., Bernard, B., Colborn, D., Rockette, H., Janosky, J., Pitcairn, D., Jurs-Lasky, M., Sabo, D., & Smith, C. (2005). Developmental outcomes after early or delayed insertion of tympanostomy tubes. *New England Journal of Medicine, 353*(6), 576–586.

Plourde, G. (2006). Preventing and managing pediatric obesity. *Canadian Family Physician, 52*, 322–328.

Prevent Blindness America. (2006). Common eye problems in children. Accessed October 8, 2006, from http://www.preventblindness.org/children/index.html.

Repka, M. X., Beck, R. W., Holmes, J. M., Birch, E. E., Chandler, D. L., Cotter, S. A., Hertle, R. W., Kraker, R. T., Moke, P. S., Quinn, G. E., & Scheiman, M. M. (2003). A randomized trial of patching regimens for treatment of moderate amblyopia in children. *Archives of Ophthalmology, 121*(5), 603–611.

Satter, E. (2005). *Your child's weight: Helping without harming.* Madison, WI: Kelcy Press.

Scheiman, M., Hertle, R., Beck, R., Edwards, A., Birch, E., Cotter, S., Crouch, E., Cruz, O., Davitt, B., Donahue, S., Holmes, J., Lyon, D., Repka, M., Sala, N., Silbert, D., Suh, D., & Tamkins, S. Pediatric Eye Disease Investigator Group. (2005). Randomized trial of treatment of amblyopia in children aged 7 to 17 years. *Archives of Ophthalmology, 123*(4), 437–447.

Sorte, J., & Daeschel, I. (2006). Health in action: A program approach to fighting obesity in young children. *Young Children, 61*(3), 40–48.

Swanwick, R., & Watson, L. (2005). Literacy in the homes of young deaf children: Common and distinct features of spoken language and sign bilingual environments. *Journal of Early Childhood Literacy, 5*(1), 53–78.

Teplin, S. W. (1995). Visual impairment in infants and young children. *Infants and Young Children, 8*(1), 18–51.

The Vision in Preschoolers Study Group. (2005). Preschool vision screening tests administered by nurse screeners compared with lay screeners in the vision in preschoolers study. *Investigative Ophthalmology & Visual Science, 46*(8), 2639–2648.

Thompson, D., McPhillips, H., Davis, R., Lieu, T., Homer, C. J., & Helfand, M. (2001). Universal newborn hearing screening: Summary of evidence. *JAMA, 286*, 2000–2010.

Topor, I. (1999). Functional vision assessments and early interventions. In D. Chen (Ed.), *Essential elements in early intervention: Visual impairment and multiple disabilities* (pp. 157–206). New York: American Foundation for the Blind.

Trahms, C. M., & Pipes, P. L. (2000). *Nutrition in infancy and childhood.* Columbus, OH: McGraw-Hill.

Trawick-Smith, J. (2006). *Early childhood develop: A multicultural perspective.* Upper Saddle River, NJ: Pearson.

U.S. Census Bureau. (2005). *How the Census Bureau measures poverty.* Housing and Household Economic Statistics Division. Accessed October 19, 2006, from http://www.census.gov/hhes/www/poverty/povdef.html.

U.S. Conference of Mayors. (2005). *A status report on hunger and homelessness in America's cities.* Accessed on October 19, 2006, from http://www.usmayors.org.

Venn, J. (2004). *Assessing students with special needs.* Upper Saddle River, NJ: Merrill.

Widen, J., Bull, R., & Folsom, R. (2003). Newborn hearing screening: What it means for providers of early intervention services. *Infants and Young Children, 16*(3), 249–257.

World Health Organization (WHO). (2006). The WHO child growth standards. Accessed on October 8, 2006, at http://www.who.int/childgrowth/en/.

HELPFUL WEB SITES

American Speech, Language, and Hearing Association (ASHA)	http://www.asha.org
Children with Special Needs	http://www.napcse.org
KidSource (Parent's guide to middle ear fluid in children)	http://www.kidsource.com
National Eye Institute	http://www.nei.nih.gov
National Institutes of Health	http://www.health.nih.gov
Prevent Blindness America	http://www.preventblindness.org

For additional health, safety, and nutrition resources, go to http://www.EarlyChildEd.delmar.cengage.com

CHAPTER 5

Conditions Affecting Children's Health

※ **OBJECTIVES**

After studying this chapter, you should be able to:

- Describe why chronic health problems are difficult to identify in young children.
- Identify the teacher's role in managing children's chronic health problems in the classroom.
- Discuss the causes of fetal alcohol syndrome (FAS) and preventive measures.
- List the symptoms of seven chronic health conditions.

※ **TERMS TO KNOW**

anaphylaxis	hormone	anemia
syndrome	hyperglycemia	endocrine
neurobiological disorder	dehydration	seizures

Today, many children with disabilities, medical problems, and chronic illnesses are enrolling in community early childhood programs. Legislative enactments, increased public awareness, research demonstrating the benefits, and improved intervention strategies have opened educational doors to all children regardless of their special needs. Consequently, teachers must be prepared to address children's learning needs as well as a range of medical and safety issues. Efforts to define the teacher's role in managing various medical procedures are beginning to receive increasing attention.

Children who develop symptoms of a chronic illness that has not yet been diagnosed present another classroom challenge (Olson, et al., 2004). These conditions may be difficult to recognize because their signs and symptoms are often less obvious than those of an acute illness. Some chronic diseases, such as sickle cell anemia and diabetes, may be present from birth. Other conditions, such as allergies and lead poisoning, may develop slowly so that their appearance is less noticeable; even the child may not be aware that anything is wrong. Also, because families see their child every day, it may be difficult for them to be objective and to recognize the early symptoms of a chronic illness.

Undiagnosed and untreated chronic illnesses can interfere with a child's overall growth and development. Teachers must work closely with families to help identify these early symptoms and assist them in obtaining appropriate medical evaluation and treatment. The earlier a chronic illness is diagnosed and treatment initiated, the less serious its impact will be on a child's developmental progress. When evaluating children for signs of chronic illness, environmental factors should also be taken into consideration. For many children, daily circumstances contribute to their health conditions and may serve as barriers to needed treatment:

- where they live—urban neighborhoods, rural areas, or without a home (homeless)
- family's financial situation, which in turn affects access to medical care, quality of nutrition, living arrangement
- exposure to environmental pollution, including air, water, noise, and chemicals
- presence of stress, trauma, violence
- disruption of the traditional family unit
- exposure to persuasive advertising

CHILDREN WITH SPECIAL NEEDS

The passage of landmark legislation, P.L. 94–457, and subsequent amendments (P.L. 99–142 in 1986; ADA in 1990) guarantees children with special needs the right to a free and appropriate public education. As a result, teachers are likely to have children with a range of disabilities, impairments, and medical problems in their programs. Many children are able to participate fully when only a few minor modifications are made to classroom environments (Figure 5–1). Others may have medical problems or disabilities that require significant teacher assistance. Health care professionals may be accessible to some programs and in some communities to train and work directly with teachers. However, in many cases these resources are not available so that teachers find themselves responsible for performing needed treatments or making their own modifications.

The inclusion of increasing numbers of children with special needs in early childhood and school-based programs means that teachers must be knowledgeable about a range of disabilities and medical problems in order to help all children succeed (Cowdery & Allen, 2005). *Children with Special Needs in Early Childhood Settings* (Paasche, Gorrill, & Strom, 2004) is an excellent teacher resource book for this purpose. The authors address the identification, intervention, and inclusion of over 65 health and developmental conditions affecting children in a quick reference format. Descriptions of several chronic health conditions that teachers are most likely to encounter in their classrooms follow.

FIGURE 5–1

Children of all abilities and disabilities attend educational programs.

ALLERGIES

Allergies are the single most common cause of chronic health problems among young children and may affect as many as one in every five children (AAFA, 2006). Continued increases in the number of children and the number of substances to which children are allergic are raising considerable concern. Although many allergies can be successfully treated and controlled, it is estimated that more than 50 percent of children with symptoms are undiagnosed. Allergic reactions range in severity from symptoms that are mildly annoying to those that can be disabling and severely restrict a child's activity and even to unexpected death.

Signs and Symptoms

A substance capable of triggering an allergic reaction is called an *allergen.* An inherited error in the body's immune system causes it to overreact to an otherwise harmless substance in the environment, such as dust, pollen, foods, or medicines (Beers, Porter, & Jones, 2006).

Allergic reactions are generally classified according to the body site where symptoms most commonly occur:

- ingestants—cause digestive upsets and respiratory problems. Common examples include foods such as milk, citrus fruits, eggs, wheat, chocolate, tree nuts, peanuts, and oral medications.
- inhalants—affect the respiratory system causing a runny nose, cough, wheezing, and itchy, watery eyes. Examples include pollens, molds, dust, animal dander, and chemicals, such as perfumes and cleaning fluids.
- contactants—cause skin irritations, rashes, hives, and eczema. Common contactants include soaps, cosmetics, dyes, fibers, latex, medications placed directly on the skin, and some plants, e.g., poison ivy, poison oak, and grass.
- injectables—trigger respiratory, digestive, and/or skin disturbances. Examples of injectables include insect bites, especially those of bees, wasps, hornets, spiders, and medications that are injected directly into the body.

Children who have chronic allergies often experience irritability and malaise in addition to the discomfort that accompanies an acute reaction. To understand how allergies affect children on a day-to-day basis, a simple comparison can be made to the generalized fatigue and uneasiness that one feels during the onset of a cold. Certainly, children cannot benefit fully from learning when they are not feeling well. For these reasons, children's allergies may be an important contributing factor in many behavior and learning problems, including disruptive behaviors, hyperactivity, chronic fatigue, disinterest, irritability, and poor concentration, and should be investigated.

Teachers can be instrumental in recognizing the early signs of children's allergic conditions. Daily observations and anecdotal records can help detect patterns of repetitious symptoms that

REFLECTIVE THOUGHTS

Examine your feelings regarding children with chronic health disorders. Are you more apprehensive about working with these children? Do you consider them to be different in some way from children who don't have long-term health problems? Do you respond to them differently in the classroom? Do you expect less of these children or are you more likely to be protective? What do you see as your role in helping children adjust to chronic health problems? Why is good communication with their families even more important in these situations?

TABLE 5-1 Cold or Allergy . . . How to Tell?

	Cold	Allergy
Time of year	more likely in fall and winter	depends on what child is allergic to—may be year round or seasonal (fall, spring)
Nasal drainage	begins clear; may turn color after 2–3 days	remains clear
Fever	common with infection	no fever
Cough	may become loose and productive	usually not productive; nasal drainage irritates throat causing frequent throat clearing and shallow cough
Itchy eyes	no	typical
Muscle aches	may be present during first 1–2 days	none
Length of illness	7–10 days	may last an entire season or year round

may otherwise be blamed on everyday childhood illnesses (Table 5–1). Common signs and symptoms of allergic disorders include:

- frequent colds and ear infections
- chronic congestion, e.g., runny nose, cough, or throat clearing; mouth-breathing
- headaches
- frequent nosebleeds
- unexplained stomachaches
- hives, eczema, or other skin rashes
- wheezing or shortness of breath
- intermittent or permanent hearing losses
- reactions to foods or medications
- dark circles beneath the eyes
- mottled tongue
- frequent rubbing, twitching, or picking of the nose
- chronic redness of the throat
- red, itchy eyes; swollen eyelids
- irritability; restlessness; lack of energy or interest

Food Allergies Allergic conditions are thought to be inherited. However, unpleasant reactions to certain foods cause many people to believe that they have food allergies. Less than 2 percent of the adult population have an immune disorder that is responsible for a true food allergy; this condition is not outgrown. An estimated 8 percent of infants and children younger than four years experience food sensitivities or intolerances which may eventually be outgrown (Asthma & Allergy Foundation of America, 2006; Wang, Visness & Sampson, 2005). Common symptoms of food allergy include:

- hives, skin rashes
- flushed or pale face
- cramps, vomiting, and/or diarrhea
- runny nose, watery eyes, congestion, and/or wheezing
- itching or swelling around the lips, tongue, or mouth
- anxiousness, restlessness
- shock
- difficulty breathing

❋ TABLE 5–2 Common Food Allergens

Foods that are most likely to trigger an allergic reaction include:
- eggs
- milk and milk products such as cheese and ice cream
- fish and shellfish
- peanuts
- tree nuts, such as almonds, cashews, and pecans
- wheat and wheat products
- soybeans

Symptoms of an allergic reaction can develop within a few minutes or several hours following the ingestion of an offending food. Foods that most commonly trigger allergic reactions are provided in Table 5–2. The Food Allergen Labeling & Consumer Protection Act (2004) currently requires manufacturers to identify if any of these foods are present in a product or if the product has been exposed to any of these ingredients during its preparation.

Because some food allergies can be severe and potentially life-threatening, programs must take steps to protect the child's well-being (Figure 5–2) (Jones & Scurlock, 2006). Teachers must work closely with the child's family to develop a plan of action in the event of an allergic reaction. An excellent food allergy action plan is available from the Food Allergy & Anaphylaxis Network or can be downloaded from their Web site (http://www.food-allergy.org). A program's plan should include emergency telephone numbers and directives for what to do in an emergency. All staff members should be aware of this plan and review it often; this step is especially important for new or substitute teachers. If injectable medications have been ordered by the child's physician, teachers should be trained to administer them properly.

Teachers must also consider children's food allergies whenever planning lessons, celebrating holidays or special occasions, or taking field trips. The cook must read food labels in detail and avoid cross-contamination (with other children's food) when preparing the child's meals. Any special food items should be labeled with the child's name and stored away from other foods. A list of children and the foods to which they are allergic should be posted inside the classroom. One teacher should be responsible for monitoring, checking, and serving all foods to children with allergies to prevent mistakes from occurring. Everyone should wash their hands carefully following a meal or snack to avoid spreading potential food allergens. Teachers should also spend time helping the other children to understand the situation and the importance of not exchanging food items.

FIGURE 5–2

Steps must be taken to protect children who have food allergies.

Management

At present, there are no known cures for allergic conditions. The types and numbers of substances which trigger allergic responses may change periodically. This may give the impression that an allergy has disappeared, only to resurface and become troublesome again at some later time.

Symptoms and complications of allergies are generally less severe and easier to control if they are identified early. Treatment is aimed at limiting a child's exposure to annoying allergens. In some instances, steps can be taken to completely remove these substances from the child's environment. For example, if a child is allergic to milk, all dairy products can be eliminated from the child's diet. If the pet dog is the cause of a child's allergies, the dog can be kept outside or at least out of the child's bedroom. In other cases, only the amount of exposure can be controlled, as in allergies to dust or pollens. Smoking must be avoided around children with respiratory allergies because it is known to aggravate and intensify their problems (Diaz-Sanchez, Rumold, & Gong, 2006; Sarna & Bialous, 2005). Left untreated, allergies can lead to more serious chronic health problems, including chronic bronchitis, permanent hearing loss, sinusitis, asthma, and emphysema.

Antihistamines, decongestants, bronchodilators, and anti-inflammatory nasal sprays are commonly used to treat the symptoms of respiratory allergies. Many children also receive medication through aerosol breathing treatments (Chipps & Spahn, 2006; Janssens & Tiddens, 2006). Although effective, most of these medications simply provide temporary relief from symptoms. Children taking antihistamines and decongestants often experience drowsiness, difficulty concentrating, and excessive thirst. They need to be supervised closely, especially during outdoor times and when activities involve risk. Some children also experience restlessness or agitation from their medications. These side effects make it particularly difficult for children to pay attention and learn, especially if the medications are prescribed for extended periods of time. Teachers must observe these children carefully and discuss any concerns about the medication's effectiveness or side effects with the child's family. A different medication with fewer side effects can sometimes be prescribed.

> *Caution:* **Teachers should always obtain approval from the child's physician and receive proper training before administering breathing treatments or any other form of medication.**

In some cases, allergy shots (desensitization therapy) are given when other forms of treatment have been unsuccessful in controlling the child's symptoms. Many children experience improvement, but the full effect may take from 12 to 18 months to achieve.

Most allergic conditions are not life threatening. However, bee stings, medications, and certain foods can lead to a condition known as **anaphylaxis** in children who have a severe allergic reaction to these substances (Table 5–3) (McIntyre, et al., 2005). This life-threatening response can cause shock and swelling of the air passages which require urgent medical attention.

> *Caution:* **An ambulance should be called at once if anaphylaxis occurs.**

Children who have a history of severe allergic reactions may keep an EpiPen at school. EpiPens are an autoinjecting device that administers a single dose of epinephrine when quickly

---

❖ TABLE 5–3 Symptoms of Anaphylaxis

Life-threatening symptoms can develop suddenly and include:
- wheezing or difficulty breathing
- swelling of the lips, tongue, throat, and/or eyelids
- itching and hives
- nausea, vomiting, and/or diarrhea
- anxiety and restlessness
- blue discoloration around the mouth and nailbeds

---

anaphylaxis – *a severe allergic reaction that may cause difficulty breathing, itching, unconsciousness, and possible death.*

FIGURE 5-3

An EpiPen auto-injector.

pressed against the skin (usually on the leg) (Figure 5–3) (*Child Health Alert*, 2005). However, this medication provides only temporary relief, so it is essential to call for emergency medical assistance.

The emotional effects of allergies on the quality of children's and families' lives cannot be overlooked (Bollinger, et al., 2006). These children are often overly protected from everyday experiences to avoid the risk of unpleasant reactions. They are continually reminded to be cautious so that exposure to offending allergens is limited. Children may also be sensitive about their appearance—frequent sneezing, runny nose, rashes, red and swollen eyes—along with feeling moody, irritable, or even depressed. In some cases, severe allergies may limit a child's participation in physical activity. Collectively, these feelings can lead to fear, withdrawn behaviors, poor self-esteem, and other maladjustment problems.

It is important that children not be allowed to use their allergies as a means of gaining attention or special privileges. Instead, they can learn to become independent and self-confident in coping with their problems. Teachers can often help children make simple adjustments in their daily lifestyles so they can lead normal, healthy lives. Also, parenting classes and individual counseling can help family members learn how to foster children's achievement of these goals. Some clinics and hospitals offer special classes to help families and children cope with allergies. A wealth of information can also be found on many professional Web sites.

ASTHMA

Asthma has become a significant health problem affecting millions of children (AAFA, 2006; Stingone & Claudio, 2006). For many young children, asthma is both a chronic and acute respiratory disorder affecting boys twice as often as girls (Joesch, et al., 2006). It is a form of allergic response and often seen in children who also have other allergic conditions. Like allergies, asthma tends to be an inherited tendency that becomes progressively worse without treatment (Burke, et al., 2003). Children who are obese also experience increased rates of asthma, raising additional concerns about their long-term health (Landrigan, et al., 2006; Ford, 2005).

A number of theories are currently being investigated to determine why the incidence of asthma is increasing at such an alarming rate. Researchers are looking at multiple factors, including the quality of indoor environments, early infant feeding practices, sanitation standards, and increased air pollution. Mothers are being encouraged to breastfeed and to withhold solid foods until infants reach six months of age to decrease the potential risk of childhood allergies (Zutavern, et al., 2004; Trahms & Pipes, 2000). Women are also being urged to not smoke during pregnancy; babies born to mothers who smoke are more likely to develop asthma later in life (Gilliland, Berhane, Li, Rappaport, & Peters, 2002). Recent studies have also found the rate of asthma to be significantly higher among minority children and those living in poverty (Claudio, Stingone, & Godbold, 2006; Davis, et al., 2006). Asthma attacks are thought to be triggered by a number of factors, including:

- airborne allergens, e.g., pollen, animal dander, dust, molds, perfumes, cleaning chemicals, paint, ozone, cockroaches (Houston, et al., 2006; Arbes, 2005; Neidell, 2004)
- foods, e.g., nuts, wheat, milk, eggs (Nicol, 2005)
- second-hand cigarette smoke
- respiratory infections, e.g., colds, bronchitis
- stress (especially anger) and fatigue
- changes in temperature, e.g., cold, rain, wind
- vigorous exercise

Signs and Symptoms

Symptoms of acute attacks include wheezing, coughing, and difficulty breathing, especially exhalation. These symptoms are caused by swelling and spasms of the respiratory tract (bronchial tubes) (Figure 5–4). As mucus collects in the airways, breathing becomes labored, and it becomes more difficult to expel air. Many children will outgrow asthma attacks as the size of their passageways increases with age.

FIGURE 5–4

Swelling and excess mucus in the airways make breathing difficult during an asthma attack.

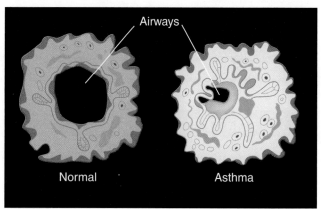

An artist's representation of bronchial tubes, or airways in the lung, in cross section. The normal airway, left, is open. The airway affected by asthma, right, is almost completely closed off. The allergic reaction characteristic of asthma causes swelling, excess mucus production, and muscle constriction in the airways, leading to coughing, wheezing, and difficult breathing.

From: http://www.niaid.nih.gov

Management

Treatment of asthma consists of identifying substances that cause flare-ups and removing them from the child's environment whenever possible. For children with airborne allergies, frequent dusting and vacuuming of the environment may be necessary. Furnace filters should be replaced on a regular basis. Furnaces can also be equipped with electrostatic air purifiers to help remove offending particles from the air. Some families find that smaller child care programs are more desirable for children with asthma because the environment can be monitored more closely and there is less exposure to respiratory infections. Medications, such as anti-inflammatory drugs and bronchodilators, may also be prescribed to decrease swelling and open air passages (Wang, Zhong, & Wheeler, 2006). These are usually administered in the form of an inhaler or aerosol breathing treatment.

A meeting should always be arranged with the family when a child with asthma is first enrolled. This enables the teacher to better understand the child's condition—what symptoms the child shows, what substances are likely to trigger an attack, what, when, and how should medications be administered, and what emergency plan of action is needed (Tables 5–4, 5–5). This information should be reviewed frequently with the child's family so that teachers are aware of any changes.

TABLE 5–4   Strategies for Managing Children's Asthma Attacks

- If you know that certain substances trigger a child's attack, remove the child from the environment (cold air, fumes).
- Encourage the child to remain quiet. Do not leave the child alone.
- Allow the child to assume a position that makes breathing easier; sitting upright is usually preferred.
- Administer any medications prescribed for the child.
- Offer small sips of room-temperature liquids (not cold).
- Contact the child's family if there is no relief from medications or if the family requests to be notified in the event of an attack.
- Do not delay calling for emergency medical assistance if the child shows any signs of struggling to breathe, fatigue, anxiety, restlessness, blue discoloration of the nail beds or lips, or loss of consciousness.
- Record your observations—child's condition prior to, during, and following an attack, factors that appeared to trigger the attack, medications that were administered, that parents were contacted.
- Stay calm; this helps put the child at ease and makes breathing easier.

REFLECTIVE THOUGHTS

Some medications used to treat the symptoms of allergies and asthma can cause undesirable side effects, including restlessness, nervousness, trembling, thirst, difficulty sleeping, drowsiness, nausea, headache, dilated pupils, difficult urination, and decreased appetite. What should you do if you observe any of these effects? What actions would you take if a child began developing difficulty breathing? How might these medications affect children's classroom behaviors and social interactions? What can teachers do to help children adjust to chronic health problems, such as asthma and allergies?

TABLE 5–5 Teacher's Checklist: Children with Allergies and Asthma

- Be familiar with the symptoms of a child's allergic reaction.
- Keep children's emergency information located where it is readily accessible; make sure that others know where to find it.
- Post emergency telephone numbers next to the telephone.
- Know where emergency medications are stored and learn how to administer them.
- Review your program's emergency policies and procedures.
- Monitor all food or other sources of allergens (e.g., animals, plants, lotions) that are brought into the classroom.
- Have the family review and update information about the child's condition periodically.

If weather triggers an attack, children may need to remain indoors on days when there are abrupt temperature changes. However, children should be encouraged to participate in regular activities as much as their condition permits. If asthma attacks are caused by strenuous play, teachers should monitor children's activity level and have them rest or play quietly until the symptoms subside. In any event, teachers should always be prepared to respond quickly if a child develops difficulty breathing (see Chapter 10).

ATTENTION-DEFICIT/HYPERACTIVITY DISORDER (AD/HD)

The current diagnostic label for this condition is now referred to as AD/HD (APA, 2000). Unfortunately, many adults continue to use this term indiscriminately to label children who are actually behaving within normal developmental limits (Biederman, 2005). Many young children are, by nature, exceedingly energetic, curious, impatient, and restless. Referring to children in this manner without professional diagnosis can have serious consequences including inappropriate treatment and altered adult expectations.

The American Psychiatric Association (APA) (2000) defines the disorder as "a **syndrome** of attention and behavior disturbances that may improve when stimulant-type drugs are administered." It is classified as a **neurobiological disorder** and is characterized by inattention, impulsivity, and hyperactivity that causes a range of behavior and learning problems, such as reading, expressive, and receptive disabilities.

Signs and Symptoms

Despite attempts to describe the condition more precisely, much controversy still remains about the causes, diagnosis, and effective management of AD/HD. Several theories are currently being investigated, including the role of genetics, prenatal exposure to smoke, alcohol and viral infections, low birth weight, environmental toxins, and biochemical disorders of the brain (Kim, et al., 2006; Deutscher & Fewell, 2005; Hudziak, et al., 2005). Boys are diagnosed with AD/HD four to five times more often than girls. However, some experts question whether the symptoms may be less exaggerated in girls and, therefore, easily overlooked. There is also a strong family tendency to this condition (Biederman, 2005).

---

syndrome – *a grouping of symptoms and signs that commonly occur together and are characteristic of a specific disease or illness.*
neurobiological disorder – *a condition of the nervous system that may be caused by genetic or biological factors.*

ISSUES TO CONSIDER • Childhood Asthma

It is 10 AM and six children are lined up on small plastic chairs in the director's office at the Wee Care 4 Kids Child Care Center. Steam hisses from clear plastic masks being held by older children over their noses and mouths while a teacher assists those who are still too young to manage the procedure alone. All of these children have one thing in common—asthma. Twice each day, teachers must administer breathing treatments to increasing numbers of young children who suffer from frequent bouts of wheezing. Unfortunately, this scene is not uncommon in many schools today as the reported incidence of childhood asthma continues to soar.

- What is asthma?
- Why are more children than ever experiencing this chronic condition?
- Why does the incidence of asthma appear to be higher among minorities and children living in poverty?
- Should teachers be responsible for administering medical procedures?
- What steps should you take to prevent administering the procedure incorrectly, and thus protect yourself from liability?

At present, there are no specific medical tests available for accurately diagnosing this disorder. However, the American Psychiatric Association (2000) has established a series of diagnostic guidelines for identifying children with AD/HD, including:

- inattention—difficulty listening; easily distracted; forgetful; has trouble completing tasks; appears not to be listening; unable to stay on task for an appropriate length of time; is careless and unable to focus on detail; avoids activities that require effort and concentration (homework)
- impulsivity—requires considerable supervision; acts before thinking; remains on task for short duration; has difficulty organizing tasks or thoughts; exceedingly impatient; has difficulty taking turns; easily frustrated; impaired performance at school, with friends, at home; frequently interrupts others; has difficulty relaxing or playing quietly
- hyperactivity—excessive motor activity (for age); constant fidgeting or moving about; has difficulty sitting, standing still, or sleeping quietly; always on the go; often talks excessively

In addition, the guidelines suggest that the behaviors must have been present before a child reaches seven years of age, be observed for at least six months, and be inconsistent with the child's expected level of development (APA, 2000).

Management

No one simple method is available to treat this disorder (Seidman, Valera, & Makris, 2005). Each child requires an individualized approach. Often a combination of methods is found to be most effective, although some are still considered to be controversial. Children's vision and hearing should also be tested to eliminate them as a potential cause of behaviors that could mimic AD/HD.

Traditional medications, such as Ritalin, Cylert, and Dexedrine as well as newer drugs such as Adderall, Concerta, and Strattera are commonly prescribed for children diagnosed with AD/HD (*Child Health Alert*, 2006; Zuvekas, Vitiello, & Norquist, 2006). These stimulant and antidepressant-type medications have a calming effect on children who have AD/HD.

The medical profession has been criticized for its overdiagnosis and overuse of medication to treat children with AD/HD (DuPaul & White, 2006). Drugs are sometimes viewed as an easy way for families, doctors, and teachers to cope with these children and are often prescribed before other forms of intervention are tried. Many of these medications cause undesirable side effects in children, including a loss of appetite, slowing of growth, sleeplessness, listlessness, depression, suicide, and stupor-like state. Furthermore, medication alone is not a cure (Kirkpatrick, 2005). The child's problem behaviors will reappear once the medication wears off or drug therapy is discontinued. However, medication is known to be beneficial for children when it is used under medical supervision, over a short period of time, and in combination with behavior management therapy (Orr, Miller, & Polson, 2005).

Behavior management and special intervention strategies have been used successfully to treat children with AD/HD. Their effectiveness can be attributed to the fact that these methods deal directly with the child's problem behaviors (DuPaul & Weyandt, 2006; Greenspan, 2006; Gigout-Hues, 2006). Through carefully planned and controlled experiences, children can learn social and academic behaviors that are acceptable and appropriate (Table 5–6).

Parenting a child with AD/HD can place a tremendous amount of strain on families (Orr, Miller, & Polson, 2005). For this reason, it is important that they also receive support and be included in children's behavioral therapy.

Implementing these strategies can provide children with opportunities to learn positive behaviors, and thus lessen the emotional problems that often accompany attention deficit disorders. Gradually, children's self-confidence will improve as they become more successful and no longer see themselves as "always bad" or "failures" at whatever they do.

Dietary management has also been suggested as a treatment (Beseler, 1999; *Child Health Alert*, 1995). The controversial Feingold diet, introduced during the 1970s, linked the elimination of sugar, artificial colors and flavorings, and foods containing an aspirin-related compound to improvements in children's behavior. Many authorities continue to question Feingold's theories and results. However, like many other forms of therapy, what works for one child may not necessarily work for another. Certainly, there is no harm in feeding children foods that are nutritious, lower in sugar, and additive-free.

TABLE 5-6 AD/HD: Strategies for Helping Children

Several basic principles can be implemented to improve children's success:
* Create a structured environment. The degree of structure depends on the type and severity of the child's problems. For example, structure for one child may involve restricting the number of furnishings in a classroom to a single table and chair. For another child, structure may be achieved by limiting the number of choices, e.g., choosing between two toys or activities.
* Establish a daily routine that is consistent and predictable. Children who have AD/DH function best when things are familiar, including a routine that is the same from day to day.
* Give directions that are clear and easy for the child to follow. Have the child look at you while you explain exactly what is expected. "Andy, I want you to put the toys in this basket." The use of repetition is also important. Modeling the desired behavior is also helpful.
* Offer praise and positive reinforcement. This is an effective means for gaining children's cooperation. It also encourages them to attempt, complete, and feel good about even simple tasks. "Good work, Nel. You put on your shoe."
* Provide challenging experiences that are within the child's skill and tolerance levels. This gives children an opportunity to be successful and avoid repeated frustration and failure.
* Provide children with opportunities for developing new interests, especially physical activities where they can channel excess energy and learn to relax.

DIABETES

Approximately 25 percent of people diagnosed with diabetes, particularly type 2, are children. However, there is growing fear that type 2 diabetes could soon reach epidemic proportions in children because it is often associated with obesity (Chia & Boston, 2006). At present, approximately 10 percent of children two and five years of age and 30 percent of children ages 6–17 are considered to be overweight. These figures reflect a 4 percent increase since 1994 and are significantly higher among minority groups (AHA, 2006; CDCa, 2007).

Teachers should be familiar with the signs, symptoms, and treatment of diabetes as many of these children will be enrolled in early childhood and after-school programs (Shipley, 2002). Treatment of childhood diabetes requires careful regulation and control. Growth, unpredictable changes in activity levels, irregular eating habits, and frequent exposure to respiratory infections often challenge successful management in children (Wong, 2001).

Signs and Symptoms

Type 1 diabetes is a chronic, incurable, and often hereditary condition that occurs when the pancreas fails to produce an adequate amount of the **hormone** insulin. Type 2 diabetes, often referred to as adult-onset diabetes, occurs when the pancreas produces an insufficient amount of insulin or when cells in the body are not able to use the insulin properly (Harrell, Jessup, & Greene, 2006). Insulin is necessary for the metabolism of carbohydrates (sugars and starches) and the storage and release of glucose (blood sugar/energy). If insulin is absent or the amount is insufficient, glucose continues to circulate freely in the bloodstream rather than being stored. This condition is known as **hyperglycemia**. Serious complications, including coma and death, can occur if it is left untreated. The onset of diabetes in children is usually rather abrupt, and includes early symptoms such as:

- rapid weight loss
- fatigue and/or weakness
- nausea or vomiting
- frequent urination

- **dehydration**
- excessive thirst and/or hunger
- dry, itchy skin

Management

Teachers must become familiar with each child's unique situation and treatment regime—whether the child has type 1 or type 2 diabetes, what dietary restrictions the child requires, and what medical treatments (urine testing, insulin injections, medications) must be administered. Children who have type 1 diabetes must be given insulin injections several times each day, have their glucose levels checked, and closely regulate their diet and activity. Some children may have an insulin pump which eliminates the need for injections. Children with type 2 diabetes may also require insulin injections, although many are able to regulate their condition through careful dietary management and/or medications to help their bodies utilize glucose. In addition to learning about and implementing children's treatment regimes, teachers must be able to recognize the signs of complications associated with diabetes. For example, a child who receives an insulin dose that is too large or too small will exhibit different symptoms and require different emergency care (see Chapter 10: see insulin shock, diabetic coma).

Arrangements should be made to meet with the families of children who are diabetic before they begin to attend an out-of-home program (ADA, 2003). Families can provide teachers with

---

hormone – *special chemical substance produced by endocrine glands that influences and regulates certain body functions.*
hyperglycemia – *a condition characterized by an abnormally high level of sugar in the blood.*
dehydration – *a state in which there is an excessive loss of body fluids or extremely limited fluid intake. Symptoms may include loss of skin tone, sunken eyes, and mental confusion.*

TABLE 5-7 Teacher's Checklist: Children with Diabetes

- Meet with the family regularly to review the child's progress and treatment procedures.
- Be familiar with the symptoms of hypoglycemia (low blood sugar) and hyperglycemia (high blood sugar) and know how to respond.
- Keep children's emergency information where it is readily accessible; make sure others also know where to find this information.
- Post emergency numbers near the telephone.
- Know where emergency medications are stored and learn how to administer them. Also learn how to check children's blood sugar and train additional staff members to perform these tests.
- Be mindful of any changes in meal schedules, length of outdoor play, or impromptu field trips that might affect the child's insulin needs.
- Review your program's emergency policies and procedures.

TABLE 5-8 Strategies for Helping Children Who Have Diabetes

Teachers can be instrumental in helping children:
- Learn about their diabetes in simple terms (and not to be ashamed, afraid, or embarrassed).
- Understand that good eating habits are important.
- Recognize the relationship between good eating habits and feeling well.
- Learn to enjoy physical activity.
- Assist with their own medical management, e.g., practice good handwashing before glucose tests (finger sticks), cleansing the injection site.
- Participate in opportunities that help build good self-esteem.

FIGURE 5-5

The diabetic child must follow special dietary restrictions.

valuable information about their child's condition and how to identify changes in behavior and appearance that may signal an impending complication. Teachers also need to be aware of dietary restrictions and medical procedures so they can be followed carefully while the child is in care (Figure 5–5). Plans for handling medical emergencies should also be worked out with families at this time and reviewed often.

Equipped with this knowledge, a teacher is better prepared to respond to children's diabetic emergencies (Table 5–7). This can be reassuring to families who may be reluctant to leave their child in the care of others. Teachers are also in a unique position to help diabetic children accept and manage their condition and to help their peers learn more about diabetes (Table 5–8).

ECZEMA

Eczema is a chronic inflammatory skin condition. Initial symptoms commonly appear in infants and children younger than five, and affect between 10 and 12 percent of all children (Wong, 2001). Eczema often disappears or significantly improves between the ages of 5 and 15 years in approximately 50 percent of these children.

Signs and Symptoms

Eczema is caused by an abnormal immune system response. It is commonly associated with allergies, especially to certain foods (e.g., eggs, wheat, milk) and substances that come in contact with the skin (e.g., wool, soaps, perfumes, disinfectants, animal dander). Often there is strong family history of allergy and similar skin problems.

Reddened patches of irritated skin may appear on an infant's or toddler's cheeks, forehead, scalp, or neck. Older children typically develop dry, itchy, scaly areas on the knees, elbows, wrists, and/or back of hands. Repeated scratching can lead to open, weeping skin that can become infected. Changes in weather can trigger an eczema flare-up or cause it to worsen, especially during summer heat or in winter cold when full-length clothing is likely to be worn. Older children may be reluctant to wear short-sleeved shirts and shorts when warmer weather arrives because of their appearance.

Management

Eczema is not curable, but can be controlled through a number of preventive measures. Eliminating environmental allergens is always the preferred and first line of defense. However, in some cases these substance may not yet be known or are difficult to eliminate, such as dust or pollen, but steps can be taken to reduce the child's exposure. Reminding children not to scratch irritated skin and keeping their skin moisturized, especially after bathing or washing is also helpful.

Limiting exposure to extreme temperature changes can also be effective for controlling symptoms. Keeping children cool in warm weather prevents sweating, which can lead to skin irritation. Reducing room temperatures, dressing infants and children in light clothing, and wiping warm areas of their body (creases in neck, elbow, knees, and face) with cool water can improve the child's comfort. Teachers may also be asked to administer antihistamines or topical cortisone ointments that the child's doctor has prescribed. Reducing stress in children's lives and helping them to develop a healthy self-image are also important strategies for reducing flare-ups.

FATIGUE

Most children enjoy a refreshing sense of energy, enthusiasm, and curiosity for life. Their stamina and intensity of play is often amazing. However, children may also experience periods of fatigue and listlessness from time to time. In most instances, both the cause and symptoms are temporary. Growth spurts, late bedtimes, moving to a new home, recovery from a recent cold, the birth of a sibling, or participation in too many activities may temporarily disrupt a child's normal sleeping pattern or increase the need for additional sleep.

TABLE 5–9 Strategies for Improving Chronic Fatigue in Children

- Help children develop good dietary habits.
- Encourage children to participate in moderate exercise, such as walking, swimming, riding bikes.
- Provide opportunities for improved sleep, e.g., earlier bedtimes, short naps during the day, a quiet sleeping area away from activity.
- Alternate periods of activity with quiet times, e.g., reading a book, playing quietly with a favorite toy, listening to music.
- Reduce environmental stress.
- Help children build effective coping skills.

Signs and Symptoms

Repeated or prolonged fatigue is not considered a normal condition for young children and should be investigated because of its potentially negative effect on growth and development. Chronic fatigue may be an indication of other health problems, including:

- poor nutrition
- chronic infection, such as otitis media
- **anemia**
- allergies
- lead poisoning
- hepatitis
- **endocrine** (hormonal) disorders, such as diabetes, thyroidism
- heart disorders

Management

Careful evaluation of the child's personal habits and lifestyle may reveal a reason for chronic fatigue. A complete medical examination may be necessary to detect any existing health problems. If no specific cause can be identified, there are several steps families and teachers can take to improve the child's general well-being (Table 5–9). Many of these measures can be built into daily classroom routines and are beneficial for all children.

FETAL ALCOHOL SYNDROME (FAS)/ FETAL ALCOHOL EFFECT (FAE)

A mother's consumption of alcohol during pregnancy has been linked directly to the preventable conditions known as fetal alcohol syndrome (FAS) and fetal alcohol effect (FAE) in the unborn child (National Center on Birth Defects and Developmental Disabilities, 2006). It is estimated that between 2,000 and 9,000 babies are born each year with fetal alcohol syndrome, although it is difficult to obtain an exact number since the signs may not be identified until after the child's first birthday (Eustace, Kang, & Coombs, 2003). How severely a child will be affected is difficult to predict, but often depends on the amount and point in the pregnancy when alcohol was ingested (Bhatara, Loudenberg, & Ellis, 2006; Gorman, 2006). Babies born to mothers who drank heavily during pregnancy are more likely to suffer from FAS; babies exposed to less alcohol typically experienced fewer and more mild abnormalities, such as difficulty with problem-solving, memory, and judgment (FAE). While alcohol can affect fetal development throughout the pregnancy, the most serious consequences tend to occur during the first three months when all major fetal organs (e.g., brain, heart, lungs, sensory and immune systems) are forming.

Signs and Symptoms

Unfortunately, the baby's brain development is most significantly affected by this syndrome—the way it develops and the way it works. Children with mild symptoms may not be diagnosed immediately, especially if their involvement is relatively mild. Fetal alcohol syndrome typically causes three major categories of disability—delayed growth, abnormalities of the brain and central

---

anemia – *a disorder of the blood commonly caused by a lack of iron in the diet, resulting in the formation of fewer red blood cells and lessened ability of the cells to carry oxygen. Symptoms include fatigue, shortness of breath, and pallor.*
endocrine – *refers to glands within the body that produce and secrete substances called hormones directly into the bloodstream.*

FIGURE 5–6

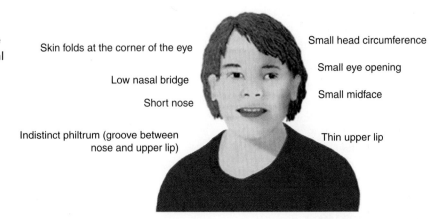

Children exposed to prenatal alcohol often have characteristic facial features.

Skin folds at the corner of the eye

Low nasal bridge

Short nose

Indistinct philtrum (groove between nose and upper lip)

Small head circumference

Small eye opening

Small midface

Thin upper lip

nervous system, and distinct facial malformations (Figure 5–6) (Kalberg, et al., 2006; Burden, Jacobson, & Jacobson, 2005). Characteristics commonly associated with FAS include:

- low birth weight
- mental retardation
- poor muscle strength and coordination
- small head circumference (microcephaly)
- heart defects
- behavior problems
- learning disabilities
- irritability; restlessness; difficulty sleeping

- droopy or short eyelids
- thin upper lip
- eyes set far apart
- ears set lower on the head
- hearing and/or vision problems
- difficulty remembering
- poor attention span

Slow growth, limited cognitive development, and numerous health problems continue to plague these children for life.

Management

FAS and FAE are entirely preventable conditions. No child would experience the physical and developmental disabilities associated with this syndrome if their mothers had avoided consumption of *all* alcohol prior to and during pregnancy. Studies have not been able to determine if any amount of alcohol is ever safe, so complete abstinence is recommended (Committee on Substance Abuse & Committee on Children with Disabilities, 2000). The incidence of FAS and FAE is considerably higher among some minority populations who may not have ready access to preventive information (Szlemko, Wood, & Thurman, 2006). Public service efforts to spread this critical message are being stepped up as a result (Ryan, Bonnett, & Gass, 2006; Project CHOICES Intervention Research Group, 2003).

Early identification and early educational and behavioral interventions for children with these syndromes are important for their long-term success (Miller, 2006; Harwood & Kleinfeld, 2002; Duckworth & Norton, 2000). Some children are able to participate in traditional learning activities, while others require considerable adaptation. A predictable routine and limited environmental distractions improve children's ability to stay focused. Educational goals should be aimed at helping children develop effective social and communication skills (oral, written, signing) and to become as independent as their disability permits (Cone-Wesson, 2005). Because these children are also prone to health problems, teachers should monitor them closely so their progress is not disrupted. Teachers must also be extremely vigilant about children's safety. Their inability to remember, difficulty in understanding cause and effect, and poor coordination place them at high risk for unintentional injury.

LEAD POISONING

Lead poisoning continues to be a major public health concern despite a significant decline in the numbers of children affected. Aggressive educational campaigns, legislation, and abatement programs have been successful in eliminating many common sources of lead contamination. Despite these efforts, the CDC estimates that approximately 434,000 U.S. children between one and five years of age have blood levels in excess of safety recommendations (CDCb, 2007).

Although lead poisoning is not a problem exclusively associated with poverty and inner-city populations, the incidence is typically higher among children living in these areas because of the lead-based paints (prior to 1978) used on houses and furniture (Table 5–10). Legislation passed in 1978 banned the production of these paints, although many existing sources still remain (AAP, 2005). Renovation of old houses can produce considerable contamination in the form of loose paint chips and paint dust that children may inhale (Lanphear, et al., 2003). Inexpensive test kits are available at hardware stores for detecting lead-based paint on surfaces.

Caution: **Use care when purchasing used toys and furniture at garage sales or from second-hand stores, as some of these items may contain lead-based paints.**

Signs and Symptoms

Young children are especially vulnerable to lead poisoning. They frequently put toys and hands in their mouths, their bodies absorb lead more readily, and their brain and nervous systems are especially sensitive to lead's harmful effects (Figure 5–7) (Mulroy, Bothell, & Gaudio, 2004; Canfield, et al., 2003). Lead gradually accumulates in the child's bones, brain, central nervous system, tissues, and kidneys (Piomelli, 2002).

Children with elevated levels of lead present a range of symptoms, including:

- irritability
- loss of appetite and nausea
- headaches
- unexplained abdominal pain, muscle aches
- constipation
- listlessness
- learning problems; short attention span; easily distracted; mental retardation
- behavior problems; aggression; impulsivity

Children younger than six years of age, living in low-income residential areas, and who consume a poor-quality diet, especially one low in vitamin C and iron, are at greatest risk for developing lead poisoning.

TABLE 5–10 Common Sources of Environmental Lead

- old lead-based house paint (prior to 1978), including dust from remodeling projects
- soil contaminated by leaded gasoline emissions and old paint chips
- plastic mini blinds (manufactured before 1996, not made in the U.S.A.)
- contaminated drinking water (from lead solder in old water pipes)
- imported dishware and crystal
- folk treatments and medications
- imported toys and metallic trinkets (MMWR, 2006)
- lead shot and fishing weights
- second-hand toys and furniture manufactured before 1978
- areas around lead smelters and mining operations
- working with or around motor vehicle batteries

FIGURE 5–7

Children's brain and nervous system are vulnerable to the effects of lead poisoning.

Management

Research has demonstrated that elevated levels of lead can lower a child's IQ by as much as 4 to 5 percent (Dugbatey, et al., 2005). Eliminating elevated levels of lead in children has thus been targeted as a primary goal of the Healthy People 2010 initiative. Consequently, the Centers for Disease Control (CDC) now recommends that all children, especially those at risk (including children who have immigrated to the United States), be screened for lead poisoning between 6 and 72 months of age (MMWR, 2000; CDC, 2007). However, a teacher who has concerns about a child's physical complaints, behavior, or learning problems and thinks there may be a risk of lead poisoning should encourage families to have their child tested.

Prevention of lead poisoning requires that environmental sources be located and removed (Sherman, 2004). Early identification of children already affected by this condition is also important so that additional exposure to lead contamination can be stopped. Children should be encouraged to practice good handwashing habits, and to keep their hands and objects out of their mouths. Children who have elevated blood levels of lead may be treated with special medications and increased dietary intake of iron and vitamin C (Burke, 2006; Chen & Rogan, 2005; Wright, et al., 2003; Simon & Hudes, 1999). Unfortunately, there is little evidence to date suggesting that educational interventions can reverse or offer any improvement in children's behavior and/or learning problems if lead has already had detrimental effects. Thus, public awareness and community education continue to be the most effective measures for combating this preventable condition (Erickson & Thompson, 2005).

SEIZURE DISORDERS

It is not uncommon to have children who experience **seizures** in early childhood or after-school settings. Unlike many other chronic health problems, terms such as seizures, convulsions, or epilepsy often arouse feelings of fear and anxiety in many adults. However, prior knowledge and planning will enable teachers to respond with skill and confidence when caring for children who experience these types of disorders (Table 5–11).

The term seizure disorder describes a cluster of symptoms rather than a particular disease. Seizures are caused by a rush of abnormal electrical impulses in the brain. This abnormal activity leads to involuntary or uncontrollable movements in various parts of the body. Their intensity and location differ, depending on the type of seizure. Some seizures involve only a momentary lapse

seizures – *a temporary interruption of consciousness sometimes accompanied by convulsive movements.*

TABLE 5-11 Strategies for Helping Children Who Experience Seizure Disorders

1. Be aware of any children with a seizure disorder in the classroom. Find out what the child's seizures are like, if medication is taken to control the seizures, and whether the child is limited in any way by the disorder.
2. Know emergency response measures. Develop guidelines for staff members to follow in the event that a child has a seizure; review the guidelines often.
3. Use the presence of a child with a seizure disorder as a learning opportunity for other children. Provide simple explanations about what seizures are; encourage children to ask questions and express their feelings. Help children learn to accept others who have special conditions.
4. Gain a better understanding of epilepsy and seizure disorders. Read books and articles, view films, and talk with health professionals and families.
5. Obtain and read the following books and pamphlets written for children. Share them with children in the classroom.
   - Gosselin, K. (2002). *Taking seizure disorders to school: A story about epilepsy.* St. Louis, MO: JayJo Books.
   - Moss, D. (1989). *Lee, the rabbit with epilepsy.* Bethesda, MD: Woodbine House.
   - Silverstein, A. (1980). *Epilepsy.* Philadelphia: J. B. Lippincott Co.
   - Young, M. (1980). *What difference does it make, Danny?* London: Andre Deutsch Limited.

of attention or interruption of thought while others may last several minutes and cause vigorous, spasmodic contractions of the entire body. Temporary loss of consciousness, frothing, and loss of bowel and bladder control may also accompany some types of seizures.

The specific cause of a seizure disorder is often difficult to determine (Cowan, 2002). Heredity is a contributing factor in some families. Children who have certain disabilities and syndromes are known to have a greater risk of experiencing a seizure disorder. However, an exact cause may never be identified. Several conditions are known to initiate seizure activity in young children:

- fevers that are high or rise rapidly (especially in infants)
- brain damage
- infections that affect the central nervous system, such as meningitis or encephalitis
- tumors
- head injuries
- lead, mercury, and carbon monoxide poisoning
- hypoglycemia (low blood sugar)
- drug reactions

Signs and Symptoms

Seizures are generally classified according to the pattern of symptoms a child presents (Friedman & Sharieff, 2006). The most common types of seizures include:

- febrile
- petit mal
- grand mal
- focal
- temporal lobe

Approximately 5 to 10 percent of infants and children under three years of age experience *febrile seizures* (Baumann, 2001). The majority of these seizures occur in infants between 6 and 12 months of age. Febrile seizures are triggered by high fever and may cause a child to lose consciousness and have involuntary jerking movements involving the entire body. They usually stop when the fever subsides, and are therefore not thought to be serious or to result in any permanent damage.

Teachers may be the first to notice the subtle, abnormal behaviors exhibited by children with *petit mal seizures* (Bishop & Boag, 2006). This type of seizure is characterized by momentary losses of attention, including:

- repeated incidences of daydreaming
- staring off into space
- a blank appearance
- brief fluttering of the eyes
- temporary interruption of speech or activity
- twitching or dropping of objects

Petit mal seizures generally occur in children 4 to 10 years of age and are characterized by a brief loss of consciousness, usually lasting 10 to 30 seconds. Children may abruptly stop an activity and resume it almost as quickly once the seizure subsides. Families should be informed of the teacher's observations and encouraged to consult the child's physician.

Grand mal seizures are the most common form of seizure disorder. Convulsive movements usually involve the entire body, often making them frightening to the observer. Some children experience an aura or warning immediately before a seizure begins. This warning may be in the form of a certain sound, smell, taste, sensation, or visual cue. Sudden rigidity or stiffness (tonic phase) is followed by a loss of consciousness and uncontrollable muscular contractions (clonic phase). When the seizure ends, children may awaken briefly and complain of a headache or dizziness before falling asleep.

Focal seizures are characterized by involuntary convulsive movements that begin at the tip of an extremity and spread toward the body trunk. The child does not always lose consciousness with this type of seizure.

Temporal lobe seizures are distinguished by spontaneous episodes of unusual behavior; the behavior is considered unusual because it is inappropriate for the circumstances. For example, a child may burst out in sudden hysterical laughter, utter unintelligible sounds, run around in circles, or cry out without apparent reason. The child may experience an aura before the seizure begins. Children who experience this type of seizure do not usually lose complete consciousness, although they may appear drowsy or momentarily confused afterward and should be encouraged to rest.

Management

Most seizures can be controlled with medication. It is vital that children take their medications every day, even after seizures are under control. Children may initially experience undesirable side effects to these drugs, such as drowsiness, nausea, and dizziness. However, these problems usually disappear after a short time. Children should be monitored closely by their physician to ensure that prescribed medications and dosages continue to be effective in controlling seizure activity and do not interfere with learning.

Whenever a child experiences a seizure, families should be notified. If the nature of the seizures changes, or if they begin to recur after having been under control, families should be encouraged to consult the child's physician. Teachers should also complete a brief, written report documenting their observations following any seizure and put it into the child's permanent health file (Table 5–12). This information may also be useful to the child's physician for diagnosing a seizure disorder and evaluating medical treatments.

Teachers play an important role in facilitating the inclusion of children with seizure disorders in early childhood and after-school programs. By arranging safe environments and mastering emergency response techniques (see Chapter 10), teachers can fully involve all children in activities (Taras & Potts-Datema, 2006). Teachers can help young children learn to accept and cope with their seizure disorder. They can also encourage children to develop positive attitudes toward people who experience seizures. A teacher's own reactions and displays of genuine acceptance can go a long way in teaching understanding and respect for anyone with special health problems.

TABLE 5–12 Information to Include in a Child's Seizure Report

- child's name
- date and time the seizure occurred
- events preceding the seizure
- how long the seizure lasted
- nature and location of convulsive movements (what parts of the body were involved?)
- child's condition during the seizure, e.g., difficulty breathing, loss of bladder or bowel control, change in skin color (pallor, blue discoloration)
- child's condition following the seizure, e.g., any injuries, complaints of headache, difficulty with speech or memory, desire to sleep
- name of person who observed and prepared the report

SICKLE CELL ANEMIA

Sickle cell anemia is an inherited disorder that interferes with the red blood cells' ability to carry oxygen (Wong, 2001). Approximately 1 out of every 400 children will be born with this genetic disease. It primarily affects the African-American population, as well as individuals of Mediterranean, Middle Eastern, and Latin American descent. Approximately 10 percent of African Americans carry the trait for sickle cell anemia but do not necessarily experience symptoms of the disease themselves; these people are called carriers. When both parents have the sickle cell trait, some of their children may be born with the actual disease, while others may be carriers.

Signs and Symptoms

The abnormal formation of red blood cells in sickle cell anemia causes chronic health problems for the child (King, et al., 2006b). Red blood cells form in the shape of a comma or sickle, rather than their typical round shape. As a result, blood flow throughout the body is slowed and occasionally blocked. Symptoms of the disease do not usually appear until sometime after the child's first birthday.

Clumping of deformed blood cells results in periods of acute illness called *crisis*. A crisis can be triggered by infection, injury, strenuous exercise, dehydration, exposure to temperature extremes (hot or cold) or, in some cases, for no known reason. Symptoms of a sickle cell crisis include fever, swelling of the hands or feet, severe abdominal and leg pain, vomiting, and ulcers (sores) on the arms and legs. Children are usually hospitalized during a crisis. Between flare-ups, they may be free from acute symptoms. These children are also at high risk for having a stroke which is characterized by muscle weakness, difficulty speaking, and/or seizures. In addition, chronic infection and anemia may cause children to be small for their age, irritable, easily tired, and at risk for cognitive delays (Smith, et al., 2006; Barden, et al., 2002; Thompson, et al., 2002). They are also more susceptible to infections, a fact that families should consider when placing young children in group care.

Management

At present there is no known cure for sickle cell anemia. Genetic counseling can assist prospective parents who are carriers in determining the probability of having a child with this condition. Hospitals in many states now screen newborns for the disease before they are sent home. Early diagnosis and medical intervention and can reduce mortality. A new drug has recently been approved to treat persons who have multiple yearly crises (Anderson, 2006). Children may be given daily antibiotics to reduce the risk of infections which are a common cause of death. Studies have also shown that frequent blood transfusions may be helpful in preventing acute crises (Miller, et al., 2001).

Children who have sickle cell disease are living longer today as the result of improved diagnosis and treatments. Although children may appear to be perfectly normal between acute episodes, they often experience a high rate of absenteeism due to flare-ups, infections, and respiratory illnesses which can interfere with their developmental and academic progress (King, et al., 2006a). Illness and discomfort may interfere with children's intake of important dietary nutrients (Kawchak, et al., 2007). When teachers understand this disease and its effects on children's health they can work with families to help children cope with the condition and continue to progress in school (Table 5–13).

TABLE 5-13 Teacher's Checklist: Children with Sickle Cell Disease

- Meet with the family regularly to review the child's progress and treatment procedures.
- Be familiar with the symptoms of acute complications, such as fever, pain, difficulty breathing, or signs of a stroke (muscle weakness, difficulty speaking, and/or seizures).
- Keep children's emergency information in a place where it is readily accessible; make sure that others know where to find this information.
- Post emergency telephone numbers near the telephone.
- Collaborate with the child's family and provide learning materials that can be used at home.
- Maintain good sanitation procedures (e.g., handwashing, sanitizing surfaces and materials) in the classroom to protect children from unnecessary infections.
- Monitor the child's physical activity and provide frequent rest periods to avoid fatigue.
- Protect the child from temperature extremes (heat or cold); arrange for the child to stay indoors when conditions are not favorable.
- Encourage children to eat a healthful diet and drink adequate fluids (allow them to use the restroom whenever necessary).
- Review your program's emergency policies and procedures.

FOCUS ON FAMILIES • Protecting Children from West Nile Virus

The West Nile virus is transmitted to humans through the bite of an infected mosquito.

Although the number of identified cases remains relatively low, the infection continues to spread. Few people who are bitten will actually develop symptoms of the disease, which include fever, headache, body aches, skin rash, and swollen lymph glands. Simple, preventive steps can be taken to protect children against this newly emerging infectious illness.

- Eliminate sources of standing water in bird baths, plants, fountains, tire swings, buckets, and wading pools.
- Keep children indoors during early-morning hours, or at dusk when mosquitoes are more active.
- Dress children in light-colored, protective clothing, such as a long-sleeved shirt, long pants, and hat.
- Apply insect repellant containing no more than 10 percent DEET sparingly to exposed skin or clothing. Do not apply around the eyes, nose, or mouth, and wash hands carefully when you are finished. Be sure to wash the repellant off when children come indoors. Do not use DEET repellants on children younger than two years or if you are pregnant.
- Install or repair screens on doors and windows.
- Keep grass cut short and eliminate areas of overgrown vegetation.
- Contact a physician if your child develops any early signs of the West Nile virus.

CASE STUDY

Read the case study and fill in the blanks with a word (or words) selected from the following list.

breathing	headache
sleep	anticonvulsants
seizure	consciousness
informed	written report
aura	time length
grand mal	involved
permanent health file	

While climbing up the playhouse ladder, Jamie let out a sudden shriek, released her grip, and fell to the ground. Her teacher quickly ran to see what had happened. Jamie lay on the ground unconscious, her arms and legs jerking. The teacher realized that Jamie was having a _____, and that it was probably a _____ type. A warning or _____ usually precedes this kind of seizure.

Jamie's teacher stood back and watched until the muscular contractions ended. In addition to the loss of consciousness, the teacher also carefully noted the exact _____ of the seizure, the parts of the body _____, and whether Jamie had any difficulty _____. Later, this information would be included in a _____, which would be placed in the child's _____.

When Jamie regained _____ she complained of a _____. The teacher encouraged her to _____ for a short while. Meanwhile, Jamie's parents were _____ of her seizure. Her mother explained that the doctor had recently prescribed a new medication and was trying to regulate the dosage. The most common group of medications used to treat seizure disorders are _____.

CLASSROOM CORNER • Teacher Activities

Everyone Is Special

Concept: People may be different, but everyone is special. (Pre-2)

Learning Objectives

- Children will learn that people are more alike than different.
- Children will learn why it is important to show others respect.

Supplies: unbreakable mirror; sheets of white paper; crayons or markers; shoebox and magazine pictures of children (different ethnicities and abilities); ball of string or yarn

Learning Activities

- Read and discuss any of the following books about children who have special qualities:
    - *That's What Friends Do* by K. Cave (general)
    - *Someone Special, Just Like You* by Tricia Brown (general disabilities)
    - *Be Quiet, Marina!* by Kristen De Bear (cerebral palsy, Down syndrome)
    - *Listen for the Bus: David's Story* by P. McMahon (vision and hearing impaired)
    - *It's Okay to Be Different* by T. Parr (general)

(continued)

CLASSROOM CORNER • Teacher Activities (continued)

- *Russ and the Firehouse* by J. E. Rikert (Down syndrome)
- *A Book of Friends* by D. Ross (diversity)
- *Any and His Yellow Frisbee* by M. Thompson (autism)
- *Susan Laughs* by Jeanne Willis (wheelchair)

■ Ask the children to help you describe the word *respect*. Have them suggest other words that mean the same thing (e.g., being kind, treating a person kindly, doing things together, not making fun of a person).

■ Have children sit in a circle. Give the first child a ball of string or yarn; ask him/her to name something special about the person sitting next to him/her. The first child should hold onto the end of the yarn and pass the ball to the person they have just described. Continue around the circle with each child describing something about the person sitting next to them and holding onto the string/yarn as it is passed to the next child. When everyone has had a turn, explain how the yarn/string illustrates that we are all connected by many of the same qualities and the things we need or like to do (we are more alike than different and that makes everyone special).

■ As a group, make a list of things that everybody likes and needs (e.g., food, sleeping, playing, having friends).

■ One at a time, have children look in a mirror and describe one quality that makes them special.

■ Place the pictures of children in a shoebox. One at a time, have children pull a picture out of the box and describe why they think this person would be special.

Evaluation

■ Children will be able to name several different ways that people are the same and different.

■ Children will be able to tell why it is important to treat all people with respect and kindness.

SUMMARY

■ Many children in group care settings are affected by chronic illness.
  - Some conditions, such as diabetes, allergies, and lead poisoning, may develop slowly and may, therefore, be difficult to recognize.
  - Families may find it difficult to acknowledge children's health problems or may not be certain where to go for help.
  - Teachers play an important role in protecting the well-being of children who have chronic diseases and helping young children cope with their conditions.

■ Allergies are another common chronic condition experienced by many young children.
  - Symptoms are caused by an abnormal response to substances called allergens and can include nasal congestion, headaches, eczema, rashes, asthma, stomachaches, and behavioral changes.
  - Treatment is often symptomatic and based on identification of offending allergens.

- AD/HD causes a variety of behavioral and learning problems.
  - Causes, diagnosis, and treatments are not clear-cut and are sometimes controversial.
  - Combinations of medication and behavior management strategies are often used to treat the disorder.
- Diabetes in children is caused by an inadequate amount or lack of the hormone insulin.
  - Early symptoms include weight loss, frequent urination, fatigue, and excessive thirst.
  - Treatment includes daily insulin injections and careful dietary regulation.
- The incidence of asthma, a form of allergic response, is increasing.
  - Many potential causes are being investigated, including exposure to chemicals and air pollution, infant feeding practices, obesity, and smoking during pregnancy.
  - Treatment is aimed at alleviating symptoms and acute attacks.
- Fetal alcohol syndrome (FAS) and fetal alcohol effect (FAE) have been linked directly to maternal alcohol consumption during pregnancy; no amount is considered safe.
  - Abnormal facial features, vision and hearing impairments, learning disabilities, and behavior problems are common.
- Lead poisoning affects thousands of children in the United States.
  - Environmental sources of lead contamination can be found in paint on older houses (prior to 1978), toys, lead shot and fishing weights, contaminated soil, and car batteries.
  - Children with elevated blood levels of lead show signs of impaired cognitive abilities, headaches, loss of appetite, fatigue, and behavior problems.

APPLICATION ACTIVITIES

1. Locate and read at least eight children's books written about the various chronic diseases discussed in this chapter.

2. Interview teachers in three different settings. Ask about the types of allergies they encounter most often and how they manage children's problems in the classroom. Develop a simple, five-day snack menu for a toddler who is allergic to milk and milk products, chocolate, and eggs.

3. Invite a speaker from the nearest chapter of the Feingold Association. Conduct an Internet search to learn more about this philosophy or read one of the following articles. Be prepared to ask questions.

   - Feingold, B. F. (1975). Hyperkinesis and learning disabilities linked to artificial food flavors and colors. *American Journal of Nursing, 75,* 797.
   - Herbert W. (1982, January 23). Hyperactivity—diet link questions. *Science News, 121,* 53.
   - Kaplan, B., McNicol, J., Conte, R., & Moghadam, H. (1989). Overall nutrient intake of preschool hyperactive and normal boys. *Journal of Abnormal Child Psychology, 17*(2), 127–132.
   - Lipton, M. A., & Mayo, J. P. (1983). Diet and hyperkinesis—an update. *Journal of the American Dietetics Association, 83*(2), 132–134.
   - Robinson, L. A. (1980). Food allergies, food additives and the Feingold Diet. *Pediatric Nurse, 6,* 38.
   - Wolraich, M. (1998). Attention deficit hyperactivity disorder. *Professional Care of Mother & Child, 8*(2), 35–37.
   - Wolraich, M., Milich, R., Stumbo, P., & Schultz, F. (1985). The effects of sucrose ingestion on the behavior of hyperactive boys. *Pediatrics, 106,* 675–682.

4. Design an educational poster on fetal alcohol syndrome prevention and display it in a prominent public area where potential mothers are likely to see it.

CHAPTER REVIEW

A. By Yourself:

1. Define the following terms:
   a. chronic
   b. orthopedic problem
   c. allergen
   d. insulin
   e. hyperglycemia
   f. allergic reaction

2. Explain why families might overlook or choose to ignore a child's health symptoms.

3. Describe the differences between febrile, petit mal, and grand mal seizures.

4. Explain why the use of medication to treat children with AD/HD has stirred so much controversy.

5. What are some of the early warning signs of diabetes? What resources are available in your community to help teachers improve their understanding of the condition and learn how to administer injections?

B. As a Group:

1. Divide into small groups. Each group should develop a case study illustrating one of the chronic health conditions described in this chapter. The case study should include a description of the condition—its cause, symptoms, effects on the child and family, and classroom strategies for assuring the child's successful inclusion. Groups should take turns reading and discussing each other's case studies.

2. Develop an emergency response plan for a child who has seizures and discuss how it would be implemented in the classroom.

3. Discuss why more children appear to be developing allergies and asthma today.

4. Discuss why many chronic health problems are difficult to identify in young children, and what the teacher's role is in this process.

5. Describe what teachers can do to help protect children from obesity.

REFERENCES

American Academy of Pediatrics (AAP). (2005). Lead exposure in children: Prevention, detection, and management. *Pediatrics, 116*(4), 1036–1046.

American Diabetes Association (ADA). (2003). Care of children with diabetes in the school and day care setting. *Diabetes Care, 26,* S131–S135.

American Heart Association (AHA). (2006). Heart disease and stroke statistics—2006 update. *Circulation, 113,* e85–e151. Accessed on December 15, 2006, from http://circ.ahajournals.org/cgi/content/short/113/6/e85.

American Psychiatric Association (APA). (2000). *Diagnostic and statistical manual of mental disorders DSM-IVTR.* (4th ed.). Washington, DC: American Psychiatric Press.

Anderson, N. (2006). Hydroxyurea therapy: Improving the lives of patients with sickle cell disease. *Pediatric Nursing, 32*(6), 541-543.

Arbes, S., Sever, M., Mehta, J., Collette, N., Thomas, B., & Zeldin, D. (2005). Exposure to indoor allergens in day-care facilities: Results from 2 North Carolina counties. *Journal of Allergy & Clinical Immunology, 116*(1), 133–139.

Asthma & Allergy Foundation of America (AAFA). (2006). Allergy facts and figures. Accessed on December 13, 2006, from http://www.aafa.org/display.cfm?id=9&sub=30.

Barden, E. M., Kawchak, D. A., Ohene-Frempong, K., Stallings, V. A., & Zemel, B. S. (2002). Body composition in children with sickle cell disease. *American Journal of Clinical Nutrition, 76*(1), 218–225.

Baumann, R. J. (2001). Prevention and management of febrile seizures. *Paediatric Drugs, 3*(8), 585–592.

Beers, M. H., Porter, R., & Jones, T. (Eds.). (2006). *Merck Manual of Diagnosis & Therapy.* Hoboken, NJ: Wiley.

Beseler, L. (1999). Effects on behavior and cognition: Diet and artificial colors, flavors, and preservatives. *International Pediatrics, 14*(1), 42–43.

Bhatara, V., Loudenberg, R., & Ellis, R. (2006). Association of attention deficit hyperactivity disorder and gestational alcohol exposure: An exploratory study. *Journal of Attention Disorders, 9*(3), 515–522.

Biederman, J. (2005). Attention-deficit/hyperactivity disorder: A selective overview. *Biological Psychiatry, 57*(11), 1215–1220.

Bishop, M., & Boag, E. (2006). Teachers' knowledge about epilepsy and attitudes toward students with epilepsy: Results of a national survey. *Epilepsy & Behavior, 8*(2), 397–405.

Bollinger, M., Dahlquist, L., Mudd, K., Sonntag, C., Dillinger, L., & McKenna, K. (2006). The impact of food allergy on the daily activities of children and their families. *Annuals of Allergy, Asthma, & Immunology, 96*(3), 415–421.

Burden, M., Jacobson, S., & Jacobson, J. (2005). Relation of prenatal alcohol exposure to cognitive processing speed and efficiency in childhood. *Alcoholism, Clinical & Experimental Research, 29*(8), 1473–1483.

Burke, B. (2006). Lead poisoning treatment. *Journal of Pediatrics, 149*(3), 428–239.

Burke, W., Fesinmeyer, M., Reed, K., Hampson, L., & Carlsten, C. (2003). Family history as a predictor of asthma risk. *American Journal of Preventive Medicine, 24*(2), 160–169.

Canfield, R. L., Henderson, C. R., Cory-Slechta, D. A., Cox, C., Jusko, T. A., & Lanphear, B. P. (2003). Intellectual impairment in children with blood lead concentrations below 10 microg per deciliter. *New England Journal of Medicine, 348*(16), 1517–1526.

Centers for Disease Control & Prevention (CDC, a). (2007). America's children in brief: Key national indicators of well-being, 2007. Accessed on September 23, 2007, from http://childstats.gov/americaschildren.

Centers for Disease Control & Prevention (CDC, b). (2007). Lead poisoning prevention program. Accessed on September 23, 2007 from http://www.cdc.gov/nceh/lead.

Chen, A., & Rogan, W. (2005). Improving behavior or lead-exposed children: Micronutrient supplementation, chelation, or prevention. *Journal of Pediatrics, 147*(5), 570–571.

Chia, D., & Boston, M. (2006). Childhood obesity and the metabolic syndrome. *Advances in Pediatrics, 53*(1), 23–53.

Child Health Alert. (2006, April). Debate over warnings for ADHD stimulants. *Child Health Alert, 24,* 1.

Child Health Alert. (2005). Epinephrine for allergic reactions in school. *Child Health Alert, 23,* 3.

Child Health Alert. (1995). Synthetic food colorings: Do they affect children's behavior? *Child Health Alert, 13,* 1.

Chipps, B., & Spahn, J. (2006). What are the determinates of asthma control? *Journal of Asthma, 43*(8), 567–572.

Claudio, L., Stingone, J., & Godbold, J. (2006). Prevalence of childhood asthma in urban communities: The impact of ethnicity and income. *Annuals of Epidemiology, 16*(5), 332–340.

Committee of Substance Abuse and Committee on Children with Disabilities. (2000). Fetal Alcohol Syndrome and alcohol-related neurodevelopmental disorders. *Pediatrics, 106,* 358–361.

Cone-Wesson, B. (2005). Prenatal alcohol and cocaine exposure: Influences on cognition, speech, language, and hearing. *Journal of Communication Disorders, 38*(4), 279–302.

Cowan, L. D. (2002). The epidemiology of the epilepsies in children. *Mental Retardation and Developmental Disabilities Research Reviews, 8*(3), 171–181.

Cowdery, G., & Allen, K. E. (2005). *The exceptional child: Inclusion in early childhood education.* Clifton Park, NY: Thomson Delmar Learning.

Davis, A., Kreutzer, R., Lipsett, M., King, G., & Shaikh, N. (2006). Asthma prevalence in Hispanic and Asian American ethnic subgroups: Results from the California Healthy Kids Survey. *Pediatrics, 118*(2), e363–370.

Deutscher, B., & Fewell, R. (2005). Early predictors of Attention-Deficit/Hyperactivity Disorder and school difficulties in low-birthweight, premature children. *Topics in Early Childhood Special Education, 25*(2), 71–79.

Diaz-Sanchez, D., Rumold, R., & Gong, H. (2006). Challenge with environmental tobacco smoke exacerbates allergic airway disease in human beings. *Journal of Allergy and Clinical Immunology, 118*(2), 441–446.

Duckworth, S. V., & Norton, T. L. (2000). Fetal alcohol syndrome and fetal alcohol effects—Support for teachers and families. *Dimensions of Early Childhood, 28*(3), 19–23.

Dugbatey, K., Croskey, V., Evans, R., Narayan, G., & Osamudiamen, O. (2005). Lessons from a primary-prevention program for lead poisoning among inner-city children. *Journal of Environmental Health, 68*(5), 15–20.

DuPaul, G., & Weyandt, L. (2006). School-based interventions for children and adolescents with attention-deficit/hyperactivity disorder: Enhancing academic and behavioral outcomes. *Education & Treatment of Children, 29*(2), 341–358.

DuPaul, G., & White, G. (2006). ADHD: Behavioral, educational, and medication interventions. *The Education Digest, 71*(7), 57–60.

Erickson, L., & Thompson, T. (2005). *Journal of Specialists in Pediatric Nursing, 10*(4), 171–182.

Eustace, L. W., Kang, D. H., & Coombs, D. (2003). Fetal alcohol syndrome: a growing concern for health care professionals. *Journal of Obstetrical, Gynecological & Neonatal Nursing, 32*(2), 215–221.

Feingold, B. F. (1975). *Why your child is hyperactive.* New York: Random House.

Ford, E. (2005). The epidemiology of obesity and asthma. *Journal of Allergy & Clinical Immunology, 115*(5), 897–910.

Friedman, M., & Sharieff, G. (2006). Seizures in children. *Pediatric Clinics of North America, 53*(2), 257–277.

Gigout-Hues, L. (2006). ADHD: A crash-free course. *Teaching PreK–8, 36*(7), 147–160.

Gilliland, F. D., Berhane, K., Li, Y. F., Rappaport, E. B., & Peters, J. M. (2002). Effects of early onset asthma and in utero exposure to maternal smoking on childhood lung function. *American Journal of Respiratory Critical Care Medicine, 167*(6), 917–924.

Gorman, C. (2006, June 5). What alcohol does to a child. *Time, 167*(23), 76–80.

Greenspan, S. (2006). Working with the child who may have ADD. *Scholastic Early Childhood Today, 21*(1), 21–22.

Harrell, J., Jessup, A., & Greene, N. (2006). Changing our future: Obesity and the metabolic syndrome in children and adolescents. *Journal of Cardiovascular Nursing, 21*(4), 322–330.

Harwood, M., & Kleinfeld, J. S. (2002). Up front, in hope: The value of early intervention for children with fetal alcohol syndrome. *Young Children, 57*(4), 86–90.

Houston, D., Ong, Pl, Wu, J., & Winer, A. (2006). Proximity of licensed child care facilities to near-roadway vehicle pollution. *American Journal of Public Health, 96*(9), 1611–1617.

Hudziak, J., Derks, E., Althoff, R., Rettew, D., & Boomsma, D. (2005). The genetic environmental contributions to attention deficit hyperactivity disorder as measured by the Conner's Rating Scales-Revised. *American Journal of Psychiatry, 162*(9), 1614–1620.

Janssens, H., & Tiddens, H. (2006). Aerosol therapy; The special needs of young children. *Paediatric Respiratory Reviews, 7*(1Suppl), S83–S85.

Joesch, J., Kim, H., Kieckhefer, G., Greek, A., & Baydar, N. (2006). Does your child have asthma? Filled prescriptions and household report of child asthma. *Journal of Pediatric Health Care, 20*(6), 374–383.

Jones, S., & Scurlock, A. (2006). The impact of food allergy: The real "fear factor." *Annuals of Allergy, Asthma, & Immunology, 96*(3), 385–386.

Kalberg, W., Provost, B., Tollison, S., Tabachnick, B., Robinson, L., Eugene, M., Hoyme, H., Trujillo, P., Buckley, D., Aragon, A., & May, P. (2006). Comparison of motor delays in young children with fetal alcohol syndrome to those with prenatal alcohol exposure and with no prenatal alcohol exposure. *Alcoholism, Clinical & Experimental Research, 30*(12), 2037–2045.

Kim, Chun-Hyung, et al. (2006). A polymorphism in the norepinephrine transporter gene alters promoter activity and is associated with attention-deficit hyperactivity disorder. *Proceedings of the National Academy of Sciences, 103*(50), 19164–19169.

King, A., Herron, S., McKinstry, R., Bacak, S., Armstron, M., White, D., & DeBaun, M. (2006a). A multidisciplinary health care team's efforts to improve educational attainment in children with sickle-cell anemia and cerebral infarcts. *Journal of School Health, 76*(1), 33–37.

King, A., Tang, S., Ferguson, K., & DeBaun, M. (2006b). An education program to increase teacher knowledge about sickle cell disease. *Journal of School Health, 75*(1), 11–14.

Kirkpatrick, L. (2005). ADHD treatment and medication: What do you need to know as an educator? *The Delta Kappa Gamma Bulletin, 72*(1), 19–24.

Kawchak, D., Schall, J., Zemel, B., Oheme-Frempong, K., & Stallings, V. (2007). Adequacy of dietary intake declines with age in children with sickle cell disease. *Journal of the American Dietetic Association, 107*(5), 843–848.

Landrigan, P., Trasande, L., Thorpe, L., Swynn, C., Liov, P., D'Alton, M., Lipkind, H., Swanson, J., Wadhwa, P., Clark, E., Rauh, V., Perera, F., & Susser, E. (2006). The National Children's Study: A 21-year prospective study of 100,000 American children. *Pediatrics, 118*(5), 2173–2186.

Lanphear, B. P., Dietrich, K. N., & Berger, O. (2003). Prevention of lead toxicity in US children. *Ambulatory Pediatrics, 3*(1), 27–33.

McIntyre, C., Sheetz, A., Carroll, C., & Young, M. (2005). Administration of epinephrine for life-threatening allergic reactions in school settings. *Pediatrics, 116*(5), 1134–1140.

Miller, D. (2006). Students with Fetal Alcohol Syndrome: Updating our knowledge, improving their programs. *Teaching Exceptional Children, 38*(4), 12–18.

Miller, S. T., Wright, E., Abboud, M., Berman, B., Files, B., Scher, C. D., Styles, L., & Adams, R. J. (2001). Impact of chronic transfusion on incidence of pain and acute chest syndrome during the Stroke Prevention Trial (STOP) in sickle-cell anemia. *Journal of Pediatrics, 139*(6), 785–789.

Morbidity & Mortality Weekly Report (MMWR). (2006). Death of a child after ingestion of a metallic charm—Minnesota, 2006. *MMWR, 55*(12), 340–341.

MMWR. (2000). Elevated blood lead levels among internationally adopted children—United States, 1998. *MMWR, 49*(5), 97–100.

Mulroy, M., Bothell, J., & Gaudio, M. (2004). First steps in preventing childhood lead poisoning: The role of child care practitioners. *Young Children, 59*(2), 20–25.

National Center on Birth Defects and Developmental Disabilities. (2006). *Fetal alcohol spectrum disorders.* Accessed on December 15, 2006, from http://www.cdc.gov/ncbddd/fas/fasask.htm#how.

Neidell, M. (2004). Air pollution, health, and socio-economic status: The effect of outdoor air quality on childhood asthma. *Journal of Health Economics, 23*(6), 1209–1236.

Nicol, A. (2005). Understanding peanut allergy: An overview of medical and lifestyle concerns. *Advanced Nurse Practitioner, 13*(10), 63–68.

Olson, A., Seidler, A., Goodman, D., Gaelic, S., & Nordgren, R. (2004). School professional's perceptions about the impact of chronic illness in the classroom. *Archives of Pediatric & Adolescent Medicine, 158*(1), 53–58.

Orr, J., Miller, R., & Polson, D. (2005). Toward a standard of care for child ADHD: Implications for marriage and family therapists. *Journal of Marital & Family Therapy, 31*(3), 191–205.

Paasche, C., Gorrill, L., & Strom, B. (2004). *Children with special needs in early childhood settings.* Clifton Park, NY: Thomson Delmar Learning.

Piomelli, S. (2002). Childhood lead poisoning. *Pediatric Clinics of North America, 49*(6), 1285–1304.

The Project CHOICES Intervention Research Group. (2003). Reducing the risk of alcohol-exposed pregnancies: A study of a motivational intervention in community settings. *Pediatrics. 111*(5), 1131–1135.

Ryan, D., Bonnett, D., & Gass, C. (2006). Sobering thoughts: Town hall meetings on fetal alcohol spectrum disorders. *American Journal of Public Health, 96*(12), e2098–3101.

Sarna, L., & Bialous, S. (2005). Children's exposure to secondhand tobacco smoke. *Public Health Nursing, 22*(6), 459–464.

Seidman, L., Valera, E., & Makris, N. (2005). Structural brain imaging of attention-deficit/hyperactivity disorder. *Biological Psychiatry, 57*(11), 1263–1272.

Sherman, M. (2004). Primary sources of lead: What can you do to minimize exposure? *Young Children, 59*(2), 26–27.

Shipley, T. E. (2002). Child care centers and children with special needs: Rights under the Americans with Disabilities Act and Section 504 of the Rehabilitation Act. *Journal of Law & Education, 31*(3), 327–349.

Simon, J. A., & Hudes, E. S. (1999). Relationship of ascorbic acid to blood levels. *JAMA, 272*, 277–283.

Smith, L., Oyeku, S., Homer, C., & Zuckerman, B. (2006). Sickle cell disease: A question of equity and quality. *Pediatrics, 117*(5), 1763–1770.

Stingone, J., & Claudio, L. (2006). Asthma and enrollment in special education among urban schoolchildren. *American Journal of Public Health, 96*(9), e1593–1598.

Szlemko, W., Wood, J., & Thurman, P. (2006). Native Americans and alcohol: Past, present, and future. *Journal of General Psychiatry, 133*(4), 435–451.

Taras, H., & Potts-Datema, W. (2005). Chronic health conditions and student performance at school. *Journal of School Health, 75*(7), 255–266.

Thompson, R. J., Gustafson, K. E., Bonner, M. J., & Ware, R. E. (2002). Neurocognitive development of young children with sickle cell disease through three years of age. *Journal of Pediatric Psychology, 27*(3), 235–244.

Trahms, C. M., & Pipes, P. L. (2000). *Nutrition in infancy and childhood.* Columbus, OH: McGraw-Hill.

Wang, J., Visness, C., & Sampson, H. (2005). Food allergen sensitization in inner-city children with asthma. *Journal of Allergy & Clinical Immunology, 115*(5), 1076–1080.

Wang, L., Zhong, Y., & Wheeler, L. (2006). Asthma medication use in school-aged children. *Journal of Asthma, 43*(7), 495–499.

Wong, D. (2001). *Wong's Essentials of Pediatric Nursing.* (6th ed.). St. Louis: Mosby.

Wright, R. O., Tsaih, S. W., Schwartz, J., Wright, R. J., & Hu, H. (2003, January). Association between iron deficiency and blood lead level in a longitudinal analysis of children followed in an urban primary care clinic. *Journal of Pediatrics, 142*(1), 9–14.

Zutavern, A., von Mutius, E., Harris, J., Mill, P., Moffatt, S., White, C., & Cullinan, P. (2004). The introduction of solids in relation to asthma and eczema. *Archives of Disease in Children, 89*(4), 303–308.

Zuvekas, S., Vitiello, B., & Norquist, G. (2006). Recent trends in stimulant medication use among U. S. children. *American Journal of Psychiatry, 163*(4), 579–585.

HELPFUL WEB RESOURCES

American Diabetes Association	http://www.diabetes.org
American Lung Association	http://www.lungusa.org
Canadian Pediatric Society	http://www.cps.ca
Centers for Disease Control and Prevention	http://www.cdc.gov
Children with Diabetes	http://www.kwd.org
Indian Health Service	http://www.ihs.gov
KidsHealth–Nemours Center for Children's Health Media	http://www.kidshealth.org
National Diabetes Information Clearinghouse	http://www2.niddk.nih.gov

For additional health, safety, and nutrition resources, go to http://www.EarlyChildEd.delmar.cengage.com

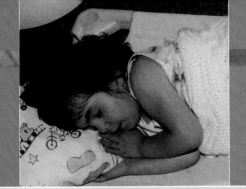

CHAPTER 6

The Infectious Process and Environmental Control

✳ OBJECTIVES

After studying this chapter, you should be able to:

- Define communicable illness.
- List the three factors that are required for an infection to be communicable.
- Name four control measures that teachers can use to reduce communicable illnesses.
- Identify the signs and symptoms of four childhood communicable diseases.
- Describe the major reasons why some children are not fully immunized.
- Discuss the family's role in controlling the spread of communicable illness.

✳ TERMS TO KNOW

antibodies	airborne transmission	convalescent
communicable	fecal-oral transmission	lymph glands
pathogen	incubation	universal infection
susceptible host	contagious	control precautions
respiratory tract	prodromal	
immunized	acute	

Young children, especially those under three years of age, are highly susceptible to communicable illness (Slack-Smith, Read, & Stanley, 2002). Frequent upper respiratory infections are common, especially during a child's first experiences in group settings (Bradley, 2003). Several factors may contribute to this increased risk. First, children with limited exposure to large numbers of children have had fewer opportunities to encounter illness and, thus, to build up **antibodies** for protection. This lowered immunity makes young children more vulnerable to germs that cause communicable and acute illnesses. Children with special needs are at an even greater risk. Physical disabilities and chronic conditions, such as diabetes, sickle cell, and asthma further reduce children's resistance and make them more susceptibile to infections.

Second, immature development of body structures contributes to a higher rate of illness. For example, shorter distances between an infant's or toddler's ears, nose, and throat encourage frequent respiratory infections.

---

antibodies – *special substances produced by the body that help protect against disease.*

FIGURE 6–1

Communicable illnesses can be spread when children mouth toys and other objects.

Third, group settings, such as home- and center-based early childhood programs, and elementary school classrooms are ideal environments for the rapid spread of illness (Brady, 2005). However, children are also exposed to communicable illnesses in many other places, including grocery stores, shopping centers, churches, libraries, and restaurants. Many of children's habits, such as sucking on fingers, mouthing toys, carelessness with bodily secretions (runny noses, drool, urine, stool), and lots of physical contact also encourage the rapid spread of communicable illness (Figure 6–1). For this reason, every attempt must be made to establish and implement policies, practices, and learning experiences that will help to protect young children from unnecessary exposure.

COMMUNICABLE ILLNESS

A **communicable** illness is an illness that can be transmitted or spread from one person or animal to another. Three factors, all of which must be present at approximately the same time, are required for this process to occur (Figure 6–2).

- a pathogen
- a susceptible host
- a method of transmission

First, a **pathogen** or disease-causing agent, such as a bacteria, virus, or parasite, must be present and available for transmission. These invisible germs are specific for each illness and are most commonly located in discharges from the respiratory (nose, throat, lungs) and intestinal tract of infected persons. They can also be found in the blood, urine, and discharges from the eyes and skin. Most pathogens require a living host for their survival. One exception, however, is the organism that causes tetanus; it can survive in soil and dust for several years.

Second, there must be a **susceptible host** or person who can become infected with the pathogen. The types of communicable illnesses experienced most often by young children generally enter their new host through either a break in the skin, the **respiratory tract**, or digestive tract. The route of entry depends on the specific illness or disease involved.

Not every child who is exposed to a particular virus or bacteria will become infected. Conditions must be favorable to allow an infectious organism to successfully avoid the body's defense systems, multiply, and establish itself. Children who are well rested, adequately nourished, **immunized**, and in a good state of health are generally less susceptible to communicable illnesses. Also, a previous case of the same illness may provide protection against additional infection. For example, an adult who had chickenpox as a child will have permanent immunity to the

---

communicable – *a condition that can be spread or transmitted from one individual to another.*
pathogen – *a microorganism capable of producing illness or infection.*
susceptible host – *an individual who is capable of being infected by a pathogen.*
respiratory tract – *pertains to, and includes, the nose, throat, trachea, and lungs.*
immunized – *a state of becoming resistant to a specific disease through the introduction of living or dead microorganisms into the body, which then stimulates the production of antibodies.*

FIGURE 6–2

Communicable illness model.

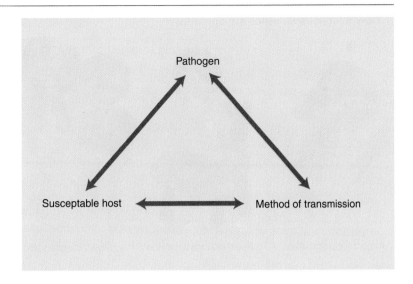

disease. However, the length of this protection varies with the illness and can range from several days to a lifetime. Children who experience a very mild or subclinical case of an illness or who are carriers of an infection are often resistant to the illness without realizing that they have actually experienced it.

Third, a method for transmitting the infectious agent from the original source to a new host is necessary to complete the communicable process (Figure 6–2). One of the most common modes of transmitting infectious agents in early education settings involves **airborne transmission**. Disease-causing pathogens are carried on tiny droplets of moisture that are expelled during coughs, sneezes, or while talking (Figure 6–3). Influenza, colds, meningitis, tuberculosis, and chickenpox are examples of infectious illnesses spread in this manner.

Fecal-oral transmission is the second most common route by which infectious illnesses are spread in group settings, particularly when there are infants and toddlers in diapers. Teachers who fail to wash their hands properly after changing diapers or helping children with toileting needs are often responsible for spreading disease-causing germs, especially if they also handle food. For this reason, it is advisable to assign diaper changing and food preparation responsibilities to different teachers. It is also critical to wash children's hands after diaper changes or after they have used the bathroom because their hands often end up in their mouths. Children must be taught appropriate handwashing procedures and monitored closely to be sure they are washing correctly. Pinworms, hepatitis A, salmonella, and giardiasis are examples of illnesses transmitted by fecal-oral contamination.

A third common method of transmission involves direct contact with body fluids, such as blood or mucus, or an area of infection on another individual. The infectious organisms are transferred directly from the original source of infection to a new host. Ringworm, athlete's foot, impetigo, Hepatitis B, and conjunctivitis (pinkeye) are a few of the conditions spread in this manner.

Communicable illnesses can also be transmitted through indirect contact. This method involves the transfer of infectious organisms from an infected individual to an intermediate object, such as water, milk, dust, food, toys, towels, eating utensils, animals, or insects, and finally

---

airborne transmission – *when germs are expelled into the air through coughs/sneezes, and transmitted to another individual via tiny moisture drops.*

fecal-oral transmission – *when germs are transferred to the mouth via hands contaminated with fecal material.*

FIGURE 6–3

How infectious illnesses are spread.

| Airborne transmission | Fecal-oral transmission | Direct transmission | Indirect transmission |

to the new susceptible host. It is also possible to infect oneself with certain viruses, such as those causing colds and influenza, by touching the moist linings of the eyes and nose with contaminated hands.

Eliminating any one of these factors (pathogen, host, or method of transmission) will prevent the spread of communicable illness. This is an important concept for families and teachers to remember when trying to control outbreaks of communicable illness, especially in group settings. It can also be beneficial for reducing the number of illnesses that teachers might carry home to their families.

STAGES OF ILLNESS

Communicable illnesses generally develop in predictable stages:

- incubation
- prodromal
- acute
- convalescence

Since many of these stages overlap, it may be difficult to identify when each begins and ends.

The **incubation** stage includes the time between exposure to a pathogen and the appearance of the first signs or symptoms of illness. During this period, the infectious organisms enter the body and multiply rapidly in an attempt to establish themselves and overpower the body's defense systems. The length of the incubation stage is described in terms of hours or days and varies for each communicable disease. For example, the incubation period for chickenpox ranges from two to three weeks following exposure, while for the common cold it is thought to be only 12 to 72 hours. Many infectious illnesses are already communicable near the end of this stage. The fact that children are often **contagious** before any symptoms are apparent makes the control of infectious illness in the classroom more difficult, despite teachers' careful observations.

The **prodromal** stage begins when an infant or young child experiences the first nonspecific signs of infection and ends with the appearance of symptoms characteristic of a particular

---

incubation – *the interval of time between exposure to infection and the appearance of the first signs or symptoms of illness.*
contagious – *capable of being transmitted or passed from one person to another.*
prodromal – *the appearance of the first nonspecific signs of infection; this stage ends when the symptoms characteristic of a particular communicable illness begin to appear.*

communicable illness (Figure 6–4). This stage may last from several hours to several days. However, not all communicable diseases have a prodromal stage. Early symptoms commonly associated with the prodromal stage may include headache, unexplained fatigue, low-grade fever, a slight sore throat, and a general feeling of restlessness or irritability. Many of these complaints are so vague that they often go unnoticed. However, because children are highly contagious during this stage, teachers and parents must recognize that these subtle changes could signal an impending illness.

During the **acute** stage an infant or child is definitely sick. This stage is marked by the onset of symptoms that are typical of the specific communicable illness. Some of these symptoms

FIGURE 6–4

Fatigue and irritability may be the first indications of a communicable illness.

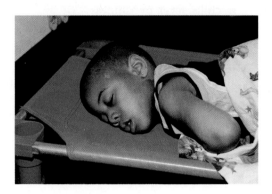

such as fever, sore throat, cough, runny nose, rash, or enlarged lymph glands are common to many infectious diseases. However, there are also characteristic patterns and variations of these symptoms that can be useful for identifying a specific communicable illness. An infant or child continues to be highly contagious throughout this stage.

The **convalescent** or recovery stage generally follows automatically unless complications develop. During this stage, symptoms gradually disappear, children begin to feel better, and they are no longer contagious.

CONTROL MEASURES

Teachers have an obligation and responsibility to help protect young children from communicable illnesses. Although many communicable illnesses are simply inconvenient, others can have serious complications. Because classrooms are ideal settings for the rapid spread of many infectious conditions, control measures must be diligently implemented to limit their spread.

Observations

Teachers' daily health observations can be effective for identifying children in the early stages of a communicable illness. By removing sick children from group settings, a direct source of infection can be eliminated. However, because many illnesses are communicable before actual symptoms appear, not all spread can be avoided. Early recognition of sick children requires that adults develop a sensitivity to changes in children's normal appearance and behavior patterns (Aronson, 2002). This process is facilitated by the fact that young children generally look and behave differently when they are not feeling well. Their actions, facial expressions, skin color, sleep habits, appetite, and comments provide valuable warnings of impending illness. Other signs may include:

- unusually pale or flushed skin
- red or sore throat
- enlarged **lymph glands**

acute – *the stage of an illness or disease during which an individual is definitely sick and exhibits symptoms characteristic of the particular illness or disease involved.*
convalescent – *the stage of recovery from an illness or disease.*
lymph glands – *specialized groupings of tissue that produce and store white blood cells for protection against infection and illness.*

- nausea, vomiting, or diarrhea
- rash, spots, or open lesions
- watery or red eyes
- headache or dizziness
- chills, fever, or achiness
- fatigue or loss of appetite

However, these same signs and symptoms may not always warrant concern in all children. For example, a teacher who knows that Tony's allergies often cause a red throat and cough in the fall, or that Shadra's recent irritability is probably related to her mother's hospitalization, would not be alarmed by these observations. Teachers must be able to distinguish between children with potentially infectious illnesses and those with health problems that are explainable and not necessarily contagious. It is also important to be alert to the signs of certain illnesses during seasons when they are more common or whenever there is known outbreak in the community.

Policies

Written policies offer another important method for controlling infectious illnesses (Copeland & Shope, 2005; Friedman, et al., 2004; Richardson, et al., 2001). Policies should be consistent with state regulations, and in place before a program begins to enroll children. Frequent review of policies with staff members assures their familiarity with the information, and that enforcement will be more consistent.

General health and exclusion policies should also be included in parent handbooks and given to families when children are accepted into a program. This enables families to know in advance what to expect if their child becomes ill and also helps to strengthen collaborative partnerships. Exclusion and inclusion policies establish clear guidelines for families and teachers to follow when deciding if children should be kept home because of illness, and when they are well enough to return (Figure 6–5).

Opinions differ on how restrictive exclusion policies should be (Lucarelli, 2002). Some experts believe that children with mild illnesses can remain in group care, while others feel that children who exhibit symptoms should not be in attendance. Because many early signs of communicable illnesses are nonspecific, teachers and families may have difficulty distinguishing between conditions that warrant exclusion and medical attention and those that do not. Consequently, programs may decide to set exclusion policies that are fairly restrictive unless they are prepared to care for sick children.

It is also important for programs to adopt policies for notifying families when children are exposed to communicable illnesses. This measure enables parents to watch for early symptoms and to keep sick children home (Figure 6–6). Immunization requirements should also be addressed in program policies, as well as actions the program will take if children are not in compliance. Local public health authorities can offer much useful information and assistance to programs when they are formulating new policies or are confronted with a communicable health problem about which they are unsure.

Guidelines for Teacher Illness   Teachers are also exposed to many infectious illnesses through their daily contact with young children. They often experience an increased incidence of

REFLECTIVE THOUGHTS

Outbreaks of communicable illnesses such as colds, flu, and head lice are common in settings where there are groups of young children. Explain why this occurs. Why is it important for teachers to understand the infectious process? What resources are available to teachers and families for improving their understanding of various childhood illnesses? Are you comfortable caring for a child who is ill?

FIGURE 6–5

Sample exclusion policy.

EXCLUSION POLICY

Control of communicable illness among the children is a prime concern. Policies and guidelines related to outbreaks of communicable illness in this center have been developed with the help of the health department and local pediatricians. In order to protect the entire group of children, as well as your own child, we ask that families assist us by keeping sick children at home if they have experienced any of the following symptoms *within the past 24 hours:*

- a fever over 100°F (37.8°C) orally or 99°F (37.2°C) axillary (under the arm)
- signs of a newly developing cold or uncontrollable coughing
- diarrhea, vomiting, or an upset stomach
- unusual or unexplained loss of appetite, fatigue, irritability, or headache
- any discharge or drainage from eyes, nose, ears, or open sores

Children who become ill with any of these symptoms will be returned home. We appreciate your cooperation with this policy. If you have any questions about whether or not your child is well enough to attend school or group care that day, please call the center *before* bringing your child.

illness—especially during the initial months of employment—that is similar to what young children do when they enroll in a new program or school. Over time, teachers gradually build up their resistance to many of these illnesses. Teachers should complete a pre-employment health assessment, have a tuberculin test, and update their immunizations to help minimize their risk of illness. However, practicing good handwashing always offers the most effective protection. Teachers who are pregnant may want to temporarily reconsider working around young children since some communicable illnesses, such as cytomegalovirus (CMV) and German measles can affect the fetus, especially during the early months.

FIGURE 6–6

Sample letter notifying families of their child's exposure.

Date_____

Dear Parent:

There is a possibility that your child has been exposed to chickenpox. If your child has not had chickenpox, observe carefully from _____ to _____ (more likely the first part of this period), for signs of a slight cold, runny nose, loss of appetite, fever, listlessness, and/or irritability. Within a day or two, watch for a spot (or spots) resembling mosquito bites on which a small blister soon forms. Chickenpox is contagious 24–48 hours before the rash appears. Children who develop chickenpox may return when all pox are covered by a dry scab (about 5 or 6 days).

If you have any questions, please call the Center before bringing your child. We appreciate your cooperation in helping us keep incidences of illness to a minimum.

When teachers are ill and trying to decide whether or not they should go to work, they must follow the same exclusion guidelines that apply to sick children. Adults who do not feel well will not be able to meet the rigorous demands necessary for working with young children. As a result, they also face an increased risk of sustaining personal injury. Programs should maintain a list of available substitute teachers so that staff members do not feel pressured to work when they are ill.

Administration of Medication The administration of medicine to young children is a responsibility that should always be taken seriously (Table 6–1). Policies and procedures for the administration of prescription and nonprescription medications, including ointments and creams, eye, ear, and nose drops, cough syrups, baby aspirin, inhalers, and nebulizer breathing treatments should be developed carefully in accordance with state licensing regulations to safeguard children, as well as teaching staff. These policies and procedures should be in writing, familiar to all staff members, filed in an accessible location, and distributed to every family (Figure 6–7).

TABLE 6–1 Guidelines for Administering Medications to Children

1. Be honest when giving children medication! Do not use force or attempt to trick children into believing that medicines are candy. Instead, use the opportunity to help children understand the relationship between taking a medication and recovering from an illness or infection. Also, acknowledge the fact that the taste of medicine may be disagreeable or a treatment may be somewhat unpleasant; offer a small sip of juice or cracker to eliminate an unpleasant taste or read a favorite story as a reward for their cooperation.
2. Designate one individual to accept medication from families and administer it to children; this could be the director or the head teacher. This step will help minimize the opportunity for errors, such as omitting a dose or giving a dose twice.
3. When medication is accepted from a family, it should be in the original container, labeled with the child's name, with the name of the drug, and include directions for the exact amount and frequency the medication is to be given.

   Caution: **NEVER give medicine from a container that has been prescribed for another individual.**

4. Store all medicines in a locked cabinet. If it is necessary to refrigerate a medication, place it in a locked box and store it on a top shelf in the refrigerator.
5. Be sure to wash your hands before and after administering medication.
6. Concentrate on what you are doing and do not talk with anyone until you are finished.
   a. Read the label on the bottle or container three times:
      - when removing it from the locked cabinet
      - before pouring it from the container
      - after pouring it from the container
   b. Administer medication on time, and give *only* the amount prescribed.
   c. Be sure you have the correct child! If the child is old enough to talk, ask "What is your name?" and let the child state his/her name.
7. Record and maintain a permanent record of each dose of medicine that is administered (Figure 6–7). Include the:
   - date and time the medicine was given
   - name of the teacher administering the medication
   - dose of medication given
   - any unusual physical changes or behaviors observed after the medicine was administered
8. Inform the child's family of the dosage(s) and time medication was given, as well as any unusual reactions that may have occurred.
9. NOTE: Adults should never take any medication in front of children.

FIGURE 6–7

Sample medication recording form.

ADMINISTRATION OF MEDICATION FORM

Child's name _____

Prescription number _____

Date of prescription _____

Doctor prescribing medicine _____

Medication being given for _____

Time medication is to be given by staff _____

Time medication last given by parent _____

Amount to be given at each time (dosage) _____

I, _____ give my permission for the staff to administer the above prescription medication (according to the above guidelines) to _____ _____ . I understand that the staff cannot be held
(child's name)
responsible for allergic reactions or other complications resulting from administration of the above medication given according to the directions.

Signed _____
(parent or guardian)

Date _____

Staff Record

Name of staff accepting medication and form _____

Is medication in its original container? _____

Is original label intact? _____

Is there written permission from the doctor attached (or the original prescription)? _____

Signature of accepting staff _____

Administration Record

DATE	TIME	AMOUNT GIVEN	STAFF ADMINISTERING	INITIALS

When children are enrolled in part-day programs, families may be able to alter medication schedules and administer prescribed medications at times when children are home. However, this option is not feasible for many children who are enrolled in full-day programs. In these instance, families will need to make prior arrangements to have the child's teachers administer prescribed medication.

Medication should never be administered by a teacher without the written consent of the child's family and written direction of a licensed physician. The label on a prescription drug is considered an acceptable directive from the physician. In the case of nonprescription medicines, families should obtain written instructions from the physician stating the child's name, the medication to be given, the dose, frequency it is to be administered, and any special precautions that may be necessary. There are risks associated with giving children over-the-counter medications that have not been authorized by a physician. Thus, to protect themselves from potential liability, teachers should not assume these risks. It is the physician's professional and legal responsibility to determine the type and exact dosage of a medication that is appropriate for an individual child.

Immunization

Immunization offers permanent protection against all preventable childhood diseases, including diphtheria, tetanus, whooping cough, polio, measles, mumps, rubella, Haemophilus influenza, and chickenpox (Figure 6–8) (Luman, et al., 2002). Yet, despite several large-scale national, state, and local campaigns, many children still are not fully immunized. At present, it is estimated that only 81 percent of young children have received all of the recommended age appropriate immunizations (CDC, 2007; Niederhauser, Walters & Ganeko, 2007). Although childhood immunization rates have improved, efforts are still needed to achieve the *Healthy People 2010* goal of 90 percent by the year 2010 (U.S. Department of Health & Human Services (DHHS), 2000).

Why are some families so seemingly complacent about having their children immunized? Perhaps they do not realize that some communicable illnesses are still life-threatening and continue to pose a threat to children who are not protected. Recent outbreaks of mumps and whooping cough, for example, have clearly demonstrated this potential (*Child Health Alert*, 2006). Some families may believe that antibiotics are available to cure any infectious illness so they are willing to take a chance. Others have expressed concern about vaccine safety and the number of immunizations that children must receive (Shui, Weintraub, & Gust, 2006; Allred, et al., 2005; Kennedy & Gust, 2005). New combined vaccines are currently being developed to reduce this number. Manufacturers have also eliminated questionable substances, such as thiomersal, from vaccines to improve their safety (Kennedy, Brown, & Gust, 2005).

Most states require children's immunizations to be current when they enter school or enroll in early childhood programs. In states where immunization laws are lax, teachers must insist that every child be fully immunized unless families are opposed on religious or medical grounds (Omer, et al., 2006). Teachers should also be diligent in keeping their own immunizations up-to-date.

Vaccines work by triggering the body's immune system to produce protective substances, called antibodies. This process is similar to what occurs when a person becomes ill with certain

FIGURE 6–8

Immunizations protect children from many preventable childhood diseases.

infectious diseases. Babies are born with a limited supply of antibodies, acquired from their mothers, which will protect them against some communicable illnesses. However, this maternal protection is only temporary and, therefore, the immunization process must be started early in a baby's life. The immunization schedule jointly recommended by the Centers for Disease Control and Protection, the American Academy of Pediatrics (AAP), and the American Academy of Family Physicians (AAFP) appears in Figure 6–9. Similar recommendations are available for Canadians and children in other countries [National Advisory Committee on Immunization (NACI), 2005].

Infants and young children, especially those in group care, are encouraged to be immunized against Haemophilus influenza Type b (Hib), an upper respiratory infection and common cause of meningitis (see Figure 6–9). Vaccines for chickenpox (varicella) and hepatitis B, a viral infection spread through contact with body secretions and feces, are also recommended for children attending early childhood programs (Zimmerman, 2003). Children who have special health needs often have a lowered resistance to communicable illnesses and are thus encouraged to be immunized against these diseases even though the immunizations may not be required. Immunizations can be obtained from most health care providers, neighborhood health clinics, or public health departments where the cost is often reduced or free.

Programs that employ more than one teacher (including aides and substitutes) are required to offer free hepatitis B immunizations to employees during the first 10 days of employment or within 24 hours following exposure to blood or body fluids containing blood (Child Care Law Center, 1994).

Environmental Control

A variety of practices and environmental changes can be used to effectively reduce the spread of most communicable illnesses (Brady, 2005; AAP, 2002; Rubino, 2002). Teachers should be familiar with these methods and understand how to implement them in their classrooms. Procedures should be written up, posted where they are visible, and reviewed periodically with all employees. Teachers must also take precautions, such as careful handwashing, to protect themselves from unnecessary exposure.

Universal Infection Control Precautions   The U.S. Department of Labor's Occupational Safety and Health Administration (OSHA) is responsible for protecting workers' safety by assuring that workplace environments and practices meet federal guidelines. Regulations passed by OSHA (1992) and amended in 2001 require child care programs (except those without paid employees) to develop and practice **universal infection control precautions** for handling contaminated body fluids (Table 6–2).

In addition, programs must also have a written plan for handling potentially infectious material, provide annual training for employees and maintain records of any exposure (OSHA, 2001; Child Care Law Center, 1994).

The purpose of universal precautions is to protect teachers from accidental exposure to blood borne pathogens, including hepatitis B and HIV/AIDS. All body fluids are considered potentially infectious and, therefore, should be treated in the same manner. Any material that has been contaminated with blood or other body fluids that might contain blood, such as urine, feces, saliva, and vomitus, must be handled with caution, regardless of whether or not a child is known to be ill.

Disposable latex gloves should always be accessible to teachers. They must always be worn whenever handling soiled objects or caring for injuries. Gloves should be removed by pulling them off inside out and carefully discarding them after use with an individual child. Thorough handwashing must follow to prevent any further spread of infection; wearing gloves does not eliminate the need for washing one's hands. Children's hands and skin should also be washed

---

universal infection control precautions – *special measures taken when handling bodily fluids, including careful hand washing, wearing latex gloves, disinfecting surfaces, and proper disposal of contaminated objects.*

FIGURE 6-9

Recommended Childhood and Adolescent Immunization Schedule—United States 2007.

FIGURE. Recommended childhood and adolescent immunization schedule, by vaccine and age — United States, 2007

Vaccine ▼ / Age ►	Birth	1 month	2 months	4 months	6 months	12 months	15 months	18 months	24 months	4–6 years	11–12 years	13–14 years	15 years	16–18 years
Hepatitis B[1]	HepB	HepB		HepB[1]		HepB					HepB Series			
Diphtheria, Tetanus, Pertussis[2]			DTaP	DTaP	DTaP		DTaP			DTaP	Tdap	Tdap		
Haemophilus influenzae type b[3]			Hib	Hib	Hib[3]	Hib								
Inactivated Poliovirus			IPV	IPV		IPV				IPV				
Measles, Mumps, Rubella[4]						MMR				MMR		MMR		
Varicella[5]						Varicella					Varicella			
Meningococcal[6]							Vaccines within broken line are for selected populations			MPSV4	MCV4	MCV4	MCV4	MCV4
Pneumococcal[7]			PCV	PCV	PCV	PCV				PCV	PPV			
Influenza[8]					Influenza (yearly)					Influenza (yearly)				
Hepatitis A[9]					HepA series					HepA series				

Legend: ▢ Range of recommended ages   ▢ Catch-up immunization   ▢ Assessment at age 11–12 years

This schedule indicates the recommended ages for routine administration of currently licensed childhood vaccines, as of December 1, 2005, for children through age 18 years. Any dose not administered at the recommended age should be administered at any subsequent visit, when indicated and feasible. ▢ Indicates age groups that warrant special effort to administer those vaccines not previously administered. Additional vaccines might be licensed and recommended during the year. Licensed combination vaccines may be used whenever any components of the combination are indicated and other components of the vaccine are not contraindicated and if approved by the Food and Drug Administration for that dose of the series. Providers should consult respective Advisory Committee on Immunization Practices (ACIP) statements for detailed recommendations. Clinically significant adverse events that follow vaccination should be reported through the Vaccine Adverse Event Reporting System (VAERS). Guidance about how to obtain and complete a VAERS form is available at http://www.vaers.hhs.gov or by telephone, 800-822-7967.

1. **Hepatitis B vaccine (HepB).** *AT BIRTH:* All newborns should receive monovalent HepB soon after birth and before hospital discharge. Infants born to mothers who are hepatitis B surface antigen (HBsAg)-positive should receive HepB and 0.5 mL of hepatitis B immune globulin (HBIG) within 12 hours of birth. Infants born to mothers whose HBsAg status is unknown should receive HepB within 12 hours of birth. The mother should have blood drawn as soon as possible to determine her HBsAg status; if HBsAg-positive, the infant should receive HBIG as soon as possible (no later than age 1 week). For infants born to HBsAg-negative mothers, the birth dose can be delayed in rare circumstances but only if a physician's order to withhold the vaccine and a copy of the mother's original HBsAg-negative laboratory report are documented in the infant's medical record. *FOLLOWING THE BIRTH DOSE:* The HepB series should be completed with either monovalent HepB or a combination vaccine containing HepB. The second dose should be administered at age 1–2 months. The final dose should be administered at age ≥24 weeks. Administering four doses of HepB is permissible (e.g., when combination vaccines are administered after the birth dose); however, if monovalent HepB is used, a dose at age 4 months is not needed. Infants born to HBsAg-positive mothers should be tested for HBsAg and antibody to HBsAg after completion of the HepB series at age 9–18 months (generally at the next well-child visit after completion of the vaccine series).

2. **Diphtheria and tetanus toxoids and acellular pertussis vaccine (DTaP).** The fourth dose of DTaP may be administered as early as age 12 months, provided 6 months have elapsed since the third dose and the child is unlikely to return at age 15–18 months. The final dose in the series should be administered at age ≥4 years. Tetanus toxoid, reduced diphtheria toxoid, and acellular pertussis vaccine (Tdap adolescent preparation) is recommended at age 11–12 years for those who have completed the recommended childhood DTP/DTaP vaccination series and have not received a tetanus and diphtheria toxoids (Td) booster dose. Adolescents aged 13–18 years who missed the age 11–12-year Td/Tdap booster dose should also receive a single dose of Tdap if they have completed the recommended childhood DTP/DTaP vaccination series. Subsequent Td boosters are recommended every 10 years.

3. **Haemophilus influenzae type b conjugate vaccine (Hib).** Three Hib conjugate vaccines are licensed for infant use. If PRP-OMP (PedvaxHIB® or ComVax® [Merck]) is administered at ages 2 and 4 months, a dose at age 6 months is not required. DTaP/Hib combination products should not be used for primary immunization in infants at ages 2, 4, or 6 months but may be used as boosters after any Hib vaccine. The final dose in the series should be administered at age ≥12 months.

4. **Measles, mumps, and rubella vaccine (MMR).** The second dose of MMR is recommended routinely at age 4–6 years but may be administered during any visit, provided at least 4 weeks have elapsed since the first dose and both doses are administered at or after age 12 months. Children who have not previously received the second dose should complete the schedule by age 11–12 years.

5. **Varicella vaccine.** Varicella vaccine is recommended at any visit at or after age 12 months for susceptible children (i.e., those who lack a reliable history of varicella). Susceptible persons aged ≥13 years should receive 2 doses administered at least 4 weeks apart.

6. **Meningococcal vaccine (MCV4).** Meningococcal conjugate vaccine (MCV4) should be administered to all children at age 11–12 years as well as to unvaccinated adolescents at high school entry (age 15 years). Other adolescents who wish to decrease their risk for meningococcal disease may also be vaccinated. All college freshmen living in dormitories should also be vaccinated, preferably with MCV4, although meningococcal polysaccharide vaccine (MPSV4) is an acceptable alternative. Vaccination against invasive meningococcal disease is recommended for children and adolescents aged ≥2 years with terminal complement deficiencies or anatomic or functional asplenia and for certain other high risk groups (see *MMWR* 2005;54[No. RR-7]); use MPSV4 for children aged 2–10 years and MCV4 for older children, although MPSV4 is an acceptable alternative.

7. **Pneumococcal vaccine.** The heptavalent pneumococcal conjugate vaccine (PCV) is recommended for all children aged 2–23 months and for certain children aged 24–59 months. The final dose in the series should be administered at age ≥12 months. Pneumococcal polysaccharide vaccine (PPV) is recommended in addition to PCV for certain high-risk groups. See *MMWR* 2000;49(No. RR-9).

8. **Influenza vaccine.** Influenza vaccine is recommended annually for children aged ≥6 months with certain risk factors (including, but not limited to, asthma, cardiac disease, sickle cell disease, human immunodeficiency virus infection, diabetes, and conditions that can compromise respiratory function or handling of respiratory secretions or that can increase the risk for aspiration), health-care workers, and other persons (including household members) in close contact with persons in groups at high risk (see *MMWR* 2005;54[No. RR-8]). In addition, healthy children aged 6–23 months and close contacts of healthy children aged 0–5 months are recommended to receive influenza vaccine because children in this age group are at substantially increased risk for influenza-related hospitalizations. For healthy, nonpregnant persons aged 5–49 years, the intranasally administered, live, attenuated influenza vaccine (LAIV) is an acceptable alternative to the intramuscular trivalent inactivated influenza vaccine (TIV). See *MMWR* 2005;54(No. RR-8). Children receiving TIV should be administered an age-appropriate dosage (0.25 mL for children aged 6–35 months or 0.5 mL for children aged ≥3 years). Children aged ≤8 years who are receiving influenza vaccine for the first time should receive 2 doses (separated by at least 4 weeks for TIV and at least 6 weeks for LAIV).

9. **Hepatitis A vaccine (HepA).** HepA is recommended for all children at age 1 year (i.e., 12–23 months). The 2 doses in the series should be administered at least 6 months apart. States, counties, and communities with existing HepA vaccination programs for children aged 2–18 years are encouraged to maintain these programs. In these areas, new efforts focused on routine vaccination of children aged 1 year should enhance, not replace, ongoing programs directed at a broader population of children. HepA is also recommended for certain high risk groups (see *MMWR* 1999;48[No. RR-12]).

The Childhood and Adolescent Immunization Schedule is approved by the Advisory Committee on Immunization Practices (http://www.cdc.gov/nip/acip), the American Academy of Pediatrics (http://www.aap.org), and the American Academy of Family Physicians (http://www.aafp.org).

TABLE 6-2 Universal Precautions for Handling Body Fluids

Whenever handling body fluids or items contaminated with body fluids, be sure to:
- Wear disposable latex gloves when you are likely to have contact with blood or other body fluids, e.g., vomitus, urine, feces, or saliva.
- Remove glove by grasping the cuff and pulling it off inside out.
- Wash hands thoroughly (lather for at least 30 seconds).
- Dispose of contaminated materials properly. Seal soiled clothing in plastic bags to be laundered at home. Dispose of diapers by tying them securely in garbage bags. Place broken glass in a designated container.
- Clean all surfaces with a disinfectant, such as a bleach solution (one tablespoon bleach/one cup water mixed fresh daily).
- Subsidize the cost of hepatitis B immunizations for all employees.

with soap and running water to remove any blood. Washable objects, such as rugs, pillows, or stuffed toys that have been contaminated with body fluids should be laundered separately from other items. Children's clothing should be rinsed out, sealed in a plastic bag, and sent home to be washed. Bloodstains on surfaces must be wiped up and disinfected with a commercial germicide or mixture of bleach and water (one tablespoon bleach to one cup water).

Handwashing Handwashing is perhaps the single most effective control measure against the spread of communicable and infectious illness in child care and school environments (Tables 6–3 and 6–4) (Kotch, et al., 2007; *Child Health Alert*, 2005; Aronson, 2003).

Frequent handwashing is especially important for infants and toddlers who are crawling on the floor, eating with their hands, or sucking their thumbs/fingers. Their hands should also be washed carefully following diaper changes. Individual washcloths moistened with soap and water can be

ISSUES TO CONSIDER • Childhood Immunizations

The number of young children who are not fully immunized against preventable communicable diseases remains relatively high (CDC, 2007). Poverty, lack of education, and poor accessibility to medical care are often cited as reasons for noncompliance. In addition, some parents have expressed concern that vaccines can make children sick. Television programs, magazine articles, and word-of-mouth have attempted to link everything from SIDS, HIV/AIDS, arthritis, multiple sclerosis, and autism to childhood vaccines. However, to date, there has been no substantiated evidence that vaccines cause any of these problems (CDC, 2006a; Doja & Roberts, 2006; Immunization Safety Review Committee, 2004). Although minor discomforts, including mild fever, achiness, and pain at the injection site may occur, vaccines are considered safe. To further improve the safety of immunizations, the American Academy of Pediatrics has urged physicians to administer the injectable form of polio vaccine (IPV), rather than the oral version (OPV), thus eliminating exposure to the live, but weakened, virus.

- As a teacher, how would you respond to families who were opposed to immunization because they felt they were unsafe?
- Where could you locate accurate information about the safety of vaccines?
- How would you handle situations where there is conflict between parental beliefs and state regulation?
- On what basis does your state grant exceptions to immunization requirements for children?

TABLE 6-3   Times when Handwashing Is Essential

Good handwashing technique should be used:
- upon arrival or return to the classroom
- before handling food or food utensils
- before and after feeding children
- before and after administering medication
- after changing diapers or handling items contaminated with mucus, urine, feces, vomitus, or blood
- after personally using the restroom
- after cleaning up from snack, play activities, or handling art materials such as clay and paint

TABLE 6-4   Correct Handwashing Technique

Following proper handwashing technique is critical for controlling the spread of infectious illnesses:
- Pull down paper towel.
- Turn on the water; wet hands and wrists under warm, running water.
- Apply soap and lather hands to loosen dirt and bacteria.
- Rub hands and wrists vigorously for a minimum of 30 seconds. Friction helps to remove microorganisms and dirt. (Have children sing the entire ABC song while rubbing their hands with soap.)
- Pay special attention to rubbing soap on the backs of hands, between fingers, and under nails.
- Rinse hands thoroughly under running water to remove dirt and soap. Keep hands lower than wrists to prevent recontamination. Leave the water running.
- Dry hand and arms carefully with paper towel.
- Use the paper towel to turn off water faucets. (This prevents hands from becoming contaminated again.)
- Open bathroom door with paper towel and discard it in an appropriate receptacle.

used for this purpose; however, infants and toddlers should also have their hands washed under running water several times a day. Preschoolers and adults should always wash with soap and running water (Figure 6–10). Children should be taught the correct procedure and supervised to be sure they continue to practice each step carefully. School-age children should be given several opportunities during the day to wash their hands, especially before and after eating. Although sanitizing hand gels are beneficial for limiting the spread of communicable illness, they are not a substitute for thorough handwashing (CDC, 2006b; Seal, Rizer, & Maas-Irslinger, 2005; Morton & Schultz, 2004).

Cleaning   Frequent cleaning of furniture, toys, and surfaces is also effective for limiting the spread of communicable illness (Reuters, 2006; Harkavy, 2002; Aronson, 2003). A solution of one-quarter cup bleach to one gallon of water (or one tablespoon/one quart) can be used for wiping off large play equipment, cribs, sleeping mats, and strollers. Tables, tops of gates, car seats, and crib rails should be scrubbed daily with soap and water and then disinfected. **Note:** *A new bleach solution must be prepared daily to maintain its disinfecting strength. Label spray bottles with the date and bleach/water ratio or purpose (e.g., general cleaning, disinfection of body fluid contamination).* Changing tables, mats, and potty chairs should be constructed of nonporous materials and free of any tears or cracks for ease of cleaning. They should be disinfected thoroughly after each use with a bleach solution that can be sprayed on and wiped off with paper towels. A stronger bleach solution (one tablespoon bleach to one cup water) should be used to disinfect surfaces contaminated with blood or large amounts of urine, stool, or vomitus. **Note**: *You will be able to smell the bleach in this stronger solution.* Several non-bleach disinfecting solutions are also available commercially.

Toys that infants have placed in their mouths should be removed for cleaning before they are used by another child. Items should be washed with soap and water, rinsed in a bleach solution, and allowed to air-dry. Some toys can also be sanitized in the dishwasher. Washable cloth and stuffed objects should be laundered between use by other children. Other surfaces, such as tables, gate tops, car seats, and crib rails that children mouth or drool on should also be scrubbed daily with soap and water and disinfected. Desktops and classroom equipment in school-age classrooms should also be wiped with a mild disinfectant at least once a week, especially during the cold and flu season.

Diapering and Toileting Areas   Children who are not toilet-trained can spread infectious illnesses through urine and feces (CDC, 2006c). Maintaining separate diapering and toileting areas can significantly reduce

FIGURE 6–10

Children's hands should be washed under running water.

contamination and the spread of infection from one child to another. Careful adherence to sanitary diapering procedures, disinfection of surfaces (free of cracks), and thorough handwashing will further reduce this risk (Table 6–5). Teachers may choose to wear disposable gloves when changing babies and/or handling soiled diapers, but this is not essential. Even if gloves are worn, meticulous handwashing must follow because they do not prevent contamination. Soiled diapers (disposable) should be placed in a covered waste container (lined with a plastic bag) that is not accessible to children. Cloth diapers must be sealed in a plastic bag and sent home for parents to launder. Babies' hands should be washed under running water.

Family preferences and cultural differences will influence when and how toilet training will be initiated (Honig, 2006; Gonzalez-Mena & Eyer, 2006, Ritblatt, Obegi, & Hammons, 2003). When toddlers are ready to begin potty training small, child-sized toilets are ideal (Table 6–6). Many states prohibit the use of shared potty-chairs in early childhood programs because they can spread infections if not properly sanitized. Families may wish to provide a chair for their child's sole use if the program's policy permits. However, teachers must still follow strict sanitizing procedures each time the chair is used. A mixture of one-quarter cup bleach to one gallon water (or one tablespoon bleach to one quart water) mixed fresh daily can be used for most disinfecting purposes. Any soiled material should first be removed with soap and water before the surface is sprayed with a disinfecting solution. Bleach solutions should remain in contact with surfaces for at least two minutes (to allow adequate disinfection) before they are wiped up; allowing sprayed surfaces to air dry is preferable. Teachers must wash their hands carefully after completing cleaning procedures and also be sure that children have washed their hands!

Room Arrangements   Simple modifications in children's environments can also have a positive effect on the control of communicable illnesses. For example, room temperatures set between 68°–70°F are less favorable for the spread of infectious illnesses and are often more comfortable for children. Their smaller body surfaces make them less sensitive than adults to cooler temperatures.

Rooms should also be well ventilated. Circulating fresh air helps to reduce the concentration of infectious organisms within a given area. Schools and large child care facilities should

TABLE 6-5   Sanitary Diapering Procedure

The consistent implementation of sanitary diapering procedures is important for reducing the spread of disease. Teachers should follow these steps:
- Organize and label all supplies.
- Have all items for diaper changing within reach.
- Place a disposable covering (paper towel, paper roll) over a firm changing surface. Do not change children on fabric chairs or sofas that could become soiled.
- If using gloves, put them on.
- Pick up the child, holding him/her away from your clothing to avoid contamination.
- Place the child on the paper surface; fasten security belt. Remove the child's clothing and/or shoes if necessary to prevent them from becoming soiled.
- Remove the soiled diaper and place in a covered, plastic-lined receptacle designated for this purpose.
- Clean baby's bottom with a disposable wipe and place in receptacle; pat skin dry.
- Remove the paper lining from beneath baby and discard.
- Wash your hands or wipe with a clean disposable wipe and discard. *Never leave the child alone.*
- Wash the baby's hands under running water.
- Diaper and redress the baby. Return baby to a play area.
- Disinfect the changing surface and any supplies or equipment that was touched with a bleach solution or other disinfectant.
- Remove gloves (if worn) and wash your hands again.

TABLE 6-6   Readiness Indicators for Toilet Training

Successful toilet training requires several things: children's bodies must reach a certain point of physical maturation and children must have basic motor and cognitive skills which permit them to participate, including:
- an ability to understand the concepts of wet and dry
- a regularity to patterns of elimination (at least during the daytime)
- language to express the need for elimination
- an ability to get clothing up and down

be equipped with an efficient mechanical ventilating system that is in good operating condition. Doors and windows can be opened for brief periods, even on cold days, to introduce fresh air. Screens should be used to prevent disease-carrying flies and mosquitoes from entering. Daily schedules that include outdoor play, even in winter, also improve children's resistance to illness.

The humidity level in rooms should also be checked periodically, especially in winter when rooms are heated and there are fewer opportunities to let in fresh air. Extremely warm, dry air increases the chances of respiratory infection by causing the mucous lining of the mouth and nose to become dry and cracked. Moisture can be added to rooms by installing a humidifier in the central heating system. A cool-mist vaporizer can also be used to increase the humidity in individual rooms. (Cool-mist units eliminate the possibility of burns.) These units should be emptied, washed out with soap and water, disinfected, and refilled with fresh distilled water each day to prevent bacterial growth. Plants or small dishes of water placed around a room will also provide increased humidity. However, they will also encourage the growth of mold spores which can aggravate children's allergies and asthma.

The physical arrangement of a classroom can also be an effective method for controlling communicable and infectious illness. For example, separating infants and toddlers who are not toilet-trained from older children can significantly reduce the spread of intestinal illnesses. Surfaces, e.g., floors, walls, counter tops, and furniture should be smooth and easy to clean. Laundry and food preparation areas should be separated from each other as well as from the classrooms. Pedal-operated sinks or faucets with infrared sensors are ideal for encouraging frequent handwashing and avoiding recontamination.

Measures taken to group children and limit the amount of close contact are also desirable. Crowding at tables or in play areas can be avoided by dividing children into smaller groups. During naptimes, children's rugs, cots, or cribs can be arranged in alternating directions, head to foot, to decrease talking, coughing, and breathing in each other's faces. Provisions should also be made for children to have individual lockers or storage space for personal items, such as blankets, coats, hats, toys, toothbrushes, and combs to reduce the transfer of communicable illnesses.

Several additional areas in children's environments deserve special attention. Sandboxes should be covered to prevent contamination from animal feces. Water tables and wading pools need to be emptied and washed out daily to prevent the spread of communicable illness; a water pH of 7.2–8.2 and chlorine level of 0.4–3.0 parts per million should be maintained in swimming pools at all times (as specified in commercial test kits). Items that children put on their heads, such as hats, wigs, and beauty parlor items can spread head lice and, therefore, may not be appropriate to use in group settings unless they can be washed or disinfected. Play clothes should be washable and laundered often.

Education

Teachers also make a valuable contribution to the control of communicable illness through the lessons they design for children. Ongoing activities that address personal health habits, exercise, and nutrition can be key factors in improving children's resistance to infectious organisms and shortening the length of convalescence (Ackerman, et al., 2001). Topics of special interest and value to young children include:

- appropriate technique and times for handwashing
- proper method for covering coughs and blowing noses
- sanitary use of drinking fountains
- not sharing personal items, e.g., drinking cups, toothbrushes, shoes, hats, towels, eating utensils
- germs
- dressing appropriately for the weather
- good nutrition
- the need for rest and exercise

Outbreaks of communicable illness provide excellent opportunities for teachers to review important preventive health concepts and practices with children. Learning is more meaningful for children when it is associated with real-life experiences, such as when a classmate has chickenpox or pinkeye. Teachers can use these opportunities to review handwashing procedures, reinforce the importance of good nutrition, conduct simple experiments illustrating how germs are spread, and model good health practices for children to imitate (children are more likely to remember what they have seen than what they have been told).

Families must be included in any educational program that is aimed at reducing the incidence of communicable illness. They should be informed of special health practices and information

REFLECTIVE THOUGHTS

Teachers who work with young children are often exposed to communicable illness in the classroom. Sometimes families unknowingly bring sick children to school or child care. How do you feel about being exposed to contagious illness? Could you care for a child who was acutely ill knowing that you too might become sick? What precautions can you take to protect yourself from such illnesses? How could you help families address the problem of bringing sick children to school? What alternative care arrangements could you suggest for a working family?

being taught to the children. Teachers can also reinforce the importance of (1) serving nutritious meals and snacks, (2) making sure that children get sufficient rest and exercise, (3) obtaining immunizations for infants, toddlers, and older children, and (4) scheduling routine medical and dental supervision. Successful control of communicable illness and the promotion of children's well-being depend on schools and families working together.

FOCUS ON FAMILIES • Giving Children Medication

Special precautions should be taken whenever administering medication to young children. Their bodies tend to be more sensitive to many medications, and they may respond differently than an adult. It is also easy to give children too much of a medication because their dosages are typically quite small. Medications left unattended may attract a curious child's attention and lead to an unintentional poisoning, so they should always be stored in a locked cabinet. Additional precautions for the safe administration of medication to children include:

- Always check with your child's physician before giving over-the-counter medications, especially to children under two years.
- Read the label carefully. Be sure you are giving the correct medication to the right child at the appropriate time interval. Also, double-check the dose that has been prescribed, and give only that amount. Make sure the medication is approved for children; many drugs are not advised for children younger than 12 years.
- Ask your pharmacist about potential drug interactions—with other medications or food—that should be avoided. Also, learn about possible reactions that should be noted before giving your child any new medication.
- Always follow the instructions for administering a medication, and finish giving the full course that has been prescribed.
- Throw away any outdated medication. Old medications may lose their effectiveness or cause unexpected reactions. Always check with a pharmacist if in doubt.
- Store medications in their original container and according to instructions.
- Never tell children medicines are "candy," and avoid taking medication in front of children.

CASE STUDY

Laura arrived at the child care center with a runny nose and cough. Her mother informed the teachers that it was probably just allergies and left before Laura could be checked in.

In addition to having a part-time job, Laura's mother is a single parent and a student at the local community college. Shortly after Laura's mother left, the teachers discovered that Laura had a fever, red throat, and swollen glands.

1. How should the teachers handle Laura's immediate situation? Should she be allowed to stay or should they try to contact Laura's mother?

2. If Laura is allowed to stay at the center, what measures can be taken to limit the risk of spreading illness to other children?

3. If this is a repeated occurrence, what steps can be taken to make sure Laura's mother complies with the center's policies?

4. How can the center help Laura's mother avoid similar situations in the future?

CLASSROOM CORNER • Teacher Activities

Those Invisible Germs...
Concept: Germs are everywhere; germs are on the things we touch. (Pre-2)

Learning Objectives
- Children will understand that germs are invisible and on most things we touch.
- Children will learn that correct handwashing removes germs.

Supplies
- baby powder or glitter; small spray bottle with water; paper towel; hand lotion

Learning Activities
- Read and discuss one of the following books:
  - *Germs Are Not for Sharing* by Elizabeth Verdick
  - *Those Mean Nasty Dirty Downright Disgusting but...Invisible Germs* by Judith Rice
  - *The Magic School Bus Inside Ralphie: A Book About Germs* (for older children) by Joanna Cole
- Ask children if they know what a germ is and if they can describe what they look like. Ask them where germs are found and what we can do to protect ourselves from them.
- Lightly spray water on the hands of half of the children; sprinkle with baby powder or glitter. Ask children to shake hands with one another and then examine their hands.
- Coat children's hands with a thin layer of hand cream (make sure no one has any allergies). Sprinkle their hands lightly with glitter. Have them attempt to brush the "germs" off by rubbing their hands together. Repeat this step using a paper towel. Finally, have children wash their hands with soap and warm water. After, ask the children which method was most effective for removing the "germs." Talk about why handwashing is important for keeping the germs away and staying healthy.
- Have children draw their own interpretations of what a germ looks like.

Evaluation
- Children can explain where germs are found and how they are spread.
- Children will demonstrate how to wash their hands correctly.

SUMMARY

- Communicable illnesses are common in group settings where there are young children. Reasons for this include children playing in close proximity, immature development of children's respiratory system, children's play and personal hygiene, adult carelessness, and poor handwashing.
- Communicable illnesses are passed from one person to another via airborne, fecal-oral, direct, or indirect methods.
- To be communicable, an illness requires a pathogen, a susceptible host, and a method for successful transmission.
- Teachers can implement practices to effectively control and manage communicable illness in group settings, including observations, health policies and sanitation procedures, enforcing immunization requirements, modifying the environment, working with families, and educating children.

APPLICATION ACTIVITIES

1. Obtain several agar growth medium plates. With sterile cotton applicators, culture one toy and the top of one table. Observe the "growth" after 24 hours and again after 48 hours. Wash the same item with a mild chlorine solution and repeat the experiment. Compare the results.

2. Contact the Office of Public Health in your state (province/territory). Obtain data on the percentage of children under six years of age who are currently immunized. How does this figure compare to the goals outlined in the *Healthy People 2010* initiative? What suggestions do you have for improving this rate? Conduct an Internet search to determine the immunization requirements for children enrolling in early childhood programs and kindergarten in your state.

3. Obtain a copy of the OSHA pamphlet on regulations and instructions for implementing a bloodborne pathogen policy (CFR 1910.1030) from your nearest regional office. Prepare a written compliance plan for an early education center.

4. Discuss how you would handle the following situations:

    a. The father of a toddler in your center is upset because his child has frequent colds.
    b. You observe your teacher covering a cough with her hand and then continuing to prepare snacks for the children.
    c. Your toddler group has experienced frequent outbreaks of strep throat in the past six months.
    d. While reviewing immunization records, you discover that one child has received only one dose of DTaP, IPV, and Hib.
    e. During health checks, Gabriel announces that he threw up all night. You notice that his eyes appear watery and his cheeks are flushed.
    f. You find that one of your aides has stored all of the children's toothbrushes together in a sealed, plastic container.
    g. Your classroom paraprofessional casually mentions that she has the stomach flu and has been throwing up all night.

5. Review and compare health care policies from an early childhood center, home-based program, Head Start program, and elementary school. How are they similar? How do they differ?

CHAPTER REVIEW

A. **By Yourself:**

1. Define each of the *Terms to Know* listed at the beginning of this chapter.

2. Describe two examples that illustrate how an illness can be spread by:
    a. airborne transmission
    b. indirect contact

3. What immunizations, and how many of each, are recommended for a 30-month-old child?

4. Where can families go to obtain immunizations for their children?

5. During what stage(s) of communicable illnesses are children most contagious?

B. **As a Group:**

1. Identify and discuss three factors that are required for an infection to be communicable.

2. What early signs would you be likely to observe in a child who was coming down with a respiratory virus?

3. Discuss specific practices that teachers can use in their classrooms to limit the spread of illnesses transmitted via:

a. the respiratory tract
   b. the fecal-oral route
   c. skin conditions
   d. contaminated objects, e.g., toys, towels, changing mats

4. Discuss when and how universal precautions should be implemented in the classroom.

5. What special accommodations would be necessary if a program wanted to include mildly ill children?

REFERENCES

Ackerman, S. J., Duff, S. B., Dennehy, P. H., Mafilis, M. S., & Krilov, L. R. (2001). Economic impact of an infection control education program in a specialized preschool setting. *Pediatrics, 108*(6), E102.

Allred, N., Shaw, K., Santibanez, T., Rickert, D., & Santoli, J. (2005). Parental vaccine safety concerns: Results from the National Immunization Survey, 2001–2002. *American Journal of Preventive Medicine, 28*(2), 221–224.

American Academy of Pediatrics (AAP). (2002). *Caring for our children: National health and safety performance standards: Guidelines for out-of-home care.* Washington, DC. Available online at http://nrc.uchsc.edu/CFOC/index.html.

Aronson, S. (2003). 2002 Update on hand hygiene in child (day) care settings. *Child Care* Information Exchange, 150, 60–62.

Aronson, S. (2002). *Healthy young children: A manual for programs* (4th ed.). Washington, DC: NAEYC.

Brady, M. (2005). Infectious disease in pediatric out-of-home child care. *American Journal of Infection Control, 33*(5), 276–285.

Bradley, R.H. (2003). Child care and common communicable illnesses in children aged 37 to 54 months. *Archives of Pediatric & Adolescent Medicine, 157*(2), 196–200.

Centers for Disease Control & Prevention (CDC). (2007). *America's Children in Brief: Key National Indicators of Well-Being, 2007.* Accessed on September 24, 2007 from http://www.childstats.gov/americaschildren/care3.asp.

CDC. (2006a). Vaccines & autism: Important conclusions form a recent report from the Institutes of Medicine. Accessed on October 19, 2006, from http://www.cdc.gov/Nip/vacsafe/concerns/autism/vacc-autism-iom_parent.pdf.

CDC. (2006b). *Stop the spread of germs.* Accessed on October 19, 2006, from http://www.cdc.gov/germstopper/home_work_school.htm.

CDC. (2006c). Outbreaks of multidrug-resistant Shigella sonnei gastroenteritis associated with day care centers—Kansas, Kentucky, and Missouri, 2005. *Morbidity & Mortality Weekly Report, 55*(39), 1068–1071.

Child Care Law Center. (1994). *Revised description of OSHA regulations on bloodborne pathogens.* San Francisco, CA.

Child Health Alert. (2006, September). Whooping cough—more common than we think. *Child Health Alert, 4.*

Child Health Alert. (2005, November). Use healthy handwashing. *Child Health Alert, 1–2.*

Copeland, K. & Shope, T. (2005). Knowledge and beliefs about guidelines for exclusion of ill children from child care. *Ambulatory Pediatrics, 5*(6), 365–371.

DHHS. (2000). *Healthy People 2010.* Accessed on September 24, 2007 from http://www.healthypeople.gov.

Doja, A. & Roberts, W. (2006). Immunizations and autism: A review of the literature. *Canadian Journal of Neurological Sciences, 33*(4), 341–346.

Friedman, J., Lee, G., Kleinman, K., & Finkelstein, J. (2004). Child care center policies and practices for management of ill children. *Ambulatory Pediatrics, 4*(5), 455–460.

Gonzalez-Mena, J., & Eyer, D. (2006). *Infants, toddlers, and caregivers.* NY: McGraw-Hill.

Harkavy, L. M. (2002). Role of surface disinfection and hand hygiene in reducing illness. *Journal of School Health,* Oct. Suppl., 27–30.

Honig, A. (2006). Infants and toddlers: Understanding confusing expressions of emotion. *Early Childhood Today, 20*(7), 17–19.

Immunization Safety Review Committee. (2004). *Immunization safety review: Vaccines and autism.* Washington, DC: National Academies Press.

Kennedy, A., Brown, C., & Gust, D. (2005). Vaccine beliefs of parents who oppose compulsory vaccination. *Public Health Report, 120*(3), 252–258.

Kennedy, A., & Gust, D. (2005). Parental vaccine beliefs and child's school type. *Journal of School Health, 75*(7), 276–280.

Kotch, J., Isbell, P., Weber, D., Nguyen, V., Savage, E., Gunn, E., Skinner, M., Fowlkes, S., Virk, J., & Allen, J. (2007). Hand-washing and diapering equipment reduces disease among children in out-of-home child care centers. *Pediatrics, 120*(1), e29-36.

Lucarelli, P. (2002). Raising the bar for health and safety in child care. *Pediatric Nursing, 28*(3), 239–241.

Luman, E. T., McCauley, M. M., Stokley, S., Chu, S. Y., & Pickering, L. K. (2002). Timeliness of childhood immunizations. *Pediatrics, 110*(5), 935–939.

Morton, J., & Schultz, A. (2004). Healthy hands: Use of alcohol gel as an adjunct to handwashing in elementary school children. *Journal of School Nursing, 20*(3), 161–167.

National Advisory Committee on Immunization (NACI). (2005). *Recommended immunization schedule for infants, children, and youth (2005)*. Accessed on October 19, 2006, from http://www.phac-aspc.gc.ca/naci-ccni/is-si/index.html.

Niederhauser, V., Walters, M., & Ganeko, R. (2007). Simple solutions to complex issues: Minimizing disparities in childhood immunization rates by providing walk-in shot clinic access. *Family & Community Health, 30*(2 Suppl), S80–91.

Occupational Safety and Health Administration (OSHA). (1992; 2001). *Bloodborne pathogens.* Washington, DC: U. S. Department of Labor, Occupational Safety and Health Administration. (As amended).

Omer, S., Pan, W., Halsey, N., Stokely, S., Moulton, L., Navar, A., Pierce, M., & Salmon, D. (2006). Nonmedical exemptions to school immunization requirements: Secular trends and association of state policies with pertussis incidence. *JAMA, 296*(14), 1757–1763.

Reuters. (2006). Cold virus lingers on common surfaces for a full day. Accessed on October 19, 2006, from http://www.nlm.nih.gov/medlineplus/news/fullstory_39415.html.

Richardson, M., Elliman, D., Macguire, H., Simpson, J., & Nicoll, A. (2001). Evidence base of incubation periods, periods of infectiousness and exclusion policies for the control of communicable diseases in schools and preschools. *Pediatric Infectious Disease Journal, 20*(2), 380–391.

Ritblatt, S., Obegi, A., & Hammons, B. (2003). Parents' and child care professionals' toilet training attitudes and practices: A comparative analysis. *Journal of Research in Childhood Education, 17*(2), 133–146.

Rubino, J. R. (2002). Economic impact of a healthy school environment. *Journal of School Health,* Oct. Suppl., 27–30.

Seal, L., Rizer, R., & Maas-Irslinger, R. (2005). A unique water optional health care personnel handwash provides antimicrobial persistence and residual effects while decreasing the need for additional products. *American Journal of Infection Control, 33*(4), 207–216.

Shui, I., Weintraub, E., & Gust, D. (2006). Parents concerned about vaccine safety: Differences in race/ethnicity and attitudes. *American Journal of Preventive Medicine, 31*(3), 244–251.

Slack-Smith, L., Read, A., & Stanley, F. J. (2002). A prospective study of absence for illness and injury in childcare children. *Child Care Health & Development, 28*(6), 487–494.

U.S. Department of Health & Human Services (HHS). (2000). *Healthy people 2010.* Office of Disease Prevention and Health Promotion. Washington, DC: U.S. Department of HHS.

Zimmerman, R. K. (2003). Recommended childhood and adolescent immunization schedule, United States, 2003 and update on childhood immunizations. *American Family Physician, 67*(1), 188, 190, 195–196.

HELPFUL WEB SITES

American Public Health Association	http://www.apha.org
Canadian Pediatric Society	http://www.cps.ca
Centers for Disease Control and Prevention (CDC) Children's Defense Fund	http://www.cdc.gov http://www.childrensdefense.org
Maternal and Child Health Bureau	http://mchb.hrsa.gov
National Center for Health Statistics	http://www.cdc.gov
National Foundation for Infectious Diseases	http://www.nfid.org
National Institutes of Health	http://www.nih.gov

For additional health, safety, and nutrition resources, go to
http://www.EarlyChildEd.delmar.cengage.com

CHAPTER 7

Communicable and Acute Illness: Identification and Management

⁜ OBJECTIVES

After studying this chapter, you should be able to:

- Identify the signs and symptoms of four common illnesses.
- Check axillary and oral temperatures with a thermometer.
- Describe basic precautions teachers should take when children in group settings show signs of communicable illness.
- Demonstrate how to correctly position babies for sleep.

⁜ TERMS TO KNOW

symptoms	abdomen	Lyme disease
asymptomatic	hyperventilation	intestinal
apnea	temperature	urination
infection	fever	salmonellosis
dehydration	tympanic	
listlessness	disorientation	

Children, especially those under three years of age, have an increased susceptibility to communicable and acute illnesses. Group settings such as schools and early childhood programs encourage the rapid transfer of these conditions among children and adults. Consequently, every effort must be made to establish policies and practices that protect young children from unnecessary exposure.

IDENTIFYING SICK CHILDREN

Teachers should be able to recognize the early signs and **symptoms** of common childhood illnesses (Figure 7–1). By doing so, they can help to limit the spread by identifying and excluding children who are sick. Teachers can also use children's illnesses to promote wellness education and strengthen healthful practices.

COMMON COMMUNICABLE ILLNESSES

Effective control and protection of children in group settings require teachers to have a sound understanding of communicable illnesses—what causes them, how they are transmitted, and how they can be controlled. Their knowledge of these illnesses and ability to implement sanitary procedures, including handwashing and disinfection, are important management skills. Table 7–1 provides brief descriptions of communicable illnesses that young children commonly experience.

Teachers should also be familiar with local public health policies regarding which communicable illnesses must be reported. Notifying health officials of existing cases enables them to monitor communities for potential outbreaks. They may also be able to provide additional information about an illness that teachers can share with families.

FIGURE 7–1

Teachers should be able to identify the early signs of childhood illnesses.

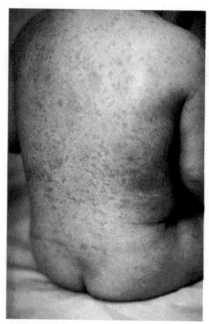

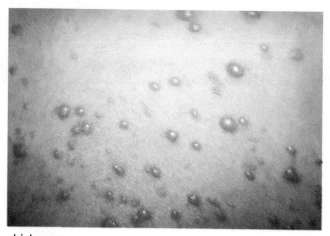

chickenpox

German measles
Source: http://phil.cdc.gov/phil

---

symptoms – *changes in the body or its functions that are experienced by the affected individual.*

TABLE 7-1 Common Communicable Illnesses

Communicable Illness	Signs and Symptoms	Infectious Agent	Methods of Transmission	Incubation Period	Length of Communicability	Control Measures
AIRBORNE TRANSMITTED ILLNESSES						
Chickenpox	Slight fever, irritability, cold-like symptoms. Red rash that develops blister-like head, scabs later. Most abundant on covered parts of body, e.g., chest, back, neck, forearm.	Virus	Airborne through contact with secretions from the respiratory tract. Transmission from contact with blisters less common.	2–3 weeks after exposure	2–3 days prior to the onset of symptoms until 5–6 days after first eruptions. Scabs are not contagious.	Specific control measures: (1) Exclusion of sick children, (2) Practice good personal hygiene, especially careful handwashing. Children can return to group care when all blisters have formed a dry scab (approximately 1 week). Immunization is now available.
Common Cold	Highly contagious infection of the upper respiratory tract accompanied by slight fever, chills, runny nose, fatigue, muscle and headaches. Onset may be sudden.	Virus	Airborne through contact with secretions from the respiratory tract, e.g., coughs, sneezes, eating utensils, etc.	12–72 hours	About 1 day before onset of symptoms to 2–3 days after acute illness.	Prevention through education and good personal hygiene. Avoid exposure. Exclude first day or two. Antibiotics not effective against viruses. Avoid aspirin products (possible link to Reye's syndrome). Watch for complications, e.g., earaches, bronchitis, croup, pneumonia.
Fifth disease	Appearance of bright red rash on face, especially cheeks.	Virus	Airborne contact with secretions from the nose/ mouth of infected person.	4–14 days	Prior to appearance of rash; probably not contagious after rash develops.	Don't need to exclude children once rash appears. Frequent handwashing; frequent washing/ disinfecting of toys/surfaces. Use care when handling tissues/nasal secretions.

(continued)

TABLE 7-1 Common Communicable Illnesses (continued)

Communicable Illness	Signs and Symptoms	Infectious Agent	Methods of Transmission	Incubation Period	Length of Communicability	Control Measures
Haemophilus influenza Type b (Hib)	An acute respiratory infection; frequently causes meningitis. Other complications include pneumonia, epiglottitis, arthritis, infections of the bloodstream and conjunctivitis.	Bacteria	Airborne via secretions of the respiratory tract (nose, throat). Persons can also be carriers with or without symptoms.	2–4 days	Throughout acute phase; as long as organism is present. Noncommunicable 36–48 hours after treatment with antibiotics.	Identify and exclude sick children. Treatment with antibiotics 3–4 days before returning to group care. Notify parents of exposed children to contact their physician. Immunize children. Practice good handwashing techniques; sanitize contaminated objects.
Measles (Rubeola)	Fever, cough, runny nose, eyes sensitive to light. Dark red blotchy rash that often begins on the face and neck, then spreads over the entire body. Highly communicable.	Virus	Airborne through coughs, sneezes and contact with contaminated articles.	8–13 days; rash develops approximately 14 days after exposure	From beginning of symptoms until 4 days after rash appears.	Most effective control method is immunization. Good personal hygiene, especially handwashing and covering coughs. Exclude child for at least 4 days after rash appears.
Meningitis	Sudden onset of fever, stiff neck, headache, irritability, and vomiting; gradual loss of consciousness, seizures, and death.	Bacteria	Airborne through coughs, nasal secretions; direct contact with saliva/nasal discharges.	Varies with the infecting organism; 2–4 days average	Throughout acute phase; noncommunicable after antibiotic treatment.	Encourage immunization. Exclude child from care until medical treatment is completed. Use universal precautions when handling saliva/nasal secretions, frequent handwashing, and disinfecting of toys/surfaces.
Mononucleosis	Characteristic symptoms include sore throat, intermittent fever, fatigue, and enlarged lymph glands in the neck. May also be accompanied by headache and enlarged liver or spleen.	Virus	Airborne; also direct contact with saliva of an infected person.	2–4 weeks for children; 4–6 weeks for adults	Unknown. Organisms may be present in oral secretions for as long as one year following illness.	None known. Child should be kept home until over the acute phase (6–10 days). Use frequent handwashing and careful disposal of tissues after coughing or blowing nose.

Disease	Symptoms	Cause	Method of Transmission	Incubation	Period of Communicability	Control Measures
Mumps	Sudden onset of fever with swelling of the salivary glands.	Virus	Airborne through coughs and sneezes; direct contact with oral secretions of infected persons.	12–26 days	6–7 days prior to the onset of symptoms until swelling in the salivary glands is gone (7–9 days).	Immunization provides permanent protection. Peak incidence is in winter and spring. Exclude children from school or group settings until all symptoms have disappeared.
Roseola Infantum (6–24 mo.)	Most common in the spring and fall. Fever rises abruptly (102°–105°F) and lasts 3–4 days; loss of appetite, listlessness, runny nose, rash on trunk, arms, and neck lasting 1–2 days.	Virus	Person to person; method unknown.	10–15 days	1–2 days before onset to several days following fading of the rash.	Exclude from school or group care until rash and fever are gone.
Rubella (German Measles)	Mild fever; rash begins on face and neck and rarely lasts more than 3 days. May have arthritis-like discomfort and swelling in joints.	Virus	Airborne through contact with respiratory secretions, e.g., coughs, sneezes.	4–21 days	From one week prior to 5 days following onset of the rash.	Immunization offers permanent protection. Children must be excluded from school for at least 7 days after appearance of rash.
Streptococcal Infections (strep throat, scarlatina, rheumatic fever)	Sudden, onset. High fever accompanied by sore, red throat; may also have nausea, vomiting, headache, white patches on tonsils, and enlarged glands. Development of a rash depends on the infectious organism.	Bacteria	Airborne via droplets from coughs or sneezes. May also be transmitted by food and raw milk.	1–4 days	Throughout the illness and for approximately 10 days afterward, unless treated with antibiotics. Medical treatment eliminates communicability within 36 hours. Can develop rheumatic fever or become a carrier if not treated.	Exclude child with symptoms. Antibiotic treatment is essential. Avoid crowding in classrooms. Practice frequent handwashing, educating children, and careful supervision of food handlers.

(continued)

TABLE 7-1 Common Communicable Illnesses (continued)

Communicable Illness	Signs and Symptoms	Infectious Agent	Methods of Transmission	Incubation Period	Length of Communicability	Control Measures
Tuberculosis	Many people have no symptoms. Active disease causes productive cough, weight loss, fatigue, loss of appetite, chills, night sweats.	Bacteria	Airborne via coughs or sneezes.	2–3 months	As long as disease is untreated; usually noncontagious after 2–3 weeks on medication.	TB skin testing, especially babies and young children if there has been contact with an infected person. Seek prompt diagnosis and treatment if experiencing symptoms; complete drug therapy. Cover coughs/sneezes. Practice good handwashing.
BLOOD BORNE TRANSMITTED ILLNESSES						
Acquired Immuno-deficiency Syndrome (AIDS)	Flu-like symptoms, including fatigue, weight loss, enlarged lymph glands, persistent cough, fever, and diarrhea.	Virus	Children acquire virus when born to infected mothers, from contaminated blood transfusions and possibly from breast milk of in-fected mothers. Adults acquire the virus via sexual transmission, con-taminated drug needles, and blood transfusions.	6 weeks to 8 years	Lifetime	Exclude children 0–5 yrs. if they have open lesions, uncontrollable nosebleeds, bloody diarrhea, or are at high risk for exposing others to blood-contaminated body fluids. Use universal precautions when handling body fluids, including good handwashing techniques. Seal contaminated items, e.g., diapers, paper towels in plastic bags. Disinfect surfaces with bleach/water solution (1:10) or other disinfectant.
Hepatitis B	Slow onset; loss of appetite, nausea, vomiting, abdominal pain, and jaundice. May also be asymptomatic.	Virus	Through contact with blood/body fluids containing blood.	45–180 days; average 60–80 days	Varies; some persons are lifetime carriers.	Immunization is preferable. Use universal precautions when handling any blood/body fluids; use frequent handwashing.

CONTACT (direct and indirect) TRANSMITTED ILLNESSES

	Signs/Symptoms	Cause	How Spread	Incubation	Period of Communicability	Control Measures
Conjunctivitis (Pinkeye)	Redness of the white portion (conjunctiva) of the eye and inner eyelid, swelling of the lids, yellow discharge from eyes and itching.	Bacteria or virus	Direct contact with discharge from eyes or upper respiratory tract of an infected person; through contaminated fingers and objects, e.g., tissues, washcloths, towels.	1–3 days	Throughout active infection; several days up to 2–3 weeks.	Antibiotic treatment. Exclude child for 24 hours after medication is started. Frequent handwashing and disinfection of toys/surfaces is necessary.
Cytomegalovirus (CMV)	Often no symptoms in children under 2 yrs.; sore throat, fever, fatigue in older children. High risk of fetal damage if mother is infected during pregnancy.	Virus	Person to person contact with body fluids, e.g., saliva, blood, urine, breast milk, in utero.	Unknown; may be 4–8 weeks	Virus present (in saliva, urine) for months following infection.	No need to exclude children. Always wash hands after changing diapers or contact with saliva. Avoid kissing children's mouths or sharing eating utensils. Practice careful handwashing with children; wash/disinfect toys and surfaces frequently.
Hand, Foot, and Mouth Disease	Affects children under 10 yrs. Onset of fever, followed by blistered sores in the mouth/cheeks; 1–2 days later raised rash appears on palms of hands and soles of feet.	Virus	Person to person through direct contact with saliva, nasal discharge, or feces.	3–6 days	7–10 days	Exclude sick children for several days. Practice frequent handwashing, especially after changing diapers. Clean/disinfect surfaces.
Herpes simplex (cold sores)	Clear blisters develop on face, lips, and other body parts that crust and heal within a few days.	Virus	Direct contact with saliva, on hands, or sexual contact.	Up to 2 weeks	Virus remains in saliva for as long as 7 weeks following recovery.	No specific control. Frequent handwashing. Child does not have to be excluded from school.

(continued)

asymptomatic – *having no symptoms.*

TABLE 7–1 Common Communicable Illnesses (continued)

Communicable Illness	Signs and Symptoms	Infectious Agent	Methods of Transmission	Incubation Period	Length of Communicability	Control Measures
Impetigo	Infection of the skin forming crusty, moist lesions usually on the face, ears, and around the nose. Highly contagious. Common among children.	Bacteria	Direct contact with discharge from sores; indirect contact with contaminated articles of clothing, tissues, etc.	2–5 days; may be as long as 10 days	Until lesions are healed.	Exclude from group settings until lesions have been treated with antibiotics for 24–48 hours. Cover areas with bandage until treated.
Lice (head)	Lice are seldom visible to the naked eye. White nits (eggs) are visible on hair shafts. The most obvious symptom is itching of the scalp, especially behind the ears and at the base of the neck.	Head louse	Direct contact with infected persons or with their personal articles, e.g., hats, hair brushes, combs, or clothing. Lice can survive for 2–3 weeks on bedding, carpet, furniture, car seats, clothing, etc.	Nits hatch in 1 week and reach maturity within 8–10 days	While lice remain alive on infested persons or clothing; until nits have been destroyed.	Infested children should be excluded from group settings until treated. Hair should be washed with a special medicated shampoo and rinsed with a vinegar/water solution (any concentration will work) to ease removal of all nits (using a fine-toothed comb). Heat from a hair dryer also helps to destroy eggs. All friends and family should be carefully checked. Thoroughly clean child's environment; vacuum carpets/ upholstery, wash/dry or dry clean bedding, clothing, hairbrushes. Seal nonwashable items in plastic bag for 2 weeks.
Ringworm	An infection of the scalp, skin, or nails. Causes flat, spreading, oval-shaped lesions that may become dry and scaly or moist and crusted. When it is present on the feet it is commonly called athlete's foot. Infected nails may become discolored, brittle, or chalky or they may disintegrate.	Fungus	Direct or indirect contact with infected persons, their personal items, showers, swimming pools, theater seats, etc. Dogs and cats may also be infected and transmit it to children or adults.	4–10 days, (unknown for athlete's foot)	As long as lesions are present.	Exclude children from gyms, pools, or activities where they are likely to expose others. May return to group care following treatment with a fungicidal ointment. All shared areas, such as pools and showers should be thoroughly cleansed with a fungicide.

Disease	Cause	Transmission	Incubation	Communicability	Management
Rocky Mountain Spotted Fever	Bacteria	Indirect transmission: tick bite.	2–14 days; average 7 days	Not contagious from person to person.	Onset usually abrupt; fever (101°–104°F); joint and muscle pain, severe nausea and vomiting, and white coating on tongue. Rash appears on 2nd to 5th day over forehead, wrist, and ankles; later covers entire body. Can be fatal if untreated. Prompt removal of ticks; not all ticks cause illness. Administration of antibiotics. Use insect repellent on clothes when outdoors.
Scabies	Parasite	Direct contact with an infected person.	Several days to 2–4 weeks	Until all mites and eggs are destroyed.	Characteristic burrows or linear tunnels under the skin, especially between the fingers and around the wrists, elbows, waist, thighs, and buttocks. Causes intense itching. Children should be excluded from school or group care until treated. Affected persons should bathe with prescribed soap and carefully launder all bedding and clothing. All contacts of the infected person should be notified.
Tetanus	Bacteria	Indirect: organisms live in soil and dust; enter body through wounds, especially puncture-type injuries, burns and unnoticed cuts.	4 days to 2 weeks	Not contagious.	Muscular spasms and stiffness, especially in the muscles around the neck and mouth. Can lead to convulsions, inability to breathe, and death. Immunization every 8–10 years affords complete protection.

(continued)

TABLE 7-1 Common Communicable Illnesses (continued)

Communicable Illness	Signs and Symptoms	Infectious Agent	Methods of Transmission	Incubation Period	Length of Communicability	Control Measures
FECAL/ORAL TRANSMITTED ILLNESSES						
Dysentery (Shigellosis)	Sudden onset of vomiting; diarrhea; may be accompanied by high fever, headache, abdominal pain. Stools may contain blood, pus or mucus. Can be fatal in young children.	Bacteria	Fecal-oral transmission via contaminated objects or indirectly through ingestion of contaminated food or water and via flies.	1–7 days	Variable; may last up to 4 weeks or longer in the carrier state.	Exclude child during acute illness. Careful handwashing after bowel movements. Proper disposal of human feces; control of flies. Strict adherence to sanitary procedures for food preparation.
E. coli	Diarrhea, often bloody.	Bacteria	Spread through contaminated food, dirty hands.	3–4 days; can be as long as 10 days	For duration of diarrhea; usually several days.	Exclude infected children until no diarrhea; practice frequent handwashing, especially after toileting and before preparing food.
Encephalitis	Sudden onset of headache, high fever, convulsions, vomiting, confusion, neck and back stiffness, tremors, and coma.	Virus	Indirect spread by bites from disease-carrying mosquitoes; in some areas transmitted by tick bites.	5–15 days	Man is not contagious.	Spraying of mosquito breeding areas and use of insect repellents; public education.
Giardiasis	Many persons are asymptomatic. Typical symptoms include chronic diarrhea, abdominal cramping, bloating, pale and foul-smelling stools, weight loss, and fatigue.	Parasite (protozoa)	Fecal-oral transmission; through contact with infected stool (e.g., diaper changes, helping child with soiled underwear), poor handwashing, passed from hands to mouth (toys, food). Also transmitted through contaminated water sources.	7–10 days average; can be as long as 5–25 days	As long as parasite is present in the stool.	Exclude children until diarrhea ends. Scrupulous handwashing before eating, preparing food, and after using the bathroom. Maintain sanitary conditions in bathroom areas.

Disease	Agent	Symptoms	Transmission	Incubation	Communicable Period	Control Measures
Hepatitis (Infectious; Type A)	Virus	Fever, fatigue, loss of appetite, nausea abdominal pain (in region of liver). Illness may be accompanied by yellowing of the skin and eyeballs (jaundice) in adults, but not always in children. Acute onset.	Fecal-oral route. Also spread via contaminated food, water, milk, and objects.	10–50 days (average range 25–30 days)	7–10 days prior to onset of symptoms to not more than 7 days after onset of jaundice.	Exclude from group settings a minimum of 1 week following onset. Special attention to careful handwashing after going to the bathroom and before eating is critical following an outbreak. Report disease incidents to public health authorities. Immunoglobulin (IG) recommended for protection of close contacts.
Pinworms	Parasite; not contagious from animals.	Irritability, and itching of the rectal area. Common among young children. Some children have no symptoms.	Infectious eggs are transferred from person to person by contaminated hands (oral-fecal route). Indirectly spread by contaminated bedding, food, clothing, swimming pool.	Life cycle of the worm is 3–6 weeks; persons can also reinfect themselves.	2–8 weeks or as long as a source of infection remains present.	Infected children must be excluded from school until treated with medication; may return after initial dose. All infected and noninfected family members must be treated at one time. Frequent handwashing is essential; discourage nail biting or sucking of fingers. Daily baths and change of linen are necessary. Disinfect school toilet seats and sink handles at least once a day. Vacuum carpeted areas daily. Eggs are also destroyed when exposed to temperatures over 132°F. Education and good personal hygiene are vital to control.
Salmonellosis	Bacteria	Abdominal pain and cramping, sudden fever, severe diarrhea (may contain blood), nausea and vomiting lasts 5–7 days.	Fecal-oral transmission: via dirty hands. Also contaminated food (especially improperly cooked poultry, milk, eggs) water supplies, and infected animals.	12–36 hours	Throughout acute illness; may remain a carrier for months.	Attempt to identify source. Exclude children/adults with diarrhea; may return when symptoms end. Carriers should not handle or prepare food until stool cultures are negative. Practice good handwashing and sanitizing procedures.

SPECIAL CONCERNS

Acquired Immunodeficiency Syndrome (AIDS)

One of the most controversial and emotionally laden communicable illnesses of recent years is HIV/AIDS (human immunodeficiency virus/acquired immunodeficiency syndrome). The Centers for Disease Control and Prevention (CDC) report that approximately 9300 U.S. children under age 13 are currently infected with the AIDS virus (CDC, 2004). However, there continues to be a significant decrease in the number of new cases diagnosed each year (MMWR, 2006).

Cause   Many children have acquired the virus from their HIV positive mothers during pregnancy, delivery, or through breastfeeding (MMWR, 2006; Nakashima & Fleming, 2003). Only a small number of children have been infected through contaminated blood transfusions. However, aggressive efforts to identify and treat mothers during their pregnancy have achieved a dramatic reduction in mother-to-infant transmissions (CDC, 2006a; Di Noia, et al., 2004).

Management   A small percentage of infants infected with the HIV virus at, or prior to, birth will develop acute symptoms of the disease within the first year. They are usually quite ill and often die before the age of five due to complications from pneumonia or a special form of cancer. However, early diagnosis and treatment with new medications is helping many children to live longer (Lee, et al., 2006). Consequently, the number of children in early education programs and schools who are HIV positive is likely to continue increasing. This can present an emotional and ethical dilemma for some teachers (AIDS InfoNet, 2006; Franks, et al., 2004; Black, 1999).

The HIV virus, which causes AIDS, is not transmitted through casual contact, such as hugging, touching, kissing, sitting next to an infected person, or even sharing his or her bathroom or eating utensils (NIAID, 2004; AAP, 2004). It is spread primarily through sexual contact with an infected individual or from blood or blood products contaminated with the HIV virus. For these reasons, the risk of HIV transmission to teachers or other children in group care is low. To date, no cases of HIV transmission are known to have occurred in child care programs. Even biting behavior does not cause the spread of HIV (Stockheim, Wilkinson, & Ramos-Bonoan, 2005).

Because teachers may not always know when HIV positive children are in attendance, they must follow universal precautions whenever handling items contaminated with blood or other body fluids, including vomit, urine, saliva, and feces (see Chapter 6, Table 6–3). Disposable gloves should always be worn when administering first aid or changing diapers, and followed by thorough handwashing (*always an effective control measure*). Contaminated surfaces, such as toilet seats, should be disinfected promptly. A solution of household bleach and water (one tablespoon bleach to one cup water) provides an inexpensive and effective disinfectant that can be used to clean up body fluids. (*Be sure to label spray bottles with the date and solution strength/purpose*). Disposable paper should be placed under children when diapers are changed; tissues and towels should also be disposable. Soiled items should be sealed in plastic bags for proper disposal. Mops should be soaked in disinfectant for 20 to 30 minutes at least once a week.

Children who are infected with HIV/AIDS are protected under the Americans with Disabilities Act (ADA) of 1990 and, therefore, cannot be denied access to educational programs (AAP, 2004; Blumenreich, 2003). Families are not required to inform school personnel about their child's condition. Some families choose to withhold this information to protect their child from potential discrimination and stigma. For the same reasons, teachers who test positive may also prefer to remain anonymous. Again, this should pose no risk to either the children or coworkers if universal precautions and strict sanitary practices are consistently followed.

The Centers for Disease Control recommends that children who are HIV positive be excluded from schools and group care settings *only* if they have open sores, uncontrollable nose bleeds, bloody diarrhea, or are at high risk for exposing others to blood-contaminated body fluids. Children who are HIV positive are actually at greater risk of contracting illnesses and infections

REFLECTIVE THOUGHTS

Teachers recognize the importance of addressing issues of diversity in their programs. However, little is often understood about how individuals from various backgrounds—cultures, recent immigrants, homeless families—view the concepts of health, illness, and traditional Western medicine. Notable differences between mainstream values, beliefs, and practices and those held by a particular group are common. Thus, teachers must make an effort to learn more about individual families and their unique beliefs and priorities in order to best serve children's health needs.

from the other children because their immune systems are compromised (Hockenberry, 2004). Many of these illnesses can be life-threatening.

Each day, more is understood about HIV and AIDS. Local health departments, medical centers, national agencies (e.g., Centers for Disease Control and Prevention, Canadian Public Health Association, American Academy of Pediatrics, National Pediatric HIV Resource Center) are valuable resources, and can provide information and guidance to early childhood programs and schools when they are establishing policies or procedures.

Sudden Infant Death Syndrome (SIDS)

Sudden infant death syndrome (SIDS) refers to the unexplainable death of a seemingly healthy infant under 12 months of age. It is a leading cause of infant death which tends to peak between the second and fourth months (National SIDS Resource Center, 2006). Deaths are more likely to occur during sleep (nighttime and naps), and especially during the fall and winter months. Despite aggressive awareness campaigns, approximately 2,000–3,000 infants continue to die each year (National Center for Health Statistics, 2006).

Cause Although no one single cause has yet been identified, several factors seem to place some babies at higher risk of dying from SIDS, including:

- premature birth
- weighing less than 3.5 pounds at birth
- being a male child
- being of African American or American Indian/Alaska Native ethnicity (Pickett, Luo, & Lauderdale, 2005)
- having a sibling who also died of SIDS
- family poverty
- prenatal exposure to illicit drugs, such as cocaine, heroin, or methadone
- maternal smoking (during and after pregnancy)
- being born to a teenage mother

Children born into families with limited education and financial resources seem to experience the highest rate of death. Their mothers often lack prenatal care and engage in poor health practices during and after their pregnancy. Many infants who die of SIDS experience repeated interruptions of breathing called **apnea**. Researchers continue to investigate possible connections between this breathing disturbance and additional circumstances (Ritz, Wilhelm, & Zhao, 2006; Shah, Sullivan, & Carter, 2006). Some of these factors include:

---

apnea – *momentary absence of breathing.*

- toxic mattress fumes
- immunizations
- use of pacifiers
- air pollution
- bedsharing with parents
- respiratory infections (such as colds and flu)

To date there has been no scientific evidence linking toxic mattress fumes or immunizations to SIDS. In fact, babies who are immunized are less likely to die from SIDS (First Candle/SIDS Alliance, 2004). Evidence regarding bedsharing practices as a risk factor remains controversial although most authorities encourage parents to place infants in their own crib (near parents) to sleep (Lahr, Rosenberg, & Lapidus, 2005).

Recent studies have established positive relationships between SIDS deaths and air pollution (Thach, 2005). These findings have lead to recommendations that families avoid exposing babies to second-hand smoke and other forms of concentrated air pollution. The use of pacifiers has also been shown to reduce SIDS deaths although there is little evidence suggesting why this practice is beneficial (Mitchell, Blair, & L'Hoir, 2006; Shah, Sullivan, & Carter, 2006).

Management   To date, a baby's sleeping position has proven to be the strongest link in preventing SIDS. This discovery lead to the launching of a nationwide "Back to Sleep" campaign in 1994 which has been credited with significantly reducing SIDS deaths. Currently, multiple child and maternal government and private agencies are promoting a continuation of this initiative called "Safe Sleep for Your Baby" (NICHD, 2006; AAP, 2006a, b). Information about SIDS and recommended infant sleeping positions—*that babies must always be placed on their backs for sleeping*—is aimed at families and teachers in early education programs (Figure 7–2). Although fewer than 16 percent of SIDS fatalities occur in child care programs, teachers must take steps to avoid any preventable death (Moon, Sprague, & Patel, 2005; Kotch, 2004; Aronson, 2003). Despite ongoing educational efforts, researchers have found that nearly one-quarter of early childhood teachers continue to place infants in unsafe conditions and sleeping positions. As a result, many states are beginning to address infant sleep position in their child care licensing regulations so that programs will no longer be able to ignore this important safety measure (Moon, Kotch, & Aird, 2006).

Initial fears that babies would be more likely to choke when placed on their back for sleeping have not proven true. It isn't clear whether back-sleeping improves babies' oxygen intake or reduces their breathing in of carbon monoxide. However, the SIDS death rate has decreased by nearly 50 percent since this practice was initially recommended (National SIDS Resource Center, 2006; NCHS, 2006).

Babies should not share a crib with another infant nor sleep in a bed with adults; both of these practices have been found to increase the risk of SIDS. However, researchers have found that placing an infant's crib in the same room with their parents can reduce this risk (McCartney, 2006). Additional guidelines for reducing the risk of SIDS are outlined in Table 7–2.

FIGURE 7–2

Putting babies to sleep on their backs significantly reduces the risk of SIDS.

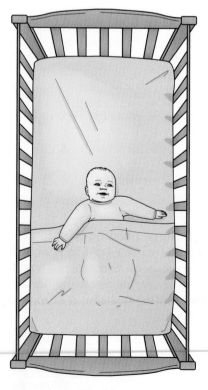

TABLE 7–2 Teacher Checklist: Practices to Reduce the Risk of Sudden Infant Death Syndrome (SIDS)

- Always put babies to sleep on their back unless a health condition prevents this.
- Use a firm mattress that fits snugly in a safety-approved crib. Never place babies on a waterbed, sheepskin, comforter, soft sofa cushions, or other soft bedding material.
- Remove pillows, thick or fluffy blankets, and soft toys from baby's bed.
- Cover babies with a thin blanket, tucking the bottom half under the mattress (Figure 7–2).
- Dress babies in light sleepwear and do not raise room temperature to avoid overheating.
- Offer a pacifier to babies who use them.
- Avoid exposing babies to second-hand smoke, car exhaust, wood smoke, and other air pollutants.
- Limit babies' exposure to persons who have colds or other respiratory infections.
- Encourage mothers to obtain professional prenatal care for themselves *and* recommended well-child checkups for their infant.
- Encourage and support breastfeeding; this may give babies extra protection against SIDS.
- Know how to respond to medical emergencies.

Because babies spend many hours sleeping on their backs it is important to change their position often during times when they are awake. Young babies have weak neck muscles and are unable to turn their head from side to side. As a result, flat spots can develop when they lay in the same position for extended periods of time. These can be prevented by changing babies' position and placing them on their tummies for brief periods throughout the day. Alternating a baby's position in the crib is also beneficial—one day the head should be placed at the head of the crib, the following day the head should be placed at the foot of the bed. This prevents the baby from consistently laying on the same side of his or her head every day.

Since there is often no identifiable cause for SIDS, families tend to blame themselves for having been negligent or using poor judgment. They believe that somehow they could have prevented this tragedy. Consequently, families who have experienced the unexpected death of an infant from SIDS require special emotional support and counseling. Siblings may also be affected by a baby's death and should be included in counseling therapy. Local chapters of several national SIDS organizations offer information and support groups to help families cope with their grief, including (see Appendix C):

- First Candle/SIDS Alliance (http://www.sidsalliance.org)
- National SIDS Resource Center (http://www.sidscenter.org)
- Association of SIDS and Infant Mortality Programs (http://www.asip1.org)
- Canadian Foundation for the Study of Infant Deaths (http://www.SIDSCanada.org)

COMMON ACUTE ILLNESSES

Children experience many forms of acute illness; however, not all of these are contagious (Bradley, 2003). Teachers must be able to distinguish conditions that are contagious from those that are limited to an individual child. *However, teachers must never attempt to diagnose children's health problems.* Their primary responsibilities include identifying children who are ill, making them comfortable until parents arrive, and advising the family to contact their health care provider. The remainder of this unit is devoted to several acute illnesses and health conditions commonly experienced by young children.

Colds

Children often experience as many as seven to eight colds during a year (Figure 7–3). This number typically decreases as children mature and their respiratory passageways lengthen, their immune systems become more effective, and they begin to develop healthy habits. Cold symptoms can range from frequent sneezing and runny nose to fever, sore throat, cough, headache, and muscle aches.

Cause   Most colds are caused by a viral **infection**, primarily rhinoviruses and coronoviruses. They spread rapidly and have a short incubation stage of one to two days.

Management   Because colds are highly contagious during the first day or two, it is best to exclude children from group-care settings. Rest, and increased intake of liquids (water, fruit juices, soups) are recommended. Nonaspirin, fever-reducing medication can be provided by the child's family and is usually adequate for treating most colds. Antibiotics are not effective against most viruses and are therefore of limited value for treating simple colds. However, a physician may prescribe antibiotics to treat complications or secondary infections that may develop.

Some children who have special needs, such as Down syndrome, leukemia, or allergies, may exhibit chronic cold-like symptoms including runny nose and a productive cough. It isn't necessary to exclude these children from school unless they develop signs of an acute infection, such as fever, red throat, white patches on their tonsils, extreme fatigue, or body aches.

Although colds themselves are not serious, complications can sometimes develop. Toddlers and preschool-aged children are often more susceptible to these complications such as earaches, bronchitis, croup, and pneumonia. Children should be observed closely and their physician contacted if any complications develop or the child does not improve within four to five days. Families should also be advised to seek immediate medical attention for children who develop white spots in their throats or on tonsils in order to rule out the possibility of strep throat.

Diaper Rash

Diaper rash is an irritation of the skin in and around the buttocks and genital area. Babies with sensitive skin are more likely to experience periodic outbreaks. Diaper rash also occurs more often in infants who are formula-fed versus breastfed (Hockenberry, 2004).

FIGURE 7–3

Children typically experience many colds during the year.

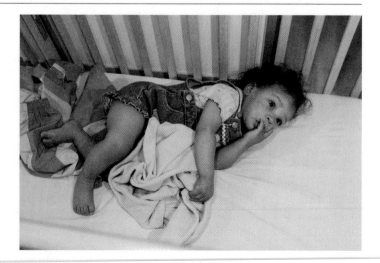

---

infection – *a condition that results when a pathogen invades and establishes itself within a susceptible host.*

Cause Prolonged contact with ammonia in urine and organic acids in stools can burn baby's skin, causing patches of red, raised areas or tiny pimples. Open, weeping areas may develop if the rash is severe, leaving irritated skin open to infection from yeast or bacteria. Reactions to fabric softeners, soaps, lotions, powders, and certain brands of disposable diapers may also cause diaper rash in some infants and toddlers. Antibiotic therapy and food changes can also trigger diaper rash.

Management Prompt changing of wet and/or soiled diapers followed by a thorough cleansing of the skin is often sufficient to prevent and treat diaper rash. Avoid using baby powders and talcs because babies are apt to inhale the fine powder (*Child Health Alert*, 1991). Also, when combined with urine, powders become good media for bacterial growth. A thin layer of petroleum jelly or zinc oxide ointment can be applied to help protect irritated areas. Allowing the infant to go without diapers (when at home) and exposing irritated skin to the air may also help speed the healing process. If the diaper rash does not improve in two or three days parents should be encouraged to contact their physician.

Diarrhea

The term diarrhea refers to frequent watery or very soft bowel movements. They may be foul-smelling and also contain particles of blood or mucus. It is not uncommon for young children to experience several episodes of diarrhea during the course of a year.

Cause Diarrhea can either be infectious or noninfectious. Infectious forms of diarrhea include:

- viral or bacterial infections, such as rotavirus, hepatitis A, or salmonellosis
- parasitic, such as giardia

Causes of noninfectious diarrhea can include:

- fruit juices containing sorbital, especially apple and pear (*Child Health Alert*, 2002)
- antibiotic therapy
- recent dietary changes
- food allergies, such as lactose intolerance
- food poisoning
- illnesses, such as earaches, colds, strep throat, or cystic fibrosis

Approximately 55,000 children are hospitalized each year as a result of diarrhea caused by rotavirus. Infants and children under age three are the most common victims of this illness. New vaccines are being developed and tested and will likely be recommended for children in group care settings (CDC, 2006b).

Frequent or prolonged diarrhea can result in **dehydration**, especially in infants and toddlers. Dehydration involves a loss of body water and can occur quickly in young children because of their small body size. Excessive dehydration can be fatal. For this reason, it is critical that teachers observe infants and young children carefully for signs of dehydration:

- dryness of the mouth
- **listlessness**
- sunken eyes
- absence of tears
- decreased or no urinary output
- rapid, weak pulse
- skin loses elasticity; doughlike

---

dehydration – *a state in which there is an excessive loss of body fluids or extremely limited fluid intake. Symptoms may include loss of skin tone, sunken eyes, and mental confusion.*
listlessness – *a state characterized by a lack of energy and/or interest in one's affairs.*

ISSUES TO CONSIDER • Implications of SARS for Children and Adults

Recent events have drawn attention to the fact that communicable illnesses of epidemic proportions are not a thing of the past. The frequency and relative ease of modern travel and dense living arrangements make it easy for a disease to spread quickly, often before its victims are even aware of exposure. Children adopted from foreign countries, for example, could potentially introduce infectious illnesses, such as SARS (severe acute respiratory syndrome) and avian flu, into the U.S. (Staat & Klepser, 2006). Scientists are working to better understand SARS, how to contain its spread, and how to treat its victims (Meissner, 2005; Lawrence, 2003; Poutanen, Low, & Henry, 2003). The appearance of SARS in many parts of the world has raised additional concerns about other new strains of viruses and bacteria that could possibly create a pandemic and threaten world health. Practicing basic sanitation measures, such as frequent handwashing, disinfection of surfaces, and improvement of personal health, affords protection against many communicable illnesses. Knowledge can also be a powerful tool for understanding these illnesses and developing appropriate preventive strategies. A wealth of information about SARS is available on many Web sites. (http://www.cdc.gov/ncidod/sars; http://www.who.int/csr/sars/en; http://www.phac-aspc.gc.ca/sars-sras/sars.html; http://www.caringforkids.cps.ca/whensick/SARSdetailed.htm). Conduct a search before considering these questions:

- What is SARS? What are its symptoms? How does it spread?
- What factors would place the children in your program at risk for exposure to SARS?
- What community resources are available to help you learn more about this disease?
- What precautionary practices would be helpful for your program to implement?
- Is SARS a reportable disease?

Management   It is important to monitor and record the frequency (number) and amount (small, large) of bowel movements. The color, consistency, and presence of any blood, mucus, or pus should also be noted. Be sure to check the child's temperature and observe for any signs of discomfort. Prompt medical advice should be sought if diarrhea is severe or prolonged, or the child becomes lethargic or drowsy. Special care should always be taken to practice meticulous handwashing by teachers and children.

Most cases of diarrhea can be treated by temporarily replacing solid foods in the child's diet with a commercially prepared electrolyte solution. This solution replaces important fluids and salts lost through the diarrhea. Liquids and soft foods can gradually be added to the diet once diarrhea has stopped. Any complaint of pain that is continuous or located in the lower right side of the **abdomen** should be reported promptly to the child's family and checked by a physician.

Children who have experienced diarrhea during the past 24 hours should be excluded from group-care settings. Exceptions to this policy would include children whose diarrhea resulted from noncontagious conditions such as food allergies, changes in diet, or recent treatment with antibiotics. However, even these children may not feel well enough to attend school or group care and participate in the day's activities. The problem and inconvenience of frequent accidental soiling may also be too time-consuming for teachers to manage.

Diarrhea lasting longer than a week should be cause for concern, especially if it is accompanied by bloating, change of appetite, or weight loss. The child should be excluded from group

---

abdomen – *the portion of the body located between the diaphragm (located at the base of the lungs) and the pelvic or hip bones.*

settings until a cause is determined, and conditions such as giardia, dysentery, or hepatitis A have been ruled out.

Dizziness

It is not unusual for children to complain of momentary dizziness or a spinning sensation after vigorous play. However, repeated complaints of dizziness should be noted and reported to the child's family. They should be advised to contact the child's physician to investigate a possible underlying cause.

Cause Dizziness can be a symptom of other health conditions, including:

- ear infections
- fever
- headaches
- head injuries
- anemia
- nasal congestion and sinus infections
- brain tumor (rare)

Management Temporary episodes of dizziness usually respond to simple first aid measures. Have the child lie down quietly or sit with head resting on or between the knees until the sensation has passed. Quiet play can be resumed when the child no longer feels dizzy. Inform parents of this experience so they can continue to monitor the child at home.

If dizziness is accompanied by any loss of balance or coordination, parents should be encouraged to check with the child's physician at once. Dizziness that results from an underlying health problem will usually not respond to most first aid measures.

Earaches

Earaches and ear infections are frequently a problem during the first three or so years of a child's life, affecting boys more often than girls (Bradley, 2003). More than half of all infants, especially those who are formula-fed versus breastfed, experience an ear infection before their first birthday (Bernius & Perlin, 2006; Smith, et al., 2006). However, by age five, children usually begin experiencing fewer ear infections as structures in the ear, nose, and throat mature (lengthen) and resistance to infection (antibody formation) improves (Figure 7–4). Children of Native American and Eskimo descent appear to experience a higher rate of ear infections, possibly related to structural differences in the ear (Curns, et al., 2002). Exposure to second-hand smoke has also been suggested as a contributing factor. Studies have also shown that children in group care tend to have a higher incidence ear infections and of otitis media than those who stay at home (Zeisel, et al., 2002).

REFLECTIVE THOUGHTS

Sometimes families knowingly or unknowingly bring sick children to school or child care. Examine your feelings about being exposed to children's communicable illnesses. Do you feel differently depending on the illness? What steps can teachers take to improve their resistance to communicable illness? How would you respond to families who repeatedly ignore a program's exclusion policies? How might cultural differences influence what parents view as illness? What could you do to help families understand and respect a program's policies?

Cause A number of conditions can cause earache in children, including:

- upper respiratory infections, such as a cold
- allergies
- dental cavities and eruption of new teeth
- excessive ear wax
- foreign objects, e.g., plastic beads, food, small toy pieces, stones
- bacterial infections, such as "swimmer's ear," otitis media
- feeding infants in a reclining position

Earaches caused by an acute bacterial infection of the middle ear are known as *otitis media*. Children who have some forms of developmental disabilities, such as Williams syndrome, Down syndrome, fragile X, autism, and cleft palate are at higher risk for developing this condition (Little, 2004). Otitis media causes an inflammation of the eustachian tube (passageway connecting the ear, nose, and throat), which can lead to a backup of fluid in the middle ear and resulting pain, fever, and temporary or chronic hearing loss (Bernius & Perlin, 2006). Often, only one ear will be affected at a time, and the infection may or may not be accompanied by fluid accumulation behind the eardrum. New research findings suggest that placing infants on their backs to sleep is also effective in decreasing the incidence of ear infection (Hunt, et al., 2003). Children, especially infants and toddlers with limited language, should be observed carefully for signs of a possible ear infection, including:

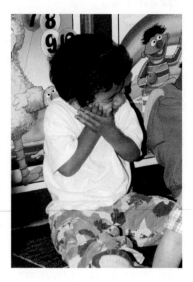

FIGURE 7–4

The frequency of ear infections decreases as children get older.

- nausea, vomiting, and/or diarrhea
- tugging or rubbing of the affected ear
- refusal to eat or swallow
- redness of the outer ear
- fever
- dizziness
- irritability
- discharge from the ear canal
- difficulty hearing
- crying when placed in a reclining position
- difficulty sleeping

Management Children who develop otitis media do not need to be excluded from group settings unless they are too ill to participate in daily activities or have other symptoms that are contagious. Teachers may be able to provide temporary relief from earache pain by having the child lie down with the affected ear on a soft blanket; the warmth helps soothe discomfort. A small, dry cotton ball placed in the outer ear may also help reduce pain by keeping air out of the ear canal. Excess wax and foreign objects should only be removed by a physician.

A child's complaints of persistent ear pain or earache should be checked by the child's health care provider if symptoms last longer than two or three days. In most cases the fluid will clear up without any further treatment. However, chronic otitis media with fluid can interfere with children's speech and language development and may therefore require medical treatment (Gravel, et al., 2006; Vernon-Feagons & Manlove, 2005).

Physicians now use several approaches to treat acute bacterial ear infections (Bauchner, et al., 2006). Current guidelines recommend taking a wait-and-see approach and limiting the use of antibiotics to reduce drug resistance. If children are placed on oral antibiotics, it is important that all medication be taken; failure to finish medication can result in a recurrence of the infection. When all medication is finished, children should be re-checked by a physician to make certain the infection is gone. In some cases, additional medication may be needed. Surgical insertion of small plastic tubes into the eardrum is sometimes recommended for children with repeated infections and chronic fluid buildup to lessen the risk of permanent hearing loss (Mui, et al., 2005). Teachers should be alert to any children with tubes in their ears. Special precautions must be taken to avoid getting water in the outer ear canal during activities that involve water play, such as swimming, bathing, or playing in pools or sprinklers. Ear plugs or a special plastic putty are commonly used for this purpose.

Fainting

Fainting, a momentary loss of consciousness, occurs when blood supply to the brain is temporarily reduced.

Cause Possible causes for this condition in young children include:

- anemia
- breathholding
- **hyperventilation**
- extreme stress, excitement, or hysteria
- drug reactions
- illness, infection, or extreme pain
- poisoning

Management Children may initially complain of feeling dizzy or weak. Their skin may appear pale, cool, and moist, and the child may collapse. If this occurs, lie the child down, elevate the legs 8 to 10 inches on a pillow or similar object, and observe breathing and pulse frequently. A light blanket can be placed over the child for extra warmth. Breathing is made easier if clothing is loosened from around the neck and waist. No attempt should be made to give the child anything to eat or drink until consciousness is regained. Parents should be notified and encouraged to consult with the child's physician.

Fever

Activity, age, eating, sleeping, and the time of day cause normal fluctuations in children's temperatures. However, a persistent elevated **temperature** is usually an indication of illness or infection, especially if the child complains of other discomforts such as headache, coughing, nausea, or sore throat (Aronson, 2000).

Cause Common causes of fever in children include:

- viral and bacterial illnesses, such as ear, skin, and upper respiratory infections
- urinary tract infections
- heat stroke and overheating

Changes in children's appearance and behavior may be an early indication of **fever**. Other indications may include:

- flushed or reddened face
- listlessness or desire to sleep
- loss of appetite
- complaints of not feeling well

hyperventilation – *rapid breathing often with forced inhalation; can lead to sensations of dizziness, lightheadedness, and weakness.*
temperature – *a measurement of body heat; varies with the time of day, activity, and method of measurement.*
fever – *an elevation of body temperature above normal; a temperature over 99.4°F or 37.4°C orally is usually considered a fever.*

- skin that is dry and warm to the touch
- "glassy" eyes

- chills
- warm, dry skin; older children may have increased perspiration

Management   Children's temperature should be checked if there is reason to believe that they may have a fever. Only digital and infrared **tympanic** thermometers are recommended for use in group-care settings because of safety and liability concerns (Table 7–3). These thermometers are quick and efficient to use, especially with children who may be fussy or uncooperative, and provide readings that are reasonably accurate (Table 7–4) (Craig, et al., 2002; Sganga, et al., 2000). Infrared forehead thermometers are currently being marketed but studies have shown them to be inaccurate. Glass mercury thermometers are considered unsafe to use with young children and also pose environmental concerns (Hoffman, Boyd, Briere, Loos, & Norton, 1999).

Children with an axillary temperature over 99.1°F (37.4°C) or a tympanic reading over 100.4°F (38°C) should be observed carefully for other symptoms of illness. Unless a program's exclusion policies require children with fevers to be sent home, they can be moved to a separate room or quiet area in the classroom and monitored. If there are no immediate indications of acute illness, children should be encouraged to rest. Lowering the room temperature, removing warm clothing, and offering extra fluids can also help make a child feel more comfortable. Fever-reducing medications should only be administered with a physician's approval. Families should also be notified so they can decide whether to take the child home or wait to see if anything further develops.

Headaches

Headaches are not a common complaint of young children. However, when they do occur, headaches are usually a symptom of some other condition. Repeated episodes of headache should be brought to families' attention.

Cause   Children may experience headaches as the result of several conditions, including:

- bacterial or viral infections
- allergies
- head injuries
- emotional tension or stress
- reaction to medication
- lead poisoning

- hunger
- eye strain
- nasal congestion
- brain tumor (rare)
- constipation
- carbon monoxide poisoning

TABLE 7–3	Preferred Methods for Checking Children's Temperature in Group Settings (in Rank Order)	
infants and toddlers	axillary
2–5 year olds	tympanic axillary oral
5 years and older	oral tympanic axillary

---

tympanic – *referring to the ear canal.*

TABLE 7-4 Comparison of Thermometer Options

Type	Advantages	Disadvantages	Normal Range	How to Use	How to Clean
Digital thermometer	Can be used to check oral and axillary temperatures Safe, unbreakable Numbers are easy to read Beeps when ready Easy to clean	Takes 1–2 minutes to obtain a reading Requires child to sit still Axillary readings are less accurate than oral Must purchase batteries and disposable covers	(Axillary) 94.5°–99.0° F (34.7°–37.2° C) (Oral) 94.5°–99.5° F (34.7°–37.3° C)	Turn switch on; wait for beep to signal ready Apply disposable sanitary cover (optional) Place under tongue (oral) or increase of armpit; hold in place; wait for beep to signal reading	Remove disposable cover. Wipe with alcohol or clean with soap and cool water.
Tympanic thermometer	Yields a quick reading Easy to use Can check child's temperature while asleep Requires limited child cooperation	Thermometer is expensive to buy (approximately $40–60) Accuracy of reading depends on correct positioning in child's ear canal (differs from child to child) Must purchase batteries and disposable ear piece coverings	96.4°–100.4° F (35.8°–38° C)	Apply disposable earpiece Turn on start button Insert probe carefully into ear canal opening; reading appears in seconds	Wipe instrument (probe) with alcohol.

Management   In the absence of any fever, rash, vomiting or **disorientation**, children who experience headaches can remain in care but should continue to be observed for other indications of illness or injury. Frequently, their headaches will disappear with rest. Patterns of repeated or intense headaches should be noted and families encouraged to discuss the problem with the child's physician.

Heat Rash

Heat rash is most commonly seen in infants and toddlers.

Cause   Heat rash is caused by a blockage in the sweat glands. It occurs primarily during the summer months, although it can occur at any other time when an infant or child is dressed too warmly. Clothing made of synthetic fabrics and overdressing can also encourage the development of heat rash, especially in young children with sensitive skin.

Management   Heat rash is not contagious. However, there are several measures that can be taken to make a child more comfortable. Affected areas can be washed with cool water, dried thoroughly, and dusted sparingly with cornstarch.

Lyme Disease

Lyme disease is a tick-borne infection most prevalent along the East Coast, although it has been identified in nearly every U.S. state and many provinces of Canada (Abbott, 2006). The number of cases continues to increase. There were over 23,300 cases reported in 2005, with children ages birth to 14 being the most common victims (CDC, 2005).

Cause   This bacterial illness is caused by the bite of a tiny, infected deer tick; however, not all deer ticks are infected, nor will everyone who is bitten develop Lyme disease. Many species of the deer tick are commonly found in grassy and wooded areas during the summer and fall months.

Management   The most effective way to prevent Lyme disease is to take preventive measures whenever children will be spending time outdoors, especially in grassy or wooded areas (Table 7–5).
Because deer ticks are exceptionally small, they are easily overlooked. Development of any unusual symptoms following a tick bite should be reported immediately to a physician. Early symptoms of Lyme disease are often confused with other illnesses and are therefore difficult to diagnose. In the early weeks following a bite, a small red, flat, or raised area may develop at the site, followed by a localized rash that gradually disappears. Flu-like symptoms, including fever, chills, fatigue, headache, and joint pain may also be experienced during this stage. If the bacterial infection is not diagnosed early and treated with antibiotics, complications, including arthritis, heart, and/or neurological problems can develop within two years of the initial bite. A blood test is available for early detection.

Sore Throat

Sore throats are a fairly common complaint among young children, especially during the fall and winter seasons. Teachers must often rely on their observations to determine when infants and toddlers may be experiencing a sore throat because children of this age are unlikely to verbalize their discomfort. Fussiness, lack of interest in food or refusal to eat, difficulty swallowing, enlarged lymph glands, fever, and fatigue may be early indications that the child is not feeling well.

---

disorientation – *lack of awareness or ability to recognize familiar persons or objects.*
Lyme disease – *bacterial illness caused by the bite of infected deer ticks found in grassy or wooded areas.*

TABLE 7-5 Measures to Prevent Tick Bites

- Encourage children to wear long pants, a long-sleeved shirt, socks, shoes, and a hat; light-colored clothing makes it easier to spot small deer ticks.
- Apply insect/tick repellent containing DEET to clothing and exposed areas of the skin (Eppes, 2003; Gayle & Ringdahl, 2001). Be sure to follow manufacturer's directions and avoid aerosol sprays that children might inhale.
- Discourage children from rolling in the grass or sitting on fallen logs.
- Remove clothing as soon as children come indoors and check all areas of the body (under arms, around waist, behind knees, in the groin, on neck) and hair.
- Bathe or shower to remove any ticks.
- Wash clothing in soapy water and dry in dryer (heat will destroy ticks).
- Continue to check children for any sign of ticks that may have been overlooked on a previous inspection.
- Promptly remove any tick discovered on the skin and wash the area carefully.

Cause Most sore throats are caused by a viral or bacterial infection. Some children may also experience a scratchy throat as the result of sinus drainage, mouth breathing, or allergies.

Management It is extremely important not to ignore a child's complaint of sore throat. A small percentage of sore throats are caused by a highly contagious streptococcal infection (Table 7–1). Although most children are quite ill with these infections, some may experience only mild symptoms, such as headache or stomachache and fever, or none at all. Unknowingly, they may become carriers of the infection and capable of spreading it to others. A routine throat culture will determine if a strep infection is present and which antibiotic will provide the most effective treatment. If left untreated, strep throat can lead to serious complications, including rheumatic fever, heart valve damage, and kidney disease (Hockenberry, 2004).

Sore throats resulting from viral infections are not usually harmful, but they can cause the child considerable discomfort. Antibiotics are not effective against most viral infections and, therefore, seldom prescribed.

Stomachaches

Most children experience an occasional stomachache from time to time. However, children may use this term to describe a range of discomforts, from hunger or a full bladder to actual nausea, cramping, or emotional upset. Teachers can use their observation and questioning skills in an effort to determine a probable cause.

Cause Children's stomachaches are often a symptom of some other condition. There are many possible causes, including:

- food allergies or intolerance
- appendicitis
- **intestinal** infections, e.g., giardiasis, salmonella, E. Coli
- urinary tract infections
- gas or constipation
- side effect to medication, especially antibiotics
- change in diet

---

intestinal – *pertaining to the intestinal tract or bowel.*

- emotional stress or desire for attention
- hunger
- diarrhea and/or vomiting
- strep throat

Management   There are several ways to determine whether or not a child's stomach pain is serious. Is the discomfort continuous or a cramping-type pain that comes and goes? Does the child have a fever? Is the child able to continue playing? If no fever is present, the stomachache is probably not serious. Encourage the child to use the bathroom and see if **urination** or having a bowel movement relieves the pain. Have the child rest quietly to see if the discomfort goes away. Check with families to determine if the child is taking any new medication or has had a change of diet. Stomach pain or stomachaches should be considered serious if they:

- disrupt a child's activity, e.g., running, playing, eating, sleeping
- cause tenderness of the abdomen
- are accompanied by diarrhea, vomiting, or severe cramping
- last longer than three to four hours
- result in stools that are bloody or contain mucus

If any of these conditions occur while the child is attending school or group care, families should be notified and advised to seek prompt medical attention for the child.

Teething

Teething is a natural process. Infants usually begin getting their first teeth around four to seven months of age. Older children will begin the process of losing and replacing their baby teeth with a permanent set about the time they reach their fifth or sixth birthday.

Cause   New teeth erupting through gum tissue can cause some children mild discomfort. However, most children move through this stage with relatively few problems.

Management   An increase in drooling and chewing activity for several days or weeks may be the only indication that an infant is teething. Some babies become a bit more fussy, run a low-grade fever (under 100°F), and may not be interested in eating. However, high fevers, diarrhea, and vomiting are usually not caused by teething, but may be an indication of illness. Chilled teething rings and firm objects for children to chew often provide comfort and relief to swollen gums.

Toothache

Toothache should not be a complaint of young children. Oral health problems can cause pain and suffering, interfere with speech and language development, make eating difficult, affect school performance and result in early tooth loss. Children should not have to forgo necessary treatment of dental problems because of limited family income (Vargas & Ronzio, 2006; Community Voices: HealthCare Underserved, 2001). Low-cost insurance (SCHIP), Medicaid, and community resources, such as clinics and dental schools, are often available to help children and families obtain essential dental care (Duderstadt, et al., 2006).

---

urination – *the act of emptying the bladder of urine.*

Teething may cause infants and toddlers some temporary discomfort. Older children may experience similar discomfort when they begin losing their baby teeth and permanent teeth erupt.

Cause Although tooth decay is the most common cause of toothache, gum disease and injury can also be painful. Children may complain of a throbbing discomfort that sometimes radiates into the ear. Redness and swelling may be observed around the gumline of the affected tooth. Foods that are hot or very sweet may intensify pain.

Management Complaints of toothache should be checked promptly by the child's dentist. In the meantime, an icepack applied to the cheek on the affected side may make the child feel more comfortable. Aspirin-free products can also be administered by the child's family for pain relief. However, prevention, including proper brushing after eating, is always the preferred approach for limiting tooth decay (Figure 7–5).

Vomiting

Vomiting can be a frightening and unpleasant experience for children. True vomiting is different from a baby who simply spits up after eating. Vomiting is a symptom often associated with an acute illness or other health problem (Hockenberry, 2004).

Cause A number of conditions can cause children to vomit, including:

- emotional upset
- viral or bacterial infection, e.g., stomach flu, strep throat
- drug reactions
- ear infections
- meningitis
- **salmonellosis**
- indigestion
- severe coughing
- head injury
- poisoning

FIGURE 7–5

Brushing teeth after eating helps to promote good oral health.

---

salmonellosis – *a bacterial infection that is spread through contaminated drinking water, food or milk, or contact with other infected persons. Symptoms include diarrhea, fever, nausea, and vomiting.*

Management The frequency, amount, and composition of vomited material is important to observe and record. Dehydration and disturbances of the body's chemical balance can occur with prolonged or excessive vomiting, especially in infants and toddlers. Children should be observed carefully for:

- high fever
- abdominal pain
- signs of dehydration
- headache

- excessive drowsiness
- difficulty breathing
- sore throat
- exhaustion

Children who continue to vomit and show signs of a sore throat, fever, or stomach pains should be sent home as soon as possible. The teacher should also advise the child's family to contact their physician for further advice.

In the absence of any other symptoms, a single episode of vomiting may simply be due to an emotional upset, dislike of a particular food, excess mucus, or reaction to medication. Usually the child feels better immediately after vomiting. These children can remain at the school and be encouraged to rest until they feel better.

In addition to not feeling well, some children are upset by the act of vomiting itself. Extra reassurance and comforting can help make the experience less traumatic. Infants should be positioned on their stomachs, with their hips and legs slightly raised to allow vomited material to flow out of the mouth and prevent choking. Older children should also be watched closely so they don't choke or inhale vomitus.

West Nile Virus

Humans have long considered mosquitoes to simply be an annoying insect that buzzes in your ear, feasts on exposed skin, and leaves an itchy raised welt as their calling card. However, the Centers for Disease Control and Protection (CDC) reported 4200 West Nile virus cases in the United States during 2006 (CDC, 2007); a total of 305 cases were reported in Canada for the same period (Public Health Agency of Canada, 2007).

A majority of persons infected with the West Nile virus will have no symptoms of the illness. Some people will experience mild flu-like symptoms while a small percent will develop symptoms that are more serious, such as high fever, muscle weakness, rash, stiff neck, tremors, disorientation, coma, and even death. Young children and the elderly are at the greatest risk for becoming ill from West Nile virus.

Cause West Nile virus is caused by the bite of an infected mosquito. The incidence is highest during the summer and fall seasons. There have also been limited reports of transmission via blood transfusion and the breast milk of an infected mother.

Management Prevention is the most important and effective strategy for avoiding this infectious illness. Eliminating any standing water found in flower pots, water fountains, bird baths, buckets, tire swings, small pools, and similar sources removes mosquito breeding sites. A number of products containing natural chemicals and bacteria are available to spray or use in ponds that cannot be drained. Additional precautionary measures include applying mosquito repellents containing DEET whenever going outdoors, wearing protective clothing (long sleeves, long pants), staying indoors during early morning and evening hours when mosquitoes are at their peak activity, and making sure that screen doors and windows are in good repair. In most cases, persons with mild symptoms will recover without medical treatment. However, prompt medical attention should be sought for prolonged illness or if any serious symptoms develop.

FOCUS ON FAMILIES • When to Call the Doctor

Frequent bouts of illness are not uncommon among young children. With time, their bodies mature, they begin to build up resistance (immunity) to many illnesses, and their immunizations will have been completed. In the meantime, families often face the difficult task of deciding at what point their child is sick enough to warrant a call to the doctor. While each child's symptoms and needs are different, there are guidelines that may be helpful in making this decision. Call the physician if your child:

- Experiences serious injury, bleeding that cannot be stopped, or excessive or prolonged pain.
- Is less than one month old and develops a fever, or is between one and three months of age and has a rectal temperature over 100.4°F.
- Has difficult, rapid, or noisy breathing.
- Experiences any loss of consciousness, including a seizure.
- Complains of unusual pain in an arm or leg. X-rays may be necessary to rule out a fracture.
- Has repeated episodes of vomiting or diarrhea and is unable to keep down liquids. Symptoms of dehydration include urination fewer than three times per day, dry lips or tongue, headache, lack of tears, excessive drowsiness, and sunken fontanel (soft spot) in infants. Young children can become dehydrated quickly.
- Develops an unusual skin rash, especially one that spreads.
- Has blood in his/her vomit, urine, or stool.
- Suffers an eye injury or develops an eye discharge. Children who have sustained an eye injury should always be seen by a physician.
- Develops stomach pain that is prolonged or interferes with appetite or activity.
- Becomes excessively sleepy and difficult to arouse.

Finally, rely on your intuition. Don't hesitate to call the doctor if you are unsure about the symptoms your child may be experiencing. Most physicians would rather be notified of a child's condition than to be called only when there is a crisis.

CASE STUDY

The teacher noticed that Kati seemed quite restless today and was having difficulty concentrating on any task that she started. She continuously squirmed, whether in her chair or sitting on the floor. On a number of occasions the teacher also observed Kati tugging at her underwear and scratching her bottom. She recalled that Kati's mother had mentioned something about getting her younger brother tested for pinworms and wondered if this might be what she was observing.

1. What action should the teacher take in this situation?
2. What control measures should be implemented? At school? At home?
3. When can Kati return to school?
4. If Kati does have pinworms, for what length of time must the teacher carefully observe the other children for similar problems?
5. What special personal health measures should be emphasized with the other children?

CLASSROOM CORNER • Teacher Activities

Move, Move, Move...

Concept: It is important to exercise to stay healthy. (Pre-2)

Learning Objectives

- Children will learn the importance of moving to stay healthy.
- Children will practice crawling, jumping, throwing, balancing, waving, and rolling.

Supplies

- gymnastic mat or a thick blanket
- balance beam
- plastic hoops or circle shapes made out of string
- tunnel or a classroom rectangular table
- bean bags or small balls
- ribbons or tissue paper strips taped together

Learning Activities

- Read and discuss one of the following books:
  - *From Head to Toe* by Nancy Eric Carle
  - *The Berenstain Bears and Too Much TV* by Stan and Jan Berenstain
- Ask the children if they know why it is important to exercise to stay healthy. Talk about different things they can do for exercise (run, ride bikes, go for a walk, play football, etc).
- Set up an obstacle course indoors or outdoors (depending on the weather). Demonstrate what movement they should do at each station (walk across a balance beam; wave ribbons quickly).
- Have children go through each obstacle several times; assist as necessary.
- Talk about which movement activities they enjoyed doing the most.

Evaluation

- Children will participate in a variety of physical activities.
- Teachers will observe children's skill levels and look for signs of possible developmental delays.

SUMMARY

- Illness is common among young children in schools and group settings.
- Teachers can help control the spread of illnesses through:
  - careful observation and early identification of sick children.
  - implementation of exclusion policies.
  - thorough handwashing.
  - environmental sanitation.
- Teachers should familiarize themselves with the causes and management strategies for common childhood illnesses and health problems.

APPLICATION ACTIVITIES

1. With a partner, practice taking each other's axillary, oral, and tympanic temperatures. Follow steps for correct cleaning of the thermometer between each use.

2. Divide the class into groups of five to six students. Discuss how each member feels about caring for children who are ill. Could they hold or cuddle a child with a high fever or diarrhea? What are their feelings about being exposed to children's contagious illnesses? How might they react if an infant just vomited on their new sweater? If they feel uncomfortable around sick children, what steps could they take to better cope with the situation?

3. Select another student as a partner and observe that person carefully for 20 seconds. Now look away. Write down everything you can remember about this person, such as eye color, hair color, scars or moles, approximate weight, height, color of skin, shape of teeth, clothing, etc. What can you do to improve your observational skills?

4. Conduct an Internet search to learn more about avian (bird flu). What is it? What steps are being taken at the national level to prevent it? What is your community doing?

CHAPTER REVIEW

A. **By Yourself:**

1. Define each of the *Terms to Know* listed at the beginning of this chapter.

2. Match each of the following signs/symptoms in column I with the correct communicable illness in column II.

Column I	Column II
1. swelling and redness of white portion of the eye	a. chickenpox
2. frequent itching of the scalp	b. strep throat
3. flat, oval-shaped lesions on the scalp, skin; infected nails become discolored, brittle, chalky, or they may disintegrate	c. head lice d. shigellosis e. conjunctivitis
4. high fever; red, sore throat	f. ringworm
5. mild fever and rash that lasts approximately three days	g. German measles
6. irritability and itching of the rectal area	h. scabies
7. red rash with blister-like heads; cold-like symptoms	i. pinworms
8. sudden onset of fever; swelling of salivary glands	j. mumps
9. burrows or linear tunnels under the skin; intense itching	
10. vomiting, abdominal pain, diarrhea that may be bloody	

B. **As a Group:**

1. Discuss what a teacher should do in each of the following situations:
   a. You have just finished serving lunch to the children, when Mara begins to vomit.
   b. The class is involved in a game of keep-away. Ted suddenly complains of feeling dizzy.
   c. During check-in, a parent mentions that his son has been experiencing stomachaches every morning before coming to school.
   d. Leandra wakes up from her afternoon nap, crying because her ear hurts.
   e. You have just changed a toddler's diaper for the third time in the last hour because of diarrhea.

f. Sami enters the classroom, sneezing and blowing his nose.

g. While you are helping Erin put on her coat to go outdoors, you notice that her skin feels very warm.

h. Richard refuses to eat his lunch because it makes his teeth hurt.

i. While you are cleaning up the blocks, Tommy tells you that his throat is sore and it hurts to swallow.

j. You have just taken Juanita's temperature (orally) and it is 102°F.

2. The concepts of illness and pain are often viewed differently by various cultural groups. Select two or three predominant cultures and research their beliefs about illness and pain. How might these differences in cultural values and beliefs influence your response in each of the situations described in Question #1?

REFERENCES

Abbott, A. (2006). Lyme disease: Uphill struggle. *Nature, 439*(7076), 524–525.

AIDS InfoNet. (2006). Children and HIV. Accessed on October 20, 2006, from http://www.thebody.com/nmai/pdfs/children.pdf.

American Academy of Pediatrics (AAP) (2006a). A child care provider's guide to safe sleep. Accessed October 20, 2006, from http://www.healthychildcare.org/pdf/SIDSchildcaresafesleep.pdf.

AAP. (2006b). A parent's guide to safe sleep. Accessed October 20, 2006, from http://www.healthychildcare.org/pdf/SIDSparentsafesleep.pdf.

AAP. (2004). *Managing infectious disease in child care and schools.* S. Aronson and T. Shope (Eds.). Elk Grove Village, IL: AAP.

Aronson, S. (2003. Sept./Oct.). Sudden infant death syndrome. *Child Care Information Exchange, 153*, 67.

Aronson, S. (2000, November). Exclusion of children with fevers from child care. *Child Care Information Exchange*, 88–89.

Bauchner, H., Marchant, C., Bisbee, A., Heeren, T., Wang, B., McCabe, M., & Pelton, S. (2006). Effectiveness of Centers for Disease Control and Prevention recommendations for outcomes of acute otitis media. *Pediatrics, 117*(4), 10009–1017.

Bernius, M., & Perlin, D. (2006). Pediatric ear, nose, and throat emergencies. *Pediatric Clinics of North America, 53*(2), 195–214.

Black, S. (1999). HIV-AIDS in early childhood centers. The ethical dilemma of confidentiality versus disclosure. *Young Children, 54*(2), 39–45.

Blumenreich, M. (2003). Confidentiality, equity, and silence: A critical look at school policy for HIV positive children. *Equity & Excellence in Education, 36*(1), 64–70.

Bradley, R. H. (2003). Child care and common communicable illnesses in children aged 37 to 54 months. *Archives of Pediatric & Adolescent Medicine, 157*(2), 196–200.

CDC. (2007). *2006 West Nile virus activity in the United States.* Accessed on April 24, 2007, from http://www.cdc.gov/ncidod/dvbid/westnile/surv&controlCaseCount06_detailed.htm.

CDC. (2006a). Revised recommendations for HIV testing of adults, adolescents, and pregnant women in healthcare settings. Accessed on October 20, 2006, from http://www.cdc.gov/hiv/topics/testing/resources/qa/print/qa_general-public.htm.

CDC. (2006b). National Center for Infectious Diseases. Accessed October 25, 2006, from http://www.cdc.gov/ncidod/dvrd/revb/gastro/rotavirus.htm.

CDC. (2005). Reported cases of Lyme disease by year, United States, 1991–2005. Accessed on October 25, 2006, from http://www.cdc.gov/ncidod/dvbid/lyme/ld_UpClimbLymeDis.htm.

CDC. (2004). *HIV/AIDS surveillance report.* Washington, DC: Centers for Disease Control and Prevention (CDC). Accessed on October 20, 2006, from http://www.cdc.gov/hiv/topics/surveillance/resources/reports/index.htm.

Child Health Alert. (2002, June). Can fruit juices cause irritable bowel syndrome? *Child Health Alert, 20*, 1.

Child Health Alert. (1991, June). Persistent hazards to young children: Inhalation of baby powder. *Child Health Alert, 20*, 1.

Community Voices: HealthCare for the Underserved. (2001). *Poor oral health is no laughing matter.* Washington, DC.

Craig, J., Lancaster, G., Taylor, S., Williamson, P., & Smyth, R. (2002). Infrared ear thermometry compared with rectal thermometry in children: A systematic review. *Lancet, 24*(360), 603–609.

Curns, A. T., Holman, R. C., Shay, D. K., Cheek, J. E., Kaufman, S. F., Singleton, R. J., & Anderson L. J. (2002). Outpatient and hospital visits associated with otitis media among American Indian and Alaska native children younger than 5 years. *Pediatrics, 109*(3), E41–1.

Di Noia, J., Schinke, S., Pena, J., & Schwinn, T. (2004). Evaluation of a brief computer-mediated intervention to reduce HIV risk among early adolescent females. *Journal of Adolescent Health, 35*(1), 62–64.

Duderstadt. K., Hughes, D., Soobader, M., & Newacheck, P. (2006). The impact of public insurance expansions on children's access and use of care. *Pediatrics, 118*(4), 1676–1682.

Eppes, S. (2003). Diagnosis, treatment, and prevention of lyme disease in children. *Pediatric Drugs, 5*(6), 363–372.

First Candle/SIDS Alliance. (2004). Immunizations and SIDS. Accessed on October 25, 2006, from http://www.firstcandle.org/FC- PDF4/Research_Position%20Statements/immunizations%20and%20sids.pdf.

Franks, B., Miller, D., Wolff, E., & Landry, K. (2004). HIV/AIDS and the teachers of young children. *Early Child Development & Care, 174*(3), 229–241.

Gayle, A., & Ringdahl, E. (2001). Tick-borne diseases. *American Family Physician, 64*(3), 461–466.

Gravel, J., Roberts, J., Roush, J., Grose, J., Besing, J., Burchinal, M., Neebe, E., Wallace, I., & Zeisel, S. (2006). Early otitis media with effusion, hearing loss, and auditory processes at school age. *Ear & Hearing Journal, 27*(4), 353–368.

Hockenberry, M. (2004). *Wong's Essentials of Pediatric Nursing.* (7th ed.). New York: Mosby.

Hoffman, C., Boyd, M., Briere, B., Loos, F., & Norton, P. J. (1999). Evaluation of three brands of tympanic thermometer. *Canadian Journal of Nursing Research, 31*(1), 117–130.

Hunt, C. E., Lesko, S. M., Vezina, R. M., McCoy, R., Corwin, M. J., Mandell, F., Willinger, M., Hoffman, H., & Mitchell, A. A. (2003). Infant sleep position and associated health outcomes. *Archives of Pediatric & Adolescent Medicine, 157*(5), 469–474.

Kotch, L. (2004). FYI. Keeping young children safe and health: SIDS in child care—What can you do? *Young Children, 59*(2), 48.

Lahr, M., Rosenberg, K., & Lapidus, J. (2005). Bedsharing and maternal smoking in a population-based survey of new mothers. *Pediatrics, 116*(4), e530–542.

Lawrence, D. (2003). Coronavirus confirmed as cause of SARS. *Lancet, 361*(9370), 1712.

Lee, G., Gortmaker, S., McIntosh, K., Hughes, M., & Oleske, J. (2006). Quality of life for children and adolescents: Impact of HIV infection and antiretroviral treatment. *Pediatrics, 117*(2), 273–283.

Little, L. (2004). *Otitis media in young children with disabilities-Practical strategies.* Online at http://www.fpg.unc.edu/~images/pdfs/snapshots/snap16.pdf.

McCartney, P. (2006). New recommendations to reduce the risk of sudden infant death syndrome. *American Journal of Maternal & Child Nursing, 31*(2), 128–137.

Meissner, H. (2005). Reducing the impact of viral respiratory infections in children. *Pediatric Clinics of North America, 52*(3), 695–710.

Mitchell, E., Blair, P., & L'Hoir, M. (2006). Should pacifiers be recommended to prevent sudden infant death syndrome? *Pediatrics, 117*(5), 1755–1758.

MMWR Weekly. (2006). Achievements in public health: Reduction in perinatal transmission of HIV infection—United States, 1995–2005. *MMWR, 55*(21), 592–597.

Moon, R., Kotch, L., & Aird, L., (2006). State child care regulations regarding infant sleep environment since the Healthy Child Care America-Back to Sleep campaign. *Pediatrics, 118*(1), 73–83.

Moon, R., Sprague, B., & Patel, M. (2005). Stable prevalence but changing risk factors for sudden infant death syndrome in child care settings in 2001. *Pediatrics, 116*(4), 972–979.

Mui, S., Rasgon, B., Hilsinger, R., Lewis, B., & Lactao, G. (2005). Tympanostomy tubes for otitis media: Quality of life improvement for children and parents. *Ear, Nose & Throat Journal, 84*(7), 420–424.

Nakashima, A. K., & Fleming, P. L. (2003). HIV/AIDS surveillance in the United States, 1981–2001. *Journal of Acquired Immune Deficiency Syndrome, 32* Suppl. 1, S68–85.

National Center for Health Statistics (NCHS). (2006). *National Vital Statistics Reports, 54*(16), 1–30.

National SIDS Resource Center. (2006). *What is SIDS? Sudden infant death syndrome: Some facts you should know, and facts about apnea and other apparent life-threatening events.* Vienna, VA.

National Institute of Allergy and Infectious Diseases (NIAID). (2004). *HIV Infection in infants and children.* Accessed October 26, 2006, at http://www.niaid.nih.gov/factsheets/hivchildren.htm.

National Institute of Child Health and Human Development (NICHD). (2006). SIDS: Back to Sleep Campaign. Accessed on October 25, 2006, at http://www.nichd.nih.gov/sids.

Pickett, K., Luo, Y., & Lauderdale, D. (2005). Widening social inequalities in risk for sudden infant death syndrome. *American Journal of Public Health, 95*(11), 1976–1981.

Poutanen, S.M., Low, D. E., Henry, B. (2003). Identification of severe acute respiratory syndrome in Canada. *New England Journal of Medicine, 348*(20), 1995–2005.

Public Health Agency of Canada. *Human West Nile virus clinical cases and infections in Canada: 2006.* Accessed on April 24, 2007, from http://www.phac-aspc.gc.ca/wnv-vwn/mon-hmnsurv-2006_e.html.

Ritz, B., Wilhelm, M., & Zhao, Y. (2006). Air pollution and infant death in southern California, 1989–2000. *Pediatrics, 118*(2), 493–502.

Sganga, A., Wallace, R., Kiehl, E., Irving, T., & Witter, L. (2000). A comparison of four methods of normal newborn temperature measurement. *The American Journal of Maternal/Child Nursing, 25*(2), 76–79.

Shah, T., Sullivan, K., & Carter, J. (2006). Sudden infant death syndrome and reported maternal smoking during pregnancy. *American Journal of Public Health, 96*(10), 1757–1759.

Smith, C., Paradise, J., Sabo, D., Rockette, H., Kurs-Lasky, M., Bernard, B., & Colborn, D., (2006). Tympanometric findings and the probability of middle-ear effusion in 3686 infants and young children. *Pediatrics, 118*(1), 1–13.

Staat, D., & Klepser, M. (2006). International adoption: Issues in infectious diseases. *Pharmacotherapy, 26*(9), 1207–1220.

Stockheim, J., Wilinson, N., & Ramos-Bonoan, C. (2005). Human bites and blood exposure in New York schools. *Clinical Pediatrics (Philadelphia), 44*(8), 699–703.

Thach, B. (2005). The role of respiratory control disorders in SIDS. *Respiratory Physiology & Neurobiology, 15*(149), 343–353.

Vargas, C., & Ronzio, C. (2006). Disparities in early childhood caries. *BMC Oral Health, 6*(1), S3.

Vernon-Feagans, L., & Manlove, E. (2005). Otitis media, the quality of child care, and the social/communicative behavior of toddlers: A replication and extension. *Early Childhood Research Quarterly, 20*(3), 306–328.

Zeisel, S. A., Roberts, J. E., Burchinal, M., Neebe, E., & Henderson, F. W. (2002). A longitudinal study of risk factors for otitis media in African American children. *Maternal & Child Health, 6*(3), 189–193.

HELPFUL WEB RESOURCES

Center for Disease Control	http://www.cdc.gov
Health Canada	http://www.hc-sc.gc.ca
Keep Kids Healthy	http://www.keepkidshealthy.com
Kid Source	http://www.kidsource.com
Morbidity & Mortality Weekly	http://www.cdc.gov
National Institutes of Health	http://www.nih.gov

For additional health, safety, and nutrition resources, go to
http://www.EarlyChildEd.delmar.cengage.com

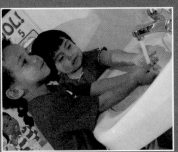

UNIT 3

Safety for the Young Child

CHAPTER 8

Creating Quality Environments

▨ OBJECTIVES

After studying this chapter, you should be able to:

- Discuss the relationship between environment and a child's growth and development.
- State the purpose of licensing requirements.
- List the necessary steps for securing a license to operate an early education program.
- Describe ways of making a child's environment safe.

▨ TERMS TO KNOW

environment	compliance	notarized
cognitive	registration	cryptospiridiosis
accreditation	developmentally	
licensing	appropriate practice (DAP)	
regulations		

Children's growth and development are continually shaped and influenced by their **environment**. Growth is enhanced through nurturing and responsive caregiving, good nutrition, homes and schools that are clean and safe, access to appropriate dental and health care, and communities that are free of drugs and violence. Opportunities for learning, experiencing new challenges, and positive social interaction are also important for promoting children's intellectual and psychological development. Thus, careful consideration must be given to all aspects of children's environments. Every effort must be made to create physical, **cognitive**, and psychological conditions that have positive effects on children's growth and development (Figure 8–1).

---

environment – *the sum total of physical, cultural, and behavioral features that surround and affect an individual.*
cognitive – *the aspect of learning that refers to the development of skills and abilities based on knowledge and thought processes.*

FIGURE 8-1

Environments should support and promote children's growth and development.

LOCATING QUALITY PROGRAMS

Demands for early childhood programs continue to increase. Locating out-of-home care for their children is a necessity for many working families. Other families simply want their children to benefit from enriching experiences and opportunities to socialize with others. Children with special developmental needs may be enrolled in early intervention programs where they can receive individualized learning experiences and special services, such as speech or physical therapy (Allen & Cowdery, 2005). Older children may require a safe, educational place to stay before and after regular school hours. Regardless of their reason, families often find the task of locating high-quality and affordable programs to be an extremely challenging one. Although many new programs and centers have opened in the rush to meet increased demand, quality has not always been a major priority.

Research continues to demonstrate that high-quality programs make a difference in children's development and family relationships (Goelman, et al., 2006; Resnick & Zurawsky, 2005; Clarke-Stewart, et al., 2002). Children enrolled in higher quality care show long-term gains in language and cognitive skills, improved readiness for school, and fewer problem behaviors (Clark-Stewart & Allhusen, 2005; Oliver & Klugman, 2002; Peth-Pierce, 2002). While most families would prefer to have their child in a quality program, the urgency and, at times, desperation of simply finding an available opening may force them to overlook this important issue. Cost and location can also be determining factors that overshadow a family's concern about quality.

It is also true that many families simply do not know how to begin evaluating the quality of a program or even what to look for. Some parents feel uncomfortable questioning teachers. Others may not be able to find a convenient high-quality program even when they are dissatisfied with poor conditions in a current arrangement.

Educating Families

Many advocacy groups and professional organizations have begun to launch national efforts to educate families about indicators that are commonly associated with quality programs and how to recognize them. Similar information is also readily available on many Web sites, making it easy for families to retrieve.

Researchers have identified three common features that are characteristic of high-quality early care and education programs (Doherty, et al., 2006; NICHD, 2004; Bredecamp & Copple, 1997):

- small group size
- low teacher–child ratio (fewer children per teacher)
- teachers who have advanced educational training in early childhood

Families should always take time to observe any new program they are considering and determine how the program measures up to these criteria. Additional areas that should also be noted include:

- physical facilities, e.g., clean, safe, spacious, licensed
- program philosophy; developmentally appropriate goals and objectives
- nutritious meals and snacks
- opportunities for family involvement
- respectful of diversity
- toys and educational activities, e.g., developmentally appropriate, variety, adequate number, organized learning experiences
- health services

Educating families about how to recognize quality in programs has obvious benefits for children. And, as demand for quality increases, some programs may be forced to improve their services or else go out of business.

Resource and Referral Services

Many communities have resource and referral agencies devoted to helping families locate center- and home-based child care. Families can request a list of available spaces based on their specific child care needs, such as location, cost, preferred hours, philosophy, and child's age. Many of these agencies were originally established as independent services but are now linked together to form state and national computerized networks; the National Association of Child Care Resource and Referral Agencies (NACCRRA) is one of the largest.

Child care resource and referral agencies may not restrict their listings to high-quality programs, so families must take time to investigate individual programs to find one that suits their needs and preferences. Some agencies will include any program with available openings, while others screen programs carefully to ensure high standards. Resource and referral agencies also play an active role in educating families about how to select quality early childhood programs. Many are also committed to providing support and ongoing inservice training for early childhood teachers.

REFLECTIVE THOUGHTS

Families are often faced with difficult choices when they try to locate child care options. Although efforts to improve the quality of early education programs continue, it is well known that not all programs reflect excellence. What does the literature suggest about how families select child care? What features distinguish quality in early childhood programs? How can communities work together to improve the overall quality of care provided in their area? What efforts are needed to improve accessibility to quality care for all children?

Professional Accreditation

A national system of voluntary **accreditation** for early childhood programs was established in 1985 by the National Association for the Education of Young Children (NAEYC). Its primary objective is aimed at promoting excellence and improving the quality of early education through a process of self-study (NAEYC, 2006a). The accreditation process identifies and recognizes outstanding early education programs and provides an added credential that recognizes their commitment to quality. Programs are accredited for three years, at which time they must reapply. NAEYC has just completed an extensive review and revision of its accreditation process and standards for evaluating quality programs (http://www.naeyc.org/accreditation).

Other organizations, such as Head Start, the National Association for Family Child Care, and the National AfterSchool Association have developed similar accreditation programs to recognize outstanding programs. Several states have also developed quality standards and voluntary systems for program accreditation (Kansas Stakeholders Advisory Committee for Early Childhood Education, 2001; Warman, 1998).

LICENSING

Licensing standards, established by individual states, represent an attempt to encourage and ensure that child care environments are safe and healthful for young children (NAEYC, 2006b). However, these standards reflect only minimal health and safety requirements and vary considerably from one state to another. They in no way guarantee quality conditions, programs, or care. This is an issue of great concern, as programs are increasingly serving infants and children with special behavior, developmental, and medical needs (Figure 8–2).

Licensing requirements serve a twofold purpose. First, they are aimed at protecting children's physical and psychological well-being by regulating the safety of environments and educational programs. Second, licensing **regulations** afford minimal protection to the program and its personnel. By complying with licensing requirements, programs are not as likely to encounter situations involving negligence.

Early attempts to regulate child care programs dealt primarily with the sanitation and safety of facilities. However, current licensing regulations often go beyond narrow concern only for the safety of physical settings. Today, teacher qualifications and the quality of educational programs planned for young children are also recognized as important elements for regulation.

Each state has a designated agency that is authorized and responsible for conducting inspections and issuing or revoking licenses to operate. This agency also oversees the review and development of licensing standards and methods for enforcing **compliance**. Again, there are

FIGURE 8–2

Licensing standards help to assure the health and safety of children's environments.

---

accreditation – *the process of certifying an individual or program as having met certain specified requirements.*
licensing – *the act of granting formal permission to conduct a business or profession.*
regulations – *standards or requirements that are set to ensure uniform and safe practices.*
compliance – *the act of obeying or cooperating with specific requests or requirements.*

significant differences in licensing standards and levels of enforcement from one state to another. This fragmented approach also lacks a system for ensuring that individual states are actually carrying out their responsibilities.

In many states, home-based child programs are governed by a separate set of regulations and often include an option of either becoming licensed or registered. Those choosing to be licensed are usually inspected by a member of the licensing agency and are expected to meet certain standards. In contrast, the requirements for **registration** are often minimal. Teachers may simply be asked to place their name on a list, complete a self-administered checklist attesting to safe conditions, or attend a brief preservice informational program. An on-site inspection of these homes is seldom conducted unless a complaint is registered. Child care programs based in churches and public schools and relative care are exempt from licensing regulation in many states.

Understandably, there is always controversy around the issue of licensing for early childhood programs. Establishing licensing requirements that adequately protect young children's health and safety—yet are realistic for teachers and programs to achieve—is a challenging task. Some people believe that too much control or standards that are set too high will reduce the number of programs. The licensing process is also costly to administer and often difficult to enforce, so that lowering the standards may be a tempting option. On the other hand, many families and teachers favor stricter regulations to ensure high-quality programs and improved respect for the early childhood profession.

Despite the ongoing controversy, licensing of early childhood programs is necessary. Ideally, licensing standards should adequately safeguard children, yet not be so overly restrictive that qualified individuals and programs are eliminated. The development of separate licensing requirements for in-home and center-based programs has been offered as one practical solution to this dilemma (Doherty, et al., 2006; Clarke-Stewart, et al., 2002).

Obtaining a License

A license permits an early education program to operate on a routine basis. As previously mentioned, the process for obtaining a license differs from state to state. However, the steps described here are generally representative of the procedure involved. In some cases, the process may require considerable time and effort, especially if major renovations must be made to the proposed facility. For others, approval may be obtained in a reasonably short time.

Those who are interested in operating an early childhood or after-school program should first contact their state or local licensing agency. Questions regarding the applicant's qualifications and specific program requirements can usually be answered at this time.

In addition to complying with state licensing regulations, child care facilities must also be in accordance with local laws and ordinances. Zoning codes must be checked to determine whether or not the location permits a program to be operated in a given neighborhood. Often this requires meeting with local planning authorities and reviewing proposed floor plans.

Buildings that house child care programs must also pass a variety of inspections to be sure they meet fire, safety, and sanitation codes. These inspections are usually conducted by personnel from the local fire and public health departments. From these inspections, it is possible to determine what, if any, renovations may be necessary in order to comply with licensing regulations. In most cases, these are relatively simple; in other cases, it may not be feasible or economical to complete all of the required changes.

Application for a permanent license can be made once all these steps have been completed. Copies of the program's plans and policies may be requested by the licensing authorities for review. Final approval usually includes an on-site inspection of the facilities to assure that all requirements and recommendations have been satisfied.

---

registration – *the act of placing the name of a child care program on a list of active providers; usually does not require on-site inspection.*

Federal Regulations

In addition to meeting state licensing requirements, early childhood programs that receive federal funds, such as Head Start, Early Head Start, and Even Start programs, must comply with an additional set of regulations. All schools and child care facilities built or remodeled after 1990 must also meet standards established by the Americans with Disabilities Act (ADA) (U.S. Department of Justice, 1997; Siegle, 1995).

FEATURES OF QUALITY PROGRAMS

Researchers are continually studying children in schools, home- and center-based programs to determine what conditions and experiences are best for promoting learning and healthy development. Through the years, they have identified several key components that distinguish high-quality programs (Doherty, et al., 2006; NICHD, 2005; Whitebrook, 2003b). The National Association for the Education of Young Children (NAEYC) (the largest organization representing early care and education in the United States) and other professional organizations have embraced these findings and incorporated them into their accreditation standards and recommended guidelines (Zaslow & Martinez-Beck, 2005; APHA & AAP, 2002; Aronson, 2002).

Teacher Qualifications

Perhaps one of the weakest areas in many state licensing regulations pertains to staff qualifications. Emphasis is usually focused on the safety of physical settings, while staff requirements such as years of experience, educational preparation, and personal qualities are often lacking or poorly defined. Even when these issues are addressed in the licensing regulations, there is little consistency from one state to another.

Research has documented a positive correlation between a teacher's educational preparation and the ability to provide high-quality early childhood education (Tout, Zaslow & Berry, 2005; Whitebrook, 2003a). Teachers who have a strong background in child development, value family involvement and communication, understand and respect diversity, and know how to create developmentally appropriate experiences are more effective in facilitating positive learning outcomes for children (Essa, 2007). As more and more children with behavior problems and disabilities are enrolled in early education programs, teachers must also be prepared to meet their special needs (Knoche, et al., 2006; Ramirez, Peek-Asa, & Kraus, 2004; Booth & Jean, 2002). In addition, teachers must also be able to work and communicate effectively with children and families of diverse backgrounds.

Unfortunately, the licensing requirements in many states do not reflect what we currently know about the importance of having teachers who have formal training in early childhood. Often, a person who is 18 years of age, has a high school diploma, and passes a background check is qualified to be hired as an early childhood teacher. As a result, they are generally not prepared to effectively handle the daily challenges involved in working with young children. This, combined with poor salaries and long hours, contributes to a high turnover rate in many programs and can have a negative effect on children's development (Booth, et al., 2003). Initiatives to improve teacher preparation and salaries are being studied, funded, and incorporated into licensing regulations in an effort to improve the quality of care and education young children receive (Ackerman, 2005; Kagan, et al., 2002; Whitebrook & Eichberg, 2002). However, teachers must also take steps to continue their education and better prepare themselves to work with young children. Many scholarship programs and professional educational opportunities are currently available, including:

- on-the-job training/inservice training
- CDA (Child Development Associates credential)
- one-year vocational training; child care or child development certificate

- two-year associate degree (A.A.) (community college)
- four-year bachelor degree
- advanced graduate training (M.A. and Ph.D.)

Although many of these degree programs are offered on traditional campuses, an increasing number are now available online.

At a minimum, all directors and head teachers should have a CDA (child development associate) credential or a two-year associate arts degree with specialized training in early childhood (Lutton, 2006). However, in many areas of the country, teachers with advanced preparation are in short supply.

Some early childhood programs include paraprofessionals as part of their teaching team. These individuals may be aides who work for wages or are unpaid volunteers. Regardless of their position or previous experience, it is essential that paraprofessionals receive a brief, but thorough, orientation to their job responsibilities and program procedures before working in the classrooms. This preparation allows paraprofessionals to be productive and effective when they begin working with the children. These are important considerations for employee retention and also benefit children in the long run.

Teachers who work in quality programs often have many special personal qualities and additional skills. They value communication and know how to develop meaningful relationships with children, families, and colleagues. They understand and respect diversity and make it a priority. They also possess qualities of warmth, patience, sensitivity to children's needs, respect for individual differences, and a positive attitude. They have the ability to plan, organize, make decisions, and resolve conflict. They also enjoy good personal health which allows them to cope with the physical and emotional demands of long, action-packed days. Individuals with these qualities are not only better teachers, but they are also more likely to have a positive effect on young children's lives.

Staffing Ratios

Staff/child ratios are determined by individual states and typically reflect only the minimal number of adults considered necessary to protect children's well-being (Vi-Nhuan, et al., 2006; Wishard, Shivers, Howes & Ritchie, 2003). However, quality learning experiences, individualized care, and maintaining conditions that safeguard children's health and safety require more teachers than is usually recommended.

Ideally, high-quality early childhood programs provide one full-time teacher for every seven to eight children three to six years of age. Programs serving children with developmental disabilities should have one teacher for every four to five children, depending on the age group and severity of their needs. If children younger than two years are included, the staff/child ratio should be no more than one full-time teacher per three to four children. A list of substitutes should also be available in the event of teacher illness or other absence.

Research suggests that small group size and low teacher/child ratios improve the quality of early education programs. However, low ratios do not always guarantee that children will be safer (Burchinal, Howes, & Kontos, 2002; Munton, Blackburn, & Barreau, 2002). Much depends on the knowledge and supervisory skills of individual teachers.

Teachers who are part of high-quality programs practice life-long learning by attending professional meetings, inservice programs, workshops, and college classes. These experiences promote continued professional growth and competence by exposing teachers to new concepts, ideas, and approaches. Teachers also have an opportunity to discuss common problems, share ideas, and discover unique solutions. This is especially important for teachers working in home-based programs who may have fewer chances to interact with other early childhood educators.

Group Size and Composition

When a license is issued to an early childhood program, specific conditions and restrictions under which it is allowed to operate are clearly defined. These conditions usually spell out:

- ages of children that can be enrolled
- group size per classroom
- maximum enrollment per program
- special populations of children to be served, e.g., children with behavior problems, children with developmental disabilities, infants, school-age, etc.

For example, a program might be licensed to provide three half-day sessions for children three to five years of age, with a maximum enrollment of 18 children per session. An in-home program might be licensed for at total of six children, ages birth to four years.

Group size is also recognized as an important indicator of quality programs (Figure 8–3) (APHA & AAP, 2002; Bredekamp & Copple, 1997). For this reason, restrictions are typically placed on the number of children a program is permitted to enroll. This figure is determined by the amount of available space, ages, and special populations of children served, as well as the number of teachers. However, it should be remembered that state regulations allow group sizes that are often much larger than is ideal for quality care.

A program's admission policies should include a description of its educational philosophy and the types of services it is able to provide. The age range, special needs, and total number of children that the program is licensed to enroll must also be clearly described to avoid parent misunderstanding.

Program Curriculum

The value of early learning experiences is well documented (Burchinal & Cryer, 2003; Clarke-Stewart, et al., 2002). Because many children spend the majority of their waking hours in out-of-home early childhood programs, it is essential that **developmentally appropriate practices (DAP)**—learning environments and enriching opportunities—be provided. Quality early education

---

FIGURE 8–3

Small group size allows children to have more individualized attention and is a feature of quality programs.

---

developmentally appropriate practices (DAP) – *learning experiences and environments that take into account children's individual abilities, interests, and diverse needs. DAP also reflects differences among families and values them as essential partners in children's education.*

programs plan learning experiences that address children's needs across all developmental areas, including:

- physical
- cognitive
- emotional
- social
- language
- self-care
- motor

It is important that the curriculum be stimulating and designed to help children acquire new skills. Time should be devoted to planning and organizing children's learning experiences and also to sharing this information with families. A schedule of daily activities and lesson plans should be posted where families can easily read them. How activities are presented throughout the day affects children's physical stamina and mental receptiveness. Fatigue and lack of interest can often be avoided by planning activities that provide alternating periods of rest and active play. For example, a long walk outdoors might be followed by a teacher-directed flannel board story or puppet show. When teachers pay careful attention to planning, they can take advantage of times when children are most likely to learn.

Health Services

Safeguarding children's health and well-being is a fundamental responsibility of teachers and school administrators (Aronson, 2002; Cryer & Phillipsen, 1997). Only when children are healthy can they fully benefit from everyday experiences and learning opportunities. Quality programs take this role seriously and address children's health needs by:

- having written policies and procedures
- maintaining comprehensive health and safety records
- training personnel to administer first aid and emergency care
- developing emergency response plans
- planning for health, safety, and nutrition education

State child care licensing regulations generally establish the types of policies and records that programs are required to maintain. Similar guidelines are issued by state departments of education for schools. Although states' requirements differ, quality programs often find it prudent to take a more comprehensive approach to recordkeeping for improved understanding and legal protection. Basic records that programs should maintain include:

- children's health assessments
- attendance
- emergency contact information
- developmental profiles
- adult health assessments
- fire and storm drills
- injuries
- daily health checks

Licensing authorities review the information in these records carefully during renewal visits.

Teachers in quality early childhood programs are trained to handle emergencies and provide first aid and emergency care to ill or injured children. They also have completed training in cardiopulmonary resuscitation (CPR). Programs choosing to meet minimal standards should have at least one staff member who is trained in these techniques and can respond immediately to emergencies.

Notarized permission forms, similar to the one shown in Figure 8–4, listing the name, address, and telephone number of the child's physician should be completed by families when the child is first enrolled. This measure grants teachers authority to administer emergency care or

---

notarized – *official acknowledgment of the authenticity of a signature or document by a notary public.*

FIGURE 8–4

Sample emergency contact information form.

EMERGENCY CONTACT INFORMATION

Child's Name _____ Date of Birth _____

Address _____ Home Phone _____

Mother's Name _____ Business Phone _____

Father's Name _____ Business Phone _____

Name of other person to be contacted in case of an emergency:

1. _____ Address _____

   Relationship (sitter, relative, friend, etc.) _____ Phone _____

2. _____ Address _____

   Relationship (sitter, relative, friend, etc.) _____ Phone _____

Authorization is hereby given for the Child Development Center Staff to release the above named child to the following persons, provided proper identification is first established (list all names of authorized persons, including immediate family):

1. _____ Relation: _____

2. _____ Relation: _____

3. _____ Relation: _____

Physician to be called in an emergency:

1. _____ Phone _____ or _____

2. _____ Phone _____ or _____

Dentist to be called in an emergency:

1. _____ Phone _____ or _____

I, the undersigned, authorize the staff of the Child Development Center to take what emergency medical measures are deemed necessary for the care and protection of my child enrolled in the Child Development Center program.

_____   _____
(Signature of Parent or Guardian/date)   Signature witnessed by:
                                                 (Notary)

_____   The above statement sworn
(Signature of Parent or Guardian/date)   before me on:

 Download this form online at http://www.EarlyChildEd.delmar.cengage.com

secure emergency medical treatment. Emergency numbers for fire, police, ambulance, and poison control should be posted next to the telephone for quick reference.

Programs that provide care for mildly ill children should develop policies that address their special health needs. Whether they remain in a separate area of the classroom away from other children or are moved to a different room, provisions should be made so they can rest and not expose other children to their illnesses. Medical supplies and equipment should be nearby so they are readily accessible.

Early childhood programs must develop emergency plans and procedures so they are prepared and able to respond to unexpected events in a prompt and organized manner (Table 8–1). These plans should outline steps for protecting children's safety in the event of fire, severe storms such as tornadoes, major disasters such as earthquakes, floods, or hurricanes, and unauthorized intruders. Representatives from local fire and law enforcement departments, the Red Cross, and emergency preparedness groups are available to assist programs in developing their emergency plans. These plans should be shared with families so they will know what to expect in the event of an emergency and can also use them to model similar procedures at home.

GUIDELINES FOR SAFE ENVIRONMENTS

Nowhere is health and safety more important than in group programs serving young children. When families enroll their children in a program, they expect them to be safe. They assume the facilities, toys, and equipment will be safe for children's use, that teachers will carefully supervise their children's activities, and that the environment and food are healthy. These expectations require teachers to be well informed and knowledgeable about how to create and maintain environments that assure children's health and safety.

As previously described, there are no national child care licensing requirements. However, several organizations have developed similar recommendations for out-of-home early childhood programs. The National Association for the Education of Young Children (NAEYC) has consistently defined and supported high standards for early-childhood programs. The American Academy of Pediatrics and the American Public Health Association prepared a document entitled *Caring for Our Children: National Health and Safety Performance Standards Guidelines for Out-of-Home Child Care Programs*, which identifies approximately 180 regulation standards and safety practices. The remainder of this chapter will address features of children's indoor and outdoor environments that require special attention.

Indoor Safety

A great deal of thought and preparation is needed to create rooms that are safe for young children. Everything from the traffic flow, placement of furniture, and choice of floor coverings to the design of changing tables and proper storage requires careful study. Knowledge of children's abilities at

TABLE 8–1 Principles of Emergency Preparedness

- Remain calm—do not panic.
- Be informed. Tune in a local station on your battery-powered radio.
- Get to a safe place. Develop and practice an appropriate disaster plan.
- Keep a first aid kit, bottled water, and flashlight handy.
- Take along children's health forms, emergency contact information, attendance records and a cell phone.
- Learn basic emergency and first aid procedures.

each stage of development plays a key role in anticipating and eliminating potential safety hazards. (Refer to Table 9–2.) A safe environment encourages children to explore and learn through play, and is also less stressful for adults.

Building and Site Location   In a time of shrinking budgets and increasing demand for child care, the selection of an appropriate building often requires a creative approach. It would be ideal to plan and design a facility specifically for this purpose. However, few programs have sufficient funds for new construction. More often, existing buildings, such as unused classrooms in public schools, older houses, unoccupied stores, church basements, or places of business such as factories or hospitals are modified or remodeled to make them suitable for early education programs. This type of work can be expensive and may not be practical in some instances. However, it may also be possible to use the talents of willing parents to help complete at least a small portion of the work and, thus, reduce the cost.

With the exception of church-based programs, home- and center-based programs are considered public facilities under the 1990 Americans with Disabilities Act (ADA) even if they are privately owned (Siegle, 1995; Surr, 1992). Consequently, they too must comply with guidelines set forth in this historical piece of legislation requiring the removal of physical barriers that would otherwise deny access to individuals with disabilities. Early childhood programs cannot refuse to admit children on the basis of their disabilities. Program directors are expected to make reasonable adjustments in policies, practices, and facilities in order to accommodate all children. Admission can be denied in special circumstances only if the required modifications are unduly difficult or costly to complete, or if there is no alternative solution to meet a child's special needs (U.S. Department of Justice, 1997). Consequently, this law has important implications throughout the site selection, building, and/or remodeling stages as more children with disabilities enroll in early childhood programs.

Location is always important to consider when selecting an appropriate site. Buildings chosen to house early childhood programs must meet local zoning requirements. These ordinances often make it difficult to locate programs in residential neighborhoods where they may be most needed. Buildings should be located away from heavy traffic, excessive noise, air pollution, animals, exposure to chemicals, bodies of water, large equipment, and other similar hazards to protect children's safety. However, these conditions may be unavoidable for programs in inner city and rural areas. It then becomes even more essential to devote time and extra effort to safety awareness, policy development, and educational programs for children, teachers, and families.

Local fire codes also affect building selection. Older buildings and those not originally designed for infants and young children may require extensive changes before they pass inspection. Rooms that children occupy must have a minimum of two exits, one leading directly outdoors. All doors should be hinged so they swing out of the room; this will prevent doors from slowing the evacuation process. Programs located on upper levels should also have an enclosed stairwell for safe escape in the event of a fire.

How much space is needed depends to some extent on the type of program and services that will be offered. Thirty-five square feet of usable floor space per child is considered an absolute minimum for adequate child care. However, teachers often find this amount of space crowded and difficult to work in. Ideally, quality programs should have 45 to 50 square feet of space per child. This amount seems to be more workable for both children and teachers. Additional space may be needed to accommodate large indoor play structures, special equipment for children with physical disabilities, or cribs for infants. However, it should also be kept in mind that spaces that are too large may be difficult to supervise. Ground floor levels are always preferable for infants and preschool-aged children, although basement areas can be used for several hours at a time provided there are at least two exits.

Space   The arrangement of space, or basic floor plan, should be examined carefully to determine the ease of conducting specific activities. For example, the traffic flow should allow ample

FIGURE 8–5

Infants need open space where they can move about and play.

room for children to arrive and depart without disturbing others who are playing. It should also accommodate separate areas for active/noisy play and quiet activities. Small rooms that lack storage space, good lighting, accessible bathrooms or adequate outdoor play areas are inconvenient and frustrating for both the staff and children.

Play spaces for infants and toddlers should be separated from those of older children to avoid injuries and confrontations. Large, open space, free of obstacles, also encourages very young children to move about and explore without hesitation (Figure 8–5).

Building Security   Added precautions should be taken to protect children from unauthorized individuals while assuring that legitimate visitors have safe access (Table 8–2). Buildings and outdoor play spaces should be evaluated carefully to determine if they are secure. Safety measures, such as locking outside doors and gates, installing key pads, or issuing card keys (used in hotels), are effective for controlling unauthorized access. Teachers and staff members should always be alert to persons entering the building and greet them as a way of acknowledging their presence. Surveillance cameras can also be installed to monitor entrances and exits. Programs should develop and review plans for handling unauthorized visitors and summoning assistance. They may also want to establish a safe area of the building where children can be moved for added protection.

REFLECTIVE THOUGHTS

As adults, we often take great efforts to create environments and rules that will protect children from harm. Yet, it can be perplexing to understand why children continue to get themselves into situations that are unsafe. Why do you think this occurs? Are adult's and children's expectations and perceptions the same? (Try getting down on your hands and knees to understand how children view their environment.) How do cultural differences affect one's definition of a safe environment?

TABLE 8-2 Inventory Checklist: Planning for Program Security

Program administrators should work closely with local law enforcement, fire, and safety officials to assess a program's risk and to develop security plans that will protect children and staff members. Critical documents should be prepared and stored in a designated folder or box. All program staff should be familiar with its location and contents for quick retrieval in the event of an emergency, such as fire, earthquake, hurricane, or unauthorized intruders. Items that should be addressed include:

- Obtaining a copy of the building floor plan or blueprint
- Preparing a list of employees by name and room, and attaching their photograph
- Preparing a roster of the children by room and attaching their photograph; note any children who have special needs
- Knowing where all shut-off valves are located and how to turn them off
- Preparing an evacuation plan with alternate exit routes
- Posting evacuation plans in each classroom and reviewing them periodically with teachers
- Conducting monthly evacuation drills with children
- Maintaining hallways and exits that are clear of obstructions
- Making copies of parent authorization forms and emergency contact information
- Compiling a list of emergency personnel and telephone numbers
- Assigning specific emergency responsibilities to individual personnel and outlining each role on a master plan
- Informing families about the program's security plans and including the information in parent handbooks
- Keeping an emergency food supply on hand

Fire Safety Local fire officials can assist schools and in-home programs in the development and review of emergency procedures. They can be invited to tour the building layout and offer expert advice about planned evacuation routes. A copy of the building floor plans can be given to local fire authorities to keep on file so they are familiar with the layout and design. This will help them to respond more efficiently in the event of an emergency.

Smoke and carbon monoxide detectors should be present in rooms occupied by children, especially where infants and young children will be sleeping. Detectors should be tested each month to make sure they are functioning properly. Additional fire safety precautions can be taken by installing flame-retardant floor coverings and draperies and having at least one multipurpose fire extinguisher available. Staff should be familiar with the location of building exits and emergency evacuation procedures. Teachers should conduct monthly fire drills with the children so they will become familiar with the routine and not be frightened in the event of a real emergency (Table 8–3). Alternate evacuation routes should be planned and practiced so that teachers will know how to get out of a building if an area is blocked by fire. Plans for evacuating children with special needs should also be given careful attention.

Extension cords should not be used in classrooms. All electrical outlets should be covered with safety caps which can be purchased in most grocery or hardware stores. However, remember that caps are only a temporary solution; they are frequently removed and not replaced, and can become a choking hazard for young children. An electrician can replace conventional outlets with childproof receptacles.

Bathroom Facilities Adequate bathroom facilities are also essential for convenience and health concerns. They should be accessible to both indoor and outdoor play areas. Installation of child-sized fixtures, including sinks, toilets, soap dispensers, and towel racks, allow children to care for their own needs (Figure 8–6). If only adult-sized fixtures are available, foot stools, large

TABLE 8-3 Teacher Checklist: How to Conduct a Fire Drill

Develop an Evacuation Plan
- Plan at least one alternate escape route from every room.
- Post a written copy of the plan by the door of each room.
- Review plans with new personnel.

Assign Specific Responsibilities
- Designate one person to call the fire department, preferably from a telephone outside of the building. Be sure to give the fire department complete information: name, address, approximate location of the fire inside the building, whether or not anyone is inside. Do not hang up until the fire department hangs up first.
- Designate several adults to assemble children and lead them out of the building; assign extra adults, e.g., cooks, secretaries, to assist with evacuation of younger children.
- Designate one adult to bring a flashlight and the notarized emergency cards or class list.
- Designate one person to turn off the lights and close the doors to the rooms.

Establish a Meeting Place
- Once outside, meet at a designated location so that everyone can be accounted for.
- DO NOT GO BACK INTO THE BUILDING!

Practice Fire Evacuation Drills
- Conduct drills at least once a month; plan some of these to be unannounced.
- Practice alternate routes of escape.
- Practice fire evacuation safety, e.g., feel closed doors before opening them, select an alternate route if hallway or stairwells are filled with smoke, stay close to the floor (crawl) to avoid heat and poisonous gases, learn the stop-drop-roll technique.
- Use a stopwatch to time each drill and record the results; strive for improvement.

wooden blocks, or platforms securely anchored to the floor will facilitate children's independence. One toilet and sink should be available for every 10 to 12 children. Programs serving children with disabilities should be designed to meet their special needs and be in compliance with ADA

FIGURE 8-6

Child-sized fixtures encourage independence.

standards (Siegle, 1995; Surr, 1992). A separate bathroom area should also be available for adults and staff members.

Handwashing facilities located near toilets and sleeping areas encourage good handwashing habits. Hot water temperatures should be maintained between 105°F (40.5°C) and 120°F (48.8°C) to protect children from accidental burns (*Child Health Alert*, 2003). Liquid or foam soap dispensers placed near sinks encourage handwashing, are easy for children to use, and are less likely (than bar soap) to end up on the floor. The use of individual paper towels and cups also improves sanitation and limits the spread of infectious illnesses. Smooth surfaces on walls and floors facilitate cleaning. Light colors, especially in bathrooms, make dirt visible and, therefore, able to be cleaned more promptly. Fixtures such as mirrors, light switches, and towel dispensers placed within children's reach, good lighting, and bright paint create a functional and pleasant atmosphere in which young children can develop self-care skills.

Surface and Furnishings   Furniture and equipment should be selected to be comfortable and safe. Children are less likely to be injured if chairs and tables are appropriately proportioned. Quality is also an important feature to consider. Furniture should be sturdy so that it can withstand hard use by groups of children and meet federal safety standards (see Chapter 9). Items with sharp corners or edges should be avoided; many manufacturers now use rounded corners on children's furniture. Bookcases, lockers, pianos, and other heavy objects should be anchored securely to the wall or floor to prevent children from pulling them over. Tall bookshelves should be replaced or cut in half to make them more child sized.

Materials used for wall and floor coverings should be easy to clean. Vinyl floor covering is a popular choice for use in early childhood centers and schools for this reason. However, they do become very slippery when wet. Care must be taken to wipe up spills immediately or to place rugs or newspapers in areas where floors are likely to get wet. Often a combination of carpeted and tiled areas is most satisfactory because it provides soft, warm surfaces where children can sit as well as surfaces that can easily be cleaned.

Each child should have an individual storage space, cubby, or locker where personal belongings can be kept (Figure 8–7). A child's private space is particularly important in group settings. It offers the psychological benefit of privacy, whereas most other classroom objects are expected to be shared. Individual cubbies help minimize the loss of prized possessions. They also are effective for controlling the spread of infectious illnesses that are transmitted through direct and indirect contact (such as head lice and pinkeye).

Other features aimed at improving the quality and safety of children's classroom environments include having locked cabinets available for storing medicines and other potentially poisonous substances, such as cleaning products and paint. A telephone should also be located conveniently in the building. A list of emergency phone numbers, including the fire department, police, hospital, ambulance, and poison control center, should be posted next to the telephone. A checklist for evaluating the safety of indoor and outdoor areas is illustrated in Table 8–4.

FIGURE 8–7

Each child should have their own space to store personal belongings.

Lighting and Ventilation Low windows and glass doors should be constructed of safety glass to prevent serious injuries if they are broken. Colorful pictures or decals placed at children's eye level also help to discourage them from accidentally walking into the glass. Doors and windows should be covered with screens to keep out unwanted insects; screens that can be locked will prevent children from falling out. Cords from draperies or blinds should be fastened up high and out of children's reach to prevent strangulation.

Good lighting is essential in classrooms and hallways. Rooms that are sunny and bright are inviting and attractive to both teachers and children. Natural light from windows and glass doors is one of the most desirable ways to supply rooms with light. Sunlight costs nothing to use and has a positive psychological effect.

Proper arrangement of artificial lighting is equally as important as the amount of brightness it produces. Areas of a room that are used for close activities, such as reading centers or art tables, require more lighting. Fluorescent lights are ideal for this purpose because they give off more light that is less glaring than incandescent bulbs. Although fluorescent lighting is initially more costly to install, it uses less electricity and is cheaper to operate.

Heating and cooling systems should be in good operating condition and maintain room temperatures between 68°F (20°C) and 85°F (29.4°C) year-round (Ferng & Lee, 2002). Classrooms should not have hot radiators, exposed pipes, furnaces, fireplaces, portable heaters, or fans that are accessible to children; if they cannot be removed, protective wire screening must be placed around them to prevent injuries.

Indoor Air Quality Every day, children are exposed to a variety of indoor air pollutants, including formaldehyde (in carpet and building materials), carbon monoxide, radon, asbestos, cigarette smoke, paint fumes, lead, numerous household chemicals, and pesticides. More studies are demonstrating a close relationship between these pollutants and an increased rate of respiratory illnesses, allergies, and asthma among children (Just, et al., 2006; Kyle, Woodruff & Axelrad, 2006; Kim, 2004). The toxic properties of these substances may pose an even greater health risk for young children due to their immature body systems and rapid growth (Table 8–5). The long-term effects of air pollutants on children's health continue to be investigated.

Although it is impossible to avoid exposure to all toxic chemicals in an environment, increased awareness and understanding of control measures can effectively reduce the risks to young children (Landrigan, et al., 2004; Daisey, Angell, & Apte, 2003). The use of aerosol sprays should always be avoided around children. Indoor air quality can be improved significantly by simply increasing ventilation (opening doors and windows daily, turning on air conditioning) and substituting alternative products for toxic chemicals. Many new building materials, often labeled "green products" or "building green," are being manufactured without toxic chemicals. The safety of existing building materials, as well as heating and ventilating systems, should be checked regularly. Labels on toys and art materials should also indicate that they are nontoxic (Figure 8–8).

Outdoor Safety

The outdoors presents an exciting environment for an endless array of imaginative play and learning opportunities for children (Rivkin, 2006; Rae, 2006; Strickland, 2005). It also has important implications for their health in terms of promoting physical activity and acquiring a lifelong appreciation for fitness and outdoor recreation. As studies continue to reveal an alarming increase in obesity among young children, the positive value of active outdoor physical activity on well-being cannot be overlooked. However, outdoor play areas are also a major source of unintentional injury for children and, therefore, require a heightened awareness of design, maintenance, and supervisory strategies (Frost, Wortham, & Reifel, 2004; Thompson & Hudson, 2000). Programs that use public parks for outdoor recreation should be particularly alert to safety hazards (CPSC, 2003).

TABLE 8–4 Teachers' Safety Checklist: Indoor and Outdoor Areas

	Date Checked	Pass/ Fail	Comments

Indoor Areas

1. A minimum of 35 square feet of usable space is available per child.
2. Room temperature is between 68°–85°F (20°–29.4°C).
3. Rooms have good ventilation:
   a. windows and doors have screens.
   b. mechanical ventilation systems are in working order.
4. There are two exits in all rooms occupied by children.
5. Carpets and draperies are fire-retardant.
6. Rooms are well lighted.
7. Glass doors and low windows are constructed of safety glass.
8. Walls and floors of classrooms, bathrooms, and kitchen appear clean; floors are swept daily, bathroom fixtures are scrubbed at least every other day.
9. Tables and chairs are child-sized and sturdy.
10. Electrical outlets are covered with safety caps.
11. Smoke detectors are located in appropriate places and in working order.
12. Furniture, activities, and equipment are set up so that doorways and pathways are kept clear.
13. Play equipment and materials are stored in designated areas; they are inspected frequently and are safe for children's use.
14. Large pieces of equipment, e.g., lockers, piano, and bookshelves, are firmly anchored to the floor or wall.
15. Cleaners, chemicals, and other poisonous substances are locked up.
16. If stairways are used:
    a. handrail is placed at children's height.
    b. stairs are free of toys and clutter.
    c. stairs are well-lighted.
    d. stairs are covered with a nonslip surface.
17. Bathroom areas:
    a. toilets and washbasins are in working order.
    b. one toilet and washbasin are available for every 10–12 children; potty chairs are provided for children in toilet training.
    c. water temperature is no higher than 120°F (48.8°C).
    d. powdered or liquid soap is used for handwashing.
    e. individual or paper towels are used for each child.
    f. diapering tables or mats are cleaned after each use.
18. At least one fire extinguisher is available and located in a convenient place; extinguisher is checked annually by fire-testing specialists.
19. Premises are free from rodents and/or undesirable insects.
20. Food preparation areas are maintained according to strict sanitary standards.

(continued)

	Date Checked	Pass/ Fail	Comments

TABLE 8–4 Teachers' Safety Checklist: Indoor and Outdoor Areas (continued)

21. At least one individual on the premises is trained in emergency first aid and CPR; first aid supplies are readily available.
22. All medications are stored in a locked cabinet or box.
23. Fire and storm/disaster drills are conducted on a monthly basis.
24. Security measures (plans, vigilant staff, key pads, locked doors, video cameras) are in place to protect children from unauthorized visitors.

Outdoor Areas

1. Play areas are located away from heavy traffic, loud noises, and sources of chemical contamination.
2. Play areas are located adjacent to the premises or within safe walking distance.
3. Play areas are well drained; if rubber tires are used for play equipment, holes have been drilled to prevent standing water.
4. Bathroom facilities and a drinking fountain are easily accessible.
5. A variety of play surfaces, e.g., grass, concrete, sand, are available; shade is provided.
6. Play equipment is in good condition, e.g., no broken or rusty parts, missing pieces, splinters, sharp edges (no open "S" hooks or protruding bolts), frayed rope.
7. Selection of play equipment is appropriate for children's ages.
8. Soft ground covers, approximately 12 inches in depth, are present under large climbing equipment; area is free of sharp debris (glass, sticks).
9. Large pieces of equipment are stable and anchored securely in the ground; finishes are non-toxic and intact.
10. Equipment is placed sufficiently far apart to allow a smooth flow of traffic and adequate supervision; an appropriate safety zone is provided around equipment.
11. Play areas are enclosed by a fence at least four feet high, with a gate and workable lock for children's security and safety.
12. There are no poisonous plants, shrubs, or trees in the area.
13. Chemicals, insecticides, paints, and gasoline products are stored in a locked cabinet.
14. Grounds are maintained on a regular basis and are free of debris; grass is mowed; broken equipment is removed.
15. Wading or swimming pools are always supervised; water is drained when not in use.

TABLE 8-5 Some Common Air Pollutants and their Health Effects

Sources
- organic particles (e.g., dust mites)
- molds
- pollen
- carbon monoxide
- formaldehyde
- insulation (e.g., asbestos, fiberglass)
- ozone

Common Health Effects
- chronic cough
- headache
- dizziness
- matigue
- eye irritation
- sinus congestion
- skin irritation
- shortness of breath
- nausea

Space   Safety must be a major consideration in the design of outdoor play areas. No less than 75–100 square feet of space per child (using it at the same time) should be available to encourage active play and decrease the potential for unintentional injury. The National Health and Safety Performance Standards recommend that play areas for infants include a minimum of 33 square feet per child; 50 square feet per child is suggested for toddlers (APHA and AAP, 2002). Ideally, play areas should be located adjacent to the building so that bathrooms are readily accessible and children are not required to walk long distances. Traveling even a short distance to playgrounds with young children requires considerable time and effort, and often discourages spontaneous outdoor play.

A fence at least four feet in height should surround the play area and include two exits with latched gates to prevent children from wandering away. Railings or slats should be spaced less than three-and-one-half inches or more than nine inches apart to prevent children's heads or bodies from becoming entrapped. Sharp wire and picket-type fences are inappropriate and should not be used around young children.

An important design element in children's play areas involves the use of space (DeBord, et al., 2002; Flynn & Kieff, 2002). Play areas should be arranged so that children are clearly visible from all directions. Large open areas encourage active play such as running and tossing balls. Hard, flat surfaces allow children to use riding toys and play outdoors during inclement weather, especially if these areas are covered. Flower beds provide children with space for gardening, while sand promotes imaginary play. Grassy areas and trees create a natural touch and offer protection from the sun. If trees are not available, large colorful awnings or tents can also be purchased from play equipment companies or home improvement stores to provide shade. Separate areas designed for quiet and

FIGURE 8–8

Children's toys should always be made from nontoxic materials.

ISSUES TO CONSIDER • Security in Early Childhood Programs

Recent media reports of school shootings, child mistreatment, and workplace violence have heightened concerns about security (Archibold & Marshall, 2006; Sander, 2006). Although many businesses have installed additional security devices in office buildings and enhanced existing security procedures, early childhood programs have been slower to respond. Routine background checks of employees, the ability of staff to recognize a child's family members, and parental authorization for releasing a child to other individuals are often the primary safety measures that programs rely on. Some centers are beginning to implement more innovative security measures, including touch key pads and Web cameras that allow families to view children on their computer screens while they are at work (Morris, 1999).

- What resources are available for learning more about appropriate steps to take?
- What workplace policies and procedures are necessary to protect the safety of children and teachers?
- Are there any disadvantages to increasing security? What might they be?
- What does the need for increased security in early childhood programs say about contemporary society?
- What newer technologies can be used to improve building security?

---

active play also help to reduce potential injuries. Always be sure to check with a local nursery or county extension office to be sure that flowers, trees, and other plantings are not poisonous to children (see Table 8–6 for a partial list, and Figure 8–9). A comprehensive listing of poisonous plants, complete with photographs, is available at http://www.ansci.cornell.edu/plants.

Designing outdoor playgrounds so they can also be enjoyed by children with developmental disabilities presents another unique and challenging opportunity. Guidelines are available for designing playgrounds that comply with the Americans with Disabilities Act (ADA) standards (http://www.access-board.gov/play/guide/intro.htm). Solid, flat surfaces that are at least three-and-one-half feet wide allow children to maneuver safely in their wheelchairs. Bright colors, textures, ramps, and handrails can easily be incorporated into play environments, improving their visibility and accessibility for children. Also, a wider selection of modified outdoor play equipment that serves the needs of all children is now available from many manufacturers.

Equipment   Each year approximately 200,000 children under the age of 12 are treated in emergency rooms as a result of playground injuries (CPSC, 2001). Because most injuries involve play equipment, careful attention must be given to its selection, placement, and maintenance (Table 8–7; also see Chapter 9). Choices of equipment should be based on:

- amount of available play space
- age and developmental appropriateness
- variety of learning experiences provided
- quality and safety of construction
- accessibility to all children, (National Center for Accessibility, 2007)

Large pieces of equipment and portable climbing structures should be firmly anchored in the ground; posts should be sunk 12 to 18 inches below ground surface if anchored with metal pins or at least six inches if set in concrete. Play equipment for preschoolers should be no taller than six feet and located at least nine feet from other equipment or surfaces such as concrete and asphalt

TABLE 8-6 Some Common Poisonous Vegetation

Vegetation	Poisonous Part	Complications
Bittersweet	Berries	Causes a burning sensation in the mouth. Nausea, vomiting, dizziness, and convulsions.
Buttercup	All parts	Irritating to the digestive tract. Causes nausea and vomiting.
Castor bean	Beanlike pod	Extremely toxic. May be fatal to both children and adults.
Daffodil, hyacinth, narcissus, jonquil, iris	Bulbs Underground roots	Nausea, vomiting, and diarrhea. Can be fatal.
Dieffenbachia	Leaves	Causes immediate burning and swelling around mouth.
English ivy	Leaves and berries	Ingestion results in extreme burning sensation.
Holly	Berries	Results in cramping, nausea, vomiting, and diarrhea.
Lily-of-the-valley	Leaves and flowers	Nausea, vomiting, dizziness, and mental confusion.
Mistletoe	Berries	Extremely toxic. Diarrhea and irregular pulse.
Oleander	Flowers and sap	Highly toxic; can be fatal. Causes nausea, vomiting, diarrhea, and heart irregularities.
Philodendron	Leaves	Ingestion causes intense irritation and swelling of the lips and mouth.
Rhubarb	Raw leaves	Can cause convulsions, coma, and rapid death.
Sweet pea	All parts, especially the seeds	Shallow respirations, possible convulsions, paralysis, and slow pulse.
Black locust tree	Bark, leaves, pods and seeds	Causes nausea and weakness, especially in children.
Cherry tree	Leaves and twigs	Can be fatal. Causes shortness of breath, general weakness, and restlessness.
Golden chain tree	Beanlike seed pods	Can cause convulsions and coma.
Oak tree	Acorns and leaves	Eating large quantities may cause poisoning. Gradually causes kidney failure.
Rhododendron	All parts	Causes vomiting, convulsions, and paralysis.
Wisteria	Seed pods	Causes severe diarrhea and collapse.
Yews	Berries and foliage	Foliage is very poisonous and can be fatal. Causes nausea, diarrhea, and difficult breathing.

to avoid injury in the event of a fall. This distance should be increased to 15 feet if the equipment has moving parts such as swings (Figure 8–10).

Because children are frequently injured on swings and teeter-totters, many states no longer permit child care programs to include them on newly constructed playgrounds (Kennedy, 2006; Tinsworth & McDonald, 2001). The Consumer Product Safety Commission (CPSC) also discourages swings in public parks (CPSC, 2003). Existing swing seats should be constructed of plastic or rubber to decrease the risk of impact injuries. If tires are used for swings, holes should be drilled

FIGURE 8-9

Examples of poisonous plants.

Oak

Lily of the Valley

Daffodil & Crocus Bulbs

English Ivy

to prevent water from collecting and allowing mosquitoes to breed. The size of any opening on equipment should also be carefully checked (openings must be less than three-and-one-half inches or greater than nine inches) so that children's heads cannot become entrapped.

Large trampolines have increased in popularity but are not appropriate in early education programs or school settings. Due to an increasing number of deaths and serious injuries, the American Academy of Pediatrics has also discouraged their use in private backyards and for athletic activities. Children under age six should not be allowed to play on trampolines (Shields, Fernandez, & Smith, 2005; American Academy of Pediatrics, 1999).

For many years, decks and children's climbing structures were constructed with chromated cooper arsenic (CCA)-treated lumber which gave it a green tint. Studies have since shown that the

TABLE 8-7 General Guidelines for Purchasing Outdoor Play Equipment

Consider:
- height of platforms and decks; these should be no higher than four–five feet for preschoolers, six feet for school-age children
- railings present on all decks and platforms, especially those higher than 30 inches above ground
- the size of all openings (including those between rungs and guardrails) should be closer than three-and-one-half inches or more than nine inches apart to prevent entrapment
- hardware such as "S" hooks, protruding nuts and bolts, or moving pieces of rope that could injure fingers or catch on clothing; rope swings that could cause strangulation
- materials used in construction. Wood/wood products require maintenance to avoid splintering and deterioration. Metal is strong, but becomes hot in sunlight and slippery when wet. Paints and chemicals used for wood treatment must be nontoxic.
- the type of surface material that will be needed under equipment
- the amount of area required for safe installation. A clearance area of nine feet is needed for stationary equipment; fifteen feet is needed for equipment with moving parts such as swings.
- ladders that are set straight up and down (vs. on an angle) encourage children to hold onto rungs when climbing

FIGURE 8–10

A safe fall zone must be established around play equipment.

arsenic compound could rub off on children's hands and potentially increase their risk of cancer (EPA, 2005). CCA-treated lumber is no longer sold, but many play structures built with this material can still be found on playgrounds and in children's backyards. Subsequent studies have determined that applying an annual coat of oil-based sealant reduces children's exposure to the arsenic-based chemicals by 86–90 percent (CPSC, 2005). The chemicals can also leach into soil surrounding the base of treated timbers and should therefore be removed periodically or covered.

Sand boxes require special care and attention to keep them safe for children (Table 8–8). Play sand, made specifically for children's sandboxes, can be purchased at garden centers or from building contractors or cement suppliers. (**Note:** Sands used in construction may contain hazardous materials, such as asbestos, and should not be used for children.) Sandboxes should have good drainage and a tightly fitting cover to keep out animals and insects. If they cannot be covered when not in use, sand should be inspected carefully for animal feces. Sand should be raked and checked each day for spiders, insects, sticks, stones, or other sharp debris before children play. Frequent sweeping of adjoining surfaces reduces the potential for slipping and falling.

Wading or swimming pools can add interest to outdoor play areas. However, they require extra supervision, safety, and sanitation precautions. Every teacher should be

Caution: **Children must never be left unattended around any source of water, including sprinklers, wading pools, water tables, puddles, ditches, fountains, buckets, or toilets.**

familiar with water safety procedures and rescue breathing procedures. At least one adult on site should be CPR certified. Limiting the number of children participating in water activities improves teachers' ability to monitor and improve safety. Safety rules should be carefully explained to the children before an activity begins and then strictly enforced.

TABLE 8–8 Teacher Checklist: Sandbox Care and Maintenance

- Purchase only special play sand for children's sandboxes.
- Make sure there is adequate drainage to prevent water from pooling.
- Rake and check sand daily for spiders, stones, and sharp objects.
- Cover sand if at all possible; if not, be sure to check for animal feces before children play.
- Sweep adjoining surfaces to prevent slipping and falling.

It is essential that pool water be disinfected prior to use by each group of children to prevent the spread of disease, such as giardia and **cyrptospiridiosis** (See Table 7–1). Inexpensive water-quality test kits are available from pool supply stores. Permanent pools and natural bodies of water must be fenced (at least five feet in height; be sure to check local codes) and have self-closing gates. Additional protection from childhood drowning can be provided by gate alarms, pool safety covers, motion alarms, and the availability of proper flotation devices.

Tricycles and other small riding toys are always children's favorites. However, they also are involved in many serious childhood injuries and a common cause of head trauma (Lalloo & Sheiham, 2003; Stanken, 2000). Children should always be required to wear bike helmets when they are riding. It is important that helmets fit properly, are worn correctly, and meet new safety standards mandated by the Consumer Product Safety Commission (Figure 8–11) (*Child Health Alert*, 2005a; Lohse, 2003). *Warning:* Children must not wear helmets while on play equipment to prevent entrapment and strangulation. A designated riding area away from where other children are playing makes riding less hazardous. It is also important to discuss rules for safe riding with children to avoid collisions and subsequent injury. Encouraging all children to ride in the same direction and allowing only one child on a bike at a time makes riding even safer.

Surface Materials   Protective materials that are soft and resilient should always be placed under play equipment to protect children from harm (Table 8–9). A minimum of 9–10 inches of sand, pea gravel, finely chopped rubber, or bark mulch will provide adequate shock resistance

FIGURE 8–11

Helmets must fit and be worn correctly to protect children from serious injury.

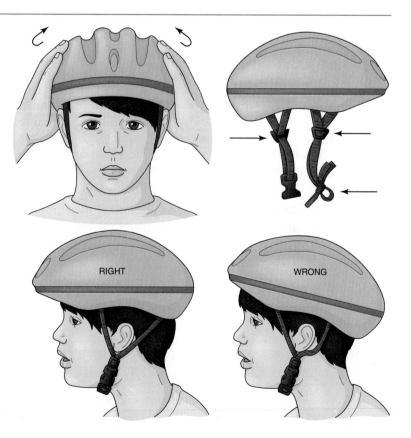

RIGHT   WRONG

---

cryptosporidiosis – *an infectious illness caused by an intestinal parasite. May be present in water (e.g., swimming pools, hot tubs, streams) contaminated with feces or from unwashed hands. Often causes severe diarrhea in children.*

TABLE 8-9 Comparison of Surfacing Materials

Material	Advantages	Disadvantages
gravel, pea (3/8 inch diameter) (6–9 inches depth)	• relatively inexpensive • readily available • long-lasting; won't decompose • drains quickly • doesn't attract animals • easy to install	• requires a barrier for containment • becomes compact if wet and freezes • must be replenished periodically; may mix with soil below • not recommended with children under 5 years; small pebbles may be thrown or stuffed into noses, ears, or mouths • not wheelchair accessible. Hazardous if gravel is scattered on hard surfaces nearby; can cause slipping and falls
gravel, medium (12 inches depth)	• qualities are similar to pea gravel	• disadvantages are similar to pea gravel • larger pieces tend to cause more superficial scrapes
bark mulch (6 inches depth)	• inexpensive • easy to install • drains quickly • readily available	• decomposes rapidly • must be contained with barriers; can wash away with heavy rains • absorbs moisture and freezes • compacts easily • difficult to find sharp objects, e.g., broken glass, sticks, nails, stones in loose mulch • prone to microbial infestations
wood chips (6 inches)	• air trapped between chips promotes cushioning effect • low in cost • accessible to wheelchairs	• washes away with heavy rains • decomposes and must be replenished to maintain cushion-effect • may be thrown about by children but not likely to cause injury
sand (coarse or masonry sand) (12 inches)	• easy to obtain • inexpensive • does not deteriorate over time • easy to install • not as prone to microbial or insect infestation • accessible by wheelchairs	• must be replenished periodically to maintain cushioning effect • may be thrown about or eaten by children • gets into shoes and clothing • hazardous when spilled onto nearby hard surfaces such as cement and tile floors; causes slipping and falls • attractive to animals, especially cats if area not covered • must be raked and sifted frequently to check for undesirable objects, e.g., sticks, broken glass, stones • requires good drainage beneath
shredded tires	• relatively low initial cost • requires good drainage system • doesn't deteriorate over time • not as likely to compact • less conducive to microbial and insect infestation • wheelchair accessible	• is flammable (10–12 inches) • may stain clothing if not treated • may contain metal particles from steel belted tires • easily thrown about by children but unlikely to cause injury

(continued)

TABLE 8-9 Comparison of Surfacing Materials (continued)

Material	Advantages	Disadvantages
rubber tiles or mat systems (check manufacturer's recommendations)	• uniform cushioning effect • easy to clean and maintain • material remains in place • foreign objects are easily noticed • good accessibility to wheelchairs	• expensive to install • requires a flat surface; difficult to use on hills or uneven area • mat or tile edges may curl up and present a tripping hazard • some materials affected by frost

Note: Suggested material depths (noncompacted) are based on shock absorbancy from falls of 6 feet.
Source: *Handbook for Public Playground Safety,* U.S. Consumer Product Safety Commission, 2003.

(Thompson & Hudson, 2003; CPSC, 2003; CPSC, 1997). However, these materials must be loosened frequently to prevent them from packing and be replaced as they deteriorate. They must also be checked frequently for any sharp debris. Special rubber matting is also an acceptable choice for fall zones and can be purchased through most outdoor equipment catalogues. Surface materials should extend approximately four feet beyond the designated fall zone to ensure children's protection.

Maintenance Hazardous conditions can often be spotted if outdoor play areas are inspected carefully each day before children begin to play. Equipment with broken pieces, jagged or sharp edges, loose screws or bolts, or missing parts should be removed or made off-limits to children. Frequent inspections of play areas for poisonous vegetation, snakes, rodents or other small animals, sharp sticks, fallen branches, broken glass, or other harmful debris can avoid unintentional injury. Wooden surfaces should be sanded and repainted regularly.

Supervision Although individuals may go to great lengths to design attractive playgrounds and safe equipment, there is without a doubt no substitution for good supervision. Children must never be left unattended. Outdoor times provide valuable opportunities for helping children learn self-protection skills that will last a lifetime. A detailed discussion of supervision and safety management will be presented in Chapter 9.

Transportation

Some early childhood programs transport children to and from other school settings or on occasional field trips. Large passenger vans are often used for this purpose, but they are not considered safe and, in the event of an accident, may actually place occupants at increased risk for serious injury (*Child Health Alert,* 2005b; National Transportation Safety Board, 2002). Vans have a tendency to roll over and offer poor structural protection to passengers. As a result, federal transportation officials currently recommend that early childhood programs replace existing passenger vans with small-scale school buses. These buses are designed with improved structural safety features (roof and fuel tanks) and, thus, offer greater protection.

Any vehicle used to transport children should be fitted with an appropriate safety restraint system (based on height, weight, and age) for each child:

■ an infant-only carrier for infants (birth–one year) weighing up to 20–22 pounds (9.1–10.0 kg) (installed facing the rear of the car) with a three- or five-point harness. A convertible safety seat for heavier infants should be purchased for babies under one year who weigh 20–35 pounds (9.1–15.9 kg).

- a child safety seat for children weighing 20–40 pounds (9.1–18.2 kg) and who are able to sit up by themselves (installed facing the front of the car)
- a booster seat used in combination with a lap belt and shoulder harness for children who have outgrown child seats and are under four foot, nine inches (57 inches; 142.5 cm) in height
- a vehicle lap belt and shoulder harness for children who are at least 55–58 inches (137.5–145 cm) in height

It is also critical that safety seats and restraints be installed according to manufacturer's specifications and used correctly whenever children are in transit:

- they must be correctly installed (facing the front or back as is appropriate) and securely anchored in the vehicle.
- they must meet federal standards for manufacturing (safety ratings of children's car seats can be accessed online at http://www.nhtsa.dot.gov/CPS/CSSRating/index.cfm).
- children must always be buckled into the seat.

Children and adults must always be buckled in securely on every trip even though it may be a time-consuming process. Young children should always ride in the back seat of a vehicle to avoid injury from airbags.

The driver of any vehicle must be a responsible individual and possess a current license appropriate for the number of passengers to be transported. Families of children who are transported on a regular basis should get to know the driver so they feel comfortable with the arrangement. Written permission and special instructions should always be obtained from each parent before children are transported.

Motor vehicles used to transport children must be in good repair. Air conditioning and heating should be operational to protect children from temperature extremes. Copies of children's health forms and emergency contact information should also be kept in the vehicle. Periodic inspections of all safety and mechanical features ensure the vehicle's safe performance. An ABC-type fire extinguisher should be secured in the front of the vehicle where it is accessible for emergencies. Liability insurance should be purchased to cover the vehicle, driver, and maximum number of passengers it will be carrying.

Special off-street areas should be designated for the sole purpose of loading and unloading children. If programs do not have adequate space to provide this feature, greater emphasis will need to be placed on safety education. Families and children should be continually reminded to use caution around traffic. Children should always enter and exit vehicles from the curbside rather than the street-side (Figure 8–12). Adequate parking for families reduces traffic congestion and improves children's safety. Families must be reminded *never* to leave children alone in a vehicle, even for just a few minutes, in order to prevent abduction and overheating. (*Note: temperatures inside of a vehicle can become dangerously high even on mild days.*)

FIGURE 8–12

Children should enter and exit from the curb-side of a car.

Families are sometimes asked to provide transportation for off-site field trips. However, this practice is risky and has the potential for creating serious legal problems in the event of an accident. Programs have no guarantee that privately owned vehicles or individual drivers meet the standards and qualifications previously discussed. As a result, programs may be even more vulnerable to lawsuits and charges of negligence. To avoid this risk, programs may want to use public transportation, such as a city bus, or contract with a private transportation company.

When private vehicles are used for transportation, several steps can be taken to protect children's safety. Travel routes should be planned in advance, reviewed with the director, and followed precisely by all drivers. Names of drivers, additional adults, and children riding in each vehicle, as well as anticipated departure and arrival times, should also be left with a program administrator. Rules for safe traveling should be reviewed with drivers and children. Plans for responding to an unplanned emergency, such as an ill child, flat tire, carjacking, or unusual weather, should also be discussed and reviewed regularly with drivers. At least one adult should have first aid and CPR training.

FOCUS ON FAMILIES • How to Choose Quality Child Care

All families want to find the best early childhood education placement for their children, but knowing what features to look for is often difficult. Small group size, a small ratio of adults to children, and teachers who have educational preparation in early childhood are three indicators commonly associated with quality programs. Families should always take time to visit a program before enrolling their children and attempt to answer some of the following questions:

- Does the environment appear to be clean, safe, and appealing to children? For example, are electrical outlets covered, are sharp items stored out of children's reach, is the carpet intact and free of snags or stains, and do children wash their hands before eating?

- Is the program accredited or licensed?

- Do the children seem happy and under control? Are children encouraged in their efforts and allowed to express their feelings? Are teachers playing and talking with the children? Do they help children solve their own problems?

- Are children treated with respect and as individuals? Is the teacher's tone of voice warm and friendly versus harsh and demanding?

- Is there adequate adult supervision? Are enough adults present to respond to an injured child or classroom emergency and to assure the safety of other children?

- Are there a sufficient number and variety of toys and materials for all children to use, or must children wait for others to finish? Are items easily accessible to children?

- Is the food served to children nutritious, age appropriate, and adequate in amount? If your child has food allergies, would his or her special needs be accommodated? Are weekly menus posted?

- Have the teachers been trained to work with young children? Do they appear to enjoy working with the children and take pride in their efforts? Are they knowledgeable about how to facilitate children's development and spot problems? Be sure to ask about their educational preparation and years of experience.

- Do you feel welcomed and encouraged to ask questions? Are there opportunities for you to become involved in your child's classroom?

FOCUS ON FAMILIES • How to Choose Quality Child Care (continued)

- Are learning experiences planned for children, or are they left to wander or watch television?
- Is a daily schedule of the children's activities posted for you to read?
- Do you agree with the program's philosophy, and is it appropriate for your child's needs?
- Have the program's policies been explained clearly, and are they acceptable to you?

CASE STUDY

Linh Nam cares for several neighborhood children while their parents work at the local meatpacking factory. In the beginning, she agreed to take in one or two children on days when their parents were unable to find other child care arrangements. However, now Linh has seven children, 19 months to six years, who show up on a regular basis. Their parents are grateful and pleased with the nurturing care Linh provides. She fears that local licensing authorities will discover her activities, but is reluctant to contact them because she has no formal training in child care and isn't sure that her house will meet safety standards. She also knows that her friends depend on her for child care and could lose their jobs if they don't have anywhere to leave their children.

1. What are Linh's options?
2. What steps can Linh take to improve her chances of becoming licensed?
3. Should licensing (or registration) be mandatory for in-home child care?
4. Should programs that don't meet state licensing standards be closed down?
5. How can increasing demands for child care be balanced against a need to improve their quality?

CLASSROOM CORNER • Teacher Activities

Recycle Everyday...

Concept: You can recycle items instead of throwing them away in the trash. (Pre-2)

Learning Objectives

- Children will learn that items can be recycled and then made into other products.
- Children will learn how to sort different items.

Supplies

- boxes (the size that reams of paper come in); newspapers, chipboard boxes, magazines/ catalogs; milk jugs and plastic bottles; cans (emptied out and clean; make sure cans don't have a sharp ring)

(continued)

CLASSROOM CORNER • Teacher Activities (continued)

Learning Activities

- Read and discuss the book:
  - *Recycle Every Day* by Nancy Elizabeth Wallace
- Decorate each box so children will know which items need to go in it (ex. picture of a milk jug, a water or soda bottle, newspaper, etc.). Children can help decorate the boxes ahead of time.
- Spread items out on the floor to show how much space discarded items take up. Talk about how items can be sorted and recycled and not thrown away.
- Demonstrate how items need to be sorted according to the pictures on the box.
- Have children come up and pick an item to place in the correct box. Sort all items. If possible, plan a field trip to a recycling center.

Evaluation

- Children can sort items.
- Children will know that items can be recycled and made into other items instead of thrown away as trash.

SUMMARY

- The environment affects all aspects of children's growth and development.
- Children's environments must be planned to be enriching and safe.
- Regulation of early childhood facilities and programs is essential for protecting children's safety.
- Adhering to licensing regulations can help protect teachers; however, not everyone agrees about how much regulation is necessary.
- Licensing procedures vary from state to state.
- The review process generally includes:
  - meeting local zoning, fire, safety, and sanitation codes.
  - review of staff qualifications and training.
  - evaluation of curriculum plans and program policies.
  - assurance that transportation, food service, and health care are adequate.
- Families can advocate for quality programs by supporting licensing and accreditation efforts, selecting quality care for their children, and being informed.

APPLICATION ACTIVITIES

1. Develop a safety checklist that teachers and families could use to inspect children's outdoor play areas for hazardous conditions. Using your list, conduct an inspection of two different play yards (for example, public vs. private), or the same play area on two separate occasions. Repeat the process for indoor areas.

2. Contact your local licensing agency. Make arrangements to accompany licensing personnel on an on-site visit of a center-based program. Be sure to review state licensing regulations

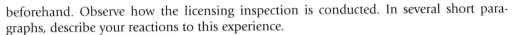
beforehand. Observe how the licensing inspection is conducted. In several short paragraphs, describe your reactions to this experience.

3. Often licensing personnel are viewed as unfriendly or threatening authority figures. However, their major role is to offer guidance and help teachers create safe environments for children. Role-play how you would handle the following situations during a licensing visit. Keep in mind the positive role of licensing personnel, e.g., offering explanations, providing suggestions, and planning acceptable solutions and alternatives:

- electrical outlets not covered
- all children's toothbrushes found stored together in a large plastic bin
- open boxes of dry cereals and crackers in kitchen cabinets
- an adult-sized toilet and wash basin in the bathroom
- a swing set located next to a cement patio
- incomplete information on children's immunization records
- a teacher who prepares snacks without first washing his or her hands

4. Obtain and read a copy of your state's licensing regulations. Organize a class debate on the topic of minimal vs. quality standards for early childhood programs.

5. Prepare a brochure or simple checklist for families describing how to select quality early education programs.

6. Learn more about the CDA credential. Research this online (http://www.cdacouncil.org) or contact the Council for Professional Recognition, 2460 16th St., NW, Washington, DC, 20009–3575; (800) 424–4310. After reading the materials, prepare a brief summary describing the program and its requirements.

7. Invite a county extension agent or florist to bring in examples or cuttings of poisonous plants. Learn to identify at least five of them.

8. Go to the U.S. Consumer Product Safety Commission Web site (http://www.cpsc.gov). Review and summarize the recommended safety standards for at least eight playground items. Prepare a handout for parents highlighting safety conditions they should observe in public play areas.

CHAPTER REVIEW

A. By Yourself

1. Match the definition in **column I** with the term in **column II**.

Column I	Column II
1. local ordinance that indicates what type of facility shall be in an area	a. regulation
2. rule dealing with procedures	b. minimal standards
3. method of action that determines present and future decisions	c. staff qualification
4. witnessed form that indicates the signature that appears on the form is really that of the person signing the form	d. notarized permissions
5. skills possessed by the people responsible for the operation of a business	e. policy
6. meeting the least possible requirements	f. zoning code

2. Identify and describe eight features of a quality early education program.

3. What steps are involved in obtaining a license to operate an early childhood program?

4. What type of car seat/restraint is appropriate for a three-year-old? What about an 11-month-old infant who weighs 27 pounds?

B. As a Group

1. Discuss the pros and cons of the following question: Should the quality of state child care licensing standards be raised?

2. How does the environment influence a child's growth and development?

3. Describe several features that make an outdoor play yard safe for young children.

4. What steps can programs take to make their facilities secure from unwanted intrusions?

5. What difference does a teacher's education preparation have on the quality of a child's experiences in an early childhood program?

REFERENCES

Ackerman, D. (2005). Getting teachers from here to there: Examining issues related to an early care and education teacher policy. *Early Childhood Research & Practice, 7*(1).

Allen, K. E., & Cowdery, G. (2005). *The exceptional child: Inclusion in early childhood education.* Clifton Park, NY: Delmar Learning.

American Academy of Pediatrics (AAP). (1999, May). Trampolines at home, school, and recreational centers. *Pediatrics, 103*(5), 1053–1056.

American Public Health Association (APHA) and American Academy of Pediatrics (AAP). (2002). *Caring for our children: National health and safety performance standards for out-of-home care.* Washington, DC.

Archibold, R., & Marshall, C. (2006, Feb.1). Ex-employee kills 5 others and herself at California postal plant. *New York Times,* A-13.

Aronson, S. (2002). *Healthy young children: A manual for programs.* (4th ed.). Washington, DC: NAEYC.

Booth, C., Kelly, J., Spieker, S., & Zuckerman, T. (2003). Toddlers' attachment security to child-care providers: The Safe and Secure Scale. *Early Education & Development, 14*(1), 83–100.

Booth, C. L., & Jean, F. (2002). Child care effects on the development of toddlers with special needs. *Early Childhood Research Quarterly; 17*(2), 171–196.

Bredekamp, S., & Copple, C. (Eds.) (1997). Developmentally appropriate practice in early childhood programs. Washington, DC: NAEYC.

Burchinal, M., & Cryer, D. (2003). Diversity, child care quality, and developmental outcomes. *Early Childhood Research Quarterly, 18*(4), 401–426.

Burchinal, M., Howes, C., & Kontos, S. (2002). Structural predictors of child care quality in child care homes. *Early Childhood Research Quarterly, 17*(1), 87–105.

Child Health Alert. (2005a, Nov.). When adults wear bike helmets, so do kids. *Child Health Alert, 23,* 2.

Child Health Alert. (2005b, Feb.). 15-Passenger vans can pose special risks. *Child Health Alert, 23,* 4.

Child Health Alert. (2003, March). Injury prevention: Accidental scald burns in skins. *Child Health Alert, 21,* 4–5.

Clarke-Stewart, A., & Allhusen, V. (2005). *What we know about childcare.* Cambridge, MA: Harvard University Press.

Clarke-Stewart, A., Vandell, D., Burchinal, M., O'Brien, M., & McCartney, K. (2002). Do regulable features of child-care homes affect children's development? *Early Childhood Research Quarterly 17*(1), 52–86.

Consumer Product Safety Commission (CPSC). (2005). Evaluation of the effectiveness of surface coatings in reducing dislodged arsenic from new wood pressure-treated with chromated cooper arsenate (CCA). Accessed on November 1, 2006, from http://www.cpsc.gov/library/foia/foia05/os/ccamitig.pdf.

CPSC. (2003). *Handbook of public playground safety.* Washington, DC.

CPSC. (2002). *Injuries and deaths associated with children's playground equipment.* Washington, DC.

CPSC. (2001). *National electronic injury surveillance system 1998–2000.* Washington, DC.

CPSC. (1997). *Playground surfacing technical information guide.* Washington, DC: U.S. Government Printing Office.

Cryer, D., & Phillipsen, L. (1997). Quality details: A close-up look at the child care program strengths and weaknesses. *Young Children, 52*(5), 51–61.

Daisey, J. M., Angell, W. J., &, Apte, M. G. (2003). Indoor air quality, ventilation and health symptoms in schools: An analysis of existing information. *Indoor Air, 13*(1), 53–64.

DeBord, K., Hestenes, L., Moore, R. C., Cosco, N., & McGinnis, J. R. (2002). Paying attention to the outdoor environment is as important as preparing the indoor environment. *Young Children, 57*(3), 32–34.

Doherty, G., Forer, B., Lero, D., Goelman, H., & LaGrange, A. (2006). Predictors of quality in family child care. *Early Childhood Research Quarterly, 21*(3), 296–312.

Environmental Protection Agency (EPA). (2005). Studies provide public with updated information on CCA-treated playground and decks. Accessed on November 1, 2006, from http://www.epa.gov/oppad001/reregistration/cca.

Essa, E. (2007). *Introduction to early childhood education.* Clifton Park, NY: Thomson Delmar Learning.

Ferng, S. F., & Lee, L. W. (2002). Indoor air quality assessment of daycare facilities with carbon dioxide, temperature, and humidity as indicators. *Journal of Environmental Health, 65*(4), 14–18, 22.

Flynn, L. L., & Kieff, J. (2002). Including everyone in outdoor play. *Young Children, 57*(3), 20–26.

Frost, J. L., Wortham, S. C., & Reifel, S. (2004). *Play and child development.* Upper Saddle River, NJ: Merrill Prentice Hall.

Goelman, H., Forer, B., Kershaw, P., Doherty, G., Lero, D., & LaGrange, A. (2006). Towards a predictive model of quality in Canadian child care centers. *Early Childhood Research Quarterly, 21*(3), 280–295.

Just, J., Nisakinovic, L., Laoudi, Y., & Grimfeld, A. (2006). Air pollution and asthma in children. *Archives of Pediatrics & Adolescent Medicine, 13*(7), 1055–1060.

Kagan, S. L., Brandon, R. N., Ripple, C. H., Maher, E. J., & Joesch, J. M. (2002). Supporting quality early childhood care and education: Addressing compensation and Infrastructure. *Young Children, 57*(3), 58–65.

Kansas Stakeholders Advisory Committee for Early Childhood Education. (2001). *Quality standards for early childhood education for children birth through eight.* Topeka, KS: Kansas State Department of Education (available online, http://www.kskits.org/html/bestpractice/qs.html). (Also available, *Quality standards in family child care homes.*)

Kennedy, M. (2006). Playgrounds. *American School & University, 78*(11), 16–18.

Kim, J. (2004). Ambient air pollution: Health hazards to children. *Pediatrics, 114*(6), 1699–1707.

Knoche, L., Peterson, C., Edwards, C., & Jeon, H. (2006). Child care for children with and without disabilities: The provider, observer, and parent perspectives. *Early Childhood Research Quarterly, 21*(1), 93–109.

Kyle, A., Woodruff, T., & Axelrad, D. (2006). Integrated assessment of environment and health: America's children and the environment. *Environmental Health Perspectives, 114*(3), 447–452.

Lalloo, R., & Sheiham, A. (2003). Risk factors for childhood major and minor head and other injuries in a nationally representative sample. *Injury, 34*(4), 261–266.

Landrigan, P., Kimmel, C., Correa, A., & Eskenazi, B. (2004). Children's health and the environment: Public health issues and challenges for risk assessment. *Environmental Health Perspectives, 112*(2), 257–265.

Lohse, J. L. (2003). A bicycle safety education program for parents of young children. *Journal of School Health, 19*(2), 100–110.

Lutton, A. (2006). NAEYC Early childhood associate degree system: Filling a gap in the U.S. teacher education system. *Young Children, 61*(5), 58–59.

Morris, B. (1999, December 2). Webcam's focus on day care. *New York Times,* G1.

Munton, A. G., Blackburn, T., & Barreau, S. (2002). Good practice in out of school care provision. *Early Child Development and Care, 172*(3), 223–230.

National Association for the Education of Young Children (NAEYC). (2006a). NAEYC Accreditation: Continuing to improve. *Young Children, 61*(5), 66–67.

NAEYC. (2006b). Licensing and public regulation of early childhood programs: NAEYC position statement (2006). Accessed online at http://www.naeyc.org/about/positions/pslicense.asp.

National Center for Accessibility. (2007). *Playgrounds for all kids!* Accessed April 25, 2007, at http://www.ncaonline.org/playgrounds/index.shtml.

National Institute of Child Health & Development (NICHD). (2005). A day in third grade: A large scale study of classroom quality and teacher and student behavior. *The Elementary School Journal, 105*(3), 305–323.

NICHD. (2004). Type of child care and children's development at 54 months. *Early Childhood Research & Practice, 19*(2), 203–230.

National Transportation Safety Board. (2002). *Evaluation of the rollover propensity of 15-passenger vans.* Washington, DC.

Oliver, S. J., & Klugman, E. (2002, May–June). Playing the day away: The importance of constructive play in early childhood settings. *Child Care Information Exchange 145,* 66–70.

Peth-Pierce, R. (2002). Early child care and children's development prior to school entry: Results from the NICHD study of early child care. *American Educational Research Journal, 39*(1), 133–164.

Rae, P. (2006). *Moving and learning across the curriculum: More than 300 activities and games to make learning fun.* Clifton Park, NY: Thomson Delmar Learning.

Ramirez, M., Peek-Asa, C., & Kraus, J. (2004). Disability and risk of school related injury. *Injury Prevention, 10*(1), 21–26.

Resnick, L., & Zurawsky, C. (2005). Early childhood education: Investing in quality makes sense. *AERA Research Points, 3*(2), 1–4.

Rivkin, M. (2006). Let's move together. *Early Childhood Today, 20*(6), 32–38.

Sander, L. (2006, Oct. 10). Missouri boy fires rifle in his school: All are safe. *New York Times,* A-18.

Shields, B., Fernandez, S., & Smith, G. (2005). Comparison of minitrampoline- and full-sized trampoline-related injuries in the United States, 1990–2002. *Pediatrics, 116*(1), 96–103.

Siegle, R. (1995, Feb.). Child care and the ADA. *Exceptional Parent,* 25, 34.

Stanken, B.A. (2000). Promoting helmet use among children. *Journal of Community Health Nursing, 17*(2), 85–92.

Strickland, E. (2005). Mindful movement. *Early Childhood Today, 19*(6), 6.

Surr, J. (1992). Early childhood programs and the American Disabilities Act (ADA). *Young Children, 47*(5), 18–21.

Thompson, D., & Hudson, S. (2003). The inside information about safety surfacing. *Young Children, 58*(2), 108–111.

Thompson, D., & Hudson, S. (2000). Children and playground injuries. In J. Frost (Ed.), *Children and injuries.* Tucson, AZ: Lawyers & Judges Publishing Co.

Tinsworth, D., & McDonald, J. (2001). *Special study: Injuries and deaths associated with children's playground equipment.* Washington, DC: U.S. Consumer Product Safety Commission.

Tout, K., Zaslow, M., & Berry, D. (2005). Quality and qualifications. In M., Zaslow & I. Martinez-Beck (Eds.). *Critical issues in early childhood professional development.* Baltimore: Brookes Publishing.

U.S. Department of Justice, (1997). Commonly asked questions about child care centers and the American with Disabilities Act. Accessed on October 30, 2006, at http://www.usdoj.gov/crt/ada/childq&a.htm.

Vi-Nhuan, L., Perlman, M., Zellman, G., & Hamilton, L. (2006). Measuring child-staff ratios in child care centers: Balancing effort and representativeness. *Early Childhood Research Quarterly, 21*(3), 267–269.

Warman, B. (1998). Trends in state accreditation policies. *Young Children, 53*(5), 52–55.

Whitebrook, M. (2003a). *Bachelor's degrees are best: Higher qualifications for pre-kindergarten teachers lead to better learning environments for children.* Washington, DC: Trust for Early Education.

Whitebrook, M. (2003b). *Early education quality: Higher teacher qualifications for better learning environments—A review of the literature.* Berkeley, CA: Center for the Study of Child Care Employment.

Whitebrook, M., & A. Eichberg. (2002). Finding a better way: Defining policies to improve child care workforce compensation. *Young Children, 57*(3): 66–72.

Wishard, A. G., Shivers, E. M., Howes, C., & Ritchie, S. (2003). Child care program and teacher practices: Associations with quality and children's experiences. *Early Childhood Research Quarterly, 18*(1), 65–103.

Zaslow, M., & Martinez-Beck, I. (Eds.). (2005). *Critical issues in early childhood professional development.* Baltimore: Brookes Publishing.

HELPFUL WEB RESOURCES

Child and Family Canada	http://www.cfc-efc.ca
Consumer Product Safety (Canada)	http://www.hc-sc.gc.ca
National Association for Family Child Care	http://www.nafcc.org
National Association for the Education of Young Children (NAEYC)	http://www.naeyc.org
National Association of Child Care Resource and Referral Agencies (NACCRRA)	http://www.naccrra.org
National Network for Child Care	http://www.nncc.org
National Program for Playground Safety	http://www.uni.edu
U.S. Product Safety Commission	http://www.cpsc.gov

For additional health, safety, and nutrition resources, go to
http://www.EarlyChildEd.delmar.cengage.com

CHAPTER 9

Safety Management

OBJECTIVES

After studying this chapter, you should be able to:
- Identify the common causes of unintentional death among young children.
- Explain why infants and toddlers are at greatest risk for unintentional injury.
- Describe the four basic principles of safety management.
- Identify two forms of negligence.
- Discuss the teacher's role in safeguarding children's safety.

TERMS TO KNOW

unintentional injury	**supervision**	**liability**
risk management	**incidental learning**	**negligence**

Unintentional injuries are the leading cause of death and permanent disability among children under the age of 14 (National Center for Health Statistics, 2006; Pan, et al., 2006). They are also responsible for thousands of nonfatal injuries and are costly in terms of time, energy, suffering, and medical expense. Although children experience many different types of injuries, the most common causes of death due to unintentional injury include (Table 9–1):

- motor vehicles—as pedestrians, riding a bicycle or wheeled toy
- drowning—in swimming pools, spas, bathtubs, ponds, toilets, buckets
- burns—from fireplaces, appliances, grills, chemicals, electrical outlets, residential fires, fireworks
- suffocation—from plastic bags, entrapment in chests or appliances, bedding, aspiration of small objects
- falls—from stairs, furniture, play equipment, windows
- poisoning—from pain relievers, carbon monoxide, cleaning products, insecticides, cosmetics

TABLE 9–1 Common Causes of Childhood Death Due to Unintentional Injury

Cause of Death	1 to 4-year-olds	5 to 9-year-olds
motor vehicle/pedestrian	36.1%	55%
drowning	27%	14.5%
fire/burns	16.3%	13.2%
suffocation	8.3%	3.2%
falls	2.0%	1.2%
poisoning	1.8%	1.2%

Source: Centers for Disease Control and Prevention (CDC) Web-based Injury Statistics Query and Reporting System (WISQARS). 2004 Unintentional Injuries Deaths, Ages, 1–4 and 5–9.

Thus, families and teachers must take extra precautions to provide environments and activities that are safe for children of all ages and stages of development.

WHAT IS UNINTENTIONAL INJURY?

The term *unintentional injury* has replaced *accidents* when referring to injuries sustained by children. This is because in most instances, factors contributing to an accident are preventable. Childhood injuries are most often attributed to environmental hazards, lack of appropriate planning and adult supervision, or a child's immature development—conditions that are all manageable with improved knowledge and awareness (Figure 9–1).

Infants and toddlers are at highest risk for sustaining life-threatening injuries and medical emergencies. Their zealous interest and curiosity in learning about their surroundings, impulsive

FIGURE 9–1

Teachers have a professional and ethical responsibility to keep children safe.

play, and immature development can unfortunately also lead children into new and unexpected dangers. Likewise, older children continue to explore their environment with an even greater sense of interest, yet still lack an adult's maturity, experience, and understanding necessary to anticipate the consequences of their behavior. Thus, assuring children's safety requires continuous awareness of children's abilities, stage of development, potential hazards, and preventive measures (Table 9–2).

Teachers and administrators assume a major role and responsibility for protecting the safety of children in their care. This can be a particularly challenging task given the ages of children typically

TABLE 9–2 Developmental Characteristics and Injury Prevention

Age	Developmental Characteristics	Hazards	Preventive Measures
Birth to 4 months	Eats, sleeps, cries. Rolls off flat surfaces. Wriggles.	Burns	Set hot water heater to a maximum of 120°F. Always keep one hand on baby.
		Falls	Never turn back or walk away from a baby who is on a table or bed.
		Toys/Choking	Select toys that are too large to swallow, too tough to break, have no sharp points or edges, and have nontoxic finishes.
		Sharp objects	Keep pins and other sharp objects out of baby's reach.
		Suffocation	Filmy plastics, harnesses, zippered bag, and pillows can smother or strangle. A firm mattress and coverings that are tucked in are safest. Babies of this age need complete protection.
4–12 months	Grasps and moves about. Puts objects in mouth.	Play areas	Keep baby in a safe place near an adult. The floor, full-sized bed, and yard are unsafe without supervision.
		Bath	Check temperature of bath water with elbow. Keep baby out of reach of faucets. *Never* leave baby alone in bath.
		Toys	Large beads on strong cord, unbreakable, rounded toys made of smooth wood or plastic are safe.
		Small objects	Keep buttons, beads, coins, and other small objects from baby's reach.
		Poisoning	Children of this age still need full-time protection.
		Falls	Don't turn your back or walk away when baby is on an elevated surface. Place gates in doorways and on stairways.
		Burns	Place guards around registers and floor furnaces. Keep hot liquids, hot foods, and electric cords on irons, toasters, and coffee pots out of baby's reach. Use sturdy and round-edged furniture. Avoid hot steam vaporizers.

TABLE 9–2 Developmental Characteristics and Injury Prevention (continued)

Age	Developmental Characteristics	Hazards	Preventive Measures
1–2 years	Investigates, climbs, opens doors and drawers; takes things apart; likes to play.	Gates, windows, doors Play areas	Securely fasten doors leading to stairways, driveways, and storage. Put gates on stairways and porches. Keep screens locked or nailed. Fence the play yard. Provide sturdy toys with no small removable parts or with unbreakable materials. Keep electric cords to coffee pots, toasters, irons, and computers out of reach.
		Water	*Never* leave child alone in tub, wading pool, or around open or frozen water. Fence and gate pools; keep locked at all times.
		Poisons	Store all medicines and poisons in locked cabinets. Store cosmetics and household products, especially caustics, out of child's reach. Store kerosene and gasoline in metal cans and out of children's reach.
		Burns	Provide guards for wall heaters, registers, and floor furnaces. Never leave children alone in the house. Close supervision is needed to protect child from injuries.
2–3 years	Fascinated by fire. Moves about constantly. Tries to do things alone. Imitates and explores. Runs and is lightening fast. Is impatient with restraint.	Traffic	Keep child away from street and driveway with strong fence and consistent discipline. Use appropriate car seats restraints.
		Water	Even shallow wading pools are unsafe unless carefully supervised.
		Toys	Large sturdy toys without sharp edges or small removable parts are safest.
		Burns	Keep matches and cigarette lighters out of child's reach. Teach them about the danger of fire. Never leave children alone in the house.
		Dangerous objects	Lock up medicine, household and garden poisons, dangerous tools, firearms, and garden equipment. Teach safe ways of handling appropriate tools and kitchen equipment.
		Playmates	Injuries happen more often when playmates are older—the two-year-old may be easily hurt by bats, hard balls, bicycles, rough play.

(continued)

TABLE 9–2 Developmental Characteristics and Injury Prevention (continued)

Age	Developmental Characteristics	Hazards	Preventive Measures
3–6 years	Explores the neighborhood. Climbs on objects. Enjoys riding tricycles. Plays and likes rough games. Frequently out of adult sight. Likes to imitate adult actions.	Tools and equipment	Store in a safe place, out of reach, and locked. Teach safe use of tools and kitchen equipment.
		Poisons and burns	Keep medicines, household cleaning products, and matches locked up. Provide nontoxic art materials.
		Falls and injuries	Check play areas for attractive hazards such as old refrigerators, deep holes, trash heaps, construction, and old buildings.
		Drowning	Teach the danger of water and begin swimming instruction.
		Traffic	Help children learn rules and dangers of traffic, insist on obedience where traffic is concerned. Use appropriate seat restraints; always buckle children in.
6–12 years	Enjoys spending time away from home. Participates in active sports, is part of a group and will "try anything once" in traffic, on foot or on a bicycle. Teaching must gradually replace supervision.	Traffic	Drive safely as an example. Use safety belts. Teach pedestrian and bicycle safety rules. Don't allow play in streets or alleys.
		Firearms	Store unloaded in a locked cabinet. Teach children to stay away from guns and tell an adult if they find one.
		Sports	Provide sound instruction, safe area, and equipment. Supervise any competition. Provide protective gear and insist that it be worn.
		Drowning	Teach swimming and boating safety.

enrolled in early education programs. However, teachers are uniquely positioned to eliminate needless tragedies and assure children's well-being with appropriate training and experience.

RISK MANAGEMENT: PRINCIPLES AND PREVENTIVE MEASURES

Prevention of **unintentional injury** requires continuous awareness and implementation of **risk management** measures (Children's Safety Network, 2005; Zavitkovsky & Thompson, 2000). Teachers and families must consider the element of safety in everything they do with young

unintentional injury – *an unexpected or unplanned event that may result in physical harm or injury.*
risk management – *measures taken to avoid an event such as an injury or illness from occurring; implies the ability to anticipate circumstances and behaviors.*

children (Table 9–2). This includes the rooms they organize, toys they purchase, and learning activities they plan. To new teachers or busy parents, this step may seem unnecessarily slow or too time-consuming. However, these are precisely the times when it is important to focus extra attention on children's safety. Any amount of time and effort is worthwhile if it spares only one child from injury!

Knowledge of developmental skills is essential for protecting children's safety (Berk, 2005). Understanding the differences in their cognitive, motor, social, and emotional abilities at various stages helps adults anticipate children's actions, and take steps to avoid unintentional injury. For example, understanding that infants put everything into their mouths should alert teachers to be extra vigilant of small items, such as a paper clip or pen cap, that might be dropped on the floor. Knowing that toddlers enjoy climbing should caution adults to securely fasten bookshelves and large pieces of play equipment to the wall or floor. Recognizing that four-year-olds' limited understanding of cause and effect makes them more vulnerable to hazardous situations in their environment is useful when designing a classroom or play yard. Or, knowing that boys are more likely to be involved in accidents than girls due to their preference for play that involves active, aggressive, and risk-taking behaviors can be used when planning large motor activities (Morrongiello, et al., 2006; Schwebel, et al., 2002; Matheny, 1991). Teachers and families will also find information about children's development helpful for:

- planning children's environments
- preparing learning activities
- selecting appropriate play equipment (indoor and outdoor)
- establishing rules
- supervising children's learning and play experiences
- developing safety education programs

An awareness of circumstances and adult behaviors that can contribute to an increased risk of unintentional injury is essential (Table 9–3).

It is also known that children in group-care settings are more likely to be injured while playing outdoors, especially on swings, climbing apparatus, and slides (Schwebel, Brezausek & Belsky, 2006; Garzon, 2005; Limbos & Peek-Asa, 2003). For this reason, some states no longer permit swings, teeter-totters, or large slides on new playgrounds. When children are at home they typically experience a higher rate of injury indoors, particularly in the kitchen and bathroom areas (U.S. Consumer Product Safety Commission, 2006).

TABLE 9-3 Conditions that Contribute to Unintentional Injury

The risk of injury is greatest when
- adults are not feeling well; suffering from symptoms of illness or discomfort or tired
- adults are angry, emotionally upset or faced with a difficult situation, such as an uncooperative child, an unpleasant conversation with a parent, a strained relationship with a staff member, or a personal problem
- new teachers, staff members, or visitors who are unfamiliar with the children and their routines are present
- conditions are rushed or planned late in the day
- there is a shortage of teachers; too few adults to provide adequate supervision
- children are not able to play outdoors due to inclement weather
- new children are included in a group and are unfamiliar with the environment, rules, and expectations
- rules have not been formulated or explained carefully to children

Teachers are exposed to children's communicable illnesses on a daily basis. Calling in sick often creates a staff shortage since substitutes may be difficult to locate. How can a teacher determine if he/she is too sick to come to work? What are the risks involved in coming to work when you are sick? How might teacher illness contribute to children's unintentional injury?

Environmental design and maintenance are also important considerations in the prevention of children's injuries. Local building codes, state child care licensing regulations, and ADA architectural requirements provide guidelines for the construction of facilities that are safe and accessible (Access Board, 2001). Consulting with licensing personnel during the planning phase of any new construction or remodeling project is helpful for identifying safety features and assuring that the facilities will comply with recommended standards. The National Association for the Education of Young Children (NAEYC) and National Association of Child Care Resource and Referral Agencies (NACCRRA) have also issued recommendations that address quality standards for children's environments.

National Health and Safety Performance Standards (*Guidelines for out-of-home child care programs*) have also been developed by the American Academy of Pediatrics and the American Public Health Association (http://nrc.uchsc.edu/national). Following the safety recommendations outlined in this document can help programs eliminate many potentially hazardous conditions in children's environments.

Despite adults' best efforts, it is not possible to prevent every childhood injury. Regardless of how much care is exercised, some circumstances will be beyond a teacher's or parent's ability to control. For example, no amount of appropriate planning or supervision can prevent a toddler from suddenly bumping into a table edge or an older child's unexpected release of a climber railing. However, the number and seriousness of injuries can be significantly reduced when basic safety principles are followed:

- planning in advance
- establishing rules
- maintaining quality supervision
- providing for safety education

Advanced Planning

Considerable thought and careful planning should go into the selection of equipment and activities that are appropriate for young children (Gestwicki, 2006; Stoecklin, 2001; Gibbs, 2000). Choices must take into account children's developmental abilities and also encourage the safe acquisition of new skills. Activities should be planned, and equipment selected to stimulate children's curiosity, exploration, and sense of independence without endangering their safety (Frost, Wortham & Reifel, 2004). When programs invest time in planning and providing a variety of developmentally appropriate learning opportunities, they typically experience a lower incidence of unintentional injury because children find the activities interesting, engaging, and suited to their abilities.

Planning for children's safety requires that teachers consider the risks involved in each activity. Many problems can easily be avoided if time is taken to examine materials, methods, and equipment before they are presented to children. This process also includes thinking through each step of an activity carefully before allowing children to begin. Advanced planning also implies that a teacher is prepared for the unexpected. This includes anticipating children's often unpredictable behaviors and developing safety rules for each activity (Figure 9–2). It also infers that adults check the safety of play equipment (indoor and outdoor) before children begin to play.

Organization is fundamental to effective advanced planning. Teachers must carefully review, from start to finish, each step of an activity before presenting it to children. Forgetting supplies or being unsure of how to proceed greatly increases the risk of unintentional injury. Thinking a project through also enables teachers to make adjustments and substitute safer alternatives for any that may be potentially hazardous.

An examination of accident records can also be useful during the planning stage. A pattern of similar injuries may suggest that teachers need to alter the way an activity is being conducted. For example, if it is noted that children are repeatedly hurt on a piece of outdoor play equipment or during a similar classroom activity, a cause must be investigated immediately. Plans to modify the rules, amount of supervision, or the equipment itself may be necessary to assure children's safety.

Establishing Rules

Rules are statements about behavior that is considered acceptable as it relates to the welfare of an individual child, concern for group safety, and respect for shared property (Table 9–4). Too often, rules only inform children about what they should not do. They leave unclear what behaviors are valued or considered acceptable. However, when rules are based on developmentally appropriate expectations, they can promote children's cooperation and understanding of how to use play equipment safely.

FIGURE 9-2

Teachers must be able to anticipate children's unpredictable behaviors.

Teachers can use rules to encourage children's appropriate behavior by stating them in positive terms, e.g., "Slide down the slide on your bottom, feet first, so you can see where you are going." The only time "no" should be used is when a child's immediate safety is endangered. To be most effective, rules should be stated clearly and in terms that are simple enough for even very young children to understand. Children are also more accepting of a rule when they have been given a brief explanation about why it is necessary.

There are no universal safety rules. Individual programs must develop their own safety guidelines and rules based on the:

- population of children being served
- type of program and equipment (indoor and outdoor)
- number of adults available for supervision
- nature of the activity involved

Programs serving very young children and children whose behavior is difficult to manage may need to establish rules and limits that are more explicit and detailed. The type of equipment and whether it is being used in the classroom, outdoors, on large school playgrounds, or in home-based settings also influences how specific rules must be to protect children from potential harm.

When rules are established, they must also be enforced consistently or children quickly learn that they have no meaning. However, a teacher must never threaten children or cause them to be afraid in order to gain compliance. Rather, children should be praised whenever they demonstrate appropriate

TABLE 9–4 General Rules for Safe Use of Play Equipment

Climbing Apparatus

Rules for Children
- Always hold on with both hands.
- Keep hands to self.
- Look carefully before jumping off equipment; be sure the area below is clear of objects and other children.
- Be extra careful if equipment or shoes are wet from snow or rain.

Guidelines for Adults
- Inspect equipment before children begin to play on it. Check for broken or worn parts and sharp edges; be sure the equipment is firmly anchored in the ground.
- Be sure the depth of surface material under equipment is adequate and free of sharp stones, sticks, and toys.
- Limit the number of children on climber at any one time.
- Always have an adult in direct attendance when children are on the equipment.
- Supervise children carefully if they are wearing slippery-soled shoes, sandals, long dresses or skirts, mittens, bulky coats, or long scarves.

Swings

Rules for Children
- Wait until the swing comes to a full stop before getting on or off.
- Always sit on the swing seat.
- Only one child per swing at any time.
- Only adults should push children.
- Stay away from moving swings.
- Hold on with both hands.

Guidelines for Adults
- Check equipment for safety, e.g., condition of chain/rope and seat, security of bolts or open-ended "S" rings; also check ground beneath swings for adequate cushioning material and sharp debris.
- Designate a "safe" area where children can wait their turn.
- An adult should be in attendance at all times.

safety behaviors. For example, a teacher might recognize a child's efforts by saying, "Carlos, I liked the way you rode your bike carefully around the other children who were playing," or "Tricia, you remembered to lay your scissors on the table before getting up to leave." Through repeated positive encouragement and adult modeling, children quickly learn appropriate safety behaviors.

Occasionally, a child will misuse play equipment or not follow directions. A gentle reminder concerning rules is usually sufficient. If this approach fails and the child continues to behave inappropriately, the teacher must remove the child from the activity or area. A simple statement such as, "I cannot allow you to hit the other children," lets the child know that this is not acceptable behavior. Permitting the child to return later to the same activity conveys confidence in the child's ability to follow expectations.

Rules never replace the need for careful adult **supervision** (Figure 9–3). Young children tend to quickly forget rules and often need to be reminded, especially when they are busy playing or excited about what they are doing. Rules should be realistic and allow children sufficient freedom to play

---

supervision – *watching carefully over the behaviors and actions of children and others.*

FIGURE 9–3

Rules never replace the need for adult supervision.

within the boundaries of safety. Rules that are overly restrictive create fear and discourage children from exploring and experimenting. The need for extensive rules can gradually be reduced as children become more dependable and aware of dangerous behaviors and situations in their environment.

Quality Supervision

Although families and teachers have many responsibilities, their supervisory role is beyond question one of the most important (Marotz, 2000). Children depend on responsible adult guidance for protection, as well as for learning appropriate safety behaviors. The younger children are, the more comprehensive and protective this supervision must be. As children gain additional motor coordination, cognitive skill, and experience in handling potentially dangerous situations, adult supervision can become less restrictive.

Quality supervision is also influenced by the nature of children's activities (Figure 9–4). For example, a cooking project involving the use of a hot appliance must be supervised more carefully than painting at an easel or putting together a puzzle. Certain pieces of play equipment may also be more challenging for some children and, thus, require close teacher supervision at all times. The nature of an activity also affects the number of children a teacher can safely manage. One adult may be able to oversee several children building with hollow blocks or riding their bikes around a play yard, while a field trip to the fire station would require the supervision of several adults.

> *Caution:* **Never leave children unattended. If a teacher must leave an area, it should be supervised by another adult.**

Occasionally, there are children who are known to be physically aggressive or who engage in behaviors that could potentially bring harm to themselves or others. Teachers are legally and ethically obligated to supervise these children more closely and to protect other children from harm. However, their responsibility goes beyond merely issuing a verbal warning to the child to stop—they must intervene and actually stop the child from continuing the dangerous activity even if it means physically removing the child from the area. Failure to intervene can result in legal action. However, there are a number of additional approaches that teachers can use to effectively manage children's disruptive behaviors (Table 9–5).

FIGURE 9–4

The amount of adult supervision required depends on the type of activity involved.

An adequate number of adults must always be available to supervise children, especially in out-of-home programs. Minimal adult/child ratios are generally established by individual state child care licensing regulations for indoor and outdoor settings. NAEYC has recommended that there never be fewer than two adults with any group of children. However, there are also considerable differences in adults' abilities to supervise and manage children's behavior. Some teachers are less effective at controlling unruly or disruptive children. In these situations, it may be necessary to have more than the required number of adults available to safely monitor children's play.

Safety Education

One of the primary methods for avoiding unintentional injury is through safety education (Schwebel, et al., 2006). Children can begin learning safe behaviors as soon as they understand the meanings of words. The earlier children learn about safety, the more naturally they will develop the attitudes and respect that lead to lifelong patterns of safe behavior.

Much safety education takes place through **incidental learning** experiences and imitation of adult behaviors. Young children who already show many safe attitudes and practices can also serve as role models for other children. For example, several children may be jumping from the top of a platform rather than climbing down the ladder. Suddenly, one child yells, "You shouldn't be doing that. You could get hurt!" As a result, the children stop and begin using the ladder. Taking advantage of teachable moments can also prove to be an effective educational tool. For example, when children stand up on a swing or run with sharp objects in their hand, teachers can use these opportunities to explain why the behavior was not appropriate and help children problem-solve safer alternatives. This form of learning is often most meaningful for young children.

TABLE 9–5 Teacher Checklist: Positive Strategies for Managing Children's Inappropriate Behavior

- Offer praise and give attention for appropriate and desired behavior.
- Redirect the child's attention to some other activity.
- Provide the child with an opportunity for choices.
- Model the appropriate and desired behavior.
- Teach and encourage children to use problem-solving techniques.
- Ignore inappropriate behaviors, unless doing so is unsafe.
- Make changes in the environment to discourage inappropriate behavior.

incidental learning – *learning that occurs in addition to the primary intent or goals of instruction.*

Safety education should also prepare children to cope with emergencies. Personal safety awareness and self-protection skills enable even young children to avoid many potentially harmful situations. Children must know what to do in an emergency and how to get help. They should learn their home address and phone number as well as how to use the telephone. Older children can also begin to learn basic first aid skills.

Teachers should not overlook their own safety in their concern for children. It is easy for adults to be careless when they are under stress or have worked long, hard hours. Sometimes, in their zealous attempts to help children, teachers take extraordinary risks; it is at these times that even greater caution must be exercised. Planning scheduled breaks and maintaining healthful eating habits will improve a teacher's alertness and ability to make sound decisions.

IMPLEMENTING SAFETY PRACTICES

Much of the responsibility for maintaining a safe environment belongs to teachers. Their knowledge of child development and daily contact with children gives them an advantageous position for identifying problem areas. However, safety must be a concern of all school personnel, including support staff such as classroom aides, cooks, housekeeping personnel, receptionists, and bus drivers. It takes only one person to identify a safety hazard that may have previously gone unnoticed.

Safety must be a continual concern. Every time teachers rearrange the classroom, take children on a field trip or walk, add new play equipment, or plan a new activity they must first stop to assess the risks involved for the children and themselves. Differences in personalities and group dynamics may also make it necessary for teachers to establish different rules for each group of children. Extra precautions may be needed when children with special needs, chronic health problems, or behavior problems are present. These children may require additional assistance and teachers may need to modify the activity or equipment to enable their full participation.

Toys and Equipment

The majority of childhood deaths and injuries related to toys and play equipment are due to choking and improper use (O'Donnell, 2006; U.S. Consumer Product Safety Commission, 2002a; Nakamura, Pollack-Nelson, & Chidekel, 2003). Many of these injuries can be prevented by carefully selecting equipment and toys that are developmentally appropriate (Stephenson, 2005; CPSC, 1997; Taylor, Morris & Rogers, 1997). Children's interests, behavioral characteristics, and developmental abilities should serve as key considerations when choosing these items (Tables 9–6 and 9–7). Age warnings on product labels do not take into account children's individual differences and, therefore, are not always reliable. Some toys on the market meet only minimal U.S. safety standards and, thus, may pose a hazard for children who are not as developmentally advanced. Injuries are also more likely to occur when children attempt to use educational materials and play equipment intended for older children, such as:

- toys that are too heavy for young children to lift
- rungs that are too large for small hands to grip securely
- steps that are too far apart
- climbing equipment and platforms that are too high above the ground
- balloons and small objects that can cause choking or suffocation (Figure 9–5)
- equipment that is unstable or not securely anchored

The opposite may also occur. When play equipment has a singular purpose or is designed for younger children, older children may misuse it in an effort to create interest and challenge.

TABLE 9-6 Teacher Checklist: Guidelines for Selecting Safe Toys and Play Equipment

1. Consider children's age, interests, and developmental abilities (including problem-solving and reasoning skills); check manufacturers' labels carefully for recommendations and warnings.
2. Choose fabric items that are washable and labeled flame-retardant or nonflammable.
3. Look for quality construction; check durability, good design, stability, absence of sharp corners or wires, and strings shorter than 12 inches (30 cm).
4. Select toys that are made from nontoxic paints and materials.
5. Avoid toys and play materials with small pieces that a child could choke on.
6. Select toys and equipment that are appropriate for the amount of available play and storage space.
7. Avoid toys with electrical parts or those that are propelled through the air.
8. Choose play materials that children can use with minimal adult supervision.

TABLE 9-7 Examples of Appropriate Toy Choices for Infants, Toddlers, and Preschoolers

Infants	Toddlers	Preschoolers
nonbreakable mirrors	peg bench	puppets
cloth books	balls	dolls and doll houses
wooden cars	records	dress-up clothes
rattles	simple puzzles	simple art materials,
mobiles	large building blocks	e.g., crayons, markers,
music boxes	wooden cars and trucks	watercolors, playdough,
plastic telephone	dress-up clothes	blunt scissors
balls	bristle blocks	books, puzzles, lacing cards
toys that squeak	large wooden beads	simple musical instruments
blocks	to string	cars, trucks, fire engines
nesting toys	cloth picture books	tricycle
teething ring	nesting cups	simple construction sets, e.g.,
washable, stuffed animals	pull and riding toys	Legos®, bristle blocks
	plastic dishes, pots and pans	play dishes, empty food
	chunky crayons and paper	containers

The amount of available classroom or play yard space will also influence choices. Equipment or toys that require a large area for their use will be a constant source of accidents if they are set up in spaces that are too small.

Quality is also very important to consider when purchasing toys. The materials and construction of toys and play equipment should be examined carefully and not purchased if they have:

- sharp wires, pins, or staples
- small pieces that could come loose, e.g., buttons, "eyes," screws, magnets
- moving parts that can pinch fingers
- pieces that are smaller than 1.5 inches (3.75 cm) or balls less than 1.75 inches (4.4 cm) in diameter (for children under three years)
- objects too heavy or large to be handled easily
- unstable bases or frames

FIGURE 9–5

Special devices can be purchased to measure the choking potential of small toys. Notice that the domino gets caught in the tube, but the die passes through the tube, indicating a choking hazard.

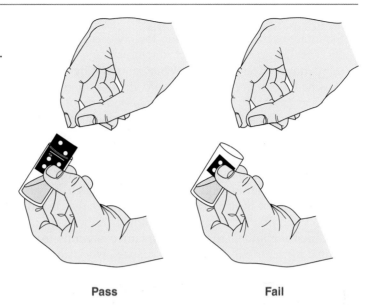

Pass   Fail

- toxic paints or materials
- sharp metal edges or rough surfaces
- defective parts or construction that will not hold up under hard use
- strings or cords (longer than 12 inches) that could cause strangulation
- parts that might cause electrical shock
- brittle plastic or glass parts that could easily break
- objects that become projectiles, such as darts, arrows, air guns

The amount of noise a toy produces should also be considered. Children's hearing is more sensitive than that of an adult's and can easily be damaged through repeated exposure to loud noises. Many children's toys emit sounds that exceed the 85-decibel threshold recommendation for safe hearing levels (ASHA, 2006; OSHA, 2003). Adults should use their judgment and be cautious in purchasing toys that produce loud music and sounds to protect young children from unnecessary hearing loss.

Not all new toys and children's products are manufactured according to U.S. safety standards, especially those that are imported (CPSC, 2007). Extreme care should also be taken when purchasing children's toys or equipment on the Internet. Hazard warnings and age recommendations may be absent, misrepresented, or not in compliance with statutory label requirements (Public Interest Research Group, 2002). Caution should also be exercised when purchasing used toys and children's equipment. Often, products that have been recalled because of hazardous features continue to appear on Web sites or in garage sales. Families and teachers should take time to inspect these items carefully and be sure they meet all current safety standards.

Toys and play equipment should be inspected on a daily basis, especially if they are used frequently by children or are located outdoors and exposed to variable weather conditions. They should always be in good repair and free of splinters, rough edges, protruding bolts or nails, and broken or missing parts. Ropes on swings or ladders should be checked routinely and replaced if they begin to fray. Large equipment should be checked often to be sure that it remains firmly anchored in the ground and that surface materials are of adequate depth and free of debris (see Chapter 8) (NPPS, 2006; Sutterby & Thornton, 2005; Frost & Sutterby, 2002).

Regularly scheduled maintenance ensures that toys and play equipment will remain in a safe condition. Equipment that is defective or otherwise unsafe for children to use should be removed promptly until it can be repaired. Items that cannot be repaired should be discarded.

■ REFLECTIVE THOUGHTS

Manufacturers are now labeling toys with age guidelines to help adults make safer choices. However, a child's chronological age does not necessarily reflect his/her developmental skills and abilities. What is meant by the term developmentally appropriate? How can a parent determine this? Why are age guidelines not always a reliable method for selecting children's toys and play equipment? Where can a parent or teacher locate information about product safety and recalls?

Special precautions are necessary whenever large equipment or climbing structures are set up indoors. Positioning equipment in an open area away from furniture or other objects reduces children's risk for injury. Mats, foam pads, or large cushions placed around and under elevated structures will also help to protect children in the event of an unexpected fall. Rules for the safe use of indoor climbers should be explained carefully to children before they begin to play. The potential for injuries can be further reduced when an adult is positioned next to the equipment and can closely monitor children's activities (Figure 9–6).

Whenever new equipment, toys, or educational materials are introduced into a classroom or outdoor setting, safety is a prime concern. Rules to safeguard children must be established and explained. However, caution should be exercised not to establish too many rules which may dampen children's enthusiasm and interest. If several new items are being introduced, it is best to do this over a period of time so that children are not overwhelmed by too many instructions.

Selection of furnishings, for example, beds, cribs, playpens, strollers, carriers, and toys for infants and toddlers, must be made with great care. As a consumer, it is important to remember that product design is often involved in childhood deaths. As a result, strict manufacturing criteria were established in 1977 by the U.S. Consumer Safety Product Commission and Canadian Consumer Corporate Affairs for the production of children's furniture (Table 9–8). Toys and furniture purchased at second-hand shops, garage sales, or on the Internet may have been manufactured before these standards went into effect and should be examined carefully. Information concerning children's toy and product recalls is available from the Consumer Product Safety Commission at (http://www.cpsc.gov) or from (http://www.safechild.net) sponsored by the Consumer Federation of America.

FIGURE 9–6

An adult should always be positioned in direct attendance when children are using playground structures.

TABLE 9-8 Infant Equipment Safety Checklist

	Yes	No

Back Carriers (not recommended for use before 4–5 months)
Carrier has restraining strap to secure child.
Leg openings are small enough to prevent child from slipping out.
Leg openings are large enough to prevent chafing.
Frames have no pinch points in the folding mechanism.
Carrier has padded covering over metal frame near baby's face.

Bassinets and Cradles
Bassinet/cradle has a sturdy bottom and a wide base for stability.
Bassinet/cradle has smooth surfaces—no protruding staples or other
   hardware that could injure the baby.
Legs have strong, effective locks to prevent folding while in use.
Mattress is firm and fits snuggly against sides of bed.
If cradle has slats, they must be spaced no more than 2 3/8 inches (6 cm) apart.

Carrier Seats
Carrier seat has a wide, sturdy base for stability.
Carrier has nonskid feet to prevent slipping.
Supporting devices lock securely.
Carrier seat has crotch and waist strap.
Buckle or strap is easy to use.

Changing Tables
Table has safety straps to prevent falls.
Table has drawers or shelves that are easily accessible without leaving
   the baby unattended.

Cribs
Slats are spaced no more than 2 3/8 inches (6 cm) apart.
No slats are missing or cracked.
Mattress fits snugly—less than two fingers width between edge of mattress
   and crib side.
Mattress support is securely attached to the head and footboards.
Corner posts are no higher than 1/16 inch (1.0 mm) to prevent entanglement.
There are no cutouts in head and footboards to allow head entrapment.
Drop-side latches cannot be easily released by a baby.
Drop-side latches securely hold sides in raised position.
All screws or bolts which secure components of crib together are present
   and tight.

Crib Toys
Crib toys have no strings longer than 7 inches (178 cm) to
   prevent entanglement.
Crib gym or other crib toy suspended over the crib must have devices that
   securely fasten to the crib to prevent it from being pulled into the crib.
Components of toys are large enough not to be a choking hazard.
Crib mobiles should be removed when baby begins to get up on hands
   and knees or turns five months of age (whichever comes first).

Gates and Enclosures
Gate or enclosure has a straight top edge.
Openings in gate are too small to entrap a child's head.
Gate has a pressure bar or other fastener so it will resist forces exerted
   by a child.

(continued)

TABLE 9–8 Infant Equipment Safety Checklist (continued)

	Yes	No

High Chairs

High chair has restraining straps that are independent of the tray.

High chair has a crotch strap; it must be used whenever baby sits
  in the high chair.

Tray locks securely.

Buckle on waist strap is easy to fasten and unfasten.

High chair has a wide base for stability.

High chair has caps or plugs on tubing that are firmly attached
  and cannot be pulled off and choke a child.

If it is a folding high chair, it has an effective locking device.

Hook-On Chairs

Hook-on chair has a restraining strap to secure the child.

Hook-on chair has a clamp that locks onto the table for added security.

Hook-on chair has caps or plugs on tubing that are firmly attached
  and cannot be pulled off and become a choking hazard.

Hook-on chair has a warning never to place chair where child can push off
  with feet.

Pacifiers

Pacifier has no ribbons, string, cord, or yarn attached.

Shield is large enough and firm enough so it cannot fit in child's mouth.

Guard or shield has ventilation holes so baby can breathe if shield does
  get into mouth.

Pacifier nipple has no holes or tears that might cause it to break off
  in baby's mouth.

Playpens

Drop-side mesh playpen or mesh crib has warning label about never
  leaving a side in the down position.

Playpens or travel cribs have top rails that automatically lock when lifted
  into the normal use position.

There are no rotating hinges in the center of the top rail.

Playpen mesh has small weave (less than 1/4–inch openings).

Mesh has no tears or loose threads.

Mesh is securely attached to top rail and floorplate.

Wooden playpen has slats spaced no more than 2 3/8 inches (6 cm) apart.

If staples are used in construction, they are firmly installed—none missing,
  or loose.

Rattles/Squeeze Toys/Teethers

Rattles and teethers have handles too large to lodge in baby's throat.

Rattles have sturdy construction that will not cause them to break apart in use.

Squeeze toys do not contain a squeaker that could detach and choke a baby.

Rattles with large, ball-like ends should not be given to babies.

Strollers

Stroller has a wide base to prevent tipping.

Seat belt and crotch strap are securely attached to frame.

Seat belt buckle is easy to fasten and unfasten.

Brakes securely lock the wheel(s).

Shopping basket low on the back and located directly over or in front
  of rear wheels.

Leg holes can be closed when used in a carriage position.

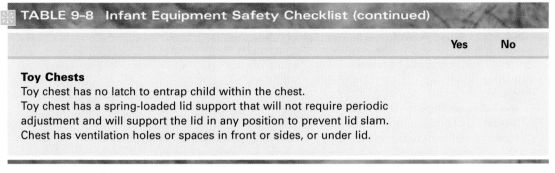

TABLE 9–8 Infant Equipment Safety Checklist (continued)

	Yes	No
Toy Chests		
Toy chest has no latch to entrap child within the chest.		
Toy chest has a spring-loaded lid support that will not require periodic adjustment and will support the lid in any position to prevent lid slam.		
Chest has ventilation holes or spaces in front or sides, or under lid.		

Adapted from *The Safe Nursery*, U.S. Consumer Product Safety Commission (CPSC), Washington, DC.

Classroom Activities

Safety must always be a priority when teachers select, plan, and implement learning activities for children. The potential for injury is present in nearly every activity, whether it is planned for indoor or outdoor settings. Even metal trucks or plastic golf clubs can cause harm when children use them incorrectly. Teachers should ask themselves the following questions when evaluating the safety of any activity:

- Is the activity age- and developmentally appropriate?
- What potential risks or hazards does this activity present?
- What special precautions do I need to take to make the activity safe?
- How should I respond if a child misuses the equipment or doesn't follow directions?
- What would I do in the event that a child is hurt while the activity is in progress?

After these questions have been given careful thought, teachers can begin to consider how basic safety principles, e.g., advanced planning, formulating rules, determining appropriate supervision, and safety education training will be applied.

Materials selected for classroom activities should always be evaluated for safety risks before they are presented to children. Added safety precautions and more precise planning may be necessary whenever the following high-risk items are used as part of an activity:

- pointed or sharp objects such as scissors, knives, and woodworking tools, e.g., hammers, nails, saws
- pipes, boards, blocks, or breakable objects
- electrical appliances, e.g., hot plates, radio, mixers
- hot liquids, e.g., wax, syrup, oil, water
- cosmetics or cleaning supplies

For added safety, projects that include any of these items should be set up in an area separated from other activities. Boundaries created with portable room dividers or a row of chairs improve a teacher's ability to closely monitor children's actions.

Restricting the number of children who can participate in an activity at any one time is another effective way to ensure safe conditions. Some activities may need to be limited to only one child. Limiting the number of children improves a teacher's ability to effectively supervise a given area. Color-coded necklaces, badges, or the number of available chairs at a table are a few methods teachers can use to control the number of children in a given area at any one time. These systems also help children determine if there is room for them to join the activity.

When electrical appliances are included in an activity, they should be inspected carefully and safety rules explained to the children (Table 9–9). Plugs and cords that are frayed should not be used. Avoid the use of extension cords that could cause children or adults to trip. Always place

> **TABLE 9-9 Teacher Checklist: Guidelines for the Safe Use of Electrical Appliances**
>
> Special precautions must be taken whenever an activity involves the use of an electrical appliance, including:
> - placing the appliance on a low table or the floor so that children can easily reach.
> - reminding children to stand back from appliances with moving parts to prevent their hair, fingers, or clothing from getting caught or burned.
> - turning handles of pots and pans toward the back of the stove or hot plate.
> - always detaching cords from the electrical outlet, never the appliance.
> - promptly replacing safety caps in all electrical outlets when the project is finished.

electrical appliances on a table nearest the outlet and against the wall for safety. Never use appliances near a source of water, including sinks, wet floors, or large pans of water.

Safety must also be a concern in the selection of art media and activities (OEHHA, 2005; CPSC, 1992). Art materials such as paints, glue, crayons, and clay must always be nontoxic when they are used by young children (Figure 9–7). Liquids, such as paints and glue, should always be stored in plastic containers to prevent the danger of broken glass. Dried beans, peas, berries, or small beads, which children can stuff into their ears or nose or swallow, should not be used. Toothpicks and similar sharp objects are also inappropriate. Fabric pieces, dried leaves or grasses, Styrofoam, packing materials, yarn, or ribbon offer safer alternatives for children's art creations. Other safe substitutions for hazardous art materials are provided in Table 9–10.

Special precautions should be taken in classrooms with hard-surfaced or highly polished floors. Spilled water, paint, or other liquids and dry materials such as beans, rice, sawdust, flour, or cornmeal cause these floors to become extremely slippery and should be cleaned up promptly. Spreading newspapers or rugs out on the floor can help prevent children and adults from slipping and falling.

Environments and activities that are safe for young children are also less stressful for adults. When classrooms and play yards are free of potential hazards, teachers can concentrate their attention on selecting safe activities and providing quality supervision. Also, being familiar with a program's safety policies and procedures and having proper emergency training, such as first aid and CPR, can increase teacher confidence and lessen stress levels.

Field Trips

Excursions away from a program's facilities can be an exciting part of children's educational experiences. However, field trips present added risks and liability concerns for schools and early education programs and therefore require that special precautions be taken (Aronson, 2001).

Most importantly, programs should have written policies outlining procedures for field trips. Families should be informed in advance of an outing and their written permission obtained for each excursion. On the day of the trip, a notice should be posted on the classroom door to remind families and staff of the children's destination and when they will be leaving and returning to the building. At least one adult accompanying the group should have first aid and CPR training. A first aid kit and cell phone should also be taken along; if a cell phone is not available, include coins for a pay phone. Tags can be pinned on children with the center's name and phone number. However, *do not* include the children's names: this enables strangers to call children by their name and makes it easier to lure them away from a group. A complete list of the children's emergency contact information, including families' telephone numbers, child's physician, and emergency

FIGURE 9–7

Children's art materials must be nontoxic.

TABLE 9–10 Teacher Checklist: Safe Substitutes for Hazardous Art Materials

Avoid	Safe Substitutes
Powders—dry tempera paints, silica, pastels, chalk, dry clay, cement. Use plaster of paris only in well-ventilated area.	Use liquid tempera paints, water colors, crayons, and nontoxic markers.
Aerosol sprays—adhesives, fixatives, paints	Use brushes or spray bottles with water-based glues, paints, and inks.
Solvents and thinners—turpentine, rubber or epoxy cements, or those containing benzene, toluene, lacquers, or varnish. Avoid enamel-based paints that require solvents for cleanup.	Select water-based paints, glues, and inks.
Permanent markers, dyes, and stains.	Prepare natural vegetable dyes (e.g., beets, walnuts, onions) or commercial cold-water dyes.
Minerals and fibers—instant paper-mache (may contain lead and asbestos fibers); glazes, printing inks (colored newsprint, magazines), paints, especially enamels (may contain lead); builder's sand (may contain asbestos).	Use black-white newspaper and water-based glue to make paper-mache; choose water-based paints and inks; purchase special sandbox sand that has been cleaned.
Photographic chemicals.	Use blueprint or colored paper set in the sun.

Additional precautions:
- Read ingredient labels carefully. Only choose materials that are labeled nontoxic. Older supplies may not comply with new federal labeling requirements and may contain harmful chemicals.
- Mix and prepare art materials (adults only) in a well-ventilated area away from children.
- Make sure children wash their hands after working with art materials.
- Keep food and beverages away from areas where art activities are in progress.

service (e.g., ambulance, fire) numbers, should also be taken along. Procedures and safety rules should be carefully reviewed with the staff and children prior to the outing.

Special consideration should also be given to the legal issues involved in conducting a field trip (Child Care Law Center, 2005). Transporting children in the private vehicles of other families, staff, or volunteers, for example, can present serious liability concerns (see Chapter 8) (NNCC, 2006; Marotz, 2000). There is almost no way of assuring that a car is safe or an adult is a good driver. Also, most states have laws that require appropriate safety restraints for each passenger, and not all vans and cars are properly equipped to provide these for multiple children. Therefore, it may be in a program's best interest not to use private vehicles for transporting children on field trips. Vehicles owned and operated by a program are usually required to carry liability insurance and are therefore preferable for transporting children. However, neighborhood walks and public bus rides are always safe alternatives.

Pets

Pets can be a special classroom addition, but care must be taken so this is also a safe experience for both the children and animals. Children's allergies should be considered before pets visit or become permanent classroom residents. Also, precautions should be taken to be sure animals are free of disease and have current immunizations (if appropriate). Some animals, such as turtles, fish, and birds, are known carriers of illnesses that are communicable to humans, such as salmonella, and are therefore not appropriate to include in the classroom (*Child Health Alert*, 2005). Instructions for an animal's care should be posted to serve as both a guideline and reminder to staff. Precautions must also be taken to protect pets from curious and overly exuberant children who may unknowingly cause harm or injury to the animal. Children must always wash their hands carefully after handling or petting animals in the classroom, zoo, or petting farm because animals are often carriers of infectious illnesses (*Child Health Alert*, 2007).

Personal Safety

Not all teachers work in classrooms. Some organizations, such as Head Start and Parents as Teachers, employ educators and other professionals to work with children and families in their homes. Opportunities to work independently and one-on-one with clients are attractive options for many teachers. However, working alone and in neighborhoods that may be unfamiliar or are noted for high crime rates may present additional risks and concerns. Organizations should establish policies and procedures in advance to protect the safety of personnel who work in these conditions. Individuals can also take steps to assure their own personal safety (Table 9–11).

LEGAL IMPLICATIONS

Safety issues generate a great deal of concern for teachers, school administrators, and program directors. Recent lawsuits, legal decisions, and increased public awareness have contributed to these feelings of uneasiness and scrutiny. As demand for early childhood programs continues to grow, interest in regulating programs and facilities has also increased. Families want and have a right to be assured that facilities are safe. Families also expect schools and early education programs to safeguard their children's well-being during the hours they are away from home.

Teachers should be familiar with the legal issues and responsibilities that affect their positions for several reasons. First, by law, teachers are expected to provide for children's safety. Second, the incidence of injury and accidents is known to be especially high among young children. Their immature developmental skills and unpredictable behavior always necessitates careful safety management.

TABLE 9-11	Teacher Checklist: Personal Safety Practices for the Home Visitor

- Check with your organization to learn about policies and/or procedures that home visitors are expected to follow.
- Become familiar with the neighborhood; visit the area and address beforehand. Learn about the community and families living there.
- Talk with local police for information about the area and to determine if your concerns or fears are warranted.
- Let a supervisor know when you leave and where you are heading; give them your planned travel route and be sure to follow it.
- Take along a cell phone or pager; carry a whistle.
- Check in frequently with your supervisor; give them your location and share any immediate safety concerns.
- Schedule visits during the daytime. If evening visits are necessary, go in teams.
- Be alert and aware of your surroundings. Listen for unusual sounds, watch for suspicious people or activity and leave if you feel uncomfortable.
- Know where to get help if something should happen.
- Complete a personal safety defense class to develop protective techniques and improve self-confidence.

The most important legal concerns for teachers center around the issue of liability (Child Care Law Center, 1992). The term **liability** refers to the legal obligations and responsibilities, especially those related to safety, that are accepted by administrators and teachers when they agree to care for children. Failure to carry out these duties in an acceptable manner is considered **negligence**.

Negligence often results from questionable safety practices and management. For legal purposes, negligent acts are generally divided into two categories according to the circumstances and resulting damages or injuries. The first category includes situations in which a teacher fails to take appropriate precautionary measures to protect children from danger. Standards for judging a teacher's actions would be set by first determining what measures a teacher with similar training and experience would be expected to take in the same situation. A teacher who failed to adhere to these standards would be considered negligent. A lack of adequate supervision, permitting children to play on equipment that is defective or in need of repair, or allowing children to engage in harmful activities such as throwing rocks or standing on swings are some examples of this form of negligence.

A second category of negligent acts includes situations in which the actions or decisions of a teacher put children at risk. An example of this type of negligence might involve a teacher making arrangements to have children transported in private vehicles that are not insured, or planning classroom activities that allow children to use poisonous chemicals or unsafe electrical equipment without proper supervision.

Prevention is always the best method for ensuring the safety of young children and avoiding unpleasant legal problems and lawsuits. However, there are steps individuals and programs can take for added protection (Marotz, 2000).

Teachers are always legally responsible for their actions. Despite careful attempts to provide safe conditions for children, at some time they may be accused of negligence or wrongdoing. For this reason, it is wise for every administrator and teacher to obtain personal liability

liability – *legal responsibility or obligation for one's actions owed to another individual.*
negligence – *failure to practice or perform one's duties according to certain standards; carelessness.*

ISSUES TO CONSIDER • Transportation Safety

Evening newscasters described the tragic death of a toddler forgotten in a child-care van. The child had been picked up from his home early that morning, placed in a car safety seat, and transported to a local child care center. However, personnel did not realize the child was missing from the center until the end of the day when it was time for the children to return home. The unconscious toddler was found still strapped in his car seat. Temperatures outside of the van had climbed into the 90s during the day. Despite emergency medical efforts, heat stroke claimed the child's life.

- What steps should have been taken to prevent this tragedy?
- What policies and procedures would keep this from happening again?
- What measures should be taken to assure children's safety during transportation? In private vehicles? In center vans?

insurance if they are not covered by their program's policy (NNCC, 2006; Child Care Information Exchange, 2002). Liability insurance can be purchased from most private insurance companies and through the National Association for the Education of Young Children (NAEYC). Accident insurance, purchased on individual children who are enrolled, also affords programs necessary protection.

Administrators and staff should not hesitate to seek legal counsel on issues related to their roles and responsibilities. Legal advice can be a valuable source of protection and be especially helpful when developing policies. Programs may wish to consider including a member of the legal profession on their board of directors or advisory council.

Teachers should always examine job descriptions carefully and be familiar with employer expectations before accepting a new position. This step helps assure that they have the appropriate qualifications and training necessary to perform all required duties. For example, if a teacher will be responsible for administering first aid to injured children, she or he should have completed basic first aid and CPR training prior to beginning employment. It is also imperative for administrators to screen potential candidates for teaching positions through careful interviewing and follow-up contacts with the individual's references. Background checks also help identify those with a history of criminal behavior. Although these steps may seem time-consuming, they will help to protect a program from hiring unqualified personnel.

Accurately maintained records, particularly accident reports, also provide added legal protection (Figure 9–8). Information in these reports can be used in court as evidence to support a teacher's or program's innocence against charges of negligence. A thorough report should be completed for each accident, regardless of how minor or unimportant it may seem at the time. This is very important because the results of some injuries are not always immediately apparent. Complications could develop years later, making it difficult for a teacher to recall the injury in sufficient detail. A special form such as the one shown in Figure 9–9 can be used for this purpose. This form should be completed by the teacher who witnessed the accident and administered first aid treatment. The information should be clear, precise, and objective. It should describe in detail the nature and location of the injury, how it occurred, the names of any witnesses, and what treatment was administered. Accident records provide a composite picture of the injury and are also useful for detecting patterns. They are considered legal documents and should therefore be kept on file for a minimum of five years.

FIGURE 9–8

A sample individual injury report form.

INDIVIDUAL INJURY REPORT FORM

Child's Name _____ Date of Injury _____

Parent _____ Time _____ AM ____ PM ____

Address _____ Parent notified _____ AM ____ PM ____

Description of injuries _____

_____

First aid or emergency treatment administered: _____

_____

Was a doctor consulted? _____ Doctor's name and address _____

Doctor's diagnosis _____

_____

Number of days child was absent as a result of injury _____

Adult in charge when injury occurred _____

Description of activity, location in facility and circumstances, immediately before and at the time of the injury

_____

_____

_____

_____

_____

_____

_____

Report prepared by (full name): _____ Date _____

FIGURE 9-9

A sample classroom injury recording form.

SUNNY DAYS CHILD CARE CENTER
Record of Children's Injuries

Date and Time	Child's Name	Nature of Child's Injuries	How the Injury Occurred	Observed By	Type of First Aid Treatment Administered	By Whom (Full name)

Download this form online at http://www.EarlyChildEd.delmar.cengage.com

FOCUS ON FAMILIES • Sun Safety

Exposure to too much sun over a lifetime can have harmful health consequences, including skin cancer, premature aging of the skin, eye damage, and interference with the immune system's ability to function. Children's skin—even that of dark-skinned children—is especially sensitive to the sun's ultraviolet (UV) rays and tends to burn quickly and easily. Steps should always be taken to protect children's skin and minimize their sun exposure. Adults should also follow these same precautions.

- Avoid going outdoors between 10 AM and 4 PM, when the sun's rays are the strongest and most damaging.

- Encourage children to play in the shade whenever possible. Rule of thumb—you shouldn't be able to see their shadow!

- Dress in protective clothing that is cool and loose fitting. Keep as much skin surface covered as possible. Children should be discouraged from wearing tank or halter tops. A hat with a brim provides shade protection for the face and eyes.

- Apply sunscreen [with a sun protection factor (SPF) of at least 15+] 30 minutes before going outdoors. Reapply every two hours or more often if children are swimming, perspiring, or drying themselves with a towel. Sunburn occurs more quickly when the skin is wet.

- Wear sunglasses to protect eyes from UV radiation. Light-colored eyes (blue, gray) are particularly sensitive to sunlight.

- Become a "SunWise" school by registering at http://www.epa.gov/sunwise/becoming. html.

CASE STUDY

Teachers at the Wee Ones Child Care Center, located in an inner-city neighborhood, know that field trips can be an important part of the curriculum. They have discussed organizing a trip to the local city zoo as part of a learning unit on animals. However, the teachers also realize the challenges involved in taking a group of 20 three- and four-year-olds on this field trip, but feel the experience is especially valuable for these children. Since the zoo is located on the other side of town, the teachers have made arrangements to ride the city bus.

1. What criteria can teachers use to determine if a field trip is worthwhile?

2. What types of planning are necessary to assure a safe and successful field trip?

3. What are the advantages/disadvantages of using public transportation?

4. What safety precautions must teachers take before leaving the premises?

5. How might visiting a site ahead of time help teachers better plan for a field trip?

6. What types of problems should teachers anticipate when taking children on field trips?

7. What information should parents be given?

8. Are off-premise field trips typically covered by liability insurance policies for early care and education programs?

CLASSROOM CORNER • Teacher Activities

Practicing Fire Drills...

Concept: It is important to know how to get out of a building in case of a fire. (Pre-2)

Learning Objectives

- Children will learn why it is important to leave the classroom in case of a fire.
- Children will practice the procedure to evacuate in case of a fire.

Supplies

- None

Learning Activities

- Read and discuss the following book:
  - *Fire! Fire!* by Gail Gibbons
- Ask children if they know why it is important to get out of a building in case of a fire. Talk to the children to let them know there really isn't a fire, but that you are going to practice just so everyone knows what to do in case there is a fire. Go over the basic rules: 1) line up quickly, 2) don't take anything with you, 3) follow the teachers, 4) sit down when you arrive at the designated area, and 5) say "here" when your name is called.
- Have children practice a fire drill following the above procedure. Take all necessary paperwork with you.
- Send home a parent letter and encourage families to have a fire evacuation plan for their family.

Evaluation

- Children will follow the fire evacuation procedure when future drills or a real evacuation occur.

SUMMARY

- Unintentional injuries are the leading cause of death for young children.
  - Children's curiosity and inability to understand cause and effect contribute to a high injury rate.
  - Adults must take steps to prevent children's injuries through advanced planning, establishing rules, providing careful supervision, and conducting safety education.
- Teachers have a professional and moral obligation to protect children's safe-being.
  - Failure to uphold this responsibility could result in charges of negligence.
  - Acts of omission involve failure to take precautionary measures.
  - Acts of commission include knowingly exposing children to elements of risk.
- Teachers can take steps to protect themselves from personal liability by purchasing liability insurance, meeting required job qualifications, completing ongoing training in CPR and first aid, and documenting all children's injuries.

APPLICATION ACTIVITIES

1. Visit an early childhood program play yard or a public playground. Select one piece of play equipment and observe children playing on or with it for at least 15 minutes. Make a list of actual or potential dangers that could result from improper use. Prepare a set of developmentally appropriate safety rules for children to follow.

2. Role-play how a teacher might handle a child who is not riding a tricycle in a safe manner.

3. You have been asked to purchase outdoor play equipment for a new child development center. Prepare a list of the safety features you would look for when making your selections. Write to several companies for equipment catalogues or go online to their Web site. Using the catalogues, select basic outdoor equipment to furnish the play yard of a small early childhood center that has two classes of 35 children each and a budget of $8,000.

4. Prepare a separate room-by-room home safety checklist for families of 1) infants, 2) toddlers, and 3) preschool-age children.

5. Survey your own or a nearby early childhood center. Following the principles outlined in this chapter, develop a building security plan.

CHAPTER REVIEW

A. **By Yourself**

1. Match the item in **column I** with those in **column II.**

Column I	Column II
1. basic element of advanced planning	a. foresight
2. legal responsibility for children's safety	b. supervision
3. the ability to anticipate	c. education
4. limits that define safe behavior	d. planning
5. failure to protect children's safety	e. rules
6. watching over children's behavior	f. safe
7. environments free of hazards	g. negligence
8. the process of learning safe behavior	h. prevention
9. a key factor in injury prevention	i. liability
10. measures taken to insure children's safety	j. organization

2. Fill in the blanks with one of the words listed below:

removed	unintentional injury	anticipate
legal	responsible	safety principles
safety education	safety	inspected

1. The leading cause of death among young children is _____.

2. Adults must be able to _____ children's actions as part of advanced planning.

3. Families expect teachers to be _____ for their child's safety.

4. Basic _____ _____ include advanced planning, establishing rules, careful supervision, and safety education.

5. Injury records are _____ records.

6. A continuous concern of teachers is _____.

7. Toys and play equipment should be _____ daily.

8. A prime method for reducing the incidence of unintentional injuries can be achieved through _____ _____.

B. As a Group

1. Discuss why rules are not a substitute for adult supervision.

2. What actions must a teacher take if he or she notices that a piece of playground equipment is broken?

3. Discuss why infants and toddlers experience the highest rate of unintentional injury.

4. What preparations should teachers make before taking children on a field trip?

5. Divide into two groups and debate the advantages and disadvantages of taking children on field trips.

REFERENCES

Access Board (2001). *Guide to ADA accessibility: Guidelines for play areas.* Available online at http://www.access-board.gov/play/guide/guide.pdf.

American Speech & Hearing Association (ASHA). (2006). *Noisy toys, dangerous play.* Accessed on November 7, 2006, from http://www.asha.org/public/hearing/disorders/noisy_toys.htm.

Aronson, S. (2001). Field trips: Planning for maximum benefit, minimum risk. *Child Care Information Exchange, 139,* 43–47.

Berk, L. (2005). *Child development.* (7th ed.). Boston, MA: Allyn & Bacon.

Centers for Disease Control and Prevention (CDC) Web-based Injury Statistics Query and Reporting System (WISQARS). 2004 Unintentional Injuries Deaths, Ages, 1-4 and 5–9. Available at: http://webappa.cdc.gov/sasweb/ncipc/leadcaus10.html. Accessed September 26, 2007.

Child Care Information Exchange. (2002, Nov.–Dec.). Does your insurance coverage fit your needs? *Child Care Information Exchange. 148,* 80–83.

Child Care Law Center. (2005). Legal issues for family child care providers: Insuring your program: Vehicle and property insurance. San Francisco, CA.

Child Care Law Center. (1992). *Legal aspects of caring for sick and injured children.* San Francisco, CA.

Child Health Alert. (2005). Add pet rodents to the list of animals that can spread salmonella. *Child Health Alert, 24,* 3.

Child Health Alert. (2007). Infection risks at petting zoos. *Child Health Alert, 25,* 1.

Children's Safety Network. (2005, Feb.). *Injury and violence prevention.* Available online at: http://www.childrenssafetynetwork.org/MonthlyBulletins/2005/february05.asp.

Frost, J. L., & Sutterby, J. A. (2002). Making playgrounds fit for children and children fit for playgrounds. *Young Children, 57*(3), 36–41.

Frost, J. L., Wortham, S. C., & Reifel, S. (2004). *Play and child development.* Upper Saddle River, NJ: Merrill Prentice Hall.

Garzon, D. (2005). Contributing factors to preschool unintentional injury. *Journal of Pediatric Nursing, 20*(6), 441–447.

Gestwicki, C. (2006). *Developmentally appropriate practice: Curriculum and development in early education* (2nd ed.). Albany, NY: Delmar.

Gibbs, C. (2000). Elementary school playground design. *School Planning & Management, 39*(7), 54–55.

Limbos, M., & Peek-Asa, C. (2003). Comparing unintentional and intentional injuries in a school setting. *Journal of School Health, 73*(3), 101–106.

Marotz, L. R. (2000). Childhood and classroom injuries. (2000). In, J. L. Frost (Ed.), *Children and injuries.* Tucson, AZ: Lawyers & Judges Publishing Co.

Matheny, A. R. (1991). Children's unintentional injuries and gender: Differentiation and psychosocial aspects. *Children's Environment Quarterly, 8,* 51–61.

Morrongiello, B., Corbett, M., McCourt, M., & Johnston, N. (2006). *Journal of Pediatric Psychology, 31*(6), 540–551.

Nakamura, S. W., Pollack-Nelson, C., & Chidekel, A. S. (2003). Suction-type suffocation incidents in infants and toddlers. *Pediatrics, 111*(1), e12–16.

National Center for Health Statistics (NCHS). (2006). *NCHS data on injuries.* Accessed on September 26, 2007 from http://www.cdc.gov/nchs/data/factsheets/injury.pdf.

National Network for Child Care (NNCC). (2006). *Child care home: Liability insurance.* Accessed on November 7, 2006, from http://www.nccc.org/Business/cch.liability.html.

National Program for Playground Safety (NPPS). (2006). *Child care—S.A.F.E. tips.* Available online at http://www.playgroundsafety.org/childcare/tips.htm.

O'Donnell, J. (2006, Nov.3). Safety issues can be ugly surprise in toys for kids. *USA Today.* Accessed on November 7, 2006, from http://www.usatoday.com/money/industries/retail/2006-11-02-mym-toy-safety-issues_x.htm.

Office of Environmental Health Hazard Assessment (OEHHA). (2005). *Guidelines for the safe use of art and craft materials.* Accessed on November 7, 2006, from http://www.oehha.ca.gov/education/art/artguide.html.

Occupational Safety & Health Administration (OSHA). (2003). Noise exposure standard, 39FR23502 (as amended) section 19010.95. U.S. Department of Labor.

Pan, S., Ugnat, A., Semenciw, R., Desmeules, M., Mao, Y., & Macleod, M. (2006). Trends in childhood injury mortality in Canada, 1979–2002. *Injury Prevention, 12*(3), 155–160.

Public Interest Research Group. (2002). *Trouble in toyland, 2002: 17th annual survey of potential toy hazards.* Accessed on June 3, 2003, at http://www.toysafety.net.

Schwebel, D. C., Speltz, M. L., Jones, K., & Bardina, L. (2002). Unintentional injury in preschool boys with and without early onset of disruptive behavior. *Journal of Pediatric Psychology, 27*(8), 727–737.

Schwebel, D., Brezausek, C., & Belsky, J. (2006). Does time spent in child care influence risk for unintentional injury? *Journal of Pediatric Psychology, 31*(2), 184–193.

Schwebel, D., Summerlin, A., Bounds, M., & Morrongiello, B. (2006). The stamp-in-safety program: A behavioral intervention to reduce behaviors that can lead to unintentional playground injury in a preschool setting. *Journal of Pediatric Psychology, 31*(2), 152–162.

Stephenson, M. (2005). Danger in the toy box. *Journal of Pediatric Health Care, 19*(3), 187–189.

Stoecklin, V. (2001). The role of culture in designing child care facilities. *Child Care Information Exchange, 139,* 60–63.

Sutterby, J., & Thornton, C. (2005). It doesn't just happen! Essential contributions from playgrounds. *Young Children, 6*(3), 26–33.

Taylor, S., Morris, V., & Rogers, C. (1997). Toy safety and selection. *Early Childhood Education Journal, 24*(4), 235–238.

U.S. Consumer Product Safety Commission (CPSC). (2006). *Childproofing your home—12 safety devices to protect your children.* Accessed on November 7, 2006, from http://www.cpsc.gov/cpscpub/pubs/grand/12steps/12steps.html.

U.S. Consumer Product Safety Commission (CPSC). (2002). *Age determination guidelines: Relating children's ages to toy characteristics and play behavior.* Washington, DC: CPSC.

U.S. Consumer Products Safety Commission (CPSC). (2007). *U.S. and Chinese product safety agencies announce agreement to improve the safety of imported toys and other consumer products.* Accessed on September 27, 2007 from http://www.cpsc.gov/cpscpub/prerel/prhtml07/07305.html.

U.S. Consumer Product Safety Commission (CPSC). *The safe nursery.* Accessed on September 27, 2007 from http://www.cpsc.gov/cpscpub/pubs/202.pdf.

U.S. Consumer Product Safety Commission (CPSC). (1992). *Labeling of hazardous art materials.* Washington, DC: CPSC.

U.S. Consumer Product Safety Commission (CPSC). (1997). *Handbook for public playground safety.* Washington, DC: CPSC.

Zavitkovsky, A., & Thompson, D. (2000). Preventing injuries to children: Interventions that really work. *Child Care Information Exchange, 100*(1), 54–56.

VIDEOS

Can be ordered online from:

- American Academy of Pediatrics (1–800–433–9016)
  - *Caring for our children: National health and safety performance standards—Guidelines for out-of-home child care*
  - *Child safety at home*
  - *Child safety outdoors*

- National Association for the Education of Young Children (NAEYC)
  - *Safe active play: A guide to avoiding play area hazards*
  - *Tools for teaching developmentally appropriate practice (series)*
  - *Nurturing growth: Child growth and development*
  - *Early intervention: Natural environments for children*

- National program for playground safety, School of Health, Physical Education and Leisure Services, University of Northern Iowa, Cedar Falls, IA, 50614–0618
  - *ABC's of supervision*
  - *Safe playgrounds*
  - *Planning safe playgrounds*
  - *The nuts and bolts of playground maintenance*

- Parents Action for Children (1–888–447–3400)
  - *Safe from the start*

HELPFUL WEB RESOURCES

American Society for Testing and Materials	http://www.astm.org
Canadian Institute of Child Health	http://www.cich.ca
Canadian Safety Council	http://www.safety-council.org
Child Care Law Center	http://www.childcarelaw.org
Injury Control Resource Information Network	http://www.injurycontrol.com
National Center for Injury Prevention and Control	http://www.cdc.gov
National Program for Playground Safety	http://www.uni.edu
Safety Link	http://www.safetylink.com
U.S. Consumer Product Safety Commission	http://www.cpsc.gov

 For additional health, safety, and nutrition resources, go to http://www.EarlyChildEd.delmar.cengage.com

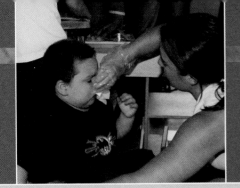

CHAPTER 10

Management of Injuries and Acute Illness

OBJECTIVES

After studying this chapter, you should be able to:

- Describe the difference between emergency care and first aid.
- Identify the ABCs for assessing emergencies.
- Name eight life-threatening conditions and state the emergency treatment for each.
- Name 10 non-life-threatening conditions and describe the first aid treatment for each.
- Discuss the teacher's role and responsibilities as they relate to management of unintentional injuries and acute illness.

TERMS TO KNOW

negligent	resuscitation	hypothermia
aspiration	paralysis	heat exhaustion
recovery position	ingested	heat stroke
sterile	alkalis	
elevate	submerge	

Prevention of unintentional childhood injuries is a major responsibility of families and teachers (Garzon, 2005; Aronson, 2002; Preboth, 2002). This goal is best achieved when programs provide safe environments, include health/safety education, and establish proper procedures for handling emergencies (Marotz, 2000).

Programs often overlook the need to develop emergency policies and plans until an unexpected event occurs. This can result in unnecessary confusion and ineffective response, and place children and adults at risk. Advanced preparation and training assures that staff will be able to respond to emergencies in a prompt and knowledgeable manner (Figure 10–1). A program's comprehensive emergency response plan should address:

- training of personnel in infant/child CPR and basic first aid techniques (Figure 10–2)
- designating staff who are responsible for administering emergency care
- obtaining notarized parental/guardian permission forms for each child that authorize emergency medical treatment

FIGURE 10–1

Planning guidelines for serious injury and emergency illness.

Serious Injury and Illness Plan

1. **Remain with the child at all times.** Keep calm and reassure the child that you are there to help. Your presence can be a comfort to the child, especially when faced with unfamiliar surroundings and discomfort. You can also provide valuable information about events preceding and following the injury/illness, symptoms the child exhibited, etc.

2. **Do not** move a child with serious injury unless there is immediate danger from additional harm, such as fire or electrical shock.

3. Begin appropriate emergency care procedures immediately. Meanwhile, send for help. Have another adult or child alert the person designated to handle such emergencies in your center.

4. **Do not** give food, fluids, or medications unless specifically ordered by the child's physician or Poison Control Center.

5. Call for emergency medical assistance if in doubt about the severity of the situation. Don't attempt to handle difficult situations by yourself. A delay in contacting emergency authorities could make the difference in saving a child's life. If you are alone, have a child dial the emergency number in your community (commonly 911).

6. If the child is transported to a medical facility before parents arrive, a teacher should accompany, and remain with the child until parents arrive.

7. Contact the child's family. Inform them of the nature of the illness/injury and the child's general condition. If the child's condition is not life-threatening, discuss plans for follow-up care, e.g., contacting the child's physician, transporting the child to a medical facility. If the family cannot be reached, call the child's emergency contact person or physician.

8. Record all information concerning serious injury/illness on appropriate forms within 24 hours; place in the child's folder and provide the family with a copy. If required, notify local licensing authorities.

FIGURE 10–2

Teachers should know the fundamentals of emergency and first aid care.

TABLE 10-1 Basic First Aid Supplies

adhesive tape—1/2- and 1-inch widths	safety pins
antibacterial soap or cleanser	scissors—blunt tipped
bandages—assorted sizes	soap—preferably liquid
blanket	spirits of ammonia
bulb syringe	splints (small)
thermometers—2	cotton balls
flashlight and extra batteries	plastic bags (sealable)
gauze pads—sterile, 2x2s, 4x4s	tongue blades
instant cold packs or plastic bags for ice cubes	towel—large and small
needle—(sewing type)	triangular bandages for slings
roller gauze—1- and 2-inch widths; stretch	tweezers
latex or vinyl gloves	first aid book or reference cards
pen and small notepad	emergency telephone numbers

- having an accessible telephone
- posting emergency telephone numbers (e.g., parents and their designated emergency contacts, hospital, fire department, emergency medical personnel (EMT), law enforcement, local poison control) next to the telephone
- making arrangements for emergency transportation
- providing a fully equipped first aid kit in each classroom or central location (Table 10–1)

Copies of a program's emergency response plans should be made available to families and reviewed on a regular basis with staff members.

Whenever emergency policies and procedures are being formulated, special attention should be given to protecting children and adults from transmissible illnesses, such as hepatitis B and C, and AIDS/HIV. Universal precautions are special infection-control guidelines that have been developed to prevent the spread of diseases transmitted via blood and other body fluids (see Chapter 6). These guidelines address several areas of precaution—barrier protection (including the use of latex/vinyl gloves and handwashing), environmental disinfection, and proper disposal of contaminated materials—and must be followed carefully whenever caring for children's injuries.

Despite careful planning and supervision, accidental injuries, and illness are inevitable. For this reason, it is important that teachers learn the fundamentals of emergency care and first aid (Table 10–2). Appropriate training and preparation allow personnel to handle emergencies with skill and confidence (Olympia, Wan, & Avner, 2005; Siwula, 2003; AAP, 2001).

Teachers are responsible for administering initial and urgent care to children who are seriously injured or acutely ill. These measures are considered to be temporary and aimed at saving lives, reducing pain and discomfort, and preventing complications and additional injury. Responsibility for obtaining additional medical treatment can then be transferred to the child's family (Marotz, 2000).

EMERGENCY CARE VS. FIRST AID

Emergency care refers to immediate treatment administered for life-threatening conditions. It includes a quick assessment of the emergency ABCs (Table 10–2). The victim is also checked and treated for severe bleeding, shock, and signs of poisoning.

TABLE 10–2	The ABCs for Assessing Emergencies
A—Airway	Make sure the air passageway is open and clear. Roll the infant or child onto his/her back. Tilt the head back by placing your hand on the child's forehead and gently push downward (unless back or neck injuries are suspected). At the same time, place the fingers of your other hand under the child's chin and lift it upward.
B—Breathing	Watch for the child's chest to move up and down. Feel and listen for air to escape from the lungs with your ear.
C—Circulation	Note the child's skin color (especially around the lips and nailbeds), and if the child is coughing or moving.

First aid refers to treatment administered for injuries and illnesses that are not considered life-threatening. Emergency care and first aid treatments are based on principles that should be familiar to anyone who works with young children including:

1. Summon emergency medical assistance (911 in many areas) for any injury or illness that requires more than simple first aid.
2. Stay calm and in control of the situation.
3. Always remain with the child. If necessary, send another adult or child for help.
4. Don't move the child until the extent of injuries or illness can be determined. If in doubt, have the child stay in the same position and await emergency medical help.
5. Quickly evaluate the child's condition, paying special attention to an open airway, breathing, and circulation.
6. Carefully plan and administer appropriate emergency care. Improper treatment can lead to other injuries.
7. Don't give any medications unless they are prescribed for certain lifesaving conditions.
8. Don't offer diagnoses or medial advice. Refer the child's family to seek professional health care.
9. Always inform the child's family of the injury and first aid care that has been administered.
10. Record all facts concerning the accident and treatment administered; file in the child's permanent folder.

In most states, legal protection is granted to individuals who administer emergency care, unless their actions are judged grossly **negligent** or harmful. This protection is commonly known as the Good Samaritan Law. Thus, teachers should not be reluctant to give needed care to an injured child for fear of being sued.

LIFE-THREATENING CONDITIONS

Situations that require emergency care to prevent death or serious disability are discussed in this section. The emergency techniques and suggestions included here are not intended as substitutes for certified first aid and cardiopulmonary resuscitation (CPR) training. Rather, they are included as a review of basic instruction and to enhance the teacher's ability to respond to children's emergencies. A course involving hands-on practice is necessary to master these skills. It is also important to take a refresher course every few years.

---

negligent – *failing to practice or perform one's duties according to certain standards; careless.*

REFLECTIVE THOUGHTS

When you place an emergency telephone call, it is important to remain calm and stay on the line. What information should you be prepared to give the dispatcher? Why shouldn't you hang up after making a report? What emergency telephone numbers should be posted in child care facilities? Where should they be posted? What emergency numbers should children learn to dial?

Absence of Breathing: Cardiopulmonary Resuscitation (CPR)

Breathing emergencies accompany many life-threatening conditions, for example, asthma, drowning, electrical shock, convulsions, poisoning, severe injuries, suffocation, choking, and Sudden Infant Death Syndrome (SIDS). Adults who work with young children should complete certified training in basic first aid and cardiopulmonary resuscitation (CPR). This training is available from most chapters of the American Red Cross and the American Heart Association or from a local ambulance service, rescue squad, fire department, high school, or community parks and recreation department.

New guidelines for cardiopulmonary resuscitation (CPR) were issued by the American Heart Association (AHA) in 2005. The changes simplified existing CPR procedures and recommended a single compression-to-ventilation rate of 30:2 for *persons of all ages* (with the exception of newborns) (AHA, 2006; 2005). A rescue breath is defined as being one second in length and sufficient to cause the chest to rise and fall. The AHA also initiated a new slogan, "push hard and push fast," to emphasize the critical importance of administering chest compressions (approximately 100 per minute) sufficient to maintain adequate blood flow. An adequate chest compression should depress the chest cavity by one-third to one-half of its depth.

It is important to remain calm while administering emergency lifesaving procedures and to perform them quickly and with confidence. Have someone call for an ambulance or emergency medical assistance while you begin mouth-to-mouth breathing. If you are alone, administer five cycles (two breaths, 30 chest compressions) before leaving the victim to call. The procedure for mouth-to-mouth breathing follows and is also illustrated in Figure 10–3.

1. Gently shake the child or infant to determine if they are conscious or asleep. If there is no response, quickly assess the child's condition and immediately begin emergency breathing procedures.
2. Position the child on his/her back on a hard surface. Using extreme care, roll an injured child as a unit, keeping the spine straight.
3. Remove any vomitus, excess mucus, or foreign objects (only if they can be seen) by quickly sweeping a finger around the inside of the child's mouth.
4. To open the airway, gently tilt the child's head up and back by placing one hand on the forehead and the fingers (not thumb) of the other hand under the chin; push downward on the forehead and lift the chin upward (head tilt-chin lift).

   Caution: **Do not tip the head back too far. Tipping the head too far can cause an obstruction of the airway. Keep your fingers on the jawbone, not on the tissue under the chin.**

5. Listen carefully for no more than 10 seconds to determine if the child is breathing: place your ear next to the child's nose and mouth and watch for a rise and fall of the chest and abdomen. If the victim is not breathing, begin CPR immediately.

FIGURE 10–3

Cardiopulmonary resuscitation (CPR) for infants and children.

(A) Only if vomitus or foreign objects are clearly visible, use the tongue-jaw lift to open the mouth. Then use a finger to quickly check for the object. Remove only if visible.

(B) Position child on his/her back. Gently tilt the head up and back by placing one hand on child's forehead and fingers of the other hand under the jawbone. Lift upwards (head tilt/chin lift). **Look** for the chest to rise/fall. **Listen** for breathing. **Feel** for breath on your cheek.

(C) *For an infant* : Place your mouth over the infant's nose and mouth creating a tight seal. Slowly and gently, give two small puffs of air (1–1 1/2 seconds), pausing between breaths. Check (look/listen) administer 30 chest compressions. Repeat cycle of 2 breaths/30 chest compressions until the child begins to breath. If air does not go in, reposition and try to breathe again.

(D) *For the child one year and older* : Place your mouth over the child's mouth forming a tight seal. Gently pinch the child's nostrils closed. Quickly give two small breaths of air (1-1 1/2 seconds per breath). If air does not go in reposition and try breathing again. Administer 30 chest compressions. Repeat cycle of 2 breaths/30 chest compressions until the child begins to breath.

(E) Lift your head and turn it to the side after each breath. This allows time for air to escape from the child's lungs and also gives you time to take a breath and to observe if the child is breathing.

6. *For an infant* (up to one year)
   a. place your mouth over the infant's nose and mouth to create a tight seal.
   b. gently give two small puffs of air (one second per breath with a short pause in between). Observe the chest (rise and fall) to be sure air is entering the lungs.

   > *Caution:* **Too much air forced into an infant's lungs may cause the stomach to fill with air (may cause vomiting and increased risk of *aspiration*). Always remember to use small, gentle puffs of air from your cheeks.**

   c. immediately administer 30 quick chest compressions by placing two fingers just below the nipple line; each compression should depress the chest by one-third to one-half of its depth.
   d. continue cycles of two breaths followed by 30 chest compressions (2:30) until the infant resumes breathing or emergency help arrives.

7. *For a child* (1 year and older):
   a. gently pinch the nostrils closed, place your open mouth over the victim's open mouth, forming a tight seal.
   b. give two small breaths of air (one second per breath), pausing between breaths to make sure air is going into the child's lungs.
   c. immediately administer 30 quick chest compressions by placing the heel of your hand over the nipple line; each compression should depress the chest by one-third to one-half of its depth.
   d. continue cycles of two breaths followed by 30 chest compressions (2:30) until the child resumes breathing or emergency help arrives.

8. DO NOT STOP OR GIVE UP! Continue administering CPR (two breaths, 30 compressions) until the child breathes alone or emergency medical assistance arrives.

If air does not appear to be entering the lungs or the chest does not rise and fall while administering CPR, check the mouth and airway for foreign objects. Only remove the object if it is clearly visible and easy to reach (refer to Airway Obstruction). If the child resumes breathing, keep him/her lying down and roll (as a unit) onto one side; this is called the **recovery position** (Figure 10–4). Maintain body temperature by covering with a light blanket and monitor the child's breathing closely until medical help arrives.

Occasionally, families of children with special medical problems or life-threatening conditions make a decision not to have their child resuscitated and will obtain a Do Not Attempt to Resuscitate (DNAR) order from their physician. A copy of this document should be kept on file and honored in the event of a breathing emergency. School personnel should also be made aware of the family's request.

FIGURE 10–4

The child should be placed in a recovery position to rest.

---

aspiration – *accidental inhalation of food, fluid, or an object into the respiratory tract.*
recovery postion – *placing an individual in a side-lying position.*

Airway Obstruction

Children under five years of age account for nearly 90 percent of deaths due to airway obstruction (National Safekids USA, 2006). More than 65 percent of the deaths occur in infants (AHA, 2005). Certain foods (Table 10–3) and small objects (Table 10–4) are common causes of aspiration and should not be accessible to children under age five. However, children with some disabilities, and older children whose development is delayed, may be more prone to choking and thus require continued supervision.

In most instances, children will be successful in coughing out an aspirated object without requiring emergency intervention. However, emergency lifesaving measures must be started immediately if:

- breathing is labored or absent
- lips and nailbeds turn blue
- cough is weak or ineffective
- the child is unable to speak
- the child becomes unresponsive
- there is a high-pitched sound when the child inhales

Respiratory infections can sometimes cause swelling and obstruction of children's airway. If this occurs, call immediately for emergency medical assistance. Time should not be wasted on attempting techniques for clearing an airway obstruction (foreign body). They are not effective and may actually cause the child more harm. Emergency techniques to relieve an airway obstruction should only be attempted if a child has been observed to be choking on an object or is unconscious and not breathing after attempts have been made to open the airway and to breathe for the child.

Different emergency techniques are used to treat infants, toddlers, and older children who are choking (AHA, 2006; 2005). Attempts to retrieve the object from the child's mouth should be made only if the object is clearly visible. Extreme care must be taken not to push the object further back into the airway.

For an infant: If the object cannot be removed easily and the infant is conscious, quickly:

- Have someone summon emergency medical assistance.
- Position the infant face down over the length of your arm, with the child's head lower than his/her chest and the head and neck supported in your hand (Figure 10–5). The infant can also be placed in your lap with its head lower than its chest.
- Use the heel of your hand to give five quick back blows between the infant's shoulder blades.

Caution: **Do not use excessive force as this could injure the infant.**

- Support and turn the infant over, face up, with the head held lower than the chest.
- Give five chest thrusts. Place two fingers just below the nipple line (Figure 10–6). Rapidly

TABLE 10–3 Teacher Checklist: Foods Commonly Linked to Childhood Choking	
raw carrots	seeds (sunflower), peanuts, and other nuts
hot dogs	chewy cookies
pieces of raw apple	cough drops
grapes (whole)	raisins
fruit seeds and pits	pretzels
gummy or hard candies	popcorn
peanut butter sandwich	chewing gum

TABLE 10-4 Objects Commonly Linked to Childhood Choking
latex balloons (uninflated or pieces)   small batteries (calculator, hearing aid)   magnets   marker or pen caps   paper clips   small objects (less than 1.5 inches; 3.75 cm) in diameter   toys with small pieces   coins   marbles   small balls, blocks, beads, or vending machine toys

compress the infant's chest approximately 1/2–1 inch (1.3–2.5 cm); release pressure completely between thrusts, allowing the chest to return to its normal position.

- Look inside the child's mouth for the foreign object. If clearly visible and reachable, remove it.
- Repeat the steps, alternating five back blows and five chest thrusts until the object is dislodged and the infant begins to cry or the infant loses consciousness.

For the child: If the object cannot be removed easily and the child is conscious, quickly:

- Summon emerge ncy medical assistance.
- Stand or kneel behind the child with your arms around the child's waist (Figure 10–7).
- Make a fist with one hand, thumbs tucked in.
- Place the fisted hand (thumb-side) against the child's abdomen, midway between the base of the rib cage (xiphoid process) and the navel.
- Press your fisted hand into the child's abdomen with a quick, inward and upward thrust.
- Continue to repeat abdominal thrusts until the object is dislodged or the child becomes unconscious.

FIGURE 10–5

The infant's head should be lower than the chest.

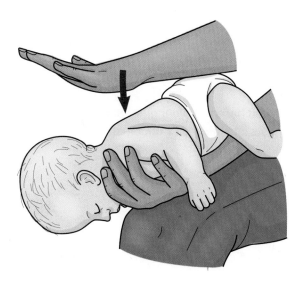

FIGURE 10–6

Location of fingers for chest compressions on an infant.

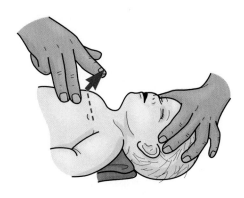

FIGURE 10–7

The Heimlich maneuver.

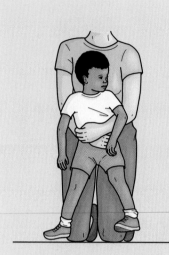

Stand or kneel behind the child with your arms around the child's waist.

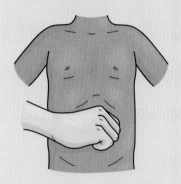

Make a fist with one hand. Place the fisted hand against the child's abdomen below the tip of the rib cage, slightly above the navel.

Grasp the fisted hand with your other hand. Press your fists into the child's abdomen with a quick upward thrust.

If the infant or child **LOSES CONSCIOUSNESS AND IS NOT BREATHING**, stop and have someone call for an ambulance or emergency medical assistance if this has not already been done. Place the child flat on the floor or other hard surface (on back, face up) and begin CPR immediately (Figure 10–8). Authorities believe that CPR chest compressions are sufficient to dislodge an object in the airway. Look inside of the child's mouth (for the foreign object) before each cycle of breaths is given.

If the infant or child begins to breathe on their own, stop CPR and continue to monitor the child closely until medical help arrives. Roll the child (as a unit) onto his/her side (recovery position). Always be sure the child receives medical attention after the object has been dislodged and breathing is restored.

Shock

Shock frequently accompanies many types of injuries, especially those that are severe, and should be anticipated. However, shock can also result from extreme emotional upset, and less severe injuries, such as bleeding, pain, heat exhaustion, poisoning, burns, and fractures. It is a life-threatening condition and requires prompt emergency treatment. Early indicators of shock include:

- skin that is pale, cool, and clammy
- confusion, anxiety, restlessness
- increased perspiration
- weakness
- rapid, shallow breathing

Signs of more serious shock may develop, and include:

- rapid, weak pulse
- bluish discoloration around lips, nails, and ear lobes
- dilated pupils
- extreme thirst
- nausea and vomiting
- unconsciousness

To treat a child in shock:

1. Have someone call for emergency medical assistance.
2. Quickly assess the ABCs. Try to identify what may have caused the shock (e.g., bleeding, poisoning) and treat the cause first.
3. Keep the child lying down.
4. Elevate the child's feet 8 to 10 inches, if there is no indication of fractures to the legs or head, or back injuries.
5. Maintain body heat by covering the child lightly with a blanket.
6. Moisten a clean cloth and use it for wetting the lips and mouth if the child complains of thirst.
7. Stay calm and reassure the child until emergency medical help arrives.
8. Observe the child's breathing closely; give mouth-to-mouth resuscitation if necessary.

Asthma

Asthma is a chronic disorder of the respiratory system characterized by periods of wheezing, gasping, and labored breathing. Numerous factors are known to trigger an acute asthma attack, including allergic

FIGURE 10–8

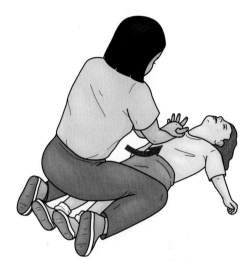

Heimlich maneuver with child lying down.

reactions, respiratory infections, emotional stress, air pollutants, and physical exertion (Stingone, & Claudio, 2006; Warman, Silver & Wood, 2006; Delfino, et al., 2003). Asthma attacks make breathing intensely difficult and, therefore, must be treated as a life-threatening event (Whaley & Wong, 2003; Slack-Smith, Read, & Stanley, 2002).

Remaining calm and confident during a child's asthmatic attack is crucial. To treat a child who is having an asthma attack:

1. Summon emergency medical help immediately if the child shows signs of anxiety, wheezing, restlessness, loss of consciousness, or blue discoloration of the nailbeds or lips. Fatigue, inability to recognize teachers, or loss of consciousness are dangerous signs of impending respiratory failure and/or cardiac arrest.
2. Reassure the child.
3. Administer any medications prescribed for the child's acute asthmatic symptoms immediately.
4. Encourage the child to relax and breathe slowly and deeply (anxiety makes breathing more difficult).
5. Have the child assume a position that is most comfortable. (Breathing is usually easier when sitting or standing up.)
6. Notify the child's family.

Bleeding

Occasionally, young children receive injuries, such as a deep gash or head laceration, that will bleed profusely. Severe bleeding requires prompt emergency treatment. Again, it is extremely important that the teacher act quickly, yet remain calm. To stop bleeding:

1. Summon emergency medical assistance immediately if bleeding comes in spurts or is profuse and cannot be stopped.
2. Follow universal precautions, including the use of latex gloves.
3. Place a pad of **sterile** gauze or clean material over the wound.
4. Apply firm pressure (5–10 minutes) directly over the site, using the flat parts of the fingers; do not let up or bleeding may begin again.
5. Place additional pads over the bandage next to the skin if blood soaks through; bleeding may restart if the wound is disturbed.
6. **Elevate** the bleeding part if there is no sign of a fracture.
7. Apply an ice pack, wrapped in a cloth or towel, to the site to help slow bleeding and decrease swelling.
8. Secure the bandage(s) in place when bleeding has stopped.
9. Locate the nearest pressure point above the injury and apply firm pressure if bleeding cannot be stopped with direct pressure and elevation (Figure 10–9).

> *Caution:* **Tourniquets should only be used as a last resort and with the understanding that the extremity will probably have to be amputated.**

Save all blood-soaked dressings. Doctors will use them to estimate the amount of blood loss. Contact the child's family when bleeding is under control and advise them to seek medical attention for the child.

Diabetes

Two potentially life-threatening emergencies associated with diabetes are hypoglycemia and hyperglycemia. Teachers must be able to quickly distinguish between these two conditions in order to

---

sterile – *free from living microorganisms.*
elevate – *to raise to a higher position.*

FIGURE 10–9

Pressure points for uncontrollable bleeding.

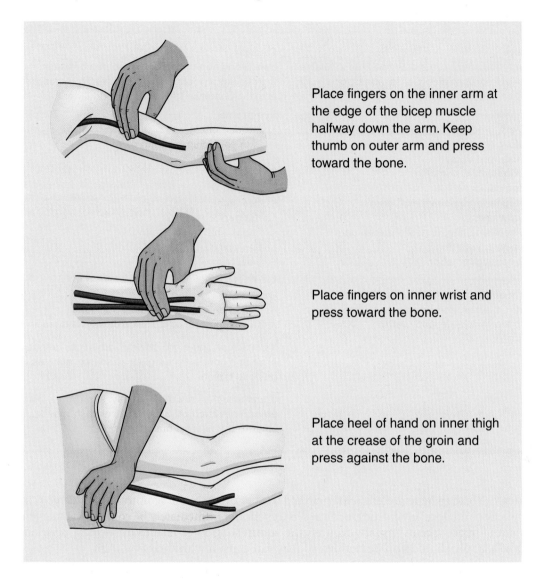

Place fingers on the inner arm at the edge of the bicep muscle halfway down the arm. Keep thumb on outer arm and press toward the bone.

Place fingers on inner wrist and press toward the bone.

Place heel of hand on inner thigh at the crease of the groin and press against the bone.

determine appropriate emergency measures (American Diabetes Association, 2003). The causes and symptoms of these complications are, in many respects, opposites of each other (Table 10–5).

Hypoglycemia, or insulin shock, is caused by low levels of sugar in the blood. It can occur whenever a diabetic child either receives an excessive dose of insulin or an insufficient amount of food. Other causes may include illness, delayed eating times, or increased activity. Similar symptoms are experienced by nondiabetic children when they become overly hungry. Hypoglycemia can often be quickly reversed by administering a sugar substance. Orange juice is ideal for this purpose because it is absorbed rapidly by the body. Concentrated glucose gel or tablets can also be purchased and used for emergency purposes. Hard candies, such as Life Savers™ or lollipops, **should not** be given because a child could easily choke.

Hyperglycemia (which can lead to diabetic coma), results when there is too much sugar circulating in the blood stream. This condition is a potential problem for every diabetic child. Illness, infection, emotional stress, poor dietary control, fever, or a dose of insulin that is too small or

TABLE 10–5 Teacher Checklist: Signs and Symptoms of Hyperglycemia and Hypoglycemia

Hyperglycemia (diabetic coma)	Hypoglycemia (insulin shock)
Causes High blood sugar caused by too little available insulin, improper diet, illness, stress, or omitted dose of insulin.	**Causes** Low blood sugar caused by too much insulin, insufficient amounts of carbohydrates, increased activity, decreased food intake, and illness.
Symptoms • Slow, gradual onset • Slow, deep breathing • Increased thirst • Skin flushed and dry • Confusion • Staggering; appears as if drunk • Drowsiness • Sweet smelling, winelike breath odor • Nausea, vomiting • Excessive urination	**Symptoms** • Sudden onset • Skin cool, clammy, and pale • Dizziness • Shakiness • Nausea • Headache • Hunger • Rapid, shallow breathing • Confusion • Seizures • Unconsciousness
Treatment Summon emergency medical assistance. Keep the child quiet and warm.	**Treatment** Summon emergency medical assistance if the child's state of consciousness is altered. If *conscious* and alert, quickly administer orange juice or a concentrated glucose source, such as glucose tablets. If *unconscious*, maintain airway, summon emergency medical assistance, or rush the child to the nearest hospital.

forgotten can lead to hyperglycemia. Whenever a teacher observes the symptoms of hyperglycemia in a diabetic child, local emergency medical services should immediately be contacted. Emergency treatment of hyperglycemia usually requires the administration of insulin by medical personnel. The child's family should also be notified so they can consult with their physician.

Drowning

Drowning is a leading cause of unintentional death among young children (Centers for Disease Control and Prevention, 2005). Even small amounts of water, such as toilet bowls, buckets, wading pools, and bathtubs, pose a serious danger. Poor muscle coordination and large upper body proportion make it difficult for young children to escape from water hazards. Older children who drown often have overestimated their swimming abilities or engaged in unsafe water activities.

Cardiopulmonary **resuscitation** must be started immediately upon rescuing a child from a drowning emergency. For this reason, every parent and teacher should complete basic CPR training.

---

resuscitation – *to revive from unconsciousness or death; to restore breathing and heartbeat.*

ISSUES TO CONSIDER • Water Safety

Several times each month, the Arizona five o'clock news and local newspapers carry heartbreaking stories of childhood drownings. More often than not, the victim is a toddler who momentarily escapes a parent's watchful eye, wanders through an unlocked gate, and falls into a residential swimming pool. Although current regulations require new houses and pool installations to meet strict building codes, many existing homes do not have these safety features in place. However, pools and spas are not the only water hazards that contribute to childhood drowning.

- What water sources are present in most homes that could contribute to a potential childhood drowning?
- What characteristics place the toddler at greater risk for drowning?
- What safety measures should be taken to protect children from drowning in residential pools or spas?
- What Web sites provide information about prevention of childhood drowning?
- How would you care for a toddler who has just been pulled from the water and is unconscious?

A child who has been rescued from drowning is likely to vomit during resuscitation attempts because large amounts of water are often swallowed. To reduce the risk of choking, the child should be placed in a recovery position (side-lying) and observed closely for signs of shock. Even if a child appears to have fully recovered from a near drowning incident, medical care should be obtained immediately. Complications, such as pneumonia, can develop from water, chemicals, or debris remaining in the lungs.

Electrical Shock

Exposure to electrical shock can be a life-threatening condition in children. Although it is natural to want to immediately grab the child, this must *never* be attempted until the source of electricity has been turned off or disconnected. This can be accomplished by unplugging the cord, removing the appropriate fuse from the fuse box, or turning off the main breaker switch. If the source cannot be located quickly, a dry nonconductive object, such as a piece of wood or plastic, a folded newspaper or magazine, or rope can be used to push or pull the child away from the current. Always be sure to stand on something dry such as a board or cardboard while attempting to rescue the child.

Severe electrical shock can cause breathing to cease, surface burns, deep tissue injury, symptoms of shock, and the heart to stop beating. To treat an infant or young child who has received an electrical shock:

1. Have someone call for emergency medical assistance while you remove the child from the source of electrical current.
2. Check the child's breathing.
3. Begin cardiopulmonary resuscitation (CPR) immediately if the child is not breathing.
4. Observe for, and treat, signs of shock and burns.
5. Have the child transported to a medical facility as quickly as possible.

REFLECTIVE THOUGHTS

It may be necessary for you to turn off the main electrical supply in a number of emergencies, such as earthquake, fire, ice storm, or tornado. Do you know where the main shut-off valve is located in your current residence? Could you locate this in your workplace?

Head Injuries

The greatest danger of severe head injuries is internal bleeding and swelling (Cook, et al., 2006; Hockenberry, 2004). Signs of bleeding and internal swelling may develop within minutes or hours following the injury, or sometimes not for several days or weeks later.

Early signs of head injury may include:

- repeated or forceful vomiting
- bleeding or clear fluid coming from nose or ears
- confusion, aggressive behavior, apathy, or loss of consciousness
- drowsiness
- severe headache

Symptoms associated with more severe head injury may appear right away or develop hours later, including:

- weakness or **paralysis**
- poor coordination or gait
- unequal size of the pupils of the eye
- speech disturbances
- double vision
- seizures
- an area of increasing swelling beneath the scalp
- unexplained restlessness or agitation

If any of these signs or symptoms develop, summon emergency medical help, and contact the child's family immediately.

Children who receive even a minor blow or bump to the head should not be moved until it can be determined that there are no fractures or additional injuries. If the injury does not appear to be serious, the child should be encouraged to rest or play quietly for the next few hours. Always inform families of any blow or injury to a child's head regardless of how insignificant it may seem at the time. It is also important to observe these children carefully during the next 24 to 36 hours for any changes in behavior or appearance that may indicate the development of complications.

Scalp wounds have a tendency to bleed profusely, causing even minor injuries to appear more serious than they actually are. Therefore, when a child receives an injury to the scalp, it is important not to become overly alarmed at the sign of profuse bleeding. Pressure applied directly over the wound with a clean cloth or gauze dressing is usually sufficient to stop most bleeding. An ice pack can also be applied to the area to decrease swelling and pain (Figure 10–10). Families should be advised of the injury so they can continue to monitor the child's condition at home.

Poisoning

Unintentional poisoning results when harmful substances have either been inhaled, ingested, touched, or injected into the body. The majority of incidences occur in children under six and

---

paralysis – *temporary or permanent loss of sensation, function, or voluntary movement of a body part.*

FIGURE 10–10

An icepack reduces the pain and swelling of bumps to the head.

involve substances that have been ingested (Mayo Clinic, 2005; Michael & Sztajnkrycer, 2004). Signs of poisoning may develop quickly or be delayed, and can include:

- nausea or vomiting
- abdominal cramps or diarrhea
- unusual odor to breath
- skin that feels cold and clammy
- burns or visible stains around the mouth, lips, or skin
- restlessness
- difficulty breathing
- convulsions
- confusion, disorientation, apathy, or listlessness
- loss of consciousness
- seizures

Emergency treatment of accidental poisoning is determined by the type of poison the child has **ingested** (Henry & Harris, 2006; Hockenberry, 2004). Poisons are divided into three basic categories: strong acids and **alkalis**, petroleum products, and all others. Examples of each type are included in Table 10–6.

---

ingested – *the process of taking food or other substances into the body through the mouth.*
alkalis – *groups of bases or caustic substances that are capable of neutralizing acids to form salts.*

REFLECTIVE THOUGHTS

Children who wear bicycle helmets are significantly less likely to experience head injury. The National Bike Safety Network (http://www.cdc.gov/ncipc/bike) and the Bicycle Helmet Safety Institute (http://www.bhsi.org) strongly urge children and adults to wear safety helmets to reduce serious head injuries. Children are also encouraged to wear helmets when riding scooters, skiing, or in-line skating (Khambalia, MacArthur & Parkin, 2005; AAP, 2007 *Child Health Alert*, 1999). How much do you know about current standards that apply to bicycle helmets? What criteria should parents use to select a helmet that is safe? Should children be required to wear helmets while attending child care programs? What are the advantages? Disadvantages?

If a child is suspected of swallowing a poisonous substance:

■ Quickly check for redness or burns around the child's lips, mouth, and tongue. These are indications of a chemical burn, usually caused by strong acids or alkalis. **Do not give the child anything to drink; do not make the child vomit.**

■ Smell the child's breath. If the poison is a petroleum product the odor of gasoline or kerosene will be present. **Do not give the child anything to drink; do not make the child vomit.**

If the child is *conscious:*

■ Quickly try to locate the container, which may provide clues about what the child has ingested.

If you cannot find a container, do not delay in calling Poison Control.

■ Call the nearest Poison Control Center (1-800-222-1222) or your city's emergency number (911 in many areas) and follow their instructions. Be sure to keep the number posted by the telephone.

■ Observe the child closely for signs of shock and/or difficulty breathing.

■ Do not give the child anything to drink.

TABLE 10–6 Poisonous Substances

Strong Acid and Alkalis	Petroleum Products	All Others
bathroom, drain, and oven cleaners	charcoal lighter	medicines
battery acid	cigarette lighter fluid	plants
dishwasher soaps	furniture polish and wax	berries
lye	gasoline	cosmetics
wart and corn remover	kerosene	nail polish remover
ammonia	naphtha	insecticides
	turpentine	mothballs
	floor wax	weed killers
	lamp oil	

If the child is *unconscious:*

- Summon emergency medical assistance immediately.
- Monitor child's airway, breathing, and circulation; administer CPR if breathing stops.
- Do not give the child anything to drink.
- Position the child in the recovery position (side-lying) to prevent choking on vomited material.
- Observe the child closely for signs of difficulty breathing.

Always check with the Poison Control Center and follow their instructions before attempting to treat childhood poisoning. If the child begins to vomit, keep his/her head lowered to prevent aspiration and choking. Contact the child's family as soon as possible.

NON-LIFE-THREATENING CONDITIONS

The majority of children's injuries and illnesses are not life-threatening but may require first aid care. Teachers who have received proper training can administer this type of care, but they are not qualified or expected to provide comprehensive medical treatment. Initial first aid treatment of children's injuries is important for reducing complications and making children feel more comfortable until their family arrives. The remainder of this chapter addresses conditions typically encountered by young children that may require first aid care.

Abrasions, Cuts, and Other Minor Skin Wounds

Minor cuts, scrapes, and abrasions are among the most common types of injury young children experience. First aid care is concerned primarily with the control of bleeding and the prevention of infection. To care for the child who has received a simple skin wound, do the following:

1. Follow universal precautions (Chapter 6), including the use of latex or vinyl gloves.
2. Apply direct pressure to the wound, using a clean cloth or sterile pad to stop any bleeding.
3. Wash the wound under running water for at least five minutes or until all foreign particles have been removed.
4. Cover the wound with a sterile bandage. A thin layer of antibiotic ointment can be applied to superficial abrasions if permitted.
5. Apply a cold pack, wrapped in a disposable paper towel or plastic bag, to the area; this can help to slow bleeding and reduce swelling.
6. Inform the child's family of the injury. Have them to check to be sure the child's tetanus immunization is current.
7. Watch for signs of infection, such as warmth, redness, swelling, or drainage.

Puncture-type wounds and cuts that are deep or ragged require medical attention because of the increased risk of infection. Stitches may be needed to close a gash greater than 1/2 inch (1.2 cm), especially if it is located on the child's face, chest, or back.

Bites

Human and animal bites are painful and can lead to serious infection (Villani, 2006). The possibility of rabies should be considered with any animal bite that is unprovoked, unless the animal is known to be free of the rabies virus. A suspected animal should be confined and observed by a veterinarian. In cases where the bite was provoked, the animal is not as likely to be rabid. First aid care for human and animal bites includes the following:

1. Follow universal precautions, including the use of latex gloves.
2. Allow the wound to bleed for a short while, if the skin is broken (this removes any saliva) before applying direct pressure to stop bleeding.
3. Cleanse the wound thoroughly with soap and water or hydrogen peroxide and cover with a clean dressing.
4. Notify the child's family and advise them to have the wound checked by the child's physician.
5. Notify local law enforcement authorities immediately if the injury is due to an animal bite; provide a description of the animal and its location (unless it is a classroom pet).

Most insect bites cause little more than local skin irritations. However, some children are extremely sensitive to certain insects, especially bees, hornets, wasps, and spiders. Signs of severe allergic reaction include:

- sudden difficulty breathing
- joint pain (delayed reaction)
- abdominal cramps
- vomiting
- fever

- red, swollen eyes
- hives or generalized itching
- shock
- weakness or unconsciousness
- swollen tongue

Allergic reactions to insect bites can be life-threatening and should be closely monitored. To treat a child for severe allergic reactions:

1. Call for emergency medical assistance (911), especially if the child has never experienced this type of reaction before.
2. Encourage the child to rest quietly. Let the child assume a position that is most comfortable for breathing.
3. Administer any medication the child may have at school for allergic reactions immediately.

First aid measures for insect bites provide temporary relief from discomfort and prevent infection. If a stinger remains in the skin, an attempt should be made to remove it quickly with tweezers. The area should then be washed and an ice/cold pack applied to decrease swelling and pain. A paste of baking soda and water applied to the area may provide temporary pain relief.

Blisters

A blister is a collection of fluid (white blood cells) that builds up beneath the skin's surface to protect the area against infection. Blisters most commonly develop from rubbing or friction, burns, or allergic reactions.

First aid care of blisters is aimed at protecting the affected skin from infection. If at all possible, blisters should not be broken. However, if they do break, wash the area with soap and water and cover with a bandage.

REFLECTIVE THOUGHTS

Risk of exposure to blood-borne diseases, such as hepatitis B and C, and HIV/AIDS, is ever present when attending to injuries that involve blood or other body fluids. What steps can teachers take to protect themselves from exposure? What additional precautions can be taken? Where can teachers locate current information about these diseases? What is OSHA? What role does it play in establishing safe workplace conditions?

Bruises

Bruises result when small blood vessels rupture beneath the skin. They are often caused by falls, bumps, and blows. Fair-skinned children tend to bruise more easily. First aid care is aimed at controlling subsurface bleeding and swelling. Apply an ice or cold pack to the bruised area for 15 to 20 minutes and repeat three to four times during the next 24 hours. Later, warm moist packs can be applied several times daily to improve circulation and healing. Alert the child's family to watch for signs of infection or unusual bleeding if the bruising is extensive or severe.

Burns

Burns result when body surfaces come in contact with heat, electrical current, or chemicals. Several factors affect the severity of an accidental burn and the need to call for emergency medical assistance, including the source, temperature of the source, affected body part or area, length of exposure, and victim's age and size (Table 10–7).

Burns that involve children are always considered more serious because of a child's smaller body surface (Hammig & Ogletree, 2006; Hockenberry, 2004). Burns caused by heat are usually classified according to the degree (depth and extent) of tissue damage.

- first degree—surface skin is red
- second degree—surface skin is red and blistered
- third degree—burn is deep; skin and underlying tissues are brown, white and/or charred. These burns require emergency medical attention—call for help immediately.

First aid care of burns (first and second) includes the following:

1. Use caution to protect yourself from the heat source.
2. Quickly **submerge** the burned areas in cool water, hold under running water, or cover with a cool, wet towel for 10 to 15 minutes. Cool water temperatures lessen the depth of burn as well as decrease swelling and pain (Figure 10–11).
3. Cover the burn with a sterile gauze dressing and tape in place. Do not use greasy ointments or creams. Dirt and bacteria can collect in the ointments and creams increasing the risk of infection.
4. Elevate the burned body part to relieve discomfort.
5. Burns that involve feet, face, hands, or genitals, cover a large area or cause moderate blistering are critical and require immediate medical attention. Parents should be advised to contact the child's health care provider.

Chemical burns should be rinsed for 10 to 15 minutes under cool, running water. Remove any clothing that might have the chemical on it. Call for emergency medical assistance or the nearest Poison Control Center for further instructions. The child's family should also be advised to contact their physician.

TABLE 10-7 Teacher Checklist: Burns—When to Call for Emergency Medical Assistance

Always call for emergency medical assistance if:

- a child or elderly person is involved
- the victim experiences any difficulty breathing
- burned areas are located on the face, head, neck, feet, hands, or genitalia
- multiple areas of the body have been burned
- chemicals, electrical current, smoke, or an explosion has caused the burn

FIGURE 10–11

Burns should be cooled under running water.

Burns caused by smoke or electrical current should not be cooled with water and require immediate medical attention.

Eye Injuries

Most eye injuries are not serious and can be treated by teachers. However, because eyes are delicate structures, it is important to know proper care strategies for different types of injuries. Also, families should always be informed of injuries involving their child's eye(s) so they can continue to observe and consult promptly with their physician.

A sudden blow to the eye from a snowball, wooden block, or other hard object is usually quite painful. First aid treatment includes the following:

1. Keep the child quiet.
2. Apply an ice pack to the eye for 15 minutes if there is no bleeding.
3. Use direct pressure to control any bleeding around the eye. Do not apply pressure to the eyeball itself. Cleanse and cover skin wounds with a sterile gauze pad.
4. Summon emergency medical assistance at once if the child complains of inability to see or is seeing spots or flashes of light.
5. Inform the child's family about any blow to the eye so they can continue to monitor the child's condition.

Foreign particles such as sand, cornmeal, or specks of dust frequently find their way into children's eyes. Although it is very natural for children to want to rub their eyes, this must be discouraged to prevent further injury to the eyeball. Often spontaneous tearing will be sufficient to wash the object out of the eye. If the particle is visible, it can also be removed with the corner of a clean cloth or by flushing the eye with warm water (*Child Health Alert*, 2002). If the particle cannot be removed easily, the eye should be covered and medical attention sought.

An object that penetrates the eyeball *must never be removed*. Place a paper cup, funnel or small cardboard box over *both* the object and the eye. Cover the uninjured eye with a gauze pad and

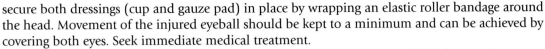

secure both dressings (cup and gauze pad) in place by wrapping an elastic roller bandage around the head. Movement of the injured eyeball should be kept to a minimum and can be achieved by covering both eyes. Seek immediate medical treatment.

A thin cut on the eye's surface can result from a piece of paper, toy, or child's fingernail. Injuries of this type cause severe pain and tearing. The teacher should cover *both* of the child's eyes with a gauze dressing. Notify the family and advise them to take the child for *immediate* medical care.

Chemical burns to a child's eye are very serious. Another staff member should call immediately for emergency medical assistance so the child can be transported to the nearest medical facility. Quickly tip the child's head toward the affected eye. Gently flush the eye with a large amount of warm water, using a small bulb syringe or bottle, for at least 15 minutes. Meanwhile, contact the child's family.

Fractures

A fracture is a break or crack in a bone. A teacher can check for possible fractures by observing the child for:

- particular areas of extreme pain or tenderness
- an unusual shape or deformity of a bone
- a break in the skin with visible bone edges protruding
- swelling
- a change in skin color around the injury site

A child who complains of pain after falling should not be moved, especially if a back or neck injury is suspected. Have someone call immediately for an ambulance or emergency medical assistance. Keep the child warm and observe carefully for signs of shock. Avoid giving the child anything to eat or drink in the event that surgery is necessary. Stop any bleeding by applying direct pressure.

If no emergency medical help is available, only persons with prior first aid training should attempt to splint a fracture. Splinting should be completed before the child is moved. Splints can be purchased from medical supply stores or improvised from items such as a rolled-up magazine or blanket, a ruler, a piece of board or a tissue box. Never try to straighten a fractured bone. Cover open wounds with a sterile pad but do not attempt to clean the wound. Elevate the splinted part on a pillow and apply an ice pack to reduce swelling and pain. Watch the child closely for signs of shock. Contact the child's family immediately and have them notify their physician.

Frostbite and Hypothermia

Frostbite results when body tissues freeze from exposure to extremely cold temperatures. Certain parts of the body are especially prone to frostbite, including the ears, nose, fingers, and toes. Wet clothing, such as mittens and shoes, can hasten the chances of frostbite. It can occur within minutes, causing the skin to take on a hard, waxy, gray-white appearance with or without blisters. Infants and young children should be watched carefully during extremely cold weather so they don't remove hats, boots, or mittens. Initially, the child may experience considerable pain or have no discomfort. However, when tissues begin to warm, there is often a tingling and painful sensation. First aid treatment for frostbite consists of the following:

- Bring the child indoors and into a warm room.
- Remove wet clothing; replace with dry clothing or wrap the child in blankets for warmth.
- Contact the child's family; have them take the child to the nearest medical facility.
- *Do not* rewarm the affected part(s) unless no medical care is available.
- Handle the frostbitten part(s) with care; avoid rubbing or massaging the area as this could further damage frozen tissue.
- Elevate the affected area(s) to ease pain and prevent swelling.

Exposure to cold temperatures can also cause **hypothermia**, a drop in body temperature that slows heart rate, respirations, and metabolism. This slowing of body functions reduces the amount of available oxygen and can lead to shivering, drowsiness, loss of consciousness, and cardiac arrest. Emergency medical personnel should be summoned at once.

Heat Exhaustion and Heat Stroke

First aid treatment of heat-related illness depends on distinguishing heat exhaustion from heat stroke. A child who has lost considerable fluid through sweating and is overheated may be suffering from **heat exhaustion**. The following symptoms would be observed:

- skin is pale, cool, and moist with perspiration
- weakness or fainting
- thirst
- nausea
- abdominal and/or muscle cramps
- headache
- normal or below normal body temperature

Heat exhaustion is not considered life-threatening. It usually occurs when a child has been playing vigorously in extreme heat or humidity. First aid treatment for heat exhaustion is similar to that for shock:

1. Have the child lie down in a cool place.
2. Elevate the child's feet 8–10 inches (20–25 cm).
3. Loosen or remove the child's clothing.
4. Sponge the child's face and body with tepid (lukewarm) water.
5. Offer frequent sips of cool water.

Heat stroke is a life-threatening condition that requires immediate treatment. The child's temperature begins to rise quickly and dangerously as perspiration stops and the body's temperature-regulating mechanism fails. For example, children left in a parked car with the windows rolled up on a warm day (70 degrees and over) can quickly develop heat stroke and die (Guard & Gallagher, 2005). Symptoms of heat stroke include:

- high body temperature ($102°$–$106°$F; $38.8°$–$41.1°$C)
- dry, flushed skin
- headache or confusion
- seizures
- diarrhea, abdominal cramps
- loss of consciousness
- shock

Emergency treatment for heat stroke is aimed at cooling the child as quickly as possible:

1. Summon emergency medical assistance at once.
2. Move the child to a cool place and remove outer clothing.
3. Sponge the child's body with cool water. The child can also be placed in a shallow tub of cool water or gently sprayed with a garden hose. Do not leave child unattended!
4. Elevate the child's legs to decrease the possibility of shock.

---

hypothermia – *below normal body temperature caused by overexposure to cold conditions.*
heat exhaustion – *above normal body temperature caused by exposure to too much sun.*
heat stroke – *failure of the body's sweating reflex during exposure to high temperatures; causes body temperature to rise.*

5. Offer small sips of cool water only if the child is fully conscious.
6. Notify the child's family.

Nosebleeds

Accidental bumps, allergies, nose picking, or sinus congestion can all cause a child's nose to bleed. Most nosebleeds are not serious and can be stopped quickly. If a nosebleed continues more than 30 minutes, get medical help. To stop a nosebleed, do the following:

1. Place the child in a sitting position, with head tilted slightly forward, to prevent any swallowing of blood.
2. Have the child breath through his/her mouth.
3. Firmly grasp the child's nostrils (lower half) and squeeze together for at least five minutes before releasing the pressure (Figure 10–12).
4. If bleeding continues, pinch the nostrils together for another 10 minutes.
5. Have the child play quietly for the hour or so to prevent bleeding from restarting.
6. Encourage parents to discuss the problem with the child's physician if nosebleeds occur repeatedly.

Seizures

Infants and young children experience seizures for a variety of reasons. Simple precautionary measures can be taken during and immediately after a seizure to protect a child from injury, and should include the following:

1. Call for emergency medical assistance if this is the first time a child has experienced a seizure. If the child has a known seizure disorder, call for emergency help if the seizure lasts longer than three to four minutes or the child experiences severe difficulty breathing or stops breathing.
2. Encourage everyone to remain calm.
3. Carefully lower the child to the floor.

FIGURE 10–12

Firmly grasp and squeeze the child's nostrils to stop a nosebleed.

4. Move furniture and other objects out of the way.
5. Do not hold the child down.
6. Do not attempt to force any protective device into the child's mouth.
7. Loosen tight clothing around the child's neck and waist to make breathing easier.
8. Watch carefully to make sure the child is breathing.
9. Place the child in the recovery position (on one side) with head slightly elevated when the seizure ends. This prevents choking by allowing oral secretions to drain out of the mouth.

When the seizure has ended, the child can be moved to a quiet area and encouraged to rest or sleep. A teacher should continue to monitor the child closely. Always notify the child's family.

Splinters

Most splinters under the skin's surface can be easily removed with a sterilized needle and tweezers (only bleach or alcohol should be used for this purpose). Clean the skin around the splinter with soap and water or alcohol before starting and after it is removed. Cover the area with a bandage. If the splinter is very deep, do not attempt to remove it. Inform the child's parents to seek medical attention. Also, make sure the child's tetanus immunization is current.

Sprains

A sprain is caused by injury to the ligaments and tissue surrounding a joint and often results in pain and considerable swelling. In most cases, only an X-ray can confirm whether an injury is a sprain or fracture. If there is any doubt, it is always best to splint the injury and treat it as if it were broken. Elevate the injured part and apply ice packs intermittently for 15 to 20 minutes at a time for several hours. Notify the child's parents and encourage them to have the child checked by a physician.

Tick Bites

Ticks are small, oval-shaped insects that generally live in wooded areas and on dogs. On humans, ticks frequently attach themselves to the scalp or base of the neck. However, the child is seldom aware of the tick's presence. Diseases, such as Rocky Mountain Spotted Fever and Lyme disease, are rare but serious complications of a tick bite. If a child develops chills, fever, or rash following a known tick bite, medical treatment should be sought at once.

Ticks should be removed carefully. Grasp the tick closely to the skin with tweezers, pulling steadily and straight out to remove all body parts; do not squeeze or twist. Wash the area thoroughly with soap and water and apply a disinfectant such as alcohol. Observe the site closely for several days and contact a physician if any signs of infection and/or rash develop.

Tooth Emergencies

The most common injuries to children's teeth involve chipping or loosening of a tooth. A tooth that has been knocked loose by a blow or fall will often retighten itself within several days. Care should be taken to keep the tooth and gum clean, avoid chewing on hard foods, and watch for signs of infection (redness, swelling).

If a tooth has been completely dislodged, the child should be seen by a dentist and monitored for signs of infection. Although dentists will seldom attempt to replace a baby tooth, they are more likely to try and reimplant children's permanent teeth. Successful reimplantation depends on prompt emergency treatment, including:

- rinsing out the tooth socket (hole remaining in the gum); apply pressure to stop bleeding
- handling the tooth with care; do not to touch the root-end

- placing the tooth in a small cup of milk; if milk isn't available, wrap the tooth in a damp cloth
- getting the child to a dentist within an hour of the injury (Krasner, 2005)

Caution: **To avoid accidental choking, do not attempt to reinsert the tooth into the socket or have a child hold the tooth in place.**

FOCUS ON FAMILIES • Poison Prevention in the Home

Children under the age of six are the most frequent victims of unintentional poisonings.

Their curiosity and limited experience often lead them unknowingly into risky situations. In many households, items such as cleaning products, garden chemicals, automobile waxes, charcoal lighter, lamp oil, and medications are commonly left in places accessible to young children. Often, simple precautions can be taken to make children's environments safe.

- Always place potentially dangerous substances in a locked cabinet. Don't rely on your child's ability to "know better."
- Supervise children closely whenever using harmful products. Take them with you if the doorbell rings or if you must leave the room.
- Teach children not to put anything into their mouths unless it is given to them by an adult.
- Test the paint on your house, walls, children's furniture, and toys to be sure it doesn't contain lead. Contact the National Lead Information Center for information (1-800-424-LEAD).
- Check before purchasing plants and flowers (indoor and outdoor) to make certain they are not poisonous.
- Insist that medications, including those purchased over-the-counter, are in child-resistant containers.
- Post the number of the nearest Poison Control Center near the telephone.
- Caution visitors to keep purses and suitcases out of children's reach.

CASE STUDY

The assistant director of the Cactus Kids Child Care Center was surprised one morning when a child care licensing surveyor from the local public health department paid an unannounced visit. She was confident that her center was in tip-top shape and would have no problem passing its annual safety inspection. As the surveyor entered one of the classrooms, she observed teachers attending to a child who appeared to be having a seizure. The director thought the child had a history of seizures, but ran back to the office to check her file.

1. What first aid measures should the teachers be administering?
2. How would their management strategies differ if the child has had no previous seizures?
3. Should the child's family be called? Why?
4. What conditions in the classroom could potentially cause a seizure?
5. If the child's seizure continues longer than five minutes, what should the teachers do?
6. What information should be recorded during and following the seizure?

CLASSROOM CORNER • Teacher Activities

Preventing Burns

Concept: There are things that are safe to touch and play with and other things that can hurt you. (Pre-2)

Learning Objectives

- Children will learn about some items that are safe to touch and other items that are not safe.
- Children will learn how to ask an adult if they aren't sure whether an item is safe to touch.

Supplies

- pictures of a stove, lighter, matches, campfire, candle, barbeque grill, ball, car, apple, crayons, a stuffed toy and a block; two pieces of string (long enough to make two big circles to sort the cards in); picture of a smiling face and a frowning face

Learning Activities

- Read and discuss one of the following books:
  - *Fire Fighters* by Robert Maass
  - *Tonka Fire Truck to the Rescue* by Ann Martin
- Tell the children you are going to talk about some items that are safe to touch and play with and others that aren't safe and can hurt them.
- Hold up the picture cards and talk about each item.
- Tell the children you are going to sort the picture cards by items that are safe to touch and those that are not. Put the smiling face in the middle of one of the circles and the frowning face in the middle of the other.
- Call a child to come up and pick a card and tell the other children if it is a safe item to touch and play with or an unsafe item. Continue until all cards have been sorted.
- Tell the children if they are not sure an item is safe or not to ask a grownup.

Evaluation

- Children will name at least two items safe to touch and two items they should not touch.
- Children will get a grownup if they are not sure whether an object is safe to touch.

SUMMARY

- Emergency care is administered for life-threatening conditions.
- First aid treatment is given for conditions that are not life-threatening.
- Early education programs should have policies and procedures in place for managing childhood emergencies, including:
  - personnel who are trained in first aid and CPR.
  - emergency contact information and telephone numbers.
  - first aid supplies.

- Teachers never offer a diagnosis or medical advice.
- Families are responsible for obtaining additional medical treatment after teachers have provided initial emergency or first aid care.

APPLICATION ACTIVITIES

1. Complete basic CPR and first aid courses.

2. Design a poster or bulletin board illustrating emergency first aid for a young child who is choking. Offer your project to a local early education center where it can be displayed for families to see.

3. Divide the class into small groups of students. Discuss and demonstrate the emergency care or first aid treatment for each of the following situations. A child:

   - burned several fingers on a hot plate
   - ate de-icing pellets
   - splashed turpentine in his/her eyes
   - fell from a climbing gym
   - is choking on popcorn
   - slammed fingers in a door
   - is found chewing on an extension cord

4. As a class project, prepare listings of emergency services and telephone numbers in your community. Distribute them to local early childhood centers or family day care homes.

CHAPTER REVIEW

A. Complete each of the given statements with a word selected from the following list. Take the first letter of each answer and place it in the appropriate space following question "j" to spell out one of the basic principles of first aid.

airway	evaluate
breathing	plans
diagnose	pressure
elevating	responsible
emergency	resuscitation

a. Always check to be sure the child is _____.
b. The immediate care given for life-threatening conditions is _____ care.
c. Early childhood programs should develop _____ for handling emergencies.
d. If an infant is found unconscious and not breathing, begin mouth-to-nose/mouth _____ _____ immediately.
e. The first step in providing emergency care is to quickly _____ the child's condition.
f. Bleeding can be stopped by applying direct _____.
g. When evaluating a child for life-threatening injuries, be sure to check for a clear _____, breathing, and circulation.
h. Families are _____ for any additional medical treatment of a child's injuries.
i. Treatment of shock includes _____ the child's legs 8 to 10 inches.
j. Teachers never _____ or give medical advice.
A basic principle of first aid is _ _ _ _ _ _ _ _ _ _.

REFERENCES

American Academy of Pediatrics (AAP). (2007). Reaffirmation of the policy on bicycle helmets. *Pediatrics, 119*(2), 405.

AAP. (2001). *Choking prevention.* Accessed on November 10, 2006, from http://www.aap.org/pubed/ZZZSE-N9YA7C.htm.

American Academy of Pediatrics (AAP) & American Public Health Association (APHA). (2002). *Caring for Our Children: National Health and Safety Performance Standards: Guidelines for Out-of-Home Child Care Programs.* Washington, DC: AAP.

American Diabetes Association. (2003). Care of children with diabetes in the school and day care setting. *Diabetes Care, 22*(1), 163–166.

American Heart Association. (2006). *2005 American Heart Association (AHA) guidelines for cardiopulmonary resuscitation (CPR) and emergency cardiovascular care (ECC) of pediatric and neonatal patients.* Accessed on November 10, 2006, from http://pediatrics.aappublications.org/cgi/content/full/117/5/e989.

American Heart Association (AHA). (2005). *2005 Guidelines for cardiopulmonary resuscitation and emergency cardiovascular care.* Dallas, TX.

Aronson, S. (2002). *Health young children: A manual for programs.* (4th ed.). Washington, DC: NAEYC.

Centers for Disease Control and Prevention (CDC). (2002). *Fact Book for 2001–2002: Water-Related Injuries.* Washington, DC: National Center for Injury Prevention and Control (NCIPC).

Centers for Disease Control and Prevention (CDCP). (2005). *Childhood drowning.* Accessed on November 10, 2006, from http://www.cdc.gov/ncipc/wisqars.

Child Health Alert. (2002, April). First aid. A clever way to remove particles from a child's eye. *Child Health Alert, 20,* 2.

Child Health Alert. (1999). Helmets recommended for skiing, snowboarding. *Child Health Alert, 18,* 2.

Cook, R., Schweer, L., Shebesta, K., Harties, K., & Falcone, R. (2006). Mild traumatic brain injury in children: Just another bump on the head? *Journal of Trauma Nursing, 13*(2), 58–65.

Delfino, R. J., Gong, H., Linn, W. S., Pellizzari, E. D., & Hu, Y. (2003). Asthma symptoms in Hispanic children and daily ambient exposures to toxic and criteria air pollutants. *Environmental Health Perspectives, 111*(4), 647–656.

Garzon, D. (2005). Contributing factors to preschool unintentional injury. *Journal of Pediatric Nursing, 20*(6), 441–447.

Guard, A., & Gallagher, S. (2005). Heat related deaths to young children in parked cars: An analysis of 171 fatalities in the United States, 1995–2002. *Injury Prevention, 11*(1), 33–37.

Hammig, B., & Ogletree, R. (2006). Burn injuries among infants and toddlers in the United States, 1997–2002. *American Journal of Health Behavior, 30*(3), 259–267.

Henry, K., & Harris, C. (2006). Deadly ingestions. *Pediatric Clinics of North America, 53*(2), 293–315.

Hockenberry, M. (2004). *Wong's essentials of pediatric nursing.* (7th ed.). New York: Mosby.

Khambalia, A., MacArthur, C., & Parkin, P. (2005). Peer and adult companion helmet use is associated with bicycle helmet use by children. *Pediatrics, 116*(4), 939–942.

Krasner, P. (2005). Reducing risk liability for dental injuries in school children. *School Nurse News, 22*(2), 19, 21–22.

Marotz, L. R. (2000). Childhood and classroom injuries. In J. L. Frost (Ed.), *Children and injuries.* Tucson, AZ: Lawyers & Judges Publishing Co.

Mayo Clinic. (2005). *Child safety: Preventing poisoning.* Accessed on November 10, 2006, from http://www.mayoclinic.com/health/child-safety/HQ01263.

Michael, J., & Sztajnkrycer, M. (2004). Deadly pediatric poisons: Nine common agents that kill at low doses. *Emergency Medical Clinics of North America, 22*(4), 1019–1050.

MMWR. (2002). Nonfatal choking-related episodes among children—United States, 2001. *Morbidity & Mortality Weekly Report (MMWR), 51*(42), 945–948.

National SafeKids USA. (2006). *Airway safety: Protecting kid from choking, suffocation and strangulation.* Accessed on November 10, 2006, from http://www.safekids.org.

Olympia R, Wan E, & Avner J. (2005). The preparedness of schools to respond to emergencies: A national survey of school nurses. *Pediatrics,* Dec;116(6): e738-745.

Preboth, M. (2002). Preventing unintentional injuries and deaths in schools. *American Family Physician, 65*(10), 2167–2170.

Siwula, C. M. (2003). Managing pediatric emergencies: No small matter. *Nursing, 33*(2), 48–51.

Slack-Smith, L. M., Read, A. W., & Stanley, F. J. (2002). Experience of respiratory and allergic illness in children attending childcare. *Child Care Health & Development, 28*(2), 171–177.

Stingone, J., & Claudio, L. (2006). Asthma and enrollment in special education among urban school children. *American Journal of Public Health, 96*(9), 1593–1598.

Villani, N. (2006). Treating dog and cat bites. *Advanced Nurse Practitioner, 14*(7), 44–45.

Warman, K., Silver, E., & Wood, P. (2006). Asthma risk factor assessment: What are the needs of inner-city families? *Annals of Allergy, Asthma & Immunology, 97*(1), 11–15.

Whaley, D., & Wong, L. (2003). *Nursing care of infants and children.* (7th ed.). St. Louis: Mosby.

HELPFUL WEB RESOURCES

Canadian Health Network	http://www.canadian-health-network.ca
Children's Safety Network	http://www.childrenssafetynetwork.org
National Safe Kids Campaign	http://www.safekids.org
National Safety Council	http://www.nsc.org
Poison Prevention.Org	http://www.poisonprevention.org
U.S. Consumer Product Safety Commission (bike helmet safety standards)	http://www.cpsc.gov

 For additional health, safety, and nutrition resources, go to http://www.EarlyChildEd.delmar.cengage.com

CHAPTER 11

Maltreatment of Children: Abuse and Neglect

OBJECTIVES

After studying this chapter, you should be able to:

- Distinguish between abuse and neglect.
- Identify three types of abuse and two types of neglect.
- Describe four strategies that teachers can use to help children who are being maltreated.
- Describe characteristics of abusive adults and maltreated children.
- Identify six sources of support and assistance for families who mistreat their children.
- Describe the teacher's legal responsibilities in a case of suspected child abuse.

TERMS TO KNOW

abuse
neglect
discipline
punishment
reprimand
intentionally

physical abuse
shaken baby syndrome
innocent
emotional abuse
verbal abuse
sexual abuse

latch-key
failure to thrive
expectations
precipitating

It is difficult, for many reasons, to determine the true extent of **abuse** and **neglect** with any degree of accuracy. More than three million cases are reported in the United States each year (Administration for Children & Families, 2004). However, it is unknown how many more instances of maltreatment go unreported. An estimated 1,000 to 2,000 children die each year as a result of maltreatment, but this number is probably much higher than the data reveal (Johnson, 2002). Thousands of additional children are known to suffer serious injuries and lifelong physical and emotional disabilities (Turner, Finkelhor, & Ormrod, 2006; Feiring & Taska, 2005).

---

abuse – *to mistreat, attack, or cause harm to another individual.*
neglect – *failure of a parent or legal guardian to properly care for and meet the basic needs of a child under 18 years of age.*

HISTORICAL DEVELOPMENTS

Accounts of child abuse date from ancient times to the present. Throughout history, young children, especially those with developmental disabilities, have suffered abusive and neglectful treatment. They have also been subjected to cultural practices that by today's standards would be considered inhumane. In many societies, children had no rights or privileges whatsoever, including the right to live.

One of the first child abuse cases in this country to attract widespread public attention involved a young girl named Mary Ellen. Friends and neighbors were concerned about the regular beatings Mary Ellen received from her adoptive parents. However, in 1874 there were no organizations responsible for dealing with the problems of child abuse and neglect. Consequently, Mary Ellen's friends contacted the New York Society for the Prevention of Cruelty to Animals on the basis that she was a human being and, therefore, also a member of the animal kingdom. Her parents were found guilty of cruelty to animals and eventually Mary Ellen was removed from their home. This incident brought gradual recognition to the fact that some form of care and protection was needed for the many maltreated and abandoned children in this country.

Although child abuse continued to be a major problem, it wasn't until 1961 that the subject once again received national attention. For a period of years, Dr. C. Henry Kempe studied various aspects of child abuse and was concerned about these children whose lives were endangered. He first introduced the phrase "battered child syndrome" in 1961 during a national conference that he organized to address problems related to the harsh treatment of children (Kempe & Helfer, 1982).

The passage of Public Law (PL) 93–247, the Child Abuse Prevention and Treatment Act (CAPTA) on January 31, 1974, signified a turning point in the history of child abuse and neglect. For the first time, national attention was drawn to the maltreatment of young children. The law also created the National Center on Child Abuse and Neglect, and required individual states to establish a central agency with legal authority to investigate and prosecute incidences of maltreatment. PL 93–247 also mandated states to develop policies, procedures, definitions, and laws that addressed the problems of child abuse and neglect. In October 1996, CAPTA was reauthorized and amended to more clearly define circumstances related to the withholding of medical treatment in life-threatening situations. Changes in the 2003 reauthorization require states to expand services for adoption, foster care, abandoned infants, and family violence prevention. Additional funding was also appropriated for child protective worker training and efforts to strengthen collaboration among various community agencies (Child Welfare Information Gateway, 2006).

Although child abuse and neglect have occurred throughout history, it is only in recent years that public attention has been drawn to the magnitude of this problem. And only now are professionals realizing the full extent and long-term effects that maltreatment can have on children's development.

DISCIPLINE VS. PUNISHMENT

The term **discipline** is derived from the word disciple and refers to the act of teaching or guiding. The appropriate use of discipline can be effective for teaching children socially acceptable ways of behaving. However, when it is used improperly or involves threats, fear, or harsh physical **punishment**, it only teaches children anger and violence.

For decades, the right to punish or discipline children as families saw fit was considered a parental privilege. Consequently, outsiders often overlooked or ignored incidences of cruelty to children so as not to interfere in a family's personal affairs. However, public attitudes regarding family privacy and

---

discipline – *training or enforced obedience that corrects, shapes, or develops acceptable patterns of behavior.*
punishment – *a negative response to what the observer considers to be wrong or inappropriate behavior; may involve physical or harsh treatment.*

the rights of families to discipline children as they wished began to change. Educators, health and law enforcement professionals, neighbors, and concerned friends grew intolerant of the abusive and neglectful treatment of young children. They began speaking out against such behavior and serving as advocates for innocent children who were being victimized by adults.

One of the most difficult aspects of this problem is deciding at what point discipline or punishment becomes maltreatment. For example, when does a spanking or verbal **reprimand** constitute abuse? Is sending a child to his room without dinner neglect? In an attempt to establish clear guidelines, federal legislation was passed forcing states to define abuse and neglect and to establish policies and procedures for handling individual cases.

ABUSE AND NEGLECT

Child maltreatment refers to any situation or environment in which a child is not safe due to inadequate protection, exposure to hazardous conditions, exploitation, mistreatment, or harm **intentionally** inflicted by adults. For legal purposes, a child is defined as an individual under 18 years of age (Figure 11–1). The most commonly recognized categories of maltreatment include:

- physical abuse
- emotional or verbal abuse
- sexual abuse
- physical neglect
- emotional or psychological neglect

Physical abuse is the most common form of abuse and is characterized by a range of visible injuries, such as cuts, burns, welts, fractures, scratches, missing hair, and other nonaccidental injuries (Figure 11–2). The explanations families provide for these injuries are often inconsistent or unreasonable based on the child's age and level of development. A combination of new and older or untreated injuries may suggest repeated abuse. In almost every instance, observable changes in the child's behavior, including shyness, fearfulness, passiveness, anger, aggression, or apprehension will accompany any physical injury (Table 11–1).

FIGURE 11–1

The legal definition of a child is an individual under 18 years of age.

---

reprimand – *to scold or discipline for unacceptable behavior.*
intentionally – *a plan of action that is carried out in a purposeful manner.*
physical abuse – *injuries, such as welts, burns, bruises, or broken bones, that are caused intentionally.*

FIGURE 11-2

Percent of abuse and neglect cases by category.

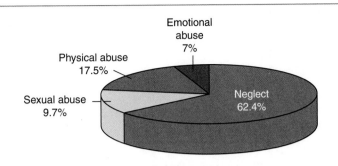

TABLE 11-1 Teacher Checklist: Identifying Signs of Abuse and Neglect

Physical Abuse
- repeated or unexplained injuries, e.g., burns, fractures, bruises, bites, eye or head injuries
- complains frequently of pain
- wears clothing to hide injuries; clothing may be inappropriate for weather conditions
- reports harsh treatment
- is often late or absent; arrives too early or stays after dismissal from school
- seems unusually fearful of adults, especially parents
- appears malnourished or dehydrated
- avoids logical explanations for injuries
- may be withdrawn, anxious, or uncommunicative or may be outspoken, disruptive, and aggressive
- lacks affection, both giving and seeking
- is given inappropriate food, beverage, or drugs

Emotional Abuse
- seems generally unhappy; seldom smiles or laughs
- is aggressive and disruptive or unusually shy and withdrawn
- reacts without emotion to unpleasant statements and actions
- displays behaviors that are unusually adultlike or childlike
- has delayed growth and/or emotional and intellectual development

Sexual Abuse
- wears underclothing that may be torn, stained, or bloody
- complains of pain or itching in the genital area
- has symptoms of venereal disease
- has difficulty getting along with other children, e.g., withdrawn, babylike, anxious
- has rapid weight loss or gain
- experiences sudden decline in school performance
- becomes involved in delinquency, including prostitution, running away, alcoholism, or drug abuse
- is fascinated with body parts, uses sexual terms and talks about sexual activities that are unfamiliar to young children

Physical Neglect
- has a bad odor from dirty clothing or hair; repeatedly arrives unclean
- is in need of medical or dental care; may have untreated injuries or illness
- is often hungry; begs or steals food while at school
- dresses inappropriately for weather conditions; shoes and clothing often sized too small or too large
- is chronically tired; falls asleep at school, lacks the energy to play with other children
- has difficulty getting along with other children; spends much time alone

(continued)

TABLE 11–1 Teacher Checklist: Identifying Signs of Abuse and Neglect (continued)

Emotional Neglect
- performs poorly in school
- appears apathetic, withdrawn, and inattentive
- is frequently absent or late to school
- uses any means to gain teacher's attention and approval
- seldom participates in extracurricular activities
- engages in delinquent behaviors, e.g., stealing, vandalism, sexual misconduct, abuse of drugs or alcohol

The **shaken baby syndrome**, another form of physical abuse, is typically seen in infants. It is caused by the vigorous shaking or tossing of an infant into the air, often because a baby won't stop crying. The resulting whiplash-like motion can cause serious bleeding and bruising in the infant's brain, death, or long-term complications, including blindness, deafness, fractures, learning disabilities, and seizures (American Academy of Pediatrics, 2006). Understanding the harmful effects of shaking a baby and recognizing that crying is a baby's main form of communication are important for preventing this senseless tragedy.

Physical abuse frequently begins as an **innocent** act of frustration or punishment. In other words, most adults do not set out to intentionally harm a child. However, during the process of disciplining the child, quick tempers and uncontrollable anger may lead to punishment that is severe and sufficiently violent to cause injuries and sometimes even death (Table 11–1). Predicting whether the abusive behavior will be repeated is often difficult, since it is more likely to occur during times when an adult has lost control (Berger, 2005). Thus, days, weeks, and even months may pass between attacks.

Emotional or **verbal abuse** occurs when caregivers repeatedly and unpredictably criticize, verbally assault, ignore, or belittle a child's behavior and/or achievements (Schneider, et al., 2005; Hamarman, Pope, & Czaja, 2002). Their demands and expectations are often unrealistic given the child's age and developmental abilities. Chronic exposure to negative statements, such as "Why can't you ever do things right?" or "I knew you were too stupid" have lifelong effects on children's emotional and intellectual development. In many cases, verbal assaults turn into physical abuse over time. Understandably, toddlers and preschoolers are the most common victims of this form of abuse.

Notable changes in a child's behavior are often an early indicator of verbal abuse. Careful observation and documentation of adult–child interactions can be useful for the early identification of potential emotional abuse. Unlike the immediate harm caused by an act of physical abuse, the effects of verbal abuse may not appear until years later. This fact makes it difficult to identify and treat before the abuse leaves permanent scars on the child's personality and development. Sadly, many of these children will experience serious psychiatric disorders later in life (Cohen, Brown, & Smaile, 2002; Feerick, Haugaard, & Hien, 2002; Johnson, 2002).

Sexual abuse includes any sexual involvement between an adult and a child, such as fondling, exhibitionism, rape, incest, child pornography, and prostitution. Such acts are

---

shaken baby syndrome – *forceful shaking of a baby that causes head trauma, internal bleeding, and sometimes death.*
innocent – *not guilty; lacking knowledge.*
emotional abuse – *repeated humiliation, ridicule, or threats directed toward another individual.*
verbal abuse – *to attack another individual with words.*
sexual abuse – *any sexual involvement between an adult and child.*

considered abuse regardless of whether or not the child agreed to participate (Kolvin & Trowell, 1996). This belief is based on the assumption that children may not be free of adult pressure or are incapable of making a rational decision in these situations. Girls are sexually abused at a rate nearly twice that of boys (Johnson, 2002; Burkhardt & Rotatori, 1995). More often, the perpetrator is male and not a stranger to the child, but rather someone the child knows and trusts, for example, a babysitter, relative, caretaker, stepparent, or teacher (Hussey, Chang, & Kotch, 2006). For this reason, the incidence of sexual abuse is probably much greater than reported and often not discovered until years later. Many victims experience delayed mental health disorders that develop in adulthood (Feiring & Taska, 2005; Fink, 2005). Victims may also be exposed to sexually transmitted diseases (STDs) and should be observed for characteristic symptoms (Table 11–2).

A caretaker's failure to provide for a child's basic needs and care is considered *physical neglect*. More than half of all substantiated cases of maltreatment involve some form of neglect, including inadequate or inappropriate food, shelter, clothing, cleanliness, or medical and dental care. Allowing children to be truant from school is also considered neglect in many states. The courts are also prosecuting adults for neglect if they supply drugs or alcohol to underage children or knowingly permit them to have access to, or use, illegal substances.

TABLE 11–2   Teacher Checklist: Identifying Symptoms of Common Sexually Transmitted Diseases (STDs)

Gonorrhea	May cause painful or burning discomfort when urinating, increased vaginal discharge (yellow, green), or vaginal bleeding. Discharge, anal itching, soreness, bleeding, or painful bowel movements are characteristic of rectal infections. May cause sore throat (oral sex). Many victims have no symptoms, but are contagious; serious complications can develop if left untreated.
Chlamydia trachomatis	May cause abnormal vaginal discharge or burning discomfort when urinating five to seven days following infection. Many victims have no symptoms; however, if left untreated it can damage a woman's reproductive organs.
Syphilis	Symptoms appear in stages following infection. Initial stage: within 10 days to 3 months a chancre (painless sore) appears at the point of contact (vagina, rectum, mouth, penis) and heals. Second stage: six weeks to six months after sore heals a generalized rash appears along with fever and enlarged lymph glands. Curable with antibiotics.
Trichomoniasis	Most common curable STD. Symptoms appear within 5 to 28 days and typically include a frothy, yellow-green, foul-smelling vaginal discharge, burning during urination, irritation, and itching around the genital area.
Genital herpes	Many victims have no symptoms. Others may develop painful blister-like sores (around vagina, rectum, penis, mouth), fever, flu-like symptoms, and swollen glands several days following infection; sores heal in two to four weeks. Reoccurrence of sores is common.
Condyloma (genital warts)	Caused by the human papilloma virus (HPV); single or clusters of warts may develop around the genital area within weeks or months following infection. Not everyone will develop symptoms. A vaccine for girls is currently available.
AIDS	Infected persons usually have no initial symptoms. Blood tests can detect the HIV virus six weeks after exposure.

Leaving young children unsupervised can also result in charges of physical neglect. The term **latch-key** was originally used to describe the large number of school-aged children who were home alone during the hours before and after school (Vail, 2004). *Self-care* children, a newer term in the literature, may more accurately describe this growing phenomenon. A shortage of programs and lack of trained personnel have made it difficult for many working families to locate adequate before- and after-school care for school-aged children. Many unanswered questions have been raised about whether these children are at greater risk for accidental injury and/or emotional distress as a result of being left alone (Lamb & Ahnert, 2006; Mayer, 1999). In the meantime, teachers can share information with families to help them decide when and if a child can be safely left home alone (Table 11–3).

Emotional or psychological neglect is perhaps the most difficult of all the types to identify and document (Feiring, 2005; Hamarman, Pope, & Czaja, 2002). For this reason, many states do not include it

---

TABLE 11–3 Tips for Determining if Children are Ready to be Left Home Alone

- Has your child expressed interest in staying home alone?
- Does your child typically understand and abide by family rules?
- Is your child reliable and able to handle responsibility in a mature manner?
- Does your child handle unexpected events in a positive way?
- Is your child able to entertain her/himself for long periods of time or does she/he require constant supervision?
- Have you rehearsed safety and emergency procedures so your child knows how to respond in the event of a fire, an unwanted telephone call, or someone knocking at the front door?
- Does your child know how to reach you if necessary? Is there another adult your child can contact if you are not available?
- Has your child experienced being home alone for short periods?
- Does your child have any fears which would be a problem if left alone?

ISSUES TO CONSIDER • Cultural Practices and Child Abuse

Members of a local Vietnamese community were irate following the arrest of a boy's 23-year-old parents for child abuse. Teachers had noted purple "bruises" on the little boy's back and chest when he arrived at school one day. The couple denied any wrongdoing, insisting they were merely performing "cao gio," a traditional Vietnamese practice used to cure fever. Following the application of medicated oil to the skin, a warm coin or spoon is scraped along the spine and chest until reddened patches appear. The boy's parents believed this would eliminate "bad winds" that had caused the fever.

- Is this abuse?
- How do cultural differences affect parental practices and values?
- Should families be expected to give up traditional cultural practices related to healing and medicine when they immigrate to this country?
- Why is it important for teachers to acquire an understanding of cultural differences?

---

latch-key – *a term that refers to school-age children who care for themselves without adult supervision before and after school hours.*

in their reporting laws. Emotional neglect reflects a basic lack of parental interest or responsiveness to a child's psychological needs and development. Parents fail to see the need, or do not know how, to show affection or converse with their child. The absence of any emotional connection, such as hugging, kissing, touching, conversation, or facial expressions revealing pleasure or displeasure, can lead to developmental delays and stunted physical growth. The term **failure to thrive** is used to describe this condition when it occurs in infants and young children. A lack of measurable gains in weight and/or height is often one of the first indicators of psychological neglect (Black, et al., 2005).

REPORTING LAWS

Reporting laws support the philosophy that parenthood carries with it certain obligations and responsibilities toward children (Figure 11–3). Therefore, punishment of abusive adults is not the primary objective. Rather, the purpose of these laws is to protect children from maltreatment and exploitation. Every attempt is made to maintain family unity by helping families find solutions to problems that may be contributing to the abuse or neglect. Contrary to common belief, removing children from their homes is not always the best solution. Criminal action against parents is usually reserved for those cases where the adults are unwilling or unable to cooperate with prescribed treatment programs.

Each case of maltreatment involves a unique and complex set of conditions, including home environments, economic pressures, individual temperaments, cultural differences, along with many other factors. For this reason, most child abuse laws and definitions are purposely written in general terms. This practice allows the legal system and social agencies greater flexibility in determining whether or not an adult has acted irresponsibly.

Laws in every state identify certain groups and professionals who are required to report suspected incidences of abuse or neglect, including:

- teachers, including assistants and student teachers
- center directors and principals
- health care providers, e.g., doctors, nurses, dentists, pharmacists, psychologists, mental health counselors

FIGURE 11–3

Parenthood involves the acceptance of certain obligations and responsibilities toward children.

---

failure to thrive – *a term used to describe an infant whose growth and mental development are severely slowed due to lack of nurturing or mental stimulation.*

REFLECTIVE THOUGHTS

Teachers (including assistants, aides, and students) are required to report suspected incidences of child abuse and/or neglect. How do you determine what to report? Should the family be informed when a report has been filed? What are your feelings about making a report when it is likely the family will know who filed the complaint? What professional responsibilities do you have to the child and family?

- law enforcement personnel
- social workers
- clergy

Program Policy

Every early childhood and after-school program should have a written plan for how suspected incidences of abuse and neglect are to be handled (Kenny, 2005). Policies and procedures should be reviewed frequently with staff to ensure their understanding and compliance. In larger programs teachers may report directly to the director, administrator, or health consultant who, in turn, contacts appropriate local authorities and files a report. However, if at any time teachers are not satisfied that their concerns have been properly reported, they are obligated by law to personally fulfill this responsibility (Kesner & Robinson, 2002). In home-based programs or smaller centers, an individual staff member may be responsible for initiating the report. Failure to do so may prolong a potentially harmful situation for the child, and can result in criminal prosecution and monetary fines for the teacher.

Initial reports are usually made by telephone and followed up with a written report that is completed several days later (Table 11–4). All information is kept strictly confidential, including the identity of the person making the report. Protection against liability and criminal charges is afforded by most reporting laws to anyone who reports abuse or neglect without deliberate intent to harm another individual.

It is not the teacher's role to prove suspicions of abuse and neglect before making a report (Pelczarski & Kemp, 2006; Kenny, 2005; Webster, et al., 2005). If there is any reason to believe that a child is being mistreated or inadequately cared for, child protective services should be contacted immediately. As long as a report is made in good faith, the teacher is merely indicating that a family may be in need of help. The law does not require that the family or adult be notified when a report is filed. In some cases, doing so could place the child in additional danger, especially if

TABLE 11–4   Teacher Checklist: What to Include in a Written Child Abuse/Neglect Report

1. The name and address of the child and the parents or caretakers (if known).
2. The child's age.
3. The nature and extent of the child's injuries or description of neglect including any evidence of previous injuries or deprivation.
4. The identity of the offending adult (if known).
5. Other information that the reporting person believes may be helpful in establishing the cause of injuries or neglect.
6. The name, address, telephone number, and professional title of the individual making the report.

sexual or harsh physical abuse is involved. Other families may experience relief when their problems are finally recognized. Therefore, the decision of whether or not to inform the family or adult may depend on the particular circumstances.

Reporting a family, colleague, or acquaintance is often difficult. However, as advocates for children's rights, teachers must always be concerned about children's well-being. Unless the child is in immediate danger, trained personnel will generally meet with the family or caregiver within a few days to evaluate circumstances surrounding the incident. Legal action may be taken depending on the seriousness of the situation. In other cases, arrangements may be made to provide family-centered support services to improve conditions for the child.

PROTECTIVE MEASURES FOR PROGRAMS AND TEACHERS

It is essential that early childhood programs and school personnel take steps to protect themselves from potential accusations of child maltreatment. Special attention should be given to careful hiring practices, policy development, and ongoing training of personnel, including:

- conducting background checks on new employees for any prior record of child abuse or felony convictions. (These are mandated in most states and conducted by state law enforcement agencies.)
- hiring individuals with formal training in early education and child development
- contacting an applicant's references (nonrelative) and requesting information about the applicant's prior performance
- reviewing an employee's past employment record, including reasons for leaving previous jobs
- establishing a code of conduct regarding appropriate child–teacher behavior (Table 11–5)
- providing continued inservice training, especially on topics related to identification of abuse/neglect, effective classroom management strategies, and teaching children self-protection skills
- establishing a policy of nontolerance toward any form of abusive behavior, including harassment and harsh discipline

There are additional measures teachers can take to protect themselves against the possibility of false accusations (Mikkelsen, 1997). By conducting daily health checks and recording the findings, a child's condition can be documented upon arrival, thus eliminating opportunities for teachers to be blamed for a bruise or scratch that may have occurred elsewhere. Teachers should also maintain careful records of children's injuries so there is factual evidence. It is also good practice not to leave a teacher alone with children. A second teacher can serve as an eyewitness to prevent any suspicions of wrongdoing. Teachers should also participate in inservice training opportunities to improve their understanding of child maltreatment and their role in intervention. Finally, teachers may want to purchase professional liability insurance unless they are covered by their employer's policy.

UNDERSTANDING THE DYNAMICS OF ABUSE AND NEGLECT

Abusive adults come from all levels of social, economic, educational, ethnic, religious, and occupational backgrounds (Hussey, Chang & Kotch, 2006; Administration for Children & Families, 2004). They live in rural areas, as well as small towns and large cities. It is a common misconception that child maltreatment is committed only by adults who are uneducated, alcoholics, drug abusers, or from poor neighborhoods. Although the incidence is significantly higher among these groups,

TABLE 11–5 Teacher Checklist: Strategies for Positive Behavior Management

- *Reinforce* desirable behaviors. Give lots of verbal praise, hugs and pats, and adult attention for things the child is doing appropriately; this reinforcement should be given often and immediately following the appropriate behavior. "I really like the way you are sharing your toys" or "That was nice of you to let Mat have a turn on the bike."

- *Redirect* the child to another activity or area when he/she is behaving inappropriately; don't comment on the inappropriate behavior. "Juan, could you come and help me set the table?" or "Let's go to the block area and build a zoo together."

- *Rules* help children understand their limits and how adults expect them to behave. Rules should be simple and state what behavior is appropriate. Limit explanations or reasons for the rule. "Mika, you need to sit on the sofa; feet go on the floor" or "We need to walk in the halls."

- *Consequences* can be used together with other management strategies. Most children understand consequences from an early age on. "When your hands are washed we can eat" or "I will have to take the ball away if you throw it at the window again."

- *Ignoring* undesirable behaviors, such as tantrums or throwing things can be effective for decreasing the attention-getting response children may be looking for. Don't look at the child or discuss the behavior with the child.

- *Practice* desirable behaviors when the child behaves inappropriately. For example, if the child scatters crayons across the floor, he/she needs to pick them up and then be praised for doing what was asked. An adult may also model the desired behavior by helping the child to pick up the crayons.

such generalizations may be overly simplistic where complex social and economic issues are involved (Schuck & Widom, 2005).

Perhaps one explanation for why a larger percentage of individuals are identified from disadvantaged families is related to their greater use of, and dependency on, public and social services. Furthermore, daily living is often more stressful for low-income families. Simply finding adequate food, clothing, housing, and transportation can become overwhelming demands (Berger, 2005; Zolotor & Runyan, 2006). In contrast, families with greater financial resources can afford private medical care, move from doctor to doctor, and even seek treatment in neighboring cities. This flexibility and inconsistent contact with a single health care provider makes it easier for families to avoid immediate suspicion and allegations of maltreatment (Freidlaender, et al., 2005). In an attempt to understand the complex nature of child abuse and neglect, three major risk factors have been identified and studied extensively:

- characteristics of adults with potential for abuse/neglect
- presence of a "special" child
- family and environmental stresses

It is believed that for abuse and neglect to take place, all three risk factors must be present at the same time.

Characteristics of Abusive/Neglectful Adults

Certain adult behaviors and predispositions are commonly associated with abusive tendencies, including:

- a history of repeated fear, anger, and rejection (Pears & Capaldi, 2001)
- low self-esteem
- difficulty in forming long-term relationships, e.g., friendships, marriage, that leads to social isolation and loneliness; looks to the child for love
- lack of trust
- early marriage and pregnancy
- maternal depression (Rinehart, et al., 2005)
- use of harsh punishment to "discipline" children
- impulsive tendencies
- low tolerance for stress
- drug and alcohol addictions
- poor problem-solving abilities

Although not every adult who exhibits these characteristics is abusive or neglectful, likewise not every abusive or neglectful caregiver will necessarily fit this description (Coates, 2006; Dixon, et al., 2005). In many cases, adults simply lack the knowledge and skills to be a successful parent. Their ignorance about children's development can lead to expectations that are often unrealistic and developmentally inappropriate based on the child's age and abilities (Milner, 2003; Baumann & Kolko, 2002). For example, a parent may become upset because a 15-month-old wets the bed, a toddler spills milk, or a seven-year-old loses a mitten. Intolerance, frustration, and uncontrolled anger can, in turn, lead to a subsequent outlash of abusive behavior. Parental addictions to drugs and alcohol further reduce their ability to be effective caregivers. Evidence also suggests that adults who grew up in abusive families are more likely to treat their own children in the same manner (Verona & Sachs-Ericsson, 2005; Feindler, Rathus, & Silver, 2003).

Presence of a "Special" Child

Occasionally an abusive or neglectful caregiver will single out a child whom they consider to be different in some way from their **expectations**. These differences may be real or only imagined, but the adult is convinced that they actually exist. Qualities that are often cited by abusive adults include a child who is:

- developmentally delayed
- disobedient or uncooperative
- physically unattractive
- unintelligent
- hyperactive
- fussy
- clumsy
- frequently ill
- very timid or weak
- resembles someone the adult dislikes

Victims of child maltreatment include an almost equal number of boys and girls. Children under three years and those with developmental disabilities, especially autism, are at highest risk for physical abuse (Figure 11–4) (Mandel, et al, 2005; Administration for Children & Families, 2004; Goldson, 1998). Infants and children over the age of six years are more likely to suffer from neglect. The risk of maltreatment is also high for children who are born out of wedlock, from unwanted or unplanned pregnancies, stepchildren, living in foster homes, or living in families where there is also domestic violence occurring.

---

expectations – *behaviors or actions that are anticipated.*

FIGURE 11–4

Children under three years are at highest risk for physical abuse.

 REFLECTIVE THOUGHTS

In many families, economic pressures contribute to the problem of child abuse and neglect. How does poverty increase the probability of child abuse? How might cultural values affect this association? What resources are available to families living in poverty to help with everyday living expenses? What potential effects might poverty and an abusive childhood have on a child's self-concept?

Family and Environmental Stresses

All individuals and families face conflict and crises from time to time. However, some are better able than others to cope with stressful events. In many maltreatment cases, stress is the **precipitating** factor. That is, conflict is sufficient to push an adult to action (abuse) or withdrawal (neglect) as a caretaker (Bugental & Shennum, 2002).

Adults who maltreat children often have difficulty discriminating between events that are significant and those that are not. Instead, they find all crises equally stressful, overwhelming, and difficult to manage. The following examples illustrate the range of personal and environmental stressors that could lead to a loss of control, especially when they occur in combination with other events that are also perceived as stressful:

- flat tire
- clogged sink
- broken window
- lost keys
- job loss
- illness, injury, or death
- financial pressures
- divorce or other marital problems
- moving
- birth of another child

Some of these events may seem trivial in comparison to others. Yet, any one may become the "straw that breaks the camel's back" and trigger abusive behavior. The adult's response may also be inappropriate or out of proportion to the actual event. It is typically at this point that anger and frustration are taken out on the child.

precipitating – *factors that trigger or initiate a reaction or response.*

THE ROLE OF THE TEACHER

Teachers are in an ideal position to identify and help children who are being maltreated (Seibel & Gillespie, 2006; Fontes, 2005; Kenny, 2004). Daily health checks and frequent interactions with children enable teachers to recognize early changes in children's behavior and appearance. Because maltreatment is often a pattern of behavior, careful written documentation of each incident is important (Crosson-Tower, 2004). Written reports should be precise and include the following information:

- the type, location, size, and severity of any injury (Figure 11–5)
- the child's explanation of how the injury occurred
- any explanation provided by the family or caretakers describing the injury occurred
- obvious signs of neglect, e.g., malnutrition, uncleanliness, inappropriate dress, excessive fatigue, lack of medical or dental care
- recent or significant changes in the child's behavior
- quality of parent/child interactions

A teacher's written observations can provide valuable evidence for child protective authorities. They may also be useful for determining which services and intervention programs are most appropriate to meet the immediate needs of children and their families.

Teachers must not ignore their professional and legal responsibilities to protect children's safety. In many cases, a teacher may be the only adult whom a child trusts enough to reveal maltreatment. Teachers must be able to identify the signs of abuse and neglect and know when and how to report suspected cases to the appropriate authorities. They must also be aware of cultural

FIGURE 11–5

A form for recording the location, size, and nature of a child's injury.

Child's Name: _____
Date: _____
Comments: _____
          Description of Injury: _____
          Location and Size of Injury: _____
          Color of Injury: _____
          Desciption of Child's Behavior: _____
Additional Comments/Concerns: _____
Reported by: _____

differences in parenting skills and expectations so as not to misinterpret what they may witness (Fontes, 2005). In addition, they must continually monitor children's school environments for unauthorized visitors and enforce school security policies and procedures.

Helping Maltreated Children

Teachers play an important role in helping maltreated children understand and cope with the effects of abuse and neglect (NAEYC, 1997). They must be positive role models and accept children for who they are, listen to their concerns without judgment, encourage their efforts, and praise their successes (Lowenthal, 1999). For many children, teachers may be the first adult who has shown a sincere interest in them without any intentions of threatening or causing them harm (Eaton, 1997).

As children begin to develop a trusting relationship, they may begin to open up and verbalize their feelings. Play therapy can be especially effective with young children by providing opportunities where they can act out anger, fears, and anxieties related to abusive treatment. Housekeeping activities and doll play are ideal activities for this purpose. Talking about how the doll (child) feels when it is mistreated can help to draw out a child's true feelings. At the same time, teachers can model good parenting skills, such as appropriate ways to talk with, treat, and care for the dolls.

Artwork can also be an effective means for helping young children express their feelings and concerns. For example, self-portraits may reveal an exaggeration of certain body parts or emotions that children have experienced. Pictures may also depict unusual practices that children have been subjected to, such as being tied up, locked in a closet, or struck with an object.

Extreme caution must always be exercised when attempting to interpret children's artwork. A child's immature drawing skills and lack of perspective can easily lead an inexperienced observer to misinterpretation and false conclusions. Therefore, it is best to view unusual items in children's drawings as additional clues, rather than absolute indicators of abuse or neglect.

Some children exhibit behaviors that adults find extremely annoying or irritating in order to gain attention. Repetitive use of such behaviors may prove especially frustrating for adults who have a low tolerance point or lack an understanding of how to manage these situations in a positive manner. In some instances, this intense frustration is sufficient to trigger an abusive response (Sprang, Clark & Bass, 2005). Teachers can be instrumental in helping children learn how to manage their anger and express feelings in ways that are both appropriate and socially acceptable. For example, a teacher might say, "Rosa, if you want another cracker, you need to use your words to ask for it. No one can understand when you whine or cry." Or, "I can't let you hit Rodney. You need to ask him for a turn on the bike."

Teachers can also be instrumental in helping children develop skills that will improve their resiliency to maltreatment (see Chapter 2). Building trusting relationships with children helps them to develop improved self-esteem and self-concept. Teachers can accomplish this through their persistent encouragement and supportive efforts to:

- respond to children in a loving and accepting manner
- set aside a private space that children can call their own
- establish gradual limits for acceptable behavior; set routines and schedules that provide order in children's lives that often have been dominated by turmoil
- let children know they are available whenever they need someone, whether it be for companionship, extra attention, or reassurance (Figure 11–6)
- take time to prepare children for new experiences; letting children know what is expected enhances the "safeness" of their environment
- encourage children to talk about their feelings, fears, and concerns

A number of educational programs and materials have been developed to help improve children's awareness and ability to respond to maltreatment (Table 11–6). Many of these resources

FIGURE 11–6

Caring adults provide children with much needed companionship, reassurance, and individualized attention.

TABLE 11–6 Teachers Checklist: Children's Books About Maltreatment

Bernstein, S., & Ritz, K. (1991). *A family that fights*. Morton Grove, IL: Albert Whitman & Co.

Dayee, F. (1985). *Private zone: A book teaching children sexual assault prevention tools*. Clayton, Victoria: Warner Books.

Fay, J., Stowell, J., & Dietzel, W. (1991). *He told me not to tell*. Spokane, WA: ACT for Kids.

Fitts, S., & Asay, D. (1999). *A stranger in the park*. Scottsdale, AZ: Agreka Books.

Foltz, L., (2003). *Kids helping kids break the silence of sexual abuse*. Lighthouse Point, FL: Lighthouse Point Press (for older children).

Freed, K. (1985). *Red flag, green flag people*. Fargo Moorhead, ND: Rape & Abuse Crisis Center.

Gil, E. (1986). *I told my secret: A book for kids who were abused*. Royal Oak, MI: Self-Esteem Shop.

Girard, L. (1992). *My body is private*. Morton Grove, IL: Albert Whitman & Co.

Girard, L. (1993). *Who is a stranger and what should I do?* New York: Concept Books.

Gross, P. (1996). *Stranger safety*. Southfield, MI: Roo Publishing.

Hindman, J., & Novak, T. (1983). *A very touching book . . . for little people and for big people*. Lincoln City, OR: Alexandria Associates.

Holmes, M., Mudlaff, S., & Pillo, C. (2000). *A terrible thing happened*. Washington, DC: Magination Books.

Johnsen, K. (1986). *Trouble with secrets*. Seattle, WA: Parenting Press.

Joyce, I. (2000). *Never talk to strangers: A book about personal safety*. Racine, WI: Golden Books Pubishing Co.

Kehoe, P. (1987). *Something happened and I'm scared to tell: A book for young victims of abuse*. Seattle, WA: Parenting Press.

Kleven, S., & Bergsma, J. (1998). *The right touch*. Bellevue, WA: Illumination Arts.

Kraizer, S. (1996). *The safe child book: A commonsense approach to protecting children and teaching children to protect themselves*. NY: Fireside Press.

Schor, H. (2002). *A place for Starr: A story of hope for children experiencing family violence*. Charlotte, NC: Kidsrights Press.

Spelman, C., & Weidner, T. (2000). *Your body belongs to you*. Morton Grove, IL: Albert Whitman & Co.

Stowell, J., & Dietzel, M. (2000). *My very own book about me: A personal safety book*. Spokane, WA: ACT for Kids.

Wachter, O. (2002). *No more secrets for me*. London: Little Brown & Co.

are available through local public libraries. Materials should be selected carefully so that they are instructive and not frightening to young children (Aronson, 2002). Social workers, nurses, doctors, mental health specialists, and public service groups can also be called upon to provide special programs for children and parents.

It is also important for all children to develop good communication and self-protection skills. Even when they do not fully understand the complexity of abuse or neglect, these skills enhance children's resilience and help them to recognize "uncomfortable" situations, how and when to tell a trusted adult, and how to assert themselves by saying no when someone attempts a behavior that is inappropriate. Informed children can be the first line of defense against abuse and neglect if they know that being beaten, forced to engage in sexual activity, or left alone for long periods is not normal or the type of treatment they deserve.

Helping Families

Raising young children is a demanding task. Many adults today have not had the same opportunities to learn parenting skills that past generations once had. They have often grown up in smaller families and had fewer opportunities to practice parenting firsthand. Their jobs frequently require relocation to distant cities and the resulting loss of immediate family support. And, more often than not, today's parents are also employed outside of the home, adding yet another challenge to the task of raising children. A lack of adequate knowledge and resources can cause some parents to react to stressful pressures by causing harm to their child. Although these circumstances in no way excuse this type of behavior, they may signal the importance of early recognition and intervention. Without sound knowledge and adequate resources, everyday stresses can lead to maltreatment of children in some families.

There are many ways teachers can help families in these situations (Seibel & Gillespie, 2006). Daily contacts provide opportunities for identifying families in crises and directing them to appropriate community services and programs, such as:

- child protective services
- day care and "crisis" centers
- family counseling
- help or "hot lines"
- temporary foster homes
- homemaker services
- transportation
- financial assistance
- parenting classes
- employment assistance
- home visitors
- self-help or support groups

Teachers can also provide families with valuable information about issues, such as child development, effective discipline, nutrition, and health to help strengthen their child-rearing skills. Teachers must, however, be sensitive to cultural differences in parenting practices that could be misinterpreted as abusive (Fontes, 2005). Establishing supportive partnerships and maintaining effective lines of communication with families are also effective strategies that teachers can use for both prevention and intervention. Teachers can also be proactive and offer seminars and workshops through local schools, child development centers, after-school programs, or community agencies on topics of interest to families, such as:

- child growth and development
- identification and management of behavior problems
- principles of good nutrition; feeding problems

- how to meet children's social and emotional needs at different stages
- preventive health care for children
- locating and utilizing community resources
- stress and tension relievers for parents
- safe environments and injury prevention
- financial planning
- organizing a family support group

Inservice Training

Teachers are morally and legally responsible for identifying the early signs of child maltreatment. However, to be effective, they must be well informed. Participation in inservice training, offered on- or off-site, can improve teachers' understanding of this problem and how to better perform their role. Appropriate topics for such inservice programs might include:

- an explanation of relevant state laws
- teachers' rights and responsibilities
- how to identify child abuse and neglect
- development of school policies and procedures for handling suspected cases
- exploration of teacher and staff reactions to abuse and neglect
- identifying community resources and services
- classroom strategies for helping abused and neglected children
- stress reduction and time management.

FOCUS ON FAMILIES • Anger Management

Being a parent has many positive rewards, but it can also be a challenging and stressful role to fulfill. At times, children are likely to behave in ways that we find upsetting and cause us to react in anger. While this behavior is understandable, it does not teach children how to handle their feelings of frustration or disappointment in a positive manner. Instead, our actions may teach children how to shout, say hurtful words, and respond in an emotional or physical manner, rather than in a rational way. When adults practice effective strategies for managing their anger, they become positive role models for children. The next time your child makes you angry, try several of the following techniques:

- Take a deep breath. Thoroughly assess the situation before you react.
- Leave the room. Take a brief "time out" and regain control of your emotions.
- Consider whether the situation or the child's behavior is actually worth your becoming upset. Could the outcome affect the long-term relationship you have with your child?
- Tell children what has upset you, and why.
- Avoid lengthy explanations and arguments with your child. Children are more likely to understand statements when they are brief and to the point.
- Learn to recognize your tolerance limits and what behaviors are most likely to make you upset.
- Always find something good to say about your child soon afterward. This helps children understand that you still love them despite their unacceptable behavior.

CASE STUDY

When it was time for snacks, four-year-old Jimmy said he wasn't hungry and refused to come over and sit down. At the teacher's gentle insistence, Jimmy reluctantly joined the other children at the table. Tears began to roll down his cheeks as he tried to sit in his chair. Jimmy's teacher watched for a few moments and then walked over to talk with him. Initially, he denied that anything was wrong, but later told the teacher that he "had fallen the night before and hurt his bottom."

The teacher took Jimmy aside and comforted him. She asked Jimmy if he would show her where he had been hurt. When Jimmy loosened his jeans, the teacher observed what appeared to be a large burn with some blistering approximately two inches in length by one inch in width on his left buttock. Several small bruises were also evident along one side of the burn. Again, the teacher asked Jimmy how he had been hurt, and again he replied that "he had fallen."

1. What actions should Jimmy's teacher take? Should she tell anyone else?
2. Would you recommend that Jimmy's teacher report the incident right away or wait until she has gathered more evidence? Why?
3. To whom should the teacher report what she observed?
4. Using the information provided, write up a complete description of Jimmy's injury.
5. If you were Jimmy's teacher, would your feelings and responses be any different if this was a first-time versus a repeated occurrence?
6. Is it necessary for the teacher to notify Jimmy's family before making a report?
7. In what ways can the teacher be of immediate help to Jimmy?
8. What should the teacher do if this happens again?

CLASSROOM CORNER • Teacher Activities

We Have Many Kinds of Feelings
Concept: We all have feelings and it is important to talk about our feelings. (Pre-2)

Learning Objectives
- Children will learn that there are many different kinds of feelings.
- Children will learn that it is important to talk about their feelings.

Supplies
- Large piece of paper to write down comments from the children; marking pen; two puppets (any kind); small pile of blocks; three small cars; box of crayons; two pieces of paper.

Learning Activities
- Read and discuss the following book:
  - *The Way I Feel* by Janan Cain
- Ask children if they have felt the same as the children in the story. Ask children to talk about what makes them feel scared, happy, angry, etc.

CLASSROOM CORNER • Teacher Activities (continued)

- Next, role-play with the puppets. Have puppet one playing with three cars and have puppet two come over to play. Have puppet one ask puppet two if she would like to play with a car. Ask the children how they think puppet two feels when she got to play with a car.

- Next, have puppet one stacking and playing with blocks. Then have puppet two come over and knock down his blocks. Ask children how they think puppet one is feeling after his block building was knocked down. Talk about what puppet two should have done differently (asked to play, asked a teacher for other blocks, etc.).

- Finally, have puppet one drawing with paper and crayons. Have puppet two come over and ask puppet one if she can play. Have puppet one say "No, I am playing with these." Ask children how puppet two is feeling, and talk about what puppet two can do to get some crayons and paper (grab them—not appropriate; ask a teacher to get them some crayons and paper—appropriate, etc.).

Evaluation

- Children will be able to name several different kinds of feelings.
- Children will be able to tell what behaviors evoke specific feelings.

SUMMARY

- Public Law 93–247, the Child Abuse Prevention and Treatment Act:
  - was the first national law that addressed the problems of child abuse and neglect
  - provides legal protection to children who are maltreated
  - requires states to pass laws, designate an investigative agency, and establish policies
  - reauthorizations of this act reflect concern about contemporary maltreatment issues, including adoption, foster care, abandoned infants, family violence, and the need for better agency collaboration
- Laws governing child abuse:
  - are developed and passed by individual states
  - are intended to preserve the family unit
  - require certain professionals, including teachers, to report suspected incidences of abuse and/or neglect
  - authorized a central agency in each state to investigate and handle child maltreatment cases
- Most states recognize four categories of abuse/neglect, including physical abuse, sexual abuse, emotional abuse, and physical neglect; emotional/psychological neglect is recognized by some states.
- Potential for abuse/neglect is thought to be greatest when three factors exist simultaneously: an adult who has abusive tendencies, a child who is viewed as "special," and environmental stressors.
- Teachers play an important role in the prevention and treatment of child abuse/neglect through early identification and reporting, providing emotional support to children, educating families, helping children learn socially acceptable behaviors, and advocating on behalf of children.

APPLICATION ACTIVITIES

1. Gather statistics on the incidence of child abuse and neglect for your city, county, and state. Compare them to the national rates.

2. Write a two-minute public service announcement for radio and television alerting the community to the problems of child abuse and neglect.

3. Locate at least five agencies or services in your community that provide assistance to abusive or neglectful families. Collect materials from these agencies and prepare a written description of their services.

4. Develop a pamphlet that illustrates self-protection skills for young children. Use it with a group of three- to four-year-olds. Evaluate their response.

5. Identify organizations in your community that work with families of sexually abused children. Do they also offer similar programs for children?

6. Develop a bibliography of resources on parenting issues.

7. Conduct a search on the Web to learn more about the CASA (Court Appointed Special Advocates) program. What role do they play in helping abused and neglected children? Is there a CASA program in your area? What qualifications are required of volunteer participants?

CHAPTER REVIEW

A. **By Yourself:**

1. Define each of the Terms to Know listed at the beginning of this chapter.

2. Select a word from the list below to complete each of the following statements.

teachers	sexual	neglect
trust	childhood	identify
physical	definition	confidential
psychological	expectations	reported

1. A child's excessive fascination with body parts and talk about sexual activities may be an indication of _____ abuse.

2. Public Law 93–247 requires states to write a legal _____ of child abuse and neglect.

3. Injury that is intentionally inflicted on a child is called _____ abuse.

4. Malnutrition, lack of proper clothing, or inadequate adult supervision are examples of physical _____.

5. Verbal abuse sometimes results because of unrealistic parent demands and _____.

6. Emotional or _____ neglect is one of the most difficult forms of neglect to identify.

7. Reporting laws usually require _____ to report suspected cases of child abuse and neglect.

8. Information contained in reports of child abuse or neglect is kept _____.

9. Many abusive adults were abused during their own _____.

10. Lack of _____ makes it difficult for many abusive and neglectful adults to form friendships.

11. Daily contact with children helps teachers to _____ children who are maltreated.

12. Suspected abuse or neglect does not have to be proven before it should be _____.

B. As a Group:

1. Describe five clues that teachers might observe in children who are being maltreated.

2. Discuss what teachers should do if they suspect that a child is being abused or neglected.

3. Describe what information should be included in both an oral and written report.

4. Discuss four ways that teachers can help abused and neglected children in the classroom.

5. Describe at least six types of services that are available in your community to help abusive or neglectful families.

6. Why does the incidence of child abuse and neglect appear to be higher among disadvantaged families?

REFERENCES

Administration for Children & Families, Children's Bureau. (2004). *Child maltreatment 2004.* Department of Health & Human Services. Accessed on October 12, 2006, at http://www.acf.hhs.gov/programs/cb/pubs/cm04.htm.

American Academy of Pediatrics (AAP). (2006). *Preventing shaken baby syndrome.* Accessed on October 12, 2006, at http://aap.org/healthtopics/childabuse/cfm.

Aronson, S. (2002). *Healthy young children: A manual for programs.* (4th ed.). Washington, DC: NAEYC.

Baumann, B. L., & Kolko, D. J. (2002). A comparison of abusive and nonabusive mothers of abused children. *Child Maltreatment, 7*(4), 369–376.

Berger, L. (2005). Income, family characteristics, and physical violence toward children. *Child Abuse & Neglect, 29*(2), 107–133.

Black, M., Dubowitz, H., Casey, P., Cutts, D., Drewett, R., Drotar, D., Frank, D., Karp, R., Kessler, D., Meyers, A., & Wright, C. (2005). Failure to thrive as distinct from child neglect. *Pediatrics, 116*(5), 1234–1237.

Bugental, D. B., & Shennum, W. (2002). Gender, power, and violence in the family. *Child Maltreatment, 7*(1), 56–64.

Burkhardt, S. A., & Rotatori, A. F. (1995). *Treatment and prevention of childhood sexual abuse.* Washington, DC: Taylor and Francis.

Child Welfare Information Gateway. (2006). *Major Federal legislation concerned with child protection, child welfare, and adoption.* Accessed on October 19, 2006, from http://childwelfare.gov/pubs/otherpubs/majorfedlegis.cfm.

Coates, T. (2006, May 8). When parents are the threat. *Time, 167*(19), 181–182.

Cohen, P., Brown, J., & Smaile, E. (2002). Child abuse and neglect and the development of mental disorders in the general population. *Developmental Psychopathology, 13*(4), 981–989.

Crosson-Tower, C. (2004). *Understanding child abuse and neglect.* (6th ed.). Boston: Allyn and Bacon.

Dixon, L., Browne, K., & Hamilton-Giachritsis, C. (2005). Risk factors of parents abused as children: A mediational analysis of the intergenerational continuity of child maltreatment (Part II). *Journal of Child Psychology & Psychiatry, 46*(1), 47–57.

Eaton, M. (1997). Positive discipline: Fostering self-esteem of young children. *Young Children, 52*(6), 43–46.

Feerick, M. M., Haugaard, J. J., & Hien, D. A. (2002). Child maltreatment and adulthood violence: the contribution of attachment and drug abuse. *Child Maltreatment, 7*(3), 226–240.

Feindler, E., Rathus, J., & Silver, L. (2003). Assessment of family violence: A handbook for researchers and practitioners. Washington, DC: American Psychological Association.

Feiring, C. (2005). Emotional development, shame, and adaptation to child maltreatment. *Child Maltreatment*, *10*(4), 307–310.

Feiring, C., & Taska, L. (2005). The persistence of shame following sexual abuse: A longitudinal look at risk and recovery. *Child Maltreatment*, *10*(4), 337–349.

Fink, P. (2005). The problem of child sexual abuse. *Science*, *309*(5738), 1182–1185.

Fontes, L. (2005). *Child abuse and culture: Working with diverse families.* New York: Guilford Press.

Friedlaender, E., Alpern, E., Mandell, D., Christian, C., & Allessandrini, E. (2005). Patterns of health care use that may identify young children who are at risk for maltreatment. *Pediatrics*, *116*(6), 1303–1308.

Goldson, E. (1998, July). Children with disabilities and child maltreatment. *Child Abuse & Neglect*, *22*(7), 663–65.

Hamarman S., Pope, K. H., & Czaja, S. J. (2002). Emotional abuse in children: variations in legal definitions and rates across the United States. *Child Maltreatment*, *7*(4), 303–311.

Hussey, J., Chang, J., & Kotch, J. (2006). Child maltreatment in the United States: Prevalence, risk factors, and adolescent health consequences. *Pediatrics*, *118*(3), 933–942.

Johnson, C. F. (2002). Child maltreatment 2002: recognition, reporting and risk. *Pediatrics International*, *44*(5), 554–560.

Kempe, C. H., & Helfer, R. (Eds.). (1982). *The battered child.* Chicago: University of Chicago Press.

Kenny, M. (2005). Teachers' attitudes toward and knowledge of child maltreatment. *Child Abuse & Neglect*, *28*(12), 1311–1319.

Kesner, J., & Robinson, M. (2002). Teachers as mandated reporters of child maltreatment: Comparisons with legal, medical, and social services reporters. *Children & Schools*, *24*(4), 222–231.

Kolvin, I., & Trowell, J. (1996). Child sexual abuse. In I. Rosen (Ed.). *Sexual deviation* (3rd.ed.). Oxford, England: Oxford University Press, 337–360.

Lamb, M., & Ahnert, L. (2006). Nonparental care. In W. Damon & R. Lerner (Eds.), *Handbook of child psychology* (6th ed.). New York: Wiley.

Mandell, D., Walrath, S., Manteuffel, B., Sgro, G., & Pinto-Martin, J. (2005). The prevalence and correlates of abuse among children with autism served in comprehensive community-based mental health settings. *Child Abuse & Neglect*, *29*(12), 1359–1372.

Mayer, D. (1999). *At home alone: Safety tips for latchkey children.* Manitoba, Canada: Manitoba Child Care Association. Child & Family Canada. Accessed on September 27, 2007 from http://www.cfc-efc. ca/docs/mcca/00001_en.htm.

Mikkelsen, E. (1997). Responding to allegations of sexual abuse in child care and early childhood programs. *Young Children*, *52*(3), 47–51.

Milner, J. S. (2003). Social information processing in high-risk and physically abusive parents. *Child Abuse & Neglect*, *27*(1), 7–20.

National Association for the Education of Young Children (NAEYC). (1997). NAEYC position statement on the prevention of child abuse in early childhood programs and the responsibilities of early childhood professionals to prevent child abuse. *Young Children*, *52*(3), 42–46.

Pears, K. C., & Capaldi, D. M. (2001). Intergenerational transmission of abuse: A two-generational prospective study of an at-risk sample. *Child Abuse & Neglect*, *25*(11), 1439–1461.

Pelczarski, Y., & Kemp, S. (2006). Patterns of child maltreatment referrals among Asian and Pacific Islander families. *Child Welfare*, *85*(1), 5–31.

Rinehart, D., Becker, M., Buckley, P., Dailey, K., Reichardt, C., Graeber, C., VanDeMark, N., & Brown, E. (2005). The relationship between mothers' child abuse potential and current mental health symptoms: Implications for screening and referral. *Journal of Behavioral Services & Research*, *32*(2), 155–166.

Schneider, M., Ross, A., Graham, J., & Zielinski, A. (2005). Do allegations of emotional maltreatment predict developmental outcomes beyond that of other forms of maltreatment? *Child Abuse & Neglect*, *29*(5), 513–532.

Schuck, A., & Widom, C. (2005). Understanding the role of neighborhood context in the long-term criminal consequences of child maltreatment. *American Journal of Community Psychology*, *36*(3–4), 207–222.

Seibel, N., & Gillespie, L. (2006, May/June). Child care as a setting for helping to prevent child abuse and neglect. *Exchange*, *169*, 16, 18–20.

Sprang, G., Clark, J., & Bass, S. (2005). Factors that contribute to child maltreatment severity: A multi-method and multidimensional investigation. *Child Abuse & Neglect*, *29*(4), 335–350.

Turner, H., Finkelhor, D., & Ormrod, R. (2006). The effect of lifetime victimization on the mental health of children and adolescents. *Social Science Medicine*, *62*(1), 13–27.

Vail, K. (2004). Millions of children are home alone after school. *The American School Board* Journal, *191*(7), 8.

Verona, E., & Sachs-Ericsson, N. (2005). The intergenerational transmission of externalizing behaviors in adult participants: The mediating role of childhood abuse. *Journal of Consulting and Clinical Psychology,* *73*(6), 1135–1145.

Webster, S., O'Toole, R., O'Toole, A., & Lucal, B. (2005). Overreporting and underreporting of child abuse: Teacher's use of professional discretion. *Child Abuse & Neglect, 29*(11), 1281–1296.

Zolotor, A., & Runvan, D. (2006). Social capital, family violence, and neglect. *Pediatrics, 117*(6), 1124–1131.

HELPFUL WEB RESOURCES

American Professional Society on Abuse of Children	http://www.apsac.org
Boys and Girls Clubs of America	http://www.bgca.org
Child Welfare Information Gateway	http://www.childwelfare.gov
Child Welfare League of America (CWLA)	http://www.cwla.org
Children's Bureau/National Center on Child Abuse and Neglect (NCCAN)	http://www.acf.dhhs.gov
Shaken Baby Alliance	http://www.shakenbaby.com

For additional health, safety, and nutrition resources, go to
http://www.EarlyChildEd.delmar.cengage.com

CHAPTER 12

Planning for Children's Health and Safety Education

OBJECTIVES

After studying this chapter, you should be able to:

- Explain the four principles of instruction.
- Develop a lesson plan for teaching health and safety concepts.
- Explain the importance of including families in children's learning experiences.
- List five health/safety topics that are appropriate for toddlers, and five that are appropriate for preschool-aged children.

TERMS TO KNOW

attitudes   inservice   retention
values   concepts   evaluation
incidental learning   objectives

Many of today's health problems result from a combination of environmental and self-imposed factors (CDC, 2006). Poor eating habits, lack of exercise, pollution, increased stress, inadequate medical or dental care, poverty, violence, and substance abuse (alcohol, drugs, and tobacco) are challenging the quality of children's health (Dunn, et al., 2006; Meeks, Heit, & Page, 2006; U.S. Department of Health & Human Services, 2000). Well-planned educational experiences help children and families to understand how these issues affect one's personal health and what behaviors can lead to improved well-being.

Education is fundamental to assuring a healthy and productive life (U.S. Department of Health & Human Services, 2005; Pressley, et al., 2005; Stein, 2005). Many health behaviors, **attitudes**, and **values** formed during the early years will be carried over into adulthood (Rae, 2006; Sorte & Daeshel, 2006; Hooper, et al., 2005). It is also a time when children are more receptive to new ideas, changes, and suggestions. Thus, it is important to help children acquire basic information and establish practices that will promote good health. This includes raising

---

attitudes – *beliefs or feelings one has toward certain facts or situations.*
values – *the beliefs, traditions, and customs an individual incorporates and utilizes to guide behavior and judgments.*

children's awareness of factors that influence health- and safety-related behaviors, encouraging positive decision-making, and motivating them to assume an active role in fostering personal well-being.

FAMILY INVOLVEMENT IN HEALTH AND SAFETY EDUCATION

Families are children's first and most important teachers. Many of children's early attitudes and health/safety practices are acquired through an ongoing combination of direct instruction, **incidental learning**, and modeling of adult behaviors. Daily activities often become important teachable moments. For example, a parent may discuss the benefits of eating fruits and vegetables while the child washes (and samples) the broccoli for tonight's dinner.

Successful health and safety education programs are built on a strong foundation of family involvement (Lundgren & Morrison, 2003; Pena, 2000; Huff & Kline, 1999; Diffily & Morrison, 1997) (Figure 12–1). When teachers collaborate with children's families they are able to discover their goals and priorities, and thus design instruction that is more responsive (Lear, Isaacs, & Knickman, 2006; Aronson, 2002). There are many resourceful ways that teachers can involve families in children's health/safety education, including:

- preparing newsletters
- accompanying children on field trips
- arranging for guest speakers
- participating in class projects, demonstrations, films, discussions
- assisting with health assessments or policy development
- sharing special talents, skills, or cultural traditions

Family involvement also provides unique opportunities for sharing health information and improving the likelihood that learning experiences will be reinforced in the child's home. It also reduces the potential frustration that children may sense if they receive information at school that is inconsistent with family values and practices. Family members may also benefit from the

FIGURE 12–1

Successful health and safety education is built on family involvement.

incidental learning – *learning that occurs in addition to the primary intent or goals of instruction.*

information and make positive changes in their own health behaviors. Additional advantages of family involvement include:

- better understanding of children's developmental needs
- improved parental esteem
- increased knowledge and competence
- reinforcement of children's learning
- strengthening positive parenting skills
- improved communication between home and school

The resources and combined efforts of families, children, and teachers can bring about meaningful improvements in health and safety behaviors.

THE ROLE OF TEACHER INSERVICE AND HEALTH AND SAFETY EDUCATION

Learning experiences that address health and safety issues are essential to include in children's educational programs. Yet, most teachers have had only limited formal training in health education and may not be adequately prepared to assume this responsibility. However, information about developmentally appropriate content and instructional techniques for teaching health and safety can be shared with teachers through **inservice** opportunities.

Inservice education should be an ongoing process and focused on expanding and updating teachers' information and skills. Many professionals in the community can be called upon to present informative inservice programs on topics, such as:

- early education programs and the law
- emergency preparedness
- identifying child abuse
- advances in health screening
- review of sanitation procedures
- stress and anger management
- working with diverse families
- infectious disease updates
- information on specific health problems, e.g., epilepsy, autism, diabetes, HIV/AIDS, allergies
- review of first aid techniques and CPR training
- health promotion practices
- nutrition education
- cultural awareness and sensitivity
- violence prevention

REFLECTIVE THOUGHTS

Historically, it was considered a family's right and responsibility to teach children values and attitudes associated with health and safety. Teachers were expected to focus their efforts on academic instruction. Is this assumption true today? What factors may be contributing to this change? How does a teacher determine what values and attitudes are important to teach young children? What steps can a teacher take to be sure that learning experiences are bias-free? What can teachers do to make sure these experiences respect a family's cultural values?

---

inservice – *educational training provided by an employer.*

It is important for all teaching and support staff to be included in inservice training opportunities. However, the diversity of participant roles and educational backgrounds make it necessary to present information and materials in a manner that is meaningful to everyone.

CURRICULUM DESIGN

Opportunities to help children develop health awareness and bring about desired changes in their behavior present exciting challenges for early education teachers. Carefully planned educational experiences prepare children to make healthy decisions that will improve the quality of their lives. The challenge becomes one of developing long-range goals and curriculum plans that will systematically build understanding and important lifelong skills.

Topic Selection

Quality health and safety education requires careful planning. Too often instruction is approached in a haphazard fashion. Topics are selected by individual teachers rather than developed according to thoughtful plans that will have long-term benefits for children. For this reason, *National Health Education Standards* have been outlined for grades K–12 to assure that children receive comprehensive health education that is also developmentally appropriate (Appendix C) (AAHPERD, 2007).

Thoughtful planning helps to assure that children's health and safety education will be instructive and meaningful (Telljohann, Symons, & Pateman, 2004). Topics and lessons should be selected to meet children's immediate and long-range developmental needs and interests. Lessons that focus on isolated information or address topics on a one-time basis are quickly forgotten (Essa, 2007). When health and safety learning experiences are integrated across the entire curriculum (e.g., dramatic play, language arts, science, math, outdoor play), children's understanding, retention, and motivation are significantly improved. This approach also helps children make important connections between what they learn in the classroom and their personal lives. Planning must also take into account the diversity of children's backgrounds and abilities and be free of any gender, cultural and/or racial bias.

Teachers can use their knowledge of children's development to provide health and safety learning experiences that are developmentally appropriate and relevant (Locke, 1998). In addition, they must be able to design activities tailored to meet a range of children's needs, abilities, and interest levels (Figure 12–2). For example, a lesson on healthy foods might include an art activity that allows some children to draw pictures of fruits and vegetables, others to create a collage of fruits and vegetables from magazine pictures, while still others may read books or help prepare a plate of fresh fruits to sample for snack.

Learning experiences should also be selected for their ability to improve the quality of children's lives. Children should understand the value of making healthful decisions and following good health and safety practices. They must be able to see the ultimate rewards and benefits for behaving in a safe and healthy manner. A simple explanation may be all that is needed, e.g., "Washing your hands gets rid of germs that can make you sick. When you are well, you can come to school and be part of the fun things we do." There are many developmentally appropriate health/safety **concepts** that can be introduced throughout the early childhood curriculum. For example, toddlers enjoy learning about:

- body parts
- growth and development
- nutritious food
- social skills/positive interaction—getting along with others

---

concepts – *combinations of basic and related factual information that represent a more generalized statement or idea.*

FIGURE 12–2

Educational activities
should reflect children's
needs and interests.

- the five senses
- personal care skills—brushing teeth, handwashing, bathing, toilet routines, dressing
- friendship
- developing self-esteem and positive self-concepts
- cooperation
- exercise/movement routines
- safe behaviors

Topics of interest to preschool children include:

- growth and development
- dental health
- safety and accident prevention—home, playground, water, firearms, traffic, poison, fire
- community helpers
- poison prevention
- emotional health—fostering positive self-image, feelings, responsibility, respecting authority, dealing with stress
- cleanliness and good grooming
- good posture
- food and good nutrition
- the values of sleep and relaxation techniques
- families
- exercise/movement activities
- control and prevention of illness
- manners
- environmental health and safety
- personal protection skills

School-aged children are eager to explore topics in greater detail, including:

- personal appearance
- dental health
- food and nutrition

- consumer health—taking medicines, understanding advertisements, reading labels, quackery
- factors affecting growth
- emotional health—personal feelings, making friends, family interactions, getting along with others, problem-solving, bullying and harassment
- roles of health professionals
- communicable illnesses and prevention measures
- safety and accident prevention—bicycle, pedestrian, water, playground and home safety, firearms, first aid techniques
- coping with stress—anger management, conflict resolution
- physical fitness

Objectives

The ultimate goal of health and safety education is the development of positive knowledge, behavior, and attitudes. Learning is demonstrated when children are able to make good decisions and carry out health and safety practices that maintain or improve their present state of health. **Objectives** describe the precise nature of change in the learner's knowledge, behavior, attitude, or values that can be observed and measured upon completion of the learning experience (Meeks, Heit, & Page, 2006).

Objectives serve several purposes:

- as a guide in the selection of content material
- to identify desirable changes in learner knowledge or behavior
- as an aid in the selection of appropriate learning experiences
- as an evaluation or measurement tool

To be useful, objectives must be written in terms that are clear and meaningful: for example, "The child will be able to select appropriate clothing to wear when it is raining." The key word in this objective is "select." It is a specific behavioral change that can be evaluated and measured. In contrast, the statement, "The child will know how to dress for the weather," is too vague and cannot be accurately assessed. Additional examples of precise and measurable terms include to:

- draw
- list
- discuss
- explain
- select
- write
- recognize

- describe
- identify
- answer
- demonstrate
- match
- compare

Measurable objectives are more difficult to develop for learning experiences that involve values, feelings, and/or attitudes. The behavioral changes associated with this type of learning are often not immediately observable. Rather, it must be assumed that at some later point, children's behaviors will reflect what they have previously learned.

Curriculum Presentation

Teachers serve as facilitators in the educational process, selecting strategies that are appropriate for children and support the stated objectives (Gordon & Browne, 2008). How a teacher presents health and safety information, skills, and values to children will depend on the instructional method that is selected. This can be one of the most challenging yet creative steps in the instructional process (Dennison & Golaszewski, 2002). When deciding on a method, teachers should consider:

---

objectives – *clear, meaningful descriptions of specific behavioral outcomes; can be observed and measured.*

- presenting only a few, simple concepts or ideas during each session
- limiting presentations to a maximum of 5–10 minutes for toddlers, 10–15 minutes for preschoolers, and 15–20 minutes for school-aged children
- class size, age group, type of materials being presented, and available resources
- emphasizing the positive aspects of concepts; avoid confusing combinations of do's and don'ts, good and bad comparisons
- learning experiences that involve children in hands-on activities with real-life materials
- ways to include simple explanations so children become familiar with common terms
- opportunities for repetition (to improve learning)
- ways to use encouragement and positive reinforcement to acknowledge children's accomplishments

There are a variety of effective methods that can be used to present health/safety instruction, including:

- group discussion
- media, e.g., filmstrips, records, models, specimens, videos and audio tapes
- demonstrations, experiments, and role play
- teacher-made displays, e.g., posters, bulletin boards, booklets, flannel boards
- art activities
- printed resource material, e.g., pamphlets, posters, charts (See Table 12–1 for ways to evaluate printed resource material.)
- puppet shows
- books and stories
- guest speakers
- personal example

Methods that actively involve young children in learning experiences are the most desirable and effective (Gordon & Browne, 2008; Essa, 2007). When learning activities involve participation, they will hold children's attention longer and improve what is remembered. Such methods are also more appealing to young children and increase their learning and **retention**. Examples of methods that actively engage children in learning include:

TABLE 12–1 Teacher Checklist: How to Evaluate Printed Resource Material
Look for materials that:
• are prepared by authorities or a reliable source • contain unbiased information; avoid promotion or advertisement of products • present accurate, up-to-date facts and information • involve the learner, e.g., suggested projects, additional reading • are thought provoking, or raise questions and answers • are attractive • add to the quality of the learning experience • are worth the costs involved • support your program's philosophy

retention – *the ability to remember or recall previously learned material.*

REFLECTIVE THOUGHTS

Planning effective learning experiences for young children requires time and effort. The Internet now offers easy access to a wealth of information, particularly in the areas of health, safety, and nutrition. Should all of this information be trusted? What criteria can you use to evaluate the accuracy of information found on Web sites? What additional steps can you take to assure that material you use for developing learning experiences is reliable?

- dramatic play, e.g., dressing up, hospital, dentist office, restaurant, traffic safety, supermarket
- field trips, e.g., visits to a hospital, dental office, exercise class, supermarket, farm
- art activities, including posters, bulletin boards, displays, pictures or flannelboards created by children
- hands-on experiences, e.g., handwashing, brushing teeth, grocery shopping, cooking projects, growing seeds, animal care, conducting simple science experiments
- puppet shows, e.g., care when you are sick, protection from strangers, health checkups, good grooming practices
- games and songs
- guest speakers, e.g., firefighter, dental hygienist, nurse, aerobics or dance instructor, nutritionist, poison control staff, mental health professional

Combinations of these approaches may also be useful for capturing and maintaining children's interest, especially when several sessions are planned on a similar topic or theme. Incorporating health and safety concepts into children's play activities reinforces learning and assures an integrated approach (Figure 12–3).

Many governmental and commercial agencies offer excellent educational materials on health, safety, and nutrition topics that are appropriate for young children. Educational materials and lesson plans are also accessible on many Web sites, including those listed at the end of this chapter. Educational materials and curriculum plans can also be obtained by writing to the organization (see Appendix C).

FIGURE 12–3

Incorporating health and safety education throughout the curriculum makes learning meaningful.

Evaluation

Ongoing **evaluation** is an integral part of the educational process and should be addressed during all stages of health/safety instruction. Evaluation provides feedback concerning the effectiveness of instruction and reveals whether or not students have learned what a teacher initially set out to teach. Evaluation procedures also help teachers determine the strengths, weaknesses, and areas of instruction that need improvement (Telljohann, Symons, & Pateman, 2004; Pealer & Dorman, 1997).

Evaluation is accomplished by measuring positive changes in children's behavior. The goals and objectives established at the onset of curriculum development are used to determine whether or not the desired behavioral changes have been achieved. Do children remember to wash their hands after using the bathroom without having to be reminded? Do children check for traffic before dashing out into the street after a runaway ball? Do children brush their teeth at least once daily? Are established rules followed by children when they are alone on the playground? In other words, evaluation is based on demonstrations of change in children's behaviors. Many of these changes can simply be observed.

Evaluation must not be looked upon as a final step. Rather, it should add a dimension of quality throughout the entire instructional program. The following criteria may be used for the evaluation process:

- Do the objectives identify areas where learning should take place?
- Are the objectives clearly stated and realistic?
- Were children able to achieve the desired objectives?
- Was the instructional method effective? Were children interested and engaged in the learning experiences?
- How could the lesson be improved?

Evaluation must not be viewed as a self-critical process even if the findings suggest that the intended learner outcomes were not achieved. Rather, the evaluation process helps to identify weaknesses in content, activity design and/or presentation. Teachers can use this information to improve future instruction.

 ISSUES TO CONSIDER • Fire Safety

The headlines read, "Three young children found dead after fire guts basement apartment." Firefighters had worked frantically, but intense flames forced them out of the burning building before the children could be located. The children had been playing with matches in their mother's closet when flames spread to nearby clothing. Smoke inhalation claimed the lives of all three children.

- What developmental characteristics might have contributed to this incident?
- What skills do young children need to learn to avoid a similar tragedy?
- What do families need to know?
- What classroom learning experiences can teachers introduce to help children respond safely in the event of a house fire?
- Describe how these learning experiences can be integrated across the curriculum.

---

evaluation – *a measurement of effectiveness for determining whether or not educational objectives have been achieved.*

ACTIVITY PLANS

A teacher's day can be filled with many unexpected events. Activity plans encourage advanced planning and organization (Figure 12–4). Time spent on advanced planning enables a teacher to be better organized, prepared, and able to focus on the learning activity.

A written format for activity plans is often as individualized as are teachers. However, activity plans for health/safety instruction should include several basic features:

- subject title or concept to be presented
- specific objectives
- materials list
- step-by-step learning activities
- evaluation and suggestions for improvement

Activity plans should contain enough information so they can be used by anyone, including a substitute teacher, classroom aide, or volunteer. Objectives should clearly indicate what children are expected to learn. Activities can then be modified to meet the needs of a particular age group. A description of materials, how they are to be used, and safety precautions required for an activity are also important to include. Examples of several activity plans follow.

Activity Plan #1: Germs and Prevention of Illness

CONCEPT   Sneezing and coughing release germs that can cause illness.

OBJECTIVES
- Children will be able to identify the mouth and nose as major sources of germs.
- Children will cover their coughs and sneezes without being reminded.
- Children will be able to discuss why it is important to cover coughs and sneezes.

MATERIALS LIST   Two large balloons and a small amount of confetti, dolls or stuffed animals, doctor kit, stethoscopes, old lab coats or men's shirt to wear as uniforms. (Note: Check before conducting this activity to be sure no one has a latex allergy.)

FIGURE 12–4

Planning is a key component of effective health and safety learning activities.

LEARNING ACTIVITIES

A. Fill both balloons with a small amount of confetti. When the activity is ready to be presented to children, carefully inflate one of the balloons by blowing into the balloon.

> *Caution:*   **Remove your mouth from the balloon each time before inhaling.**

When it is inflated, quickly release pressure on the neck of the balloon, but do not let go of the balloon itself. Confetti will escape as air leaves the balloon, imitating germs as they leave the nose and mouth during coughs and sneezes. Repeat the procedure. This time, place your hand over the mouth of the balloon as the air escapes (as if to cover a cough or sneeze). Your hand will prevent most of the confetti from escaping into the air.

B. Discuss the differences between the two demonstrations with the children: "What happens when someone doesn't cover their mouth when they cough?" "How does covering your mouth help when you cough or sneeze?"

C. Include a discussion of why it is important to stay home when you are sick or have a cold.

D. Help children set up a pretend hospital where they can care for "sick" dolls or animals. Encourage children to talk about how it feels to be sick or when they must take medicine. Reinforce the importance of covering coughs and handwashing to keep from getting sick.

E. Have several books available for children to look at and discuss:

Berger, M. (1995). *Germs make me sick.* New York: HarperCollins.
Capeci, A. (2001). *The giant germ (Magic School Bus Chapter Book 6).* New York: Scholastic.
Katz, B. (1996). *Germs! Germs! Germs!* New York: Cartwheel Books.
Rice, J. (1997). *Those mean, nasty, dirty, downright disgusting but invisible germs.* St. Paul, MN: Redleaf Press.
Romanek, T. (2003). *Achoo: The most interesting book you'll read about germs.* Toronto, ON: Kids Can Press.

EVALUATION

- Children can begin to describe the relationship between germs and illness.
- Children can identify coughs and sneezes as a major source of germs.
- Children voluntarily cover their own coughs and sneezes.

Activity Plan #2: Handwashing

CONCEPT   Germs on our hands can make us sick and/or spread illness to others.

OBJECTIVES

- Children can describe when it is important to wash their hands.
- Children can demonstrate the handwashing procedure without assistance (Figure 12–5).
- Children will value the concept of cleanliness as demonstrated by voluntarily washing their hands at appropriate times.

MATERIALS LIST   Liquid or bar soap, paper towel, sink with running water.

LEARNING ACTIVITIES

A. Present the fingerplay, "Bobby Bear and Leo Lion." Have children gather around a sink to observe a demonstration of the handwashing procedures as the story is read.

One bright, sunny morning, Bobby Bear and Leo Lion (make a fist with each hand, thumbs up straight), who were very good friends, decided to go for a long walk in the woods (move fists in walking motion). They walked and walked, over hills (imitate walking

FIGURE 12–5

Children should learn to wash their hands correctly.

motion raising fists) and under trees (imitate walking motion lowering fists) until they came to a stream where they decided to cool off.

Bobby Bear sat down on a log (press palm of hand on faucet with adequate pressure to release water) and poured water on Leo Lion. Leo Lion danced and danced under the water (move hand and fingers all around underneath the water) until he was all wet. Then it was Bobby Bear's turn to get wet, so Leo Lion (hold up other fist with thumb up) sat down on a log (press palm of hand on faucet with adequate pressure to release water), and Bobby Bear danced and danced under the water until he was all wet (move other hand under water).

This was so much fun that they decided to take a bath together. They found some soap, picked it up (pick up bar of soap), put a little on their hands (rub a little soap on hands), then laid it back down on the bank (place soap in dish on side of sink). Then they rubbed the soap on their fronts and backs (rub hands together for 30 seconds) until they were all soapy.

After that, Bobby Bear jumped back on his log (press faucet) and poured water on Leo Lion until all his soap was gone (move hand under water). Then Leo Lion jumped back on his log (press other faucet) and poured water on Bobby Bear and rinsed him until all his soap was gone (move other hand under water).

Soon the wind began to blow and Bobby Bear and Leo Lion were getting very cold. They reached up and picked a leaf from the tree above (reach up and take a paper towel from the dispenser) and used it to dry themselves off (use paper towel to dry both hands). When they were all dry, Bobby Bear and Leo Lion carefully dropped their leaves into the trash can (drop paper towel into wastebasket). They joined hands (use fists, thumbs up and joined; walking motion, rapidly) and ran merrily back through the woods.[1]

[1] The author would like to acknowledge Rhonda McMullen, a former student and graduate of the Early Childhood Program, University of Kansas, for sharing her delightful story and creative ways with young children.

B. Discuss the proper handwashing procedure with small groups of children. Ask simple questions and encourage all children to contribute to the discussion.

- "When is it important to wash our hands?"
- "What do we do first? Let's list the steps together."
- "Why do we use soap?"
- "Why is it important to dry our hands carefully after washing them?"

C. Talk with children about the importance of washing hands after blowing their nose, coughing into their hands, playing outdoors, using the bathroom, and before eating. Model these behaviors and set a good example for children.

D. Set up a messy art activity, e.g., fingerpaint, clay, glue, gardening. Practice handwashing. Have children look at their hands before and after washing them. Point out the value of washing hands carefully.

E. Have children practice washing their hands for as long as it takes them to sing the complete ABC song.

F. Read and discuss with the children several of the following books:

Adams, P. (1990). *Six in a bath.* New York: Child's Play International.
Boynton, S. (2007). *Bath time!* New York: Workman Publishing Company.
Cobb, V. (1989). *Keeping clean.* New York: HarperCollins Children's Books.
Edwards, F. B. (2000). *Mortimer Mooner stopped taking a bath.* Kingston, Ontario: Pokeweed Press.
Gerver, J. (2005). *Bath time.* New York: Children's Press.
Katz, A. (2001). *Take me out of the bathtub, and other silly dilly songs.* New York: Scholastic.
Ross, R. (2000). *Wash your hands!* LaJolla, CA: Kane/Miller Book Publishers.
Showers, P. (1991). *Your skin and mine.* New York: HarperCollins Juvenile Books.
Woodruff, E. (1990). *Tubtime.* New York: Holiday House, Inc.

G. Observe children washing their hands from time to time to make sure they continue to follow good procedures.

H. Observe children at different times throughout the day to determine if they are using correct technique and washing hands at appropriate times.

EVALUATION

- Was the fingerplay effective for demonstrating the handwashing technique?
- Can children wash their hands correctly and alone?
- Do children wash their hands at the appropriate times, without being prompted?

Activity Plan #3: Dressing Appropriately for the Weather

CONCEPT   Clothing helps to keep us healthy.

OBJECTIVES

- When given a choice, children will be able to match appropriate items of clothing with different kinds of weather, e.g., rainy, sunny, snowy, hot, cold.
- Children will be able to perform two of the following dressing skills: button a button, snap a snap, or zip up a zipper.
- Children will demonstrate proper care and storage of clothing by hanging up their coats, sweaters, hats, etc., at least two out of three days.

MATERIALS LIST Items for a clothing store, such as clothing, cash register, play money, mirror; old magazines and catalogues containing pictures of children's clothing, paste, and paper or newspaper; buttons, snaps and zippers sewn on pieces of cloth; dolls and doll clothes; books and pictures.

LEARNING ACTIVITIES

A. Read and discuss with the children several of the following books:

Andersen, H. C. (2002). *The emperor's new clothes.* New York: North South Winds Press.
Calder, L. (1991). *What will I wear?* Racine, WI: Western Publishing Co.
Jennings, P. (1996). *What should I wear?* New York: Random House.
Neitzel, S. (1994). *The jacket I wear in the snow.* New York: Morrow Books.
Scarry, R. (2002). *Richard Scarry's what will I wear?* New York: Random House.
Watanabe, S. (1992). *How do I put it on?* New York: Collins.

B. Help children set up a clothing store. Provide clothing appropriate for boys and girls. Include items that could be worn for different types of weather conditions. Talk about the purpose of clothing and how it helps to protect our bodies. Help children identify qualities in clothing that differ with weather conditions, e.g., short sleeves vs. long sleeves, light colors vs. dark colors, lightweight fabrics vs. heavyweight fabrics, etc.

C. Have children select two different seasons or weather conditions. Give children old magazines or catalogues from which they can choose pictures of appropriate clothing. Display completed pictures where families can see them. Younger children can point to and name various items of clothing.

D. Provide children with pieces of cloth on which a button, zipper, and snap have been sewn. Working with a few children at a time, help each child master these skills. Have several items of real clothing available for children to practice putting on and taking off.

EVALUATION

- Children can select at least two appropriate items of clothing for three different types of weather.
- Children can complete two of the following skills—buttoning a button, snapping a snap, zipping a zipper.
- Children hang up their personal clothing, e.g., hats, coats, sweaters, raincoats, at least two out of three days.

Activity Plan #4: Dental Health

CONCEPT Good dental care helps to keep teeth healthy.

OBJECTIVES

- Children will be able to identify at least two purposes that teeth serve.
- Children can name at least three foods that are good for healthy teeth.
- Children can describe three ways to promote good dental health.

MATERIALS LIST Gather men's old shirts (preferably white) to use as dental uniforms, stuffed animals, tongue blades, children's books on dental health, old magazines, plastic fruits and vegetables, and gardening tools.

LEARNING ACTIVITIES

A. Locate learning and resource materials about children's dental care on the following Web sites:

American Dental Association (http://www.ada.org); American Academy of Pediatric Dentistry (http://www.aapd.org); National Head Start Oral Health Resource Center (http://www.mchoralhealth.org/HeadStart/index.html); Health Resources & Services Administration (http://www.hrsa.gov).

B. Read one or more of the following books during group time. Talk with the children about the role teeth play (e.g., for chewing, speech, smiling, a place for permanent teeth) and why it is important to take good care of them.

Dowdy, L. (1997). *Barney goes to the dentist.* Allen, TX: Barney Publications.
Frost, H. (1999). *Going to the dentist.* Mankato, MN: Pebble Books.
Mercer, M. (2001). *Just going to the dentist.* New York: Golden Books.
Schoberle, C. (2000). *Open wide! A visit to the dentist.* New York: Simon Spotlight.
Showers, P. (1991). *How many teeth?* New York: Harper Collins Juvenile Books.
Smee, N. (2000). *Freddie visits the dentist.* Hauppauge, NY: Barrons Educational Series.

C. Set up a "dentist" office for dramatic play. Have old white shirts available for children to wear as uniforms. Place stuffed animals in chairs so children can practice their "dentistry" skills using wooden tongue blades and cotton balls.

D. Spread out plastic fruits, vegetables, child-sized gardening tools, and baskets on the floor. Have children plant a garden with foods that are healthy for their teeth.

E. Discuss ways children can help to keep their teeth healthy, e.g., daily brushing with a fluoride toothpaste; regular dental checkups; eating nutritious foods/snacks (especially raw fruits, vegetables); avoiding chewing on nonfood items, e.g., pencils, spoons, keys; limiting sweets.

F. Help children construct "good food" mobiles. Use old magazines to cut out pictures of foods that are good for healthy teeth. Paste pictures on paper, attach with string or yarn and tie to a piece of cardboard cut in the shape of a smile.

G. Have children help plan snacks for several days; include foods that are nutritious and promote healthy teeth.

EVALUATION
- Children can identify at least two functions that teeth serve.
- Children can name at least three foods that are good for healthy teeth.
- Children can describe three good dental health practices that help to keep teeth healthy.

Activity Plan #5: Toothbrushing

CONCEPT   Teeth should be brushed after meals and snacks to stay white and healthy.

OBJECTIVES
- Children can state appropriate times when teeth should be brushed.
- Children can demonstrate good toothbrushing technique.
- Children can describe one alternate method for cleaning teeth after eating.

MATERIALS LIST   One white egg carton per child, cardboard, pink construction paper; several old toothbrushes, cloth, and grease pencil. Toothpaste and toothbrushes (donated).

LEARNING ACTIVITIES
A. Invite a dentist or dental hygienist to demonstrate toothbrushing to the children. Ask the speaker to talk about how often to brush, when to brush, how to brush, alternate ways of cleaning teeth after eating, what type of toothpaste to use, and care of toothbrushes. This may also be a good opportunity to invite families to visit so they can reinforce toothbrushing skills at home.

FIGURE 12–6

A set of "egg carton" teeth.

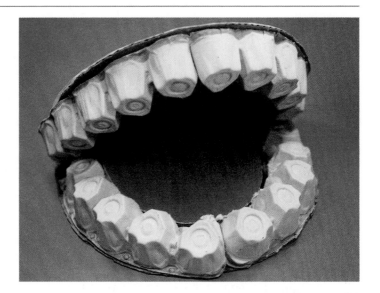

B. Help children construct a set of model teeth from egg cartons (Figure 12–6). Cut an oval approximately 14 inches in length from lightweight cardboard; crease oval gently along the center. Cut the bottom portion of an egg carton lengthwise into two strips. Staple egg carton "teeth" along the small ends of the oval. Glue pink construction paper along the edges where "teeth" are fastened to form "gums." Also cover the backside of the oval with pink construction paper. Use a grease pencil to mark areas of plaque on the teeth. Cover the head of an old toothbrush with cloth and fasten. With the toothbrush, have children demonstrate correct toothbrushing technique to remove areas of plaque (grease pencil markings).

C. Obtain pamphlets on children's dental health from your local dental health association. Prepare a newsletter article reinforcing the concepts children have been learning.

D. Send a note home to families and request that children bring a clean toothbrush to school. (Local dentists and dental associations may be willing to donate brushes.) Practice step-by-step toothbrushing with small groups of children.

E. Older children will enjoy designing posters or bulletin board displays that reinforce good dental hygiene.

F. Read and discuss with children several of the following books:

McGuire, L. (1993). *Brush your teeth please.* New York: Reader's Digest.
Keller, L. (2000). *Open wide: Tooth school inside.* New York: Henry Holt & Co.
Luttrell, I. (1997). *Milo's toothache.* New York: Puffin Books.
Quinlan, P. (1992). *Brush them bright.* Toronto, Ontario: Somerville House.
West, C. (1990). *The king's toothache.* New York: HarperCollins.

EVALUATION

- Children can identify times when teeth should be brushed.
- Children can demonstrate good toothbrushing technique.
- Children can correctly identify at least one alternate method for cleaning their teeth after eating.

Activity Plan #6: Understanding Feelings (Mental Health)

CONCEPT   Feelings affect the state of one's mental as well as physical well-being.

OBJECTIVES
- Children will be able to name at least four feelings or emotions.
- Children can express their feelings in words.

MATERIALS LIST   Old magazines, glue, paper; large, unbreakable mirror; shoe boxes.

LEARNING ACTIVITIES

A. Read and discuss with the children several of the following books:

Anglund, J. (1993). *A friend is someone who likes you.* San Diego, CA: Harcourt, Brace, Jovanovich.

Bang, M. (1999). *When Sophie gets angry—Really, really, angry.* New York: Scholastic.

Blumenthal, D. (1999). *The chocolate-covered-cookie tantrum.* New York: Clarion Books.

Carle, E. (2000). *The grouchy ladybug.* New York: Scholastic.

Carle, E. (2000). *The very lonely firefly.* New York: Scholastic.

Carlson, N. (1998). *I like me.* New York: Scholastic.

Crary, E. (1996). *I'm scared.* Seattle, WA: Parenting Press.

Crary, E. (1996). *I'm mad.* Seattle, WA: Parenting Press.

Gainer, C. (1998). *I'm like you, you're like me: A child's book about understanding and celebrating each other.* Minneapolis, MN: Free Spirit Publishing.

Lewis, P. (2002). *I'll always love you.* Wilton, CT: Tiger Tales.

Spelman, C. M. (2000). *When I feel angry.* Morton Grove, IL: Albert Whitman & Co.

Thomas, P. (2000). *Stop picking on me.* Hauppaugne, NY: Barron's Juveniles.

B. During large or small group time, encourage children to talk about different feelings people experience. Stress that many of these feelings are normal and that it is important to learn acceptable and healthy ways of expressing them. Ask children, one at a time, to name a feeling, e.g., happy, sad, tired, bored, special, excitement, surprise, fear, lonely, embarrassed, proud, or angry (Figure 12–7). Have children act out the feeling. Encourage children to observe the expressions of one another. Help children learn to recognize these feelings. "Have you ever seen someone look like this?" "Have you ever felt like this?" "What made you feel like this?" Discuss and role-play healthy ways to cope with these feelings.

C. Place an unbreakable mirror where children can see themselves. Encourage them to imitate some of the feelings they have identified and observe their own facial expressions.

D. Make a collage of feelings using pictures of people from old magazines. Help children identify the feelings portrayed in each picture.

E. Construct "I Am Special" boxes. Have children decorate old shoe boxes with pictures of things that reflect their individuality, such as favorite foods, activities, toys, etc. Have children fill their boxes with items that tell something special about themselves; for example, a hobby, favorite toy, photograph, souvenirs from a trip, pet, picture of their family. Children can share their boxes and tell something special about themselves during "Show and Tell" or large group time.

F. Older children can be involved in role play. Write out problem situations on small cards; for example, "You and another child want the same toy," "Someone knocks down the block structure you just built," "Another child pushes you," "A friend says he/she doesn't like you anymore." Have pairs of children select a card and act out acceptable ways of handling their feelings in each situation. Discuss their solutions.

FIGURE 12–7

Have children role play different emotions.

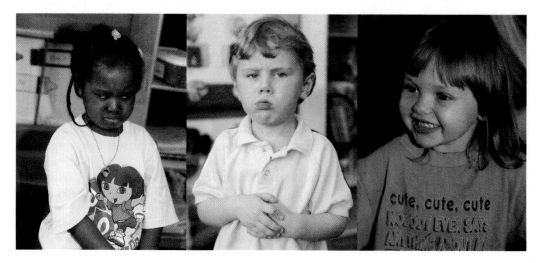

EVALUATION

■ Children can name at least four different feelings or emotions.
■ Children begin using words rather than physical aggression to handle difficult or emotional situations.

Activity Plan #7: Safety in Cars

CONCEPT   Safety rules are important to follow in and around vehicles.

OBJECTIVES

■ Children will begin to understand the purpose and importance of wearing seat belts or sitting in an appropriate safety car seat.
■ Children can name at least one important safety rule to follow in and around cars.

MATERIALS LIST   Order, or download from the Internet, pamphlets about seat belt restraints and car safety from the National Passenger Safety Association (1050 17th Street, N.W., Suite 770, Washington, DC 20036) or from the National Highway Traffic Safety Administration (U.S. Department of Transportation, 400 Seventh Street, S.W., Washington, DC 20590). Prepare photographs of children demonstrating the following safety rules:

a. Always hold an adult's hand when going to and from the car; never dash ahead.
b. Always get in and out of a car on the curbside.
c. Open and close car doors properly. Place both hands on the door handle to reduce the possibility of getting fingers caught in the door.
d. Sit in the car seat; never ride standing.
e. Put on seat belt or use safety car seat.
f. Lock all car doors before starting out.
g. Ride with arms, legs, head, and other body parts inside the car.
h. Don't play with controls inside of the car.
i. Ride quietly so as not to disturb the driver.

LEARNING ACTIVITIES

A. Discuss with the children information found in the pamphlets. Stress the importance of wearing seat belts or riding in an appropriate car seat restraint. Later, have children take the pamphlets home to share with families.

B. Mount photographs of safety rules on posterboard or display on a table. Encourage children to identify the safe behavior demonstrated in each picture (Figure 12–8).

C. Use large group time to discuss with the children the importance of each safety rule pictured in the photographs.

D. For dramatic play, use large wooden blocks, cardboard boxes or chairs, and a "steering wheel" to build a pretend car. Have children demonstrate the car safety rules as they play.

E. Prepare a chart with all of the children's names. Each day, have children place a checkmark next to their name if they rode in a car seat and wore their seat belt on the way to school.

F. Establish a parent committee to plan a "Safe Riding" campaign. On randomly selected days, observe parents and children as they arrive and depart from the center; record whether or not they were wearing seat belt restraints. Enlist children's artistic abilities to design and make awards to be given to families who ride safely. Repeat the campaign again in several months.

EVALUATION

- Children can be observed wearing seat belts or sitting in a proper safety car seat.
- Children can name one safety rule to observe when riding in a car.

TEACHER RESOURCES

Seat Belts Activity Book (Teacher's Guide). U.S. Department of Transportation, National Highway Traffic Safety Administration, Washington, DC 20590.

We Love You, Buckle Up (Preschool curriculum kit on use of seat belt restraints). Order from NAEYC, 1834 Connecticut Avenue, N.W., Washington, DC 20009.

FIGURE 12–8

Children can begin to learn about safety signs.

Activity Plan #8: Pedestrian Safety

CONCEPT Young children can begin to learn safe behaviors in and around traffic and a respect for moving vehicles.

OBJECTIVES
- Children will be able to identify the stop, go, and walk signals.
- Children can describe two rules for safely crossing streets.
- Children will begin to develop respect for moving vehicles.

MATERIALS LIST Flannelboard and characters; cardboard pieces, poster paint, wooden stakes; masking tape, yarn or string; six-inch paper plates; red, green, and yellow poster paint; black marker.

LEARNING ACTIVITIES

A. Obtain the booklets (series of 5): *Preschool Children in Traffic* from the American Automobile Association, 1000 AAA Drive, Heathrow, FL 32746. NAEYC also has the following booklets available: *Walk in Traffic Safely; We Cross the Street Safely: A Preschool Book on Safety;* and *When We Cross the Street: A First Book on Traffic Safety.* Also read:

Berenstain, S., & Berenstain, J. (1999). *My trusty car seat: Buckling up for safety.* New York: Random House.
Committee, C. B. (2000). *Buckles buckles everywhere.* Palmetto Bookworks.
Mattern, J. (2007). *Staying safe in the car.* New York: Weekly Reader Early Learning.
Rathmann, P. (1995). *Officer Buckle and Gloria.* New York: Putnam Publishing Group.

B. Discuss rules for safely crossing streets:

    a. always have an adult cross streets with you (this is a must for preschool children)
    b. only cross streets at intersections
    c. always look both ways before stepping out into the street
    d. use your ears to listen for oncoming cars
    e. don't walk out into the street from between parked cars or in the middle of a block
    f. ask an adult to retrieve balls and toys from streets
    g. always obey traffic signs

C. Introduce basic traffic signs (only those that have meaning to young pedestrians), e.g., stop, go, walk, pedestrian crossing, one-way traffic, bike path, railroad crossing. Help children learn to recognize each sign by identifying certain features, such as color, shape, location.

D. Help children to construct the basic traffic signs using cardboard and poster paint. Attach signs to wooden stakes. Set up a series of "streets" in the outdoor play yard using string, yarn or pieces of cardboard to mark paths; place traffic signs in appropriate places. Select children to ride tricycles along designated "streets" while other children practice pedestrian safety.

E. Prepare a flannelboard story and characters to help children visualize pedestrian safety rules.

F. Help children construct a set of stop-go-walk signs. Have each child paint three paper plates—one red, one green, one yellow. On a plain white plate, write the word WALK. Fasten all four plates together with tape or glue to form a traffic signal.

EVALUATION
- Children respond correctly to the signals stop, go, walk.
- Children can state two rules for safely crossing streets. (Puppets can be used to ask children questions.)
- Children demonstrate increased caution in the play yard while riding tricycles and other wheeled toys and also as pedestrians.

Activity Plan #9: Poisonous Substances—Poison Prevention

CONCEPT Identification and avoidance of known and potentially poisonous substances.

OBJECTIVES
- Children will be able to name at least three poisonous substances.
- Children can identify at least one safety rule that will help prevent accidental poisoning.

MATERIALS LIST Old magazines; large sheet of paper; glue; small squares of paper or self-adhesive labels; marking pens.

LEARNING ACTIVITIES
A. Invite a guest speaker from your local hospital emergency room or Public Health Department to talk with the children about poison prevention.
B. Show children pictures and/or real labels of poisonous substances. Include samples of cleaning items, personal grooming supplies, medicines, perfumes, plants, and berries.
C. Discuss rules of poison prevention:

   a. Only food should be put into the mouth (Figure 12–9).
   b. Medicine is not candy and should only be given by an adult.
   c. An adult should always inform children that they are taking medicine, not candy.
   d. Never eat berries, flowers, leaves, or mushrooms before checking with an adult.

D. Make a wall mural for the classroom displaying pictures of poisonous substances. Be sure to include a sampling of cleaning products, personal grooming supplies, medicines, plants; products commonly found in garages, such as insecticides, fertilizers, gasoline, and automotive fluids. Glue pictures of these products on a large sheet of paper. Display the mural where parents and children can look at it.

EVALUATION
- Children can point to or name at least three poisonous substances.
- Children can state and role-play at least one safety rule that can help prevent accidental poisoning.

TEACHER RESOURCES

Common poisonous plants and mushrooms of North America, by Turner, N., & Szczawinski, A. (1995). Portland, OR: Timber Press.

Poison: Keeping your family safe (booklet). Channing Bete, 200 State Road, South Deerfield, MA 01373; 800-628-7733.

Protect your child from poisons in your home. (2000). Washington, DC: U.S. Department of Health & Human Services. Available online at http://www.fda.gov.

Teacher's guide to poison prevention. (2002). Obtain a free copy from Washington Poison Center at 1-800-222-1222; or write to the Washington Poison Center, 155 NE 100th St., Suite 400, Seattle, WA 98125–8012.

FIGURE 12–9

Children must learn that only food belongs in their mouths.

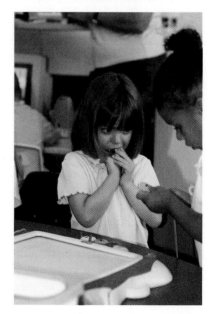

Activity Plan #10: Fire Safety

CONCEPT   Fire safety rules are important to know in the event of a fire.

OBJECTIVES

- Children can describe what they would do if there was a fire at their house or school.
- Children can demonstrate stop, drop, and roll.
- Children can state what a firefighter does and how they put out fires.

MATERIALS LIST   Large cardboard boxes; posterboard; photograph of each child; chalk and paint in fire colors (red, orange and yellow); small spray bottles; paper and plastic wrap; rolling pin; tape.

LEARNING ACTIVITIES

A. Invite a firefighter to the classroom. Ask the speaker to discuss important safety skills such as stop-drop-and-roll crawling on the floor to stay away from smoke and heat, and having alternative evacuation routes.

B. Construct a fire obstacle course. Build a tunnel out of cardboard boxes. Establish a "designated meeting place" at the end of the tunnel by displaying a poster with children's photographs. Have children begin the obstacle course by demonstrating the correct stop, drop, and roll technique. Next, have children crawl through the tunnel on their hands and knees; this shows children the appropriate way for navigating through a smoke-filled room before arriving at the designated safe area. Be sure to encourage and reinforce children's efforts.

C. Take cardboard boxes outside and have the children decorate them to look like buildings. Have children draw fire on the buildings using red, yellow, and orange chalk. Children can then use small spray bottles filled with water to put out the fire.

D. Add firefighter figures, ladders, fire trucks, and other fire-related materials to the block area.

E. Create a fire painting. Have the children paint a picture with red and yellow paint. While the paint is still wet, cover with plastic wrap and secure to the back of the painting with tape. Have the child use a rolling pin to roll out their painting.

EVALUATION

- Children can describe how they would get out of their house or school safely during a fire and where they would go once outside the building.
- Children can demonstrate stop, drop, and roll.
- Children can state what firefighters do and how they put out fires.[2]

[2] The author would like to thank Allison Moore, a former student and graduate of the Early Childhood program, Department of Human Development and Family Life, University of Kansas, for her innovative lesson plan.

FOCUS ON FAMILIES • Evaluating Health-Safety Information on the Internet

The Internet has substantially increased consumer access to health and safety information. As a result, we are often more aware of current developments and better able to make informed decisions. However, the lack of any regulatory control has also allowed considerable misinformation to be posted on Web sites, particularly in the areas of health and safety. Thus, consumers must approach such information with caution. Consider:

- What individual or group is responsible for this site? Check the URL (Web address): information on sites maintained by the government (http://www.gov) and educational institutions (http://www.edu) is generally considered more reliable.
- Are the individuals who prepared and run the site qualified? (Often the credentials of advisory board members or the Webmaster will be included.)
- Who is the intended audience? Is the purpose to entertain, inform, or educate?
- Judging this can be helpful in determining whether a site is a source of legitimate information.
- Is the site current? How recently was the information updated? It may be difficult to know if the date posted on a Web page refers to when the information was originally written, last revised, or actually posted.
- Does the information appear to be objective and free of bias? Sites run by private individuals or commercial groups may reflect personal opinion or attempt to sell a product. Facts and figures should include a reference to the original source of information.
- What links are included? Anyone can establish a link to any other Web page, so this may not prove to be a valid strategy for evaluating a site's credibility.
- Does the site include a way to contact the owner if you have questions or wish further information?

CASE STUDY

Eduardo, a new assistant, was asked by his head teacher to develop a lesson on "Healthy Eating Helps Us Grow." Although eager to be given this assignment, Eduardo was also apprehensive about planning something that four-year-olds would enjoy. He arrived early that morning and set up a grocery store for dramatic play, books about food for the children to read, and magazine pictures of foods for the children to sort into categories using the Food Pyramid. The children played "grocery shopping" for a while, looked at several of the books, but weren't interested in the sorting activity.

1. Were the activities Eduardo planned appropriate for four-year-olds?
2. How effective was this lesson for teaching children about healthy eating habits?
3. What are some realistic learning objectives that Eduardo might have established in preparation for this lesson?
4. How would Eduardo evaluate what the children may have learned from these activities?
5. What changes would you make in Eduardo's instructional strategies?

SUMMARY

- Poor lifestyle practices and attitudes contribute to many of today's health problems.
- Education is a key element in reducing health problems.
  - It raises individual awareness and ability to make informed decisions.
  - Education enables individuals to begin assuming some responsibility for personal health.
  - It contributes to improved health and safety behaviors and quality of life.
- Effective health and safety education requires long-range planning to ensure that children receive comprehensive instruction.
- Objectives describe the changes in an individual's behavior that can be expected as the result of instruction.
  - They can be used to identify appropriate content material and learning experiences for children.
  - They should be used to evaluate the effectiveness of instruction and behavioral outcomes.
- Including families in children's health and safety education encourages consistency between school and home.
  - When families are informed about what children are learning at school, they can reinforce the same information, practices, and values at home.
  - When teachers are aware of differences (e.g., cultural, linguistic, ethnic) in families' values regarding health, they will be able to create learning experiences that are more responsive to children's needs.
- Ongoing inservice opportunities help teachers stay informed, especially in the areas of health and safety, where new developments and information appear frequently.

APPLICATION ACTIVITIES

1. Interview a teacher of toddler or preschool children and a first or second grade teacher. Ask them to describe the health and safety concepts that are emphasized with each group. Arrange to observe one of the teachers conducting a health/safety session with children. What were the teacher's objectives? Was the instructional method effective? Did the teacher involve children in learning activities? Were the children attentive? Were the objectives met?

2. Visit several Web sites that provide information about appropriate child seat belt restraints and car safety seats. Read and compare the information. Do all statements agree? Do the statements disagree? For what audience is the material written, e.g., families, children, teachers and other professionals?

3. Develop a lesson plan for a unit on "What Makes Us Grow?" Include objectives, time length, materials, learning activities, measures for evaluation, and any teacher resource information. Exchange lesson plans with another student; critique each other's plan for clarity of ideas, thoroughness, and creativity.

4. Select, read, and evaluate three children's books from the reference lists provided in this unit.

CHAPTER REVIEW

A. **By Yourself:**

1. Match each of the following definitions in **Column I** with the correct term in **Column II**.

Column I

1. to assess the effectiveness of instruction
2. favorable changes in attitudes, knowledge and/or practices
3. a sharing of knowledge or skills
4. ideas and values meaningful to a child
5. subject or theme
6. feeling or strong belief
7. occurs in conjunction with daily activities and routines
8. the end product of learning

Column II

a. education
b. outcome
c. positive behavior changes
d. attitude
e. relevance
f. topic
g. incidental learning
h. evaluation

2. The following is a list of suggested health/safety topics. Place an A (appropriate) or NA (not appropriate) next to each of the statements. Base your decision on whether or not the topic is suitable for preschool-aged children.

_____ dental health
_____ feelings and how to get along with others
_____ primary causes of suicide
_____ consumer health, e.g., understanding advertisements, choosing a doctor, medical quackery
_____ eye safety
_____ the hazards of smoking
_____ how to safely light matches
_____ physical fitness for health
_____ cardiopulmonary resuscitation
_____ the values of rest and sleep
_____ safety at home
_____ animal families

B. **As a Group:**

1. Discuss why health and safety education are so important during a child's early years.

2. Describe what purpose evaluation serves in health and safety education. How can this information be used to improve future lessons?

3. Debate the pros and cons of including families in children's health and safety instruction.

4. Discuss the purpose of long-range planning in children's health and safety education.

5. Discuss how teachers can determine if health and safety resource materials are reliable.

REFERENCES

American Alliance for Health, Physical Education, Recreation and Dance (AAHPERD). (2007). *National Health Education Standards.* Accessed on April 27, 2007, from http://www.aahperd.org/aahe/pdf_files/standards.pdf.

Aronson, S. (2002). *Healthy young children: A manual for programs.* (4th ed.). Washington, DC: NAEYC.

Centers for Disease Control & Prevention (CDC). (2006). Chronic disease prevention. Accessed on November 10, 2006, from http://www.cdc.gov/nccdphp.

Dennison, D., & Golaszewski, T. (2002). The activated health education model: Refinement and implications for school health education. *Journal of School Health, 72*(1), 23–26.

Diffily, D., & Morrison, K. (Eds.). (1997). *Family-friendly communication for early childhood programs.* Washington, DC: NAEYC.

Dunn, C., Thomas, C., Ward, D., Pegram, L., Webber, K., & Cullitan, C. (2006). Design and implementation of a nutrition and physical activity curriculum for child care settings. *Prevention of Chronic Disease* (e-Pub), *3*(2), A58.

Essa, E. (2007). *Early childhood education.* (5th ed.). Clifton Park, NY: Thomson Delmar Learning.

Browne, K., & Gordon, A. (2008). *Beginnings and beyond.* (7th ed.). Clifton Park, NY: Thomson Delmar Learning.

Hooper, C., Munoz, K., Gruber, M., & Nguyen, K. (2005). The effects of a family fitness program on the physical activity and nutrition behaviors of third-grade children. *Research Quarterly for Exercise & Sport, 76*(2), 130–139.

Huff, R., & Kline, M. (1999). Promoting health in multicultural populations: A handbook for practitioners. San Francisco, CA: Sage Publications.

Lear, J., Isaacs, S., & Knickman, J. (Eds.). (2006). *School health services and programs.* San Francisco, CA: Jossey-Bass.

Locke, D. (1998). *Increasing multicultural understanding.* Thousand Oaks, CA: Sage.

Lundgren, D., & Morrison, J. W. (2003). Involving Spanish-speaking families in early education programs. *Young Children, 58*(3), 88–95.

Meeks, L., Heit, P., & Page, R. (2006). *Comprehensive school health education.* New York: McGraw-Hill.

Pealer, L. N., & Dorman, S. M. (1997). Evaluating health related web sites. *Journal of School Health Education, 67*(6), 232–235.

Pena, D. (2000). Parent involvement: Influencing factors and implications. *Journal of Educational Research, 94*, 42–54.

Pressley, J., Barlow, B., Durkin, M., Jacko, S., Dominquez, D., & Johnson, L. (2005). A national program for injury prevention in children and adolescents: The injury free coalition for kids. *Journal of Urban Health, 82*(3), 389–402.

Rae, P. (2006). Physical fitness and the early childhood curriculum. *Young Children, 61*(3), 12–19.

Sorte, J., & Daeshel, I. (2006). Health in action: A program approach to fighting obesity in young children. *Young Children, 61*(3), 40–48.

Stein, K. (2005). Nutrition quality and education in K-12 schools. *Journal of the American Dietetic Association, 105*(3), 334–336.

Telljohann, S., Symons, C., & Pateman, B. (2004). *Health education: Elementary and Middle School applications.* New York: McGraw-Hill.

U.S. Department of Health & Human Services. (2000). *Healthy people 2010.* Washington, DC: National Center for Chronic Disease Prevention and Health Promotion.

U.S. Department of Health & Human Services. (2005). *Preventing chronic disease through healthy lifestyles.* Washington, DC: U.S. Government Printing Office.

HELPFUL WEB SITES

American Automobile Association	http://www.aaa.com
American Dental Association	http://www.ada.org
American Heart Association	http://www.amhrt.org
Awesome Library	http://www.neat-schoolhouse.org
Canadian Childcare Resource & Research Unit	http://www.childcarecanada.org
Center for Disease Control & Protection	http://www.cdc.gov
Children, Stress, & Natural Disasters; University of Illinois	http://www.ag.uiuc.edu
Consumer Product Safety Commission	http://www.cpsc.gov
Dole Food Company	http://www.dole5aday.com
Environmental Protection Agency	http://www.epa.gov
KidSource Online	http://www.kidsource.com
National Dairy Council	http://www.nationaldairycouncil.org
National Fire Protection Association	http://www.nfpa.org
National Highway Traffic Safety Administration	http://www.nhtsa.dot.gov
National Institutes of Health	http://www.nih.gov
National Safety Council	http://www.nsc.org
PE (physical education) Central	http://www.pecentral.org
Service Canada	http://www.servicecanada.gc.ca
The Weather Channel on the Web	http://www.weatherclassroom.com

*For additional health, safety, and nutrition resources, go to
http://www.EarlyChildEd.delmar.cengage.com*

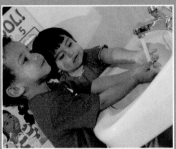

Foods and Nutrients: Basic Concepts

CHAPTER 13

Nutritional Guidelines

❈ OBJECTIVES

After studying this chapter, you should be able to:

- Outline the steps required to evaluate the nutrient content of a meal or meals.
- Use the Dietary Guidelines for Americans to achieve your personal nutritional goals.
- Classify foods according to the Food Guide Pyramid.
- Identify nutrient strengths for each major food group in the Food Guide Pyramid.
- Evaluate the nutritional quality of a food from its package label.

❈ TERMS TO KNOW

nutrition	essential nutrient	protein
nutrients	Dietary Reference Intake (DRI)	Percent Daily Values (%DV)
malnutrition	Dietary Guidelines for Americans	nutrition claims
undernutrition	calcium	

Good nutrition affects the health and well-being of individuals of all ages. It is important to note that all persons throughout life need the same nutrients, but in varying amounts. Young children have a greater need for nutrients that support growth and provide energy; older children and adults require nutrients to maintain and repair body tissue and to provide energy.

To teach good food habits, teachers and families must first set a good example. Children are more likely to model behaviors they observe in people they love and admire. To set a good example, adults must be knowledgeable about basic nutrition and understand how to maintain healthy eating habits. The ability to apply this knowledge to the care of children will hopefully follow.

Nutrition is the study of food and how it is used by the body. Nutritionists study foods because foods contain **nutrients**, which are chemical substances that serve specific purposes. Nutrients meet the body's need for:

- sources of energy
- materials for growth and maintenance of body tissue
- regulation of body processes

---

nutrition – *the study of food and how it is used by the body.*
nutrients – *the components or substances that are found in food.*

TABLE 13–1 Nutrients: Their Functions

	Calories per Gram	Energy	Build/Maintain Body Tissues	Regulators
carbohydrates	4	X		
fats	9	X		
proteins (needed for every function)	4	X	X	X
minerals			X	X
water			X	X
vitamins				X*

*are required in a regulatory role only.

Table 13–1 shows the relationship between nutrients and their functions.

Nutrients are needed in adequate amounts for normal body function to take place. An inadequate supply or poor utilization of nutrients may lead to **malnutrition** or **undernutrition** and result in abnormal body function and general poor health. Malnutrition may also result from excessive intake of one or more nutrients. This, too, may interfere with normal body functions and contribute to health problems. For example, there is currently much concern about excessive consumption of dietary fats and cholesterol and of self-supplementation with minerals and vitamins.

Approximately 50 nutrients are known to be essential for humans. An **essential nutrient** is one that must be provided by food substances, as the body is unable to manufacture it in adequate amounts. Persons of all ages require the same essential nutrients, only in different amounts. Factors, such as age, activity, gender, health status, and lifestyle determine how much of a particular nutrient is needed. Information regarding the amounts of nutrients found in specific foods can be found online (http://www.nal.usda.gov/fnic/foodcomp/search) and in many books.

A healthful diet is based on a daily intake of nutritious foods and meals. What to eat? What not to eat? How much to eat? The answers to these important questions have led to the development of a number of nutritional tools and guidelines. Each provides information that will promote healthful eating habits; the choice lies with the individual and may depend on time available, ease of use, and interest.

Regardless of the guideline selected, the common factor necessary for good nutrition is the inclusion of a wide variety of foods. Some foods contain many nutrients, while others contain only a few. No single food includes enough of all nutrients to support life. The only exception is breast milk, which contains all the nutrients known to be needed by an infant until about six months of age. Consuming a wide variety of foods improves the likelihood that all essential nutrients will be obtained.

---

malnutrition – *prolonged inadequate or excessive intake of nutrients and/or calories required by the body.*
undernutrition – *an inadequate intake of one or more required or essential nutrients.*
essential nutrient – *nutrient that must be provided in food because it cannot be synthesized by the body at a rate sufficient to meet the body's needs.*

DIETARY REFERENCE INTAKES (DRIs)

The "master guideline" for nutrition planning in the United States and Canada is the **Dietary Reference Intakes (DRIs)**. Known since 1941 as the Recommended Daily Dietary Allowances (RDA), the most recent revision of this plan has brought about major changes in both format and philosophy. Emphasis is now placed on the relationship between dietary intake, health, and the lowered risk of chronic disease. The updated guideline, released over a period of several years, is presented as four components. Table 13–2 illustrates the first two portions of the new document. The DRIs consist of:

- Recommended Daily Allowance (RDA)—goals for nutrient intake by individuals.
- Adequate Intake (AI)—goals for nutrient intake when an RDA has not been determined.
- Estimated Average Requirement (EAR)—amount of a nutrient that is estimated to meet the requirements of 50 percent of the individuals in a given life-stage or gender group; this number is used to establish the RDAs.
- Tolerable Upper Intake Level (UL)—the highest intake level that is likely to pose no health risk; exceeding this limit could cause potential toxicity and health risks.

The DRIs are used to set national nutritional policy as well as for *assessing* the nutrient intakes of individuals/groups and *planning* diets for individuals/groups (Murphy & Barr, 2006; Murphy, Guenther, & Kretsch, 2006). They are also used for determining the nutrient information present on food labels (Yates, 2006). It is suggested that RDAs, AIs, and ULs be used in planning diets for individuals, while the EAR is more useful in planning for groups. EARs are believed to be important in the assessment of intakes of both individuals and groups (Yates, 2006; Institute of Medicine, 2003).

For the Dietary Reference Intake guidelines to be meaningful, the nutrient content of foods must be known. (See the references at the end of this chapter.) To evaluate a diet by means of the Dietary Reference Intake guidelines, the following steps are required:

1. List the amounts of all foods and beverages consumed during one 24-hour period.
2. Use nutrient value tables or a computer program to determine the nutrient content of each food and beverage consumed.
3. Total the amount of each nutrient consumed during the day.
4. Determine if the amount of nutrients consumed are sufficient by comparing the total amount of each nutrient consumed with the Dietary Reference Intake for the appropriate age and sex group (Table 13–2).

DIETARY GUIDELINES FOR AMERICANS

The National Nutrition Monitoring and Related Research Act of 1990 requires the Secretaries of Health and Human Services (HHS) and the U.S. Department of Agriculture (USDA) to issue a joint report, called the **Dietary Guidelines for Americans**, at least every five years. The Dietary Guidelines Advisory Committee (DGAC) released the latest version of the *Guidelines* in January 2005, (Figure 13–1). New recommendations are based on current scientific knowledge about the role nutrition plays in maintaining health and minimizing disease risks.

At this time, the *Dietary Guidelines* has come to serve as the basis for nearly all nutrition information in the United States. While the Dietary Reference Intakes (DRIs) only address

---

Dietary Reference Intake (DRI) – *a plan that presents the recommended goals of nutrient intakes for various age and gender groups.*

Dietary Guidelines for Americans – *report that provides recommendations for daily food choices, to be balanced with physical activity, to promote good health and reduce certain disease risks.*

FIGURE 13–1

Dietary Guidelines for Americans.

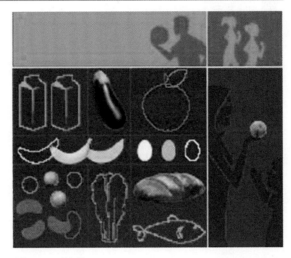

Source: From http://www.healthierus.gov/dietaryguidelines.

specific nutrients, the *Dietary Guidelines* focus on eating and activity behaviors and their impact on health for persons two years and older. Key recommendations include:

- **Adequate nutrients within calorie needs**—including a wide variety of nutrient-dense foods in one's diet while limiting fats, cholesterol, sugars, salt, and alcohol.
- **Weight management**—maintaining a healthy balance of calories consumed (food and beverages) with calories burned through physical activity to lower the risk of becoming overweight or obese.
- **Physical activity**—keeping physically active each day. The American Academy of Pediatrics (AAP), National Association for Sport & Physical Education (NASPE), and Canadian Academy of Sport Medicine (CASM) support this recommendation and encourage children of all ages to engage in moderate to vigorous activity daily (AAP, 2006; NASPE, 2006; CASM, 2006) (Figure 13–2). Excess weight and a sedentary lifestyle have been linked to many chronic diseases. Teachers have a responsibility to plan appropriate physical activities for children and to model their own enjoyment and participation in these activities.
- **Food groups to encourage**—consuming more fruits, vegetables, whole grain products, and low-fat dairy products is strongly encouraged. Important vitamins and nutrients in these foods are often lacking in children's diets today. Many children fail to consume the recommended number of daily servings from each of these groups (Guenther, et al., 2006). Two cups of fruit, two and one-half cups of vegetables, three or more ounce-equivalents of whole-grain products, and three cups of fat-free or low-fat dairy products are recommended; smaller servings are appropriate for children who consume fewer than 2000 calories/day. Whole grains are an excellent source of fiber and other nutrients essential to a balanced diet and are also low in fat. Fruits and vegetables are rich sources of many vitamins and minerals and are also naturally high in fiber.
- **Fats**—high fat intake is associated with the development of some chronic diseases and, when combined with minimal physical activity, can promote obesity. Total fat intake should be limited to 20–35 percent of one's daily calories. Less than 10 percent of these calories should come from saturated (animal) fats. Cholesterol intake should be limited to less than 300 mgs. per day. Choose meat and dairy products that are low-fat and avoid trans fats in processed foods.
- **Carbohydrates**—are an important source of energy and fiber. However, foods high in added sugar should be limited. Include adequate servings of fruits, vegetables, and whole grain products each day.

TABLE 13-2 Dietary Reference Intakes (DRIs): Recommended Intakes for Individuals Vitamins
Food and Nutrition Board, Institute of Medicine, National Academies

Life Stage Group	Vit A (µg/d)[a]	Vit C (mg/d)	Vit D (µg/d)[b,c]	Vit E (mg/d)[d]	Vit K (µg/d)	Thiamin (mg/d)	Riboflavin (mg/d)	Niacin (mg/d)[e]	Vit B6 (mg/d)	Folate (µg/d)[f]	Vit B12 (µg/d)	Pantothenic Acid (mg/d)	Biotin (µg/d)	Choline[g] (mg/d)
Infants														
0–6 mo	400*	40*	5*	4*	2.0*	0.2*	0.3*	2*	0.1*	65*	0.4*	1.7*	5*	125*
7–12 mo	500*	50*	5*	5*	2.5*	0.3*	0.4*	4*	0.3*	80*	0.5*	1.8	6*	150*
Children														
1–3 y	300	15	5*	6	30*	0.5	0.5	6	0.5	150	0.9	2*	8*	200*
4–8 y	400	25	5*	7	55*	0.6	0.6	8	0.6	200	1.2	3*	12*	250*
Males														
9–13 y	600	45	5*	11	60*	0.9	0.9	12	1.0	300	1.8	4*	20*	375*
14–18 y	900	75	5*	15	75*	1.2	1.3	16	1.3	400	2.4	5*	25*	550*
19–30 y	900	90	5*	15	120*	1.2	1.3	16	1.3	400	2.4	5*	30*	550*
31–50 y	900	90	5*	15	120*	1.2	1.3	16	1.3	400	2.4	5*	30*	550*
51–70 y	900	90	10*	15	120*	1.2	1.3	16	1.7	400	2.4[h]	5*	30*	550*
>70 y	900	90	15*	15	120*	1.2	1.3	16	1.7	400	2.4[h]	5*	30*	550*
Females														
9–13 y	600	45	5*	11	60*	0.9	0.9	12	1.0	300	1.8	4*	20*	375*
14–18 y	700	65	5*	15	75*	1.0	1.0	14	1.2	400[i]	2.4	5*	25*	400*
19–30 y	700	75	5*	15	90*	1.1	1.1	14	1.3	400[i]	2.4	5*	30*	425*
31–50 y	700	75	5*	15	90*	1.1	1.1	14	1.3	400[i]	2.4	5*	30*	425*
51–70 y	700	75	10*	15	90*	1.1	1.1	14	1.5	400	2.4[h]	5*	30*	425*
>70 y	700	75	15*	15	90*	1.1	1.1	14	1.5	400	2.4[h]	5*	30*	425*

(continued)

TABLE 13-2 Dietary Reference Intakes (DRIs): Recommended Intakes for Individuals Vitamins Food and Nutrition Board, Institute of Medicine, National Academies (continued)

Life Stage Group	Vit A (μg/d)[a]	Vit C (mg/d)	Vit D (μg/d)[b,c]	Vit E (mg/d)[d]	Vit K (μg/d)	Thiamin (mg/d)	Riboflavin (mg/d)	Niacin (mg/d)[e]	Vit B_6 (mg/d)	Folate (μg/d)[f]	Vit B_{12} (μg/d)	Pantothenic Acid (mg/d)	Biotin (μg/d)	Choline[g] (mg/d)
Pregnancy														
14–18 y	750	80	5*	15	75*	1.4	1.4	18	1.9	600[i]	2.6	6*	30*	450*
19–30 y	770	85	5*	15	90*	1.4	1.4	18	1.9	600[i]	2.6	6*	30*	450*
31–50 y	770	85	5*	15	90*	1.4	1.4	18	1.9	600[i]	2.6	6*	30*	450*
Lactation														
14–18 y	1,200	115	5*	19	75*	1.4	1.6	17	2.0	500	2.8	7*	35*	550*
19–30 y	1,300	120	5*	19	90*	1.4	1.6	17	2.0	500	2.8	7*	35*	550*
31–50 y	1,300	120	5*	19	90*	1.4	1.6	17	2.0	500	2.8	7*	35*	550*

Note: This table (taken from the DRI reports, see www.nap.edu) presents Recommended Dietary Allowances (RDAs) in bold type and Adequate Intakes (AIs) in ordinary type followed by an asterisk(*). RDAs and AIs may both be used as goals for individual intake. RDAs are set to meet the needs of almost all (97 to 98 percent) individuals in a group. For healthy breastfed infants, the AI is the mean intake. The AI for other life stage and gender groups is believed to cover needs of all individuals in the group, but lack of data or uncertainty in the data prevent being able to specify with confidence the percentage of individuals covered by this intake.

[a] As retinol activity equivalents (RAEs). 1 RAE=1 μg retinol, 12 μg β-carotene, 24 μg α-carotene, or 24 μg β-cryptoxanthin. The RAE for dietary provitamin A carotenoids is twofold greater than retinol equivalents (RE), whereas the RAE for performed vitamin A is the same as RE.

[b] As cholecalciferol, 1 μg cholecalciferol = 40 IU vitamin D.

[c] In the absence of adequate exposure to sunlight.

[d] As α-tocopherol. α-Tocopherol includes *RRR*-α-tocopherol, the only form of α-tocopherol that occurs naturally in foods, and the *2R*-stereoisomeric forms of α-tocopherol (*RRR*-, *RSR*-, *RRS*-, *RRS*-α-tocopherol) that occur in fortified foods and supplements. It does not include the *2S*-stereoisomeric forms of α-tocopherol (*SRR*-, *SSR*-, *SRS*-, and *SSS*-α-tocopherol), also found in fortified foods and supplements.

[e] As niacin equivalents (NE). 1 mg of niacin = 60 mg of tryptophan; 0–6 months = performed niacin (not NE).

[f] As dietary folate equivalents (DFE). 1 DFE = 1 μg food folate = 0.6 μg of folic acid from fortified food or as a supplement consumed with food = 0.5 μg of a supplement taken on an empty stomach.

[g] Although AIs have been set for choline, there are few data to assess whether a dietary supply of choline is needed at all stages of the life cycle, and it may be that the choline requirement can be met by endogenous synthesis at some of these stages.

[h] Because 10 to 30 percent of older people may malabsorb food-bound B_{12} it is advisable for those older than 50 years to meet their RDA mainly by consuming foods fortified with B_{12} or a supplement containing B_{12}.

[i] In view of evidence linking folate intake with neural tube defects in the fetus, it is recommended that all women capable of becoming pregnant consume 400 μg from supplements or fortified foods in addition to intake of food folate from a varied diet.

[j] It is assumed that women will continue consuming 400 μg from supplements or fortified food until their pregnancy is confirmed and they enter prenatal care, which ordinarily occurs after the end of the periconceptional period—the critical time for formation of the neural tube.

Copyright 2004 by the National Academy of Sciences. All rights reserved.

FIGURE 13-2

Physical activity recommendations for children.

The American Academy of Pediatrics (AAP), National Association for Sport & Physical Education (NASPE), and Canadian Academy of Sport Medicine (CASM) encourage daily physical activity for children of all ages:

– *infants* should have ample opportunities to explore their environment and should not be confined to a stroller or carrier for longer than 60 minutes/day.

– *toddlers* should accumulate at least 30 minutes of structured, vigorous physical activity and at least 60 minutes or more of free play.

– *preschoolers and school-age children* should participate in at least 60 minutes of structured physical activity during the day. They should also be given opportunities to engage in several hours of unstructured physical activity.

- **Sodium and potassium**—high sodium (salt) and low potassium intake has been linked to high blood pressure in some individuals. Although it is essential for life, most people get enough sodium from food without adding extra salt. Sodium intake should be limited to 2300 mgs. (approximately 1 teaspoon) or less per day. Fruits, vegetables, and whole grains in their simplest forms contain little sodium and are ideal for including in one's diet; many are also good sources of potassium. Most processed foods and fast foods are quite high in sodium and salt and their consumption should be limited.

- **Alcoholic beverages**—persons who choose to consume alcohol should do so in moderation (one drink/day for women, two drinks/day for men). Women who are pregnant or breastfeeding should avoid alcohol.

- **Food safety**—young children are at a higher risk for food-borne illnesses. Washing hands, keeping food preparation areas clean, cooking food to proper temperatures, storing foods in proper refrigeration, and following food labels are key tips to reducing food-borne illness.

Canada has developed similar guidelines, entitled *Canada's Food Guide*. The newest version of this document was released in 2007 and encourages citizens to follow healthy eating patterns. A companion document, *Canada's Physical Activity Guide to Healthy Active Living* stresses the importance of establishing daily activity practices.

Other Nutrition Guidelines

Healthy People 2010 originated with the U.S. Public Health Service. Some of the statements that address children's needs include:

- reducing the prevalence of growth retardation to less than 5 percent among low-income children age five years or younger
- increasing the proportion of persons aged two years and older who consume no more than 30 percent of calories from total fat
- increasing the proportion of persons aged two years and older who consume at least six daily servings of grain products, with at least three being whole grain
- increasing the proportion of consumers who follow key food safety practices

Several non-profit organizations, including the American Heart Association and the National Cancer Institute, also advise similar healthy eating and physical activity behaviors. Their guidelines call for reducing fat, cholesterol, sodium, and alcohol in the diet and increasing vegetable, fruit, and whole grain consumption.

ISSUES TO CONSIDER • Food Guide Pyramid

The Food Guide Pyramid, developed by the U.S. Department of Agriculture, was initially designed as a teaching tool to be used in conjunction with the Dietary Guidelines for Americans. Although the Dietary Guidelines are reviewed and updated every five years, the original Pyramid had not been reevaluated since it was first released. The Pyramid has become part of a growing controversy questioning some of the nutritional recommendations it promotes. For example, one such criticism is that the Pyramid recommendations for the Milk group may be too high (Mitka, 2005).

- What additional criticisms of the new Food Guide Pyramid might be raised?
- Would you consider the new Food Guide Pyramid to be an effective guideline for healthy eating given the increasing rates of child and adult obesity?
- How might you change the Pyramid (e.g., design, nutritional information) to make it a more effective consumer education tool?

THE FOOD GUIDE PYRAMID

The graphic illustration of the Dietary Guidelines for Americans is the Food Guide Pyramid (Figure 13–3), which was revised in 2005 to reflect more flexibility in its recommendations for individuals of different ages, gender, and activity levels (U.S. Department of Agriculture, 2005a,b). The new pyramid stresses the importance of physical activity in conjunction with a well-balanced and healthy diet. The vertical stripes on the pyramid represent the essential food groups:

- orange for grains
- green for vegetables
- red for fruits
- yellow for oils
- blue for milk
- purple for meats and beans

The varying widths of the pyramid's stripes indicate the relative proportion of each food group that should be included in daily meals. However, each individual will require different amounts of

FIGURE 13–3

MyPyramid is an interactive, Internet-based tool designed to promote healthy eating habits.

foods from each group according to age, gender, and level of physical activity. The Pyramid conveys the importance of a daily meal pattern that includes a wide variety of foods (represented by the various color bands) and moderation of eating that is balanced with physical activity. The interactive Web site (http://www.mypyramid.gov) offers weekly menus and also allows individuals to plan, record, and monitor their food intake and daily activity (U.S. Department of Agriculture, 2005c).

Grains

Foods such as breads, breakfast cereals, pastas, and rice make up the Grains group. Food choices from this group provide complex carbohydrates and should be whole grain or enriched products. Whole grain products retain all of the grain and are a good source of fiber. Enriched breads and cereals are products that have been processed and then fortified with specified amounts of certain vitamins and minerals that are equivalent to those found in the whole grain. Nutrients which are commonly added include iron, calcium, thiamin, riboflavin, and niacin. Most grain products are also being fortified with folacin (folic acid) which reduces the incidence of spina bifida, cleft lip and cleft palate birth defects (Carmichael et al., 2007).

A typical serving from this group consists of one slice of bread, one cup of dry, ready-to-eat cereal, or one-half cup of cooked rice, cereal, or pasta. As with the other groups, the child's serving is one-half the size of the adult serving. The Pyramid plan recommends that adults eat a minimum of six ounces of grain products daily; children require three to four ounces. At least half of the servings should be whole grain.

Vegetables

The Vegetable group contributes notable amounts of minerals, vitamins, and fiber to one's diet. This group represents a wide range of color and variety food options. Daily choices should include dark green vegetables such as broccoli and leafy greens as well as orange-colored foods such as sweet potatoes, squash, and carrots which are rich in Vitamin A (Table 13–3). Dry beans and peas should also be consumed more often. The Pyramid plan recommends that adults eat two and one-half cups of vegetables every day (based on a 2000 calorie intake); children only need one to one and one-half cups depending on their age.

The health benefits of dietary fiber are receiving increased attention. Many children fail to consume adequate fiber because their intake of fruits and vegetables is limited (Kranz, 2006; Kranz, et al., 2005). However, very high fiber intake in childhood can interfere with the absorption of essential vitamins and minerals. A practical recommendation for fiber intake for children over two years of age is the "age plus 5" rule. For example, Tasha, age three years, would require eight grams of fiber/day. See Table 13–4 for food sources and amounts of fiber.

Fruits

The Fruit group is a major contributor of vitamins, especially Vitamins A and C, and fiber (*American Dietetic Association*, 1997) (Table 13–3). At least one Vitamin C-rich and one Vitamin A-rich selection should be included every day (Table 13–5).

Oils

The thin yellow line on the Pyramid represents the Oils group. This group consists of fats that are liquid at room temperature, such as the vegetable (plant) oils (canola, corn, cottonseed, olive, sunflower) used in cooking, as well as the oils from fish. Plant oils contain no cholesterol and are considered to be beneficial. Foods such as nuts, olives, and avocados also have a naturally high oil content but this is a healthy form of fat. Some oils are used mainly as flavorings, such as walnut oil and sesame oil. Mayonnaise, certain salad dressings, and soft (tub or squeeze) margarine with no

TABLE 13-3 Good to Excellent Sources of Vitamin A

cantaloupe	winter squash
carrots	greens
pumpkin	apricots
sweet potatoes	watermelon*
spinach	broccoli

*May cause allergic reactions.

TABLE 13-4 Dietary Fiber Content of Some Commonly Eaten Foods

Food	Amount	Fiber (gram)
cheerios	1/2 cup	1.5
raisin bran	1/2 cup	2.5
oatmeal	1/4 cup	1.9
macaroni, enriched	1/2 cup	1.3
bread, whole wheat	1/2 slice	0.9
bread, white	1/2 slice	0.6
graham crackers	1 square	0.5
orange sections	1/2 cup	2.2
banana, sliced	1/2 cup	1.9
apple with skin	1/2 cup	1.3
acorn squash	1/4 cup	2.3
green peas	1/4 cup	2.2
corn, frozen	1/4 cup	1.0
pinto beans	1/2 cup	5.5
black beans	1/2 cup	7.5

TABLE 13-5 Good to Excellent Sources of Vitamin C

orange*	tomatoes*
orange juice*	grapefruit*
strawberries*	mustard greens
cauliflower	spinach
broccoli	cabbage
sweet peppers, red or green	tangerine*

*May cause allergic reactions.

trans fats are considered oils. Solid fats are also included in the Oils group. Some are made from animal sources (butter) while others (stick and soft margarine) are converted from a liquid to a solid form by a process called hydrogenation. In general, the nutrient contribution of this group is low and the calorie content is high.

Milk

This group includes milk and foods made from it that retain their calcium content, such as home-made puddings, frozen yogurts, and ice creams; hard cheeses like Swiss and cheddar; soft cheeses like ricotta and cottage cheese; and all yogurts. Dairy products that provide little or no calcium include butter, cream cheese, and cream; thus, they are not considered part of the Milk group. Foods that provide **calcium** equal to that in one cup of milk are:

1 1/2 ounces cheddar cheese	1 2/3 cup cottage cheese
1 cup pudding	1 1/4 ounces mozzarella cheese
1 3/4 cups ice cream	1 cup plain yogurt

The Milk group is a major source of dietary calcium but a poor source of iron and vitamins A and C. Children should consume a total of two cups of milk or the equivalent from this group daily; adults should have three cups. Servings may be divided into one-half cup portions in consideration of children's smaller appetites and capacity. Because foods in the Milk group tend to be high in fat and cholesterol, reduced- and low-fat products are preferred choices. However, children should not be given low-fat milk and dairy products prior to the age of two. Infants and toddlers require the additional fats and fat-calories for energy and healthy nervous system development.

Meat and Beans

Beef, veal, pork, lamb, fish, and poultry are included in the Meat and Beans group. Other foods included in this group are eggs, legumes such as dry peas and beans, nuts, and nut butters such as peanut butter. Cheese may also be substituted for meats; however, it should be remembered that cheeses are high in cholesterol and do not contain iron, which is a nutrient strength of this group. The Meat and Beans group is also a major source of dietary protein and B-vitamins.

The recommended daily amount from the Meat and Beans group, as with the other groups, varies by individual, based on age, gender, and physical activity. Children two- to three-years-old require approximately two ounce equivalents daily; children four and older require three to four ounce equivalents. The following foods contain **protein** that is approximately equal to that in one ounce of meat, poultry or fish:

1 egg
1 ounce of cheese
1/4 cup cottage cheese
1/4 cup cooked dried peas or beans
2 tablespoons peanut butter

Discretionary Calories

Foods consumed from each of the Pyramid groups provide calories for energy. How many calories an individual needs to take in varies according to age, gender, and level of physical activity (Figure 13–4). The new interactive Food Pyramid offers tools that help a person determine how many calories are needed each day (http://www.mypyramid.gov).

Discretionary calories represent the difference between the number of calories a person takes in from the recommended servings in each food group and one's ideal or target caloric goal. They can be compared to discretionary income: just as your budget contains discretionary or extra income to cover special expenses like vacation trips or DVDs, your diet may contain a small number of discretionary calories that can be "spent" on foods that may be higher in fats, added sugar,

---

calcium – *mineral nutrient; a major component of bones and teeth.*
protein – *class of nutrients used primarily for structural and regulatory functions.*

FIGURE 13–4

Eating a variety of foods supplies the greatest number of nutrients.

and alcohol. Persons who are relatively sedentary will have, on the average, between 100–300 discretionary calories each day depending on the foods they have chosen to consume from each of the food groups.

Adding a large number of foods that contain discretionary calories can dilute the healthful quality of a person's diet (Kranz, Smicikilas-Wright & Francis, 2006). For example, the Vitamin C contribution of an apple is altered significantly when sugars and fats are added, Table 13–6. The calorie content also increases with the addition of sugar, flour, and fat in making an apple pie.

NUTRITIONAL LABELING

The Nutritional Labeling and Education Act, passed in 1990, resulted in many changes in the labeling of food products. The food label, regulated by the Food and Drug Administration (FDA) and the U.S. Department of Agriculture (USDA), underwent a major revision in 1994 (Figure 13–5). This resulted in the current label that provides:

- Easy-to-read nutrition information on packaged foods.
- Serving sizes in commonly consumed amounts. This prevents using small serving sizes to make food products that are high in fat, cholesterol, sodium, or calories look better than they are.
- A list of all ingredients (in decreasing order relative to amount) on their label.

TABLE 13-6 How Added Sugar and Fats Alter a Food's Calories and Nutrient Contribution

	Calories	Potassium	Vitamin C
banana, 1/2 cup sliced	67	268 mg	6.5 mg
banana chips, 1 ounce	147	152 mg	1.8 mg
banana pudding, 1/2 cup	72	62 mg	0.3 mg
banana bread, 1 slice	196	80 mg	1.0 mg
banana cream pie, 1/8 pie	387	238 mg	2.3 mg
banana waffle, 1 small round	212	140 mg	1.1 mg

FIGURE 13–5

A typical food label.

Nutrition Facts

Serving Size 3/4 cup (30g)
Servings Per Container about 15

Amount Per Serving	Cereal	Cereal with 1/2 cup Skim Milk
Calories	100	140
Calories from Fat	5	5

	% Daily Value**	
Total Fat 0.5g*	**1**%	**1**%
Saturated Fat 0g	**0**%	**0**%
Polyunsaturated Fat 0g		
Monounsaturated Fat 0g		
Cholesterol 0mg	**0**%	**0**%
Sodium 220mg	**9**%	**12**%
Potassium 190mg	**5**%	**11**%
Total Carbohydrate 24g	**8**%	**10**%
Dietary Fiber 5g	**21**%	**21**%
Soluble Fiber 1g		
Insoluble Fiber 4g		
Sugars 6g		
Other Carbohydrate 13g		
Protein 3g		

Vitamin A	15%	20%
Vitamin C	0%	2%
Calcium	0%	15%
Iron	45%	45%
Vitamin D	10%	25%
Thiamin	25%	30%
Riboflavin	25%	35%
Niacin	25%	25%
Vitamin B$_6$	25%	25%
Folate	25%	25%
Vitamin B$_{12}$	25%	35%
Phosphorus	15%	25%
Magnesium	15%	20%
Zinc	10%	15%
Copper	10%	10%

*Amount in Cereal. One half cup skim milk contributes an additional 40 calories, 65mg sodium, 200mg potassium, 6g total carbohydrate (6g sugars), and 4g protein.

**Percent Daily Values are based on a 2,000 calorie diet. Your daily values may be higher or lower depending on your calorie needs.

	Calories:	2,000	2,500
Total Fat	Less than	65g	80g
Saturated Fat	Less than	20g	25g
Cholesterol	Less than	300mg	300mg
Sodium	Less than	2,400mg	2,400mg
Potassium		3,500mg	3,500mg
Total Carbohydrate		300g	375g
Dietary Fiber		25g	30g

FIGURE 13–6

Commonly used food labeling terms defined.

WHAT SOME CLAIMS MEAN

high-protein: at least 10 grams (g) high-quality protein per serving

good source of calcium: at least 100 milligrams (mg) calcium per serving

more iron: at least 1.8 mg more iron per serving than reference food. (Label will say 10 percent more of the Daily Value for iron.)

fat-free: less than 0.5 g fat per serving

low-fat: 3 g or less fat per serving. (If the serving size is 30 g or less or 2 tablespoons or less, 3 g or less fat per 50 g of the food.)

reduced or fewer calories: at least 25 percent fewer calories per serving than the reference food

sugar-free: less than 0.5 g sugar per serving

light (two meanings):

■ one-third fewer calories or half the fat of the reference food. (If 50 percent or more of the food's calories are from fat, the fat must be reduced by 50 percent.)

■ a "low-calorie," "low-fat" food whose sodium content has been reduced by 50 percent of the reference food.

Source: Courtesy of FDA Consumer, September 1995.

REFLECTIVE THOUGHTS

The use of the Pyramid as a guide for making healthy food choices requires an understanding that individual foods within a food group can vary greatly in nutrient content relative to sugar, fat, and calories. Choose different foods within a given Pyramid food group and assign them to one of the following groups:

a. unrestricted—eat any amount every day (high nutrient content but low in fat and sugar)

b. moderately restricted—eat only one to three times per day (moderately high in fat and/or sugar)

c. very restricted—eat only two to three times per week (high in fat and/or sugar and calories)

- **Percent Daily Values (%DV)** that show how a serving of food fits into a total day's diet. (This replaces the previously used U.S. RDA.)
- **Nutrition claims** that mean the same on every product (Figure 13–6).
- Voluntary information for the most commonly eaten fresh fruits and vegetables, raw fish, and cuts of meat. This information may appear on posters or in brochures in the same area as the food is sold.

Recent amendments now require food manufacturers to list trans fats (liquid oils that have been converted into solid fats, such as margarine) as well as saturated fats and cholesterol on their labels. Food allergens (milk, eggs, tree nuts [such as almonds, walnuts], peanuts, shellfish [such as shrimp, crab, lobster], fish, wheat and soy) that could potentially cause life-threatening reactions must also be disclosed (U.S. Food & Drug Administration, 2004). Manufacturers are allowed to list health claims on their labels, such as "may reduce the risk of heart disease," as long as there is scientific evidence to back up the statement.

CALORIES FROM FAT

Labels now provide the amounts of fat, saturated fat, and trans fats. The number of calories from fat are also listed. With the amount of fat and calories from fat identified on the label, determining the percent of calories from fat is simple

$$\text{Percent of calories from fat} = \frac{\text{fat calories/serving}}{\text{total calories/serving}} \times 100$$

To calculate the number of calories from fat, use this formula:

calories from fat = grams (g) of fat/serving $\times$ 9 (cal/g)

The following calculations of percent of calories from fat in some selected foods will show how fat content reports on labels may be misleading:

Cheddar cheese—1 ounce = 115 calories and 9 g of fat:
Calories from fat = 9 $\times$ 9 = 81
Percent calories from fat = 81/115 $\times$ 100 = 70%

Eggs—one egg = 75 calories and 6 g of fat:
Calories from fat = 6 $\times$ 9 = 54
Percent calories from fat = 54/75 $\times$ 100 = 72%

Percent Daily Values (%DV) – *measures of the nutritional values of food; used in nutrition labeling.*
nutrition claims – *statements of reduced calories, fat, or salt on the food labels.*

90% fat-free ground beef—3 ounces = 185 calories and 10 g of fat:
 Calories from fat = 10 × 9 = 90
 Percent calories from fat = 90/185 × 100 = 49%

For all of these examples, the grams of fat (9, 6, and 10) are low, yet they all presented more than 30 percent of calories from fat.

The recommendation that only 30 percent of calories should come from fat does not mean that all healthy food choices must derive less than 30 percent of their calories from fat. This would virtually eliminate all red meat and most dairy products. However, it does mean that if you eat a lean hamburger with 49 percent fat-calories, it might be better to skip the French fries at 47 percent fat-calories and substitute an apple, banana, or orange with less than 10 percent of calories from fat.

The calculations for percent of fat-calories may seem tedious at first, but after a few calculations you will find that you can skim a label and judge its nutrient density or fat-calorie level. You will not need to take a calculator with you when you go grocery shopping.

FOCUS ON FAMILIES • Dietary Guidelines for Americans

The *Dietary Guidelines for Americans* encourages a diet that is moderate in sugar consumption. Many foods such as milk/dairy products and fruit have naturally occurring sugar. Foods that have sugar added in processing or preparation add unnecessary calories and are often low in many vitamins and minerals. Sugar is thought not to be harmful if it is used in limited amounts in the diet.

- Know your food labels: A *reduced sugar* food item contains at least 25 percent less sugar than the reference food. *No added sugar* or *without added sugar* foods indicate that no sugars were added during processing or packaging. *Sugar-free* foods contain less than 0.5 grams sugar per serving.

- The following terms, if listed as the first or second ingredient of a food label, indicate the food is likely high in sugar: Brown sugar, corn sweetener or corn syrup, fructose, fruit juice concentrate, glucose, dextrose, high-fructose corn syrup, honey, lactose, maltose, molasses, raw sugar, table sugar (sucrose), syrup.

- Major food sources of sugar in the United States are sodas, cakes, candy, cookies, pies, fruit drinks and punches, and dairy desserts such as ice cream. Healthy foods that contain added sugar should be limited in the diet: chocolate milk, presweetened cereals, and fruits packed in syrup. If these foods are eaten, do so in moderation and choose smaller serving sizes (a serving of soda in the 1950s was 6.5 ounces compared to a 20-ounce serving today!).

CASE STUDIES

1. Betsy, age three-and-one-half, drinks milk to the exclusion of adequate amounts of food from other food groups. What nutrient is Betsy receiving in excess? What two nutrients are most likely to be deficient?

2. Jason, age four, refuses to eat fruit. He will occasionally accept a small serving of applesauce and a few bites of banana but little else. What two nutrients are probably deficient in Jason's diet?

CASE STUDIES (continued)

3. Jeremy, age three, is allergic to milk and dairy products. What nutrient is deficient in Jeremy's diet?

4. Tommy, age two, by choice will eat only high carbohydrate foods, preferably those that are sweet. He rejects high-protein, high-fat foods such as meats and cheese. How would you change his diet to provide adequate protein and fat for normal growth and nerve development without increasing his carbohydrate intake with high-fat pastries, cakes, etc.?

5. Mary, age four, refuses milk and all milk products; she likes to drink a variety of juices. How would you adjust her diet to assure that she meets her calcium requirement?

CLASSROOM CORNER • Teacher Activities

Tasting a Rainbow...
Concept: Fruits and vegetables are healthy foods to eat and we should eat a variety of them. (Pre-2)

Learning Objectives

- Children will learn that fruits and vegetables are healthy foods to eat.
- Children will experience tasting a variety of fruits and vegetables.

Supplies

- one red fruit and vegetable (apple, strawberry, tomato, watermelon, red pepper)
- one orange fruit and vegetable (orange, acorn squash, orange pepper, cantaloupe, yam, carrot)
- one green fruit and vegetable (grape, lime, spinach, honey dew, green pepper, apple, pear, broccoli, bean, pea, kiwi)
- one yellow fruit and vegetable (banana, pineapple, lemon, yellow squash, corn)
- one purple fruit and vegetable (purple grape, purple cabbage)
- one blue fruit (blueberry)
- hand wipes; plates; forks

Learning Activities

- Read and discuss one of the following books:
  - *Give me 5 a day* by Kathy Reeves, Brenda Crosby, Jennifer Hemphill, and Elizabeth Hoffman
  - *I Will Never Not Ever Eat a Tomato* by Lauren Child
- Tell children that bodies need healthy foods, like fruits and vegetables, to keep us healthy and help us grow. Show children a picture of a rainbow; tell them that fruits and vegetables have many colors like a rainbow.

(continued)

CLASSROOM CORNER • Teacher Activities (continued)

- Have all children wash their hands with wipes. Hand each child a plate with fruit, a plate with vegetables, and a fork. Make sure all the fruits and vegetables are cut into bite-sized pieces to prevent choking. Talk about how the colors of the food on their plates are the same colors that make up a rainbow.

- Give children an opportunity to taste each item and talk about how each tastes. Focus the activity on the importance of tasting a variety of fruits and vegetables instead of on children's likes and dislikes.

Evaluation

- Children will name several kinds of fruits and vegetables.
- Children will taste a variety of fruits and vegetables.

SUMMARY

- The study of nutrition is concerned with what nutrients are, why the human body needs them, how much of each is needed, and where they may be obtained from foods.

- Food Guidelines are provided to aid in making food choices that assure meeting the essential nutrients in adequate amounts without consuming excesses of nutrients that might be unhealthful.

- The most practical guide for making healthful food choices is the Pyramid, which groups foods that contain similar kinds and amounts of nutrients.

- Dietary Reference Intakes (DRIs) gives a more precise evaluation of nutrient needs for persons in various age and sex groups.

- The *Dietary Guidelines for Americans* advises on food selections that meet nutrient needs and avoids known harmful effects of over consumption of some nutrient groups.

- *Healthy People 2010* is a comprehensive set of disease-prevention and health-promotion objectives for the U.S. to achieve over the first decade of the century.

- Eating a variety of foods from all food groups is the best assurance of consuming a health-promoting diet.

APPLICATION ACTIVITIES

1. Record your personal food intake for the past 24 hours. Go to MyPyramid.gov and generate "My Pyramid Plan" by entering your age, gender, and activity level. Analyze the results of your 24-hour food intake by comparing it with the Pyramid Plan recommendations.

2. Plan a day's menu for a four-year-old girl who does an extra 45 minutes of activity each day. Include the recommended amounts from each food group, the calorie pattern on which the recommendations are based, and the number of oils/discretionary calories recommended per day from My Pyramid Plan.

3. Assume that a child is allergic to citrus fruit and strawberries (common food allergies). What fruit and/or vegetable choices could be substituted to provide adequate vitamin C?

4. The next time you eat pizza, note the amount that you ate. Use the Pyramid as a guide to evaluate the number of servings that you received from each of the different food groups.

If you had a green salad with your pizza, what nutrients did it add? Estimate how many one-cup servings the salad would have yielded.

CHAPTER REVIEW

A. **By Yourself:**

1. Match the foods in **column I** to the appropriate food group in **column II**. Some foods may include more than one food group.

Column I	Column II
1. navy beans	a. Milk group
2. rice	b. Meat and Beans group
3. spaghetti	c. Grain group
4. hamburger pizza	d. Vegetable group
5. macaroni and cheese	e. Fruit group
6. peanut butter sandwich	f. Oils group
7. French fries	g. Discretionary calories
8. ice cream	
9. popcorn	
10. carbonated beverages	

B. **As a Group:**

1. Describe where the source of energy is in food. What nutrients yield energy?

2. Discuss how an individual might use the Dietary Guidelines for Americans to improve their personal well-being.

3. Describe what dietary reference intakes are and what purpose(s) they might serve for an individual.

4. Debate the merits and limitations of the current Food Pyramid.

REFERENCES

American Academy of Pediatrics. (2006). Active healthy living: Prevention of childhood obesity through increased physical activity. *Pediatrics, 117*(5), 1834–42.

American Dietetic Association. (1997). Vegetarian diets. *Journal of the American Dietetic Association, 97,* 1317–21.

Canadian Academy of Sport Medicine. (2006). *Position statement: Physical inactivity in children and adolescents.* Accessed on November 15, 2006, from http://www.casm-acms.org/forms/statements/final_inactivity_position.pdf.

Carmichael, S., Yang, W., Herring, A., Abrams, B., & Shaw, G. (2007). Maternal food insecurity is associated with increased risk of certain birth defects. *Journal of Nutrition, 137*(9), 2087–92.

Guenther, P., Dodd, K., Reedy, J., & Krebs-Smith, S. (2006). Most Americans eat much less than the recommended amounts of fruits and vegetables. *Journal of the American Dietetic Association, 106*(9), 1364–68.

Kranz, S. (2006). Meeting the dietary reference intakes for fiber: Sociodemographic characteristics of preschoolers with high fiber intakes. *American Journal of Public Health, 96*(9), 1538–42.

Kranz, S., Mitchell, D., Siega-Riz, A., & Smicikilas-Wright, H. (2005). Dietary fiber intake by American preschoolers is associated with more nutrient-dense diets. *Journal of the American Dietetic Association, 105*(2), 221–225.

Kranz, S., Smicikilas-Wright, H., & Francis, L. (2006). Diet quality, added sugar, and dietary fiber intakes in American preschoolers. *Pediatric Dentistry, 28*(2), 164–171.

Institute of Medicine, Food & Nutrition Board. (2003). *Dietary Reference Intakes: Applications in Dietary Planning*. Washington, DC: National Academies Press.

Mitka, M. (2005). Government unveils new food pyramid: Critics say nutrition tool is flawed. *Journal of the American Medication Association, 1*(293), 2581–82.

Murphy, S., & Barr, S. (2006). Recommended Dietary Allowances should be used to set daily values for nutrition labeling. *American Journal of Clinical Nutrition, 83*(5), 1223S–1227S.

Murphy, S., Guenther, P., & Kretsch, M. (2006). Using the dietary reference intakes to assess intakes of groups: Pitfalls to avoid. *Journal of the American Dietetic Association, 106*(10), 1550–1553.

National Association for Sport & Physical Education. (2006). Active start: A statement of physical activity guidelines for children birth to five years.

Physical activity for children: A statement of guidelines for children ages 5–12, 2nd Edition. Accessed on November 15, 2006, from http://www.aahperd.org/naspe/template.cfm?template=ns_active.html.

U.S. Department of Agriculture. (2005a). *Dietary Guidelines*. Accessed on November 15, 2006, from http://www.mypyramid.gov/guidelines/index.html.

U.S. Department of Agriculture. (2005b). Inside the Pyramid. Accessed on November 15, 2006, from http://www.mypyramid.gov/pyramid/index.html.

U.S. Department of Agriculture. (2005c). *Tips and Resources*. Accessed on November 15, 2006, from http://www.mypyramid.gov/tips_resources/index.html.

U.S. Food & Drug Administration. (2004). Food Allergen Labeling and Consumer Protection Act of 2004. Accessed on November 15, 2006, from http://www.cfsan.fda.gov/~dms/alrgact.html.

Yates, A. (2006). Which dietary reference intake is best suited to serve as the basis for nutrition labeling for daily values? *Journal of the American Dietetic Association, 136*(10), 2457–62.

HELPFUL WEB RESOURCES

Canada's Food Guide to Healthy Living	www.hc-sc.gc.ca
Federal Citizen Information Center	http://www.pueblo.gsa.gov
Food and Drug Administration (FDA) (Food labels)	http://www.cfsan.fda.gov
Food Guide Pyramid for Kids	http://www.mypyramid.gov
Tufts University Center on Nutrition Science and Policy	http://nutrition.tufts.edu
United States Department of Agriculture (USDA) News Site	http://www.usda.gov
United States Department of Agriculture MyPyramid.gov	http://www.mypryamid.gov

For additional health, safety, and nutrition resources, go to http://www.EarlyChildEd.delmar.cengage.com

CHAPTER 14

Nutrients that Provide Energy (Carbohydrates, Fats, and Proteins)

※ OBJECTIVES

After studying this chapter, you should be able to:

- Identify the three classes of nutrients that supply energy.
- State the amount of energy supplied by each class of nutrients.
- List three factors that determine individual energy requirements.
- Identify foods containing good sources of energy-supplying nutrients.
- Calculate daily caloric requirements of a child based on the child's weight.
- Plan a day's diet that eliminates refined sucrose.
- Plan a day's diet that meets the recommended 30 percent of calories from fat, and is low in saturated fatty acids and cholesterol.

※ TERMS TO KNOW

energy	basal metabolic rate (BMR)	linolenic acid
calories	thermic energy of food	trans fats
enzymes	digest (digestion)	MUFAs
coenzymes	absorb (absorption)	PUFAs
gram	metabolize (metabolism)	
milligram	linoleic acid	

Energy is generally defined as the ability to do work. Examples of work performed by the body are (1) moving the body, (2) building new tissues, (3) maintaining body temperature, and (4) digesting, absorbing, and metabolizing food. Energy is required for all body functions. In terms of survival, the need for energy is second only to the need for oxygen and water.

The amount of potential energy in a food is expressed in **calories**; for example, a one-cup serving of ice cream supplies 185 calories. The energy cost of a given activity is also measured and expressed in calories; for example, swimming for 30 minutes expends about 150 calories.

---

energy – *power to perform work.*
calories – *units used to measure the energy value of foods.*

Carbohydrates, fats, and proteins found in foods supply energy for the body's activities. Vitamins, minerals, and water do not supply calories but they are essential for the functioning of **enzymes**, **coenzymes**, and hormones. Enzymes and coenzymes are vitamin-containing substances that initiate and participate in the many metabolic reactions that are necessary for the release of energy from carbohydrates, fats, and proteins. Hormones, such as thyroxin and insulin, while not directly involved in energy-releasing reactions, do regulate many of these reactions. For example, several are required to maintain a blood sugar level that provides an adequate supply of energy for all body needs. The caloric value of any given food is determined by its carbohydrate, fat, and protein content. The relative numbers of calories contained in carbohydrates, fats, and proteins are:

- carbohydrates—four calories per gram
- fat—nine calories per gram
- proteins—four calories per gram

A **gram** is a metric unit of measurement for weight. The symbol for gram is "g." There are 28 grams in one ounce, and 454 grams in one pound. A metal paper clip weighs about one gram. A **milligram** is a metric unit of weight that is equal to one-thousandth of a gram: there are one thousand milligrams in a gram. The symbol for milligram is "mg."

Every individual has different energy requirements. These requirements vary slightly on a day-to-day basis and are determined by a combination of:

- basal metabolic rate (BMR)
- physical activity
- energy spent to release energy from food (thermic energy of food)

The term **basal metabolic rate (BMR)** describes the energy needed just to carry on vital involuntary body processes, such as blood circulation, breathing, cell activity, body temperature maintenance, and heartbeat. The BMR varies little from day to day. A child's BMR will be higher than an adult's due to a faster heart beat, respiratory rate, and additional energy required for growth. BMR does not reflect voluntary activity. However, physical activity to the aerobic level will increase heart beat and breathing rates which will temporarily increase the BMR. For most children and adults, the energy required to meet basal metabolic needs is greater than energy expended for voluntary physical activity.

Physical activity is the aspect of an individual's energy need that is subject to the greatest conscious control. For instance, participation in tennis or swimming as a recreational activity requires far more energy than reading or watching television (Figure 14–1). Children should be encouraged to participate in vigorous physical activity on a daily basis. The benefits of physical activity include improved motor development, opportunities for socialization, a sense of personal accomplishment, improved physical and mental health, and increased fitness. The additional calories required by increased physical activity provide the opportunity to increase food intake and thus make it easier to meet other nutrient requirements.

Thermic energy of food refers to the energy required to **digest**, **absorb**, transport, and **metabolize** nutrients in food. This factor accounts for approximately 10 percent of an individual's total energy requirement.

---

enzymes – *proteins that catalyze body functions.*
coenzymes – *a vitamin-containing substance required by certain enzymes before they can perform their prescribed function.*
gram – *a metric unit of weight (g); approximately 1/28 of an ounce.*
milligram – *a metric unit of weight (mg); approximately 1/1000 of a gram.*
basal metabolic rate (BMR) – *minimum amount of energy needed to carry on the body processes vital to life.*
thermic energy of food – *energy required to digest, absorb, transport, and metabolize nutrients in food.*
digestion – *the process by which complex nutrients in foods are changed into smaller units that can be absorbed and used by the body.*
absorption – *the process by which the products of digestion are transferred from the intestinal tract into the blood or lymph or by which substances are taken up by the cells.*
metabolism – *all chemical changes that occur from the time nutrients are absorbed until they are built into body tissue or are excreted.*

FIGURE 14–1

Quiet activities burn fewer calories.

FIGURE 14–2

The energy needs of active, growing children are considerably greater than those of an adult.

Growing children need more energy per unit of body weight than do adults (Figure 14–2) (Fox, et al., 2006). Growth requires energy for division and/or enlargement of existing cells (Brown, 2005). Physical activity and body mass also affect the amount of energy an individual child needs. Daily caloric requirement is calculated on the basis of normal body weight. For example, a four-year-old child needs approximately 40 calories per pound of body weight. (The energy needs of infants are detailed in Chapter 17.) For comparison, a moderately active adult female requires approximately 18 calories per pound; a moderately active adult male needs approximately 21 calories per pound. (Moderately active has been described as equal time "on the feet and on the seat.") Males have a higher BMR than do females due to their greater muscle-to-fat ratio. Muscle tissue requires BMR energy, while fat needs zero energy for storage or retrieval.

Balancing the number of calories eaten with the number of calories expended results in a stable body weight (see *Dietary Guidelines for Americans* in Chapter 13). Eating fewer calories than are needed leads to weight loss. The result of eating too few calories is more serious in growing children than in adults. Too few calories can result in a slowed growth rate because body tissue must be utilized to meet energy demands. Children need sufficient calories from carbohydrates and fat to spare protein that is needed for growth. Children, as well as adults, should get one-half or more of their daily calories from carbohydrates; starch is the preferred carbohydrate because its food sources contribute needed vitamins, minerals, and fiber as well as energy.

TABLE 14–1 Tips for Managing an Overweight Child

- Increase the amount of physical activity in which a child participates. This is often the most effective approach to weight control.
- Make slight changes in a child's meals and snacks to help a child control weight. For example, offer fat-free animal crackers or fresh fruit rather than a chocolate cookie or chips.
- Encourage water consumption and reduce a child's intake of sweetened beverages.
- Avoid clean plate requirements.
- Substitute fresh fruit or low-fat, low-sugar, dairy-based desserts for high calorie desserts. Do not exclude desserts; this only increases their importance for the child.
- Be a good role model for children and follow healthy eating and physical activity habits.

Too many calories consumed over a period of time may lead to obesity. Obese children are often less active than their slimmer playmates and may require fewer calories due to their reduced activity level. The obese child's bulkier body may make coordinated movements more difficult, and thus increase the risk of accidental injury. This may also contribute to the obese child's reluctance to engage in play that involves much physical activity, which can lead to additional weight gain. It is important to stop this vicious cycle during the child's early years because there is strong evidence that child obesity results in adult obesity. There are also many known health risks associated with being overweight or obese. Obese children are often teased by their playmates and excluded from play activities. Exclusion from play groups often adds to problems encountered by the obese child, such as poor self-image, decreased fitness level, and fewer opportunities for socialization. Children who have a weight problem should be encouraged to become more active and to eat a healthful diet of nutrient-dense foods (Table 14–1) (Davis, Northington & Kolar, 2000). Calories should never be drastically reduced as this can cause a reduction of essential nutrients (Faith & Kerns, 2005; Satter, 2005). A safer approach is to adjust calorie intake to keep body weight stable while the child grows taller. Over time, this will bring the weight:height ratio (also known as body mass index, or BMI) back into a normal range.

According to the 2005 *Dietary Guidelines for Americans*, children need sufficient food to ensure proper growth. Physical activity, not food restriction, is recommended to encourage weight loss. Children on weight-reduction programs must be under a physician's supervision to make sure their nutritional needs are being met.

CARBOHYDRATES AS ENERGY SOURCES

Carbohydrates yield four calories per gram and should be a child's primary sources of energy. At least half the energy required by a child should be derived from carbohydrates. For example, a child who requires 1,600 calories should get at least 800 calories from carbohydrates; 800 calories are supplied by 200 grams of carbohydrates. Many experts recommend that adults consume a minimum of 125 grams (500 calories) of carbohydrates daily. Children require more, but the exact minimum amount needed is not known. The majority of one's carbohydrates should be from complex (starch) sources with no more than 10 percent of calories coming from refined sugar.

Foods that contain complex and unprocessed carbohydrates are wise choices for children's snacks. Fresh fruits and vegetables, fruit and vegetable juices, and whole grain products such as breads, cereals, and crackers are nutritious and readily accepted snack foods for growing children.

Consumption of refined sugar has increased since 1900; the use of complex carbohydrates, such as starches, has dropped during that same period. Current nutrition recommendations suggest increased amounts of complex carbohydrates and decreased amounts of refined sugars. This

> ### ISSUES TO CONSIDER • Are We Having an Obesity Epidemic?
>
> The media tell us almost daily that we are fat and getting fatter. Depending upon the source, the story will be that "30–50 percent of all Americans are obese," or 20 percent above their normal body weight. The message will then proceed to tell us that obesity increases our risk for several diseases.
>
> - Why do Americans not take these warnings seriously enough to really try to achieve and maintain body weight and thus reduce risk of disease?
> - How much attention is or should be given to helping children balance energy input with energy output so they will not be as likely to experience an obesity problem?
> - Discuss the importance of including physical activity as routine programming in child care and school programs.
>
> It is reported that families with young children are eating away from home and at fast-food restaurants more often.
>
> - What are the common menu choices for children and adults in these restaurants?
> - Consider the amount of high fat foods available, the lack of fruit, vegetables, and milk as menu items, and the average total calorie count of fast-food offerings.
> - Could the accelerated use of fast-food offerings be contributing to the increase of obesity in children and adults?

simply means less sugar and more starch and fiber from the grain, vegetable, and fruit groups. Three general classes of carbohydrates are found in foods: simple sugars, compound sugars, and complex carbohydrates.

Simple Sugars

Simple sugars consist of one sugar unit that needs no further digestion prior to absorption. Examples of simple sugars are:

- glucose
- fructose
- galactose

Glucose is the form in which sugar is used by body cells. However, most glucose in the blood is a result of digestion of more complex carbohydrates (starches).

Fructose is present in honey and high-fructose corn syrup; it is sweeter than all other sugars. In some cases, smaller amounts of fructose may be used to give a desired degree of sweetness.

Galactose is not found free in foods but results from the digestion of "milk sugar."

Compound Sugars

Compound sugars are made up of two simple sugars joined together. Compound sugars must be digested to their component simple sugars before they can be absorbed and utilized by the body. Two important examples of compound sugars are:

- sucrose
- lactose

In its refined form, sucrose is commonly known as table sugar. Sucrose is found in sugar beets and sugar cane and in fruits, vegetables, and honey. When sucrose occurs in fruits and vegetables, it is accompanied by other essential nutrients such as vitamins, minerals, and water

FIGURE 14–3

The sugars in fruits are accompanied by other essential nutrients.

(Figure 14–3). Refined sucrose, or table sugar, is the cause of concern in several aspects of health. Refined table sugar contributes no nutrients—only calories. For this reason, calories from table sugar are frequently called "empty calories." Eating too many empty calories can lead to obesity accompanied by a deficiency of some essential nutrients. Children who are allowed to eat too many foods containing refined sugar may not be hungry for more healthful foods containing the nutrients they need.

Refined sucrose has also been linked to tooth decay in children. Other important factors contributing to tooth decay are the stickiness of the food containing the sugar, the frequency and timing of eating, the frequency of tooth brushing, whether the sugar is contained in a meal with other foods or in a snack, and whether the sugar-containing food is accompanied by a beverage.

Lactose, commonly referred to as "milk sugar," is found in milk and dairy products including many processed foods. It is the only carbohydrate found in an animal-source food. Lactose occurs in the milk of mammals, including human breast milk. It is the least sweet of all common sugars which explains why one cup of 2 percent milk with the equivalent of one tablespoon of sugar in the form of lactose does not taste sweet. It has advantages over other sugars in that lactose aids in establishing and maintaining beneficial intestinal bacteria. Calcium is used more efficiently by the body if lactose is also present. Fortunately, calcium and lactose occur in the same food—milk.

Although lactose is usually a beneficial sugar, it can present problems for some individuals. Some persons do not produce the enzyme lactase needed to break lactose down to its component simple sugars so that it can be absorbed. This condition is commonly referred to as lactose intolerance, and may cause considerable intestinal discomfort, cramping, gas, and diarrhea. Some individuals can tolerate small amounts of milk (one to two cups a day) if it is consumed in several smaller feedings. Dairy products such as yogurt and buttermilk are often better tolerated than milk. Lactose intolerance is more common among certain racial and ethnic populations, including persons of Native American, Asian American, Mexican American, African American and Jewish descent (Jackson & Savaiano, 2001). Adults are also more likely to develop the condition and to experience troublesome symptoms.

Complex Carbohydrates

Complex carbohydrates are composed of many units of simple sugar joined together. Complex carbohydrates must be broken down to their component simple sugars before the body can absorb, use, and store them. The digestion of only one complex carbohydrate often results in thousands of simple sugars. Complex carbohydrates that are important to human nutrition are:

- starch
- cellulose
- glycogen

Starches are the only digestible form of complex carbohydrates found in foods. They are available in large amounts in grains, legumes (peas, dried beans), and root vegetables such as potatoes, sweet potatoes and carrots. The starches in these foods are often accompanied by a host of vitamins and minerals that the body needs, and are therefore desirable components of a healthful diet.

Cellulose is an indigestible complex carbohydrate. Because humans are unable to digest cellulose, it cannot be absorbed and used by body cells, and therefore does not contribute any calories. Although it cannot be absorbed, cellulose is a good source of insoluble fiber that increases the rate of food transit through the intestinal tract and increases the frequency of elimination of intestinal waste material. This action by cellulose results in decreased time for digestion and absorption of food components and cholesterol. Rapid transit of materials through the gastrointestinal tract has also been shown to reduce absorption of substances that may cause cancer formation. It is also thought to provide some detergent effect to teeth, thus aiding good dental health. Cellulose is found in whole grains, nuts, fruits, and vegetables.

Another complex carbohydrate of physiological importance is glycogen. Glycogen is often referred to as animal starch. It is the form in which carbohydrate is stored in the body for future conversion into sugar and subsequent energy.

The use of artificial sweeteners to replace sugar as a means of reducing calorie intake has become a common practice. The four FDA-approved artificial sweeteners are saccharin, aspartame (Nutrasweet), acesulfame potassium (Sunett), and Sucralose (Splenda, approved in 1998) (American Dietetic Association, 2004). Used in moderation, these sweeteners are accepted as safe for adult consumption. The herbal sweetener Stevia has not received FDA approval but is currently being sold as a dietary supplement (U.S. News World Report, 2001). Adequate evidence has not been received by the FDA to designate Stevia as a safe food additive (U.S. Food and Drug Administration, 1999). The use of the non-calorie artificial sweeteners in a child's diet is questionable because foods containing them are usually poor sources of important nutrients. Also, most children have from birth a strong preference for a sweet taste that does not need to be enhanced by "fake" sweets. Children with phenylketonuria (PKU), a genetic disease characterized by an inability to properly metabolize the essential amino acid phenylalanine, must not use aspartame because it contains phenylalanine. Accumulation of this toxic substance may cause severe and irreversible brain damage.

FATS AS ENERGY SOURCES

For the past several decades, fats have been given much "bad press" and the food market has been deluged with low-fat and fat-free foods. However, fat is an essential nutrient for the young child. It is required for growth and production of body regulators as well as being the most concentrated dietary source of energy. Because young children have a small stomach capacity, fats play an important role in meeting their high energy needs.

Fats are the richest food source of energy, supplying nine calories per gram consumed. Foods in which fats are readily identified are butter, margarine, cheese, shortening, oils, and salad dressings. Less obvious sources of fats are meats, whole milk, egg yolks, nuts, and nut butters. Fruits

REFLECTIVE THOUGHTS

Fat intake seems to be a prime dietary concern of most Americans, and yet American children have higher blood cholesterol levels than children anywhere else in the world. How can we reduce cholesterol, a fatlike substance found only with animal-source fats, without limiting food fat for children who still need more fat for growth and brain development?

The American Academy of Pediatrics (AAP) recommends that fat intake not be reduced before two years of age because infants and young children need 50 percent of their energy from fat to assure normal growth and brain development. After the child has reached age two, the AAP recommends a gradual decrease in fat to result in 30 percent of energy from fat by age four or five years. This fat reduction is particularly important for children in families with a history of early heart disease.

- Which of the Pyramid food groups would contribute the most animal fat and cholesterol?
- Which three food groups contribute little fat and no cholesterol?
- How could a green vegetable become a source of fat and cholesterol?

and vegetables contain little fat, with the exception of the avocado, which is quite rich in good fats. Bread and cereal products are naturally low in fat. However, baked goods such as cakes, pies, doughnuts, and cookies are high in added fat. Although some dietary fat is required for good health, recommendations have been made to reduce average fat intake to about 30 percent of total daily calories. However, the American Academy of Pediatrics and the American Heart Association recommend that there should be no dietary fat restriction for children under two years of age (AAP, 2006; AHA, 2006). The 2005 *Dietary Guidelines for Americans* advises that total fat intake be maintained "between 30 to 35 percent of calories for children two to three years of age and between 25 to 35 percent of calories for children and adolescents 4 to 18 years of age," with most fats coming from fish, nuts, and vegetable oils. For a child requiring 1,600 calories, this means 480 calories or 50–55 grams of fat in the diet. This is equivalent to approximately four tablespoons of butter or oil.

Although they provide more than twice as much energy per gram as do carbohydrates, fats are a less desirable energy source for children. They are more difficult for children to digest than carbohydrates and are accompanied by fewer essential nutrients. However, fats should not be reduced below 30 percent of a child's daily calories because they perform important functions for the child:

- allow normal growth and development of brain and nerve tissues
- provide the essential fatty acids (**linoleic** and **linolenic**)
- are carriers of the required fat-soluble vitamins
- allow infants and children with limited stomach capacity to meet their calorie needs

The practice of lowering a very young child's fat intake through the use of skim milk is not an acceptable safe choice. Most authorities believe that this practice may lead to insufficient calorie intake and essential fatty acid (EFA) deficiency. In addition, infants and young children (under two years of age) who consume the same amount or more of skim milk as they previously consumed of breast milk or formula will receive a higher and possibly excessive amount of protein and minerals. These excesses require the body to excrete greater amounts of waste and minerals,

linoleic acid – *a polyunsaturated fatty acid, which is essential (must be provided in food) for humans.*
linolenic acid – *one of the two polyunsaturated fatty acids that are recognized as essential for humans.*

which the child's kidneys may not be mature enough to handle (Insel, Turner, & Ross, 2006). Low fat (2 percent) milk may be given to children older than two years and may be advised if there is a strong family history of cardiovascular disease (CVD).

Fats must undergo digestion and absorption into the body before their energy can be released. Digestion of dietary fats produces:

- fatty acids
- glycerol

The resulting fatty acids and glycerol can be absorbed for use by the body. Fatty acids in foods are either saturated or unsaturated.

Fats found in animal-source foods such as meat, milk, cheese and eggs contain fatty acids that are saturated (Figure 14–4). Fats containing predominantly saturated fatty acids are usually solid at room temperature and are often accompanied by cholesterol. Cholesterol and saturated fats have been extensively investigated as undesirable dietary components. However, after years of study, few definite conclusions have been reached regarding the role of dietary cholesterol in cardiovascular disease or the advisability of lowering the saturated fatty acid and cholesterol intake of children. However, the American Heart Association (AHA) recommends that dietary intake of

FIGURE 14–4

Comparison of saturated fat values in foods.

Food Category	Portion	Saturated Fat Content (grams)	Calories
Cheese			
• Regular cheddar cheese	1 oz	6.0	114
• Low-fat cheddar cheese	1 oz	1.2	49
Ground beef			
• Regular ground beef (25% fat)	3 oz (cooked)	6.1	236
• Extra lean ground beef (5% fat)	3 oz (cooked)	2.6	148
Milk			
• Whole milk (3.25%)	1 cup	4.6	146
• Low-fat (1%) milk	1 cup	1.5	102
Breads			
• Croissant (med)	1 medium	6.6	231
• Bagel, oat bran (4")	1 medium	0.2	227
Frozen desserts			
• Regular ice cream	½ cup	4.9	145
• Frozen yogurt, low-fat	½ cup	2.0	110
Table spreads			
• Butter	1 tsp	2.4	34
• Soft margarine with zero *trans fats*	1 tsp	0.7	25
Chicken			
• Fried chicken (leg with skin)	3 oz (cooked)	3.3	212
• Roasted chicken (breast no skin)	3 oz (cooked)	0.9	140
Fish			
• Fried fish	3 oz	2.8	195
• Baked fish	3 oz	1.5	129

Accessed from http://www.health.gov/DietaryGuidelines/dga2005/document/pdf/chapter6.pdf.

saturated and **trans fats** be limited (AHA, 2006). It is important to remember that cholesterol is found only in animal-source food fats. However, do not equate high fat with high cholesterol. For example, coconut derives 83 percent of its calories from fat, and 89 percent of its fatty acids are saturated, but it has no cholesterol.

Unsaturated fats are usually soft at room temperature or are in oil form. Monounsaturated fatty acids (**MUFAs**), which have only one point of unsaturation, are currently being reported to be most effective in controlling the kind and amount of fat and cholesterol circulating in the blood. Thus olive oil and canola oil, high in MUFA, are recommended for use by CVD-prone persons.

Fats found in plant-source foods such as corn oil or sunflower oil contain mostly unsaturated fatty acids. Many plant oils are polyunsaturated, which means the fatty acids contain numerous unfilled attachment sites. Polyunsaturated fatty acids are often called **PUFAs**. Linoleic and linolenic acids are polyunsaturated fatty acids that are essential for all humans, but are needed in greater amounts for infants and children than for adults. These essential fatty acids cannot be produced by the body and so must be obtained from food sources. Plant-source foods are better sources of these essential fatty acids than animal-source foods and do not contain cholesterol. Protein links with fat to produce lipoproteins, which are involved in the transport of fat and cholesterol in the blood. A high blood level of high density lipoproteins (HDLs), which have a high ratio of protein to fat, are currently thought to reduce the risk of cardiovascular disease. Physical activity has been identified as the most effective way to increase HDL (good cholesterol) levels in blood.

PROTEINS AS ENERGY SOURCES

Proteins are the third class of nutrients that the body can use as an energy source. Proteins supply four calories per gram; the same amount of energy that is derived from carbohydrates. Although they both yield the same number of calories per gram, proteins are generally a more expensive form of energy than are carbohydrates. "Eating protein to meet energy needs . . . represents a waste like burning furniture for heat when firewood is available" (Longacre, 1976).

Proteins must be digested into their component amino acids prior to absorption and utilization by the body. Each protein is unique in the number, arrangement, and specific amino acids from which it is built. Since proteins (amino acids) function as materials to build body tissues and as regulators of body functions, they will be discussed in detail in subsequent chapters.

FOCUS ON FAMILIES • Healthy Families

Calculate and graph your child's body mass index (BMI) using the following method: (Teachers can provide families with a BMI table from the CDC Web site: http://www.cdc.gov.)

Example: Height: 4 ft. 0 in.   Weight: 75 lbs.

1. Multiply weight (pounds) by 703: $75 \times 703 = 52,725$
2. Multiply height (inches) by 48 (inches): $48 \times 48 = 2,304$
3. Divide the answer in step 1 by the answer in step 2: $52,725/2,304 = 23$

---

trans fats – *unsaturated fats that have been converted to a solid by a process of hydrogenation.*
MUFAs – *monounsaturated fatty acids; fatty acids that have one double hydrogen bond; nuts, avocados, and olive oil are high in this form of fat.*
PUFAs – *polyunsaturated fatty acids; fatty acids that contain more than one bond that is not fully saturated with hydrogen.*

FOCUS ON FAMILIES • Healthy Families (continued)

The higher a child's BMI, the greater the risk for certain health-related diseases. Regardless of where a child's BMI appears on the graph, all families should consider adopting the following lifestyle changes.

- Sit as a family at mealtime. All distractions such as televisions, video games, and computers should be turned off. Mealtime is the time to begin healthy, nonstressful conversations with your family.

- Use the Food Guide Pyramid to guide your food choices and to incorporate a wide variety of foods into your family's diet. Choose the majority of foods from the fruits, vegetables and grains groups. Use My Pyramid Plan to choose the right foods and amounts for each family member.

- Encourage healthy snacking at planned times. Empty-calorie snacking throughout the day will cause a child to eat poorly at meals.

- Shop sensibly and avoid purchasing "junk" food. If those foods are readily available, it is difficult to engage in healthy snacking.

CASE STUDY

Terry, age five, has several decayed teeth. His dentist has suggested a program of good dental hygiene plus limiting his intake of refined sucrose.

Plan a day's menu for Terry that contains at least 150 grams of carbohydrates without any refined sucrose (table sugar). Use the following average amounts of carbohydrates:

bread, cereals, pastas	15 grams/slice or ounce
fruits and juices	10 grams/½ adult serving
starchy vegetables	10 grams/½ adult serving
milk	6 grams/½ cup

CLASSROOM CORNER • Teacher Activities

Roll the Cube and Move...
Concept: Food gives us energy and energy is what helps us move. (Pre–2)

Learning Objectives

- Children will learn that eating food gives the body energy to move.
- Children will practice different movement activities: clapping, jumping, stomping, running, touching their toes, and tossing a bean bag.

Supplies

- Cube or small box with pictures representing each of the above actions; bean bags (one per child)

(continued)

CLASSROOM CORNER • Teacher Activities (continued)

Learning Activities

- Talk about the importance of eating healthy foods such as fruits, vegetables, whole grains, meats, dairy, and proteins to give our body energy. Explain that energy is what makes the body be able to move.
- Explain the movement cube. Demonstrate the actions represented by each picture on the cube (hands together—clapping; toes—touch your toes, etc).
- Have children take turns rolling the cube and performing the appropriate action.

Evaluation

- Children can name some foods that give them energy.
- Children can perform a variety of movement activities.

SUMMARY

- Energy is needed to do the work of the body, including internal involuntary activity and voluntary physical activity.
- A person's total energy need is a composite of (a) basal metabolic need, (b) voluntary physical activity, and (c) metabolism to release energy for activities (a) and (b) above.
- During periods of active growth, children need energy for the increase in body size.
- The nutrient classes that yield energy are carbohydrates (four calories/gram), proteins (four calories/gram), and fats (nine calories/gram).
- Carbohydrates come in different forms: simple sugars (glucose and fructose), compound sugars (sucrose and lactose), and complex carbohydrates (starch). Cellulose is a carbohydrate that does not give energy but is important as a source of fiber.
- The fatty acids of different fats may be saturated or unsaturated and all yield nine calories per gram.
- Two unsaturated fatty acids (linoleic and linolenic) are very important for children because they are essential for growth.
- Cholesterol (a fatlike substance) and saturated fats, if consumed in generous amounts, are believed to increase risk of cardiovascular disease (CVD).
- Proteins are inefficient sources of energy and are not usually burned for energy unless there are not enough carbohydrates and fats available to meet energy needs.

APPLICATION ACTIVITIES

1. Using the cereal label in Figure 14–5, determine the following: a) the number of calories derived from carbohydrates; b) the approximate percentage of total calories derived from sucrose and other sugars
2. Which of the nutrient contributions of this cereal are increased by the addition of milk?
3. a. Explain why cereal with milk has a higher carbohydrate value than cereal alone.

   b. Is this cereal predominantly starch or sucrose.

   c. Do starches and complex carbohydrates increase with the addition of milk?

FIGURE 14–5

Cereal label.

Nutrition Facts
Serving Size 3/4 cup (30g)
Servings Per Container about 15

Amount Per Serving	Cereal	Cereal with 1/2 cup Skim Milk
Calories	100	140
Calories from Fat	5	5

		% Daily Value**
Total Fat 0.5g*	**1%**	**1%**
Saturated Fat 0g	**0%**	**0%**
Polyunsaturated Fat 0g		
Monounsaturated Fat 0g		
Cholesterol 0mg	**0%**	**0%**
Sodium 220mg	**9%**	**12%**
Potassium 190mg	**5%**	**11%**
Total Carbohydrate 24g	**8%**	**10%**
Dietary Fiber 5g	**21%**	**21%**
Soluble Fiber 1g		
Insoluble Fiber 4g		
Sugars 6g		
Other Carbohydrate 13g		
Protein 3g		
Vitamin A	15%	20%
Vitamin C	0%	2%
Calcium	0%	15%
Iron	45%	45%
Vitamin D	10%	25%
Thiamin	25%	30%
Riboflavin	25%	35%
Niacin	25%	25%
Vitamin B$_6$	25%	25%
Folate	25%	25%
Vitamin B$_{12}$	25%	35%
Phosphorus	15%	25%
Magnesium	15%	20%
Zinc	10%	15%
Copper	10%	10%

*Amount in Cereal. One half cup skim milk contributes an additional 40 calories. 65mg sodium. 200mg potassium. 6g total carbohydrate (6g sugars). and 4g protein.

**Percent Daily Values are based on a 2.000 calorie diet. Your daily values may be higher or lower depending on your calorie needs.

		Calories:	2.000	2.500
Total Fat	Less than		65g	80g
Saturated Fat	Less than		20g	25g
Cholesterol	Less than		300mg	300mg
Sodium	Less than		2.400mg	2.400mg
Potassium			3.500mg	3.500mg
Total Carbohydrate			300g	375g
Dietary Fiber			25g	30g

4. Calculate the caloric requirement of a four-year-old child who weighs 42 pounds.

5. Determine the number of calories in a serving of food that contributes the following: carbohydrate—12 grams; protein—8 grams; fat—10 grams.

CHAPTER REVIEW

A. **By Yourself:**

1. Match the terms in **column II** to the correct phrase in **column I.**

   Column I

   1. a simple sugar
   2. digestible complex carbohydrate
   3. found in meats, dairy products, legumes, and eggs
   4. building blocks of proteins
   5. found in grains, fruits, vegetables, and milk products
   6. richest source of energy
   7. indigestible complex carbohydrate
   8. table sugar (complex sugar)

   Column II

   a. amino acids
   b. cellulose
   c. protein
   d. carbohydrate
   e. glucose
   f. fats
   g. starch
   h. sucrose

2. Explain why fat intake must not be restricted for children younger than two years.

3. Give two examples of saturated and unsaturated fats.

4. Discuss the factors that determine how many calories an individual requires.

B. **As a Group:**

1. Conduct an online search of scholarly articles on childhood obesity. Why are more children overweight or obese today? In what ways can teachers begin to address this problem in their programs?

2. Discuss the cause of lactose intolerance, which groups of children are more likely to experience this condition, and what dietary modifications would need to be made.

3. Prepare a convincing argument to counter the statement, "Carbohydrates are bad for you."

4. Discuss whether all fats are unhealthy and should thus be eliminated from one's diet.

REFERENCES

American Academy of Pediatrics (AAP). (2006). Dietary recommendations for children and adolescents: A guide for practitioners. *Pediatrics, 117*(2), 544–559.

American Dietetic Association. (2004). Position of the American Dietetic Association: Use of nutritive and nonnutritive sweeteners. *Journal of the American Dietetic Association, 104*(2), 255–275.

American Heart Association (AHA). (2006). *Dietary guidelines for healthy children.* Accessed on November 16, 2006, from http://www.americanheart.org/presenter.jhtml?identifier=4575.

Brown, J. (2005). *Nutrition through the life cycle.* Belmont, CA: Thomson Wadsworth.

Davis, S., Northington, L., & Kolar, K. (2000). Cultural considerations for treatment of childhood obesity. *Journal of Cultural Diversity, 7*(4), 128–132.

Faith, M. & Kerns, J. (2005). Infant and child feeding practices and childhood overweight: The role of restriction. *Maternal & Child Nutrition, 1*(3), 164–168.

Fox, M., Reidy, K., Novak, T., & Ziegler, P. (2006). Sources of energy and nutrients in the diets of infants and toddlers. *Journal of the American Dietetic Association, 106*(1 Suppl.), 28s–42s.

Insel, P., Turner, R., & Ross, D. (2006). *Discovering nutrition.* American Dietetic Association. Boston, MA: Jones & Bartlett Publishers.

Jackson, K. & Savaiano, D. (2001). Lactose maldigestion, calcium intake and osteoporosis in African-, Asian-, and Hispanic-Americans. *Journal of the American College of Nutrition, 20*(2), 198s–207s.

Longacre, D. J. (1976). *More-with-less cookbook.* Scottsdale, PA: Herald Press.

Morris, H. (2001). Stevia adds sweetness, but don't call it a sweetener. *U.S. News World Report, 131*(5), 50.

Satter, E. (2005). *Your child's weight: Helping without harming.* Madison, WI: Kelcy Press.

U.S. Department of Health & Human Services and U.S. Department of Agriculture. (2000). *Dietary guidelines for Americans.* Washington, DC.

U.S. Food and Drug Administration (1999). Sugar substitutes: Americans opt for sweetness and lite. *FDA Consumer.* College Park, MD.

HELPFUL WEB RESOURCES

Canadian Council of Food & Nutrition   http://www.ccfn.ca

Center for Science in Public Interest (CSPI)   http://www.cspinet.org

Health-Kids.gov   http://www.kids.gov

Women, Infants, and Children (WIC)   http://www.fns.usda.gov

WebMD   http://www.webmd.com

United States Department of Agriculture MyPyramid.gov   http://www.mypyramid.gov

For additional health, safety, and nutrition resources, go to http://www.EarlyChildEd.delmar.cengage.com

CHAPTER 15

Nutrients That Promote Growth of Body Tissues

(Proteins, Minerals, and Water)

❋ OBJECTIVES

After studying this chapter, you should be able to:

- Describe how growth occurs.
- Name three classes of nutrients that promote growth of body tissue and list food sources for each.
- Explain the role that proteins, minerals, and water play in body growth.
- Differentiate between nonessential and essential amino acids.
- Identify food sources for complete protein and for incomplete protein.
- Identify examples of complementary incomplete protein combinations.

❋ TERMS TO KNOW

amino acids
nonessential amino acids
essential amino acids
complete protein

incomplete proteins
complementary proteins
supplementary proteins
minerals

collagen
hemoglobin
iron-deficiency anemia

Growth may be defined as an increase in physical size of either the entire body or of any body part. Growth may occur by 1) an increase in the number of cells, or by 2) an increase in the size of individual cells. At various stages of the child's life, either or both types of growth may be occurring. Although young children are continually growing, the rate of growth is often irregular. They will grow linearly (taller) for a period of time and then stop and just gain weight for a while. Their appetite and need for nutrients is greatest during the linear growth phase. Failure to meet nutrient needs for growth may result in a small-for-age child, who has decreased resistance to disease, poor utilization of food eaten, and delays in expected physical and mental development.

Infancy and early childhood are periods of rapid growth (Figure 15–1). During the first six months of life, infants will typically double their birth weight and triple it by the end of the first

FIGURE 15–1

Infancy is a period of rapid growth.

year. Their birth length should increase by 50 percent by the first birthday. Birth weight and length are the baselines for evaluating infant growth. Head circumference is another measure used to evaluate a child's growth and development.

PROTEINS FOR GROWTH

Proteins play an important role in growth. Protein is the material from which all body cells are built. Approximately 15 percent of body weight consists of protein which is concentrated in muscles, glands, organs, bones, blood, and skin (Figure 15–2).

Proteins are composed of hundreds of individual units called **amino acids**. The human body is able to manufacture some of the amino acids needed to build proteins; these amino acids are termed **nonessential amino acids**. Amino acids that the body cannot manufacture in needed amounts must be provided by proteins in foods; these amino acids are termed **essential amino acids**.

When all essential amino acids occur in adequate amounts in food protein, that protein is said to be a **complete protein**. Complete proteins typically occur in animal-source foods such as meats, milk, eggs, and cheese.

Incomplete proteins are those that lack adequate amounts of one or more essential amino acids. Proteins from plant sources such as grains, legumes, and vegetables are incomplete proteins.

---

amino acids – *the organic building blocks from which proteins are made.*
nonessential amino acids – *amino acids that are produced in the body.*
essential amino acids – *amino acids that can only be obtained from protein food sources.*
complete protein – *protein that contains all essential amino acids in amounts relative to the amounts needed to support growth.*
incomplete proteins – *proteins that lack required amounts of one or more essential amino acids.*

FIGURE 15–2

How protein is distributed in the body.

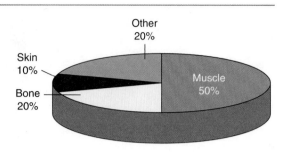

One exception is the soybean, which supplies adequate amino acids to support growth in young children. However, soybean consumption in large amounts can decrease iron absorption. Gelatin, an animal-source food, is also an incomplete protein.

Complete protein intake may be achieved by combining two or more incomplete proteins that are complementary. A food that supplies an amino acid that is absent or in low quantities in another food is said to complement that food. For example, wheat, which is deficient in lysine, may be combined with peanuts, which contain adequate amounts of lysine but lack another essential amino acid provided by wheat (Insel, Turner & Ross, 2006). The resulting combination of wheat and peanuts contains all the essential amino acids and is equivalent to a complete protein. For example, the wheat-peanut combination could be served as a peanut butter sandwich or a peanut sauce on pasta. Plant proteins tend to be less costly than complete animal proteins. However, a greater amount of incomplete protein is needed to achieve the equivalent of a complete protein. For instance, one cup of beans will complement two and two-thirds cups of rice to form a complete protein.

Essential amino acids resulting from the digestion of food protein must be used within a short time, as they are not stored for future use. All essential amino acids must be available several times each day to form the complete proteins needed to support rapid growth.

Young children may have difficulty consuming the larger quantities of food (incomplete proteins) necessary to meet protein requirements given their smaller stomach capacity. However, most children are able to achieve normal growth and development as long as careful attention is paid to planning a well-balanced diet (ADA & Dietitians of Canada, 2003; Dunham & Kollar, 2006). Children who follow this type of diet often have a BMI that is closer to normal (Insel, Turner, & Ross, 2006).

Many favorite dishes are good examples of combinations of incomplete proteins that result in the equivalent of a complete protein. Foods may be combined in either of two ways to obtain adequate protein for less money than most animal-based proteins cost:

- **complementary proteins**—incomplete protein combined with another incomplete protein to equal complete protein.
  Examples: peanut butter sandwich, beans and rice, chili, peas and rice, macaroni salad with peas, lentil soup with crackers, navy beans with cornbread, baked beans and brown bread

- **supplementary proteins**—incomplete protein combined with a small amount of complete protein to equal complete protein.
  Examples: macaroni and cheese, rice pudding, egg salad sandwich, cheese pizza, cereal and milk

---

complementary proteins – *proteins with offsetting missing amino acids; complementary proteins can be combined to provide complete protein.*

supplementary proteins – *a complete protein mix resulting from combining a small amount of a complete protein with an incomplete protein to provide all essential amino acids.*

Protein Requirements

The total amount of protein needed daily is based on desirable body weight. Because infants are growing at an extremely rapid rate, their protein needs are greater, relative to their size, than at any other period of life (see Figure 13–2, Chapter 13). Children's need for protein per pound of body weight continues to remain high during the preschool years due to continued growth. For example, an eight-month-old infant needs approximately 13.5 grams of protein daily; a two-year-old requires 13 grams and a four-year-old needs 19 grams. Although school-age children are growing at a slower rate, they continue to need approximately 35–40 grams of good quality protein. To be meaningful, these figures can be considered in terms of amounts of food. The following selection of foods illustrates how easy it is for children to get adequate protein:

Food	Protein
2 cups of milk	16 grams
1 slice whole wheat bread	2.7 grams
1 ounce meat	7 grams
1 slice provolone cheese	7 grams
1 egg	5.5 grams
3 wheat crackers	.5 grams
2 oz. cooked pasta	7 grams
	TOTAL = 45.7 grams

Table 15–1 shows a menu for one day that would provide more than the daily recommended amount of protein for a four- to six-year-old child.

MINERALS FOR GROWTH

Minerals are inorganic elements that help to regulate body functions and build body tissue. The following discussion deals with minerals that help to build body tissue. The regulatory functions performed by minerals will be covered in Chapter 16. (Check Table 16–4, the mineral summary, for more detailed information.)

Minerals provide no energy and are required in far smaller amounts than are energy-producing nutrients. For example, the RDA for protein is 19 grams for a four-year-old child; this amount is slightly more than two and one-half servings of meat. In contrast, the RDA for calcium for that same child is 0.8 gram. Other minerals are required in even smaller amounts.

Growth involves creating increased amounts of body tissue, which requires adequate amounts of specific minerals. Two types of body tissues most dependent on minerals for growth are bones and teeth, and blood.

Building Bones and Teeth

Calcium and phosphorus are the major minerals found in bones and teeth (Figure 15–3). Bones are formed by the deposition of phosphorus and calcium crystals on **collagen**, a flexible protein base composed of amino acids. Young children's bones are soft and pliable; as growth occurs, the

---

minerals – *inorganic chemical elements that are required in the diet to support growth and repair tissue and to regulate body functions.*

collagen – *a protein that forms the major constituent of connective tissue, cartilage, bone, and skin.*

TABLE 15–1   Menu Supplying Recommended Daily Allowances of Protein for Four- to Six-Year-Olds

Breakfast	Grams of Protein
1/2 c fruit juice or 1/2 medium banana	trace
1/2 c dry oat cereal	1
1/2 c milk*	4
Midmorning Snack	
1/2 c milk*	4
1/2 slice buttered toast	1
Lunch	
1/2 fish taco (1/2 tortilla, 1 1/2 ounces tilapia)	15
4 cherry tomatoes	.5
1/2 medium apple	trace
1/2 c milk*	4
Midafternoon Snack	
1/2 c fruit juice	trace
2 rye crackers	1
Dinner	
1 chicken leg (1 oz)*	6
1/4 c rice	1
1/4 c broccoli	trace
1/4 c strawberries	trace
1/2 c milk*	4
TOTAL:	41.5 grams of protein

*Complete protein.

amount of calcium and phosphorus deposited in their bones increases, resulting in larger, denser bones. Although bones appear to be solid and unchanging, calcium and phosphorus move in and out and are continually being replaced. The calcium content of adult bone, for example, is thought to be replaced every five years. Children need calcium not only for bone growth but also for replacement of existing bone. Adults require calcium only for replacement. Other minerals are also needed for normal bone and tooth formation, but they are rarely limiting factors in the development of these tissues.

Sources of Calcium   Milk and milk products are the major food source of calcium. With the exception of vegetables such as broccoli, collard greens, kale, and Chinese cabbage, or the soy products tofu, miso, and tempeh, there are no rich food sources of calcium other than milk and dairy products. A one-cup serving of the vegetables and soy products listed above will only provide about one-half the amount of calcium available in one cup of milk. Milk, cheese, and yogurt are excellent sources of calcium. Custards, pudding, and ice cream provide calcium, but they also contain varying amounts of added sugar and fat, which reduce their nutrient density relative to calcium.

The calcium content of many dishes may be increased by the addition of nonfat dry milk or cheese. Adding these foods to casseroles, cooked cereals, breads, salads, and ground meat dishes not only increases the amount of calcium and protein but also improves the quality of the incomplete proteins in pastas, cereals, or flours. Calcium is currently being added to all flours and some brands of orange juice. This is a good combination; the vitamin C in the orange juice aids

FIGURE 15–3

Calcium and phosphorus are essential for healthy teeth and bones.

in calcium absorption. Many additional food products, such as breads, cereals, and soy milks are also being fortified with calcium.

Sources of Phosphorus Phosphorus is also found in milk and milk-containing foods as well as other high-protein and whole grain foods. Good sources of phosphorus are milk, meats, fish, eggs, and grain products. Calcium and phosphorus occur in approximately equal amounts in milk. It is easier to obtain phosphorus than calcium, since it occurs in more kinds of foods. The balance between calcium and phosphorus may be upset if a child is permitted to drink large amounts of carbonated beverages that contain phosphorus. If the child drinks more carbonated beverages than milk, phosphorus in the diet outweighs calcium, and calcium absorption may be impaired (Fiorito, et al., 2006). This could result in reduced deposition of calcium in the bones and, in extreme cases, withdrawal of calcium from the bones. When carbonated beverages are substituted for milk as a child's beverage, the potential calcium available for consumption is further reduced (Marshall, et al., 2003).

The Role of Fluoride Fluoride should be considered in connection with bone and tooth formation. Many communities add fluoride to the community water supply in an effort to reduce tooth decay in children. Fluoride-containing toothpastes are also recommended for use by children. Fluoride incorporated into a growing tooth from drinking water makes the tooth harder and more resistant to decay. Fluoride applied to the exterior surface of the tooth is less effective in hardening of the tooth, but it is also thought to reduce the incidence of decay (Tinanoff, Kanellis, & Vargas, 2002). Excess amounts of fluoride may cause mottling and brown-staining of the teeth. Children who are drinking fluoridated water should be taught not to swallow toothpaste after brushing to prevent possible excess consumption that could result in tooth discoloration.

The most consistent source of fluoride is the local water supply, either as naturally occurring fluorine or as fluoride added to a level of one p.p.m. (one part fluoride per million parts of water). Food sources of fluoride are variable and depend on the fluorine content of the soil where grown.

ISSUES TO CONSIDER • Nutrient-Fortified Foods

A thought-provoking question posed by the National Dairy Council asks, "Calcium-fortified foods: Is there a reason for concern?" (National Dairy Council, 2002). Our common current concern with not meeting our calcium needs makes us vulnerable to advertisements of extra calcium sources. As yet, the answer to this question is "no," but this could change if food industry competition in this area continues to escalate. Already one bakery is making a claim that its bread is better than another because two slices of its bread have the same amount of calcium as one glass of milk. Several fruit juices are now fortified with enough calcium to make them nearly equivalent to milk.

- Does this mean that fortified products can be substituted for milk?
- Do these fortified foods give us the protein and vitamins A and D that milk does?

The upper, adult tolerable level for calcium intake is 2,500 milligrams per day. An amount above this limit may increase the risk for kidney stone formation. Children's smaller bodies may reduce their tolerance level.

- Is there a need to regulate the types and amounts of nutrients used to fortify foods?
- What foods might be fortified with the least danger of exceeding tolerance levels?

Building Blood

Iron is a mineral that is essential to the formation of hemoglobin and healthy blood. **Hemoglobin** is the iron-containing protein in red blood cells that carries oxygen to the cells and removes waste (carbon dioxide) from the cells. Normal growth depends on a healthy blood supply to nourish an increasing number of cells.

Iron-deficiency anemia is caused by inadequate intake of dietary iron and is more common in children one to three years of age. It is characterized by low levels of hemoglobin in red blood cells, which reduces the cells' ability to carry oxygen to tissues. The end result is decreased growth rate, fatigue, lack of energy, possible reduction in learning ability, and reduced resistance to infections (Taras, 2005).

Sources of Iron   The Meat and Beans group and the iron-fortified grain group are the best sources of iron. Liver is an especially rich source of iron, but is also high in cholesterol (and it is not a food that is well-accepted by most adults or children). Milk, which is usually a major part of children's diets, contains very little iron. Consequently, a child who drinks large amounts of milk to the exclusion of iron-containing foods may not receive enough iron to support a growing blood supply.

Studies of children's nutritional status have repeatedly found that intakes of calcium and iron are inadequate (Fiorito, et al., 2006; Skalicky, et al., 2006; Schneider, et al., 2005). There may be several reasons for this. One reason may be that neither calcium nor iron are widely distributed in foods. Also, many factors affect the absorption of calcium and iron. Therefore, the presence of either mineral in foods does not always assure that the mineral will be absorbed for use by body cells. Additionally, many foods containing calcium or iron are expensive (Brotanek, et al., 2005; Schrader, Blue, & Horner, 2005).

hemoglobin – *the iron-containing, oxygen-carrying pigment in red blood cells.*
iron-deficiency anemia – *a failure in the oxygen transport system caused by too little iron.*

Factors That Affect Absorption of Calcium and Iron

Calcium	Factor	Iron
↑	Adequate Vitamin C	↑
↑	Increased Need	↑
↓	Large Dose	↓
↓	Fiber (Bulk) in Diet	↓
↓	High Protein Level	↑

Factors that *increase* the absorption of calcium and iron:

- Vitamin C aids in keeping calcium and iron more soluble, and therefore more readily absorbed by the body.
- Vitamin C maximizes the absorption of iron in foods when it is consumed in the same meal.
- Calcium and iron absorption increases at times when the body requires more calcium, such as when intake is inadequate or during periods of rapid growth.

Factors that *decrease* the absorption of calcium and iron:

- Large single doses of calcium and iron are not as well-absorbed as several smaller doses.
- Large amounts of fiber in the diet speed intestinal movement, decreasing the time calcium and iron are in contact with absorption surfaces.

Proteins aid the overall absorption of iron. The iron in meats (known as heme iron) is especially high in red meats such as beef; it is more readily absorbed than the iron in grains and other nonmeat foods. However, young children often refuse this type of meat because it is more difficult to chew.

Although the child has a significant need for the minerals calcium, phosphorus, and iron, smaller amounts of "trace" minerals are also required for growth. Because the amounts of these minerals are quite small, they can usually be met with the average diet—one that includes variety and adequate calories. Zinc and selenium are two of these minerals that continue to attract media attention.

THE ROLE OF WATER

Water is an important constituent of all body tissues. An infant's body weight is nearly 70–75 percent water; approximately 60 percent of normal adult body weight is water. This percentage gradually declines throughout the life cycle. Water is essential for survival; humans can survive much longer without food than they can without water. The need for water is affected by body surface area, environmental temperature, and activity. Water is supplied to the body through drinking water and other beverages, solid foods, and the water that results from energy metabolism.

Vomiting and diarrhea cause an excess loss of water that can rapidly cause dehydration. This is especially threatening to infants, toddlers, and young children, since the amount of water loss necessary to produce dehydration is small in comparison to that of an adult.

Children experience more rapid loss of water through evaporation and dehydration than do adults. When children are busily involved in activities, they may need periodic reminders to drink fluids (Figure 15–4). This is important at any time but especially during periods of vigorous physical activity and when the weather is hot or humid. Children and adults should be encouraged to drink water rather than sugared beverages, since the presence of sugar is known to slow the absorption of water (AAP, 2001). Many children request fruit juice instead of water to drink but this practice should be discouraged. Although 100% fruit juices contribute important nutrients to a healthy diet, excess intake can lead to a number of problems in children, including:

FIGURE 15–4

Children absorbed in active play may need to be reminded to drink fluids.

- Stunted growth. Toddlers who fill up on fruit juice may not get the fuel they need to grow (Dennison, Rockwell, & Baker, 1997). They will have less room for milk and other foods that are richer in calories and other important nutrients, including protein and fat, which should not be restricted in very young children.
- Diarrhea. Too much fluid in itself can cause loose stools. Some juices, notably apple juice, also contain sorbitol, a natural sugar that can be difficult to digest in large quantities, compounding that effect. Some children who drink a lot of juice may experience occasional loose stools while others may develop diarrhea.
- Tooth decay. Toddlers sometimes use a bottle more for comfort than nourishment or refreshment. Overreliance on a bottle, especially as a way to fall asleep, can lead to baby bottle tooth decay (BBDT)—a form of dental decay resulting from prolonged exposure to sugars in juice or in milk (Marshall, et al., 2003; King, 1998).
- Excess weight gain. Children who consume large quantities of fruit juices are at risk for becoming overweight. Natural sugars in fruit juices can contribute to excess energy intake and resulting weight gain (O'Connor, Yang, & Nicklas, 2003).

THE ROLE OF VITAMINS

Vitamins are not structural parts of growing tissue; however, some of them play critical roles in the use of minerals and proteins as building material for the body. For example, bones could not be properly formed or maintained without vitamins A, D, and C, and blood components could not be produced without vitamins C, B_6, B_{12}, and folic acid. (See Chapter 16, Table 16–1.) Vitamins, although not structural parts of any of the growth products, are essential for cell division for new cells and for increase in mass of all cells.

REFLECTIVE THOUGHTS

Single nutrients are often discussed as if functioning alone. Actually a single nutrient can rarely complete any function alone. A look at the critical needs of an actively growing child shows many nutrient dependencies. A protein deficiency is often looked upon as the only cause of retarded growth in children in some poor, underdeveloped countries. If that is true, how can their protein deficiency and growth retardation be so easily corrected by feeding the children generous amounts of flour and sugar? When a child is provided with sufficient energy, the small amounts protein in their diet can be used for growth.

- How does vitamin C help maximize the availability of calcium from food sources?
- Why is growth depressed when a diet has adequate protein but lacks folic acid or vitamin B_{12}?
- Lack of a single vitamin can keep carbohydrates from yielding energy. Explain how this can happen.
- How is calcium dependent upon vitamin D?
- Make a list of as many nutrient interdependencies that you can.

FOCUS ON FAMILIES • Nutrients that Promote Growth

Calcium is a major mineral found in bones and teeth and is needed in the diet to support normal bone formation. Children ages one through eight require 500 to 800 mg of calcium daily to meet nutritional needs. The calcium requirement for school-age children (9–12 years) increases to approximately 1300 mg. daily. Teachers can support calcium intake by regularly including calcium-rich foods into meal patterns and by encouraging parents to provide these foods in the child's diet. Some excellent sources of calcium are:

Milk Group	Serving Size	Calcium (mg)
yogurt	1 cup	452
cheese (cheddar, Swiss)	1 1/2 oz.	300–400
milk	8 oz.	300
calcium-fortified orange juice	8 oz.	300
lasagna	1 cup	286
calcium-fortified cereal	1 cup	250
cheese pizza	1 slice	220
string cheese	1 ounce (1 slice)	214
cheeseburger	1	182
macaroni and cheese	1/2 cup	180

CASE STUDY

The following chart shows a fairly typical daily intake for Timothy, age four and a half. Consider this daily pattern in terms of balance between calcium and phosphorus.

Breakfast:
   1 slice of toast
   1 scrambled egg
   1/2 cup orange juice

Midmorning Snack:
   2 graham crackers (milk offered but refused)

Lunch:
   2 fish sticks
   1/4 cup peas
   1/2 slice bread
   water (milk offered but refused)

Midafternoon Snack:
   1 small soft drink

Dinner:
   hamburger
   French fries
   1 small soft drink

1. Which foods provide calcium?
2. Which foods provide phosphorus?
3. Change the above menu to eliminate the phosphorus/calcium imbalance.
4. What other foods would improve Timothy's calcium intake if he refuses to drink milk?

CLASSROOM CORNER • Teacher Activities

Calcium Helps to Make Strong Bones and Teeth...
Concept: Some foods have calcium and calcium is important for strong bones and teeth. (Pre–2)

Learning Objectives

■ Children will learn that they need to eat foods with calcium for strong bones and teeth.
■ Children will experience tasting a variety of yogurts and learn that yogurt is a good source of calcium.

Supplies

■ One small container each of strawberry, blueberry, lemon, and peach yogurt; hand wipes; plates; spoons; a graph with pictures of a lemon, blueberry, strawberry, and peach

---

CLASSROOM CORNER • Teacher Activities (continued)

Learning Activities

- Discuss why bodies need calcium to help build strong bones and teeth. Tell children that yogurt is a food that has calcium and that it comes in many different flavors.
- Show children the graph and ask them to name each of the fruits.
- Have children clean their hands with wipes and then pass out a plate with a small taste of each kind of yogurt.
- Have children taste each of the flavored yogurts; discuss how each is different.
- Have children place an "x" on the graph next to their favorite flavor.

Evaluation

- Children can name one food that is a good source of calcium.
- Children will eat foods with calcium to develop strong bones and teeth.

SUMMARY

- Growth is an increase in size of the entire body or any part of the body.
- Growth occurs first by an increase in the number of cells. This type of growth has a definite time schedule for each organ; a lack of nutrients during this time schedule cannot be corrected later.
- Growth by an increase in the size of cells continues during most of the total growth period. Deficiency of nutrients during this period may be reversed later.
- The nutrients most needed during the growth periods are protein, minerals, and water. Proteins are components of all living cells; the amino acids that they provide are critically needed for synthesis of specific cellular proteins.
- The best sources of protein that provide all of the amino acids required for growth are meat, fish, poultry, and dairy products.
- Calcium and phosphorus, major components of bones and teeth, crystallize upon a protein base. As they are deposited, the bones and teeth harden.
- Calcium is found primarily in dairy products, while phosphorus is found in milk and in meats, grains, beans, nuts, and cereal products.
- Iron is a part of hemoglobin, a protein found in red blood cells that is necessary for the carrying of oxygen to all body cells.
- Best food sources of iron are red meats and iron-fortified breads and cereals.
- Many factors can interfere with the absorption of both calcium and iron.
- The limited sources of iron and calcium and their absorption problems means that special attention must be given to food choices to assure that adequate amounts of these minerals are provided for the growing child.
- Water is a major constituent of all living body cells; 60 to 75 percent of total body weight is water. Water need is first in line for survival of body cells. During active growth periods, water is a most critical need.

APPLICATION ACTIVITIES

1. Compare the nutrition information labels from several prepared cereals. Common iron content levels are 98 percent daily value, 45 percent daily value, and 25 percent daily value. After reviewing the "Factors That Affect Absorption of Calcium and Iron," discuss which cereal(s) would be the wisest choice in terms of iron absorption. What other step(s) could be taken to increase the absorption of iron available in the cereal?

2. Explain why early childhood is a time of risk for iron-deficiency anemia. Consider factors such as food groups in which iron occurs, typical food preferences, and relative ease of eating various foods.

3. Determine the amount of protein recommended for a child who weighs 42 pounds.

CHAPTER REVIEW

A. By Yourself:

1. Match the terms in **column II** with the definition in **column I**. Use each term in **column II** only once.

Column I	Column II
1. an essential amino acid	a. calcium
2. a nutrient class that functions both to build tissues and provide energy	b. milk group
3. the mineral component of hemoglobin	c. iron
4. the mineral that is a major component of bones and teeth	d. meat and beans group
5. the food group that provides the greatest amounts of calcium	e. lysine
6. the food group that provides the greatest amounts of iron	f. minerals
7. a nutrient class that helps to regulate body processes and also helps to build body tissue	g. protein
8. comprises approximately 60 percent of normal adult body weight	h. water

2. Identify three food sources that are incomplete proteins.

3. Explain how supplementary proteins can be used to provide a complete protein.

4. List at least three non-dairy sources of complete protein.

5. Locate information about vegetarian diets on the Internet. Can all of a child's protein, iron, and calcium needs be met if he or she follows this type of dietary pattern?

B. As a Group:

1. Explain why an infant's and toddler's protein need is greater than that of an adult's.

2. Discuss why children are at-risk for developing iron deficiency anemia?

3. What problem(s) can occur from an excess intake of fluoride?

4. How could you provide calcium to a child who is allergic to milk and dairy products?

REFERENCES

American Academy of Pediatrics (AAP). (2001). The use and misuse of juices in pediatrics. *Pediatrics, 107*(55), 1210–1213.

American Dietetic Association & Dietitians of Canada. (2003). Position of the American Dietetic Association and Dietitians of Canada: Vegetarian diets. *Journal of the American Dietetic Association, 103*(6), 748–765.

Brotanek, J., Halterman, J., Auinger, P., Flores, G., & Weitzman, M. (2005). Iron deficiency, prolonged bottle-feeding, and racial/ethnic disparities in young children. *Archives of Pediatrics & Adolescent Medicine, 159*(11), 1038–1042.

Dennison, B. A., Rockwell, H. L., & Baker, S. L. (1997). Excessive fruit juice consumption by preschool-aged children is associated with short stature and obesity. *Pediatrics, 99,* 15–22.

Dunham, L., & Kollar, L. (2006). Vegetarian eating for children and adolescents. *Journal of Pediatric Health Care, 20*(1), 27–34.

Fiorito, L., Mitchell, D., Smiciklas-Wright, H., & Birch, L. (2006). Dairy and dairy-related intake during middle childhood. *Journal of the American Dietetic Association, 106*(4), 534–542.

Insel, P., Turner, R., & Ross, D. (2006). *Discovering nutrition.* American Dietetic Association. Boston, MA: Jones & Bartlett Publishers.

King, K. (1998). Healthy smiles: A multidisciplinary baby bottle tooth decay prevention program. *Journal of Health Education, 29*(1), 4–8.

Marshall, T., Levy, S., Broffitt, B., Warren, J., & Eichenberger-Gilmore, J. (2003). Dental caries and beverage consumption in young children. *Pediatrics, 112*(3), e184–191.

National Dairy Council. (2002, Jan./Feb.). *Calcium-fortified foods: Is there a reason for concern?* Accessed on November 16, 2006, from http://www.nationaldairycouncil.org/NationalDairyCouncil/Health/Digest/dcd73_1Page1.htm.

O'Connor, T., Yag, S., & Nicklas, T. (2003). Beverage intake among preschool children and its effect on weight status. *Pediatrics, 118*(4), 1010–1018.

Schneider, J., Fujii, M., Lamp, C., Lonnerdal, B., Dewey, K., & Kidenberg-Cherr, S. (2005). Anemia, iron deficiency, and iron deficiency anemia in 12–36 mo-old children from low income families. *American Journal of Clinical Nutrition, 82*(6), 1269–1275.

Schrader, S., Blue, R., & Horner, A. (2005). Better Bones Buddies: An osteoporosis prevention program. *Journal of School Health, 21*(2), 106–114.

Skalicky, A., Meyers, A., Adams, W., Yang, Z., Cook, J., & Frank, D. (2006). Child food insecurity and iron deficiency anemia in low-income infants and toddlers in the United States. *Maternal & Child Health, 10*(2), 177–185.

Taras, H. (2005). Nutrition and student performance at school. *The Journal of School Health, 75*(6), 199–213.

Tinanoff, N., Kanellis, M., & Vargas, C. (2002). Current understanding of the epidemiology mechanisms, and prevention of dental caries in preschool children. *Pediatric Dentistry, 24*(6), 543–551.

HELPFUL WEB RESOURCES

American Academy of Pediatrics	http://www.aap.org
American Dietetic Association	http://www.eatright.org
Child Health Alert	http://www.childhealthalert.com
Food and Nutrition Information Center	http://nal.usda.gov
National Association for the Education of Young Children (NAEYC)	http://www.NAEYC.org
U.S. Department of Agriculture MyPyramid.gov	http://www.mypyramid.gov
Vegetarian Resource Group	http://www.vrg.org

 For additional health, safety, and nutrition resources, go to
http://www.EarlyChildEd.delmar.cengage.com

CHAPTER 16

Nutrients that Regulate Body Functions

(Proteins, Minerals, Water, and Vitamins)

✳ OBJECTIVES

After studying this chapter, you should be able to:

- Name the general body functions regulated by nutrients.
- Identify nutrients that perform regulatory functions in the body.
- List at least one specific function performed by each of the four nutrient classes identified as regulators.

✳ TERMS TO KNOW

milligram (mg)	fat-soluble vitamins	microcytic anemia
microgram (mcg)	water-soluble vitamins	coenzymes
neuromuscular	synthesis	adenosine triphosphate (ATP)
megadose	DNA	hormones
macrocytic anemia	RNA	
toxicity	catalyzes (catalyst)	

All body functions are subject to regulation by nutrients. For example, energy cannot be produced or released from carbohydrates, proteins, and fats without specific nutrients catalyzing sequential steps. New tissues such as bone, blood, or muscles cannot be formed unless specific vitamins, minerals, and proteins are available to perform their primary functions in each of these processes. Nerve impulses will not travel from one nerve cell to another, nor will muscles contract, unless the required nutrients are available in adequate amounts at the appropriate times. The regulation of some body functions involves more than one or two nutrients and reactions. Many other functions involve intricate sequences of reactions that require many nutrients.

The regulation of body functions is an extremely complex process. While much has been learned about the role of nutrients in regulation, there is still much that is unknown. It is important to remember that nutrients and functions are intricately interrelated. No single nutrient can function alone; thus, regulation of body functions often depends on many nutrients. This unit briefly discusses four nutrient classes involved in regulating body functions:

- vitamins
- minerals
- proteins
- water

Protein has been discussed earlier in terms of both energy and growth. Minerals and water were introduced as tissue-building nutrients and will now be considered as regulatory nutrients. Vitamins are able to perform only regulatory functions. They do not yield energy directly, nor do they become part of body structure. However, no energy can be released or any tissue built without benefit of the specific regulatory activities performed by vitamins.

Vitamins and minerals are needed in extremely small amounts. In Chapter 13, Table 13–2, you will find that their RDAs are measured in **milligrams (mg)**, which are one-thousandth of a gram, and in **micrograms (mcg)**, which are one-millionth of a gram. One standard size metal paper clip weighs approximately one gram. Imagine that you smash that paper clip into 1,000 pieces or 1,000,000 pieces and try to envision one milligram or one microgram. Would you expect to see a particle that was one microgram in size?

The regulatory functions discussed in this chapter are crucial to children's normal growth and development (Table 16–1 and Table 16–4). Generally these functions are:

- energy metabolism
- cellular reproduction and growth
- bone growth
- **neuromuscular** development and function
- blood composition control

Although a number of additional functions are involved in the growth process, only those listed above will be discussed because of their critical relationship to children's health and learning potential.

VITAMINS AS REGULATORS

Vitamins are needed in extremely small amounts, but they are essential for normal body function (West, 2003). Each vitamin plays a specific role in a variety of body activities (Table 16–1). Vitamins frequently depend upon one another to perform their functions. For example, the vitamins thiamin and niacin are both needed as crucial coenzymes for the release of energy, but thiamin cannot function in the place of niacin, nor can niacin function in the absence of thiamin's action in a prior step. Study Table 16–1 and note that most vitamins are involved in several different functions; vitamin E may be one exception. It has only one main purpose, but this function is performed in almost every cell in the body.

Vitamins are required and used in specific amounts. Large excesses do not serve any useful function and in some instances are known to be harmful. For example, toxic effects have long been identified for excesses of vitamin A and vitamin D (Brown, 2005). Recent research has described neurological damage resulting from large amounts of vitamin B_6. Kidney stone formation and destruction of vitamin B_{12} stores as a result of a **megadose** of vitamin C (ascorbic acid) have also been described. Megadoses are usually defined as 10 times the recommended daily amount for an

---

milligram (mg) – *a metric unit of measurement; one milligram equals one-thousandth of a gram.*
microgram (mcg) – *a metric unit of measurement; one microgram equals one-millionth of a gram.*
neuromuscular – *pertaining to control of muscular function by the nervous system.*
megadose – *an amount of a vitamin or mineral at least 10 times that of the RDA.*

TABLE 16-1 Vitamin Summary

Vitamin	Functions	Sources	Deficiency Symptoms	Toxicity Symptoms
Fat-soluble Vitamins vitamin A	maintenance of: • remodeling of bones • all cell membranes • epithelial cells; skin • mucous membranes, glands regulation of vision in dim light	liver, whole milk, butter, fortified margarine, orange and dark green vegetables, orange fruits (apricots, nectarines, peaches)	depressed bone and tooth formation, lack of visual acuity, dry epithelial tissue, increased frequency of infections related to epithelial cell vulnerability	headaches, nausea, vomiting, fragile bones, loss of hair, dry skin infant: hydrocephalus, hyperirritability
vitamin D	regulates calcium/phosphorus absorption mineralization of bone	vitamin D fortified milk, exposure of skin to sunlight	rickets (soft, easily bent bones), bone deformities	elevated blood calcium; deposition of calcium in soft tissues resulting in cerebral, renal, and cardiovascular damage (Dubick & Rucker, 1983)
vitamin E	antioxidant	vegetable oils, wheat germ, egg yolk, leafy vegetables, legumes, margarine	red blood cell destruction; creatinuria	fatigue, skin rash, abdominal discomfort
vitamin K	normal blood coagulation	leafy vegetables, vegetable oils, liver, pork; synthesis by intestinal bacteria	hemorrhage	none reported for naturally occurring vitamin K
Water-soluble Vitamins vitamin C (ascorbic acid)	formation of collagen for: • bones/teeth • intercellular cement • wound healing aid to calcium/iron absorption conversion of folacin to active form neurotransmitter synthesis	citrus fruits, strawberries, melons, cabbage, peppers, greens, tomatoes	poor wound healing, bleeding gums, pinpoint hemorrhages, sore joints, scurvy	nausea, abdominal cramps, diarrhea precipitation of kidney stones in susceptible person; "conditioned scurvy" (Dubick & Rucker, 1983)

TABLE 16–1 Vitamin Summary (continued)

Vitamin	Functions	Sources	Deficiency Symptoms	Toxicity Symptoms
thiamin	carbohydrate metabolism energy metabolism neurotransmitter synthesis	whole or enriched grain products, organ meats, pork	loss of appetite, depression, poor neuromuscular control, beriberi	none reported
riboflavin	metabolism of carbo-hydrates, fats, and proteins energy metabolism	dairy foods, meat products, enriched or whole grains, green vegetables	sore tongue, cracks at the corners of the mouth (cheilosis)	none reported
niacin	carbohydrate, protein, and fat metabolism; energy metabolism; conversion of folacin to its active form	meat products, whole or enriched grain products, legumes	dermatitis, diarrhea, depression, and paranoia	flushing, itching, nausea, vomiting, diarrhea, low blood pressure, rapid heart beat, low blood sugar, liver damage (Dubick & Rucker, 1983)
pantothenic acid	energy metabolism; fatty acid metabolism; neuro-transmitter synthesis	nearly all foods	uncommon in humans	none reported
vitamin B$_6$ (Pyridoxine)	protein and fatty acid synthesis; neurotrans-mitter synthesis; hemoglobin synthesis	meats, organ meats, whole grains, legumes, bananas	nervous system: • irritability • tremors • convulsions } infants	unstable gait, numbness, lack of coordination (Schaumberg et al., 1983)

(continued)

TABLE 16-1 Vitamin Summary (continued)

Vitamin	Functions	Sources	Deficiency Symptoms	Toxicity Symptoms
folacin	synthesis of DNA and RNA; cell replication protein synthesis	liver, other meats, green vegetables	macrocytic anemia characterized by unusually large red blood cells; sore tongue, diarrhea	none reported (large amount may hide a B_{12} deficiency)
vitamin B_{12} (Cobalamin)	synthesis of DNA and RNA; conversion of folacin to active form; synthesis of myelin (fatty covering of nerve cells); metabolism of carbohydrates for energy	animal foods, liver, other meats, dairy products, eggs	macrocytic anemia, nervous system damage, sore mouth and tongue, loss of appetite, nausea, vomiting (pernicious anemia results from faulty absorption of B_{12})	none reported
biotin	carbohydrate and fat metabolism; amino acid metabolism	organ meats, milk, egg yolk, yeast; synthesis by intestinal bacteria	nervous disorders, skin disorders, anorexia, muscle pain	none reported

macrocytic anemia – *a failure in the oxygen transport system characterized by abnormally large immature red blood cells.*

adult. There is not enough information to define toxic doses of all vitamins for young children; however, it is certainly smaller than the amount required to produce **toxicity** symptoms in an adult. Therefore, extreme caution should be used if giving children vitamin supplements without a physician's advice. The most common nutrient toxicities in children involve iron. Iron is found in many vitamin supplements and excess intake can cause serious illness or death. "If a little bit is good, a lot is better" is a dangerous practice relative to vitamins.

Vitamins have been the subject of much attention in the press, having been promoted as "cures" for numerous conditions including cancer, common colds, fatigue, depression, and mental illness (Consumers Union, 1998). Many people take vitamins and give them to their children as an "insurance policy" (Gardiner, Dvorkin, & Kemper, 2004). Vitamins can supplement a "hit-or-miss" diet but should not be considered a substitute for adequate nutrient intake. There are a number of reasons why supplements, by themselves, cannot compensate for an inadequate diet. Vitamin and/or mineral supplements do not provide all of the nutrients known to be needed by humans, nor do they provide any calories which are essential for children (Briefel, et al., 2006). Poor diets often lack adequate fiber, essential amino acids, and/or essential fatty acids. These deficiencies cannot be corrected by vitamin/mineral supplements. Also, there may be substances as yet unknown, but essential, which are derived from foods that are not included in vitamin/mineral preparations. The 2005 *Dietary Guidelines for Americans* states, "Because each food group provides a wide array of nutrients in substantial amounts, it is important to include all food groups in the daily diet."

Vitamins are classified as fat-soluble (dissolved in or carried in fats) or water-soluble (dissolved in water). **Fat-soluble vitamins** differ from **water-soluble vitamins** both chemically and functionally. Consuming large doses of fat-soluble vitamins in supplements can cause toxicity because these substances are absorbed and stored in the body for later use. Fat-soluble vitamins are found in many high-fat foods, such as meats, milk and milk products, nuts, avocados, and vegetable oils. Water-soluble vitamins dissolve in water and are absorbed directly into the blood stream and cells. The body is not able to store these vitamins so they are not toxic. Consequently, deficiencies of water-soluble vitamins can develop within a few days if they are not consumed on a regular basis. Water-soluble vitamins are readily available in fruits, vegetables, whole grain products, milk and milk products, and many meats. Table 16–2 provides a summary of the characteristics of these two classes of vitamins.

TABLE 16–2 Characteristics of Vitamins

	Fat-soluble Vitamins	Water-soluble Vitamins
examples	A, D, E, K	vitamin C (ascorbic acid), thiamin, niacin, riboflavin, pantothenic acid, B_6 (pyridoxine), biotin, folacin, B_{12} (cobalamin)
stored in body	yes	no (B_{12} is an exception)
excreted in urine	no	yes
needed daily	no	yes
deficiency	develop slowly (months, years)	develop rapidly (days, weeks)

toxicity – *a state of being poisonous.*
fat-soluble vitamins – *vitamins that are dissolved, transported and stored in fat.*
water-soluble vitamins – *vitamins that are dissolved and transported in water/fluids; cannot be stored.*

Vitamins in Energy Metabolism

A slow steady release of energy is important to body needs. If energy is released in a haphazard fashion, much of it is lost as heat. Since young children require greater amounts of energy per pound, they cannot afford to lose energy in such a fashion. The primary vitamins involved in the regulation of metabolism for the release of energy are:

- thiamin
- niacin
- riboflavin
- pantothenic acid

These four vitamins are important coenzyme components that act as a team to release energy from carbohydrates and fats. However, they are not the only nutrients involved in this process; all of the other required nutrients must also be available in adequate amounts at the time needed.

Vitamins in Cellular Reproduction and Growth

Two vitamins that are absolutely essential for cell growth are folacin and cobalamin (B_{12}). Both vitamins participate in the **synthesis** of **DNA** and **RNA**, which are the chemicals that provide the pattern for cell division and growth. So crucial are these vitamins for cell division and growth that deficiencies are quickly noticeable in tissues that are frequently replaced, such as red blood cells or the cells lining the intestine.

Young children may be considered at risk for both folacin and B_{12} deficiency; both of these vitamins are necessary for the synthesis of protein. Requirements for these nutrients are always increased during periods of rapid growth. The fact that B_{12} is found only in food derived from animal sources must also be considered. Parents must plan children's vegetarian meals carefully to be sure they include adequate vitamin B_{12} and other critical nutrients (Table 16–3) (ADA, 2003). Vitamin B_{12} supplementation is usually recommended when no animal products are included in children's diet.

⊞ TABLE 16–3 Replacing Animal Sources of Nutrients

Vegetarians who eat no animal products need to be more aware of nutrient sources. Nutrients most likely to be lacking and their nonanimal sources are:

- **vitamin B$_{12}$**—fortified soy beverages and cereals
- **vitamin D**—fortified soy beverages and sunshine
- **calcium**—tofu processed with calcium, broccoli, seeds, nuts, kale, bok choy, legumes (peas and beans), greens, lime products, and orange juice enriched with calcium
- **iron**—legumes, tofu, green leafy vegetables, dried fruit, whole grains, and iron-fortified cereals and breads, especially whole-wheat (Absorption is improved by vitamin C, found in citrus fruits and juices, tomatoes, strawberries, broccoli, peppers, dark-green processed tortillas, and soy beverages, grain, leafy vegetables, and potatoes with skins.)
- **zinc**—whole grains (especially the germ and bran), whole-wheat bread, legumes, nuts, and tofu
- **protein**—tofu and other soy-based products, legumes, seeds, nuts, grains, and vegetables

Courtesy of *FDA Consumer*, October 1995.

---

synthesis – *the process of making a compound by the union of simpler compounds or elements.*
DNA – *deoxyribonucleic acid; the substance in the cell nucleus that codes for genetically transmitted traits.*
RNA – *ribonucleic acid; the nucleic acid that serves as messenger between the nucleus and the ribosomes where proteins are synthesized.*

Vegetarian diets are classified by the extent to which the diet includes animal foods:

- lacto-ovo-vegetarian—diary foods and eggs included
- lacto-vegetarian—dairy foods included, but no eggs
- vegan—no animal source foods included, including items such as honey

It was formerly thought that vegan diets could not adequately meet children's nutrient needs. In a 1997 position paper on vegetarianism, the American Dietetic Association stated that, "because vegan diets tend to be high in bulk, care should be taken to ensure that calorie intakes are sufficient to meet every need." Infants and children who consume well-planned vegetarian diets can generally meet all of their nutritional requirements for growth. Table 16–3 lists those nutrients most likely to be deficient in the vegetarian diet and includes alternative (nonanimal) sources.

Some general recommendations for assuring that children obtain the vitamins needed for optimal growth include:

- Minimize intake of less nutritious foods such as sweets and fatty foods.
- Choose whole or unrefined grain products instead of refined products.
- Choose a variety of nuts, seeds, legumes, fruits, and vegetables, including good sources of vitamin C to improve iron absorption.
- Choose low fat varieties of dairy products, if they are included in the diet.
- Vegans should use properly fortified sources of vitamin B_{12}, such as fortified soy beverages or cereals, or take a supplement (FDA Consumer, October 1995).

Cellular reproduction and growth are dependent on proteins, folacin and B_{12}. One vitamin that is essential to the metabolism of proteins is pyridoxine (B_6). Pyridoxine **catalyzes** the chemical changes that permit the building of proteins from amino acids or the breakdown of proteins to provide needed amino acids.

Vitamins That Regulate Bone Growth

The minerals calcium and phosphorus are the major structural components of bones and teeth. However, bone growth also depends on a number of other nutrients as regulators, including vitamins A, C, and D (Figure 16–1).

FIGURE 16–1

Many nutrients are involved in the regulation of body functions.

---

catalyzes – *accelerates a chemical reaction.*

Vitamin A regulates the destruction of old bone cells and their replacement by new ones. This process is known as "remodeling."

Vitamin C functions in two ways in the formation of bone tissue:

- maintains the solubility of calcium, making it more available for absorption
- aids in the formation of collagen, the flexible protein foundation upon which phosphorus and calcium are deposited

Vitamin D is necessary for the absorption of calcium and phosphorus, the major constituents of bones and teeth. It is also needed to assure blood levels of calcium and phosphorus that allow for deposition of these minerals in bones and teeth.

Vitamins That Regulate Neuromuscular Function

Vitamins play a role in neuromuscular functioning either through the synthesis of neurotransmitters (chemical messengers) or through growth or maintenance of nerve cells.

Vitamin B_6 and vitamin C, thiamin, and niacin catalyze the synthesis of neurotransmitters that carry messages to all organs and regulate nerve-muscle activities. Deficiencies of these vitamins result in neurological abnormalities.

Vitamins B_6 and B_{12} are necessary for the formation and maintenance of the myelin sheath, the insulative layer surrounding nerve cells, and are therefore especially critical for developing infants and young children. Faulty myelin sheath formation and maintenance results in abnormal passage of nerve impulses, which may result in numbness, tremors, or loss of coordination.

Recent research has determined that maternal deficiency of folacin may result in cleft lip, cleft palate, and neural tube defects that develop during the first months of fetal life (Anthony, 2007; Carmichael, et., al, 2007; Leung & Ernest, 2007; Pitkin, 2007). Neural tube defects, commonly known as spina bifida, result in an incomplete formation of the spinal column (nerves and bone) and brain. Folacin is readily found in fruits, vegetables, dried beans and legumes, and fortified whole grain products. Prenatal vitamins contain folacin; however, neural tube defects often occur before the mother realizes that she is pregnant. Consequently, many foods and grain products are now being fortified with folacin.

Vitamins That Regulate Blood Formation

Some vitamins play an important role in the formation of blood cells and hemoglobin. Hemoglobin, the red pigment of the red blood cells, carries oxygen to all cells of the body and carries the waste product, carbon dioxide, away from the cells to the lungs. Vitamins needed for the production of red blood cells and hemoglobin are:

- vitamin E
- pantothenic acid
- vitamin B_6 (pyridoxine)
- folacin
- vitamin B_{12} (cobalamin)

MINERALS AS REGULATORS

Many body functions require the presence of specific minerals (Table 16–4). The amounts of minerals required for regulatory purposes are smaller than those needed for building or repairing body tissue. Minerals used by the body for regulatory purposes are usually parts of enzymes or coenzymes or may catalyze their action.

TABLE 16-4 Mineral Summary

Mineral	Functions	Sources	Deficiency Symptoms	Toxicity Symptoms
calcium	major component of bones and teeth; collagen formation; muscle contraction; secretion/release of insulin; neurotransmitters; blood	dairy products, turnip or collard greens, canned salmon or sardines, soybeans or soybean curd (tofu)	poor growth, small adult size, fragile and deformed bones, some form of rickets	unlikely: absorption is controlled; symptoms usually result from excess vitamin D or hormonal imbalance
phosphorus	major component of bones and teeth; energy metabolism; component of DNA and RNA	dairy products, meats, legumes, grains; additive in soft drinks	rare with normal diet	large amounts may depress calcium absorption
magnesium	major components of bones and teeth; activator of enzymes for ATP use; required for synthesis of DNA and RNA and for synthesis of proteins by RNA	nuts, seeds, green vegetables, legumes, whole grains	poor neuromuscular coordination, tremors, convulsions	unlikely
sodium	nerve impulse transmission; fluid balance; acid-base balance	meats, fish, poultry, eggs, milk, (naturally occurring sodium); many processed and cured foods (added sodium), salt, MSG	rare (losses from sweat may cause dizziness, nausea, muscle cramps)	linked to high blood pressure in some persons; confusion; coma

(continued)

TABLE 16-4 Mineral Summary (continued)

Mineral	Functions	Sources	Deficiency Symptoms	Toxicity Symptoms
potassium	nerve impulse transmission; fluid balance; acid-base balance	fruits (bananas, orange juice), vegetables, whole grains, fresh meats, fish	weakness, irregular heartbeat	unlikely from food sources
iron	component of hemoglobin; enzymes involved in oxygen utilization	liver, oysters, meats, enriched and whole grains, leafy green vegetables	microcytic anemia (characterized by small, pale red blood cells), fatigue, pallor, shortness of breath	unlikely (may be due to genetic defect)
zinc	component of many enzymes involved in: protein metabolism, DNA/RNA synthesis collagen formation wound healing	liver, oysters, meats, eggs, whole grains, legumes	retarded growth, loss of senses of taste and smell, delayed wound healing	excess supplementation may interfere with iron/copper metabolism nausea, vomiting, diarrhea, gastric ulcers
iodine	component of thyroxin, which regulates basal metabolic rate; regulates physical and mental growth	iodized salt, seafoods, many processed foods	goiter, physical dwarfing, cretinism if deficiency occurs during fetal life	iodism; rashes; bronchitis

microcytic anemia – *a failure in the oxygen transport system characterized by abnormally small red blood cells.*

> ## REFLECTIVE THOUGHTS
>
> What are your thoughts about vitamin and/or mineral pills? They are staples in the lives of millions of Americans, but are they necessary? Vitamin/mineral pills are safe for adults if they provide no more than 100 percent daily RDAs.
>
> - Are they a good buy if they only have a placebo affect?
> - Would you recommend vitamin/mineral pills for young children?
>
> Think about the risks involved in giving vitamin/mineral supplements to children. Because they often look and taste like candy, it is easy for children to ingest an amount of supplements that could cause toxic symptoms and even death. However, there are circumstances when supplements can be beneficial for adults and children.
>
> - Think of the benefit risk ratio for both children and adults.

Minerals in Energy Metabolism

Minerals also play an important role in the steady, efficient release of energy. This process of energy metabolism (production, storage, and release) depends on adequate amounts of:

- phosphorus
- magnesium
- iodine
- iron

Phosphorus is necessary for the production of enzymes and **coenzymes** required for energy-releasing metabolism, and also for the formation of **adenosine triphosphate (ATP)**, the chemical substance in which potential energy is stored in body cells. Another mineral, magnesium, is necessary for both the storage and the release of the energy trapped in ATP. Iron functions as part of one of the key enzyme systems in the final stages of energy metabolism. Iodine is a component of the hormone thyroxin. As such, iodine aids in the control of the rate at which the body uses energy (the basal metabolic rate) for involuntary activities.

Minerals in Cellular Reproduction and Growth

Minerals required for cellular reproduction and growth include:

- phosphorus
- magnesium
- zinc

Phosphorus is a structural component of both DNA and RNA. Magnesium is required both for the synthesis of DNA and for synthesis of proteins from the pattern provided by DNA. Zinc functions as part of an enzyme system that must be active during DNA and RNA synthesis. DNA allows cells to reproduce and to synthesize proteins needed for growth.

A lack of adequate zinc can result in stunted growth, decreased acuity of taste and smell that may further decrease food intake, and delayed sexual maturity. Zinc is chemically related to iron so that its absorption is affected by many of the same factors. Excessive supplementation with calcium and/or iron can also seriously reduce the availability of zinc.

---

coenzymes – *a vitamin-containing substance required by certain enzymes before they can perform their prescribed function.*
adenosine triphosphate (ATP) – *a compound with energy-storing phosphate bonds that is the main energy source for all cells.*

Minerals That Regulate Neuromuscular Function

Passage of nerve impulses from nerve cell to nerve cell or from nerve cell to muscle is dependent on the presence of:

- sodium
- potassium
- calcium
- magnesium

Sodium and potassium act to change the electrical charge on the surface of nerve cells, allowing the passage of nerve impulses. Calcium is required for the release of many neurotransmitters from nerve cells. The passage of a nerve impulse to a muscle cell causes the contraction of muscles. Calcium is required for the actual contraction of a muscle, while ATP, which contains phosphorus as a structural component, provides the energy for the contraction to take place. Sodium and potassium promote the relaxation phase of muscle contraction. Magnesium also helps to regulate neuromuscular activity and causing muscle relaxation.

Minerals in Blood Formation

Blood is the medium responsible for transporting all regulatory minerals. Iron is a structural part of hemoglobin and an important component of blood. Copper aids with the absorption of iron and its incorporation into hemoglobin. Calcium is also necessary for the production of substances required to trigger blood coagulation.

❖ PROTEINS AS REGULATORS

Proteins are the only class of nutrients that can perform all three general functions of nutrients. They build and repair body tissue, regulate body functions, and provide energy.

 ISSUES TO CONSIDER • Food Supplement Safety

"Food supplements" are appearing in the food market in increasing numbers and are often in the news. Traditionally, food supplements were made of one or more essential nutrients believed to be needed in the diet in greater amounts, or they were promoted as cures for some disease or health condition. Now the term has been broadened to include products that are ingested to supplement one's diet, such as herbs and other plant-derived substances that might improve health. The magic of using the term "food supplement" is that it can be used to advertise a substance as a cure for a condition or disease without demonstrating any proof. Manufacturers do not have to submit their product to the Food and Drug Administration (FDA) for testing and approval before it can be offered for sale. Promoting herbs, often as pills, for the cure of many conditions is a concern of nutritionists, professional health care personnel, and pharmacists. A food supplement must now carry on its label the statement: "This product is not approved by the FDA."

- Will this label serve as a warning that this may not be a safe product to use?
- Does using the term "natural" give assurance that a product is safe?
- Why is it important that a person check with his or her doctor and pharmacist before using any of these products?
- Why is there so much concern about the increasing use of herbs as food supplements?

Proteins in Energy Metabolism and Growth Regulation

Proteins (amino acids) are important components of enzymes and some hormones and thus play a major role in the regulation of energy metabolism. The body must have an adequate supply of protein in order to produce these important enzymes and hormones.

All body functions are dependent on the presence and activity of enzymes. Enzymes are defined as protein catalysts. A catalyst is a substance that regulates a chemical reaction without becoming part of that reaction. The sequential metabolism for release of energy requires many steps; each step requires at least one enzyme specific for the particular reaction. Many enzymes require vitamin-containing coenzymes to enable them to catalyze their specific chemical reactions.

Hormones are substances that are secreted by glands for action on tissue elsewhere in the body. As such, they regulate many body functions. Although not all hormones are composed of amino acids, two amino-acid dependent hormones, thyroxin and insulin, are required in energy metabolism.

Thyroxin regulates the rate at which energy is used for involuntary activities. It is secreted by the thyroid gland. Insulin is secreted by the pancreas. Its presence is necessary for glucose to be absorbed by the body cells so that it may be used as an energy source for cellular activity. Insulin and adrenalin (another amino acid-dependent hormone) act together to maintain normal blood glucose levels.

WATER AS A REGULATOR

The initial step of processing food for use by the body is digestion. Digestion is the process by which food is broken down mechanically and chemically into nutrients that can be used by the body. Food composition is changed during chemical digestion through the breakdown of nutrient molecules by the addition of water. Water is added at appropriate places in the molecules of protein, fats, and carbohydrates to break them into units small enough to be absorbed and used by the cells. Water is essential for many processes as the medium in which chemical reactions take place (Figure 16–2).

After food is digested, nutrients are absorbed and carried in solution via the blood and lymph to the cells. Again, water serves as the main transporting agent and comprises all body fluids including blood, lymph, and tissue fluid. It also is the major component of body secretions such as salivary juice, gastric juice, bile, perspiration, and expirations from the lungs. Water also plays a major role in ridding the body of waste material. Soluble body waste is carried out in urine, which is 95 percent water. Water also regulates body temperature during changes in environmental temperature and activity-related heat production. It is important that children be given plain water rather than juice or other sweetened beverages because sugar greatly reduces water absorption.

SUMMARY FOR UNIT 4

Approximately 40 nutrients are recognized as essential for providing energy, allowing normal growth for the child and maintenance for the adult. Each nutrient has its special function(s). Some nutrients share functions and in many cases the function of any given nutrient is dependent upon one or more other nutrients being present. The purpose of the following summary chart is to help you understand some of these functional interrelationships and reduce some confusion about what nutrients really do in the body. You might make this a personal study by associating each functional unit with the part of your own body. For example, when listing nutrient needs for bones and teeth, envision your own bones and teeth and what these nutrients are doing for them.

---

hormones – *special chemical substances produced by endocrine glands that influence and regulate certain body functions.*

FIGURE 16-2

Water is necessary for the regulation of many body functions.

Summary of Biological Functions of Nutrients

Functional Unit	Nutrients Involved	Specific Function
blood formation and maintenance	calcium vitamin K protein	blood clotting
	iron copper vitamin B_6 folacin	hemoglobin production
	folacin vitamin B_{12}	production of red blood cells

Summary of Biological Functions of Nutrients (continued)

Functional Unit	Nutrients Involved	Specific Function
bone and teeth development	calcium phosphorus magnesium	components of bones and teeth
	vitamin C vitamin A vitamin D	building and remodeling of bones
nerve-muscle development and activity	vitamin C thiamin niacin vitamin B_6 pantothenic acid calcium potassium	transmission of nerve impulses
	calcium magnesium potassium sodium thiamin pantothenic acid	regulates muscle contraction and relaxation
growth and maintenance of body parts	protein phosphorus zinc selenium vitamin B_6 folacin	regulates cell division and synthesis of needed cell proteins
	iodine	regulates physical and mental growth
availability of energy for cellular activity	carbohydrates fats proteins	may be "burned" to release energy
	phosphorus magnesium thiamin riboflavin niacin pantothenic acid biotin	roles in enzyme and coenzyme production to release energy
	iodine	regulates basal metabolic energy needs

FOCUS ON FAMILIES • Nutrients That Regulate Body Functions

Water is essential for the regulation of body functions. Although water is abundantly available, getting children and adults to consume adequate amounts continues to be a challenge. Water has many competitors such as sodas, fruit drinks, fruit beverages, sport drinks, and fruit ades that children often find more appealing. These beverages, however, provide little nutritional value while adding large amounts of calories and sugar. Given the continuing increases in childhood obesity and dental caries, it is important that families and teachers encourage children to drink more water and set a good example for them to follow.

- Limit or avoid purchasing sweetened beverages. If these items are not readily available in the home, your child is more likely to drink water and other nutritious beverages such as milk and 100 percent fruit juice.

- Keep a pitcher of water available in the refrigerator with small cups within the child's reach. Smaller cups are less intimidating and more manageable.

- When traveling from home or participating in physical activities, encourage your child to carry a water bottle to quench his or her thirst. This is more economical than purchasing beverages from vending machines or convenience stores and will provide more health benefits in comparison to sodas, fruit drinks, fruit beverages, and fruit ades.

CASE STUDY

Tony, age four-and-one-half, is allergic to citrus fruits. Even a few drops of juice cause him to break out in hives.

1. For what nutrient should Tony's diet be closely monitored?

2. a. If Tony's diet is actually deficient in this nutrient, would symptoms appear rapidly or slowly?

   b. Why?

3. Suggest foods other than citrus fruits that could also provide this nutrient.

4. List two symptoms of deficiency that you might anticipate Tony to display.

5. a. Should Tony be given supplements of this nutrient to offset possible deficiencies?

   b. Why or why not?

CLASSROOM CORNER • Teacher Activities

Let's Make Pizza

Concept: Pizza can provide many of the nutrients your body needs. (Pre–2)

Learning Objectives

- Children will learn how to make pizza.

- Children will learn pizza can be a healthy food.

- Child will learn the names of the ingredients.

CLASSROOM CORNER • Teacher Activities (continued)

Supplies

- English muffins (one-half per child); one can of pizza sauce; one red pepper; one green pepper; one package pepperoni or diced ham; one can of black olives; one can of pineapple chunks; one bag of mozzarella cheese; two cookie sheets; seven plastic spoons; hand wipes

Learning Activities

- Read and discuss one of the following books:
  - *Pizza Party* by Grace Maccarone
  - *Pizza Pat* by Rita Golden Gelman
  - *Pizza* by Saturnino Romay
- Tell children they are going to make pizza. Ask children what kind of pizza they like to eat. Explain the process for making pizza (first get an English muffin, spread on pizza sauce, add remaining ingredients, cover with cheese). Have children name each ingredient.
- Set up ingredients on a table and have several children come up at a time to make their pizzas. Once pizzas are made, put them on a cookie sheet (be sure to identify each child's pizza so they can eat their own).
- Talk about different ingredients they put on their pizza and how each can help their body.

Evaluation

- Children will be able to follow the process on making a pizza.
- Children will know pizza can be a healthy food choice.
- Children can name some ingredients used to make pizza.

SUMMARY

- Proteins, minerals, and vitamins are nutrient classes that regulate body activity.
- Vitamins function only as regulators, but they are essential for reactions involved with energy release, growth by cell division, bone and blood formation, and brain and nerve activities.
- Minerals are required for the same regulatory functions as vitamins in addition to regulating water balance in the body.
- Proteins, in addition to providing energy and supporting growth, function in many regulatory reactions.
- Enzymes are special proteins needed in the many stages of metabolism to provide energy to all body cells.
- Proteins, or their amino acids, are parts of hormones that control the rate of many reactions that release energy for body use.
- Water, as the medium in which most nutrient functions take place, regulates a majority of nutrient activity and transports all nutrients after they enter the body. Water is also the prime regulator of body temperature.

APPLICATION ACTIVITIES

1. Using the vitamin and mineral summaries in Tables 16–1 and 16–4, list two specific foods or types of foods that are rich sources of each of the following nutrients:

   magnesium   thiamin
   calcium   riboflavin

   a. What foods are good sources of more than one of these nutrients?
   b. Which nutrients occur in the same types of foods?
   c. Which nutrients do not occur in the same types of foods?
   d. Which nutrients are found mostly in animal-source foods?
   e. Which nutrients are found mostly in plant-foods?

CHAPTER REVIEW

A. **By Yourself:**

   1. What two minerals are required for energy metabolism?

   2. What two minerals are required for cellular division and growth?

   3. Name an important nutrient component of enzymes and some hormones.

   4. Which nutrient is the prime regulator of body temperature?

   5. What role(s) does water play in the body?

B. **As a Group:**

   1. Read the position statement, "Vegetarian Diets," issued by the American Dietetic Association (http://www.eatright.org) & Dietitians of Canada (http://www.dietitians.ca) (2003). What are the benefits and limitations of a vegetarian diet for young children?

   2. Discuss the role fluoride plays in the formation and maintenance of tooth enamel.

   3. Identify five non-dairy sources of calcium. Are they an adequate substitute?

   4. Discuss why vitamins A and C are considered to be at-risk vitamins for young children.

   5. React to the statement, "I take vitamins just to be sure I get everything I need."

REFERENCES

American Dietetic Association (ADA). (2003). Vegetarian diets (revised statement). *Journal of the American Dietetic Association, 103*(6), 748–765.

ADA. (1997). Vegetarian diets. *Journal of the American Dietetic Association, 97,* 1317–1321.

Anthony, A. (2007). In utero physiology: Role of folic acid in nutrient delivery and fetal development. *American Journal of Clinical Nutrition, 85*(2), 598S–603S.

Briefel, R., Hanson, C., Fox, M., Novak, T., & Ziegler, P. (2006). Feeding infants and toddlers study: Do vitamin and mineral supplements contribute to nutrient adequacy or excess among US infants and toddlers? *Journal of the American Dietetic Association, 106*(1), 52–65.

Brown, J. (2005). *Nutrition now.* Belmont, CA: Thomson Wadsworth.

Carmichael, S., Yang, W., Herring, A., Abrams, B., & Shaw, G. (2007). Maternal food insecurity is associated with increased risk of certain birth defects. *Journal of Nutrition, 137*(9), 2087–2092.

Consumers Union. (1998, April). *Consumer reports on health—1998: Vitamins and minerals and herbs.* Yonkers, NY: Consumers Union.

FDA Consumer Publication. (1995, October). *More people trying vegetarian diets.* Washington, DC: U.S. Department of Agriculture.

Gardiner, P., Dvorkin, L., & Kemper, K. (2004). Supplement use growing among children and adolescents. *Pediatric Annals, 33*(4), 227–232.

Leung, D. & Ernest, J. (2007). Pre-conceptual folic acid supplementation in uninsured pregnant Hispanic women. *Southern Medical Journal, 100*(1), 85–96.

Pitkin, R. (2007). Folate and neural tube defects. *American Journal of Clinical Nutrition, 85*(1), 285S–288S.

West, K. (2003). Vitamin A deficiency disorders in children and women. *Food & Nutrition Bulletin, 24*(4), 78–90.

HELPFUL WEB RESOURCES

Federal Citizen Information Center	http://www.pueblo.gsa.gov
Mayo Clinic Health Letter	http://www.mayoclinic.com
Tufts University Nutrition Science and Policy	http://www.nutrition.tufts.edu
United States Department of Agriculture (USDA)	http://www.fns.usda.gov

For additional health, safety, and nutrition resources, go to http://www.EarlyChildEd.delmar.cengage.com

Nutrition and the Young Child

CHAPTER 17

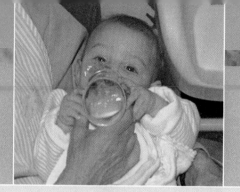

Infant Feeding

❊ OBJECTIVES

After studying this chapter, you should be able to:

- Discuss the advantages of breastfeeding.
- Describe the proper way to bottle-feed an infant.
- Describe ways to feed the breast-fed infant in a child care setting.
- Identify the appropriate ages at which to introduce semi-solid foods to infants.
- Name recommended safe foods to use as first semi-solid foods.
- Give criteria for selecting nutritious solid food for the baby and evaluate benefits of commercial versus home-prepared semi-solid food.
- Evaluate nutrient contributions of different types of commercial baby food and make appropriate choices.

❊ TERMS TO KNOW

prenatal	distention	palmar grasp
low-birthweight (LBW) infant	regurgitation	pincer grip
antibodies	developmental readiness or	type 1 diabetes
aseptic procedures	physiological readiness	electrolyte(s)

❊ PROFILE OF AN INFANT

During the first year of a child's life, the rate of growth and development is more rapid than at any other period in the life cycle (Allen & Marotz, 2007). Infants will double their weight during the first five to six months and will approximately triple their birth weight by the end of the first year. Birth length may be expected to increase by 50 percent by the child's first birthday.

Infants are totally dependent upon their families and teachers to protect them from environmental hazards, such as temperature change and pathogenic organisms, and to provide the necessary nutrients in a safe and useable form. The giving of food must be coupled with socializing and much tender loving care (TLC). Without TLC, infants' growth and development can be seriously delayed even when they are receiving all of the nutrients they need (Black, et al., 2006; Robinson, 2002; Weiss, et al., 2001). Infants require physical and emotional stimulation to help them learn. Food and the feeding relationship can help to meet many of the infant's needs by providing a variety of tastes, colors, temperatures, textures, physical contact, and visual and social interaction.

TABLE 17-1 Infant Feeding Guidelines

Food	Age (months)					
	0–2	2–4	4–6	6–8	9–10	11–12
human milk/formula (oz)	18–28	25–32	27–45	24–32	24–32	24–32
iron-fortified cereal (tbsp)			4–8	4–6	4–6	4–6
zwieback, dry toast				1	1	1–2
vegetable, plain, strained (tbsp)				3–4	6–8	7–8 (soft, chopped)
fruit, plain, strained (tbsp)				3–4	6–8	8 (soft, cooked, chopped)
meat, plain, strained (tbsp)				1–2	4–6	4–5 (ground or chopped)
egg yolk (tbsp)					1	1
fruit juice (oz)				2–4	4	4
potato, rice, noodles (tbsp)						8

Reprinted by permission from Morrison Management Specialists, *Manual of clinical nutrition management*. Atlanta, GA, 2003.

Within the first 12 months, infants will progress from a diet that consists solely of breast milk or formula to one that gradually includes semi-solid foods and finally to a modified adult diet that includes them in the family meal time (Table 17–1).

MEETING NUTRITIONAL NEEDS OF THE INFANT

The rapid rate of growth and development that is characteristic of infancy must be supported by adequate nutrient intake—protein, carbohydrates, and fat. An infant's nutrient and calorie needs are especially high during this first year, but their stomach capacity is quite small. This explains the infant's need for frequent feedings of nutrient-dense food.

The infant's needs for all nutrients remain high in proportion to their body size throughout the first year. However, their social and emotional needs must also be met to ensure optimal growth and development (Feldman, et al., 2004). The growth rate is especially rapid during the first four months which accounts for the infant's very high energy needs. For example, a newborn requires approximately 50 calories per pound of body weight daily until five to six months of age. One-fourth to one-third of these calories are used for growth. As the infant progresses through the first year and becomes more mobile, fewer calories are needed for growth and more are required for physical activity (Figure 17–1). By six months of age the infant requires only 40–45 calories per pound.

An infant's nutritional needs may be conditioned by the mother's nutritional status during pregnancy. A common consequence of poor **prenatal** (conception to birth) nutrition is a

---

prenatal – *the period from conception to birth of the baby.*

FIGURE 17–1

Older infants require fewer calories for growth but more for physical activity.

low-birthweight (LBW) infant. The incidence of serious illness and death is very high for low-birthweight infants during their first year. In addition, LBW infants often experience a high rate of serious health problems such as:

- poor regulation of body temperature
- increased susceptibility to infection
- difficulty in metabolizing carbohydrates, fats, and proteins
- delayed development of kidneys and digestive organs
- poorly calcified bones—reduced bone density
- poor iron stores resulting in neonatal anemia
- presentation of vitamin deficiencies during neonatal period (birth to 28 days): vitamin E, folacin, and pyridoxine deficiencies are most common

Infants at highest risk for these problems are those born to teen-age mothers who must meet their own high nutrient needs for growth in addition to providing nutrients for the developing fetus. Common prenatal nutritional deficiencies that produce low-birthweight babies are:

- protein
- energy
- folacin
- vitamin D
- pyridoxine

Prenatal nutrient deficiencies may be partially corrected, but rarely totally reversed, by supplementing for the baby's deficient nutrient needs immediately after birth. The WIC (Women, Infants, and Children) program, which provides food supplements for pregnant and breastfeeding women, infants, and children up to the age of five, has been very effective in reducing the incidence of prenatal, infant, and child malnutrition (Black, et al., 2004). WIC currently serves approximately 45 percent of all infants born in the United States and provides nutrition and child care information in a number of languages (Figure 17–2).

---

low-birthweight (LBW) infant – *an infant who weighs less than 5.5 pounds (2,500 grams) at birth.*

FIGURE 17–2

WIC provides nutrition and child care information in several languages.

Cómo Atender A Un Bebé Molesto

Cargar y abrazar a su bebé es muy importante y le dará la seguridad y el amor que ella necesita para crecer. **Esto NO la va a malcriar.**

Si su bebé esta molesta, o llora mucho, ella posiblemente . . .

. . . tenga hambre.

Dé pecho cada vez que ella tenga hambre. Signos de que el bebé tiene hambre incluyen: chuparse las manos, o mamar y mover la cabeza como si buscara el pecho.

. . . necesite atención.

"Abrace" a su bebé en vez de usar un portador de bebés.

. . . esté muy agitada o muy cansada.

♥ Cálmela meciéndola suavemente de lado a lado, muchísimo contacto de piel con piel, baños tibios, luces bajas y música suave.

. . . esté teniendo un periodo de crecimiento rápido.

♥ A las 2, 6, y 12 semanas su bebé puede que tenga hambre más seguido porque está creciendo más rápido. Aliméntela cuando ella parezca que tenga hambre.

. . . puede ser sensible a la cafeína.

♥ Trate de no tomar café, refrescos de cola ó té.

. . . está enferma.

♥ llame al doctor, especialmente si tiene fiebre, y siga dando pecho.

El Programa WIC es un empleador y proveedor de igualdad de oportunidad

Developed by South Los Angeles Health Projects, REI WIC Program FB5/03s

The First Six Months

During the first six months, the infant's nutritional needs can be met solely with breast milk or formula. Breast milk and formula are both high in fat and provide approximately 650 calories per quart to meet the infant's energy needs. The full-term infant is born with a temporary store of iron and vitamin A that lasts approximately five to six months. However, a premature infant may require supplements of these nutrients during this period. No semi-solid foods are needed or advisable until the infant is at least five months of age. Younger infants are not developmentally or physiologically ready to ingest solid foods (this is discussed later in the chapter).

The benefits of breastfeeding continue to gain increased attention and support. The American Academy of Pediatrics urges mothers to breastfeed infants exclusively during the first six months and continue until one year of age if possible (AAP, 2005). Scientific evidence demonstrates a positive relationship between breastfeeding and a reduced risk of some childhood health problems, including SIDS, ear infection (otitis media), allergies and asthma, diabetes, and bacterial meningitis (Chantry, Howard, & Auinger, 2006; Nelson, Yu, & Williams, 2005; Pettigrew, et al., 2003; Duffy, et al., 1997). In addition, researchers have found that some children show small gains in development and intellectual function (Gibson-Davis & Brooks-Gunn, 2006; Jensen, et al., 2005; Slykerman, et al., 2005). A summary of the advantages of breast milk are presented in Table 17–2. Breastfeeding also requires that mothers increase some nutrients in their own diet (Table 17–3).

Some mothers may elect formula feeding as the best approach after giving careful consideration to their health and lifestyle factors. Conditions that might cause a mother to choose formula feeding are:

- illness of the mother
- mother needs to take medications
- mother needs to be away from the child for long periods of time

TABLE 17–2   Advantages of Breastfeeding

Breast Milk:
- has all of the nutrients needed by the infant for the first six months
- contains proteins that are more digestible than cow's milk protein
- contains lactose, the main carbohydrate component, which aids in calcium absorption and in establishing beneficial intestinal flora
- provides **antibodies** (immunoglobulins) that protect the infant from some infectious illnesses
- has a higher content of the essential fatty acids
- provides taurine*
- provides dietary nucleotides**
- is less likely to cause food allergies
- reduces the risk of bacteria entering the infant's body from unsanitary formula preparation
- is inexpensive, convenient, and always available at the correct temperature
- contains less sodium (salt) than formulas
- fosters emotional bonding between mother and infant
- is a biologically active substance, changing in nutrient composition to meet the infant's changing needs

*Taurine is a free amino acid (not found in proteins) that is particularly important for the normal growth and development of the central nervous system. It is now added to some formulas, especially those for premature infants.
**Dietary nucleotides play a role in the infant's ability to produce antibodies in response to exposure to infectious organisms. The American Academy of Pediatrics currently recommends that these be added to all prepared formulas.

antibodies – *special substances produced by the body that help protect against disease.*

> ❋ **TABLE 17-3 Breastfeeding and a Mother's Dietary Needs**
>
> Mothers who are breastfeeding need to increase their daily intake of some nutrients, including:
> - approximately 500 additional calories
> - 15–20 grams of protein
> - vitamins A, C, and folacin
> - calcium (equivalent of one extra serving)
> - an additional four cups of fluids
> - vitamin B_{12} and D (if no animal products are consumed)

- mother prefers not to nurse
- mother uses addictive drugs, including tobacco

Regardless of the feeding method that is chosen, teachers must be accepting and willing to assist families in meeting their infants' nutritional needs. Mothers should never be made to feel guilty or that they have made the wrong decision.

The Teacher and the Breastfeeding Mother

The mother who is employed outside the home may choose to continue breast-feeding. She may use a breast-pump or hand express her milk and refrigerate or freeze it so that caregivers can feed it to her baby while she is at work. Breast milk can be refrigerated (40°F) in a sterile container and used within 48 hours; it can also be frozen (0°F), preferably in hard plastic containers (to avoid breakage or tears) and used within three months from the time it was expressed. Frozen breast milk must never be refrozen once it has been thawed. Containers should be clearly labeled with the date and the baby's name.

Teachers should also be supportive and willing to assist the mother who is able to come and nurse her infant during the day (Aird, 2002; Morris, 1995) (Table 17–4).

Safe Handling of Breast Milk Human milk varies in color, consistency, and odor, depending on the mother's diet and storage container used. Since breast milk is not homogenized, the cream may rise to the top of the container. Shaking it briefly before feeding helps to remix the layers. Safe handling by the teacher includes following these steps:

- Wash hands well before touching any milk containers. Avoid touching the inside of bottles or caps.
- Request that mothers label containers with the date when milk was collected; use the oldest milk first.

> ❋ **TABLE 17-4 Teacher Checklist: Support for Nursing Mothers**
>
> Early childhood programs can provide an environment that will support mothers who wish to nurse their infants at the facility by:
> - creating a private area that is quiet and comfortable
> - having a place where mothers can wash their hands before and after nursing
> - providing a comfortable chair (a rocking chair if possible) and a foot rest to relieve back strain
> - making water or other fluids available for mothers to drink
> - having the infant ready (e.g., awake, diapers changed, infant's hands cleaned) when mother arrives

TABLE 17–5 Thawing Frozen Breast Milk Safely

1. Wash your hands with soap and water before touching the breast milk container.
2. Place the sealed container of breast milk in a bowl of warm water for about 30 minutes, or hold the container of four ounces of human milk under warm running water for approximately four minutes. **NEVER MICROWAVE BREAST MILK!** Microwaving can alter the nutritional composition of breast milk and also cause burns to the baby due to uneven heating.
3. Swirl the container to blend any fat that may have separated and risen during thawing.
4. Feed thawed milk immediately or store in the refrigerator for a maximum of 24 hours.
5. **NEVER REFREEZE BREAST MILK.**

- If breast milk is to be stored for more than 48 hours, it should be frozen. (See Table 17–5 for safe thawing instructions.)
- Frozen breast milk may be safely stored in a freezer ($0°F$) for up to three months.

The Teacher and the Formula-Fed Infant

Although breastfeeding offers important benefits, many infants in child care programs will be formula fed. The infant's family and health care provider will determine which formula is best for the infant. Commercial infant formulas are prepared to closely resemble breast milk in composition relative to the amount of protein, carbohydrate, and fat. Most infant formulas are made from modified cow's milk or soy products and are available in powder, liquid concentrates, or as ready-to-feed liquids. Infants who have difficulty tolerating milk-based formulas may be switched to one that is soy-based. Although they are considered to be safe, there has been some concern expressed about the plant-based estrogens in soy and their effect on infant growth. Soy can also cause allergic reactions in some babies (Strom, et al., 2001; Setchell, et al., 1998). Unmodified cow's milk should not be given to infants prior to one year of age because it often causes digestive disorders including intestinal bleeding. Goat's milk is also not recommended as it does not contain adequate nutrients.

Preparation of Formula

Safe preparation of formula is primarily dependent on two factors:

1. Sanitation—Sanitary formula preparation using **aseptic procedures** prevents serious illness that could result when bacteria are introduced into the formula. This requires careful sanitizing of all utensils used in preparing formula and thorough handwashing prior to mixing the formula. When preparing formula from a powdered concentrate, the water to be used for dilution must be sterilized (boiled); bottled (sterile) water can also be purchased and used for this purpose. Honey should never be added to a formula for an infant less than one year of age.

   Caution: **Honey contains *Clostridium botulinum* spores, which, in an infant's intestine, can produce a dangerous, life-threatening toxin.**

   Infant formulas are packaged in different forms. Families can choose from ready-to-feed (RTF), concentrated liquid, or powder formulas. Each formula type requires different preparation techniques as specified on the product label.

aseptic procedure – *treatment to produce a product that is free of disease-producing bacteria.*

2. Accuracy—Accurate measuring and mixing of formula (according to directions) assures that the infant will receive needed calories and nutrients in the amounts required for optimal growth and development. Adding too much water dilutes the formula and the amount of nutrients the infant receives and will cause malnutrition. Adding too little water results in an "over-rich" formula that may cause digestive problems. If given over a long period of time, this rich formula results in excessive caloric intake and obesity. Skim or low-fat milk should not be used in formula preparation because infants need fat to meet their calorie needs within the volume of feedings that can be comfortably taken in each day. Adequate fat in the diet is also a critical need relative to normal nerve development; fat is needed to form the myelin sheath, or the insulation, around new nerve fibers. It is recommended that 40 to 50 percent of the infant's calories come from fat. The fat in the formula must also provide the essential fatty acids (linolenic and linoleic) that are required for cell growth. The equivalent of one tablespoon of a polyunsaturated fat, such as corn oil or safflower oil, will meet the infant's need for essential fatty acids. Table 17–6 provides a summary of the formulas available for infants.

FEEDING TIME FOR THE INFANT

How frequently a baby is fed is determined by the family, infant, and health care provider. For the first four months it is generally considered best to feed an infant on demand. Infants vary greatly as to how much food they can comfortably handle at one time, and thus how often they require

TABLE 17–6 Examples of Infant Formulas

Standard Formulas

Enfamil with Iron	20 cal/oz	modified cow's milk
Enfamil	20 cal/oz	modified cow's milk
Similac with Iron	20 cal/oz	modified cow's milk
Similac	20 cal/oz	modified cow's milk
SMA	20 cal/oz	modified cow's milk
SMA Lo Iron	20 cal/oz	modified cow's milk
Carnation Good Start	20 cal/oz	modified cow's milk

Soy Formulas

Isomil	20 cal/oz	hypoallergenic formula
Nursoy	20 cal/oz	hypoallergenic formula
ProSobee	20 cal/oz	hypoallergenic formula
Soyalac	20 cal/oz	hypoallergenic formula
Carnation Alsoy	20 cal/oz	hypoallergenic formula
Gerber Soy Formula	20 cal/oz	hypoallergenic formula

Therapeutic Formulas

Nutramigen	20 cal/oz	hypoallergenic formula
Pregestimil	20 cal/oz	hypoallergenic formula
Alimentum	20 cal/oz	hypoallergenic formula
Lofenalac	20 cal/oz	for phenylketonurics (PKU)
Pedialyte	3 cal/oz	electrolyte/fluid replacement
Mead Johnson Lactofree	20 cal/oz	lactose-free milk
Lactose-Free (Ross)	20 cal/oz	lactose-free milk
Enfamil Premature	20 or 24 cal/oz	premature infant formula
Enfamil 22	22 cal/oz	premature infant formula
Similac Special Care	20 or 24 cal/oz	premature infant formula
Similac NeoSure Advance	22 cal/oz	premature infant formula

food. The individual infant will signal when he/she needs food and is therefore the best source of information about when to feed or not to feed. It is important that parents and teachers learn to read a baby's cues because not all crying indicates a need for food (Soltis, 2004; Wood & Gustafson, 2001). Noting the baby's body language as well as the tone, intensity, and length of crying can be helpful in determining if the infant is indeed hungry, is distressed about a wet diaper, or simply wants to be picked up and held. Although the frequency and amount of feeding varies from infant to infant, typical guidelines suggest:

0–1 months	6 feedings of 3–4 oz/feeding
1–2 months	6 feedings of 3–5 oz/feeding
2–3 months	5 feedings of 4–6 oz/feeding
4–5 months	5 feedings of 5–7 oz/feeding
6–7 months*	5 feedings of 6–8 oz/feeding
8–12 months*	3 feedings of 8 oz/feeding

*Also taking solid foods

An infant who is consuming adequate formula (liquids) will usually have at least six or more wet diapers a day.

How to feed a baby involves much more than getting the nipple into the mouth. Cleanliness at feeding time is of prime importance. The teacher's hands must be soap-washed prior to every feeding. Formula should not be too warm or too cold. If it feels slightly warm when tested against the inside of the wrist, it is the right temperature.

> *Caution:* **Infant formula in the bottle should not be heated in a microwave. The fluid formula may become dangerously hot while the outside of the bottle feels cool. This method of heating has severely burned some infants.**

Feeding time should be relaxed and preceded by a few minutes of talking and playing with the infant. When adults cuddle, maintain eye contact, and talk with the infant they are satisfying critical social and emotional needs. The feeding experience also meets the infant's need for close human contact (bonding) (Figure 17–3).

The infant should be held in a sitting position with his/her head resting against the teacher's upper arm. The bottle should be tilted slightly upward to keep the nipple full of formula and prevent the baby from swallowing excess air which can cause gas and **distention**. (See Figure 17–4 for examples of different nipples that can be used for bottle feeding.) Allow at least 20 minutes per

FIGURE 17–3

Feeding time encourages infant-parent bonding.

---

distention – *stretched or enlarged.*

FIGURE 17–4

Different types of nipples.

   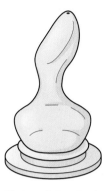

Regular nipple
Available in slow,
medium,
and fast flow

Newborn nipple

Orthodontic Nipple

Cleft-palate nipple

feeding to avoid hurrying the infant. Babies will usually signal when they have had enough to eat by turning their head away, releasing or playing with the nipple, or pushing away from the adult. It is important to recognize these cues and not force the infant to take additional milk.

Burping   Because babies naturally swallow air when sucking, they should be burped two or three times during the feeding and again when they have finished eating (Figure 17–5). The infant can be placed either in an upright position over the adult's shoulder or face-down across the lap while the adult gently pats or rubs the baby's back. It is also normal for babies, especially those who are formula-fed, to experience **regurgitation** and spit up small amounts of their feeding. The frequency and amount that an infant spits up tends to decrease with age.

> *Caution:* **An infant's bottle should never be propped up, nor should the baby ever be left unattended while feeding. Infants do not have sufficient motor control to remove the bottle from their mouth and may aspirate the formula after they fall asleep. This practice also increases the risk of baby bottle tooth decay (BBTD) and ear infections.**

Water   Until solid foods are added, breast milk or formula should meet the baby's water requirements. However, since the infant has a great need for water and is prone to dehydration, it is not safe to assume that formula will always meet the infant's needs. A thirsty baby acts much like a hungry baby. So, if the baby appears hungry shortly after feeding, a small amount of unflavored water can be offered. Water sweetened with sugar or flavored drinks should not be given to babies. Waters with special electrolytes (salts and minerals) should only be given with a doctor's recommendation. A baby's daily water intake should be limited to no more than four ounces so that it does not replace their consumption of milk.

Supplements   Vitamin and/or mineral supplements are sometimes recommended for infants. In general, breast milk or formula is adequate to meet most of the infant's nutritional needs with the exception of vitamin D and the mineral fluoride. Breast-fed infants are usually given a vitamin D supplement; however, the formula-fed infant receives adequate amounts of this vitamin

---

regurgitation – *the return of partially digested food from stomach to mouth.*

FIGURE 17–5

Babies should be burped during and after feedings.

and should not be supplemented. Although fluoride is not added to infant formulas and is only present in scant amounts in breast milk, the American Academy of Pediatric Dentists (AAPD) does recommend supplementation before six months of age. Excess fluoride can have toxic effects and cause tooth discoloration. It should only be prescribed by the child's health care provider or dentist. Infants who are breast fed longer than six months may require supplementation with iron because milk is a poor source of this mineral. Introducing iron-fortified foods is also beneficial.

> *Caution:* **Fluoride supplements combined with vitamin D are not safe to use with the formula-fed infant. That is because formulas are already supplemented with vitamin D and excessive intake of this vitamin may have serious consequences for the infant.**

INTRODUCING SEMI-SOLID (PUREED) FOODS

The teacher, family, and health care professional must cooperate closely when infants are introduced to semi-solid foods. Finely cut, pureed foods high in fluid content, such as cereals, and pureed fruits and vegetables, can be introduced between five and six months of age. Introducing semi-solid foods prior to five months of age is inappropriate because the infant does not demonstrate **developmental or physiological readiness**.

Developmental Readiness

At approximately five months of age, the baby changes from only being able to suck to now being able to move food to the back of the mouth and to swallow without an initial sucking action. At this point, the baby is able to chew, to sit with some comfort, and to lean forward toward the spoon. At four to five months, the infant shows interest in touching, holding, and

developmental or physiological readiness – *growth (both physical and cognitive) and chemical processes that lead to the ability to perform a function.*

FIGURE 17–6

Babies begin to show interest in picking up foods at about four or five months of age.

tasting objects—food and otherwise (Figure 17–6). It is important to note that at this age the baby can turn his head away from food when satisfied, signaling a desire to stop eating. This signal should be watched for, respected, and the offering of food should be stopped.

Physiological Readiness

By five to six months of age, the infant's digestive system has matured and is able to metabolize complex carbohydrates and proteins other than milk protein. This is also about the time that the iron stores which were present at birth are nearly depleted. Semi-solid foods such as iron-enriched cereals and pureed vegetables and fruits can gradually be introduced into the infant's diet. High protein meat products should not be added until the infant is approximately six to eight months of age. Prior to this time, the infant's kidneys are not sufficiently developed to handle the nitrogen-containing wastes that result from high protein digestion.

Table 17–7 presents age-related, developmental factors that may influence infant feeding behavior. However, it is important to remember that infants vary greatly in their rate of development

REFLECTIVE THOUGHTS

Missy T. is the mother of six-week-old Hayden. Hayden is Missy's first child. Missy's mother lives nearby and is happy to help with Hayden's care. Missy complains of being tired and mentions to her mother that Hayden had awakened several times during the night acting hungry. Her mother advises her to add cereal to his bedtime bottle in order to "fill him up so he will sleep through the night." She also advises cutting larger holes in the nipple so the cereal won't clog it.

- Should Missy follow her mother's advice?
- What are the dangers, if any, of feeding a six-week-old baby cereal from the bottle?
- Do child care practices change from generation to generation?
- Consider possible short- and long-term outcomes of feeding semi-solid food from a bottle.
- How would you respond if you were the teacher and a parent requested that you feed an infant in this manner?

TABLE 17–7 Age-Related Infant Eating Behaviors

Age	Common infant behaviors
1–3 months	• becomes fussy when hungry • turns face toward nipple • sucks vigorously but may choke on occasion
4–6 months	• assumes more symmetrical sitting position • grasps for objects • puts objects in mouth • may close hands around bottle • turns head away from food when no longer hungry • leans toward food-containing spoon
6–7 months	• teeth erupt • shows up and down chewing motions • grasps finger foods using entire hand (**palmar grasp**) and gets them to mouth • drinks small amounts of liquid from a cup • holds bottle with both hands
7–8 months	• sits alone with little support • uses finger and thumb (**pincer grip**) to pick up small food pieces • can better manipulate food in the mouth • more successful when drinking from a cup • begins self-feeding with help
9–12 months	• can more precisely grasp and release objects • reaches for the spoon • feeds self with some help • drinks successfully from a cup • more aware of environment • mimics motions and activities observed

(Allen & Marotz, 2007). Infants who have developmental delays or special needs may take longer to develop these skills. Differences in cultural practices may also influence when children are encouraged to attempt self-feeding. That is why there is no need for concern if a baby presents some of these behaviors ahead of or behind schedule. Foods should be introduced according to the individual baby's abilities, interests and needs.

New foods should be introduced slowly with only a few baby spoonfuls offered one or two times daily. The food may be thinned with formula, breast milk, or water to make it more acceptable to the infant. Semi-solid foods should be fed with a spoon rather than in a bottle. Iron-fortified infant cereal is usually the first addition. Rice or barley cereals are less likely to cause allergic reactions, and are therefore wise choices for the first semi-solid food offered.

A suggested sequence for introducing solid foods is:

5–6 months	iron-enriched cereals
6–8 months	vegetables, followed by fruits
8–9 months	meat and meat substitutes

Initially, it is better to offer individual foods rather than mixtures. If an allergy or sensitivity develops, the offending food can be readily identified. Sugar, salt, and butter should not be added

palmar grasp – *using the entire hand to pick up objects.*
pincer grip – *using the thumb and finger to pick up an object.*

to an infant's food. When an infant begins to eat semi-solid food, parents may choose to prepare pureed foods at home or use commercially prepared food. Either is acceptable as long as the foods are nutritionally adequate. Table foods (removed before they have been seasoned for the rest of the family) can be pureed in a blender. For example, if the family is having baked chicken, peas, and rice, an appropriate serving for the infant might be two tablespoons chicken, two tablespoons peas, and one-quarter cup rice (all pureed). Preparing food in this manner can expose the infant to a wider variety of items and allows families to have more control over what will be offered. Initially, it may be wise to limit high-fiber foods. Home-prepared pureed food may be frozen in ice cube trays; when frozen, the cubes can be removed, stored in the freezer in a tightly sealed container, and thawed and used as needed.

If the decision is to use commercially prepared baby food, it is better to use plain fruits, vegetables, and meats rather than "dinners," or "desserts," which are often extended with starches and other additives. Information on the labels of commercially prepared infant and toddler foods should be read carefully in order to make healthful selections (Figure 17–7). Remember, ingredients on food labels are listed in descending order according to the amount present. The first ingredient in an acceptable infant food should be fruit, vegetable, or meat, not water or starch. When feeding a child prepared baby food, it is better to remove the small portion that you will use, put it in a bowl, and return the rest of the jar's contents to the refrigerator. This will reduce the chance of contaminating the remaining food with bacteria and enzymes found in the saliva; these enzymes can also cause the food to break down and become "watery."

Infants may begin to drink small amounts of liquid from a cup at about six to seven months of age. They like to help hold their cup and bring it to their mouth although many spills should be expected. By six to seven months they can pick up and chew on finger foods (Figure 17–8). Teeth are also beginning to erupt at this age, and the provision of "chew foods" such as dry toast or baby biscuits helps the teething process. (Refer to Table 17–1.)

Infants with Special Needs

Although eating appears to be a natural process, infants who are born prematurely or who have a range of health problems, including genetic disorders and congenital malformations, may present special feeding challenges and nutritional needs. For example, infants born with Down syndrome

FIGURE 17–7

Special labeling rules.

Nutrition Facts
Serving Size 1 jar (140g)

Amount Per Serving
Calories 110

Total Fat	0g
Sodium	10mg
Total Carbohydrate	27g
Dietary Fiber	4g
Sugars	18g
Protein	0g

% Daily Value

Protein 0%	•	Vitamin A 6%
Vitamin C 45%	•	Calcium 2%
Iron 2%		

Nutrition Label for
Foods for Children
Under Four Years Old.

Nutrition Facts
Serving Size 1 jar (140g)

Amount Per Serving
Calories 110   Calories from Fat 0

Total Fat	0g
Saturated Fat	0g
Cholesterol	0mg
Sodium	10mg
Total Carbohydrate	27g
Dietary Fiber	4g
Sugars	18g
Protein	0g

% Daily Value

Protein 0%	•	Vitamin A 6%
Vitamin C 45%	•	Calcium 2%
Iron 2%		

Nutrition Label for
Foods for Children Two
to Four Years Old.

FIGURE 17–8

The six- to eight-month-old infant enjoys finger foods.

GRACO

typically have weak facial muscles which make sucking difficult and less efficient. Later, these children have a tendency to overeat and to gain excessive weight. Some infants may have conditions that require surgery which can increase their need for certain nutrients at a time when they may not be feeling or eating well. It is especially important that infants with special needs obtain

---

 ISSUES TO CONSIDER • Does Infant Formula Cause Type 1 Diabetes?

Recent reports have questioned a possible link between formula feeding and an increased incidence of **type 1 diabetes**. The implication is that protein in cow's milk might precipitate type 1 diabetes; children who developed diabetes have shown elevated levels of antibodies to these proteins. A recent report stated that to date, studies have failed to take into consideration the wide variety of formulas on the market. However, the American Academy of Pediatrics strongly encourages breastfeeding and avoidance of cow's milk and products containing cow's milk proteins during the first year, especially for infants with a strong family history of type 1 diabetes. The concern is even greater for infants who may have a sibling with diabetes.

- What implications does this study have for breastfeeding recommendations?
- If a family prefers to bottle feed an infant, what formula options are available?
- Why do you think the American Academy of Pediatrics recommends avoidance of cow's milk protein for just the first year?

Source: Marincic, P. Z., McCune, R. W., & Hendricks, D. G. (1999). Cows-milk-based infant formula: Heterogeneity of bovine serum albumin content. *Journal of the American Dietetic Association*, 99, 1575–1578.

---

type 1 diabetes – *a disease distinguished by a lack of insulin production; usually diagnosed in childhood or young adulthood.*

all of the nutrients necessary for healthy growth and brain development during the months following birth.

An infant's eating behaviors may be further challenged by infection, medication side effects, unpleasant medical treatments, swallowing difficulties, dental problems, special diets, and fatigue. These factors may make it difficult for the infant with special needs to eat and maintain an interest in food. Families may be referred to a feeding clinic where the infant's physical and nutritional needs can be evaluated and where they can receive assistance. Nutritional services are also available through Early Head Start, IDEA (Individuals with Disabilities Education Act, Part C), WIC (Special Supplemental Feeding Program for Women, Infants, and Children), hospital clinics, and other community-based programs.

Many infants with special needs are enrolled in early childhood programs today. Teachers must work closely with their families to learn as much about the child's condition, medical treatments, nutritional needs, and ways that they can collaborate to assure the infant's healthy development.

Some Common Feeding Concerns

Allergies The most common chronic condition affecting infants is allergies. Allergic responses to food may cause a variety of symptoms such as runny nose, diarrhea, constipation, bloating, vomiting, hives, and eczema (Ziegler, 2003). These symptoms are not specific for any given food and should be discussed with the infant's physician.

If a family has a history of allergies, it is recommended that the introduction of semi-solid foods be delayed until the infant is at least six months of age (Fiocchi, Assa'ad, & Bahna, 2006). Certain foods such as citrus juice(s), egg, cereal products other than rice, chocolate, nuts and nut butters, and fish/shellfish are common allergens. Their addition to the baby's diet should be delayed until late infancy.

If allergic reactions seem to be linked with a specific food, the food should be eliminated from the diet and reintroduced at a later time. If a milk-based formula seems to be the offending food, it may be necessary to replace it with one formulated from modified proteins or soybeans.

Colic Some seemingly healthy infants may develop colic, which causes abdominal discomfort, cramping, and prolonged periods of intense crying (Lobo, et al., 2004; St James-Roberts, 1999). The distress occurs most often in late afternoon and evening and at approximately the same time each day. Consoling these infants is difficult and typically ineffective. The exact cause of colic is unknown. Changing the type of formula may relieve unpleasant symptoms for some infants. Mothers who are breastfeeding should continue to do so, but may want to monitor their diet for highly spiced or strongly flavored foods that may contribute to the infant's problem. Fortunately, most infants outgrow colic at about three to four months of age.

Vomiting and Diarrhea Infants may experience vomiting or diarrhea for numerous reasons. Some common causes include:

- food allergies or food sensitivities
- overfeeding
- infections: systemic or food-borne
- eating food that the baby is not yet ready for
- incorrect formula preparation
- use of fruit juice
- swallowed air
- reflux

When vomiting and diarrhea occur, the primary concern is to replace fluid and **electrolytes** that have been lost. The child with diarrhea should receive a liquid intake of approximately three ounces of fluid per pound of body weight. There are numerous RTF rehydrating formulas available for use (Pedialyte, Infalyte, and Rehydralyte); parents should check with their health care provider before giving these solutions to an infant. Fruit juices, carbonated beverages, tea, or adult electrolyte formulas are not recommended because of their high sugar and low electrolyte content. The goal is gradual progression or return to the infant's normal diet.

Acute diarrhea due to an infection, and characterized by accompanying fever, must be attended to immediately. The infant's physician should be contacted and immediate and consistent attention should be given to replacing lost fluids and electrolytes.

Anemia   Inadequate iron intake can result in low-hemoglobin type anemia that may delay the growth process and cause the infant to be lethargic (Skalicky, et al., 2006). The iron stores present at birth are usually exhausted by six months of age unless the infant is on an iron-fortified formula. Some infants may experience intestinal problems if placed on an iron-fortified formula. Adding iron-enriched cereals to an infant's diet at about fix to six months of age is usually sufficient to prevent anemia.

Baby Bottle Tooth Decay (BBDT)   Babies who are allowed to recline or sleep with a bottle or breast in their mouth may develop bottle-mouth syndrome. This condition is characterized by a high rate of tooth decay caused by the pooling of sugar-containing formula, breast milk, or juices in the baby's mouth. Weaning infants to a cup at about eight months of age also reduces the risk of developing this problem.

Ear Infection   Propping the bottle up so the infant may lie down and feed without being held can lead to a higher rate of ear infections (Tully, 1998). A child should be held in a semi-seated position during feedings to prevent milk from traveling back into the eustachian tubes and ear canals.

Obesity   Obesity results when energy intake exceeds an infant's need for energy for growth, maintenance, and activity. Some infant feeding practices that are thought to play a role in obesity are overeating during bottle feeding, too early introduction of semi-solid foods, and feeding cereal in the bottle (Burdette, et al., 2006, 2005).

It is important to be alert to signs that a baby is satisfied. Stopping periodically during the feeding gives the infant a chance to assess his/her own hunger and respond appropriately when the bottle is again offered. It is important to respect an infant's judgment of the amount of food needed at a given time.

Since the parent or teacher receives visual indicators of how much the child has drunk from a bottle, the bottle-fed infant is frequently urged to finish the feeding. In so doing, the parent or teacher may ignore the infant's signs of fullness. Such signs include:

- closing the mouth or turning away from the bottle
- falling asleep
- fussing at repeated attempts to continue feeding
- biting or playing with the nipple

Some authorities believe that continuously ignoring these signs may cause the infant to stop giving these signals, thus ending a means of regulating food intake. This could have serious consequences later for the toddler, the preschooler, and the adult who does not know when to stop eating. To establish the point at which the infant is satisfied, the teacher might stop after a few minutes of solid-food feeding and play with the child before offering food again. This helps determine whether the infant is eating because of hunger or to get attention.

---

electrolytes – *substances which, when in solution, become capable of conducting electricity; examples include sodium and potassium.*

Introducing semi-solid foods to the infant before they are needed or giving foods that are too high in sugar or fat may lead to babies taking more calories than they need with the consequence of obesity (Mannella, et al., 2006). Continuing to offer solid food after the baby seems satisfied also contributes to obesity and may set the stage for overeating later in life.

Choking This can be avoided during breast or bottle feeding by holding the child properly with the head elevated as previously described. Allowing the infant to lie down with the bottle propped up greatly increases the danger of choking. The six- to seven-month-old infant wants and should be given finger foods such as dry bread, crackers, or dry cereal. However, the infant should be monitored closely because these foods may increase the risk of choking. This danger can be minimized by having the child sit in an upright position and breaking foods into small pieces that are easy for the infant to chew and swallow. Offering semi-solid food that is finely ground and somewhat diluted will also minimize choking. Due to the high incidence of choking among infants, CPR training for parents and teachers is vitally important.

Teething Teeth begin to erupt around six months of age. This can be a stressful period for some infants and may temporarily disrupt their feeding pattern. As a result, some infants may begin to wean themselves from breast or bottle feedings. They may prefer foods that can be chewed such as dry toast or teething biscuits. Diarrhea accompanying teething is usually due to infectious organisms and is not caused by the teething process. Appropriate toys and food items should be made available to discourage infants from picking up and chewing on inappropriate or unsafe objects. In an early childhood program, it is important to ensure that toys are frequently sanitized to reduce the risk of spreading infectious organisms.

Constipation Breast-fed infants are generally not troubled by constipation. Because breast milk is so easily digested, only a small amount of waste product remains to be excreted. Infants who are formula-fed, especially with soy-based products, may experience more problems with constipation. Giving them additional water is often sufficient to address the problem. However, if the formula-fed infant fails to have a bowel movement for more than three or four days, the family should contact their health care provider for advice.

FOCUS ON FAMILIES • Infant Feeding

A majority of food preferences carried into adulthood evolve from childhood and childhood eating experiences. Birth (or before) is the ideal time to begin addressing a child's nutritional well-being.

- Breast milk and/or infant formula is recommended as the infant's primary source of nutrition for the first year. Cow's milk cannot meet the nutritional requirements needed for the rapid growth rate of an infant and should not be offered during the first year.

- Always hold and bond with an infant during feedings. This is essential in preventing choking and bottle-mouth syndrome.

- The first food that should be introduced into an infant's diet is a single-grain iron-fortified cereal. Introduce foods one at a time in order to detect possible allergies/intolerances.

- Be wary of food additives, especially in commercially produced baby food. "Desserts" and "dinners" often contain additives and offer less nutritional value than plain cereal, vegetables, fruits, and meats.

- 100 percent fruit juice can be introduced at approximately six to seven months of age.

- Avoid fruit beverages, fruit drinks, sodas, and tea.

- Avoid foods that cause choking: grapes, peanuts, hotdogs, and popcorn.

CASE STUDY

Lindsey, five months old, has been brought to child care as her mother has returned to work. Lindsey was started on cereal mixed with pureed fruit prior to entering child care. Lindsey's mother pumps her breast milk and delivers it to child care frozen to be thawed and fed to Lindsey as needed. The infant is now experiencing some diarrhea and apparent abdominal pain.

1. What are some possible causes of Lindsey's discomfort?
2. Do you know how the breast milk is handled at home?
3. What are safe procedures for handling breast milk at child care?
4. Given Lindsey's age, is she ready to have fruit added to her diet?
5. What other food/liquids could be used to mix in her cereal; what type of cereal should she be fed?

CLASSROOM CORNER • Teacher Activities

Planning Healthy Snacks...
Concept: Healthy food choices provide important energy. (Pre–2; school-age)

Learning Objectives

- Children will learn to plan healthy snacks.
- Children will identify foods their bodies need to stay healthy.

Supplies

- Paper; crayons or markers; computer and Internet access (for older children); Food Guide Pyramid poster (can be printed from http://www.mypyramid.gov); magazine pictures of healthy snack items; glue stick.

Learning Activities

- Discuss the importance of choosing healthy snacks (e.g., growth, energy, staying healthy/not sick). Use the Food Guide Pyramid to talk about foods that are considered healthy and why it is important to select a variety of foods from each group, including some that are new.
- Draw a grid on a large sheet of paper (for each day of the week). Have younger children plan a week's worth of afternoon snacks; teachers can fill in the grid with foods that children name or children can glue food pictures onto the grid. Older children can explore the Pyramid online and learn about healthy food options before writing out their menu. Have the cook use this menu to prepare snacks for the week; older children may be able to prepare their own snacks each day.

Evaluation

- Children are able to make healthy food choices and understand why this is important.
- Children understand what a menu is and how it works.

SUMMARY

- The first year of an infant's life is one of very rapid growth and change.
  - The baby will have tripled its birth weight; its length will have increased by 50 percent.
- Good nutrition is a major factor contributing to physical growth.
  - Breast milk is the preferred nutrition for the first four to six months.
  - Formula is an acceptable alternate when breastfeeding is not feasible.
  - Unmodified cow's or goat's milk should not be given during the first year.
- The infant is developmentally and physiologically ready for semi-solid foods at about five to six months.
  - Single grain cereals are the first semi-solid foods added.
  - Vegetables, fruits, and meats are added over the next three months.
- Social aspects of infant feeding are important.
  - The infant should be held when feeding.
  - Cuddling, eye-contact, and talking should be part of the infant feeding experience.
  - Feeding is a key aspect of the infant–parent bonding.

APPLICATION ACTIVITIES

1. Mrs. Jones, mother of two-month-old Kelly, has been on maternity leave from her job. At present, she is breast-feeding Kelly. She is preparing to return to work and place Kelly with a teacher. She is concerned that she must switch Kelly to formula, although she has found breastfeeding quite rewarding. What feeding options can her teacher offer her?

2. Visit the baby food section of the local grocery store and read the ingredients listed on the labels. Based on the ingredients listed, select several kinds of foods that are good choices to feed to a young infant.

3. Plan an instructional package that could be given to a new employee in an infant care facility. What social aspects of infant feeding should be included in addition to nutritional and infant-handling factors?

4. If applicable, review state regulations for early childhood teachers relating to infant feeding.

5. Review the common problems associated with low-birthweight infants and report the prenatal nutrient deficiencies that most frequently result in the birth of low-birthweight infants.

CHAPTER REVIEW

A. **By Yourself:**

1. Provide a rationale for why an infant's bottle should not be propped up during a feeding.

2. In what order should the following foods be introduced?

   pureed peas   pureed meat products   iron-fortified cereal
   crisp toast   pureed peaches

3. At approximately what age should each of these foods be introduced?

4. Describe three social factors that make feeding time more enjoyable for an infant.

5. Explain why unmodified cow's or goat's milk should not be given to an infant before one year of age.

6. Why should caregivers hold and talk to an infant while he/she is being fed?

B. As a Group:

1. Discuss why it is important not to feed babies semi-solid foods before five to six months of age.

2. Debate the advantages/disadvantages of breastfeeding versus formula feeding.

3. Describe several feeding practices that are considered to contribute to infant obesity.

4. Discuss baby bottle tooth decay (BBDT) and feeding practices that will prevent this condition.

5. Discuss why reduced fat or skim milk should not be used in preparing an infant's formula feeding.

REFERENCES

Aird, L. (2002). Breastfeeding promotion in child care. *Child Care Information Exchange, 145*(May/June), 46–48.

Allen K. E. & Marotz, L. (2007). *Developmental profiles: Pre-birth through twelve.* Clifton Park, NY: Thomson Delmar Learning.

American Academy of Pediatrics (AAP). (2005). Breastfeeding and the use of human milk. Policy Statement. *Pediatrics, 115*(2), 496–506.

Black, M., Dubowitz, H., Casey, P., & Cutts, D. (2006). Failure to thrive as distinct from child neglect. *Pediatrics, 117*(4), 1456–1460.

Black, M., Cutts, D., Frank, D., Geppert, J., Skalicky, A., Levenson, S., Casey, P., Berkowitz, C., Zaldivar, N., Cook, J., Meyers, A., & Herren, T. (2004). Special Supplemental Nutrition Program for Women, Infants, and Children participation and infants' growth and health: A multisite surveillance study. *Pediatrics, 114*(1), 169–176.

Burdette, H., Whitaker, R., Hall, W., & Daniels, S. (2006). Breastfeeding, introduction of complementary foods, and adiposity at 5 years of age. *American Journal of Clinical Nutrition, 83*(3), 550–558.

Burdette, H., Whitaker, R., Hall, W., & Daniels, S. (2005). Maternal infant-feeding style and children's adiposity at 5 years of age. *Archives of Pediatric & Adolescent Medicine, 160*(5), 513–520.

Chantry, C., Howard, C., & Auinger, P. (2006). Full breastfeeding duration and associated decrease in respiratory tract infection in US children. *Pediatrics, 117*(2), 425–432.

Duffy, L., Faden, H., Wasielewski, R., Wolf, J., & Krystofik, D. (1997). Exclusive breastfeeding protects against bacterial colonization and day care exposure to otitis media. *Pediatrics, 100*(4), E7.

Feldman, R., Keren, M., Gross-Rozval, O., & Tyano, S. (2004). Mother-child touch patterns in infant feeding disorders: Relation to maternal, child, and environmental factors. *Journal of the American Academy of Child & Adolescent Psychiatry, 43*(9), 1089–1097.

Fiocchi, A., Assa'ad, A., & Bahna, S. (2006). Food allergy and the introduction of solid foods to infants: A consensus document. *Annals of Allergy, Asthma & Immunology, 97*(1), 10–20.

Gibson-Davis, C. & Brooks-Gunn, J. (2006). Breastfeeding and verbal ability of 3-year-olds in a multicity sample. *Pediatrics, 118*(5), e1444–1151.

Jensen, C., Voight, R., Prager, T., Zou, Y., Fraley, J., Rozelle, J., Turcich, M., Llorente, A., Anderson, R., & Heird, W. (2005). Effects of maternal docosahexaenoic acid intake on visual function and neurodevelopment in breastfed term infants. *American Journal of Clinical Nutrition, 82*(1), 125–132.

Kurtzweil, P. (1995, May). Labeling rules for young children's food. *FDA Consumer.*

Lobo, M., Kotzer, A., Keefe, M., Brady, E., Deloian, B., Froese-Fretz, A., & Barbosa, G. (2004). Current beliefs and management strategies for treating infant colic. *Journal of Pediatric Health Care, 18*(3), 115–122.

Mannella, J., Ziegler, P., Briefel, R., & Novak, T. (2006). Feeding Infants and Toddlers Study: The types of foods fed to Hispanic infants and toddlers. *Journal of the American Dietetic Association, 106*(1 Suppl.), S96–106.

Marincic, P. Z., McCune, R. W., & Hendricks, D. G. (1999). Cows-milk-based infant formula: Heterogeneity of bovine serum albumin content. *Journal of the American Dietetic Association, 99*, 1575–1578.

Morris, S. (1995). Supporting the breastfeeding relationship during child care: Why is it important? *Young Children, 50*(2), 59–62.

Nelson, E., Yu, L., & Williams, S. (2005). International Child Care Practices study: Breastfeeding and pacifier use. *Journal of Human Lactation, 21*(3), 289–295.

Pettigrew, M., Khodaee, M., Gillespie, B., Schwartz, K., Bobo, J., & Foxman, B. (2003). Duration of breast-feeding, daycare, and physician visits among infants 6 months and younger. *Annals of Epidemiology, 13*(6), 431–435.

Robinson, J. (2002). Attachment problems and disorders in infants and young children: Identification, assessment, and intervention. *Infants & Young Children, 14*(4), 6–18.

Setchell, K., Zimmer-Nechemias, L., Cai, J., & Heubi, J. (1998). Isoflvone content of infant formulas and the metabolic fate of these phytoestrogens in early life. *American Journal of Clinical Nutrition, 68*(6), 1453–1461.

Skalicky, A., Meyers, A., Adams, W., Yang, Z., Cook, J, & Frank, D. (2006). Child food insecurity and iron deficiency anemia in low-income infants and toddlers in the United States. *Maternal & Child Health Journal, 10*(2), 177–185.

Slykerman, R., Thompson, J., Becroft, D., Robinson, E., Pryor, J., Clark, P., Wild, C., & Mitchell, E. (2005). Breastfeeding and intelligence of preschool children. *Acta Paediatrics, 94*(7), 832–837.

Soltis, J. (2004). The signal functions of early infant crying. *The Behavior & Brain Sciences, 27*(4), 443–458.

St James-Roberts, I. (1999). What is distinct about infants' "colic" cries? *Archives of Disease in Children, 80*(1), 56–61.

Strom, B., Schinnar, R., Zieglar, E., Barnhart, K., Sammuel, M., Macones, G., Stallings, V., Drulis, J., Nelson, S., & Hanson, S. (2001). *JAMA, 286*(7), 807–814.

Tully, S. (1998). The right angle. Otitis media and infant feeding position. *Advance for Nurse Practitioners, 6*(4), 44–48.

Weiss, S., Wilson, P., Seed, M., & Paul, S. (2001). Early tactile experience of low birth weight children: Links to later mental health and social adaptations. *Infant & Child Development, 10*(3), 93–115.

WIC Program, Research & Education Institute, Inc., Harbor-UCLA Medical Center. (1990). *Nutrition and child care information.* Los Angeles, CA.

Wood, R. & Gustafson, G. (2001). Infant crying and adults' anticipated responses: Acoustic and contextual influences. *Child Development, 72*(5), 1287–1300.

Ziegler, R. (2003). Food allergen avoidance in the prevention of food allergy in infants and children. *Pediatrics, 111*(6), 1162–1171.

HELPFUL WEB RESOURCES

Child Care Bureau	http://www.acf.dhhs.gov
Keep Kids Healthy	http://www.keepkidshealthy.com
La Leche League	http://www.lalecheleague.org
National Network for Childcare	http://www.nncc.org
The National Women's Health	http://www.4woman.gov
Public Health Agency of Canada	http://www.phac-aspc.gc.ca

For additional health, safety, and nutrition resources, go to
http://www.EarlyChildEd.delmar.cengage.com

CHAPTER 18

Feeding Toddlers and Young Children

❋ OBJECTIVES

After studying this chapter, you should be able to:

- Outline three of the teacher's major responsibilities in feeding the toddler.
- Estimate appropriate serving sizes of food for toddlers, preschoolers, and school-age children.
- Describe the possible consequences of overreliance on milk as a food for toddlers.
- List two strategies that will enable the teacher to promote good eating habits.
- Name three health problems that are thought to be related to unhealthy eating habits acquired at an early age.

❋ TERMS TO KNOW

neophobic	Prader-Willi syndrome	hypertension
individuality	reward(s)	refusal
Down syndrome	dental caries	

❋ PROFILE OF TODDLERS, PRESCHOOLERS, AND SCHOOL-AGED CHILDREN

Toddlers (one- to two-and-a-half-year-olds) are a challenge! They want to assert their independence yet need and want limits. As they become increasingly mobile and active, they need to be protected from environmental hazards while learning personal safety skills. They have an insatiable curiosity and are continuously on the move.

Many toddlers spend considerable time each day in early education programs with teachers and other children because their parents work. These opportunities expose children to social and eating experiences that may differ from those in their home. As a result, the child begins to learn that different people do things in different ways.

Many toddlers also become avid television watchers. What they see will affect their behavior, including their reactions to food. The hours spent sitting in front of the television reduce valuable time that should be spent in physical activity (Figure 18–1). This inactivity reduces the child's caloric needs and can ultimately contribute to child obesity problems. There is also cause for concern about the foods advertised during children's prime television time. Recent research shows that many commercials create a desire for foods that are high in refined sugars and fat (Jenvey, 2007; Connor, 2006; Nestle, 2006).

Although toddlers grow at a slower rate than do infants, they continue to have a significant need for calories and essential nutrients. However, their limited stomach capacity and attention span make this a challenging task. The infant was best fed on demand, but the toddler needs a consistent schedule for eating. In their struggle for independence, toddlers may resist this schedule and frequently reject the food served. They have learned the power of the word "no" and use it constantly. They quickly learn to shape adults' behavior by refusing to eat or, at other times, by eating to gain adult favor.

The toddler is described as being **neophobic**—having a fear of anything new (Satter, 2000). This may interfere with the child's willingness to eat an increasing variety of foods. However, recognizing that this behavior is characteristic of toddlers should help families and teachers be a bit more patient and ingenious as they introduce new foods.

Preschool-aged children (two-and-a-half- to six-year-olds) are generally easier to manage. They are relaxed, willing to listen, and usually follow adult directions. Although they still assert their independence, they want to please adults and begin to express their **individuality** in ways that are more appropriate. Preschoolers continue to need structure and respect it more than toddlers do. However, they do not suddenly become overly compliant, and are still somewhat hesitant to accept new things. They want to do things for themselves and may need a bit of adult assistance to be successful. Many of these changes will be reflected in the preschool-aged child's responses to food and eating.

School-aged children are becoming increasingly aware of a much bigger world. They are energetic, curious, eager to learn, and able to understand situations that are more complex. Friends and friendships gradually replace time spent with family, although school-aged children still need and find comfort in knowing they can rely on their parents. Watching television, playing electronic games, and participating in active outdoor play now consume more of their time.

Family and friends continue to influence the school-aged child's eating behaviors. Family practices and food preferences reflect cultural variations and, in turn, shape children's eating habits (Kittler & Sucher, 2003). However, the favorite foods of friends and peers also begin to influence food choices. School-aged children enjoy helping with meal preparation and shopping. Their appetite is generally good, but tends to fluctuate with growth spurts and activity levels.

FIGURE 18-1

Engaging children in physical activity helps to prevent obesity.

THE CHALLENGE OF FEEDING A TODDLER

Toddlers, in asserting their independence, begin to make their preferences known. This includes their firm announcement of what foods they will or will not eat. Fortunately, their "will" and "will not" foods change almost daily. Great care must be taken so that the parent or teacher does not become involved in a battle of wills over what the toddler will eat and when it will be eaten.

neophobic – *fear of things that are new and unfamiliar.*
individuality – *qualities that distinguish one person from another.*

Basic to minimizing this friction is a clear understanding of the primary responsibilities of parent/teacher and child in the feeding relationship (Satter, 2000). The teacher is responsible for:

- serving a variety of nutritious foods
- deciding when food is offered
- setting a good example by eating a variety of foods

The child is responsible for:

- choosing what foods will be eaten from those that have been offered
- deciding how much of the offered food to eat

What Foods Should Be Served and How Much

Families and teachers have a responsibility to provide a variety of nutritious foods each day. As discussed in Chapter 13, the Food Guide Pyramid guidelines are easy to follow and ensure meeting daily nutritional needs. To review the Food Guide Pyramid groups and recommended daily servings for toddlers, see Figure 18–2 or visit www.MyPyramid.gov/kids.

- Grains – 3 ounces
- Vegetables – 1 cup
- Fruits – 1 cup
- Milk – 2 cups
- Meat and Beans – 2 ounces
- Oils (use sparingly)

Foods from all food groups should be offered at each meal. They may be offered individually:

- Ground beef patty
- Broccoli
- Whole grain bread
- Diced peaches
- Milk

Or be combined in one main dish:

- Spaghetti with meat sauce
- Green Beans
- Diced pineapple
- Milk

Toddlers usually prefer foods presented individually. Toddler serving sizes are approximately one-fourth that of an adult serving for each food group with the exception of the milk group (see Figure 18–3 on page 432).

- Milk – 1/2 cup
- Meat – 1 ounce
- Fruits and Vegetables – 2 tablespoons
- Breads and Cereals – 2 tablespoons rice, cereal, or pasta; 1/2 slice bread

When feeding a toddler, it is preferable to serve slightly less than what the teacher thinks the child will eat and let the child ask for more. In this way toddlers are not overwhelmed by the serving size and are allowed to assert their independence by asking for more. The toddler's decreased rate of growth typically causes a decrease in appetite and lack of interest in food. This often causes parents and teachers great concern. However, it is important that this concern does not lead to begging, nagging, or forcing children to eat more food than they want or need.

Table 18–1 presents some age-related eating behaviors that may be helpful in understanding children's changing responses to food. Adults can use this knowledge to help maximize positive feeding experiences at different ages.

FIGURE 18–2

Food guide pyramid for children.

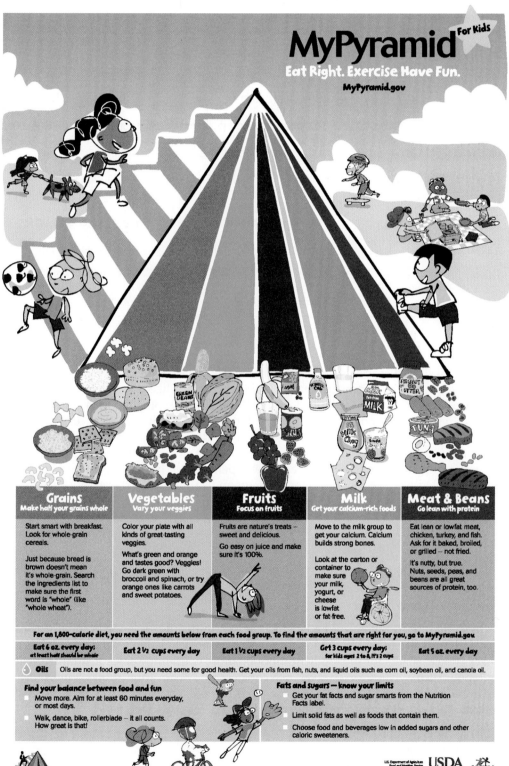

MyPyramid For Kids

Eat Right. Exercise Have Fun.

MyPyramid.gov

Grains Make half your grains whole	**Vegetables** Vary your veggies	**Fruits** Focus on fruits	**Milk** Get your calcium-rich foods	**Meat & Beans** Go lean with protein
Start smart with breakfast. Look for whole-grain cereals. Just because bread is brown doesn't mean it's whole-grain. Search the ingredients list to make sure the first word is "whole" (like "whole wheat").	Color your plate with all kinds of great-tasting veggies. What's green and orange and tastes good? Veggies! Go dark green with broccoli and spinach, or try orange ones like carrots and sweet potatoes.	Fruits are nature's treats — sweet and delicious. Go easy on juice and make sure it's 100%.	Move to the milk group to get your calcium. Calcium builds strong bones. Look at the carton or container to make sure your milk, yogurt, or cheese is lowfat or fat-free.	Eat lean or lowfat meat, chicken, turkey, and fish. Ask for it baked, broiled, or grilled — not fried. It's nutty, but true. Nuts, seeds, peas, and beans are all great sources of protein, too.

For an 1,800-calorie diet, you need the amounts below from each food group. To find the amounts that are right for you, go to MyPyramid.gov.

Eat 6 oz. every day; at least half should be whole	**Eat 2½ cups every day**	**Eat 1½ cups every day**	**Get 3 cups every day;** for kids ages 2 to 8, it's 2 cups	**Eat 5 oz. every day**

Oils Oils are not a food group, but you need some for good health. Get your oils from fish, nuts, and liquid oils such as corn oil, soybean oil, and canola oil.

Find your balance between food and fun
- Move more. Aim for at least 60 minutes everyday, or most days.
- Walk, dance, bike, rollerblade — it all counts. How great is that!

Fats and sugars — know your limits
- Get your fat facts and sugar smarts from the Nutrition Facts label.
- Limit solid fats as well as foods that contain them.
- Choose food and beverages low in added sugars and other caloric sweeteners.

MyPyramid.gov STEPS TO A HEALTHIER YOU

U.S. Department of Agriculture
Food and Nutrition Service
September 2005
FNS-581

USDA

USDA is an equal opportunity provider and employer.

FIGURE 18-3

A sample menu for toddlers.

BREAKFAST	LUNCH	DINNER
Whole milk (1/2 cup)	Whole milk (1/2 cup)	Whole milk (1/2 cup)
Cream of wheat (1/4 cup)	Beef patty (1 oz)	Finely diced chicken (1 oz)
or	Broccoli (2 tbsp)	Cooked carrots (2 tbsp)
Whole wheat toast (1/2 slice)	Diced watermelon (2 tbsp)	Diced plums (2 tbsp)
Jam or Jelly (1 tsp)	Whole wheat bread (1/2 slice)	Rye bread (1/2 slice)
Diced peaches (1/4 cup)	Margarine (1 tsp)	Margarine (1 tsp)
MIDMORNING SNACK	**MIDAFTERNOON SNACK**	**EVENING SNACK**
Vanilla wafers (3)	Cheese cube (1/2 oz)	Applesauce (1/2 cup)
Orange juice (1/2 cup)	Whole wheat crackers (2)	Graham crackers (2)
	Water	Water

When to Serve Food

The timing of meals and snacks is important when feeding the toddler. Too much time between feedings will result in an overhungry, cranky child who is less likely to accept food when it is presented. Meals and snacks spaced too closely will not allow ample time for a child to become hungry, again resulting in a poor eating response. Most young children also eat better at meals if they are not overly tired and if they have been given a little warning so that they can "wrap up" their current play activity. Allowing time for reading a quiet story just before a meal may set the stage for a pleasant and more satisfying meal-time experience for both child and teacher.

Because toddlers have a critical need for nutrients and a small stomach capacity, they must eat more often than the three-meal family pattern. A good eating pattern is:

- breakfast
- midmorning snack
- lunch
- midafternoon snack
- dinner
- bedtime snack, if needed

Snacks should be chosen from the Food Guide Pyramid and be planned carefully as part of the day's total nutrient intake. If a food is appropriate to be included in a child's meal, it is also a good snack choice. Snacks for the toddler cannot be those commonly promoted on television as "snacks." Foods such as chips, snack cakes, rich cookies, candy bars, fruit "drinks," and sodas have no place in the toddler's daily food plan. These foods contain empty calories, which provide little if any nutritional value. Examples of healthy food choices for snacks are:

- cheese cubes and pita wedges
- crackers with peanut butter or hummus
- 100 percent fruit juice—orange or other juices fortified with vitamin C
- raw vegetables—cucumber slices, cherry tomatoes cut in half, sliced mushrooms, zucchini rounds, red and orange pepper strips

TABLE 18-1 Expected Eating Behaviors According to Age Behavior

Age	Behavior
12–24 months	has a decreased appetite sometimes described as a finicky or fussy eater; may go on food jags uses spoon with some degree of skill helps feed self
2-year-old	appetite is fair often has strong likes and dislikes; may go on food jags likes simple food, dislikes mixtures, wants food served in familiar ways learns table manners by imitating adults and older children
3-year-old	appetite is fairly good; prefers small servings; likes only a few cooked vegetables feeds self independently, if hungry uses spoon in semi-adult fashion; may spear with fork and spread with a blunt knife (Figure 18–4) dawdles over food when not hungry
4- to 5-year-old	eats well, but not at every meal may develop dislikes of certain foods and refuse them to the point of tears if pushed; often adapts to preferences of family and teachers likes to help with meal preparation uses all eating utensils; becomes skilled at spreading jelly or peanut butter, pouring milk on cereal, or cutting soft foods such as bread
6- to 7-year-old	has good appetite; eats most foods willingness to try new foods is unpredictable able to use eating utensils, but not always correctly easily distracted; has difficulty sitting through a meal
8- to 9-year-old	usually has a good appetite; boys eat more than girls prefers to eat when hungry rather than at specified times open to trying new foods, but prefers certain "favorites" enjoys cooking eats quickly so they can resume previous activity
10- to 12-year-old	always hungry; seems to eat non-stop and large amounts at one time needs a big snack after school dislikes few foods; interested in trying foods from other cultures and those seen on television seems to forget manners that were previously learned

Adapted from Allen, K. E., & Marotz, L. R. (2007). *Developmental profiles: Pre-birth to twelve.* (5th ed.). Clifton Park, NY: Delmar Learning.

- lightly cooked vegetables—broccoli flowerettes, green beans, carrots, edamame
- fruits—apple and orange wedges, bananas, applesauce, diced peaches/pears/plums
- whole grain crackers or breads
- dry, nonsweetened cereal
- yogurt

How to Make Eating Time Comfortable, Pleasant, and Safe

Children are more likely to eat in comfortable surroundings. Furniture should be of an appropriate size; table height should be a comfortable height for children and chairs should allow their feet to rest

FIGURE 18–4

Three-year-olds can learn to spread and cut with a plastic knife.

flat on the floor. If a highchair or youth chair is used, it must allow support for the child's feet and have a comfortable eating tray. Eating utensils should be child-sized and nonbreakable. An upturned rim around plates provides a means of "trapping" elusive bits of food. Use of plates that are divided into two or three compartments may help reduce frustration for toddlers as they develop their feeding skills. Small (4–6 ounce) plastic cups with broad bases are easy for children to hold and reduce spilling. Forks chosen for children should have short, blunt tines and broad, short, easy-to-grasp handles. Spoons should also have short, blunt handles and shallow bowls for easy use.

Toddlers are developing improved fine motor skills and hand/eye coordination. This enables them to better handle utensils and to feed themselves. Toddlers should be encouraged to practice these skills but should not be given too many hard-to-manage foods at one time. Serving finger foods along with those foods that require using a fork or spoon reduces mealtime frustration.

Finger foods encourage self-feeding and are usually well accepted and easy to handle. Meats and cheeses may be cut into cubes or strips, vegetables into sticks, and fruits into slices. Toddlers enjoy turning some nonfinger foods into finger foods and often accept them better because it was their individual choice. An adult may not think peas, mashed potatoes, and rice are finger foods, but toddlers do. A little flexibility in the choice of eating methods often pays off in the toddler's increased willingness to try eating by conventional methods.

Sanitation is an important consideration in feeding the toddler. The aseptic environment required when feeding infants is not necessary or possible to maintain with toddlers. However, cleanliness is of prime importance when preparing, serving, and eating food. The teacher and toddler must thoroughly wash their hands before handling or eating food and again after eating or before returning to work or play (Figure 18–5). Handwashing is mandatory since this age group does a lot of eating with their hands.

FIGURE 18–5

Children must wash their hands before handling food.

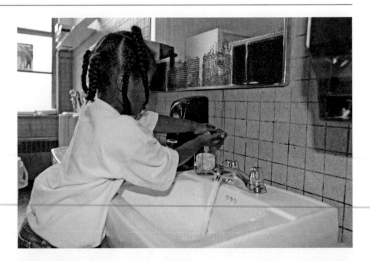

AS THE TODDLER BECOMES A PRESCHOOLER

As children grow older, they begin to eat more willingly. However, preschoolers will have even firmer ideas of what they will and will not eat. The preschooler grows in "spurts" that are followed by periods of little or no growth, only weight gain. During active growth periods the child's appetite and food acceptance is usually good. However, as growth slows, so does the child's appetite. It is during this latter stage that parents and teachers often are unduly concerned. (This concern can have the consequence of establishing a food–emotion link that can lead to long-lasting feeding problems.) There is no real cause for concern; a growing, energetic child will never starve. Remember that during this age, food should be offered frequently. If the child does not eat a good lunch, it will soon be snack time and he or she can get the needed nutrients then. The important thing is to remember that snack foods are always of high nutritious quality.

Attitudes formed about food and eating patterns during the preschool years will be carried into adulthood. Teachers and families share responsibilities for promoting healthful eating practices and helping young children form positive feelings about food. Preschoolers like rules even though they may resist them. Rules about acceptable eating behavior should be enforced consistently but also allow some flexibility for both the adult and child in order to avoid stressful eating situations.

Guidelines for Feeding the Preschooler

As with toddlers, the Food Guide Pyramid provides a simple guideline for feeding preschoolers (Figure 18–6). The main difference is in amount of food served. Suggested serving sizes for the preschooler are:

1/2 to 3/4 cup milk
1/2 to 1 slice of bread

FIGURE 18–6

A sample menu for preschool-aged children.

BREAKFAST	LUNCH	DINNER
2% milk (3/4 cup)	2% milk (3/4 cup)	2% milk (3/4 cup)
Cream of wheat (1/4 cup)	Beef patty (1 1/2 oz)	Diced chicken (1 1/2 oz)
or	Broccoli (1/4 cup)	Cooked carrots (1/4 cup)
Whole wheat toast (1/2 slice)	Diced watermelon (1/4 cup)	Diced plums (1/4 cup)
Jam or Jelly (1 tsp)	Whole-wheat bread (1/2 slice)	Rye bread (1/2 slice)
Diced peaches (1/2 cup)	Margarine (1 tsp)	Margarine (1 tsp)
MIDMORNING SNACK	**MIDAFTERNOON SNACK**	**EVENING SNACK**
Vanilla wafers (3)	Cheese cube (1 1/2 oz)	Applesauce (1/2 cup)
Orange juice (1/2 cup)	Whole wheat crackers (2)	Graham crackers (2)
	Water	Water

FIGURE 18–7

Children enjoy preparing some of the food that they will eat.

1 tbsp for each year of age for:
  fruits (approximately 1/4 cup)
  vegetables (approximately 1/4 cup)
  meats and meat alternates (approximately 1 1/2 ounces)

Serving the preschooler a little less than you expect them to eat does not overwhelm them but rather gives them an opportunity to ask for more. Three- to five-year-old children are also very aware of the appearance of food. Attention should be given to presenting a variety of colors, shapes, and textures in a meal. Doing so makes the food more attractive and increases its acceptance. At this age the child prefers foods that are lukewarm. Hot or cold foods are often rejected or played with until they reach an acceptable temperature. Involving children in meal preparation often improves their interest in eating a food or meal they have helped to fix (Figure 18–7).

The same rules for making mealtime comfortable for the toddler also apply for the preschooler. Although many three- to five-year-olds still have trouble managing eating utensils, they will gradually become more adept with continued use and encouragement. For example, children can begin learning how to spread and cut bread using a plastic knife. Young children may also be more cooperative and willing to eat if some finger foods are included and unintentional messes are ignored.

Nutrient Needs of School-Aged Children

Although energy expenditures and growth rates are highly variable from child to child, the need for a well-balanced diet continues to be critical for school-aged children. For the most part, they are eager eaters and open to trying new foods. Peers and groups outside of the child's family, including school and television, begin to compete with long-standing family eating patterns and food preferences. However, families still play an important role in terms of their expectations, the foods they make available at home, and the importance they place on eating meals together.

School-aged children tend to eat more at one sitting and require fewer in-between-meal snacks than when they were younger. Many children consume a portion of their daily nutrients from meals eaten at school. However, they are usually eager for, and need, a substantial after-school snack. Having access to a supply of healthy foods allows children to independently select and prepare a nutritious snack and also reinforces healthful eating habits. Appropriate serving sizes for school-aged children are:

  1 cup milk (2%)
  1 slice bread or 3/4 cup dry cereal
  1/2 to 3/4 cup fruits/vegetables
  1 ounce meat or meat alternate (snack); 2 ounces (meals)

The Food Guide Pyramid serves as an effective tool for assuring that all essential nutrients are included in children's meals and snacks.

Children With Special Needs

Children who have developmental disabilities or delays may present a range of different nutritional needs and feeding challenges. Impaired motor abilities may make self-feeding and/or swallowing difficult. Medications, such as some antibiotics and those taken for seizure disorders, can increase a child's need for certain nutrients. Some genetic conditions, such as **Down syndrome** and **Prader-Willi syndrome** increase the tendency for obesity, and thus make it necessary to monitor children's food intake carefully. Other children may have difficulty recognizing and communicating when they are hungry or have had enough to eat. Some children with autism will only eat a few food items and may require considerable coaxing before they will even take a few bits. Food allergies are also quite common among this population.

Since nutrition is essential to good health and maximizing developmental potential, careful attention must be paid to identifying and meeting each child's unique nutrient needs. Teachers must work closely with the child's family to determine how the child's condition may affect eating ability and nutrient requirements. Teachers should also monitor children's growth patterns to make sure they continue to stay within healthy limits. Families can keep teachers informed of any changes in the child's medical condition or treatments that might affect eating behavior. Teachers should not hesitate to call on nutrition professionals for advice and assistance with children's feeding problems.

GOOD EATING HABITS

Life-long eating habits are often formed between the ages of one to five years. This makes the feeding of toddlers and young children an important task. Families and teachers can promote good eating habits in two ways:

- serving a variety of nutritious foods
- eating with the children and modeling an enjoyment of a variety of nutritious foods

One of the most important goals in developing good eating habits is to gain the child's acceptance of a variety of foods from each of the food groups. It is especially important to cultivate children's interest in the fruit and vegetable groups because the nutrient contributions within each of these groups vary significantly. Children should also be encouraged to try a variety of new foods and familiar foods that have been prepared in different ways.

Toddlers and preschoolers often have a strong preference for sweet foods and a dislike for most vegetables. Families and teachers can address this challenge by downplaying sweets and increasing children's interest in vegetables. For example, children might help grow vegetables in containers or a small garden, harvest the mature vegetables, and prepare them for a meal. Teachers should also eat a variety of vegetables in front of the children, comment on how delicious they are, and display pleasure (such as smiling). This power of suggestion can have a contagious effect on children's willingness to at least try a few bites.

Children are often avid mimics of adults they admire and of their peers in group settings. Consequently, it is particularly important that adults sit with the children at mealtime, engage in pleasant conversation, show enjoyment when eating all kinds of food, and never exhibiting dislike for a food. Children quickly pick up on any negative reactions to foods and begin to imitate them. Table 18–2 provides some suggestions for introducing new foods to young children that may increase their acceptance.

Older children enjoy being involved in meal planning and preparation. For example, children in an after-school program might develop the weekly snack menu from a list of healthy food items

---

Down syndrome – *a genetic disorder that is characterized by unique facial features, mental retardation, and motor delays.*
Prader-Willi syndrome – *a chromosomal disorder that causes learning and behavior problems, overeating that can lead to obesity, poor muscle tone, and short height.*

TABLE 18-2 Introducing New Food

1. Introduce only one new food at a time.
2. Serve new food with familiar foods.
3. Serve only small amounts of the new food—begin with one teaspoonful.
4. Introduce new food only when the child is hungry.
5. Talk about the new food—taste, color, texture, etc.
6. Let the child help prepare the new food.
7. Encourage the child to taste the new food. If rejected, accept the refusal and try again later. As foods become more familiar, they are more readily accepted.
8. Find out what is not liked about a rejected food. The food may be accepted if it is prepared in a different way.
9. Let the child see you eat the new food and enjoy it!

Adapted from: *Food for Preschoolers*. (2002). Washington State University Cooperative Extension Service.

the teacher provides. They can also be assigned specific meal preparation roles and trusted to perform them with skill and confidence. Not only does this acknowledgement appeal to the school-aged child's sense of responsibility, but it also fosters positive self-esteem. Involving school-aged children in food-related activities also provides opportunities for learning about foods and reinforcing healthy eating and activity habits. This is important since school-aged children are especially vulnerable to conflicting messages about body image and weight control. It also helps them to understand the connections between health and eating behaviors.

Rewards should not be offered for trying a new food. Also, foods should never be used as a reward for any type of behavior. Studies with preschool children have shown that rewards for trying new foods increased the frequency of tasting a new food but did not increase its long-term acceptance. Adults are often tempted to use food (especially dessert or popular sweet snacks) as a reward for eating nutritious foods presented in the meal. This practice makes these foods assume undue importance for the child. Appropriate desserts should be nutritious (nutrient dense) and planned as an essential part of the meal. For example, a zucchini or carrot bar or muffin may disguise vegetables that a child might otherwise refuse. Also, a child should never be asked to present a "clean plate" before receiving their dessert. This is one sure way to start the child on a road to obesity or eating disorders (Stang, Rehorst, & Golicic, 2004).

HEALTH PROBLEMS RELATING TO EATING HABITS

Teaching children healthful eating practices can have lifelong positive benefits. A number of health problems are now thought to be directly or indirectly related to foods eaten. Examples are:

- **dental caries** (tooth decay)
- obesity (excess body fat)
- **hypertension** (high blood pressure)
- cardiovascular disease (CVD)
- diabetes mellitus
- some cancers

rewards – *things given for appropriate behavior.*
dental caries – *tooth decay.*
hypertension – *elevation of blood pressure above the normally accepted values.*

The occurrence of dental caries may be affected by sugar in the diet (Kranz, Smiciklas-Wright, & Francis, 2006; Kranz, et al., 2005). However, the type of sugar (soluble or not), the form it is in (adheres to tooth surface or not), and the time it is eaten (meals versus snacks) determine the decay potential more than does total sugar intake. Providing sugar in the form of fruits and vegetables may give protection from tooth decay and also provide needed nutrients for the actively growing child.

Prevention of obesity should start with infant feeding. Look for the infant's signals of satiety and stop feeding when they occur. The toddler and preschooler will usually signal or stop eating when they have had enough food, unless eating or not eating is their best way to get attention. Forcing children to continue eating interferes with their ability to recognize when they are full and can contribute to obesity. A genetic potential for obesity exists in some families; this does not mean that obesity is inevitable for all family members. Children with one or two obese parents should be helped during early childhood years to make wise choices of nutrient-dense foods. Approximately 16 percent of children are currently overweight (American Heart Association & Stroke Statistics Subcommittee, 2006). This rate of overweight has tripled in the last 20 years. Serving children nutritious foods, involving them in physical activity and limiting their sedentary activities, such as television viewing and computer/video games is critical for maintaining normal body weight and reducing the risk of short- and long-term health problems (Lindsay, et al., 2006; Mann, 2005) (Figure 18–8).

FIGURE 18–8

The Physical Activity Pyramid is designed to help children get fit and stay healthy.

© 1999 University of Missouri-Columbia, MU Extension GH 1800

For many years hypertension (high blood pressure) has been correlated with a high intake of salt (sodium) (Karppanen & Mervaala, 2006). Children from families where hypertension is common are at high risk and may benefit from reducing their intake of salt. Although sodium is an essential nutrient for infants and young children, this need can easily be met without the use of the salt shaker. The increased consumption of convenience, processed, and fast foods, which are often high in sodium, may be contributing to a significant increase in the salt intake of many adults and children.

Cardiovascular disease (CVD) is most often associated with high levels of certain fatty substances in the blood. Cholesterol is most often associated with CVD; however, a high intake of saturated fatty acids and/or total fat are primary contributors to CVD. Sixty percent of overweight children ages 5 to 10 will already have one risk factor for heart disease (AHA, 2006; CDC, 2000).

The possible health benefit of testing and monitoring blood cholesterol levels in young children remains controversial issue. The American Academy of Pediatrics recommends that no cholesterol testing be done before the child is two years old. The two- to eight-year-old child should be tested for cholesterol only if there is a strong family history of cardiovascular disease before the age of 55 years.

Fats, including cholesterol, should not be restricted in the diet of the infant or toddler; fats are a source of essential fatty acids and are required for normal nerve development.

The diet for a child with high blood cholesterol levels should be carefully monitored to include no more than 30 percent of calories from fat, and have 10 percent or less calories from saturated fat. If a child's diet must be adjusted for any reason, the first priority must be that it meets all of the nutrient requirements for normal growth and development. Involving the child in more physical activity may also lower blood cholesterol.

While type 1 diabetes is not caused by the child's diet, the disease does have a profound effect on the diabetic child's eating habits and growth (Hockenberry, 2004). There is no one "diabetic diet." The primary goal in feeding a child with diabetes is to provide food to meet his/her nutritional needs. The purpose is to find a balance between food, medication (insulin), and activity to achieve normal blood sugar levels.

Typical meal plans for diabetic children include limitation of concentrated sugars, meals planned with food exchanges, and matching the amount of medication taken to the amount of carbohydrates in meals and snacks. It is important that children with diabetes be able to eat foods similar to their peers so they don't feel that they are "different."

It had been thought that type 1 diabetes occurred only in children and young adults, while type 2 diabetes occurred primarily in overweight, middle-aged, and older adults. Recent years have seen a dramatic increase in type 2 diabetes in younger children due to the epidemic of childhood obesity (Bindler & Bruya, 2006). According to the American Academy of Pediatrics, research shows that 30 to 50 percent of children newly diagnosed with diabetes have type 2 diabetes. This figure was less than 4 percent in 1990 (*Food Insight*, 2000).

Some Common Feeding Concerns in Younger Children

Consuming Excessive Amounts of Milk The child who drinks milk to the exclusion of other foods may be at risk for iron-deficiency anemia and vitamin C (ascorbic acid) deficiency. Milk is very deficient in iron and in vitamin C. The child who drinks more than 16–24 ounces of milk daily usually does not consume enough foods from the other food groups to adequately meet nutrient needs. Offering the child water between meals to satisfy thirst may help in solving this problem. Including iron-rich foods in the child's daily meals will also protect against iron-deficiency anemia. Examples of good food sources of iron are presented in Table 19–1 on page 450.

Child's Refusal to Eat Toddlers and preschoolers may occasionally refuse food either because they are not hungry or because they are asserting their newly found independence. Whatever the cause, the best response is to ignore it. Remember that active growing children will not let themselves starve—they will get hungry and eat. If nutritious food is provided for meals and snacks and if families and teachers do not give in to substituting the less nutritious foods that the child requests, hunger will eventually win over the challenge of **refusal**. However, it is important that the teacher does not "try too hard" or attempt to coax or convince children to eat. This can lead to unpleasant battles and emotion-packed feeding sessions.

Dawdling and Messiness These are the trademarks of young children and cannot be avoided; however, they can be controlled. Children dawdle for various reasons—they have eaten enough, they'd rather eat something else, or they have learned that it gets attention. Establishing mealtime rules and consistently enforcing them will usually end dawdling. The teacher should decide upon an appropriate length of time for eating (approximately 20–25 minutes), warn the child when there is not much time left, and then remove the child from the table. This may result in some temporary unhappiness, but the young child quickly learns that they must eat when given the opportunity. However, it is always important to avoid hurrying children at mealtime and to allow sufficient time for eating.

Children need to learn to feed themselves and manage proper eating utensils, even though some foods may present a real challenge. This results in understandable and forgivable messiness and should be ignored. Attention-getting messiness should be ignored also; otherwise, the behavior will be reinforced and likely continued. However, the teacher has some rights too, and continuous, avoidable messiness may be handled by removing the child from the table.

Food Jags This problem can best be solved by prevention. Foods served to young children should be chosen so that a specific food does not appear too frequently. This helps to avoid the child getting fixed on a given food. Food jags occur when children consume a limited variety of foods and eventually results in a deficient intake of certain nutrients. Fortunately, children usually tire of these limited foods and will usually return to their normal eating behaviors.

REFLECTIVE THOUGHTS

Many families report that their children are allergic to specific foods. However, actual documented food allergies are reported to affect up to 8 percent of children. Foods most commonly responsible for nearly 90 percent of all allergic reactions include milk, eggs, soy, peanuts, tree nuts (cashews and almonds), wheat, fish, and shellfish (The Food Allergy & Anaphylaxis Network, 2006). However, not all food-related reactions are caused by allergies; some result from food intolerances. Many symptoms of food intolerance are identical to allergic symptoms.

- How can you tell the difference between food allergies and food intolerances?
- Is the difference important in terms of meal planning?
- Review the list of common foods causing allergic reactions. What similarities do you see between those foods and substances used to make infant formula?

---

refusal – *the act of declining or rejecting.*

Inconsistencies in Adult Approaches to Feeding Problems   This concern relates to several problems already cited. It is very important that families and teachers communicate and agree on a consistent approach to handling certain food-related problems. It doesn't matter if the problem is weaning from excessive milk intake, decreasing dawdling and messiness behaviors, refusal to eat, or dealing with food jags. What is essential is that an intervention or procedure designed to address the problem behavior is established and carried out consistently by the teachers and family. The child cannot be expected to learn acceptable behavior if the rules constantly change.

Food Additives and Hyperactivity   Since 1973, when the Feingold diet was initially published, there has been considerable interest in the possible link between food additives and behavior problems, particularly hyperactivity and AD/HD (see Chapter 5). Several early double-blind studies failed to show a link between additives and/or sugar and hyperactivity; however, more recent studies of specific additives have indicated some responses related to the amount of the additive given (Wolraich, 1996). Research has still not provided clear-cut answers. No doubt some children may be affected by certain additives in an allergic-type reaction. For these children, the offending agent should be eliminated from their diet. Sugar has also been thought to be a cause of hyperactivity, but this, too, has been unproven. Restricting a child's sugar intake has not been shown to improve behavior or learning. Actually, a biochemical case can be made for sugar as a calming and sleep-inducing agent (Sizer & Whitney, 1999). Avoidance of additives or dyes is certainly not harmful if the diet still includes sufficient amounts of foods from all food groups.

Fast-Food Consumption   The current cultural pattern of increased numbers of two-working-parent and single-parent families has changed family eating practices. More meals are eaten outside of the home, especially in fast-food restaurants. There is growing concern about the repeated and long-term consumption of fast food and its effect on young children. Most fast foods are very high in calories, cholesterol, fat, and salt. Over time, these can contribute to significant health problems such as cardiovascular disease, hypertension, diabetes, and/or obesity. Fast foods are also low in vitamins A and C and calcium, unless milk is the selected beverage. A too-frequent scenario is a mother and young child at a fast-food restaurant. The mother shares a few bites of her hamburger with the child, whose meal is rounded out with French fries and a small cola. An occasional fast-food meal for children is not a problem if care is taken when food selections are made and nutrients that may be lacking are made up at other times in the day.

Effect of Television on Food Preferences and Food Choices   Television advertising exerts a major effect on children's attitudes toward food (Figure 18–9). Many children spend more time watching television than they spend in school. It is estimated that a child is

FIGURE 18–9

Television commercials influence children's ideas about food.

exposed to three hours of commercials per week and to 19,000–22,000 commercials each year (Strasburger, 2001). Over one-half of these commercials are for food. Cereals (mostly sweetened), cookies, candy, sweetened beverages, and fast-food offerings are the most frequently advertised foods (Harrison & Marske, 2005; Story & French, 2004). Many of these foods are high in sugar or fat and are too calorie-dense to be healthful choices for young children. An additional concern is the extent to which adult food choices are influenced by the child's food preferences that were learned from television food commercials.

ISSUES TO CONSIDER • "Surfing the Web" for Information

Many of us "surf the Web" for information. A report in the *American Journal of Public Health* noted that 40 percent of Americans access the Internet to obtain medical information (Baker, et al., 2003).

- Do you think all the information available on the Internet is factual or reliable?
- Do you believe that you can judge which is factual and which is not?
- Where would you turn for guidance?

Clues to unreliable sources include

- information based on testimonials.
- information provided by someone who stands to profit.
- unpublished information available only on the Internet.

FOCUS ON FAMILIES • Feeding Toddlers and Young Children

Mealtimes with children can be filled with many emotions and learning experiences. It can be a joyful time for families to form strong positive bonds, or it can be a time when conflicts erupt and eating no longer becomes a pleasurable experience. Many families are faced with the latter if they have a picky eater in the family. It is challenging, but not impossible, to get picky eaters to explore and accept new foods in their diet. With careful planning, families can work to make their eating experiences positive ones.

- Let children help with menu planning. Take them to the grocery store to help pick out fresh fruits and vegetables. Challenge them to find a new item to try.
- Serve foods that a child does not like with a favorite food they are familiar with.
- Use different preparation techniques to prepare food in a fun way. For example, try freezing fresh fruit or incorporating vegetables into muffins and cookie bars.
- Do not give up on a food if your child does not accept it the first time. It can take 10 to 15 exposures to an unfamiliar food before a child may accept it.
- Serve regular meals and snacks. Children are more likely to eat better if their meals and snacks are adequately spaced apart.
- Avoid sharing and passing your own food dislikes to your child.
- Finally, most children will get what they need nutritionally. Continue offering a wide variety of colorful foods and making mealtime a positive, pleasant experience.

CASE STUDY

Maria, age seven years, is new to the community and has recently enrolled in your after-school program. She and her parents speak Portuguese, but very little English. The other children are intrigued with Maria and her "different" language. They eagerly attempt to teach her some English words by pointing to and repeating the names of foods and objects with exaggerated clarity. Although Maria seems to enjoy their attention and is responding to their efforts, you are concerned that she still eats very little during snack time.

1. Why should you be concerned that Maria is not eating?
2. What steps can you take to learn more about her family's food preferences?
3. Where might you access information about foods and food preferences native to Maria's culture?
4. Where might you access materials to aid in Maria's care and communication with her family?
5. How/where might you locate an interpreter for assistance?

CLASSROOM CORNER • Teacher Activities

Tasting Pears...
Concept: The same food can have different tastes and textures. (Pre–2)

Learning Objectives
- Children will learn that pears come in a variety of tastes.
- Children will experience tasting three kinds of pears.

Supplies
- two Anjou pears; two Bosc pears; two Bartlett pears; hand wipes; small plates; napkins

Learning Activities
- Read and discuss the following book:
  - *Too Many Pears!* by Jackie French
- Tell children there are different varieties of pears. Talk about the importance of eating fruit each day.
- Have children wash their hands with wipes and then pass around each pear for children to feel and look at the differences and similarities. Have children describe each pear's color, texture, shape and talk about differences.
- Next pass out a napkin and a plate to each child. Place a small bite of each pear on a plate for children to taste; this can be done one at a time or the plate can have a sample of each pear on it.
- Give children an opportunity to taste each pear and talk about how each one tastes. Talk about the different tastes and textures.

Evaluation
- Children will know that pears are a healthy food choice.

SUMMARY

- After the first birthday:
  - physical growth rate slows.
  - behavioral change is rapid.
- Food can serve as a source of friction. The adult's responsibility is to:
  - serve a *variety* of nutritious foods.
  - decide when to offer food.
  - set a good example by eating a variety of nutritious foods.
- The child will decide:
  - what to eat.
  - how much to eat.
- Long-term food habits are formed during the preschool years.
  - Make self-feeding as successful as possible to foster self-esteem.
  - Make feeding as nutritious as possible to minimize food-related health problems such as obesity, anemia, and hypertension.

APPLICATION ACTIVITIES

1. Eighteen-month-old Jason has recently been enrolled in an all-day early childhood program. His health assessment reveals that he is anemic. Observations of his eating habits suggest that he dislikes meat and vegetables but eats large quantities of fruits and drinks at least two cups of milk at every meal and snack. What changes in eating habits should the teacher try to foster to improve Jason's iron status?

2. Formulate plans for the dining area of an early childhood program that will help to foster children's self-feeding skills. Include a discussion of appropriate furniture and eating utensils. Plan a menu for one day (one meal and two snacks) that will further enhance the child's self-feeding skills.

3. Four-year-old Traci arrives at her child care provider's home every morning with a bag of doughnuts. Her mother informs the provider that it is okay for Traci to eat the doughnuts since she doesn't like what is being served for breakfast. The other children have also begun to ask for doughnuts. How should the provider handle this situation? What factors must be considered?

CHAPTER REVIEW

A. **By Yourself:**

1. Name three ways that mealtimes can be made pleasant for children.

2. Explain the teacher's major responsibilities in toddler feeding situations.

3. Suggest serving sizes for a two-year-old and a four-year-old for each of the following foods: bread, peas, applesauce, orange juice, banana, cooked chicken, noodles, baked beans

B. **As a Group:**

1. Watch one hour of Saturday morning cartoons on television and discuss the following:
   a. What foods were presented in the majority of commercials?
   b. What adjectives were used in describing foods that were advertised?

c. Imagine that you are a four-year-old. On your next trip to the grocery store with your mother, what products would you want her to buy?

2. Go to a fast-food restaurant featuring hamburgers and observe the following:
   a. How many toddlers and preschoolers are there?
   b. What are the children eating and drinking?
   c. What foods might have been ordered from the menu to provide a more nutritious, healthier meal?
   d. Ask the restaurant for nutritional information or visit its Web site.

3. Go to the local supermarket and observe advertising techniques geared toward children's foods.
   a. What cereals are shelved at a child's eye level?
   b. What types of foods are displayed at the end of aisles?
   c. What food items are typically displayed at the checkout counter?
   d. What types of free food samples are offered by the store to young children?

REFERENCES

Allen, K. E., & Marotz, L. R. (2007). *Developmental profiles: Pre-birth through twelve* (5th ed.). Clifton Park, NY: Delmar Learning.

American Heart Association (AHA). Statistics Committee and Stroke Statistics Subcommittee. (2006). Heart disease and stroke statistics – 2006 update. *Circulation, 113*(6), e85–151. Accessed December 5, 2006, from http://circ.ahajournals.org/cgi/reprint/113/6/e85.pdf.

Baker, L., Wagner, T., Singer, S., & Bundorf, M. (2003). Use of the Internet and E-mail for health care information. *JAMA, 289*(18), 2400–2406.

Bindler, R. & Bruya, M. (2006). Evidence for identifying children at risk for being overweight, cardiovascular disease, and type 2 diabetes in primary care. *Journal of Pediatric Health Care, 20*(2), 82–87.

Centers for Disease Prevention & Control (CDC). (Winter, 2000). Preventing obesity among children. *Chronic Disease Notes and Reports, 13,* 1.

Connor, S. (2006). Food-related advertising on preschool television: building brand recognition in young viewers. *Pediatrics, 118*(4), 1478–1485.

Harrison, K. & Marske, A. (2005). Nutritional content of foods advertised during television programs children watch most. *American Journal of Public Health, 95*(9), 1568–1574.

Hockenberry, M. (2004). *Wong's essentials of pediatric nursing.* St. Louis, MO: C.V. Mosby.

International Food Information Council Foundation. (2003, January/February). The challenge of type 2 diabetes in children. *Food Insight.* Accessed on December 6, 2006, from http://www.ific.org/foodinsight/2003/jf/diabetesfi103.cfm.

Jenvey, V. (2007). The relationship between television viewing and obesity in young children: A review of existing explanations. *Early Child Development and Care, 177*(8), 809–820.

Karppanen, H. & Mervaala, E. (2006). Sodium intake and hypertension. *Progress in Cardiovascular Disease, 49*(2), 59–75.

Kittler, P. & Sucher, K. (2003). *Food and culture.* St. Paul, MN: Brooks Cole.

Kranz, S., Smiciklas-Wright, H., & Francis, L. (2006). Diet quality, added sugar, and dietary intakes in American preschoolers. *Pediatric Dentistry, 28*(2), 164–171.

Kranz, S., Smiciklas-Wright, H., & Francis, Siega-Riz, A., & Mitchell, D. (2005). Adverse effect of high added sugar consumption on dietary intake in American preschoolers. *Journal or Pediatrics, 146*(1), 105–111.

Lindsay, A., Sussner, K., Kim, J., & Gortmaker, S. (2006). The role of parents in preventing childhood obesity. *The Future of Children, 16*(1), 169–186.

Mann, C. (2005). Provocative study says obesity may reduce U.S. life expectancy. *Science, 307*(5716), 1716–1717.

Nestle, M. (2006). Food marketing and childhood obesity—a matter of policy. *New England Journal of Medicine, 354*(24), 2527–2529.

Satter, E. (2000). *How to get your child to eat . . . But not too much.* Palo Alto, CA: Bull Publishing Co.

Sizer, F., & Whitney, E. (1999). *Nutrition concepts and controversies* (8th ed.). Belmont, CA: Wadsworth/Thomson Learning.

Stang, J., Rehorst, J., & Golicic, M. (2004). Parental feeding practices and risk of childhood overweight in girls: Implications for dietetics practice. *Journal of the American Dietetic Association, 104*(7), 1076–1079.

Strasburger, V. (2001). Children and TV advertising: Nowhere to run, nowhere to hide. *Journal of Developmental & Behavioral Pediatrics, 22*(3), 185–187.

Story, M. & French, S. (2004). Food advertising and marketing directed at children and adolescents in the U.S. *International Journal of Behavioral Nutrition & Physical Activity, 1*(1), 1479–1486.

The Food Allergy & Anaphylaxis Network. (2006). Accessed on December 5, 2006, from http://www.foodallergy.org/allergens/index.html.

Washington State University Cooperative Extension Service. (2002). *Food for preschoolers.* Pullman, WA.

Wolraich, M. L. (1996). Diet and behavior: What the research shows. *Contemporary Pediatrics, 13*(12), 29–39.

HELPFUL WEB RESOURCES

American Diabetes Association   http://www.diabetes.org

American Heart Association   http://www.americanheart.org
(childhood obesity)

Council for Exceptional Children   http://www.cec.sped.org

Food & Nutrition Information Center   http://www.nal.usda.gov
(Education materials; cultural and
ethnic foods)

For additional health, safety, and nutrition resources, go to
http://www.EarlyChildEd.delmar.cengage.com

CHAPTER 19

Planning and Serving Nutritious and Economical Meals

OBJECTIVES

After studying this chapter, you should be able to:

- Identify the criteria for adequate menus for young children.
- Describe where information can be obtained regarding licensing requirements for food and nutrition services.
- Plan meals and snacks for toddlers, preschoolers, and school-aged children that meet their nutritional requirements.
- Outline a simple cost control plan.

TERMS TO KNOW

sensory qualities
ethnic
weekly menus
cycle menus
odd-day cycle menus

whole grains
enriched
full-strength
fruit drinks

cost control
(First-In-First-Out) FIFO
    inventory method
procurement

Nourishment is essential for human life. Eating is a sensory, emotional, and social experience that most children and adults enjoy. Many young children spend a portion of their time in early childhood or after-school programs. As a result, teachers have many opportunities to help children establish positive attitudes toward eating. This can be accomplished by planning nourishing meals that are acceptable to children and serving these meals and snacks in a pleasant atmosphere.

MEAL PLANNING

A menu is a list of foods that are to be served; it is the basis of any food service. Menu planning requires time and a careful evaluation of the physical, developmental, and social needs of those for whom it is planned. Thoughtful planning is necessary whether the menu is designed to feed a family of three or designed for an institution serving thousands of meals a day. The difference between the two situations is largely one of scale. The same careful planning must be applied to the development of menus suitable in each setting. An adequate menu that is planned for children must

- meet children's nutritional needs.
- meet any existing funding or licensing requirements.
- be appealing (have taste, texture, and eye appeal).
- make children comfortable by including familiar foods.
- encourage healthy food habits by introducing new foods.
- provide safe food and be served in clean surroundings.
- stay within budgetary limits.
- provide alternatives for children with food allergies, eating problems, and special nutritional needs.

A Good Menu Meets Nutritional Needs

The primary criterion for a good menu is nutritional adequacy. A menu must meet the nutritional needs of the children for whom it is intended (Figure 19–1). When planning menus for young children it is important to first determine what portion of the day's total nutrient requirements will be provided. To determine children's nutritional needs, the Food Guide Pyramid and/or the *Dietary Guidelines for Americans* for that age group should be reviewed.

Iron, calcium, and vitamins A and C are nutrients for which young children are most at risk; these nutrients should be provided daily. Tables 19–1 through 19–4 provide examples of food sources for these nutrients and suggestions for preparation.

Early childhood programs participating in federally funded food programs for children are required to provide at least one-third of the recommended daily requirements for calcium, iron,

FIGURE 19–1

A good menu meets children's nutrient needs.

 REFLECTIVE THOUGHTS

The Food Pyramid represents an idea that has become very popular. Review the new Food Guide Pyramid illustrated on page 000 in Chapter 13. The Pyramid has now been modified so that it is interactive and can be personalized based on an individual's age, gender, and level of physical activity.

- What aspects of the new Pyramid do you personally find most useful?
- Do you think people will be more or less likely to use this new model?
- What changes do you plan to make in your daily life/work based on the new Pyramid?
- How will you use the Pyramid to plan your diet?
- What portion of your Pyramid do you have the greatest difficulty achieving?

TABLE 19-1 Sources of Iron and Suggested Preparation

Liver
strips, baked
braised, with apple slices and onion

Beef
ground beef patty
meat loaf
roast beef
roast beef sandwich
beef stew
meatballs or meat sauce and spaghetti

Dried Peas, Beans, and Lentils
with rice
with small amounts of meat
with vegetables
in soup or salad
in a tortilla

Pumpkin or Squash Seed Kernels, Roasted

Ham
ham salad
ham and sweet potato casserole
scalloped ham and potatoes
sliced baked ham
ham sandwich

Prunes
stewed
whip
fruit soup

Chicken
chicken and rice
chicken and noodles
creamed chicken
baked chicken
chicken salad

Grain Products (Whole or Enriched)
fortified ready-to-eat cereals
pasta with tomato or meat sauce
gingerbread
bran or cornmeal muffins
tortillas
rice pudding

Raisins
in bread or rice pudding
plain
in cereals or breads

Spinach
raw
salad with onions and bacon
cooked and tossed
    with parmesan cheese
    with hard cooked eggs
    with cheese sauce

TABLE 19-2 Sources of Calcium and Suggested Preparation

Milk
plain
in custards
in puddings

Cheese
in sandwiches
in cream sauce
cubes
in salads

Yogurt
plain
with fruit
as dip for fruits or vegetables
frozen

Salmon, or Trout
patties
loaf

Soy
milk, fortified
tofu, fortified

Vegetables
broccoli stir-fried; with cheese sauce
Chinese cabbage stir-fried or in salads
cauliflower, cooked, raw or in salads

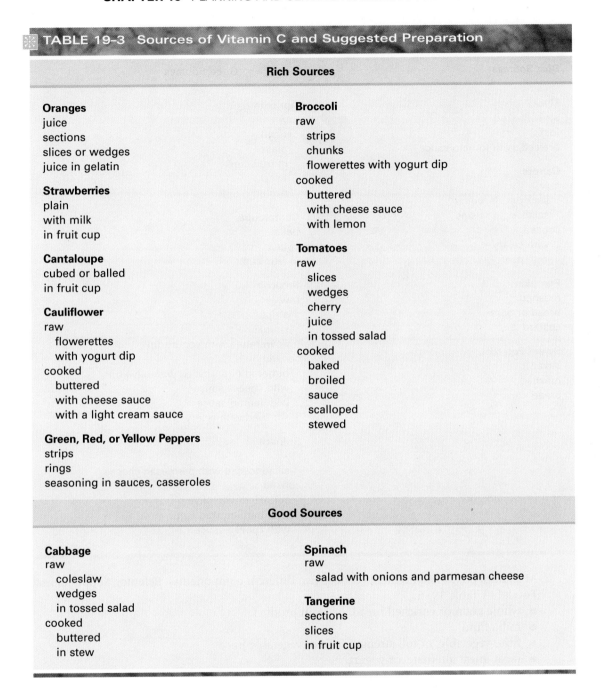

TABLE 19–3 Sources of Vitamin C and Suggested Preparation

Rich Sources

Oranges
juice
sections
slices or wedges
juice in gelatin

Strawberries
plain
with milk
in fruit cup

Cantaloupe
cubed or balled
in fruit cup

Cauliflower
raw
　flowerettes
　　with yogurt dip
cooked
　buttered
　with cheese sauce
　with a light cream sauce

Green, Red, or Yellow Peppers
strips
rings
seasoning in sauces, casseroles

Broccoli
raw
　strips
　chunks
　flowerettes with yogurt dip
cooked
　buttered
　with cheese sauce
　with lemon

Tomatoes
raw
　slices
　wedges
　cherry
　juice
　in tossed salad
cooked
　baked
　broiled
　sauce
　scalloped
　stewed

Good Sources

Cabbage
raw
　coleslaw
　wedges
　in tossed salad
cooked
　buttered
　in stew

Spinach
raw
　salad with onions and parmesan cheese

Tangerine
sections
slices
in fruit cup

vitamin A, and vitamin C; meeting one-half of a children's daily nutrient requirements is ideal. Federal Child and Adult Care Food Program (CACFP) guidelines require early childhood programs to follow a basic meal pattern that ensures minimum nutritional adequacy:

1. Minimum Breakfast Requirement
   - whole grain or enriched bread or grain alternate
   - fruit, vegetable, or full-strength fruit or vegetable juice
   - milk, fluid

TABLE 19-4   Sources of Vitamin A and Suggested Preparation

Rich Sources	Good Sources

Liver
strips, baked
loaf
braised, with tomato sauce
 	
Carrots
raw
  sticks, curls, coins
  salad, with raisins
cooked
  with celery
  with peas
 	
Pumpkin
mashed
bread or bars
custard
 	
Sweet Potatoes
baked
mashed
bread
	Apricots
	raw
	canned
	  plain
	  in fruit cup
	  whip
	  nectar
	
	Cantaloupe
	balls
	cubes
	in fruit cup
	
	Broccoli
	raw
	  strips
	  chunks
	  flowerettes with yogurt dip
	cooked
	  buttered or sprinkled with olive oil
	  with cheese sauce
	  with lemon sauce
	  stir-fried with celery, onions
	
	Spinach
	raw
	  salad tossed with parmesan cheese
	cooked
	  sprinkled with olive oil
	  with hard cooked eggs
	  with cheese sauce

2. Minimum Snack Requirement (choose two different components). Refer to "Supplemental Foods" in Table 19–5.
   - whole grain or enriched bread, or grain product
   - milk, fluid
   - fruit, vegetable, or full-strength fruit or vegetable juice
   - meat, meat alternate, or yogurt
3. Minimum Lunch or Supper Requirement
   - meat or meat alternate
   - fruits and/or vegetables (two or more different kinds)
   - whole grain or enriched bread, or grain product
   - milk, fluid

Minimum serving sizes are determined by the child's age in categories of one to three years, three to six years, and six to twelve years (USDA, 2005).

A Good Menu Meets Funding or Licensing Requirements

Many child care organizations depend on some form of government monies for their funding. Perhaps the best known of these government programs is the Child and Adult Care Food Program (CACFP).

TABLE 19-5 CACFP Meal Requirements for Children Ages One Through Twelve

Child Meal Pattern - Breakfast
Select All Three Components for a Reimbursable Meal

Food Components	Ages 1–2	Ages 3–5	Ages 6–12[1]
1 milk			
fluid milk	1/2 cup	3/4 cup	1 cup
1 fruit/vegetable			
juice,[2] fruit and/or vegetable	1/4 cup	1/2 cup	1/2 cup
1 grains/bread[3]			
bread or	1/2 slice	1/2 slice	1 slice
cornbread or biscuit or roll or muffin or	1/2 serving	1/2 serving	1 serving
cold dry cereal or	1/4 cup	1/3 cup	3/4 cup
hot cooked cereal or	1/4 cup	1/4 cup	1/2 cup
pasta or noodles or grains	1/4 cup	1/4 cup	1/2 cup

[1] Children age 12 and older may be served larger portions based on their greater food needs. They may not be served less than the minimum quantities listed in this column.
[2] Fruit or vegetable juice must be full-strength.
[3] Breads and grains must be made from whole-grain or enriched meal or flour. Cereal must be whole-grain or enriched or fortified.

Child Meal Pattern - Lunch or Supper
Include Foods from All Four Components for a Reimbursable Meal.

Food Components	Ages 1–2	Ages 3–5	Ages 6–12[1]
1 milk			
fluid milk	1/2 cup	3/4 cup	1 cup
2 fruits/vegetables			
juice,[2] fruit and/or vegetable	1/4 cup	1/2 cup	3/4 cup
1 grains/bread[3]			
bread or	1/2 slice	1/2 slice	1 slice
cornbread or biscuit or roll or muffin or	1/2 serving	1/2 serving	1 serving
cold dry cereal or	1/4 cup	1/3 cup	3/4 cup
hot cooked cereal or	1/4 cup	1/4 cup	1/2 cup
pasta or noodles or grains	1/4 cup	1/4 cup	1/2 cup
1 meat/meat alternate			
meat or poultry or fish[4] or	1 ounce	1 1/2 ounces	2 ounces
alternate protein product or	1 ounce	1 1/2 ounces	2 ounces
cheese or	1 ounce	1 1/2 ounces	2 ounces
egg or	1/2 egg	3/4 cup	1 egg
cooked dry beans or peas or	1/4 cup	3/8 cup	1/2 cup
peanut or other nut or seed butters or	2 Tbsp.	3 Tbsp.	4 Tbsp.
nuts and/or seeds[5] or	1/2 ounce	3/4 ounces	1 ounces
yogurt[6]	4 ounces	6 ounces	8 ounces

[1] Children age 12 and older may be served larger portions based on their greater food needs. They may not be served less than the minimum quantities listed in this column.
[2] Fruit or vegetable juice must be full-strength.
[3] Breads and grains must be made from whole-grain or enriched meal or flour. Cereal must be whole-grain or enriched or fortified.
[4] A serving consists of the edible portion of cooked lean meat or poultry or fish.
[5] Nuts and seeds may meet only one-half of the total meat/meat alternate serving and must be combined with another meat/meat alternate to fulfill the lunch or supper requirement.
[6] Yogurt may be plain or flavored, unsweetened or sweetened.

(continued)

TABLE 19–5 CACFP Meal Requirements for Children Ages One Through Twelve (continued)

Child Meal Pattern - Snack
Select Two of the Four Components for a Reimbursable Snack

Food Components	Ages 1–2	Ages 3–5	Ages 6–12[1]
1 milk			
fluid milk	1/2 cup	1/2 cup	1 cup
1 fruit/vegetable			
juice,[2] fruit and/or vegetable	1/2 cup	1/2 cup	3/4 cup
1 grains/bread[3]			
bread or	1/2 slice	1/2 slice	1 slice
cornbread or biscuit or roll or muffin or	1/2 serving	1/2 serving	1 serving
cold dry cereal or	1/4 cup	1/3 cup	3/4 cup
hot cooked cereal or	1/4 cup	1/4 cup	1/2 cup
pasta or noodles or grains	1/4 cup	1/4 cup	1/2 cup
1 meat/meat alternate	1/2 ounce	1/2 ounce	1 ounce
meat or poultry or fish[4] or	1/2 ounce	1/2 ounce	1 ounce
alternate protein product or	1/2 ounce	1/2 ounce	1 ounce
cheese or	1/2 ounce	1/2 ounce	1 ounce
egg[5] or	1/2 egg	1/2 egg	1/2 egg
cooked dry beans or peas or	1/8 cup	1/8 cup	1/4 cup
peanut or other nut or seed butters or	1 Tbsp.	1 Tbsp.	2 Tbsp.
nuts and/or seeds or	1/2 ounce	1/2 ounce	1 ounce
yogurt[6]	2 ounces	2 ounces	4 ounces

[1] Children age 12 and older may be served larger portions based on their greater food needs. They may not be served less than the minimum quantities listed in this column.
[2] Fruit or vegetable juice must be full-strength. Juice cannot be served when milk is the only other snack component.
[3] Breads and grains must be made from whole-grain or enriched meal or flour. Cereal must be whole-grain or enriched or fortified.
[4] A serving consists of the edible portion of cooked lean meat or poultry or fish.
[5] One-half egg meets the required minimum amount (one ounce or less) of meat alternate.
[6] Yogurt may be plain or flavored, unsweetened or sweetened.

Source: Food and Nutrition Service, United States Department of Agriculture, 2007.

This program reimburses participating centers and home-based programs for meals served to the children. The per meal/snack rate compensates programs, in part, for their food, labor, and administrative expenses. Funds are provided by the Food and Nutrition Service of the U.S. Department of Agriculture; in most states, the program is administered by the Department of Education. The meal plan cited in Table 19–5 reflects the minimum that must be served in order to qualify for reimbursement under this program. At this time, meals are planned using food-based menu planning, using Nutrient Standard or Assisted Nutrient Standard Menu Planning, or adopting an alternate menu planning approach developed by a state agency or by the school food authority with state agency approval. The guidelines are quite specific as to the minimum amounts of food required to fulfill a serving. Guidelines are also available listing specific foods that are permitted as alternatives within each food group (Table 19–6). The menu planner working within these guidelines must take great care to keep up with the current information as this program undergoes frequent and sometimes sweeping changes. The National School Lunch Act requires that school meals comply with the *Dietary Guidelines for Americans*.

Early childhood programs must be licensed to participate in the CACFP program. The National School Lunch Act requires that school meals comply with the *Dietary Guidelines for Americans*. Licensing of child care facilities is administered by state agencies, usually the Department of Health.

TABLE 19-6 Acceptable Bread and Bread Alternates

Important Notes:
- All products must be made of whole grain or enriched flour or meal.
- Serving sizes listed below are specified for children under six years of age.
- A *"full"* serving (defined below) is required for children six years of age and older.
- USDA recommends that cookies, granola bars, and similar foods be served in a snack no more than twice a week. They may be used for a snack only when:
  - whole grain or enriched meal or flour is the predominant ingredient as specified on the label or according to the recipe; and
  - the total weight of a serving for children under six years of age is a minimum of 18 grams (0.6 ounces) and for children over six years, a minimum of 35 grams (1.2 ounces).
- To determine serving sizes for products in Group A that are made at child care centers, refer to "Cereal Products" in FNS–86, "Quantity Recipes for Child Care Centers."
- Doughnuts and sweet rolls are allowed as a bread item in breakfasts and snacks only.
- French, Vienna, Italian, and Syrian breads are commercially prepared products that often are made with unenriched flour. Check the label or manufacturer to be sure the product is made with *enriched* flour.
- The amount of bread in a serving of stuffing should weigh at least 13 grams (0.5 ounces).
- Whole grain, enriched, or fortified breakfast cereals (cold, dry, or cooked) may be served for breakfast or snack only.

Group A
When you obtain these items commercially, a *full* serving should have a minimum weight of 20 grams (0.7 ounces). The serving sizes specified below should have a minimum weight of 10 grams (0.5 ounces).

Item	Serving Size
bread sticks (hard)	2 sticks
chow mein noodles	1/4 cup
crackers (saltines and snack)	4 squares
lavosh	1/2 serving
melba toast	3 pieces
pretzels (hard)	1/2 serving
stuffing (bread)	1/2 serving

Group B
When you obtain these items commercially, a *full* serving should have a minimum weight of 25 grams (0.9 ounces). The serving sizes specified below should have a minimum weight of 13 grams (0.5 ounces).

Item	Serving Size
bagels	1/2 bagel
biscuits	1 biscuit
breads (white, rye, whole-wheat, raisin, French)	1/2 slice
buns (hamburger, hot dog)	1/2 bun
cookie-crackers (graham, animal)	
egg roll/wonton wrappers	1 serving
English muffins	1/2 muffin
pita bread	1/2 round
muffins	1/2 muffin
pizza crust	1 serving
pretzels, (soft)	1 pretzel
rolls and sweet rolls (unfrosted)	1/2 roll
taco shells (whole, pieces)	1 shell
tortillas	1/2 tortilla

(continued)

TABLE 19-6 Acceptable Bread and Bread Alternates (continued)

Group C

When you obtain these items commercially, a *full* serving should have a minimum weight of 31 grams (1.1 ounces). The serving sizes specified below should have a minimum weight of 16 grams (0.6 ounces).

Item	Serving Size
cookies	1/2 serving
cornbread	1 piece
croissants	1/2 croissant
pie crust (meat or meat alternate pies)	1/2 serving
popovers	1/2 popover
waffles	1/2 serving

Group D

When you obtain these items commercially, a *full* serving should have a minimum weight of 50 grams (1.8 ounces). The serving sizes specified below should have a minimum weight of 25 grams (0.9 ounces).

Item	Serving Size
doughnuts (all types)	1/2 doughnut
granola bars (plain)	1/2 serving
hush puppies	1/2 serving
muffins/quick breads (all except corn bread)	1/2 serving
sopapillas	1/2 serving
sweet roll (unfrosted)	1/2 serving
toaster pastry (unfrosted)	1/2 serving

Group E

When you obtain these items commercially, a *full* serving should have a minimum weight of 63 grams (2.2 ounces). The serving sizes specified below should have a minimum weight of 31 grams (1.1 ounces).

Item	Serving Size
cookies (with nuts, raisins, chocolate pieces, fruit purees)	1/2 serving
doughnuts (all kinds)	1/2 serving
French toast	1/2 serving
fruit grain bars/granola bars (with fruit, nuts, chocolate pieces)	1/2 serving
sweet rolls	1/2 serving
toaster pastry (frosted)	1/2 serving

Group F

When you obtain these items commercially, a *full* serving should have a minimum weight of 75 grams (2.7 ounces). The serving sizes specified below should have a minimum weight of 38 grams (1.3 ounces).

Item	Serving Size
coffee cake	1/2 serving

Group G

When you obtain these items commercially, a *full* serving should have a minimum weight of 115 grams (4 ounces). The serving sizes specified below should have a minimum weight of 58 grams (2 ounces).

Item	Serving Size
Brownies	1/2 serving

TABLE 19-6 Acceptable Bread and Bread Alternates (continued)

Group H
When you serve these items, a *full* serving should have a minimum of 1/2 cup cooked product.
The serving sizes specified below are the minimum half servings of a cooked product.

Item	Serving Size
barley	1/4 cup
breakfast cereals (cooked)	1/4 cup
bulgur or cracked wheat	1/4 cup
couscous	1/4 cup
macaroni (all shapes)	1/4 cup
masa	1/4 cup
noodles (all varieties)	1/4 cup
pasta (all shapes)	1/4 cup
ravioli (noodle only)	1/4 cup
rice (enriched white or brown)	1/4 cup

Courtesy of USDA, 2005.

Each state has its own licensing requirements with regard to nutrition and food service. Teachers who provide food for children should be familiar with the licensing requirements for their particular state. Nutrition related areas that are often addressed in licensing regulations include:

1. Administration and record keeping
   - sample menus and appropriate menu substitutions
   - production records
   - number of meals served daily

2. Food service
   - specifications for kitchens and equipment
   - sanitation of dishes, utensils, and equipment
   - requirements for transport of food when kitchen facilities are not available
   - feeding equipment required for specific age groups

3. Staffing
   - requirements of person in charge of food service

4. Nutrition policies
   - number of meals and snacks to be served within the current week
   - posting of menus and their availability to families

ISSUES TO CONSIDER • Benefits of CACFP

A recent study concluded that meals provided by the CACFP have the potential to improve the diets (and health) of young children. Children attending a center that was participating in the CACFP were shown to have fewer sick days than children in a center that was not participating in CACFP. The study also found that nearly one-fourth of the children in the study were overweight and were almost equally distributed between the center not receiving CACFP funding and the center which did.

- Consider the practical implications of this study for families of children in child care.

- Of what importance are the results of this study to menu planners?

- What is the "take home lesson" from this study for families and/or teachers?

FIGURE 19–2

Slice apples horizontally for a
novel and magical surprise!

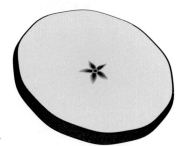

- color
- flavor (strong or mild; sweet or sour)
- texture (crisp or soft)
- shape (round, cubed, strings)
- temperature (cold or hot)

- seating of adults at the table with children
- posting of food allergies in kitchen and eating area

A Good Menu Is Appealing

The French say, "We eat with our eyes." Menu planners who take into consideration how food will look on a plate are likely to develop meals that are more appealing and acceptable to children. Figure 19–2 illustrates another way to slice apples that offers a surprise and may make them more appealing to children. Appeal can be increased by contrasting the following **sensory qualities**:

These sensory qualities play an important part in children's choice and acceptance of foods (de Wijk, et al., 2004; Dansby & Bovell-Benjamin, 2003). Toddlers and young children think of foods in terms of color, flavor, texture, and shape rather than the nutrient content. Using sensory qualities of food to appeal to young children takes advantage of their developmental abilities to interpret their environment through their physical senses.

A comparison of the following two menus illustrates how color can make a meal more visually appealing:

Menu #1
Grilled Cheese Sandwiches
Celery Sticks
Banana Chunks
Milk

Menu #2
Grilled Cheese Sandwiches
Buttered Broccoli
Plums
Milk

Menu #1 is essentially tones of yellow and light brown. Substituting broccoli for celery sticks adds more color and increases the amount of vitamins A and C. Substituting plums for bananas improves color contrast and adds another texture.

The sensory qualities of a meal also provide opportunities for adults to expand children's language development. Children can be encouraged to identify foods and describe their features such as round, rectangular, red, yellow, hot or cold, smooth or crisp.

Although color is an important element in food appeal, other aspects also contribute to its acceptability. Young children often prefer mildly flavored, simple foods. Softer textured foods such as chicken or ground meats are more likely to be eaten because they are easier for children to chew and swallow. Young children also prefer plain foods that do not touch each other as opposed to mixed dishes. They also have a preference for sweet foods. Since the basis for this preference may

sensory qualities – *aspects that appeal to sight, sound, taste, feel, and smell.*

be biological, care should be taken to limit their availability and offer fruits and nutritious whole grain baked products instead.

A Good Menu Includes Familiar Foods and New Foods

Although it is important to introduce children to new foods, it is also important to serve some foods that are familiar. Familiarity influences children's food choices and their acceptance of foods (Wardle et al., 2003a; Young, Anderson, & Beckstrom, 2003). Much of this familiarity is learned from family eating practices (Addessi, et al., 2005; Fisher, et al., 2002). Sharing information, menu plans, and recipes with families can be helpful for expanding children's food choices.

When introducing new foods, it is a good idea to include them along with familiar ones. This ensures that if the new food is not well-accepted, children will not leave the table hungry. (See Table 18–2 on page 438 for suggestions on introducing new foods to young children.) The menu planner might also consider introducing unfamiliar foods at snack time, which avoids the new food being labeled a "breakfast food" or "lunch food." New foods should be introduced with little fanfare. Involving children in the preparation of an unfamiliar food often enhances its acceptance (Hermann, Parker, & Brown, 2006).

When feeding young children, it is also wise to include a number of finger foods (Table 19–7). Children who may have difficulty managing eating utensils will find the presence of some finger foods comforting.

Children from a variety of cultural and ethnic groups are present in most classrooms today. A good menu planner draws on this wealth of backgrounds and includes foods that are familiar to a variety of cultures (Algert, 2003). The inclusion of **ethnic** foods serves several purposes:

- Children from the featured culture are likely to be familiar with these foods. Their acceptance and enjoyment may encourage other children to try foods that are unfamiliar.
- Foods that are representative of different cultural groups add variety and interest to children's meals. They can also be used to help children learn about other cultures.
- Serving ethnic food helps the teacher establish rapport with the children and their families. This may foster increased family participation in the program's activities.
- Educating children about various cultures fosters greater respect for children who are from a culture different from their own.
- The sharing of food is often an effective way of helping children from different cultures and ethnicities gain acceptance and feel more comfortable in an unfamiliar group.

TABLE 19-7 Suggested Finger Foods

apricot pieces	grapefruit sections (seeded)
banana chunks	green grapes (halved)
blueberries	melon cubes
cauliflower buds	nectarines
cheese cubes	orange sections
cherry tomatoes	red and green pepper sticks
crackers	pineapple chunks
cucumbers	sliced mushrooms
diced fresh peaches	string cheese
diced fresh pears	strawberries, diced
kiwi slices	zucchini sticks

ethnic – *pertaining to races or groups of people who share common traits or customs.*

Steps in Menu Planning

Menu planning should be organized so that it may be completed efficiently and effectively. Materials that are helpful in menu planning include:

- menu forms
- a list of foods on hand that need to be used
- a list of children's allergies
- recipe file
- old menus with notes and suggestions
- calendar with special events and holidays noted
- grocery ads for short-term planning
- USDA list of available commodity foods

The menu form shown in Figure 19–3 can be used by a large center or small home-based program. It can be modified to include only the meals that will be served.

Step 1 List the main dishes to be served for lunch during the week. These should include a meat or meat alternate. Be sure to note children's food allergies and plan for appropriate substitutes. Combinations of whole grain products (see Chapter 13), such as dried peas, beans, lentils, cheese, nuts, or nut butters are acceptable protein-source substitutes for meat, poultry, eggs, or fish. However, many of these combinations do not contribute as much iron as does meat. Care must be taken when planning menus with non-meat proteins to include iron-rich foods so that children's iron needs will be met.

Bean burrito with cheese	BBQ beef	Scrambled eggs	Chili	Macaroni and cheese	Protein

Step 2 List vegetables and fruits, including salads, for the main meal. Be sure to use fruits and vegetables in season. Fresh produce in season is often less expensive, more nutritious, and contributes more fiber than canned and frozen foods. Fresh fruits and vegetables also offer excellent materials for learning activities. If menus are planned months in advance, local County Extension Offices can provide information concerning seasonal produce and predicted supplies.

Zucchini Orange wedges	Broccoli Mango slices	Cherry tomatoes 1/2 banana	Carrots and celery Plum slices	Green beans Apple wedges	Fruits and Vegetables

Step 3 Add enriched or whole grain breads and cereal products.

Whole wheat tortilla	Enriched bun	Whole wheat toast	Corn muffin	Enriched macaroni (in casserole)	Bread

Step 4 Add beverage. Be sure to include the required amount of milk.

Milk	Milk	Milk	Milk	Milk	Milk

FIGURE 19-3

A sample menu-planning form.

		Monday	Tuesday	Wednesday	Thursday	Friday
Breakfast	Fruit/Vegetable Bread Milk					
Snack (supplement)	Bread Fruit/Vegetable or Milk					
Lunch	Protein Fruit/Vegetable Fruit/Vegetable Bread Milk					
Snack (supplement)	Bread Fruit/Vegetable or Milk					
Notes	# Served					

Step 5 Plan snacks to balance the main meal. Especially check for vitamin C, vitamin A, iron, and calcium.

PM Snack	Watermelon Wheat crackers Water	Cheese crackers Peanut butter Milk	Pizza biscuits Pineapple juice	Oatmeal cookies Milk	Brown-white sandwich Apricot-orange juice
AM Snack	Prepared oat cereal Milk	Bran muffin Apple juice	Pumpkin bread Milk	Raisin toast Orange juice	Rye crackers Milk

Step 6 Review your menu. Be sure it includes the required amounts from the Food Guide Pyramid.
- Does it meet funding or licensing requirements?
- Does it include a variety of contrasting foods?
- Does it contain familiar foods?
- Does it contain new foods?

Step 7 Note changes on the menu and post it where it can be viewed by teachers and families (Figure 19–4). The menu serves as an important form of communication between the early childhood program and families and helps to ensure that children's daily and weekly nutrient needs are being met.

Step 8 Evaluate the menu. Did the children appear to eat and enjoy the foods that were served? Was there much plate waste? Remember, do not eliminate a food from the menu because it resulted in too much plate waste. Repeated exposures to rejected foods have been shown to

FIGURE 19–4

Menus should be made available to families.

WEEKLY MENUS					
Week of _____					
Lunch and Snacks					
	Monday	**Tuesday**	**Wednesday**	**Thursday**	**Friday**
Snack	Bagel with cream cheese Orange juice	Blueberry muffin Milk	Mixed fresh veggies & dip Corn muffin Water	Waffles Applesauce Milk	Graham crackers Cranberry juice
Lunch	Turkey with gravy Mashed sweet potatoes Peas Apple slices Bread & butter Milk	Macaroni & cheese Broccoli Watermelon Milk	Scrambled eggs Green beans Plums Biscuits Milk	Beef barbecue Cooked carrots Whole wheat bread Pears Milk	Spaghetti with meat sauce Tossed salad Bread sticks Honeydew melon Milk
Snack	Peanut butter Bananas Milk	Yogurt Pineapple Smoothies Water	Cheese cubes Whole wheat crackers Grape juice	Oatmeal cookies Milk	Mini pitas Hummus Tomato juice

improve children's acceptance over time (Wardle, et al., 2003b). Children's likes and dislikes are continually changing and the rejected food of this week may become a favorite in a week or two. However, be sure to note children's likes and dislikes on your copy and keep for future reference.

WRITING MENUS

There are several approaches to menu-writing that the planner may wish to consider: weekly menus, cycle menus, and odd-day cycle menus. The program's scheduled hours of operation, personnel who will be preparing the food, and method of purchasing food and supplies will all influence the choice of menu preparation that is most functional. **Weekly menus** list foods that are to be prepared and served for one week at a time. This is a time-consuming approach. Preparing two or three weeks' worth of menus simultaneously is often a more efficient use of the menu planner's time. It also allows utilization of larger, more economical amounts of food. The menu planner is also better able to evaluate the menu's nutrient contributions over a period of time and avoid frequent repetitions of the same foods.

Cycle menus incorporate a series of weekly menus that are reused or recycled over a two- or three-month period. Cycle menus are usually written to parallel the seasons and incorporate fruits and vegetables that are most available and affordable. A well-planned cycle menu requires a greater initial time investment, but saves time in the long run. Food ordering also becomes less time-consuming and more efficient. However, the planner should not hesitate to change parts of the cycle that prove difficult to prepare or that are not well accepted by the children. Seasonal cycle menus may be used for a period of years with timely revisions.

Odd-day cycle menus involve planning menus for any number of days other than a week (e.g., four days, six days, nine days). This type of cycling avoids the association of specific foods with certain days of the week. It also requires careful planning to avoid serving dishes or foods that require advance preparation in Monday-to-Friday programs.

NUTRITIOUS SNACKS

Snacks can be effective for meeting some of children's daily nutrient needs as long as the food choices are nutrient-dense (Bernath & Masi, 2006). Snacks should contribute vitamins, minerals, and other nutrients important in health, growth, and development (Figure 19–5). Nutrient-dense foods can supply nutrients that may be missing or not adequately consumed in previous meals. Calorie-dense snacks, high in sugar and fat, are not appropriate choices for young children.

Foods that are new or unfamiliar to children are best introduced at snack time. Tasting parties and learning experiences designed around new foods also help to increase children's interest and willingness to try something different.

Snacks can also be useful for meeting children's high energy needs. Their small stomach capacities and short attention spans often make it difficult for them to eat enough at one meal to sustain them until the next. One and one-half or two hours between meals seems to be the best spacing for most children in order to prevent them from becoming too hungry or spoiling their appetite for the next meal.

---

weekly menus – *menus that are written to be served on a weekly basis.*
cycle menus – *menus that are written to repeat after a set interval, such as every three to four weeks.*
odd-day cycle menus – *menus planned for a period of days other than a week that repeat after the planned period; cycles of any number of days may be used. These menus are a means of avoiding repetition of the same foods on the same day of the week.*

FIGURE 19–5

Snacks suggestions for school-aged children.

Active days and growing bodies make after-school snacks a must. Plan snacks that children can help to make. Encourage children to drink water—thirst may be disguised as hunger.

- Banana chunks dipped in yogurt and crispy rice cereal; freeze
- Yogurt "sundaes"—layer flavored yogurt with fruit pieces and granola
- Bagel melts—low-fat cheese slice on bagel half; microwave
- Baked pita chips (make your own) with salsa
- Tortilla rollups—roll a low-fat cheese and ham slice up in a tortilla; serve with fat-free ranch dip
- Fruit smoothies—blend yogurt with favorite fruits
- Trail mix—combine various cereals, dried fruit, and mini marshmallows
- Whole wheat tortilla spread with peanut butter and cinnamon sugar
- Raw veggies with homemade hummus
- Oatmeal raisin cookies or pumpkin bread (a great cooking activity)
- Egg salad on wheat crackers
- Apple wedges with peanut butter dip
- Chocolate tofu pudding

Suitable Snack Foods

A wide variety of raw fruits and vegetables are ideal for snack foods. They are excellent sources of vitamin C, vitamin A, and fiber (which aids elimination) and should be included often. Fruits and vegetables should be sectioned, sliced, or diced into small pieces to prevent choking and make it easier for children to chew. The crispness of fruits and vegetables helps to remove food clinging to the teeth and stimulates the gums so they stay healthy. Children also seem to enjoy the subtle flavors of many different fruits and vegetables.

Whole grains or enriched breads and grain products are also good high-fiber snack foods. The variety and flavors of **whole grains** also add interest to children's diets. **Enriched** breads and cereals are refined products to which iron, thiamin, niacin, riboflavin, and folic acid are added in amounts equal to the original whole grain product.

Unsweetened beverages such as **full-strength** fruit and vegetable juices also make good choices for snacks. Juices made from oranges, grapefruit, tangerines, and tomatoes are rich in vitamin C. Vitamin C may also be added to apple, grape, cranberry and pineapple juices. Check the labels of these juices to determine if they are fortified with vitamin C. Carbonated beverages, **fruit drinks**, fruit ades, and fruit punches are unacceptable options. These beverages contain large amounts of sugar, water, and no other nutrients, except perhaps some added vitamin C.

- Fruit juice must be 100 percent juice.
- Juice drink may have as little as 39 percent fruit juice.
- Fruit drink has from 0–10 percent real juice.

Water is also essential for good health; children should drink six to eight small glasses of water a day (Figure 19–6). Water should be available to children at all times and may be served with their

---

whole grains – *grain products that have not been refined; they contain all parts of the kernel of grain.*
enriched – *adding nutrients to grain products to replace those lost during refinement; thiamin, niacin, riboflavin, and iron are nutrients most commonly added.*
full-strength – *undiluted fruit or vegetable juice.*
fruit drinks – *products that contain 10 percent fruit juice, added water, and sugar.*

meals and snacks. Allowing children to pour the water from a pitcher, as they want it, may encourage them to drink more water. Special attention should be given to water intake after a period of physical activity and when the environmental temperature is high (Shu, 2007). A good plan might be to stop at the drinking fountain on the way in after a period of active outdoor play.

SERVING MEALS

A nutritious meal is of no value to a child if it is not eaten and enjoyed. The atmosphere in which meals are served can either forestall or further contribute to eating problems. All meals should be served in a relaxed, social atmosphere (see Figure 19–7 on page 466). The classroom should be straightened up prior to mealtimes to eliminate the distraction of scattered toys or an unfinished game. The resulting uncluttered environment provides a more restful atmosphere in which to eat.

The table should also be made attractive. Child-made placemats add interest to the meal and give children an opportunity to contribute to the meal. Centerpieces may be constructed during art or assembled from objects gathered on field trips or nature hikes. Plates, cups, utensils, and napkins should be laid out neatly and appropriately. Setting the table offers children a positive learning experience, improves their interest in the meal, and enhances self-esteem. Foods served in an attractive manner have increased appeal. Using proper cooking techniques helps to retain food's color and shape. Arranging them neatly in serving dishes or on plates also improves visual appeal. (White or warm-hued plates enhance natural food colors; cool-hued plates tend to detract from most food colors.) Fresh, edible garnishes may be used if time and budget permit. Contrived or "cute" foods are time-consuming to prepare and may actually result in the children wanting to save them as "souvenirs" rather than eating them.

Food may be served in a variety of styles:

- plate service
- family-style service
- combination of the above

Plate service involves placing food on plates in the kitchen before serving. This style is the best option for **cost control** as it permits the greatest degree of portion control and fewer leftover foods.

In family-style service, the food is placed on the table in serving dishes. Children are able to help themselves and pass the dish to the next child. Beverages are placed in small, easily managed pitchers, and each child pours the amount desired before passing it to the next child. While this method does not permit the same degree of portion control as plate service, it does promote children's problem-solving and decision-making skills. Because children determine how

FIGURE 19–6

Children should be encouraged to drink six to eight glasses of water daily.

---

cost control – *reduction of expenses through portion control inventory and reduction of waste.*

FIGURE 19–7

Mealtimes should be a pleasant social experience for children.

much food to take and to eat, they are also gaining independence and learning important self-regulation skills. They are also practicing motor skills used to dip, serve, pass, and pour, as well as social skills such as cooperating and sharing. Many teachers feel that the positive aspects of family-style service outweigh the benefits of smaller portions and cost control of plate service.

Positive aspects of both styles of service may lead the teacher to choose a combination of the two. For example, the teacher may place servings of the entree on the plates (the amount is determined by each child's request) while the children pass the bread, fruit, and vegetables. This style of service allows portion control, a very positive aspect since the entree is the most expensive item on the menu, and safety, since the entree is usually a hot food. If the vegetables are hot, they may also be served by the teacher.

It is important that adults eat meals with children. Adults serve as role models for appropriate behavior and attitudes concerning foods (Hendy & Raudenbush, 2000). Mealtime should be a time when teachers sit and engage in pleasant conversions about things of interest to the children. Children should also be encouraged to talk with one another. Dwelling on table manners and behavior during meals should be avoided as much as possible. Only positive reinforcement of good behavior should be mentioned. Problem eaters need special positive reinforcement of good eating behavior; if possible, negative behavior should be ignored during mealtime. Table 19–8 offers some additional suggestions for making mealtimes happy times.

THE MENU MUST STAY WITHIN THE BUDGET

While the menu lists what foods are to be served, the budget defines the resources allotted for menu preparation. Items that must be included in the budget are food, personnel, and equipment. The food budget can be controlled through careful attention to:

- menu planning
- food purchasing
- food preparation
- food service
- recordkeeping

Cost control is essential if a food service is to stay within the budget. The goal is to feed the children appetizing, nutritious meals at a reasonably low cost. However, cost control should never be the defining factor at the expense of good nutrition.

TABLE 19–8 Making Mealtime a Happy Time

Creating a positive eating environment makes mealtime an enjoyable experience for children if you:

- provide meals that are nutritious, attractive and tasty.
- provide a transition or quiet time just before meals so children are relaxed.
- avoid delays so children do not have to wait.
- have children help set the table, put food on the table, or help clean up after eating.
- make sure the room is attractive, clean, and well lit; limit distractions.
- get to know each child's personality and reaction to foods.
- provide tables, chairs, dishes, glassware, eating, and serving utensils that are appropriate for children.
- support and encourage children's efforts to feed themselves.
- avoid making children feel rushed or pressured. Allow plenty of time for children to eat.
- never force children to eat. They can be picky eaters.
- offer a variety of foods in different ways.
- encourage social interaction.

Adapted from USDA, 2007.

Menu Planning

Cost control begins at the menu-planning stage. To plan menus that stay within a budget, it is important to begin by including inexpensive foods. To do so, the planner must be aware of current prices and seasonal supplies.

To lower food costs, the menu planner should make careful use of supplies on hand and leftovers. (Note: *leftovers must be refrigerated promptly and cannot be reclaimed for reimbursement.* To ensure that quality foods are selected from supplies on hand, the **First-In-First-Out (FIFO) inventory method** should be used. This food storage system places newly purchased foods at the back of storage and older foods at the front so they can be used first. This method of rotating stocks of food can be facilitated by dating all supplies as they come into the storage area.

Food Purchasing

Food purchasing, or **procurement**, is a crucial step in cost control. Lowering food costs during the purchasing phase can be accomplished by utilizing food from local suppliers, using USDA donated foods, and keeping abreast of price trends and the market availability of various foods. Purchasing too much food or inappropriate foods can turn a menu that is planned around inexpensive foods into an expensive menu. The key step is to determine as accurately as possible the amount of food that is needed to feed everyone an adequate amount. The use of standardized recipes can be a great help in determining how much and what kinds of food are needed. The U.S. Department of Agriculture has developed a set of such recipes for use in school lunches and Child Care Food Programs (FNS–304,). These recipes provide a list of ingredients and quantities required to serve groups of 25 or 50 individuals.

First-In-First-Out (FIFO) inventory method – *a method of storage in which the items stored for the longest time will be retrieved first.*

procurement – *the process of obtaining services, supplies, and equipment in conformance with applicable laws and regulations.*

Before purchasing food, a written food order should be prepared. Written product specifications are used to clarify the following information:

- name of product
- federal grade
- packaging procedures and type of package
- test or inspection procedures
- market units—ounces, pounds, can size, cases, etc.
- quantity (number) of units needed
- style of food desired—pieces, slices, halves, chunks, etc.

If foods are purchased from local retail stores, a simple form that follows the store's floor plan will make the task easier and more efficient. When completing the market order, list the items that must be purchased for the entire menu period (e.g., one week, four weeks) in the following order:

- main dishes
- breads, cereals, pastas
- fruits and vegetables
- dairy products

Frozen foods should be selected last to minimize thawing between store freezer and food service freezer.

Food Preparation

Appropriate methods of preparation help to retain a food's nutritional quality and control costs. Fruits and vegetables should be peeled only if necessary, as more nutrients are retained if the skin is left intact. If peeling is necessary, as it may be for very young children, only a thin layer of skin should be removed.

Correct heat and cooking times are important factors in cost control as well as nutrient retention. Foods cooked too long or at excessively high heat may undergo shrinkage or be burned. In either case, food costs increase because burned food is not usable and shrinkage results in fewer portions than originally planned. Nutrients, such as thiamin and vitamin C, are readily destroyed when exposed to heat.

Standardized recipes, as previously described, help to ensure that correct amounts of ingredients are purchased and leftovers are minimized. Leftover foods that have not been placed on the table may be promptly frozen and used when serving the same dish again. Leftovers should be reheated in a separate pan and not mixed with freshly prepared portions. They should never be reheated more than once.

Food Service

If the recipe specifies a serving size, that amount should be served, for example, "one-half cup or 1 1/2" × 1 1/2" square." When a family-style service is used in early childhood programs and schools, the staff serve children standard portions as a means of portion control. In programs where children are encouraged to serve themselves, each child should be asked to take only as much as can be eaten.

Serving utensils that are made to serve specific portions are an aid to portion and cost control. Examples of such utensils are soup ladles and ice cream scoops, which are available in a number of standardized sizes. These tools are available at restaurant supply companies.

Recordkeeping

Records documenting the amount of money spent on food and the number of children and staff served daily must be maintained. These records provide accurate information about whether the amount of money spent on food is within the projected budget.

A record of expenses for each month should also be kept. For further accuracy, an inventory of foods on hand should be done and the cost of the inventory determined and deducted from the raw food cost for that month. (If inventories tend not to differ much from month to month, this last step may be omitted.) At the end of each month

- calculate the total number of individuals served.
- calculate the total food bills.
- divide the total dollars spent by the total number served to determine monthly food costs per person.

FOCUS ON FAMILIES • Meal Planning

Families should use the Food Guide Pyramid as the basis for planning healthy, nutritious meals. Meal planning may require additional time, but proves to be worthwhile for the following reasons:

1. You can ensure that all food groups from the Pyramid are included.

2. It helps you to balance meals (serving meat that is high in salt, such as ham, with foods that do not contain large amounts of salt, such as steamed vegetables).

3. By using a grocery list, you will make fewer unnecessary trips to the store and be less likely to buy foods on impulse.

Preparing a grocery list for the first time may feel overwhelming, but following these principles can help get you started:

- Build the main part of your meal around complex carbohydrates (rice, pastas, other grains).

- Add variety and try different ethnic cuisines.

- Use planned leftovers to save time and money. (Serve half of a beef pot roast for one meal and use the other half in a stew or for BBQ sandwiches.) If time allows, cook a double batch of your family's favorite dish and freeze part for later use.

- Avoid purchasing foods high in fat (and trans fats) such as doughnuts, croissants, pastries, snack cakes, high-fat cookies, high-fat crackers, and chips.

- Try purchasing these foods for healthy, nutritious snacks: animal crackers, fig bars, Cheerios, graham crackers, whole wheat pitas or tortillas, pretzels, breadsticks, fresh fruits and vegetables.

CASE STUDY

Ms. R. is responsible for planning menus at an early childhood center that enrolls 50 children. She wants to plan a menu according to the Food Guide Pyramid featuring a variety of foods from each section of the Pyramid. Her purpose is to introduce new or unusual foods to the children. She starts with the grain group and features bagels, tortillas, fried rice, hush puppies, and pita bread. The next group she considers includes vegetables.

1. Suggest some unusual vegetables to prepare.

2. How can these vegetables be prepared and presented to increase their acceptance?

3. How should refusals be handled?

4. What food group would you highlight next? Why?

CLASSROOM CORNER • Teacher Activities

Exploring Pumpkins

Concept: Pumpkins are kind of food that are abundant in the fall. You can eat their seeds or use them to make many other foods items. (Pre-2)

Learning Objectives

- Children will learn about and explore pumpkins.
- Children will be given an opportunity to try two pumpkin products.

Supplies

- 1 large pumpkin; knife (teacher use only); newspaper; medium-sized bowl for seeds; baking pan; oil; pumpkin muffin recipe and ingredients; muffin tins; hand wipes

Learning Activities

- Read and discuss one of the following books:
  - *Pumpkin Day, Pumpkin Night* by Anne Rockwell
  - *Pumpkins* by Melvin and Gilda Berger
  - *The Berenstain Bears and the Prize Pumpkin* by Stan and Jan Berenstein
  - *Pumpkin Pumpkin* by Jeanne Titherington
- Show the children a pumpkin and ask children to help describe its appearance. Ask children questions about the pumpkin (color, size, shape, what can be done with a pumpkin, if it is a vegetable, and if it can be eaten).
- Tell the children you are going to cut open the pumpkin and see what is inside. While the teacher cuts open the pumpkin, have children clean their hands with wipes. Call children up one at a time to put their hands in the pumpkin and remove some of the seeds. After everyone has had a turn, put the seeds aside; let children know that you will wash the seeds and bake them in the oven later.
- Next have the children help make pumpkin muffins. They can add ingredients, stir, spoon batter into muffin cups, etc.
- Serve the pumpkin seeds and muffins for snack with a glass of milk.

Evaluation

- Children will be able to name some characteristics and uses for pumpkins.
- Children will name at least two foods that can be made from a pumpkin.

SUMMARY

- The menu is the basic tool of food service.
  - The menu should meet the nutritional needs of those served.
  - The menu should introduce new foods.
  - Familiar, well-liked foods should be served frequently.
  - Foods should be cooked and served in sanitary surroundings.
  - Menus should be planned within budgetary limits.

- Careful menu planning is essential to cost control.
  - Including seasonal foods in the menu lowers costs.
  - Using good quality food products appropriate to menu items saves money.
  - Prompt storage of food at the correct temperature limits waste.
  - Use of standardized recipes and appropriate serving sizes controls costs.
  - Accurate recordkeeping enables the menu planner to be aware of food costs.

APPLICATION ACTIVITIES

1. Plan a five-day menu appropriate for four-year-old children that includes morning snack, lunch, and afternoon snack. The menu should provide one-half of the foods needed according to the Food Guide Pyramid. Provide one good source each of vitamin C, calcium, and iron daily. Provide at least three good sources of vitamin A during the five-day period.

2. Four-year-old Jamie often comes to school without having had breakfast at home. (Both of his parents work so he leaves home early every day.) By mid-morning, Jamie is often inattentive, lethargic, and seems to be off "in his own world." He seldom plays games with the other children and spends most of his recess just standing around. At lunchtime, Jamie tends to select only milk and breads and is resistant to eating most vegetables and meats.

   a. What may be the cause of Jamie's mid-morning behavior?

   b. How would you characterize Jamie's nutritional status?

   c. What eating patterns need to be corrected?

   d. What steps should be taken to improve Jamie's participation in activities, as well as his nutritional patterns and status?

3. Review the criteria given for menus. Rank the criteria as you perceive their degree of importance. Are there other factors that you feel should also be considered in planning adequate menus? Consider the needs of individual early childhood programs, home-based programs, or family homes. Are the important factors the same or different for each situation?

4. Three-year-old Eiswari is allergic to eggs. Explain how this affects menu planning.

5. Plan a daily menu that would meet all of the nutrient needs of a child who follows a vegan vegetarian diet. Modify the menu for a child who is a lacto-ovo-vegetarian. Include appropriate sizes of servings (refer to Chapter 16).

6. The following weekly menu is planned for an early childhood program during the month of January:

Meat loaf	Whole wheat roll with margarine
Fresh asparagus	Watermelon-blueberry fruit cup
Milk	

   a. Evaluate this menu and suggest changes that could make it less expensive but equally or more nutritious.

   b. How would the cost of this menu served in January compare to the cost of the same menu served in June?

CHAPTER REVIEW

A. By Yourself:

1. State the appropriate serving size for a child three- to five-years-old for each of the following foods:

   a. milk   d. vegetable
   b. dry cereal   e. bread
   c. fruit

2. Where can information relative to licensing requirements for nutrition and food services for young children be obtained?

3. Name four sensory qualities that improve food's appeal.

4. What are two reasons for using fresh fruits and vegetables in season?

5. List two strategies that the menu planner can use to control food costs.

B. As a Group:

1. Outline three ways to control food costs when preparing food.

2. Discuss how environment affects children's eating behaviors. Identify steps that adults can take to create a positive eating atmosphere for children.

3. Discuss how you might handle the following mealtime behaviors:
   - child refuses to eat any vegetables
   - child eats only the macaroni and cheese on his plate and then asks for more
   - child belches loudly to make the other children laugh
   - child is too busy talking to finish eating by the time others are done

4. Evaluate and comment on the quality of the following snacks:
   - cheese pizza and water
   - oatmeal/raisin cookie and milk
   - grape juice and pear slices
   - fruit drink and graham crackers
   - apricot jam and whole wheat toast

REFERENCES

Addessi, E., Galloway, A., Visalberghi, E., & Birch, L. (2005). Specific influences on the acceptance of novel foods in 2–5-year-old children. *Appetite, 45*(3), 264–271.

Algert, S. (2003). Teaching elementary school children about healthy Native American foods. *Journal of Nutrition Education & Behavior, 35*(2), 105–106.

Bernath, P. & Masi, W. (2006). Smart school snacks: A comprehensive preschool nutrition education program. *Young Children, 61*(3), 20–24.

Dansby, M., & Bovell-Benjamin, A. (2003). Physical properties and sixth graders' acceptance of extruded ready-to-eat sweet potato breakfast cereal. *Journal of Food Science, 68*(8), 2607–2612.

de Wijk, R., Polet, I., Engelen, L., van Doorn, R., & Prinz, J. (2004). Amount of ingested custard dessert as affected by its color, odor, and texture. *Physiology & Behavior, 82*(2–3), 397–403.

Fisher, J., Mitchell, D., Smickiklas-Wright, & Birch, L. (2002). Parental influences on young girls' fruit, vegetable, micronutrient, and fat intakes. *Journal of the American Dietetic Association, 1999*(69), 1264–1272.

Hendy, H. & Raudenbush, B. (2000). Effectiveness of teacher modeling to encourage food acceptance in preschool children. *Appetite, 34*(1), 61–76.

Hermann, J., Parker, S., & Brown, B. (2006). After-school gardening improves children's reported vegetable intake and physical activity. *Journal of Nutrition Education & Behavior, 38*(3), 201–202.

Shu, J. (2007). Focus on fitness. *Early Childhood* Today, 21(7), 10.

State of Florida Department of Citrus. (1976). *The sunshine cookbook.* Lakeland, FL: Florida Department of Citrus.

U.S. Department of Agriculture, Food and Nutrition Service. (2005). *Child and adult care food program.* Washington, DC: FNS.

Wardle, J., Herrera, M., Cooke, L., & Gibson, E. (2003a). Modifying children's food preferences: The effects of exposure and reward on acceptance of an unfamiliar vegetable. *European Journal of Clinical Nutrition, 57*(2), 341–348.

Wardle, J., Cooke, L., Gibson, E., Sapochnik, M., Sheiham, A., & Lawson, M. (2003b). Increasing children's acceptance of vegetables: A randomized trial of parent-led exposure. *Appetite, 40*(2), 155–162.

Young, L., Anderson, J., & Beckstrom, L. (2003). Making new foods fun for kids. *Journal of Nutrition Education & Behavior, 35*(6), 337–348.

PAMPHLETS

Conserving the Nutritive Value in Foods, USDA Home and Garden Bulletin No. 90. Superintendent of Documents, U.S. Government Printing Office, Washington, DC 20402.

Food is More than Just Something to Eat, Nutrition, Pueblo, CO 81009.

Growing Up with Breakfast, Kellogg Company, Department of Home Economics Services, 235 Porter Street, Battle Creek, MI 49016.

Buying Food, Superintendent of Documents, U.S. Government Printing Office, Washington, DC 20402.

Fun with Good Foods, USDA, PA-1204. Superintendent of Documents, U.S. Government Printing Office, Washington, DC 20402.

VIDEO

The Child and Adult Care Food Program. *Nutrition guidance for child care.* (1992). Washington, DC: United States Department of Agriculture. Running Time: 30 minutes.

HELPFUL WEB RESOURCES

American Dietetic Association	http://www.eatright.org
Child and Adult Care Food Program	http://www.cacfp.org
FDA—Center for Food Safety and Applied Nutrition	http://vm.cfsan.fda.gov
USDA—Center for Nutrition Policy and Promotion	http://www.usda.gov
USDA—Food and Nutrition Service	http://www.fns.usda.gov

For additional health, safety, and nutrition resources, go to http://www.EarlyChildEd.delmar.cengage.com

CHAPTER 20

Food Safety

✳ OBJECTIVES

After studying this chapter, you should be able to:

- State aspects of personal hygiene that relate to food safety.
- Describe proper ways to store food.
- Describe methods of sanitizing food preparation areas and equipment.
- Identify proper dishwashing practices.
- Explain how to prevent contamination of food.
- Cite examples of food-borne illnesses.

✳ TERMS TO KNOW

food-borne illness
food-borne illness outbreak
HACCP—Hazard Analysis
  Critical Control Point
critical control point

pasteurized
sanitized
disinfected
bacteria
viruses

parasites
irradiation
food infections
food intoxications

This unit introduces factors other than the menu that contribute to effective food service in schools and early childhood settings. The success of a carefully planned menu depends upon the food being safe to eat.

✳ FOOD SAFETY DEPENDS ON SANITATION

The safety of meals prepared for young children is of equal importance to the nutritional value. Food-borne illness is a major public health issue; food illnesses are dangerous and may be fatal to young children (McCabe-Sellers & Beattie, 2004). A **food-borne illness** is a disease or illness that is carried or transmitted by food.

---

food-borne illness – *a food infection due to ingestion of food contaminated with bacteria, viruses, some molds, or parasites.*

A **food-borne illness outbreak** occurs when two or more people become ill after ingesting the same food and a laboratory analysis confirms that food was the source of the illness. The United States Centers for Disease Control (CDC) estimates that 76 million people become ill each year as a result of food-borne illnesses (CDC, 2005). This accounts for 325,000 hospitalizations and 5,000 deaths yearly. Those groups at greatest risk are:

- infants and children
- pregnant women
- elderly individuals
- persons with chronic diseases
- persons with weakened immune systems

While food-borne illness outbreaks associated with fast-food chains and manufactured foods receive media coverage, most cases are caused by home-cooked meals. (Remember the Thanksgiving when the whole family had "the flu" after the holiday dinner?) The connection between food and illness is often overlooked because the symptoms are similar to those experienced with other common conditions. As a result, the true extent of food-borne illness in this and other countries is unknown.

Causes of Food-Borne Illness

Food can become unsafe in several ways. Hazards to food are present in the air, in water, in other foods, on work surfaces, and on food service workers' hands and bodies. These hazards can be divided into three categories (Figure 20–1):

- biological
- chemical
- physical

FIGURE 20–1

Examples of food hazards.

Hazard	Examples
Biological	Bacteria
	Parasites
	Viruses
	Molds, yeasts
Chemical	Pesticides
	Metals
	Cleaning chemicals
Physical	Dirt
	Hair
	Broken glass
	Metal shavings
	Plastic
	Bones
	Rodent droppings

food-borne illness outbreak – *two or more persons become ill after ingesting the same food. Laboratory analysis must confirm that food is the source of the illness.*

Bacteria present in the environment pose the greatest threat to food safety. Some bacteria can cause serious and dangerous illnesses while others are beneficial (e.g., blue cheese, yogurt, etc.). The risk of environmental contamination of foods can be reduced through two basic approaches:

- following good personal health and cleanliness habits
- maintaining a sanitary food service operation

Hazard Analysis and Critical Control Point (HACCP)

- HACCP, or **Hazard Analysis and Critical Control Point**, is a food safety and self-inspection system that highlights potentially hazardous foods and how they are handled in the food service environment. The U.S. Food and Drug Administration (FDA) recommends implementation of HACCP because it is one of the most effective and efficient ways to ensure that food products are safe (Food Safety & Inspection Service, USDA, 2006; Griffith, 2006). A sound HACCP plan is based on seven principles (Soriano, Molto, & Manes, 2002):

1. **Conducting a hazard analysis**. In this phase, a HACCP team is assembled. The team should list all food items used in the establishment with the product code, preparation techniques, and storage requirements for each one. A flow chart should be developed that follows the food from receiving to serving in order to identify potential hazards during each step of this process (Figure 20–2).
2. **Determining the critical control point (CCP)**. These are points during food preparation where hazards are identified and can be prevented or controlled (i.e., cooking foods to appropriate temperatures; using proper thawing techniques; maintaining proper refrigerator/freezer temperatures).
3. **Establishing critical limits.** Procedures and operating guidelines are developed to help prevent or reduce hazards in the food service area. Requirements should be established and monitored to ensure that they are being met.
4. **Establishing monitoring procedures.** This principle needs to be accomplished through consistent documentation in temperature logs, observation and measurement of requirements, and frequent feedback and monitoring by the food service manager.
5. **Establishing corrective actions.** Specific actions need to be developed and implemented if a critical control point procedure is not being met. These episodes should be accurately documented so that future occurrences can be prevented.
6. **Establishing recordkeeping and documentation procedures.** Records of importance include recipes, time/temperature logs, employee training documentation, cleaning schedules, and job descriptions.
7. **Establish verification procedures.** Management must be diligent in observing staff members' routine behaviors and provide continued training to address any deficiencies.

For the HACCP plan to be successful in any food service establishment, continuous monitoring and improvement are essential (U.S. Department of Health & Human Services, 2001; 2003).

Personal Health and Cleanliness

Persons who are involved in food preparation and service must take great care to maintain a high level of personal health. Food handlers must meet health standards set by health department and child care licensing agencies in each state. Personnel who work in licensed early childhood or school-based

---

Hazard Analysis Critical Control Point (HACCP) – *a food safety and self-inspection system that highlights potentially hazardous foods and how they are handled in the food service department.*
critical control point (CCP) – *a point or procedure in a specific food system where loss of control may result in an unacceptable health risk.*

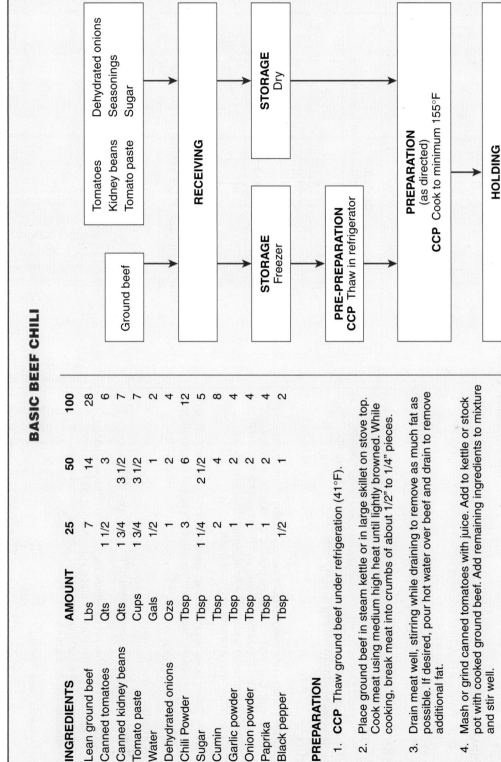

FIGURE 20-2

Recipe flow charts identify potential hazards in a food service establishment.

BASIC BEEF CHILI

INGREDIENTS	AMOUNT	25	50	100
Lean ground beef	Lbs	7	14	28
Canned tomatoes	Qts	1 1/2	3	6
Canned kidney beans	Qts	1 3/4	3 1/2	7
Tomato paste	Cups	1 3/4	3 1/2	7
Water	Gals	1/2	1	2
Dehydrated onions	Ozs	1	2	4
Chili Powder	Tbsp	3	6	12
Sugar	Tbsp	1 1/4	2 1/2	5
Cumin	Tbsp	2	4	8
Garlic powder	Tbsp	1	2	4
Onion powder	Tbsp	1	2	4
Paprika	Tbsp	1	2	4
Black pepper	Tbsp	1/2	1	2

PREPARATION

1. **CCP** Thaw ground beef under refrigeration (41°F).

2. Place ground beef in steam kettle or in large skillet on stove top. Cook meat using medium high heat until lightly browned. While cooking, break meat into crumbs of about 1/2" to 1/4" pieces.

3. Drain meat well, stirring while draining to remove as much fat as possible. If desired, pour hot water over beef and drain to remove additional fat.

4. Mash or grind canned tomatoes with juice. Add to kettle or stock pot with cooked ground beef. Add remaining ingredients to mixture and stir well.

5. **CCP** Simmer chili mixture for 1 hour, stirring occasionally. Temperature of cooked mixture must register 155°F or higher.

Flow chart boxes:

Ground beef → RECEIVING

Tomatoes, Kidney beans, Tomato paste, Dehydrated onions, Seasonings, Sugar → RECEIVING

STORAGE Freezer

STORAGE Dry

PRE-PREPARATION **CCP** Thaw in refrigerator

PREPARATION (as directed) **CCP** Cook to minimum 155°F

HOLDING **CCP** Cover and maintain minimum 140°F

(continued)

FIGURE 20-2

Recipe flow charts identify potential hazards in a food service establishment (continued).

BASIC BEEF CHILI (cont'd)

SERVICE
CCP Maintain above 140°F

↓

COOLING
CCP Chill quickly to 41°F or lower

↓

STORAGE
CCP Cover, label, and date
Refrigerate up to 7 days
Freeze up to 3 months

↓

REHEATING
CCP Thaw in refrigerator
Heat to minimum 165°F internal temperature

PREPARATION (cont'd)

6. **CCP** Remove from heat and portion into service pans. Cover and hold for service (140°F).

7. Portion: 1 cup (8 ounces) per serving

SERVICE

1. **CCP** Maintain temperature of finished product above 140°F during entire service period. Keep covered whenever possible. Take and record temperature of unserved product every 30 minutes. Maximum holding time, 4 hours.

STORAGE

1. **CCP** Transfer unserved product into clean, 2-inch deep pans. Quick-chill. Cooling temperature of product must be as follows: from 140°F to 70°F within 2 hours and then from 70°F to 41°F or below, within an additional 4 hour period. Take and record temperature every hour during chill-down.

2. **CCP** Cover, label, and date. Refrigerate at 41°F or lower for up to 7 days (based on quality maintained) or freeze at 0°F for up to 3 months.

REHEATING:

1. **CCP** Thaw product under refrigeration, if frozen (41°F).

2. **CCP** Remove from refrigeration, transfer into shallow, 2-inch deep pans and immediately place in preheated 350°F oven, covered. Heat for 30 minutes or until internal temperature reaches 165°F or above.

Discard unused product.

Reprinted by permission from La Vella Food Specialists, *HACCP for Food Service, Recipe Manual and Guide,* 1998.

Download this form online at http://www.EarlyChildEd.delmar.cengage.com

programs are usually required to provide written documentation that they are currently free of tuberculosis; this proof can be in the form of a negative skin test or chest X-ray. Food handlers should also undergo periodic physical examinations to document their state of general health.

Everyone who is involved in food preparation and service should also be free of communicable diseases. Those suffering from colds, respiratory or intestinal types of influenza, hepatitis, gastrointestinal upsets, or severe throat infections should not be involved in food handling. People who are experiencing mild forms of these conditions often feel that they are well enough to work but in doing so they may transmit their illness to others. People should refrain from handling food until their symptoms have subsided (Figure 20–3). An emergency store of simply prepared foods can solve the problem of what to feed the children when the cook is ill. Foods that could be available for emergency use include:

- canned soups
- peanut butter
- canned or frozen fruits and vegetables
- tuna or chicken, canned
- cheese (can be frozen)
- dried beans and pastas

An adequate supply of these foods can provide meals that require a minimum of time or cooking skill to prepare.

Food handlers should wear clean, washable clothing and should change aprons frequently if they become soiled. Hair should be covered by a net, cap, or scarf while the worker is handling food.

FIGURE 20–3

Food handlers' health and transmission of food-borne illness.

Condition	Guidelines
Abscess or skin infections	Avoid food preparation if lesions are open or draining. Plastic/latex gloves should be worn if sores are present on hands.
Cough, cold, or respiratory infection (without fever)	Avoid handling or working with food if coughing is uncontrollable or nose-blowing is frequent. Wash hands often and step out of food preparation areas when coughing or sneezing.
Cuts or burns (not infected)	Keep affected area(s) bandaged. Wear plastic/latex gloves if injuries are on hands or lower arms.
Diarrhea	Avoid contact with food, children and other personnel until 24 hours after diarrhea ends. Medical evaluation should be obtained for diarrhea lasting longer than 48 hours to rule out infectious diseases such as E. coli, giardia, salmonella, hepatitis A, and campylobacter. Contact local health department authorities if tested positive for any of these.
HIV/AIDS	No restrictions are necessary. Food handlers should practice good handwashing and personal hygiene.
Respiratory infections (with fever)	No contact should be had with food or food preparations until 24 hours after the fever ends. A throat culture may be needed to rule out strep infections.
Vomiting	Avoid contact with food, children, and other personnel until 24 hours after the vomiting ends.

Head coverings should be put on and shoulders checked carefully for loose hair prior to entering the kitchen. Fingernails should be properly maintained and no polish or artificial nails should be allowed. Jewelry should not be worn with the exception of a plain ring, such as a wedding band.

Food handlers should refrain from chewing gum or smoking while working with food. Both practices can introduce saliva to the food handling area.

The Importance of Handwashing

Handwashing is of utmost importance to personal cleanliness (Figure 20–4). Hands should be washed thoroughly:

- before work
- before putting on gloves to work with food
- before touching food
- after handling nonfood items, such as cleaning or laundry supplies
- between handling different food items
- after using the bathroom
- after coughing, sneezing, or blowing the nose
- after using tobacco, eating, or drinking
- after touching bare body parts (face, ears) or hair

Hands should be washed thoroughly after handling raw foods, such as fish, shellfish, meat and poultry, and before handling other foods. The use of gloves offers an additional measure of protection but hands must still be washed carefully following their removal. Current recommendations suggest that soap and water remains the accepted method of cleaning hands in non-health care settings (Patil, Cates, & Morales, 2005; Hillers, et al., 2003). Waterless, alcohol-based gels are increasingly used in health care settings but are not a substitute for proper handwashing. However, they may not be a sensible choice in early childhood settings because these gels can be potentially toxic if ingested by children. If alcohol-based sanitizing hand gels are used, they must be made inaccessible. To encourage young children to thoroughly wash their hands, have them count to 20 and then say their full name or sing the entire alphabet song while washing their hands. If the food handler has cuts or abrasions on hands or arms, the cuts should be bandaged and gloves

FIGURE 20–4

Hands should be washed thoroughly before handling food.

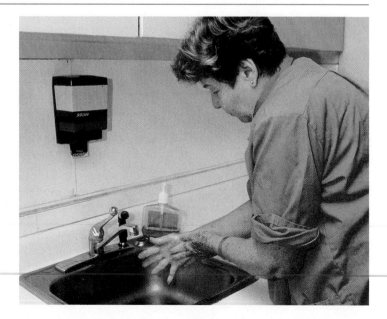

FIGURE 20–5

Proper handwashing technique.

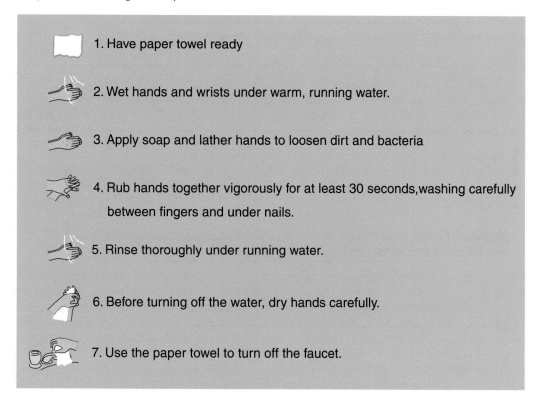

1. Have paper towel ready

2. Wet hands and wrists under warm, running water.

3. Apply soap and lather hands to loosen dirt and bacteria

4. Rub hands together vigorously for at least 30 seconds, washing carefully between fingers and under nails.

5. Rinse thoroughly under running water.

6. Before turning off the water, dry hands carefully.

7. Use the paper towel to turn off the faucet.

should be worn. Gloved hands should be washed as often as bare hands because the gloves can also pick up bacteria. See Figure 20–5 for an example of proper handwashing technique.

Safe and Sanitary Food Service

The way in which food is handled, stored, transported, and prepared ultimately affects the health of those who consume it. Understanding how each of these steps may become a potential source of contamination is critical. Food preparers should develop and practice safe food handling techniques to minimize the risk of food-borne illness.

Food   All raw produce should be inspected for spoilage upon delivery and should be thoroughly washed before use. Fresh fruits and vegetables can carry bacteria and pesticide residues (Sivapalasingam, et al., 2004). Produce that won't be peeled, such as strawberries, potatoes, and green onions, can be washed with plain water. If necessary, use a small brush to remove surface dirt. Lettuce leaves should be washed individually. Produce that will be peeled should be rinsed well to prevent spreading bacteria from the peel or rind to the hands and edible parts of the fruit or vegetable. All dairy products must be **pasteurized**. Tops of cans should be washed before opening; contaminants on cans can be passed to other cans or work surfaces by a dirty can opener. The can opener should also be washed daily. Food in cans which "spew" when opened should be discarded immediately. All other food packages should be in good condition (e.g., no broken film on meat packages, no dented cans) to protect the integrity of the product.

pasteurized – *heating a food to a prescribed temperature for a specific time period to destroy disease-producing bacteria.*

After washing raw meat, fish, or poultry, rinse the sink with hot, soapy water. The kitchen sink and faucet handles should be sanitized frequently. The sink drain should also be sanitized weekly. Food particles trapped in the drain and disposal along with moisture in the drain provide an excellent environment for bacterial growth. A disinfecting solution (one tablespoon of chlorine bleach per one quart of water) can be poured down the drain.

Food Storage   Careful storage and handling of food at appropriate temperatures are essential food safety measures. Refrigerators should be maintained at 38°F to 40°F. A thermometer hung from a shelf in the warmest area of the refrigerator can be used to check whether appropriate temperatures are being maintained. Freezers should be maintained at 0°F or below. Frozen foods should only be thawed:

- in the refrigerator
- in cold water (place food in watertight, plastic bag; change water every 30 minutes)
- in a microwave oven
- while cooking

> *Caution:* **Frozen food should never be thawed at room temperature! Once thawed, food should be used and never refrozen.**

Transport   Food should be covered or wrapped during transport. Covering provides additional temperature control and avoids the possibility of contamination during transport. When serving foods, each serving bowl, dish, or pan should have a spoon; spoons should not be used to serve more than one food. Caution should also be used not to touch serving spoons to a person's plate to prevent contamination from saliva.

Food Service   Food that has been on the tables should not be saved. The exception to this rule are fresh fruits and vegetables that may be washed after removal from the table and served later or incorporated into baked products such as muffins. Food that has been held in the kitchen at safe temperatures (160°F for hot food or 40°F or below for cold foods) may be saved. Food should not be held at these temperatures longer than two hours. Foods that are to be saved should be placed in shallow (three inches or less) pans and refrigerated or frozen immediately. Spreading food in a thin layer in shallow pans allows it to cool more rapidly.

Foods such as creamed dishes, meat, poultry, or egg salads are especially prone to spoilage and should be prepared from chilled ingredients as quickly as possible and served or immediately refrigerated in shallow containers. All such foods should be maintained at temperatures below 40°F until cooked or served.

Sanitation of Food Preparation Areas and Equipment

The cleanliness of the kitchen and kitchen equipment is a vital factor in assuring food safety. Traffic through the kitchen should be minimized to reduce the amount of dirt and bacteria that are brought in. All areas of the kitchen should be cleaned on a regular basis. A schedule, such as that shown in Figure 20–6, is helpful for making sure that floors, walls, ranges, ovens, and refrigerators are routinely cleaned. Equipment used in the direct handling of food must also receive extra care and attention. Countertops and other surfaces on which food is prepared should be **sanitized** or **disinfected** with a chlorine bleach solution each time a different food is prepared on it. Disinfecting may be done with

---

sanitized – *cleaned or sterilized.*
disinfected – *killed pathogenic organisms.*

FIGURE 20–6

Kitchen sanitization depends on frequent, systematic cleaning.

CLEANING SCHEDULE

Daily
- ▼ Cutting boards sanitized after each use
- ▼ Counter tops washed and sanitized between preparation of different foods
- ▼ Tables washed with sanitizing solution
- ▼ Can openers washed and sanitized
- ▼ Range tops cleaned
- ▼ Floors damp mopped

Weekly
- ▼ Ovens cleaned
- ▼ Refrigerator cleaned and rinsed with vinegar water

As Needed
- ▼ Refrigerator/freezer defrosted
- ▼ Walls washed
- ▼ Floors scrubbed

---

a liquid chlorine bleach solution (one-quarter cup bleach to a gallon of water or one tablespoon per quart of water). A fresh solution must be mixed daily to retain its disinfecting strength.

> *Caution* **Never mix bleach with anything other than water—A poisonous gas can result!**

Cutting boards should be nonporous and always washed with hot, soapy water and sanitized with bleach solution after each use. Designating separate cutting boards for different food

 REFLECTIVE THOUGHTS

How safe is your personal kitchen? Although regulations are written for organizational kitchens, what about the kitchens in our homes?

Do you:

- sanitize counter surfaces and cutting boards? Do you use an antibacterial product or dilute chlorine bleach?
- sanitize utensils? Do you immerse them in hot (170°F) water for at least 30 seconds? Do you wash them in the dishwasher?
- wash your hands frequently? Wash briskly with soap? Dry them with a clean towel or paper towels?
- sanitize spills from raw meats, fish, seafood, and poultry?
- avoid using sponges, or wash/sanitize them regularly?
- wash fruits and vegetables thoroughly?
- cook foods to proper temperatures?
- ensure refrigerators/freezers are maintained at appropriate temperatures?

preparations (e.g., meat, raw poultry, salad, fresh fruits) reduces the risk of cross contamination. Cutting boards can be labeled or color coded to indicate their specific purpose.

Dishwashing Dishes may be washed by hand or with a mechanical dishwasher. If washing by hand:

- wash dishes with hot water and detergent
- rinse dishes in hot, clear water
- sanitize dishes with chlorine bleach solution or scald with boiling water
- air dry (not dried with a towel) all dishes, utensils, and surfaces

If a mechanical dishwasher is used to wash dishes, the machine must meet local health department standards. Some state licensing regulations provide guidelines as to the method of dishwashing that is to be used based on the number of persons served.

Sanitation of Food Service Areas

The eating area also requires special attention. Cleanliness of the tables can be a problem, especially if they are also used as classroom tables. In order to maintain adequate sanitation, the tables should be washed with a chlorine bleach solution:

- before each meal
- after each meal
- before each snack
- after each snack (Figure 20–7)

Children should be taught to wash their hands carefully before eating. Adults must also do the same, especially before they begin to set the table or prepare/serve food. Children should also be taught that serving spoons are used to serve food and then replaced in the serving dishes. Children should never be allowed to eat food directly from serving dishes or to eat from the serving utensils.

The guidelines shown in Figure 20–8 provide a useful tool for ongoing assessment of food service conditions.

FIGURE 20–7

Tables should be washed and disinfected before and after meals.

FIGURE 20–8

Guidelines for evaluating sanitary conditions.

SANITATION EVALUATION

	EX	GOOD	FAIR	POOR

FOOD

1. Supplies of food and beverages must meet local, state, and federal codes.

2. Meats and poultry must be inspected and passed for wholesomeness by federal or state inspectors.

3. Milk and milk products must be pasteurized.

4. Home-canned foods must not be used.

FOOD STORAGE

1. Perishable foods are stored at temperatures that will prevent spoilage:
   a. Refrigerator temperature: 40°F (4°C) or below
   b. Freezer temperature: 0°F (-18°C) or below

2. Thermometers are located in the warmest part of each refrigerator and freezer and are checked daily.

3. Refrigerator has enough shelves to allow space between foods for air circulation to maintain proper temperatures.

4. Frozen foods are thawed in refrigerator or quick-thawed under cold water for immediate preparation, or thawed as part of the cooking process. (Never thawed at room temperature.)

5. Food is examined when brought to center to make sure it is not spoiled, dirty, or infested with insects.

6. Foods are stored in rodent-proof and insect-proof covered metal, glass, or hard plastic containers.

7. Containers of food are stored above the floor (6 inches) on racks that permit moving for easy cleaning.

Continued

FIGURE 20–8

Guidelines for evaluating sanitary conditions (continued).

SANITATION EVALUATION

	EX	GOOD	FAIR	POOR
8. Storerooms are dry and free from leaky plumbing or drainage problems. All holes and cracks in storeroom are repaired.				
9. Storerooms are kept cool: 50°F to 70°F (10°C to 21°C)				
10. All food items are stored separately from nonfood items.				
11. Inventory system is used to be sure that stored food is rotated.				
FOOD PREPARATION AND HANDLING				
1. All raw fruits and vegetables are washed before use. Tops of cans are washed before opening.				
2. Thermometers are used to check internal temperatures of: a. Poultry—minimum 170°F (74°C)				
b. Pork and pork products— minimum 160°F (66°C).				
3. Meat salads, poultry salads, potato salads, egg salad, cream-filled pastries and other potentially hazardous prepared foods are prepared from chilled products as quickly as possible and refrigerated in shallow containers or served immediately.				
4. All potentially hazardous foods are maintained below 40°F (4°C) or above 140°F (60°C) during transportation and holding until service.				
5. Foods are covered or completely wrapped during transportation.				
6. Two spoons are used for tasting foods.				
7. Each serving bowl has a serving spoon.				
8. Leftover food from serving bowls on the tables is not saved. An exception would be raw fruits and vegetables that could be washed. Food held in kitchen at safe temperatures is used for refilling bowls as needed.				

Continued

FIGURE 20–8

Guidelines for evaluating sanitary conditions (continued).

SANITATION EVALUATION

	EX	GOOD	FAIR	POOR
9. Food held in the kitchen at safe temperatures is reused.				
10. Foods stored for reuse are placed in shallow pans and refrigerated or frozen immediately.				
11. Leftovers or prepared casseroles are held in refrigerator or frozen immediately.				
STORAGE OF NONFOOD SUPPLIES 1. All cleaning supplies (including dish sanitizers) and other poisonous materials are stored in locked compartments or in compartments well above the reach of children and separate from food, dishes, and utensils.				
2. Poisonous and toxic materials other than those needed for kitchen sanitation are stored in locked compartments outside the kitchen area.				
3. Insect and rodent poisons are stored in locked compartments in an area apart from other cleaning compounds to avoid contamination or mistaken usage.				
CLEANING AND CARE OF EQUIPMENT 1. A cleaning schedule is followed: a. Floors are wet mopped daily, scrubbed as needed.				
b. Food preparation surfaces are washed and sanitized between preparation of different food items (as between meat and salad preparation).				
c. Cutting boards are made of hard nontoxic material, and are smooth and free from cracks, crevices, and open seams.				

Continued

FIGURE 20–8

Guidelines for evaluating sanitary conditions (continued).

SANITATION EVALUATION

	EX	GOOD	FAIR	POOR
d. After cutting any single meat, fish, or poultry item, the cutting board is thoroughly washed and sanitized.				
e. Can openers are washed and sanitized daily.				
f. Utensils are cleaned and sanitized between uses on different food items.				
2. Dishwashing is done by an approved method:				
a. *Hand washed*—3-step operation including sanitizing rinse.				
b. *Mechanical*—by machine that meets local health department standards.				
3. Range tops are washed daily and as needed to keep them clean during preparation.				
4. Ovens are cleaned weekly or as needed.				
5. Refrigerator is washed once a week with vinegar.				
6. Refrigerator is defrosted when there is about 1/4" thickness of frost.				
7. Tables and other eating surfaces are washed with a mild disinfectant solution before and after each meal.				
8. All food contact surfaces are air-dried after cleaning and sanitizing.				
9. Cracked or chipped utensils or dishes are not used; they are disposed of.				
10. Garbage cans are leakproof and have tight-fitting lids.				
11. Garbage cans are lined with plastic liners and emptied and cleaned frequently.				
12. There is a sufficient number of garbage containers available.				

Continued

FIGURE 20–8

Guidelines for evaluating sanitary conditions (continued).

SANITATION EVALUATION

	EX	GOOD	FAIR	POOR

INSECT AND RODENT CONTROL

1. Only an approved pyrithren base insecticide or fly swatter is used in the food preparation area.

2. The insecticides do not come in contact with raw or cooked food, utensils, or equipment used in food preparation and serving, or with any other food contact surface.

3. Doors and windows have screens in proper repair and are closed at all times. All openings to the outside are closed or properly screened to prevent entrance of rodents or insects.

PERSONAL SANITATION

1. Health of food service personnel meets standards:
   a. TB test is current.
   b. Physical examination is up to date.

2. Everyone who works with or near food is free from communicable disease.

3. Clean washable clothing is worn.

4. Hairnets or hair caps are worn in the kitchen.

5. There is no use of tobacco or chewing gum in the kitchen.

6. Hands are washed thoroughly before touching food, before work, after handling nonfood items, between handling of different food items, after using bathroom, after coughing, sneezing, blowing nose.

FOOD-BORNE ILLNESSES

Food poisoning refers to a variety of food-borne illnesses that may be caused by the presence of **bacteria**, **viruses**, **parasites**, or some forms of molds growing on foods (Table 20–1). Foods that are visibly molded, soured, or beginning to liquefy should not be used; nor should food from bulging cans or cans in which the liquid is foamy or smells strange. However, foods containing most food poisoning organisms carry few signs of spoilage. The food usually appears and smells safe, but still can cause severe illness. Proper sanitation procedures, preparation, and food handling should prevent most food-borne illnesses (Kotch, et al., 2007; Cody, 2002).

| FIGURE 20–9

Irradiated foods must display this radura symbol.

The introduction of **irradiation** as a food preservation technique may in time reduce the incidence of food-borne disease. Irradiation has been approved by the Food and Drug Administration (FDA) as an "additive" for destroying illness-producing microorganisms, such as salmonella and E. coli, in food. It is also used to eliminate parasites and insects in food, slow the sprouting process (as in potatoes), delay ripening, and decrease spoilage. This procedure involves exposing food to low levels of gamma radiation; the amount of exposure and the types of foods that can be irradiated are regulated by the FDA (Parnes & Lichtenstein, 2004). Irradiated foods must carry the symbol and message shown in Figure 20–9. Irradiation is allowed in nearly 40 countries and is endorsed by the World Health Organization, the American Medical Association, and the CDC, among others.

The use of irradiation as a preservative for food is still controversial, and some people feel uncomfortable consuming food preserved in this manner. Irradiated foods are not radioactive nor do they retain any radioactivity. In some cases, there may be a loss of some nutrients; vitamins A, E, and C, beta carotene, and thiamin are particularly vulnerable to destruction by irradiation. However, the American Dietetic Association suggests that the amount of nutrient loss is less than the loss that results during conventional food preservation methods (Wood & Bruhn, 2000). Recently, the USDA released specifications for the purchase of irradiated ground beef through the National School Lunch Program. It became available for schools to purchase in January 2004.

Irradiation is not as dangerous as its critics claim, but neither is it the solution to all food-borne illness problems as its promoters claim. Probably the most serious concerns should be that irradiation could be used to cover up unsanitary food processing procedures or that consumers will rely too much upon irradiation protection and become careless in the handling of food. Until more is known about the safety of irradiation and the degree of protection that it affords, it is important that the prescribed procedures for sanitary handling of food be consistently and carefully practiced.

Steam pasteurization is another technique developed to produce safer meat products. In this process the carcass is exposed to pressurized steam for six to eight seconds (McCann, et al., 2006). This technique covers the entire carcass, killing all bacteria uniformly.

Researchers are also looking at spraying baby chicks with antibiotic mist to reduce *salmonella* infections in poultry. Other research is looking at changing cattle feeding practices immediately before slaughter to control E. coli in beef. Undoubtedly, new strategies for controlling and managing

---

bacteria – *one-celled microorganisms; some are beneficial for the body but pathogenic bacteria cause diseases.*
viruses – *any of a group of submicroscopic infective agents, many of which cause a number of diseases in animals and plants.*
parasites – *organisms that live on or within other living organisms.*
irradiation – *food preservation by short-term exposure of the food to gamma ray radiation.*

TABLE 20–1 Food-Borne Illnesses

Disease And Organism That Causes It	Source Of Illness	Symptoms	Prevention Methods
salmonellosis *Salmonella* (bacteria; more than 1,700 kinds)	May be found in raw meats, poultry, eggs, fish, milk, and products made with them. Multiplies rapidly at room temperature.	Onset: 12–48 hours after eating. Nausea, fever, headache, abdominal cramps, diarrhea, and sometimes vomiting. Can be fatal in infants, the elderly, and the infirm.	• Handling food in a sanitary manner • Thorough cooking of foods • Prompt and proper refrigeration of foods
E. coli E. coli 0157:H7	May occur in beef (primarily ground beef) unpasteurized apple cider, raw milk, raw potatoes, mayonnaise. Organism is naturally present in food animals.	Onset: 12–72 hours. Watery, profuse diarrhea, fever. Diarrhea may be bloody.	• Cooking ground meats to 165°F. This temperature is high enough to inactivate E. coli. • Pasteurization
staphylococcal food poisoning staphylococcal enterotoxin (produced by *Staphylococcus aureus* bacteria)	The toxin is produced when food contaminated with the bacteria is left too long at room temperature. Meats, poultry, egg products; tuna, potato and macaroni salads; and cream-filled pastries are good environments for these bacteria to produce toxin.	Onset: 1–8 hours after eating. Diarrhea, vomiting, nausea, abdominal cramps, and prostration. Mimics flu. Lasts 24–48 hours. Rarely fatal.	• Sanitary food handling practices • Prompt and proper refrigeration of foods
botulism botulinum toxin (produced by *Clostridium botulinum* bacteria)	Bacteria are widespread in the environment. However, bacteria produce toxin only in an anaerobic (oxygen-less) environment of little acidity. Types A, B, and F may result from inadequate processing of low-acid canned foods, such as green beans, mushrooms, spinach, olives, and beef. Type E normally occurs in fish.	Onset: 8–36 hours after eating. Neuro-toxic symptoms, including double vision, inability to swallow, speech difficulty, and progressive paralysis of the respiratory system. OBTAIN MEDICAL HELP IMMEDIATELY. BOTULISM CAN BE FATAL.	• Using proper methods for canning low-acid foods • Avoidance of commercially canned low-acid foods with leaky seals or with bent, bulging, or broken cans • Toxin can be destroyed after a can is opened by boiling contents hard for 10 minutes—NOT RECOMMENDED

(continued)

TABLE 20-1 Food-Borne Illnesses (continued)

Disease And Organism That Causes It	Source Of Illness	Symptoms	Prevention Methods
Listeriosis *Listeria* monocytogenes	Raw animal products and dairy foods, contaminated water.	Mild fever and diarrhea, severe sore throat, meningitis, encephalitis, still birth, or abortion.	• Pasteurization • Sanitation • Hygiene
parahaemolyticus food poisoning *Vibrio parahaemolyticus* (bacteria)	Organism lives in salt water and can contaminate fish and shellfish. Thrives in warm water.	Onset: 15–24 hours after eating. Abdominal pain, nausea, vomiting, and diarrhea. Sometimes fever, headache, chills, and mucus and blood in the stools. Lasts 1–2 days. Rarely fatal.	• Sanitary handling of foods • Thorough cooking of seafood
gastrointestinal disease enteroviruses, rotaviruses, parvoviruses	Viruses exist in the intestinal tract of humans and are expelled in feces. Contamination of foods can occur in three ways: (1) when sewage is used to enrich garden/farm soil, (2) by direct hand-to-food contact during the preparation of meals, and (3) when shellfish-growing waters are contaminated by sewage.	Onset: After 24 hours. Severe diarrhea, nausea, and vomiting. Usually lasts 4–5 days but may last for weeks.	• Sanitary handling of foods • Use of pure drinking water • Adequate sewage disposal • Adequate cooking of foods
hepatitis hepatitis A virus	Chief food sources: shellfish harvested from contaminated areas, and foods that are handled a lot during preparation and then eaten raw (such as vegetables).	Jaundice, fatigue. May cause liver damage and death.	• Sanitary handling of foods • Use of pure drinking water • Adequate sewage disposal • Adequate cooking of foods
mycotoxicosis mycotoxins (from molds)	Produced in foods that are relatively high in moisture. Chief food sources: beans and grains that have been stored in a moist place.	May cause liver and/or kidney disease.	• Checking foods for visible mold and discarding those that are contaminated • Proper storage of susceptible foods

TABLE 20-1 Food-Borne Illnesses (continued)

Disease And Organism That Causes It	Source Of Illness	Symptoms	Prevention Methods
giardiasis *Giardia lamblia* (flagellated protozoa)	Protozoa exist in the intestinal tract of humans and are expelled in feces. Contamination of foods can occur in two ways: (1) when sewage is used to enrich garden/farm soil, and (2) by direct hand-to-food contact during the preparation of meals. Chief food sources: foods that are handled a lot during preparation.	Diarrhea, abdominal pain, flatulence, abdominal distention, nutritional disturbances, "nervous" symptoms, anorexia, nausea, and vomiting.	• Sanitary handling of foods • Avoidance of raw fruits and vegetables in areas where the protozoa is endemic • Proper sewage disposal
amebiasis *Entamoeba histolytica* (amoebic protozoa)		Tenderness over the colon or liver, loose morning stools, recurrent diarrhea, change in bowel habits, "nervous" symptoms, loss of weight, and fatigue. Anemia may be present.	• Sanitary handling of foods • Avoidance of raw fruits and vegetables in areas where the protozoa is endemic • Proper sewage disposal
perfringens food poisoning *Clostridium perfringens* (rod-shaped bacteria)	Bacteria are widespread in environment. Generally found in meat and poultry and dishes made with them. Multiply rapidly when foods are left at room temperature too long. Destroyed by cooking.	Onset: 8–22 hours after eating (usually 12). Abdominal pain and diarrhea. Sometimes nausea and vomiting. Symptoms last a day or less and are usually mild. Can be more serious in older or debilitated people.	• Sanitary handling of foods especially meat and meat dishes and gravies • Thorough cooking of foods • Prompt and proper refrigeration
shigellosis (bacillary dysentery) *Shigella* (bacteria)	Food becomes contaminated when a human carrier with poor sanitary habits handles liquid or moist food that is then not cooked thoroughly. Organisms multiply in food stored above room temperature. Found in milk and dairy products, poultry, and potato salad.	Onset: 1–7 days after eating. Abdominal pain, cramps, diarrhea, fever, sometimes vomiting, and blood, pus, or mucus in stools. Can be serious in infants, the elderly, or debilitated people.	• Handling food in a sanitary manner • Proper sewage disposal • Proper refrigeration of foods
campylobacterosis *Campylobacter jejuni* (rod-shaped bacteria)	Bacteria found on poultry, cattle, and sheep that can contaminate the meat and milk of these animals. Chief food sources: raw poultry and meat and unpasteurized milk.	Onset: 2–5 days after eating. Diarrhea, abdominal cramping, fever, and sometimes bloody stools. Lasts 2–7 days.	• Thorough cooking of foods • Handling of food in a sanitary manner • Avoid unpasteurized milk

(continued)

TABLE 20-1 Food-Borne Illnesses (continued)

Disease And Organism That Causes It	Source Of Illness	Symptoms	Prevention Methods
gastroenteritis *Yersinia enterocolitica* (non-spore-forming bacteria)	Ubiquitous in nature; carried in food and water. Bacteria multiply rapidly at room temperature, as well as at refrigerator temperatures of 39.2°F (4° to 48.2°F (4° to 9°C). Generally found in raw vegetables, meats, water, and unpasteurized milk.	Onset: 2–5 days after eating. Fever, headache, nausea, diarrhea, and general malaise. Mimics flu. An important cause of gastroenteritis in children. Can also infect other age groups, and, if not treated, can lead to other more serious diseases (such as lymphadenitis, arthritis, and Reiter's syndrome).	• Thorough cooking of foods • Sanitizing cutting instruments and cutting boards before preparing foods that are eaten raw • Avoidance of unpasteurized milk and unchlorinated water
cerus food poisoning *Bacillus cereus* (bacteria and possibly their toxin)	Illness may be caused by the bacteria, which are widespread in the environment, or by an enterotoxin created by the bacteria. Found in raw foods. Bacteria multiply rapidly in foods stored at room temperature.	Onset: 1–18 hours after eating. Two types of illness: (1) abdominal pain and diarrhea, and (2) nausea and vomiting. Lasts less than a day.	• Sanitary handling of foods • Thorough cooking of foods • Prompt and adequate refrigeration
cholera *Vibrio cholera* (bacteria)	Found in fish and shellfish harvested from waters contaminated by human sewage. (Bacteria may also occur naturally in Gulf Coast waters.) Chief food sources: seafood, especially types eaten raw (such as oysters).	Onset: 1–3 days. Can range from "subclinical" (a mild uncomplicated bout with diarrhea) to fatal (intense diarrhea with dehydration). Severe cases require hospitalization.	• Sanitary handling of foods • Thorough cooking of seafood

Courtesy of "Who, Why, When, and Where of Food Poisons (And What to Do About Them)." FDA Consumer, July–August 1982.

ISSUES TO CONSIDER • An E. coli Outbreak

E. coli 0157:H7 is a deadly bacteria that is frequently in the news. It is commonly associated with outbreaks of contaminated and undercooked meats—especially ground beef. However, they are not always the only sources of this infectious agent. A recent outbreak occurred at a popular water park when one of the children in attendance accidentally defecated in the wading pool. It was later determined that the chlorine levels had not been maintained at a level sufficient to destroy the bacteria. This incident resulted in 26 cases of illness reported in several surrounding states. One child ultimately died from the effects of E. coli 0157:H7 poisoning.

- Are your sanitation procedures adequate to prevent illnesses, such as E. coli, from spreading through water play?

- Are your food preparation and service methods safe?

- What sanitation precautions should you observe when taking children on an outing to prevent this type of illness?

---

food contamination will continue to be developed. In the meantime, consumers must follow good sanitation and food handling practices to protect themselves and others.

CONDITIONS FOR BACTERIAL GROWTH

Since our environment contains numerous bacteria, why do food-borne illnesses not occur even more frequently than they do? For illness to occur the following conditions must be present:

- *Potentially hazardous food*—bacteria generally prefer foods that are high in protein; such as meat, poultry, eggs, and dairy products.
- *Oxygen*—some bacteria require oxygen. Others cannot tolerate oxygen. Other bacteria can grow in environments with or without oxygen.
- *Temperature*—temperature is probably the most critical factor in bacterial growth. The hazard zone of 41°F–140°F is the range in which bacteria grow most rapidly.
- *Time*—a single bacterial cell can multiply into one million cells in five hours under ideal conditions.
- *Water*—bacteria grow in foods with a higher moisture content.
- *Acidity*—bacteria prefer conditions that are near neutral (pH 7.0).

Food infections result from ingestion of large amounts of viable (live) bacteria in foods that cause infectious disease. Salmonella, E. coli, and campylobacter are examples of such bacteria. Symptoms usually develop relatively slowly (12–24 hours) since incubation of the bacteria takes time.

Food intoxications result from eating food containing toxins that are produced in the food by bacterial growth. Symptoms usually develop more rapidly (within 1–6 hours) than those associated with infections except for botulinum toxins, which produce symptoms much later (8–36 hours) (Schlenker & Long, 2006).

The incidence of food-borne illnesses appears to be on the rise and is a frequent cause of illness among infants and toddlers in early childhood programs. The most common food carriers of infectious agents and/or toxins are protein-based foods such as milk, eggs, meat, fish, and

---

food infections – *illnesses resulting from ingestion of live bacteria in food.*
food intoxications – *illnesses resulting from ingestion of food containing residual bacterial toxins in the absence of viable bacteria.*

poultry. Poultry products are one of the most frequent causes of food poisoning, which explains the recommendation that a separate cutting board be provided for poultry and raw meat products (Tauxe, 2002). An additional reason for concern is that the U.S. Department of Agriculture has relaxed its inspection rules, has no standards for bacterial contamination, and allows federal inspectors of poultry products only two seconds to examine each bird. Since bacteria are not visible to the human eye, the results of any "inspection" are questionable. Thus, the consumer must assume full responsibility for choosing, storing, and preparing these products so they do not cause illness. Safe-handling instructions attached to packaging can aid the consumer in safely preparing these foods if they are followed carefully (Figure 20–10). Very thorough cooking of poultry, eggs, and other meat products will destroy bacteria and most toxins. It is NEVER safe to allow young children to eat raw or poorly cooked eggs, meat products, fish, or seafood. Their less than fully developed immune systems leave them more vulnerable to, and less able to cope with, a food-borne illness (Kendall, et al., 2003). It is important to remember that cold temperature **STOPS** bacterial growth. Heat **KILLS** bacteria. Figure 20–11 outlines safe cooking temperatures.

FIGURE 20–10

Safe handling instructions are present on every package of meat and poultry.

SAFE-HANDLING INSTRUCTIONS

THIS PRODUCT WAS PREPARED FROM INSPECTED AND PASSED MEAT AND/OR POULTRY. SOME FOOD PRODUCTS MAY CONTAIN BACTERIA THAT COULD CAUSE ILLNESS IF THE PRODUCT IS MISHANDLED OR COOKED IMPROPERLY. FOR YOUR PROTECTION, FOLLOW THESE SAFE-HANDLING INSTRUCTIONS.

KEEP REFRIGERATED OR FROZEN. THAW IN REFRIGERATOR OR MICROWAVE.

 KEEP RAW MEAT AND POULTRY SEPARATE FROM OTHER FOODS. WASH WORKING SURFACES (INCLUDING CUTTING BOARDS), UTENSILS, AND HANDS AFTER TOUCHING RAW MEAT OR POULTRY.

COOK THOROUGHLY.

KEEP HOT FOODS HOT. REFRIGERATE LEFTOVERS IMMEDIATELY OR DISCARD.

FOCUS ON FAMILIES • Handwashing

Food safety is everyone's responsibility, and it is never too early to introduce children to safe hygiene behaviors. Handwashing is the single-most effective tool for reducing illness by germs transferred from people and surroundings. Teaching children the art of correct handwashing is an essential component of teaching them about sound eating behaviors and practices. As the primary role model for children, parents and teachers should consistently practice good handwashing techniques and be active in getting children to adopt this behavior.

- Children should wash their hands with warm, soapy water before eating, after using the toilet, after playing with a pet, and after nose blowing.
- Keep a step stool nearby to make it easier for the child to reach the sink.

FIGURE 20–11

Safe cooking temperatures.

Product	Fahrenheit	Product	Fahrenheit
Eggs and Egg Dishes		**Poultry**	
Eggs	Cook until yolk and white are firm	Chicken, whole	180
		Turkey, whole	180
Egg dishes	160	Poultry breasts, roast	170
Ground Meat and Meat Mixtures		Poultry thighs, wings	Cook until juices run clear
Turkey, chicken	165		
Veal, beef, lamb, pork	160	Stuffing (cooked alone or in bird)	165
Fresh Beef		Duck and goose	180
Medium rare	145	**Ham**	
Medium	160	Fresh (raw)	160
Well done	170	Pre-cooked (to reheat)	140
Fresh Veal		**Seafood**	
Medium rare	145	Fin fish	145
Medium	160	Minced fish such as fish sticks, fish or seafood patties	155
Well done	170	Stuffed fish or seafood stuffing	165
Fresh Lamb		Oysters, clams, mussels	165
Medium rare	145	Shrimp, lobster, crab or other seafoods	145
Medium	160		
Well done	170		
Fresh Pork			
Medium	160		
Well done	170		

Source: USDA. (1996, November).

Download this form online at http://www.EarlyChildEd.delmar.cengage.com

FOCUS ON FAMILIES • Handwashing (continued)

- Post a chart near the sink and make a mark for every time hands are washed. Praise your child for a job well done.

- Make handwashing fun. Hand and soap dispensers are available in different shaped bars/bottles.

- Be creative . . . create your own song using the melodies from favorite childhood songs or nursery rhymes such as "Row, row, row your boat" or "Old McDonald had a farm." Have your child wash hands for the entire length of the song. This will be fun and ensure that the appropriate amount of time is spent properly cleaning hands.

CASE STUDY

The health department is investigating an outbreak of food poisoning at a local child care center. The children were served a menu that included tacos, tossed lettuce salad, fresh melon cubes, and milk. Annie, the cook, had forgotten to put the ground beef in the refrigerator to thaw a few days earlier, so she allowed it to thaw on the counter overnight. After dividing the partially thawed raw ground beef with her bare hands, she continued preparations for lunch and chopped the ingredients for the tossed salad. Using the same knife that she used to open the packages of ground beef, she cut the melon into cubes for the fruit salad.

1. What is the likely cause of this food-borne illness outbreak?
2. In what ways did the cook contribute to this situation?
3. How could this outbreak have been prevented?

 CLASSROOM CORNER • **Teacher Activities**

Cleaning and Setting the Table. . .
Concept: Cleaning the table before eating and touching the correct parts of cups, plates, and silverware when placing them on the table can prevent the spread of germs. (Pre–2)

Learning Objectives
- Children will learn how to clean classroom tables before meals.
- Children will learn how to properly place cups, plates, and silverware on the table.

Supplies
- Soapy water and disinfectant water in spray bottles; one dishcloth per table; one paper towel per table; silverware, cups, plates, and napkins for meal time.

Learning Activities
- Chose one helper per table and demonstrate how a table is to be washed and set for meal time.
- Have each child wash their hands carefully before starting.
- Give each child a spray bottle filled with soapy water. Have them spray the table and wipe the surface with a dishcloth or paper towel. Next, the teacher should spray the disinfectant (bleach mixture or commercial product) and wipe it off.
- Have children wash their hands after cleaning the tables; tell them that hands get dirty after touching a dirty table.
- Next show children how to put one plate by each chair; they should only touch the outside rim of each plate.
- Next show children how to handle silverware by only touching the handles, not the eating portion.
- Finally show children how to touch the lower part of the cup, not the rim. Have children place silverware, cups, and napkins at each place.
- Have children rewash their hands if they scratch their nose, cover a cough, etc., while setting the table.
- Discuss how washing hands, cleaning the tables, and handling eating utensils correctly help to prevent the spread of germs.

CLASSROOM CORNER • Teacher Activities (continued)

Evaluation

- Children will be able to follow the steps to clean off the tables.
- Children will set the tables correctly touching the plates, cups and silverware appropriately.

SUMMARY

- Basic food safety is an integral factor in the quality of a food service.
    - Wash hands before and after preparation of food.
    - Keep raw meats and poultry separate from other foods.
    - Clean and disinfect cutting boards and kitchen surfaces after preparing food.
    - Keep hot foods hot and cold foods cold.
    - Do not leave food out at room temperature for longer than two hours.
    - Refrigerate leftovers promptly in shallow containers or tightly wrapped bags.
    - Meat and poultry should be cooked all the way through until the juices run clear.
    - Hamburgers should be cooked to a temperature of 165°F and should be brown inside, not pink.
    - Do not taste or eat raw, rare, or even pink ground meat or poultry in any form. When eating out, order ground meats thoroughly cooked.
    - Cook seafood until it is opaque and flaky. Do not eat raw shellfish, such as oysters or clams, even if marinated.
    - Cook eggs thoroughly; they should be firm and not runny.
    - Avoid eating other foods that contain raw or undercooked eggs, such as Caesar salad dressing or cookie dough.
- HACCP (Hazard Analysis and Critical Control Point) is a food safety and self-inspection system that highlights potentially hazardous foods and how they are handled in the food service environment.
- Food safety depends on personal cleanliness and careful food handling.
- Personal health and cleanliness includes:
    - negative tuberculosis test.
    - periodic physical examinations.
    - clean work clothing.
    - head coverings.
    - frequent, thorough handwashing.
- Sanitation of the food service area requires systematic attention including:
    - cleaning schedules.
    - spot cleaning spills as they happen.
    - thorough daily cleaning.
- Safe food handling requires temperature control.
    - Temperature above 140°F to kill bacteria.
    - Temperature below 40°F to prevent bacterial growth.

APPLICATION ACTIVITIES

1. The cook at your early childhood center has strep throat. Using the emergency stock discussed in this chapter, plan a menu for lunch that will meet the CACFP menu-planning guidelines outlined in Chapter 19.

2. Invite a laboratory technician to class to make culture plates of a:

   a. hand before washing.

   b. hand after washing with water only.

   c. hand after washing with soap and water.

   d. strand of hair.

   The technician should then return to the class with the cultures after they have incubated for two to three days.

   a. Is there bacterial growth on any of the culture plates?

   b. Which cultures have the most bacterial growth?

   c. Discuss how these results could be best utilized in terms of:

      1. food preparation and service.

      2. early childhood center meal and snack times.

3. Visit a local early childhood center or public school. Use the sanitation checklist in Figure 20–8 to evaluate the kitchen. Develop suggestions for correcting any problems noted. Share the results with the program director.

CHAPTER REVIEW

A. **By Yourself:**

   1. List three means of keeping the food preparation area clean and germ-free.

   2. Describe the care, uses, and handling of cutting boards necessary for safe food service.

   3. How could ground meat be safely thawed if there is not time to thaw it in the refrigerator?

   4. Terry, a cook, has a cut on her hand. John, a cook, has just developed a sore throat and constant cough. Hanna, a cook, has been experiencing unexplained diarrhea for several days. What precautions should each of these cooks take?

B. **As a Group:**

   1. Explain what the term HACCP refers to. Develop your own HACCP plan—from the time you purchase a pound of ground beef until it shows up as a hamburger on your plate.

   2. Identify and describe the personal sanitation practices that would be important to review with a new cook.

   3. Set up a debate, with one side arguing on behalf of irradiation while the other side argues against this procedure.

   4. Describe the audiences most likely to be sickened by food-borne illnesses and explain why they are at greater risk.

REFERENCES

Centers for Disease Control & Prevention (CDC). (2005). Foodborne illness. Accessed on November 27, 2006, from http://www.cdc.gov/ncidod/dbmd/diseaseinfo/foodborneinfections_g.htm.

Cody, M. (2002). *Food safety for professionals.* (2nd ed.). Chicago: The American Dietetic Association.

Food Safety and Inspection Service, USDA. (2006). The use of ingredients of potential public health concern. Compliance with the HACCP system regulations and request for comment. *Federal Registry, 71*(88), 26677–26679.

Griffith, C. (2006). HACCP and the management of healthcare associated infections: Are there lessons to be learnt from other industries? *International Journal of Health Care Quality Assurance Incorporating Leadership in Health Services, 19*(4–5), 351–367.

Hillers, V., Medeiros, L., Kendall, P., & DiMascola, S. (2003). Consumer food-handling behaviors associated with prevention of 13 foodborne illnesses. *Journal of Food Protection, 66*(10), 1893–1899.

Kendall, P., Medeiros, L., Hillers, V., Chen, G., & DiMascola, S. (2003). Food handling behaviors of special importance for pregnant women, infants and young children, the elderly, and immune-compromised people. *Journal of the American Dietetic Association, 102*(12), 1646–1649.

Kotch, J., Isbell, P., Weber, D., Nguyen, V., Savage, E., Gunn, E., Skinner, M., Fowlkes, S., Virk, J., & Allen, J. (2007). Handwashing and diapering equipment reduces disease among children in out-of-home child care centers. *Pediatrics, 120*(1), e29–36.

McCabe-Sellers, B. & Beattie, S. (2004). Food safety: Emerging trends in foodborne illness surveillance and prevention. *Journal of the American Dietetic Association, 104*(11), 1708–1717.

McCann, M., Sheridan, J., McDowell, D., & Blair, I. (2006). Effects of steam pasteurisation on *Salmonella* Typhimurium DT104 and *Escherichia coli* O157:H7 surface inoculated onto beef, pork and chicken. *Journal of Food Engineering, 76*(1), 32–40.

Parnes, R. & Lichtenstein, A. (2004). Food irradiation: A safe and useful technology. *Nutrition in Clinical Care, 7*(4), 149–155.

Patil, S., Cates, S., & Morales, R. (2005). Consumer food safety knowledge, practices, and demographic differences: Findings from a meta-analysis. *Journal of Food Protection, 68*(9), 1884–1894.

Schlenker, E. & Long, S. (2006). *William's essentials of nutrition and diet therapy.* (9th ed.). St. Louis, MO: Mosby.

Sivapalasingam, S., Friedman, C., Cohen, L., & Tauxe, R. (2004). Fresh produce: A growing cause of outbreaks of foodborne illness in the United States, 1973 through 1997. *Journal of Food Protection, 67*(10), 2342–2353.

Soriano, J., Molto, J., & Manes, J. (2002). Development of a nutritional HACCP plan. *Journal of the American Dietetic Association, 102*(10), 1399–1401.

Tauxe, R. (2002). Emerging foodborne pathogens. *International Journal of Food Microbiology, 78*(1–2), 31–41.

U.S. Department of Health and Human Services (HHS). Public Health Service. Food & Drug Administration. (2001; 2003). *2001 Food Code & 2003 Supplement.* Accessed on November 27, 2006, from http://www.cfsan.fda.gov/~dms/fc01toc.html.

Wood, O. & Bruhn, C. (2000). Position of the American Dietetic Association: Food irradiation. *Journal of the American Dietetic Association, 100*(2), 246–253.

HELPFUL WEB RESOURCES

Centers for Disease Control and Prevention	http://www.cdc.gov
Fight Bac!	http://www.fightbac.org
Food and Drug Administration	http://www.fda.gov
Gateway to Government Food Safety Information	http://www.FoodSafety.gov
The National Food Safety Database Recall Information: USDA	http://www.fsis.usda.gov
University of Nebraska (Food Safety and Self-Inspection for Child Care Facilities)	http://www.ianr.unl.edu

For additional health, safety, and nutrition resources, go to http://www.EarlyChildEd.delmar.cengage.com

CHAPTER 21

Nutrition Education Concepts and Activities

OBJECTIVES

After studying this chapter, you should be able to:

- Identify the primary goal of nutrition education for young children.
- List four basic concepts important to nutrition education.
- Explain the various roles that teachers play in children's nutrition education.
- Describe four ways that nutrition education activities contribute to child development.
- Describe the general safety principles that must be observed in planning children's nutrition education activities.

TERMS TO KNOW

nutrition education	hands-on	objectives
concepts	serrated	attitudes
sensorimotor	preplan	peer
harvest	evaluation	

In the simplest of terms, **nutrition education** is any activity that tells a person something about food. These activities may be structured, planned activities, or very brief, informal happenings. The primary goals of nutrition education designed for young children are to introduce them to a few basic nutrition principles and to encourage them to eat and enjoy a variety of nutritious foods.

BASIC CONCEPTS OF NUTRITION EDUCATION

Some basic **concepts** for teaching young children that nutrition is important for good health are:

1. Children must have food to grow and to have healthy bodies.

- All animals and plants need food.
- Eating food helps children grow, play, learn, and be happy.

---

nutrition education – *activities that impart information about food and its use in the body.*
concepts – *combinations of basic and related factual information that represent a more generalized statement or idea.*

- Many different foods are good for us.
- Eating food makes us feel good.

2. Nutrients come from foods. It is these nutrients that allow children to grow and be healthy.
   - After food is eaten these nutrients are set free to work in our bodies.
   - Nutrients do different things in our bodies.
   - Many different nutrients are needed each day.
   - Foods are the sources of all of the nutrients that are needed.

3. A variety of foods should be eaten each day. No one food provides all of the needed nutrients.
   - Different foods provide different nutrients so we need to eat many kinds of food.
   - Nutrients need to work together in our bodies; we need many different nutrients each day.
   - Children should be introduced to a variety of foods from each of the Food Guide Pyramid groups and be encouraged to at least try a small bite.
   - Children should explore how foods differ relative to color, shape, taste, and texture. They can learn to group and to identify certain kinds of foods such as fruits, breads, and meats.

4. Foods must be carefully handled before they are eaten to ensure that they are healthful and safe.
   - Cleanliness of all foods and people who handle foods is important.
   - Hands should always be washed carefully before eating or touching food.
   - Some foods need to be cooked and eaten hot.
   - Some foods must be kept refrigerated and may be served cold.
   - Involving children with food handling helps them learn about the preparation that must be done to foods before they are eaten.
   - Eating food that has not been handled properly can make children very ill.

These conceptual points require that the people responsible for nutrition education have a basic knowledge of nutrition, in relation to both foods and nutrients.

Families often have nutrition-related questions that may either be about their child or something they have read in a magazine or on the Internet. It is important that teachers provide accurate information. Although teachers may not always know the correct answer, there are many community resources and allied health professionals (e.g., dietitians, health department personnel, USDA extension service, health educators) to which parents can be referred.

Teachers will also find an abundance of printed materials that can be used for planning classroom nutrition activities or distributing to families. However, these materials must be evaluated carefully to be sure they are accurate, free of bias, and appropriate for the purpose intended. Questions to consider include:

1. Is the resource known for its reliability in reporting?
2. What are the professional credentials of the author(s)?
3. Is the resource accurate and does it address nutritional facts rather than theories or biased opinion?
4. Are unsubstantiated health claims presented?
5. Is the resource trying to sell something?
6. Is the material presented at the appropriate level or is it adaptable?
7. Are the suggested nutrition education projects healthful?
8. Are the projects safe?

RESPONSIBILITY FOR NUTRITION EDUCATION

An effective nutrition education program involves the cooperative efforts of directors or administrators, teachers, cooks or food service personnel, and children's families (see Figure 21–1 on page 504). Although the organizational structure may vary from program to program, everyone makes important direct and indirect contributions to children's nutrition education.

FIGURE 21–1

Effective nutrition education requires the cooperative efforts of school personnel.

Directors often play a supportive and influential role in this process. The value a director places on nutrition education can send a powerful message to teachers and food service personnel. For example, a director who considers children's nutrition education a priority will make sure that financial support is available. In contrast, a director who considers this unimportant may also care little about the nutritious quality of children's meals and snacks or whether teachers include any nutrition education in the curriculum.

Teachers are usually responsible for planning and executing nutrition education experiences in the classroom and for creating a pleasant atmosphere for meals and snacks. For this reason, teachers should be familiar with the conceptual framework behind nutrition education. They should be aware of the nutritional value of foods and how to foster children's healthy eating behaviors. Teachers should also be knowledgeable about appropriate instructional methods, able to establish achievable objectives, and responsible for evaluating the results of nutrition activities.

Food service personnel are responsible for preparing and serving meals that are nutritious and appealing, and, in some programs, they may also plan the menu. Including foods on the menu that reinforce classroom nutrition activities is an effective strategy for improving what children are learning. Teachers should work closely with food service personnel so they are aware of nutrition activities and can have the appropriate food items and equipment on hand.

Underlying the effectiveness of all nutrition education for young children is one very simple, basic concept: *Set a good example.* Children who observe a teacher eating and enjoying a variety of nutritious foods will learn to eat more nutritiously than children who observe adults drinking soft drinks and consuming other calorie-dense junk foods.

Family Involvement in Nutrition Education

Family involvement is vital to children's nutrition education. Teachers play an important role in this process by helping families understand why good nutrition is necessary, how to meet children's nutrient needs, how to shape their eating habits, and how to encourage healthy activity patterns (Simpson, Swicegood, & Gaus, 2006; Hindin, Contento, & Gussow, 2004). Families can be encouraged to reinforce what children are learning at school when teachers establish and maintain open communication. Teachers can also achieve a true commitment to family involvement in children's nutrition education by:

- posting weekly menus and including suggestions for foods that provide nutritional complements to each menu.

- providing families with a report of, and recipes for, new foods that their children have recently been introduced to and tasted.
- sharing information about nutrition education learning activities and food experiences with families; requesting feedback on the child's reaction to these experiences.
- presenting some evening meetings or workshops for families. These could include talks or questions/answer sessions with local health agency personnel, demonstrations of food preparation by a local chef, or presentations by a parent who may have some food or nutrition experience to share.
- inviting families to accompany children on food-related field trips.
- encouraging families to join their children for lunch on occasion.
- having a family volunteer to assist with menu planning.
- asking families to share special recipes that are nutritious and family favorites.
- inviting families to share ethnic or traditional foods with the class.
- requesting that families assist with and observe one food experience activity with their child.
- soliciting volunteers to help develop guidelines/policy for acceptable foods that families can bring for birthday or holiday celebrations.

Regardless of the degree of involvement chosen by individual teachers and families, the overriding common goal is children's optimal growth and development. Such a goal can best be met when open, understanding, two-way communication exists between teacher and families.

RATIONALE FOR NUTRITION EDUCATION IN THE EARLY YEARS

Young children are in the process of forming lifelong eating habits, and are thus more receptive to new ideas about food and food-related practices. Basic principles of good nutrition and how they relate to children's health can be effectively taught through nutrition education. Unplanned opportunities also provide "teachable moments." Nutrition education should be integrated across the curriculum to help children understand the relevance of good nutrition to their daily lives. This approach also promotes children's development in other areas including:

- *Promotion of language development and listening skills*
  Children learn and use food names, food preparation terms, and names of utensils. Children also use language to communicate with their peers and teachers throughout the nutrition activity. A variety of children's literature and music can also be introduced to reinforce language, listening, and motor skills as well as nutrition concepts.
- *Promotion of cognitive development*
  Children learn to follow step-by-step directions in recipes. Math concepts are learned through activities that involve measurement of food (cups, ounces, teaspoons), counting, and time periods. Science concepts, such as changes in form (e.g., solids, liquids, gases), are reinforced through activities that involve heating, mixing, cooking, or chilling of foods. Children also begin to learn respect for other cultures, different food practices, where foods come from, and the ways in which foods are grown or produced.
- *Promotion of **sensorimotor** development*
  Hand and finger dexterity are developed through measuring, cutting, mixing, spreading, and serving food. Sensory experiences involving shapes, textures, and colors are learned through an introduction to a wide variety of foods.

---

sensorimotor – *Piaget's first stage of cognitive development, during which children learn and relate to their world primarily through motor and sensory activities.*

■ *Promotion of social/emotional development*

Through nutrition activities, children learn to work as part of a team in either large or small groups. Their knowledge and acceptance of cultural differences is also enhanced by activities that feature ethnic foods and eating customs. In addition, children gain self-confidence and improved self-concept when they master such skills as pouring juice into a glass, serving their own vegetables, or cutting up a sandwich by themselves. Problem-solving skills can also be enhanced.

PLANNING A NUTRITION EDUCATION PROGRAM

The nutrition education program should be part of a coordinated plan that consists of well-designed activities leading to specific outcomes. (A list of resources for children's activities involving nutrition education is provided in Figure 21–2.) Educational experiences should be planned to meet specified goals rather than simply being a way to fill time or keep children busy. Measur-

---

FIGURE 21–2

Resources for teaching nutrition education.

Action for Healthy Kids. http://www.actionforhealthykids.org

Albyn, C. & Webb, L. (1993). *The multicultural cookbook for students* (ages 9–12). Phoenix, AZ: Oryx Press.

American Heart Association. www.americanheart.org

American Dietetic Association. *Five a day for children up to 2 years.* http://www.eatright.org

D'Amico & Drummond, K. (1996). The science chef travels around the world: Fun food experiments and recipes for kids. San Francisco, CA: Jossey-Bass.

Eat Healthy. Play Hard. Read More. Family Bookbag (Web site; includes lessons and family education information). Michigan State University Extension, Family & Consumer Sciences (FCS) Program. http://www.familybookbag.fcs.msue.msu.edu

Evers, C. (2006). *How to teach nutrition to kids.* Tigard, OR: 24 Carrot Press.

Food for Thought. University of Illinois Extension. http://www.urbanext.uiuc.edu/foodforthought

Health Teacher (lesson plans for K–12) http://www.healthteacher.com

HeartPower Online. American Heart Association (lesson plans for pre-K through first grade; in English and Spanish). http://www.americanheart.org/presenter.jhtml?identifier= 3003345

KidsHealth in the Classroom. The Nemours Foundation. Weekly newsletter for educators with lesson plans. http://classroom.kidshealth.org

Berman, C. & Fromer, J. (2006). *Meals without squeals: Child care feeding guide & cookbook.* Boulder CO: Bull Publishing.

MyPyramid for Kids. http://www.MyPyramid.gov

National Gardening Association. Kids Gardening (lesson plans and projects) http://www.kidsgardening.org

National Dairy Council. *Nutrition Explorations.* http://www.nutritionexplorations.org

National Network for Child Care. Cooking with children: Kids in the kitchen. http://www.nncc.org/Curriculum/fc46_cook.kids.html

Nutrition Education of Texas (extensive lesson plans and resources for teaching nutrition education to children grades pre-K through high school) http://netx.squaremeals.org

Smart Snack for Healthy Teeth. National Institute of Dental and Craniofacial Research. http://www.nidcr.nih.gov/HealthInformation/DiseasesAndConditions/Childrens OralHealth

Berman, C. & Fromer, J. (2002). *Teaching children about food: A teaching and activities guide (family & child care).* Boulder CO: Bull Publishing.

able objectives should be developed and serve as guides in the selection of content, instructional method, assessment process, and desired behavioral outcomes.

The overall program should be planned around some or all of the four basic nutrition education concepts described at the beginning of this chapter. Concepts and content should be appropriate for the age and developmental abilities of children in the group. For example, young children are able to comprehend that food is good and that eating many different types of foods is important for staying healthy. They are also able to learn that common foods can be prepared in a variety of ways. The three-year-old, for example, may not yet realize that a head of lettuce, a leaf of lettuce on a sandwich, and lettuce in a salad are all the same food. Tasting parties are easy ways to introduce children to new foods or different forms of the same food. Older children are able to understand the concept of food groups based on similar nutrient contributions and their relationship to good health.

Teachers must plan to evaluate their nutrition lessons to determine if they have been effective in achieving the desired outcomes. Learning objectives which describe expected behavioral changes are useful for this purpose. Figures 21–3 and 21–4 illustrate how a nutrition concept can

FIGURE 21–3

Sample outline for incorporating nutrition education concept #1 into children's learning experiences.

CONCEPT: CHILDREN NEED FOOD TO GROW AND HAVE HEALTHY BODIES

OBJECTIVES: The children should learn that
▼   all living things need food
▼   food is important for growth and for good health

SUGGESTED ACTIVITIES
▼   caring for animals in the classroom with special attention to their diets
▼   taking field trips to the zoo or farm to learn what animals eat
▼   caring for plants in the classroom
▼   planting a vegetable garden in containers or a small plot of ground
▼   weighing and measuring the children periodically
▼   tracing outlines of each child on large sheets of paper

QUESTIONS FOR EXTENDING LEARNING EXPERIENCES
▼   What do animals eat?
▼   Do all animals eat the same foods?
▼   Do animals eat the same foods as people?
▼   Do animals grow faster or slower than people?
▼   What do plants eat?
▼   Can people see plants eating?
▼   Do plants eat the same foods as people?
▼   What does it mean to be healthy?
▼   Do people need food to be healthy?
▼   Do children need food to grow?

EVALUATION
▼   Children can name what animals and plants eat.
▼   Children can describe some effects of not feeding plants and animals.

FIGURE 21–4

Sample outline for incorporating nutrition education concept #4 into children's learning experiences.

CONCEPT: FOODS MUST BE CAREFULLY HANDLED BEFORE THEY ARE EATEN

OBJECTIVES: Children should understand
▼ where foods come from
▼ how foods are handled

SUGGESTED ACTIVITIES
▼ Grow, **harvest**, and prepare foods from a garden.
▼ Sprout alfalfa, radishes, or bean seeds.
▼ Discuss and illustrate the different parts of plants used as food (leaves, roots, fruit, seeds).
▼ Conduct simple experiments that show change in color or form of food.
▼ Play "store" or "farm."
▼ Take children on a field trip to a farm, dairy, bakery, or grocery store.

QUESTIONS FOR EXTENDING LEARNING EXPERIENCES
▼ Where does food come from?
▼ Where do grocery stores get food?
▼ Is food always eaten the way it is grown?
▼ Who prepares different foods?
▼ Does all food come from the store?

EVALUATION
▼ Children can name sources of specific foods.
▼ Children can name who handles such foods as bread, milk, etc.

---

be outlined and developed into learning experiences for children. However, it should be remembered that an activity does not have to be conducted in a rigid manner just because you have established a plan. As in any other curricular activity, children's developmental interests and abilities should be the governing factors for planning and extending learning activities.

✳ GUIDELINES FOR NUTRITION EDUCATION ACTIVITIES

Nutrition education activities should contribute to children's improved understanding and practice of healthy behaviors. In addition, lessons should reflect children's unique developmental needs, abilities, and interests.

1. Nutrition activities should be suitable for the children's developmental skills and abilities. Teachers should modify activities so that all children, including those who have special needs, can fully participate.

> *Caution:* **Special consideration should be given to children's chewing ability, especially when fresh fruits, peanut butter, or raw vegetables are to be used in the activity.**

---

harvest – *to pick or gather fruit or grains.*

FIGURE 21–5

Hands-on experiences foster children's positive feelings about food.

2. Actual foods should be used in nutrition projects as often as possible. These may be accompanied by pictures, games, and stories to reinforce what is being learned. Special consideration must be given to food safety, funding, available equipment, and any known food allergies when planning educational experiences that involve real food.

   Caution: **The teacher should always check for allergies to any foods (or similar foods) that will be used in the nutrition activity.**

3. The foods used should be nutritious. A variety of healthy foods should be chosen from the various Food Guide Pyramid groups. Foods (such as cakes, pies, doughnuts, and cookies) that are typically high in fat, sugar, and calories are usually not as nutritious and should be limited.

FIGURE 21–6

Foods prepared during nutrition activities should be eaten soon after the activity has been completed.

hands-on – *active involvement in a project; actually doing something.*

4. The end products of a nutrition activity should be edible and eaten by the children on the same day to effectively reinforce learning concepts. Pasta collages, vegetable prints, and chocolate pudding finger paintings are not suitable nutrition projects since it is not possible to eat the end product. These activities say to the child that it is okay to play with or waste food; this is not a desirable behavior for children to develop.

5. Children should be involved in the actual food preparation. **Hands-on** experiences such as cleaning vegetables, rolling dough, spreading butter, and cutting biscuits increase learning and help to develop a child's positive feelings about food (Figure 21–5). These activities not only enhance food experiences, but aid in the development of other skills such as manual dexterity, counting, problem-solving, and learning to follow directions. Children will often accept new, unfamiliar foods more readily if they have helped in the preparation (Girard, 2005).

6. Once the nutrition activity is completed, the food should be eaten within a short period of time (Figure 21–6). Delays between the completion of the activity and use of the food lessen the activity's impact.

SAFETY CONSIDERATIONS

Attention to the following points can contribute to the increased success and safety of all food experiences.

Basic Guidelines

- Be aware of all food allergies identified in children. Post a list of the children's names along with the foods they cannot eat. Some of the more common foods to which children may be allergic are: wheat; milk and milk products; juices with a high acid content such as orange or grapefruit; strawberries; chocolate; eggs; soy; shellfish; and nuts.
- Avoid serving foods such as nuts, raw vegetables, peanut butter, and popcorn that may cause younger children to choke. These foods should not be given to children who have problems with chewing or swallowing, either. Peanut butter and raw fruits and vegetables are appropriate to serve to older children under close adult supervision.
- Children should always sit down to eat.
- Use low work tables and chairs.
- Use unbreakable equipment whenever possible.
- Supply enough tools and utensils for all of the children in the group.

REFLECTIVE THOUGHTS

Americans are heavy and getting heavier. Our supermarket shelves provide the widest selection of foods in the world. Low-fat, fat-free, and sugar-free foods are available in increasing numbers. Books, magazines, and newspapers feature the "Diet of the Week/Month/Year."

- What nutrition education experiences and activities could you provide to promote children's healthy eating habits?
- What types of foods or eating patterns should be stressed?
- What additional lifestyle factors may contribute to obesity?
- Review the Issues to Consider from Chapter 19 on page 457. What implications does that study have for planning nutrition education experiences?

- Use blunt knives or **serrated** plastic knives for cutting cooked eggs, potatoes, bananas, etc. Vegetable peelers should be used only under supervision and only after demonstrating their proper use to the children.
- Have only the necessary tools, utensils, and ingredients at the work table. All other materials should be removed as soon as they are no longer needed. Plan equipment needs carefully to avoid having to leave the work area during an activity. The teacher should never leave the activity area when there are utensils or foods present that may cause injury.
- **Preplan** the steps of the cooking project; discuss these steps with the children before beginning. Children should understand what they are expected to do and what the adults will do before the cooking materials are made available to them.
- Long hair should be pulled back and fastened; floppy or cumbersome clothing should not be worn. Aprons are not essential, but may help keep clothes clean.
- Hands should be washed carefully before beginning the activity.
- Begin with simple recipes that require little cooking. Once the children feel comfortable with those cooking projects, move on to slightly more complex ones.
- Allow plenty of time for touching, tasting, looking, and comparing as well as for discussion. Use every step in the cooking project as an opportunity to expand the learning experience for the children.

Food Safety

- Wash hands before and after a cooking project; this applies to teachers as well as children.
- Children and adults with colds should not help with food preparation.
- Children and adults with cuts or open sores on their hands should have them properly covered during food preparation.
- Keep all cooking utensils clean. Have extra utensils available in case one is dropped or a child puts one into his/her mouth.
- Teach children how to taste foods that are being prepared. Give each child a small plate and spoon to use. Never let the children taste foods directly from the bowl or pan in which the foods are being prepared.
- Avoid using foods that spoil rapidly. Keep sauces, meats, and dairy products refrigerated.

Cooking Safety

- Match the task to the children's developmental levels and attention spans.
- Instruct children carefully regarding the safe use of utensils.
- Emphasize that all cooking must be supervised by an adult.
- Adults should do the cooking over stove burners. Always turn pot handles away from the edge of the stove.
- Use wooden utensils or utensils with wooden handles for cooking. (Metal utensils conduct heat and can cause painful burns.)

DEVELOPING ACTIVITY PLANS FOR NUTRITION ACTIVITIES

The success of each classroom activity as it contributes to the total nutrition education program depends on careful planning. The principles of curriculum design, including topic selection,

---

serrated – *saw-toothed or notched.*
preplan – *outline a method of action prior to carrying it out.*

development of objectives, instructional procedures, and **evaluation** are covered in depth in Chapter 12. Reviewing this material will be helpful in planning nutrition education activities. Some special considerations when developing plans for an effective nutrition program are:

- The title (subject) and **objectives** chosen for each activity should contribute to the understanding of one or more of the four nutrition concepts considered appropriate for children.
- Classroom activities that involve hands-on experience with real food are most effective in teaching children about nutrition.
- Careful preplanning is essential for making each activity safe as well as a good learning experience. Most plans need a cautions list.
- Preplanning allows a sequencing of activities so that each new activity reinforces things that have been learned from prior lessons.
- Evaluation, in addition to giving feedback on the current activity, should be used in planning future activities.

Activity Plan #1 Weighing and Measuring Children

CONCEPT   Weighing and Measuring Children

LEARNING OBJECTIVES

- Children will be able to discuss how eating healthy foods helps them to grow.
- Children can explain how growth is determined by measurements of height and weight.
- Children will be able to recognize that people come in different sizes.

SUPPLIES   a balance-beam scale or bathroom scale; yardstick; large sheets of paper and markers or crayons; samples of nutritious fruits or vegetables for children to taste

LEARNING ACTIVITIES

A. Weigh and measure each child. Encourage children to assist the teacher in reading his/her height and weight measurements. Record the information. Repeat this activity periodically to monitor each child's rate of growth and to make comparisons. Use this activity to reinforce the importance of healthy eating and activity habits.

B. Trace an outline of each child on large sheets of paper. Have children color their paper "selves."

C. Discuss individual differences among children, such as concepts of tall and short. (The discussion should be positive—these differences are what make each child special.)
   – Does everybody weigh the same?
   – Is everyone the same height?
   – Do children stay the same size? Do adults?
   – What makes children grow?

D. Prepare samples of several nutritious fruits or vegetables for children to taste. Use the activity to reinforce the concept that nutritious foods help children grow.

EVALUATION

- Each child can tell the teacher his/her height and weight.
- Children can name nutritious foods that contribute to good health and growth.
- Children will be able to discuss why some people are taller or shorter than others.

evaluation – *a measurement of effectiveness for determining whether or not educational objectives have been achieved.*
objectives – *a clear and measurable description of a specific behavior that an individual is expected to learn.*

Activity Plan #2 Making Hummus and Pitas

CONCEPT   People from other cultures eat foods that may be different from those we typically eat.

LEARNING OBJECTIVES

- Children will learn that people from other cultures may eat different types of foods.
- Children will be able to correctly describe the items used to make hummus and why they are considered to be healthy.

SUPPLIES   bowl, measuring spoons, spatula; potato masher; blender or food processor; ingredients (see recipe); fresh vegetables; pocket pitas or flatbread cut into small wedges

LEARNING ACTIVITIES

A. Be sure teachers and children have washed their hands before proceeding. To make the hummus, assemble the equipment and all the ingredients.
   (For a picture recipe to use in the classroom, see Figure 21–7 on page 518.)

   1 15-ounce can chickpeas (garbanzo beans), drained
   2–3 tablespoons warm water
   2 tablespoons olive oil
   2 tablespoons lemon juice
   1 garlic clove, crushed
   salt to flavor
   2 tablespoons sesame seeds or 3 tablespoons peanut butter (optional)

An assortment of raw vegetables (such as carrot and celery sticks, red/orange/yellow pepper strips, broccoli pieces) and pita wedges, pieces of flatbread, or crackers for dipping

Drain chickpeas; place them in a small bowl with the water, olive oil, and lemon juice. Let children take turns mashing the beans using the potato masher. After each child has had a turn, the teacher can scrape the mixture into a blender and add the remaining ingredients, blending until smooth. Place the hummus in a small bowl and serve with raw vegetables, pita wedges, pieces of flatbread, or crackers.

> *Caution:*   **Be sure to check for any food allergies before beginning this project.**

B. Read one or more of the following books and discuss the concept that people may eat many different kinds of foods:

   Everybody Cooks Rice by Norah Dooley
   Dumpling Soup by Jama Kim Rattigan
   Dim Sum For Everyone by Grace Lin
   The Tortilla Factory by Gary Paulsen

C. Have each child name his/her favorite food. Discuss how families eat foods that are the same and different.

EVALUATION

- Children will be able to name foods that are commonly eaten by people from different cultures.
- Children recognize that people eat foods that may be different from those that they typically eat.

FIGURE 21-7

Picture recipe for making hummus.

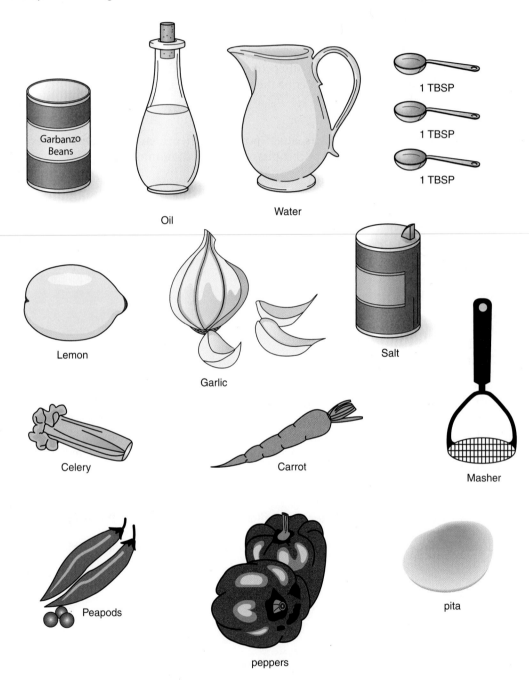

Garbanzo Beans

Oil

Water

1 TBSP

1 TBSP

1 TBSP

Lemon

Garlic

Salt

Celery

Carrot

Masher

Peapods

peppers

pita

Activity Plan #3 Tasting Party

CONCEPT   "Tasting Party for Dairy Foods."

LEARNING OBJECTIVES

- Children will learn that common foods may be served in a variety of ways.
- Children will be able to identify foods that belong to the milk group.
- Children will be able to state why it is important for them to drink milk.

SUPPLIES   small pitcher of milk; unflavored yogurt; cottage cheese; cheddar cheese; ice cream; one pint of whipping cream; small plastic jar with lid; plastic knives

LEARNING ACTIVITIES

A. Be sure teachers and children have washed their hands before beginning.
   Place the pitcher of milk, unflavored yogurt, cottage cheese, cheddar cheese (cut into small cubes), and ice cream on the table. Encourage children to describe the appearance and texture of each item. Do they look alike? Is cottage cheese like cheddar cheese? How is it different? Point out that each food began as milk and has been changed as the result of different preparation methods. Have the children sample each food. Do they all taste alike? Why were these foods chilled before preparation and why should they be eaten immediately? Why is it important to drink milk and eat milk-based products?

B. Pour the whipping cream into a small, clean plastic jar, filling it only half full. Add a few dashes of salt and tighten the jar lid. Let the jar sit until the cream reaches room temperature. Have children take turns shaking the jar until the butter separates from the milk. When it is finished, pour away the milk and remove the butter. Let children spread the butter on a small cracker to taste.

   Caution: **Check beforehand for any milk or dairy product allergies. Provide alternative foods if necessary. Stress that refrigeration and sanitation are very important when working with protein foods such as milk and milk products.**

C. Read and discuss one or more of the following books:
   No Moon, No Milk by Chris Babcock
   No Milk by Jennifer Ericsson
   Milk: From Cow to Carton by Aliki
   From Milk to Ice Cream by Stacy Taus-Bolstad

D. Additional activities can be planned, including making yogurt or cheese from milk, preparing fruit smoothies, and/or making ice cream.

EVALUATION
- Children can identify foods made from milk.
- Children will taste each food served.
- Children will be able to describe where milk and butter come from.

Activity Plan #4 Trip to the Grocery Store

CONCEPT   Children will learn that many different types of fruits and vegetables are available.

LEARNING OBJECTIVES
- Children are encouraged to make decisions about foods and to taste a variety of foods.
- Children will buy a fruit or vegetable with which they may not be familiar.
- Children will be able to name three new fruits or vegetables.

SUPPLIES   local newspaper with weekly food advertisements; paper and pencil; plastic foods; grocery bags; cash register and play money

LEARNING ACTIVITIES

A. Have children look at the produce section in the weekly food advertisements. Ask them to name the fruits and vegetables. Find out if children have ever tasted each of the items and whether or not they liked them.

B. Plan a field trip to the grocery store. Be sure to secure parental permission in advance. Give each child a small piece of paper on which the name of a different fruit or vegetable is written. At the grocery store, help children locate their assigned fruit or vegetable. After purchasing the items and returning to the classroom, ask the children to help describe each food—its color, shape, whether it has seeds, how it grows, and if the skin is peeled or eaten. Finally, ask the cook to prepare the fruits or vegetables for the children to eat: a mixed fruit salad, a vegetable plate, or vegetable soup.

> *Cautions:*
> **Permission must be obtained from families before taking the field trip.**
> **Fasten restraints if driving to the store.**
> **If walking to store, review safety rules for walking, crossing streets, etc.**
> **Check for allergies and provide alternatives if necessary.**

C. Provide the children with various props—plastic foods, empty food containers, grocery bags, cash register and play money—to create their own grocery store. Have some children act as grocers, some as clerks, and others as shoppers.

EVALUATION

- Children are able to identify two varieties of red fruit.
- Children taste each of the prepared fruits or vegetables.
- Children can name and describe three different fruits and/or vegetables.

Activity Plan #5 Safe Lunches

CONCEPT
How to pack lunches that are safe and healthy.

LEARNING OBJECTIVES

- Children will learn how to select and eat food safely.
- Children will select at least one food with which they are not familiar.
- Children will include a variety of nutritious foods in their lunch.

SUPPLIES
empty lunch box with thermos; obtain foods that may be available in school cafeteria/kitchen as examples of items that children can pack in a lunchbox (e.g., sandwich, milk, juice, soup, carrot sticks, cheese cubes, tortilla, apple, banana, yogurt, salad, etc.)

LEARNING ACTIVITIES

A. Display the food choices on a table. Have children wash their hands prior to selecting food. In groups of two, have children choose foods from those provided that they would pack in a lunchbox to bring to school. Encourage children to choose a variety of foods based on the Food Guide Pyramid. After each child has packed his/her lunch, have a discussion about the foods that were chosen. Let children eat the foods they have packed in their lunchboxes. Extend the discussion by asking:

- Which foods need to be kept cold?
- Which foods need to be kept hot?
- Which foods need to be wrapped or stored in special containers to be kept safe?
- Which foods need to be washed before they are eaten?
- Are there any other foods you would choose for your lunch box that are not included here?

> *Cautions:*
> **Check for children's food allergies prior to activity.**
> **Recommend sampling only those foods that do not require storage at extreme temperatures to avoid illness (i.e., avoid milk, yogurt, ice cream, soup).**

B. Take children on an actual picnic lunch. Let them help with the preparation and safe storage of foods for the event.

EVALUATION

- Children are able to participate in choosing their own food at mealtime.
- Children select a variety of healthful foods from each of the Food Guide Pyramid groups.
- Children are able to explain how foods must be handled and stored to prevent illness.

Activity Plan #6 Eating Five Fruits and Vegetables Daily

CONCEPT It is important to eat at least five fruits and vegetables each day.

LEARNING OBJECTIVES

- Children will learn that there are many different types of fruits and vegetables.
- Children will learn that a particular fruit or vegetable may be prepared and eaten in a variety of different ways.
- Children will understand that fruits and vegetables taste good and keep us healthy.

SUPPLIES disposable plates and napkins; a variety of fruits that represent different sizes, colors, and shapes (e.g., apples, bananas, oranges, kiwi, melons, star fruit, mangos, etc.); a variety of vegetables, emphasizing different preparation techniques (e.g., baked potato, mashed potato, French fries, scalloped potatoes)

LEARNING ACTIVITIES

A. Be sure that adults and children wash their hands prior to handling the food. Lay out the assortment of fruits and vegetables (that have been cut into small pieces) on a table. Give children a paper plate and allow them to select a total of five fruits and vegetables. Encourage children to select a variety of different foods, particularly those they have never eaten before. Have the children sample each of the foods they have selected. As a group, discuss these questions:

- What are some of the different colors of fruits and vegetables?
- What are the different ways of preparing the same food? Do you know of any more?
- Is there a food you tried today that you have never eaten before? Will you try it again?
- Did you know that if you eat a total of five fruits and vegetables every day, it can keep you from getting sick? Discuss.

> *Cautions:*
> **Check beforehand for children's food allergies.**
> **Maintain foods at appropriate temperatures to avoid illness.**

B. On another day, have the cook prepare some of the same vegetables. Discuss how cooking affects the color, texture, and flavor of different vegetables.
C. Take the children to visit a local supermarket. Call the store manager prior to the visit. He/she may be able to arrange for a special tour which may include food sampling in the produce department.

EVALUATION

- Children can explain why it is important to include a variety of fruits and vegetables in their daily diet.
- Children select a variety of different fruits and vegetables to eat at mealtime.
- Children understand that eating five fruits and vegetables daily can prevent disease.

OTHER SOURCES OF INFORMATION ABOUT FOOD

Children learn about food from informal sources as well as from planned programs of instruction. Their families, their teachers, other children, and television serve as additional sources of information about food and all have an effect on children's eating habits (Folta, Goldberg, & Economos, 2006; Weber, Story, & Harnack, 2006) (Figure 21–8).

The Family

A family's food preferences and **attitudes** are of primary importance in the child's formation of food preferences and attitudes about food. Family food choices are subject to cultural influences, money available for food, educational level, and specific preferences of family members (Briefel, et al., 2006; Di Noia, Schinke, & Contento, 2005; Patrick & Nicklas, 2005). Children become familiar and comfortable with certain foods through repeated exposures. Since familiarity is one of the most influential factors affecting food choices, children who come from families that eat a wide variety of foods are often more willing to try new foods.

Teachers

Teachers also exert considerable influence over children's attitudes about food. For this reason, teachers should display a positive attitude, through their actions and words, and a willingness to try new foods.

FIGURE 21–8

Additional sources of influence on children's eating habits.

ADDITIONAL FACTORS THAT INFLUENCE CHILDREN'S EATING HABITS:

▼ Families of children who have a strong preference for high-fat foods have higher BMI scores than parents who do not have a strong preference for high-fat foods.

▼ Children are more likely to eat a certain food if they observe adults eating it.

▼ There is a strong relationship between the food preferences of toddlers and their mothers, fathers, and older siblings.

▼ Involving families in children's nutrition education programs increases the diversity and quality of student's diets.

▼ Involving families in children's nutrition education programs increases the diversity and quality of student's diets. In general, the more hours women work outside the home, the fewer hours they spend preparing meals, and the more meals their children eat away from home.

▼ The nutrition knowledge and practices of food service personnel in child care centers has a major influence on the quality of menus served (Escobar, 1999).

---

attitudes – *beliefs or feelings one has toward certain facts or situations.*

ISSUES TO CONSIDER • Food Trend Predictions

Food corporations are continuously engaged in developing and marketing new items aimed at the health-conscious consumer. Organic foods, herbal supplements, oxygenated waters, low- and fat-free foods, foods enhanced with phytochemicals for added health benefits, and nutrition products that can be eaten on the run, such as juice bars, energy shakes, and protein smoothies are predicted to be hot products.

- Do you perceive these trends to be positive or negative?
- What effect(s) might these trends have on families' ideas about what children should be eating?
- How might these trends influence children's ideas about nutritious food?
- How will these trends affect children in your care?

Other Children

Children's food choices are frequently made on the basis of approval or disapproval of others in their group. A child with a strong personality who eats a variety of foods can be a positive influence on other children. On the other hand, children who are "picky eaters" can also spread their negative influence. A simple statement from the teacher, such as, "You don't have to eat the broccoli, Jamie, but I can't allow you to spoil it for Tara and Pablo," should be effective in curbing this negative influence. Younger children may base their choices on familiarity of food and its taste. Older children (five and up) are more subject to **peer** influence when deciding whether or not to eat a food.

Television

Television is a major source of information and misinformation about food for many children and their families (Wansink, 2006). Unfortunately, nutrient-dense foods are rarely featured on television (Nestle, 2006). Rather, those foods that taste good, are chocolaty, highly-sugared or loaded with fat, are really fun, or come with a prize appear most often. The influential role television plays in determining children's food choices is discussed in Chapter 18. Families and teachers can help to counteract television's influence by monitoring the programs that children view and by pointing out differences between programs and commercials (Hindin, Contento, & Gussow, 2004). Children need to understand that the purpose of a commercial is to sell a product that may not always be good for them.

FOCUS ON FAMILIES • 5 a Day for Better Health

Families can take an active part in ensuring that their child consumes a total of five fruits and vegetables daily. Consuming five to nine servings of fruits and vegetables daily can improve health and reduce the risk of cancer, heart disease, hypertension, diabetes, and obesity.

Families can create activities that help to convey this important health message.

- Prepare homemade vegetable soup or a fresh fruit salad. Have your child name each vegetable or fruit contained in the recipe. This increases your child's awareness of how fruits and vegetables can be included in daily meal plans while providing a nutritious meal or snack.

(continued)

---

peer – *one of the same rank; equal.*

FOCUS ON FAMILIES • 5 a Day for Better Health (continued)

- Visit the nearest farmer's market. Not only will your child develop an appreciation for fresh produce, but it will also stimulate curiosity and questions for learning.
- Teach your child the importance of eating seasonal fruits and vegetables not only for the taste, but also the cost savings it can provide for your family. Below is a sampling of some fruits and vegetables you will find plentiful every season.

  Spring: apples, grapefruits, pears, strawberries, broccoli, cabbage, carrots, asparagus
  Summer: berries, cantaloupes, melons, peaches, corn, green beans, cucumbers, okra

  Fall: oranges, peaches, prunes, plums, brussels sprouts, tomatoes, peppers, zucchini
  Winter: apples, grapefruit, oranges, beets, cauliflower, potatoes, spinach, squash

- Try planting one of the foods listed above. Your child will learn about the growing process and realize that foods do not always originate in the supermarket.

CASE STUDY

Marcus, age four years, has been ill several times this spring with upper respiratory infections. His mother mentions that she is now giving him an herbal supplement to "boost his immune system" so that he won't be ill as often. She asks you if you think the supplement will help Marcus and if you feel it is safe for Marcus to take.

1. What information do you need to know before answering her questions?
2. What resources are available to find the necessary information?
3. How will you determine if the information available to you is accurate and reliable?
4. Are you qualified to advise Marcus's mother on this issue?

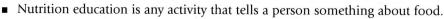

SUMMARY

- Nutrition education is any activity that tells a person something about food.
  - Children must have food for growth and healthy bodies.
  - Nutrients come from food.
  - A variety of foods must be eaten to provide needed nutrients.
  - Foods must be handled carefully to be safe to eat.
- Nutrition education must be appropriate for the persons being taught.
  - Nutrition activities should promote skills in all developmental areas.
  - Activities should illustrate basic nutrition concepts.
- The primary goal of nutrition education is to teach children to choose a healthful diet.
  - Food used in activities should be nutritious.
  - The end product should be edible.
  - All activities should be planned with an emphasis on safety.

APPLICATION ACTIVITIES

1. Prepare lesson plans for a two-day nutrition education activity. Plans may be for two consecutive days or for any two days within one week. The lesson plan for each day should be in the format presented in this unit.

2. Outline an equipment list and safety plan for a food experience in which four- and five-year-olds make pancakes in the classroom. Cooking will be done in an electric skillet on a table. What precautions should be taken? How should the room be safely arranged? What instructions should be given to the children?

3. Select 15 to 20 library books appropriate for young children. Note those instances where food is portrayed either in the story or pictures. What types of foods are shown? Chart these foods according to the Food Guide Pyramid. What percentage of foods were noted within each group? What was the general message about food presented in these books?

4. Watch one hour of children's television programs on Saturday morning.

   a. Determine the percent of observed advertisements that featured "sweets" (gum, candy, soft drinks, snack cakes, and pre-sweetened cereals). Calculate the percentage of advertisements featuring fast foods or those especially high in fat.

   b. Which food groups were least represented in these commercials?

5. Review an article about nutrition from a popular magazine. Apply the suggested criteria for a good nutrition resource. Is this a good article? Why or why not?

CHAPTER REVIEW

A. **By Yourself:**

   1. Explain how children typically form their food preferences.

   2. Describe how program directors, teachers, and families collectively contribute to children's nutrition education.

   3. What role do teachers play in developing and implementing nutrition education for children?

   4. What fundamental principles should guide nutrition education activities conducted with children?

B. **As a Group:**

   1. Discuss the ways in which nutrition education experiences can promote children's development in other areas.

   2. What criteria should be used for choosing appropriate nutrition education concepts for children?

   3. Describe four ways that programs can involve families in children's nutrition education.

   4. Why is it important to include nutrition education during children's early years?

   5. What safety issues must teachers consider when conducting classroom food activities?

REFERENCES

Briefel, R., Ziegler, P., Novak, T., & Ponza, M. (2006). Feeding Infants and Toddlers Study: Characteristics and usual nutrient intake of Hispanic and non-Hispanic infants and toddlers. *Journal of the American Dietetic Association, 106*(1 Suppl.), S84–95.

Di Noia, J., Schinke, S., & Contento, I. (2005). Dietary patterns of reservation and non-reservation Native American youths. *Ethnicity & Disease, 15*(4), 705–712.

Folta, S., Goldberg, J., & Economos, C. (2006). Food advertising targeted at school-age children: A content analysis. *Journal of Nutrition Education & Behavior, 38*(4), 244–248.

Girard, B. (2005). Fruits and vegetables galore: Helping kids eat more. *Journal of Nutrition Education and Behavior, 37*(4), 221–223.

Hindin, T., Contento, I., & Gussow, J. (2004). A media literacy nutrition education curriculum for Head Start parents about the effects of television advertising on their children's food requests. *Journal of the American Dietetic Association, 104*(2), 192–198.

Nestle, M. (2006). Food marketing and childhood obesity—a matter of policy. *New England Journal of Medicine, 354*(24), 2527–2529.

Patrick, H. & Nicklas, T. (2005). A review of family and social determinants of children's eating patterns and diet quality. *Journal of the American College of Nutrition, 24*(2), 83–92.

Simpson, C., Swicegood, P., & Gaus, M. (2006). Nutrition and fitness curriculum: Designing instructional interventions for children with developmental disabilities. *Teaching Exceptional Children, 38*(6), 50–53.

Wansink, B. & American Dietetic Association. (2006). Position of the American Dietetic Association: Food and nutrition misinformation. *Journal of the American Dietetic Association, 106*(4), 601–607.

Weber, K., Story, M., & Harnack, L. (2006). Internet food marketing strategies aimed at children and adolescents: A content analysis of food and beverage brand web sites. *Journal of the American Dietetic Association, 106*(9), 1463–1466.

HELPFUL WEB RESOURCES

5 a Day for Better Health	http://www.5aday.com
American Dietetic Association	http://www.eatright.org
U.S. Food and Drug Administration	http://www.fda.gov
Healthy People 2010	http://www.healthypeople.gov
Journal of Nutrition Education & Behavior	http://www.jneb.org
PE Central	http://www.pecentral.org
Teaching Strategies, Inc.	http://www.teachingstrategies.com
U.S. Department of Agriculture	http://www.usda.gov

 For additional health, safety, and nutrition resources, go to http://www.EarlyChildEd.delmar.cengage.com

Epilogue

✳ LOOKING AHEAD . . . MAKING A DIFFERENCE

As promised, this book has taken you on a journey. You have had an opportunity to learn about many topics that are important to children's health, safety, and nutrition. The new skills that you have developed will improve your abilities to observe children and to detect the early signs of acute and chronic developmental conditions and impending illness. You should be more aware of children's health problems, including childhood obesity, communicable illness, and sensory impairments, and their impact on learning and development. You have learned how to modify children's environments in order to protect them from unintentional injury and unnecessary illness. Your knowledge of children's critical nutrient needs and ways to satisfy them through thoughtful planning has also undoubtedly improved.

Most importantly, you have gained a better understanding of the preventive health concept, not only as it applies to the care and education of young children, but also its application to your own personal life. Knowing there are many things one can do to improve the quality of his or her well-being becomes a powerful incentive to help children establish healthful eating and physical activity habits at an early age. We must also serve as positive role models because we know that children look up to adults and often model their behaviors. As stated throughout the book, teachers are in an ideal position to promote children's health, safety, and nutrition and to make that a priority. Their dedicated efforts to achieving this goal and their commitment to family involvement will make a difference in children's lives.

The ultimate goal and true mark of learning is change . . . change in the way one thinks, change in one's behavior. Undoubtedly, your journey through this book has changed you in some way—to question, think, and/or act differently. However, the journey does not end here. New discoveries that affect our understanding of chronic diseases, nutrition, and safety practices are revealed almost daily. Our ideas and best practices for promoting children's lifetime wellness are continually being reshaped by this information. Some of the areas receiving special attention include:

- Improving the quality of early childhood programs.
- Planning and serving meals/snacks that provide essential nutrients, reduce unnecessary fat and calories, and are respectful of cultural differences.
- Reducing the incidence of childhood obesity.
- Maintaining the safety of food and food environments.
- Addressing and responding to the needs of children with special medical and developmental challenges.
- Building children's resiliency to stress, bullying, and everyday environmental pressures.
- Improving communication and partnerships with families.
- Increasing awareness and sensitivity to child and family differences.
- Recognizing environmental contaminants and their effect on children's health.
- Addressing the need for more family education.
- Encouraging physical activity as a lifestyle practice.

- Addressing the issues of child abuse and domestic violence.
- Advocating on behalf of children's interests.
- Improving children's access to medical and dental care.
- Reducing poverty and food insecurity.

This list is not inclusive. Some issues may be of greater concern and interest to particular communities or regions. Others have an appeal that is more universal and likely to affect the welfare of children everywhere. In either case, the future of children's well-being offers unique opportunities for innovative solutions and teacher commitment.

Continue this journey. Keep learning about new developments as they unfold, explore topics that peak your curiosity, and become an advocate for children's health, safety, and nutrition. Accept the challenge . . . look ahead and make a difference!

APPENDICES

APPENDIX A
Nutrient Information: Fast-Food Vendor Websites

Arby's	http://www.arbys.com
A&W	http://www.awrestaurants.com
Back Yard Burgers	http://www.backyardburgers.com
Baja Fresh	http://www.bajafresh.com
Blimpie	http://www.blimpie.com
Burger King	http://www.burgerking.com
Carl's Jr.	http://www.carlsjr.com
Chick-fil-A	http://www.chick-fil-a.com
Chipotle Mexican Grill	http://www.chipotle.com
Church's Fried Chicken	http://www.churchs.com
Dairy Queen	http://www.dairyqueen.com
Domino's Pizza	http://www.dominos.com
El Pollo Loco	http://www.elpolloloco.com
Einstein Bros. Bagels	http://www.einsteinbros.com
Hardee's	http://www.hardees.com
In-and-Out Burger	http://www.in-n-out.com
KFC	http://www.kfc.com
Krystal	http://www.krystal.com
Little Caesars	http://www.littlecaesars.com
Long John Silvers	http://www.ljsilvers.com
McDonald's	http://www.mcdonalds.com
Pizza Hut	http://www.pizzahut.com
Quiznos Sub	http://www.quiznos.com
Sonic Drive-in	http://www.sonicdrivein.com
Steak 'n Shake	http://www.steaknshake.com
Subway	http://www.subway.com
Taco Bell	http://www.tacobell.com
Wendy's	http://www.wendys.com
White Castle	http://www.whitecastle.com

*For more information on food and nutrition, visit the Food and Nutrition Information Center at http://www.nal.usda.gov/fnic.

APPENDIX B
Growth and BMI Charts for Boys and Girls

Instructions for Using Charts:

1. Locate the child's age along the bottom of the chart.
2. Locate the child's height/weight along the right-hand side of the chart.
3. Place an X at the point where the two lines cross. This point represents a percentile (child's height/weight ranked in comparison to other children of the same age). For example: A five-year-old male who is 43.3 inches tall is ranked at the fiftieth percentile. This means that approximately 50 percent of five-year-old males are taller; 50 percent are shorter.
4. Body mass index is a relatively accurate measure of body fat and risk of obesity. To calculate BMI, use the following formula:

weight (pounds) ÷ height (inches) ÷ height (inches) × 703.

Plot the result on the graphs that follow.

Source: Developed by the National Center for Health Statistics in collaboration with the National Center for Chronic Disease Prevention and Health Promotion (2000).

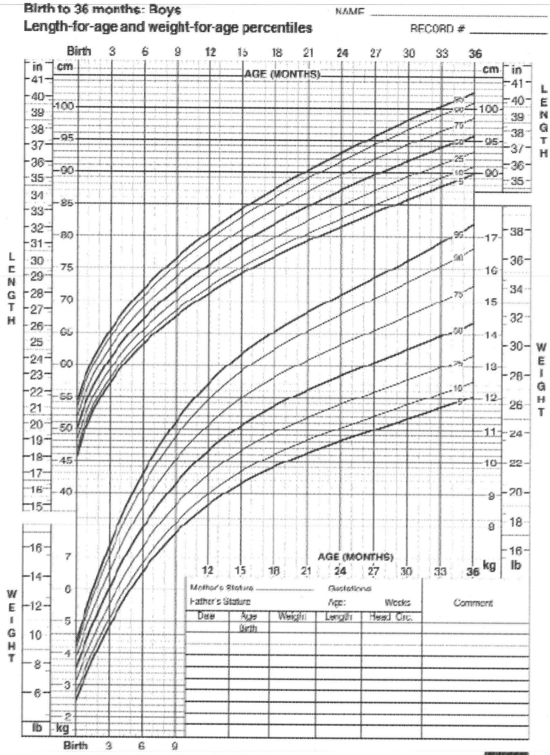

Birth to 36 months: Boys
Length-for-age and weight-for-age percentiles

NAME _____

RECORD # _____

2 to 20 years: Boys
Stature-for-age and weight-for-age percentiles

NAME

RECORD #

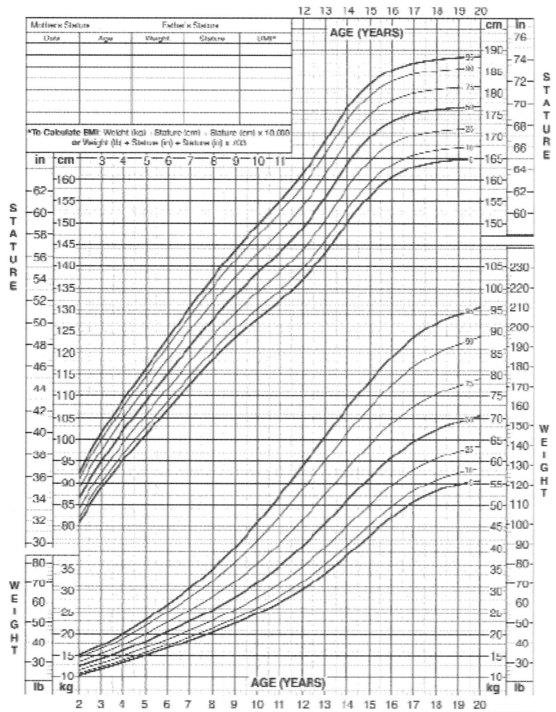

Published May 30, 2000 (modified 11/21/00).
SOURCE: Developed by the National Center for Health Statistics in collaboration with
the National Center for Chronic Disease Prevention and Health Promotion (2000).
http://www.cdc.gov/growthcharts

2 to 20 years: Boys
Body mass index-for-age percentiles

NAME _____

RECORD # _____

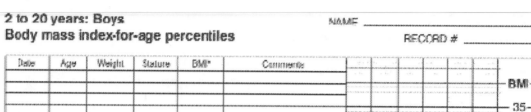

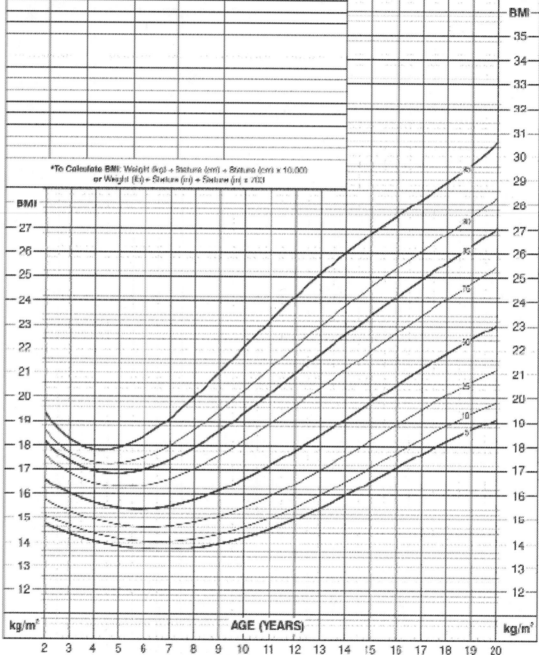

SOURCE: Developed by the National Center for Health Statistics in collaboration with
the National Center for Chronic Disease Prevention and Health Promotion (2000).
http://www.cdc.gov/growthcharts

Birth to 36 months: Girls
Length-for-age and weight-for-age percentiles

NAME

RECORD #

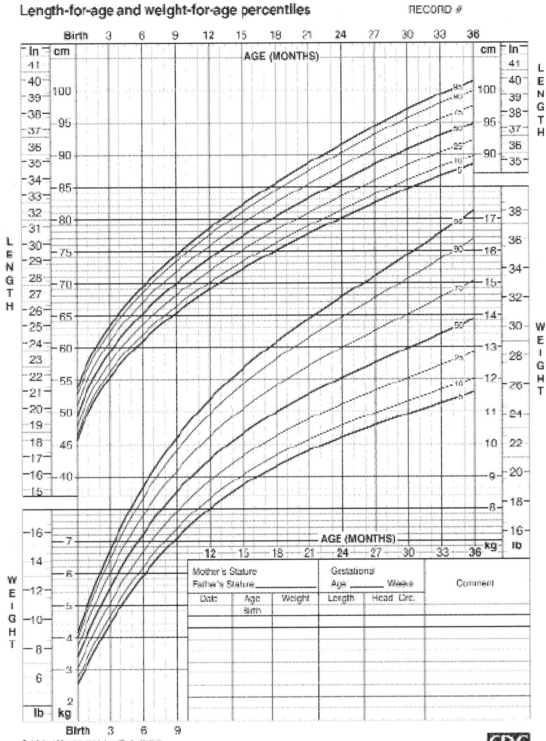

Published May 30, 2000 (modified 4/20/01).
SOURCE: Developed by the National Center for Health Statistics in collaboration with
the National Center for Chronic Disease Prevention and Health Promotion (2000).
http://www.cdc.gov/growthcharts

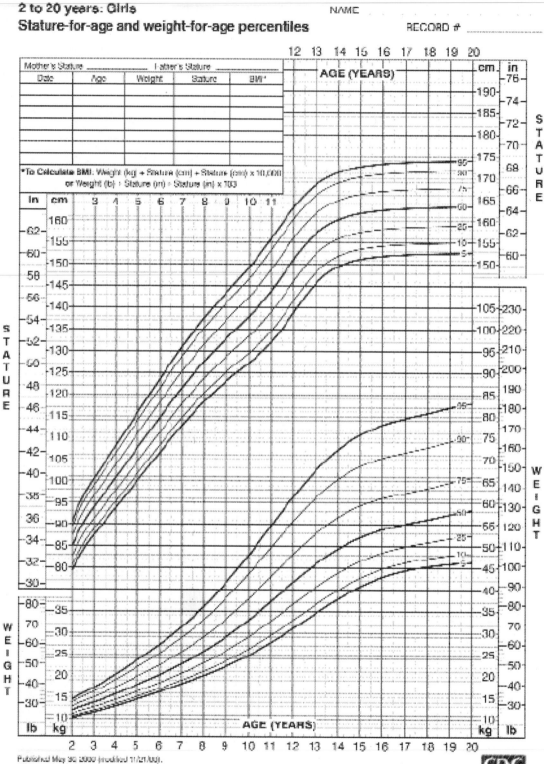

2 to 20 years: Girls
Stature-for-age and weight-for-age percentiles

NAME

RECORD #

Published May 30 2000 (modified 11/21/00).
SOURCE: Developed by the National Center for Health Statistics in collaboration with
the National Center for Chronic Disease Prevention and Health Promotion (2000)
http://www.cdc.gov/growthcharts

2 to 20 years: Girls
Body mass index-for-age percentiles

NAME _____

RECORD # _____

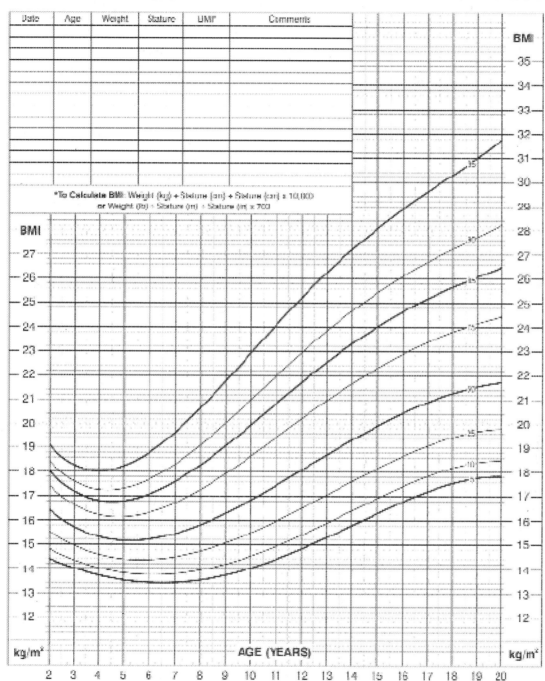

Published May 30, 2000 (modified 10/16/00).
SOURCE: Developed by the National Center for Health Statistics in collaboration with
the National Center for Chronic Disease Prevention and Health Promotion (2000).
http://www.cdc.gov/growthcharts

APPENDIX C
National Health Education Standards for Students (Grades K-4)

The standards listed below are an excerpt from the document, *National Health Education Standards: Achieving Health Literacy* produced by the Joint Committee on National Health Education Standards. The full document and specific performance indicators for each standard can be accessed online at: http://www.aahperd.org/aahe/pdf_files/standards.pdf.

Health Education Standard 1: Students will comprehend concepts related to health promotion and disease prevention.

Health Education Standard 2: Students will demonstrate the ability to access valid health information and health-promoting products and services.

Health Education Standard 3: Students will demonstrate the ability to practice health-enhancing behaviors and reduce health risks.

Health Education Standard 4: Students will analyze the influence of culture, media, technology, and other factors on health.

Health Education Standard 5: Students will demonstrate the ability to use interpersonal communication skills to enhance health.

Health Education Standard 6: Students will demonstrate the ability to use goal setting and decision-making skills to enhance health.

Health Education Standard 7: Students will demonstrate the ability to advocate for personal, family, and community health.

APPENDIX D
Federal Food Programs

Federal food programs are funded and regulated by the U.S. Department of Agriculture and administered at the state level by the U.S. Department of Education or the Public Health Department. Information about food programs available in a given locality may be obtained from city or county health departments, state public health departments, or the state departments of education.

CHILD NUTRITION PROGRAMS

Child nutrition programs provide cash and/or food assistance for children in public schools, nonprofit private schools, early education centers, home-based child care programs, and summer day camps.

National School Lunch Program (NSLP)

The National School Lunch Program (NSLP) is the oldest and largest federal child feeding program in existence, both in terms of number of children reached and dollars spent. The NSLP is administered at the national level by the U.S. Department of Agriculture (USDA) and at the state level by the U.S. Department of Education. The USDA reimburses the states for nutritionally adequate lunches served according to federal regulations. The amount of money received per meal depends upon whether the student must receive free meals or is able to pay either full or reduced price. The families of those students receiving free or *reduced price meals* must submit statements of income and meet family size and income guidelines to be eligible. These guidelines are adjusted periodically according to national *poverty guidelines*. Statements of family income must be submitted to the local school district at the beginning of each school year.

Meals funded by NSLP include five food components: meat or meat alternatives, such as peanut butter, eggs, or beans, two or more servings of fruits and/or vegetables, bread, and milk. The meals must provide at least one-third of the recommended daily dietary allowances (RDAs) for the age group served.

School Breakfast Program (SBP)

The School Breakfast Program was authorized by the Child Nutrition Act of 1966. This program also makes provision for free or reduced price meals along with full price meals. The same income eligible guidelines are used for the School Breakfast Program as for the School Lunch Program. The School Breakfast Program is available to schools and public or licensed nonprofit residential child care facilities.

Child and Adult Care Food Program (CACFP)

The Child and Adult Care Food Program provides money for food and commodities for meals served to children in licensed early childhood centers, home-based child care programs, and adults in adult care programs. The program benefits children 12 years old and under, disabled persons in an institution serving a majority of persons 18 years old and under, migrant children 15 years old and younger, and adults with disabilities. Infant meal patterns are different, and include infant formula, milk, and other foods. The CACFP program is administered by the U.S. Department of Agriculture's Food and Nutrition Service (FNS). In most states it is administered by the Department of Education.

Reimbursement is for two meals and one snack or one meal and two snacks. Reimbursements are determined by income eligibility. The meal pattern is the same as that required in the National School Lunch Program, adjusted by age in categories of infants 1–2 years of age, children 3–5 years and 6–12 years of age, and adults.

Family Nutrition Programs

Two governmental programs that help provide the family with adequate food are the Special Supplemental Program for Women, Infants and Children, better known as WIC, and the Food Stamp Program.

Special Supplemental Nutrition Program for Women, Infants, and Children (WIC)

The WIC program may be operated by either public or nonprofit health agencies. It provides nutrition counseling and supplemental foods rich in protein, iron, and vitamin C to pregnant or lactating women, infants, and children up to five years of age who are determined to be at risk by professional health assessment. Participants receive specified amounts of the following foods:

- iron-fortified infant formula
- iron-fortified cereal
- fruit/vegetable juices high in vitamin C
- fortified milk
- cheese
- eggs
- peanut butter
- dried beans and legumes

The Food Stamp Program

The Food Stamp Program may be administered by either state or local welfare agencies. It is the major form of food assistance in the United States. Its purpose is to increase the food purchasing power of low-income persons. Those who meet eligibility standards may buy stamps that are worth more than the purchase price. The very poor receive stamps free. Stamps may be used to buy *allowed foods* or seeds from which to grow foods. Items not allowed include soap, cigarettes, paper goods, alcoholic beverages, pet foods, or deli foods that may be eaten on the premises.

APPENDIX E
Monthly Calendar: Health, Safety & Nutrition Observances

Teachers may find the following list helpful for developing educational lessons and activities that focus on national observances of children's health, safety and nutrition concerns. Additional resources and information can be accessed on many websites, including those that follow.

January

Healthy weight week	National Heart Lung & Blood Institute: *We Can* campaign http://wecan.nhlbi.nih.gov
Poverty awareness month	Children's Defense Fund http://www.childrensdefense.org

February

American Heart month	American Heart Association http://www.americanheart.org
Burn awareness week	Burn Prevention Foundation http://www.burnprevention.org
Children's dental health month	American Dental Association http://www.ada.org
Child passenger safety week	National Highway Traffic Safety Administration http://www.nhtsa.dot.gov
Girls and women in sports day	National Association for Girls and Women in Sports http://www.aahperd.org
	National Council of Youth Sports http://www.ncys.org

March

Brain injury awareness month	Brain Injury Association of America http://www.biausa.org
Diabetes awareness	American Diabetes Association http://www.diabetes.org
Inhalants and poisons awareness	National Inhalant Prevention Coalition http://www.inhalants.org
Nutrition month	American Dietetic Association http://www.eatright.org
Poison prevention month	Poison Prevention Week Council http://www.poisonprevention.org
Save your vision month	American Optometric Association http://www.aoa.org
School breakfast week	School Nutrition Association http://www.schoolnutrition.org

April

Autism awareness month	Autism Society of America http://www.autism-society.org
Child abuse prevention month	Children's Bureau Administration for Children and Families http://www.childwelfare.gov
National playground safety week	National Program for Playground Safety http://www.uni.edu
National SAFE KIDS week	Safe Kids Worldwide http://www.safekids.org
Sports eye safety month	American Academy of Ophthalmology http://www.aao.org
Youth sports safety month	National Youth Sports Safety Foundation http://www.nyssf.org

May

Allergy and asthma awareness month	Asthma and Allergy Foundation of America http://www.aafa.org http://www.foodallergy.org
Better hearing and speech month	American Speech-Language-Hearing Association (ASHA) http://www.asha.org
Better sleep month	Better Sleep Council http://www.bettersleep.org
Bike safety month	League of American Bicyclists http://www.bikeleague.org
	Pedestrian and Bicycle Information Center http://www.bicyclinginfo.org
	Safe Kids U.S.A. http://www.usa.safekids.org
Buckle up America week	National Highway Traffic Safety Administration http://www.nhtsa.dot.gov
Clean air month	American Lung Association http://www.lungusa.org
Healthy vision month	American Optometric Association http://www.aoa.org
Lyme Disease awareness month	Lyme Disease Foundation http://www.lyme.org
Mental health month	National Mental Health Association http://www.nmha.org
Melanoma/skin cancer detection and prevention month	American Academy of Dermatology http://www.aad.org
Physical fitness and sports month	President's Council on Physical and Sports Fitness http://www.fitness.gov

June

Fireworks eye safety month

Prevent Blindness America
http://www.preventblindness.org

Home safety month

Home Safety Council
http://www.homesafetycouncil.org

National safety month

National Safety Council
http://www.nsc.org

Sun safety week

Sun Safety Alliance
http://www.sunsafetyalliance.org

July

UV (ultra violet) eye safety month

American Academy of Ophthalmology
http://www.aao.org

August

Children's eye health and safety month

Prevent Blindness America
http://www.preventblindness.org

Immunization awareness month

National Immunization Program
Centers for Disease Control and
Prevention
http://www.cdc.gov

September

America on the move

America On the Move Foundation
http://www.americaonthemove.org

Baby safety month.

U.S. Consumer Product Safety
Commission
http://www.cpsc.gov

Family health and fitness

Shape Up America
http://www.shapeup.org

Fruit and vegetable month

Fruit and Vegetable Program Office
Centers for Disease Control and
Prevention/Produce for Better Health
Foundation
http://www.5ADay.gov

Head lice prevention month

National Pediculosis Association
http://www.headlice.org

National Preparedness month

National Safety Council
http://www.nsc.org

Sickle cell awareness month

Sickle Cell Disease Association
of America, Inc.
http://www.sicklecelldisease.org

October

Dental hygiene month

American Dental Hygienists' Association
http://www.adha.org

Eye injury prevention month

American Academy of Ophthalmology
http://www.aao.org

Fire prevention week	National Fire Protection Association http://www.firepreventionweek.org
Halloween safety month	Prevent Blindness America http://www.preventblindness.org
Health education week	National Center for Health Education Society for Public Health Education http://www.nche.org
Health literacy month	National Institutes of Health (NIH) http://www.nih.gov
School bus safety week	New York State Department of Motor Vehicles http://www.nysgtsc.state.ny.us
SIDS awareness month	First Candle/SIDS Alliance http://www.firstcandle.org

November

American diabetes awareness month	American Diabetes Association http://www.diabetes.org
Epilepsy awareness month	Epilepsy Foundation http://www.epilepsyfoundation.org
National adoption awareness month	National Council for Adoption Infant Adoption Awareness Program www.adoptioncouncil.org
National healthy skin month	American Academy of Dermatology http://www.aad.org

December

National handwashing awareness week	Henry the Hand Foundation http://www.henrythehand.com
National safe toys and celebrations month	Consumer Product Safety Commission http://www.cpsc.gov
Safe toys and gifts month	Kids Health http://www.kidshealth.org

APPENDIX F
One-Week Sample Menu

	Breakfast	Lunch	Snack (Supplement)
Monday	muffin 100% fruit juice milk	spaghetti with meat sauce green beans diced peaches milk	applesauce graham crackers water
Tuesday	dry cereal banana milk	baked chicken mashed potatoes green peas whole grain bread milk	saltines cheese slices water
Wednesday	waffle sticks syrup 100% fruit juice milk	hamburger patty baked sweet potato broccoli whole grain bread milk	mixed raw vegetables & dip pita bread wedges water
Thursday	cinnamon toast 100% fruit juice milk	turkey tetrazzini carrots diced pears milk	yogurt blueberries water
Friday	pancakes strawberries milk	vegetable soup PB/J sandwich sliced plums milk	cheese cubes whole wheat tortilla water

APPENDIX G
Children's Book List

Dental Health

Civardi, A. (1992). *Going to the Dentist.* Usborne, London: E. D. C. Publications.
Dowdy, L. (1997). *Barney Goes to the Dentist.* New York: Lyrick.
Frost, H. (1999). *Going to the Dentist.* Mankato, MN: Pebble Books.
Keller, L. (2000). *Open Wide: Tooth School Inside.* New York: Henry Holt & Company.
Lewison, W. (2002). *Clifford's Loose Tooth.* New York: Scholastic.
Mayer, M. (2001). *Just Going to the Dentist.* New York: Golden Books.
McGuire, L. (1993). *Brush Your Teeth Please.* New York: Reader's Digest.
Minarik, E. (2002). *Little Bear's Loose Tooth.* New York: HarperFestival.
Munsch, R. (2002). *Andrew's Loose Tooth.* New York: Scholastic.
Murkoff, H. (2002). *What to Expect When You Go to the Dentist.* New York: HarperFestival.
Rogers, R. (1989). *Going to the Dentist.* New York: G. P. Putman & Sons.
Schoberle, C. (2000). *Open Wide! A Visit to the Dentist.* New York: Simon Spotlight.
Showers, P. (1991). *How Many Teeth?* New York: HarperCollins.
Smee, N. (2000). *Freddie Visits the Dentist.* Hauppauge, NY: Barrons Educational Series.

Illness/Germs

Berger, M. (1995). *Germs Make Me Sick!* New York: HarperCollins.
Berger, M. (2002). *Why I Sneeze, Shiver, Hiccup, & Yawn.* New York: HarperCollins.
Capeci, A. (2001). *The Giant Germ.* New York: Scholastic Paperbacks.
Cole, J. (1995). *The Magic School Bus Inside Ralphie: A Book About Germs.* New York: Scholastic.
Cote, P. (2002). *How Do I Feel?* New York: Houghton Mifflin. (Spanish & English).
Dealey, E. (2002). *Goldie Locks Has Chicken Pox.* New York: Scholastic.
Demuth, P. (1997). *Achoo!: All About Colds.* New York: Grosset & Dunlap.
Katz, B. (1996). *Germs! Germs! Germs!* New York: Cartwheel Books.
O'Brien-Palmer, M. (1999). *Healthy Me: Fun Ways to Develop Good Health and Safety Habits: Activities for Children 5–8.* Chicago, IL: Chicago Review Press.
Rice, J. (1997). *Those Mean, Nasty, Dirty, Downright Disgusting but Invisible Germs.* St. Paul, MN: Redleaf Press.
Romanek, T. (2003). *Achoo: The Most Interesting Book You'll Ever Read About Germs.* Kids Toronto, CA: Can Press.
Ross, T. (2000). *Wash Your Hands!* New York: Kane/Miller.
Showers, P. (1991). *Your Skin and Mine.* New York: HarperCollins.
Wenkman, L. (1999). *Body Buddies Say . . . "Wash Your Hands!"* Bloomington, IN: Sunrise Publications.

Mental Health (feelings)

Agassi, M. (2000). *Hands Are Not for Hitting.* Minneapolis, MN: Free Spirit Publishing.
Anglund, J. (1993). *A Friend Is Someone Who Likes You.* New York: Harcourt Brace Jovanovich.
Anholt, C. (1998). *What I Like.* Cambridge, MA: Candlewick Press.
Anholt, C. (1998). *What Makes Me Happy?* Cambridge, MA: Candlewick Press.
Baker, L. (2001). *I Love You Because You're You.* New York: Cartwheel Books.
Bang, M. (1999). *When Sophie Gets Angry—Really, Really Angry.* New York: Scholastic.
Blumenthal, D. (1999). *The Chocolate-Covered-Cookie Tantrum.* New York: Clarion Books.
Cain, J. (2000). *The Way I Feel.* Seattle, WA: Parenting Press.

Carle, E. (1999). *The Very Lonely Firefly*. New York: Philomel Books.

Carle, E. (2000). *The Grouchy Ladybug*. New York: Scholastic.

Carlson, N. (1990). *I Like Me!* Parsippany, NJ: Pearson Learning.

Carlson, N. (1997). *How to Lose All Your Friends*. New York: Puffin Books.

Cole, J. (1997). *I'm a Big Brother*. New York: William Morrow & Co.

Cole, J. (1997). *I'm a Big Sister*. New York: William Morrow & Co.

Crary, E. (1992). *I'm Mad*. Seattle, WA: Parenting Press.

Crary, E. (1996). *I'm Scared*. Seattle, WA: Parenting Press.

Cruz, R. (1992). *Alexander and the Terrible, Horrible, No Good, Very Bad Day*. New York: Aladdin.

Cutis, J. L. (1998). *Today I Feel Silly: And Other Moods That Make My Day*. New York: HarperCollins.

Cutis, J. L. (2002). *I'm Gonna Like Me: Letting Off a Little Self-Esteem*. New York: Joanna Cotler.

Demi. (1996). *The Empty Pot*. New York: Henry Holt & Co.

Eisenberg, P. (1992). *You're My Nikki*. New York: Dial Books for Children.

Gainer, C. (1998). *I'm Like You, You're Like Me: A Child's Book About Understanding and Celebrating Each Other*. Minneapolis, MN: Free Spirit Publishing.

Hammerseng, K. (1996). *Telling Isn't Tattling*. Seattle, WA: Parenting Press.

Henkes, K. (1996). *Chrysanthemum*. New York: HarperTrophy.

Hudson, C., & Ford, B. (1990). *Bright Eyes, Brown Skin*. Just Us Books.

Krasny, L., & Brown, M. (2001). *How to Be a Friend: A Guide to Making Friends and Keeping Them*. Boston, MA: Little Brown & Co.

Kubler, A., & Formby, C. (1995). *Come Play with Us*. Ashworth Road, Bridgemead, Swindon, Wiltshire, SN5 7YD: Child's Play International, Ltd.

Lachner, D. (1995). *Andrew's Angry Words*. New York: North South Books.

Lalli, J. (1997). *I Like Being Me: Poems for Children, About Feeling Special, Appreciating Others, and Getting Along*. Minneapolis, MN: Free Spirit Publishing.

Lewis, J. (1993). *Claire and Friends*. Brookline, MA: Creative License Press.

Lewis, P. (2002). *I'll Always Love You*. Wilton, CT: Tiger Tales.

Lovell, P. (2001). *Stand Tall, Molly Lou Melon*. New York: Scholastic.

Naylor, P. (1994). *King of the Playground*. New York: Aladdin.

O'Neill, A. (2002). *The Recess Queen*. New York: Scholastic.

Parr, T. (2001). *It's Okay to be Different*. Boston, MA: Little, Brown.

Payne, L. (1994). *Just Because I Am: A Child's Book of Affirmation*. Minneapolis, MN: Free Spirit Publishing.

Payne, L. (1997). *We Can Get Along: A Child's Book of Choices*. Minneapolis, MN: Free Spirit Publishing.

Pinkney, A., & Pinkney, B. (1997). *Pretty Brown Face*. Lake Worth, FL: Red Wagon Books.

Spelman, C. (2000). *When I Feel Angry*. New York: Albert Whitman & Co.

Thomas, P. (2000). *Stop Picking on Me*. Hauppauge, NY: Barrons.

Vail, R. (2002). *Sometimes I'm Bombaloo*. New York: Scholastic.

Viorst, J. (1992). *The Good-bye Book*. New York: Aladdin.

Weninger, B., & Marks, A. (1995). *Good-bye Daddy*. New York: North-South Books.

Personal Health & Self-Care

Aliki. (1991). *My Five Senses*. New York: HarperCollins.

Aliki. (1992). *I'm Growing*. New York: HarperCollins.

Brown, M. (1991). *Good Night Moon*. New York: HarperFestival.

Cazet, D. (1992). *I'm Not Sleepy*. New York: Orchard Books.

Edwards, F. (1990). *Mortimer Mooner Stopped Taking a Bath*. Kingston, Ontario: Pokeweed Press.

Fox, M. (1997). *Time for Bed*. Lake Worth, FL: Red Wagon Books.

Gordon, J. R. (1991). *Six Sleepy Sheep*. New York: St. Martin's Press.

Himmelman, J. (1995). *Lights Out!* Mahwah, NJ: Troll.

Katz, A. (2001). *Take Me Out of the Bathtub*. New York: Scholastic.

Keats, E. J. (1992). *Dreams*. New York: Aladdin Books.

Leonard, M. (1998). *Getting Dressed*. New York: Bantam Books.

Murkoff, H. (2000). *What to Expect at Bedtime*. New York: HarperFestival.

Murkoff, H. (2000). *What to Expect When You Go to the Doctor*. New York: HarperFestival.

Pfeffer, W. (1999). *Sounds All Around*. New York: HarperCollins.

Reidy, H. (1999). *What Do You Like to Wear?* New York: Larousse Kingfisher Chambers.

Rowland, P. (1996). *What Should I Wear?* New York: Random House.

Showers, P. (1990). *Ears Are for Hearing*. New York: Ty Crowell Co.

Showers, P. (1993). *The Listening Walk*. New York: HarperTrophy.

Showers, P. (1997). *Sleep Is for Everyone*. New York: HarperCollins.

Sykes, J. (1996). *I Don't Want to Go to Bed*. Wilton, CT: Tiger Tales.

Time-Life. (1993). *What Is a Bellybutton?* Alexandria, VA: Time-Life Books.

Watanabe, S. (1992). *How Do I Put It On?* New York: Philomel.

Wood, A. (1996). *The Napping House*. San Diego, CA: Harcourt Brace & Co.

Safety

Berenstain, S., & Berenstain, J. (1999). *My Trusty Car Seat: Buckling Up for Safety*. New York: Random House.

Best, C. (1995). *Red Light, Green Light, Mama and Me*. New York: Orchard Books.

Boxall, E. (2002). *Francis the Scaredy Cat*. Cambridge, MA: Candlewick Press.

Committee, C. B. (2000). *Buckles Buckles Everywhere*. Columbia, SC: Palmetto Bookworks.

Cuyler, M. (2001). *Stop, Drop, Roll*. New York: Simon & Schuster.

Dubowski, C. (1990). *Fire Engine to the Rescue*. New York: McClanahan Book Company.

Girard, L. (1987). *My Body Is Private*. Morton Grove, IL: Albert Whitman & Co.

Hayward, L. (2001). *A Day in the Life of a Firefighter*. New York: Dorling Kindersley Publisher.

Hindman, J. (1986). *A Very Touching Book . . . for Little People and Big People*. Alexandria, VA: Alexandria Press.

Johnsen, K. (1986). *Trouble with Secrets*. Seattle, WA: Parenting Press.

MacLean, C. K. (2002). *Even Firefighters Hug Their Moms*. New York: Dutton.

Mitton, T. (2001). *Down by the Cool of the Pool*. New York: Orchard Books.

Palatini, M. (2002). *Earthquack!* New York: Simon & Schuster.

Prigger, M. (2002). *Aunt Minnie and the Twister*. New York: Clarion.

Rathmann, P. (1995). *Officer Buckle and Gloria*. New York: Putnam.

Reasoner, C. (2003). *Bee Safe (The Bee Attitudes)*. Los Angeles, CA: Price Stern Sloan Publishers.

Rylan, C. (1991). *Night in the Country*. New York: Aladdin.

Schwartz, L. (1995). *The Safety Book for Active Kids: Teaching Your Child How to Avoid Everyday Dangers*. Santa Barbara, CA: Learning Works.

Tekavec, H. (2002). *Storm Is Coming!* New York: Dial.

Weeks, S. (2002). *My Somebody Special*. San Diego, CA: Harcourt, Inc.

Weidner, T. (1997). *Your Body Belongs to You*. Morton Grove, IL: Albert Whitman & Co.

Special Needs

Aseltine, L., Mueller, E., & Tait, N. (1987). *I'm Deaf and It's Okay*. Morton Grove, IL: Albert Whitman & Co.

Bunnett, R. (1996). *Friends at School*. Long Island City, NY: Star Bright Books.

Fassler, J. (1987). *Howie Helps Himself.* Morton Grove, IL: Albert Whitman & Co.

Gosselin, K. (1996). *Zooallergy: A Fun Story About Allergy and Asthma Triggers.* Valley Park, MO: JayJo Books.

Gosselin, K. (1998). *Taking Diabetes to School.* Valley Park, MO: JayJo Books.

Harrison, T. (1998). *Aaron's Awful Allergies.* Buffalo, NY: Kids Can Press.

Lakin, P. (1994). *Dad and Me in the Morning.* Morton Grove, IL: Albert Whitman & Co.

London, J. (1997). *The Lion Who Had Asthma.* Morton Grove, IL: Albert Whitman & Co.

Maguire, A. (2000). *Special People, Special Ways.* Arlington, TX: Future Horizons.

Mayer, G., & Mayer, M. (1993). *A Very Special Critter.* New York: Golden Books.

Millman, I. (2000). *Moses Goes to School.* New York: Frances Foster Books/Farrar, Straus & Giroux.

Nausau, E. (2001). *The Peanut Butter Jam.* Albuquerque, NM: Health Press.

Powers, M. (1987). *Our Teacher's in a Wheelchair.* Morton Grove, IL: Albert Whitman & Co.

Shriver, M. (2001). *What's Wrong with Timmy?* New York: Little Brown & Co.

Smith, N. (1999). *Allie the Allergic Elephant: A Children's Story of Peanut Allergies.* Jungle Communications, Inc.

Stuve-Bodeen, S. (1998). *We'll Paint the Octopus Red.* Woodbine House.

Weiner, E. (1999). *Taking Food Allergies to School.* Valley Park, MO: JayJo Books.

White Pirner, C. (1994). *Even Little Kids Get Diabetes.* Morton Grove, IL: Albert Whitman & Co.

Nutrition

Appleton, J. (2001). *Do Carrots Make You See Better?* St. Paul, MN: Red Leaf Press.

Barkan, J. & Wheeler, J. (1989). *My Measuring Cup.* New York: Warner Juvenile Books.

Berenstain, S., & Berenstain, J. (1995). *The Berenstain Bears and Too Much Junk Food.* New York: Random House.

Carle, E. (1986). *The Very Hungry Caterpillar.* New York: Putnam.

Carle, E. (1998). *Pancakes, Pancakes!* New York: Aladdin Books.

Cole, J. (1990). *The Magic School Bus: Inside the Human Body.* New York: Scholastic.

Compestine, Y. (2001). *The Runaway Rice Cake.* New York: Simon & Schuster.

French, V. (1998). *Oliver's Fruit Salad.* New York: Orchard Books.

Geeslin, C. (1999). *How Nanita Learned to Make Flan.* New York: Atheneum.

Gershator, D. (1998). *Bread Is for Eating.* New York: Henry Holt.

Hall, Z. (1996). *The Apple Pie Tree.* New York: Scholastic.

Harms, T. (1981). *Cook and Learn: Nutritious Foods from Various Cultures.* St. Paul, MN: Red Leaf Press.

Katzen, M. (1994). *Pretend Soup and Other Real Recipes: A Cookbook for Preschoolers and Up.* Berkeley, CA: Tricycle Press.

Krauss, R. (1989). *The Carrot Seed.* New York: HarperTrophy.

Lin, G. (1999). *The Ugly Vegetables.* Watertown, MA: Charlesbridge Publishing.

Lin, G. (2001). *Dim Sum for Everyone.* New York: Knopf.

Loreen, L. (1996). *The Edible Pyramid: Good Eating Every Day.* New York: Holiday House.

Mayer, M. (1998). *The Mother Goose Cookbook: Rhymes and Recipes for the Very Young.* New York: William Morrow & Co.

McGinley, N. (1999). *Pigs in the Pantry: Fun with Math and Cooking.* New York: Simon & Schuster.

Paulsen, G. (1998). *The Tortilla Factory.* San Diego, CA: Harcourt Brace.

Peterson, C. (1996). *Harvest Year.* Homedale, PA: Boyd Mill Press.

Priceman, M. (1996). *How to Make an Apple Pie and See the World.* New York: Knopf.

Reiser, L. (1998). *Tortillas and Lullabies.* New York: Greenwillow Books.

Rockwell, L. (1999). *Good Enough to Eat: A Kid's Guide to Food and Nutrition.* New York: HarperCollins.

Sanger, A. (2001). *First Book of Sushi*. Berkeley, CA: Tricycle Press.

Sharmat, M. (1989). *Gregory, the Terrible Eater*. New York: Scholastic.

Swain, G. (1999). *Eating*. St. Paul, MN: Red Leaf Press.

Wells, P. (2003). *Busy Bears: Breakfast with the Bears*. London, England: Sterling Publications.

Westcott, N. (1998). *Never Take a Pig Out to Lunch and Other Poems*. New York: Orchard Books.

Woods, D., & Woods, A. (2000). *The Big Hungry Bear*. Swindon, England: Child's Play Publishers.

abdomen – the portion of the body located between the diaphragm (located at the base of the lungs) and the pelvic or hip bones.

absorption – the process by which the products of digestion are transferred from the intestinal tract into the blood or lymph or by which substances are taken up by the cells.

abuse – to mistreat, attack, or cause harm to another individual.

accident – an unexpected or unplanned event that may result in physical harm or injury.

accreditation – the process of certifying an individual or program as having met certain specified requirements.

acuity – sharpness or clearness, as in vision.

acute – the stage of an illness or disease during which an individual is definitely sick and exhibits symptoms characteristic of the particular illness or disease involved.

adenosine triphosphate (ATP) – a compound with energy-storing phosphate bonds that is the main energy source for all cells.

AIDS (acquired immunodeficiency syndrome or acquired immune deficiency syndrome) – a disease caused by the human immunodeficiency virus (HIV).

airborne transmission – when germs are expelled into the air through coughs/sneezes, and transmitted to another individual via tiny moisture drops.

alignment – the process of assuming correct posture or of placing various body parts in proper line with each other.

alkalis – groups of bases or caustic substances that are capable of neutralizing acids to form salts.

allowed foods – foods that are eligible for reimbursement under School Lunch or Child Care Food Program Guidelines.

amblyopia – a condition of the eye commonly referred to as "lazy eye"; vision gradually becomes blurred or distorted due to unequal balance of the eye muscles. The eyes do not present any physical clues when a child has amblyopia.

amino acids – the organic building blocks from which proteins are made.

anaphylaxis – a severe allergic reaction that may cause difficulty breathing, itching, unconsciousness, and possible death.

anecdotal – a brief note or description that contains useful and important information.

anemia – a disorder of the blood commonly caused by a lack of iron in the diet, resulting in the formation of fewer red blood cells and lessened ability of the cells to carry oxygen. Symptoms include fatigue, shortness of breath, and pallor.

anthropometric – pertains to measurement of the body or its parts.

antibodies – special substances produced by the body that help protect against disease.

apnea – momentary absence of breathing.

appraisal – the process of judging or evaluating; to determine the quality of one's state of health.

aseptic procedure – treatment to produce a product that is free of disease-producing bacteria.

Note: Definitions are based on usage within the text.

aspiration – accidental inhalation of food, fluid, or an object into the respiratory tract.

assessment – appraisal or evaluation.

asymptomatic – having no symptoms.

attitudes – beliefs or feelings one has toward certain facts or situations.

atypical – unusual; different from what might commonly be expected.

audiologist – a specially prepared clinician who uses nonmedical techniques to diagnose hearing impairments.

autonomy – a state of personal or self-identity.

bacteria – one-celled microorganisms; some are beneficial for the body, but pathogenic bacteria cause diseases.

basal metabolic rate – minimum amount of energy needed to carry on the body processes vital to life.

biochemical – pertains to chemical evaluation of body substances such as blood, urine, etc.

bonding – the process of establishing a positive and strong emotional relationship between an infant and his or her parent; sometimes referred to as attachment.

bottle-mouth syndrome – a pattern of tooth decay, predominantly of the upper teeth, that develops as the result of permitting a child to go to sleep with a bottle containing juice, milk, or any other caloric liquid that may pool in the mouth.

calories – units used to measure the energy value of foods.

calcium – mineral nutrient; a major component of bones and teeth.

catalyst – a substance that speeds up the rate of a chemical reaction but is not itself used up in the reaction.

catalyzes – accelerates a chemical reaction.

characteristics – qualities or traits that distinguish one person from another.

cholesterol – a fat-like substance found in animal-source foods that is synthesized by humans and performs a variety of functions within the body.

chronic – frequent or repeated incidences of illness; can also be a lengthy or permanent status, as in chronic disease or dysfunction.

clinical – pertains to evaluation of health by means of observation.

coenzymes – a vitamin-containing substance required by certain enzymes before they can perform their prescribed function.

cognitive – the aspect of learning that refers to the development of skills and abilities based on knowledge and thought processes.

collagen – a protein that forms the major constituent of connective tissue, cartilage, bone, and skin.

communicable – a condition that can be spread or transmitted from one individual to another.

complementary proteins – proteins with offsetting missing amino acids; complementary proteins can be combined to provide complete protein.

complete proteins – proteins that contain all essential amino acids in amounts relative to the amounts needed to support growth.

compliance – the act of obeying or cooperating with specific requests or requirements.

concepts – combinations of basic and related factual information that represent more generalized statements or ideas.

conductive hearing loss – affects the volume of word tones heard, so that loud sounds are more likely to be heard than soft sounds.

contagious – capable of being transmitted or passed from one person to another.

contrasting sensory qualities – differing qualities pertaining to taste, color, texture, temperature, and shape.

convalescent – the stage of recovery from an illness or disease.

cost control – reduction of expenses through portion control, inventory, and reduction of waste.

criteria – predetermined standards used to evaluate the worth or effectiveness of a learning experience.

critical control point (CCP) – a point or procedure in a specific food system where loss of control may result in an unacceptable health risk.

cryptosporidiosis – an infectious illness caused by an intestinal parasite. May be present in water (e.g., swimming pools, hot tubs, streams) contaminated with feces or from unwashed hands. Often causes severe diarrhea in children.

cycle menus – menus that are written to repeat after a set interval, such as every three to four weeks.

Daily Value (DV) – a term the FDA has proposed to replace the USDA RDA values in the new nutrition food labels.

deciduous teeth – a child's initial set of teeth; this set is temporary and gradually begins to fall out at about five years of age.

dehydration – a state in which there is an excessive loss of body fluids or extremely limited fluid intake. Symptoms may include loss of skin tone, sunken eyes, and mental confusion.

dental caries – tooth decay.

dermatitis – inflammation or irritation of the skin, such as in rashes and eczema.

development – commonly refers to the process of intellectual growth and change.

developmental norms – the mean or average age at which children demonstrate certain behaviors and abilities.

developmental or physiological readiness – growth (both physical and cognitive) and chemical processes that lead to the ability to perform a function.

developmentally appropriate practice (DAP) – learning experiences and environments that take into account each child's abilities, diverse needs, and individual interests. DAP also reflects differences among families and values them as essential partners in children's education.

diagnosis – the process of identifying a disease, illness, or injury from its symptoms.

Dietary Guidelines for Americans – a report that gives recommendations for daily food choices, to be balanced with physical activity, and to assure good health and reduce certain disease risks.

dietary nucleotides – amino acid combinations found to increase an infant's ability to produce antibodies in response to exposure to disease.

Dietary Reference Intake (DRI) – a plan that presents the recommended goals of nutrient intakes for various age and gender groups.

digestion – the process by which complex nutrients in foods are changed into smaller units that can be absorbed and used by the body.

digestive tract – pertains to and includes the mouth, throat, esophagus, stomach, and intestines.

direct contact – the passage of infectious organisms from an infected individual directly to a susceptible host through methods such as coughing, sneezing, or touching.

discipline – training or enforced obedience that corrects, shapes, or develops acceptable patterns of behavior.

disinfected – killed pathogenic organisms.

disorientation – lack of awareness or ability to recognize familiar persons or objects.

distention – stretched or enlarged.

DNA (deoxyribonucleic acid) – the substance in the cell nucleus that codes for genetically transmitted traits.

Down syndrome – a genetic disorder that is characterized by unique facial features, mental retardation, and motor delays.

elevate – to raise to a higher position.

electrolytes – substances which, when in solution, become capable of conducting electricity; examples include sodium and potassium.

emotional abuse – repeated humiliation, ridicule, or threats directed toward another individual.

endocrine – refers to glands within the body that produce and secrete substances called hormones directly into the blood stream.

energy – power to perform work.

enriched – adding nutrients to grain products to replace those lost during refinement; thiamin, niacin, riboflavin, and iron are nutrients most commonly added.

environment – the sum total of physical, cultural, and behavioral features that surround and affect an individual.

enzymes – proteins that catalyze body functions.

epithelial tissue – specialized cells that form the skin and mucus linings of all body cavities, such as the lungs, nose, and throat.

essential amino acids – amino acids that can only be obtained from protein food sources.

essential nutrient – a nutrient that must be provided in food because it cannot be synthesized by the body at a rate sufficient to meet the body's needs.

ethnic – pertaining to races or groups of people who share common traits or customs.

evaluation – a measurement of effectiveness for determining whether or not educational objectives have been achieved.

expectations – behaviors or actions that are anticipated.

failure to thrive – a term used to describe an infant whose growth and mental development are severely slowed due to lack of nurturing or mental stimulation.

family nutrition programs – nutrition programs that focus on the family unit. Examples are Food Stamps, WIC, and the Food Distribution Program.

fecal-oral transmission – when germs are transferred to the mouth via hands contaminated with fecal material.

fever – an elevation of body temperature above normal; a temperature over 99.4°F or 37.4°C orally is usually considered a fever.

First-In-First-Out (FIFO) – a method of storage in which the items stored for the longest time will be retrieved first.

food-borne illness – a food infection due to ingestion of food contaminated with bacteria, viruses, some molds, or parasites.

food-borne illness outbreak – when two or more people become ill after ingesting the same food. Laboratory analysis must confirm that food is the source of the illness.

food infections – illnesses resulting from ingestion of live bacteria in food.

food insecurity – uncertain or limited access to a reliable source of food.

food intoxications – illnesses resulting from ingestion of food containing residual bacterial toxins in the absence of viable bacteria.

food pyramid – a guide to daily food choices developed by the USDA.

fortified food – food with vitamins and/or minerals added that were not found in the food originally, or that are added in amounts greater than occur naturally in the food.

fruit drinks – a product that contains 10 percent fruit juice, added water, and sugar.

full-strength juice – undiluted fruit or vegetable juice.

giardiasis – a parasitic infection of the intestinal tract that causes diarrhea, loss of appetite, abdominal bloating and gas, weight loss, and fatigue.

gram – a metric unit of weight; approximately 1/28 of an ounce.

growth – increase in size of any body part or of the entire body.

habits – unconscious repetitions of particular behaviors.

hands-on – active involvement in a project; actually doing something.

harvesting – picking or gathering fruit or grains.

Hazard Analysis Critical Control Point (HACCP) – a food safety and self-inspection system that highlights potentially hazardous foods and how they are handled in the food service department.

head circumference – the distance around the head obtained by measuring over the forehead and bony protuberance on the back of the head; it is an indication of normal or abnormal growth and development of the brain and central nervous system.

health – a state of wellness. Complete physical, mental, social, and emotional well-being; the quality of one element affects the state of the others.

health assessment – the process of gathering and evaluating information about an individual's state of health.

health promotion – engaging in behaviors that help maintain and enhance one's health status; includes concern for certain social issues affecting the diet and environment.

heat exhaustion – above normal body temperature caused by exposure to too much sun.

heat stroke – failure of the body's sweating reflex during exposure to high temperatures; causes body temperature to rise.

hemoglobin – the iron-containing, oxygen-carrying pigment in red blood cells.

hepatitis – an inflammation of the liver.

heredity – the transmission of certain genetic material and characteristics from parents to child at the time of conception.

high-density lipoproteins (HDL) – a protein-fat combination with a high protein to fat ratio, which is formed in the blood to aid in fat transport; a high HDL blood value may decrease risk of cardiovascular disease.

high-fructose corn syrup – a frequently used sweetener produced by exposing corn starch to acid and enzyme action to increase the fructose content; it is much sweeter than sucrose.

HIV (human immunodeficiency virus) – the virus that causes AIDS.

hormone – a special chemical substance produced by endocrine glands that influences and regulates certain body functions.

hyperactivity – a condition characterized by attention and behavior disturbances, including restlessness, impulsivity, and disruptive behaviors. True cases of hyperactivity respond to the administration of stimulant-type medication.

hyperglycemia – a condition characterized by an abnormally high level of sugar in the blood.

hyperopia – farsightedness; a condition of the eyes in which an individual can see objects clearly in the distance but has poor close vision.

hypertension – elevation of blood pressure above the normally accepted values.

hyperventilation – rapid breathing often with forced inhalation; can lead to sensations of dizziness, light-headedness, and weakness.

hypothermia – below normal body temperature caused by overexposure to cold conditions.

immunized – a state of becoming resistant to a specific disease through the introduction of living or dead microorganisms into the body, which then stimulate the production of antibodies.

impairment – a condition or malfunction of a body part that interferes with optimal functioning.

incidental learning – learning that occurs in addition to the primary intent or goals of instruction.

incomplete proteins – proteins that lack required amounts of one or more essential amino acids.

incubation – the interval of time between exposure to infection and the appearance of the first signs or symptoms of illness.

indirect contact – transfer of infectious organisms from an infected individual to a susceptible host via an intermediate source such as contaminated water, milk, toys, utensils, or soiled towels.

individuality – qualities that distinguish one person from another.

infection – a condition that results when a pathogen invades and establishes itself within a susceptible host.

ingested – the process of taking food or other substances into the body through the mouth.

innocent – not guilty; lacking knowledge.

inservice – educational training provided by an employer.

intentional – a plan of action that is carried out in a purposeful manner.

intentionally – to do on purpose.

intervention – practices or procedures implemented to modify or change a specific behavior or condition.

intestinal – pertaining to the intestinal tract or bowel.

iron-deficiency anemia – a failure in the oxygen transport system caused by too little iron.

irradiation – food preservation by short-term exposure of the food to gamma ray radiation.

judicious – wise; directed by sound judgment.

lactating – producing and secreting milk.

language – form of communication that allows individuals to share feelings, ideas, and experiences with one another.

latch-key – a term that refers to school-aged children who care for themselves without adult supervision before and after school hours.

lethargy – a state of inaction or indifference.

liability – legal responsibility or obligation for one's actions owed to another individual.

licensing – the act of granting formal permission to conduct a business or profession.

linoleic acid – a polyunsaturated fatty acid, which is essential (must be provided in food) for humans.

linolenic acid – one of the two polyunsaturated fatty acids that are recognized as essential for humans.

lipoprotein – protein linked with fat to aid in the transport of various types of fat in the blood.

listlessness – a state characterized by a lack of energy and/or interest in one's affairs.

low-birthweight (LBW) infant – an infant who weighs less than 5.5 pounds (2500 grams) at birth.

low-density lipoproteins (LDL) – a lipoprotein with a low protein to fat ratio that contains a high level of cholesterol; high blood levels of LDL may signal increased risk for heart disease.

Lyme disease – bacterial illness caused by the bite of infected deer ticks found in grassy or wooded areas.

lymph glands – specialized groupings of tissue that produce and store white blood cells for protection against infection and illness.

macrocytic anemia – a failure in the oxygen transport system characterized by abnormally large immature red blood cells.

malnutrition – prolonged inadequate or excessive intake of nutrients and/or calories required by the body.

mandatory – something that is required; no choices or alternatives available.

megadose – an amount of a vitamin or mineral at least ten times that of the RDA.

meningitis – a disease, often caused by bacteria, that leads to inflammation of the brain and spinal cord.

metabolism – all chemical changes that occur from the time nutrients are absorbed until they are built into body tissue or are excreted.

microcytic anemia – a failure in the oxygen transport system characterized by abnormally small red blood cells.

microgram – a metric unit of measurement; one-millionth of a gram.

milligram – a metric unit of measurement; one-thousandth of a gram.

minerals – inorganic chemical elements that are required in the diet to support growth and repair tissue and to regulate body functions.

misarticulation – improper pronunciation of words and word sounds.

mixed hearing loss – a disorder that involves a combination of conductive and sensorineural hearing losses

mold – a fuzzy growth produced by fungi.

monounsaturated fatty acid (MUFA) – a fatty acid that has only one bond in its structure, and that is not fully saturated with hydrogen.

mottling – marked with spots of dense white or brown coloring.

myopia – nearsightedness; an individual has good near vision but poor distant vision.

neglect – failure of a parent or legal guardian to properly care for and meet the basic needs of a child under eighteen years of age.

negligent – failing to practice or perform one's duties according to certain standards; careless.

neophobic – fear of things that are new and unfamiliar.

neural tube deficit – a birth defect involving damage to the brain and spinal cord.

neurobiological disorder – a condition of the nervous system that may be caused by genetic or biological factors.

neurological – pertaining to the nervous system, which consists of the nerves, brain, and spinal column.

neuromuscular – pertaining to control of muscular function by the nervous system.

nonessential amino acids – amino acids that are produced in the body.

normal – average; a characteristic or quality that is common to most individuals in a defined group.

norms – an expression (e.g., weeks, months, years) of when a child is likely to demonstrate certain developmental skills.

notarized – official acknowledgment of the authenticity of a signature or document by a notary public.

nutrients – components or substances that are found in food.

nutrient intake – consumption of foods containing chemical substances (nutrients) essential to the human body.

nutrient strengths – nutrients that occur in relatively large amounts in a food or food group.

nutrient weaknesses – nutrients that are absent or occur in very small amounts in a food or food group.

nutrition – the study of food and how it is used by the body.

nutrition claims – statements of reduced calories, fat, or salt on the food labels.

nutrition education – activities that impart information about food and its use in the body.

obesity – a condition characterized by an excessive accumulation of fat.

objectives – clear and meaningful descriptions of what an individual is expected to learn as a result of learning activities and experiences.

observations – to inspect and take note of the appearance and behavior of other individuals.

odd-day cycle menus – menus planned for a period of days other than a week that repeat after the planned period; cycles of any number of days may be used. These menus are a means of avoiding repetition of the same foods on the same day of the week.

ophthalmologist – a physician who specializes in diseases and abnormalities of the eye.

optometrist – a specialist (non-physician) trained to examine eyes and prescribe glasses and eye exercises.

overweight – weight that exceeds (by 20 percent or less) the recommendations for "desirable" body weight.

pallor – paleness.

palmar grasp – using the entire hand to pick up objects.

parallel play – a common form of play among young children in which two or more children, sitting side by side, are engaged in an activity but do not interact or work together to accomplish a task.

paralysis – temporary or permanent loss of sensation, function, or voluntary movement of a body part.

parasites – organisms that live on or within other living organisms.

pasteurized – heating a food to a prescribed temperature for a specific time period to destroy disease-producing bacteria.

pathogen – a microorganism capable of producing illness or infection.

peers – one of the same rank; equals.

Percent Daily Value (%DV) – a measure of the nutritional value of food; used in nutrition labeling.

personal sanitation – personal habits, such as handwashing, care of illness, cleanliness of clothing.

physical abuse – injuries, such as welts, burns, bruises, or broken bones, that are caused intentionally.

pincer grip – using the thumb and finger to pick up an object.

poverty guidelines – family-size and income standards for determining eligibility for free or reduced-price meals under the National School Lunch Program.

Prader-Willi syndrome – a chromosomal disorder that causes learning and behavior problems, overeating that can lead to obesity, poor muscle tone, and short height.

precipitating – factors that trigger or initiate a reaction or response.

predisposition – having an increased chance or susceptibility.

prenatal – the period from conception to birth of the baby.

preplan – outline a method of action prior to carrying it out.

prevention – measures taken to avoid an event such as an accident or illness from occurring; implies the ability to anticipate circumstances and behaviors.

preventive health – engaging in behaviors that help to maintain and enhance one's health status; includes concern for certain social issues affecting the population's health and environment.

primary goal – the aim that assumes first importance.

procurement – the process of obtaining services, supplies, and equipment in conformance with applicable laws and regulations.

prodromal – the appearance of the first nonspecific signs of infection; this stage ends when the symptoms characteristic of a particular communicable illness begin to appear.

protein – class of nutrients used primarily for structural and regulatory functions.

PUFA (polyunsaturated fatty acids) – fatty acids that contain more than one bond that is not fully saturated with hydrogen.

punishment – a negative response to what the observer considers to be wrong or inappropriate behavior; may involve physical or harsh treatment.

radura symbol – a required symbol placed on all food that has been treated with irradiation.

RDA (Recommended Daily Dietary Allowances) – suggested amounts of nutrients for use in planning diets. RDAs are designed to maintain good nutrition in healthy persons. Allowances are higher than requirements in order to afford a margin of safety.

receptive loss – hearing loss that affects the range of tones heard, so that high tones are more likely to be heard than low tones.

recovery position – placing an individual in a side-lying position.

reduced-price meals – a meal served under the Child Care Food Program to a child from a family which meets income standards for reduced-price school meals.

referrals – directing an individual to other sources, usually for additional evaluation or treatment.

refusal – the act of declining or rejecting.

registration – the act of placing the name of a child care program on a list of active providers; usually does not require on-site inspection.

regulations – standards or requirement that are set to ensure uniform and safe practices.

regurgitation – the return of partially digested food from stomach to mouth.

reimplanted – replaced a part from where it was removed, such as a tooth.

reprimand – to scold or discipline for unacceptable behavior.

resilient – the ability to withstand or resist difficulty.

resistance – the ability to avoid infection or illness.

respiratory diseases – disease of the respiratory tract, such as colds, sore throats, flu.

respiratory tract – pertains to, and includes, the nose, throat, trachea, and lungs.

resuscitation – to revive from unconsciousness or death; to restore breathing and heartbeat.

retention – the ability to remember or recall previously learned material.

rewards – things given for appropriate behavior.

Reye's syndrome – an acute illness of young children that severely affects the central nervous system; symptoms include vomiting, coma, and seizures.

RNA (ribonucleic acid) – the nucleic acid that serves as messenger between the nucleus and the ribosomes where proteins are synthesized.

Salmonella – a bacteria that can cause serious food-borne illness.

salmonellosis – a bacterial infection that is spread through contaminated drinking water, food, or milk or contact with other infected persons. Symptoms include diarrhea, fever, nausea, and vomiting.

sanitized – cleaned or sterilized.

sanitizing solution – a solution of diluted chlorine bleach (one-quarter cup chlorine to one gallon of water), used to sanitize utensils and work surfaces.

saturated fatty acid (SFA) – a fatty acid that has all carbon bonds satisfied by hydrogen.

scald – to rinse with boiling water.

sedentary – unusually slow or sluggish; a lifestyle that implies a general lack of physical activity.

seizures – a temporary interruption of consciousness sometimes accompanied by convulsive movements.

self-care children – children left to care for themselves.

sensorimotor – Piaget's first stage of cognitive development, during which children learn and relate to their world primarily through motor and sensory activities.

sensorineural loss – a type of hearing loss that occurs when sound impulses cannot reach the brain due to damage of the auditory nerve, or cannot be interpreted because of prior brain damage.

sensory qualities – aspects that appeal to sight, sound, taste, feel, and smell.

serrated – saw-toothed or notched.

sexual abuse – any sexual involvement between an adult and child.

shaken baby syndrome – forceful shaking of a baby that causes head trauma, internal bleeding, and sometimes death.

skeletal – pertaining to the bony framework that supports the body.

skinfold – a measurement of the amount of fat under the skin; also referred to as fat-fold measurements.

speech – the process of using words to express one's thoughts and ideas.

spina bifida – a birth defect in which incomplete formation of the body vertebrae allows a portion of the spinal cord to be exposed to the outside. Varying degrees of paralysis and lack of function are common in the portion of the body below the defect.

standardized recipe – a recipe that has been tested to produce consistent results.

Staphylococcus – a bacteria that can cause serious food-borne illnesses.

sterile – free from living microorganisms.

strabismus – a condition of the eyes in which one or both eyes appear to be turned inward (crossed) or outward (walleye).

submerge – to place in water.

supervision – watching carefully over the behaviors and actions of children and others.

supplementary proteins – a complete protein mix resulting from combining a small amount of a complete protein with an incomplete protein to provide all essential amino acids.

susceptible host – an individual who is capable of being infected by a pathogen.

symptoms – changes in the body or its functions that are experienced by the affected individual.

syndrome – a grouping of symptoms and signs that commonly occur together and are characteristic of a specific disease or illness.

synthesis – the process of making a compound by the union of simpler compounds or elements.

taurine – a free amino acid needed by infants for normal growth and development of the central nervous system.

tax exempt – excused from taxation, often on the basis of nonprofit status.

temperature – a measurement of body heat; varies with the time of day, activity, and method of measurement.

thermic energy of foods – energy required to digest, absorb, transport, and metabolize nutrients in food.

toxicity – a state of being poisonous.

trans fats – unsaturated fats that have been converted to a solid by a process of hydrogenation.

tuberculosis – an infectious disease caused by the tubercle bacillus, characterized by the production of lesions.

tympanic – referring to the ear canal.

type 1 diabetes – a disease distinguished by a lack of insulin production; usually diagnosed in childhood or young adulthood.

universal infection control precautions – special measures taken when handling bodily fluids, including careful handwashing, wearing latex gloves, disinfecting surfaces, and proper disposal of contaminated objects.

urination – the act of emptying the bladder of urine.

values – the beliefs, traditions, and customs an individual incorporates and utilizes to guide behavior and judgments.

verbal assault – to attack another individual with words.

viruses – any of a group of submicroscopic infective agents, many of which cause a number of diseases in animals and plants.

vitamins – organic substances needed in very small amounts to regulate many metabolic functions in the body.

weekly menus – menus that are written to be served on a weekly basis.

well child – a child in a good physical, mental, social, and emotional state.

whole grains – grain products that have not been refined; they contain all parts of the kernel of grain.

WIC (Women, Infants, and Children) – a federal program that provides food supplements for pregnant women, infants, and children to age five.

Note: tables, figures/illustrations, and boxes are denoted by a *t, f,* or *b* respectively, following the page number

Note: tables, figures/illustrations, and boxes are denoted by a *t*, *f*, or *b* respectively, following the page number

Note: tables, figures/illustrations, and boxes are denoted by a t, f, or b respectively, following the page number

Note: tables, figures/illustrations, and boxes are denoted by a *t*, *f*, or *b* respectively, following the page number

Note: tables, figures/illustrations, and boxes are denoted by a *t*, *f*, or *b* respectively, following the page number

Note: tables, figures/illustrations, and boxes are denoted by a *t, f,* or *b* respectively, following the page number

Note: tables, figures/illustrations, and boxes are denoted by a *t*, *f*, or *b* respectively, following the page number

Note: tables, figures/illustrations, and boxes are denoted by a *t*, *f*, or *b* respectively, following the page number

Note: tables, figures/illustrations, and boxes are denoted by a *t*, *f*, or *b* respectively, following the page number